The Second Red Scare and
the Unmaking of the New Deal Left

Politics and Society in Twentieth-Century America

Series Editors

WILLIAM CHAFE, GARY GERSTLE, LINDA GORDON, AND JULIAN ZELIZER

A list of titles in this series appears at the back of the book

The Second Red Scare and the Unmaking of the New Deal Left

Landon R. Y. Storrs

PRINCETON UNIVERSITY PRESS

Princeton & Oxford

Copyright © 2013 by Princeton University Press

Published by Princeton University Press, 41 William Street,
Princeton, New Jersey 08540

In the United Kingdom: Princeton University Press, 6 Oxford Street,
Woodstock, Oxfordshire OX20 1TW

press.princeton.edu

LIBRARY OF CONGRESS CATALOGING-IN-PUBLICATION DATA
Storrs, Landon R. Y.
  The second Red Scare and the unmaking of the New Deal left / Landon
R. Y. Storrs.
     p. cm. — (Politics and society in twentieth-century America)
Includes bibliographical references and index.
  ISBN 978-0-691-15396-4 (hardcover : acid-free paper) 1. Anti-
communist movements—United States—History—20th century. 2. New
Deal, 1933–1939. 3. Conservatism—United States—History—20th
century. 4. Liberalism—United States—History—20th century. 5. United
States—Officials and employees—Biography. 6. United States—Officials
and employees—Political activity—History—20th century. 7. Criminal
investigation—Political aspects—United States—History—20th century. 8.
Allegiance—United States—History—20th century. 9. Internal security—
United States—History—20th century—Juvenile literature. 10. United
States—Politics and government—1933–1945. I. Title.
  E743.5.S86 2013
  973.91—dc23   2012014277

British Library Cataloging-in-Publication Data is available

This book has been composed in Sabon and Archer

Printed on acid-free paper

Printed in the United States of America

10 9 8 7 6 5 4 3 2 1

For Mason

Contents

Illustrations

Abbreviations

AAA	Agricultural Adjustment Administration
AAUW	American Association of University Women
ADA	Americans for Democratic Action
AFDC	Aid to Families with Dependent Children
AFL	American Federation of Labor
ALPD	American League for Peace and Democracy
APWA	American Public Welfare Association
CEA	Council of Economic Advisers
CIO	Congress of Industrial Organizations
CNF	Consumers' National Federation
CP	Communist Party USA
CR	Consumers' Research
CSC	Civil Service Commission
ECA	Economic Cooperation Administration (Marshall Plan agency)
ECOSOC	Economic and Social Council of the United Nations
EEOC	Equal Employment Opportunity Commission
EO	Executive Order
FBI	Federal Bureau of Investigation, Department of Justice
FERA	Federal Emergency Relief Administration
FFR	Fund for the Republic, Ford Foundation
FSA	Federal Security Agency (1939–53)
HEW	Department of Health, Education, and Welfare (1953–80)
HUAC	House Un-American Activities Committee
ILO	International Labor Organization
IOELB	International Organizations Employee Loyalty Board
IRA	Indian Reorganization Act
LID	League for Industrial Democracy
LWS	League of Women Shoppers
MSA	Mutual Security Agency
NAACP	National Association for the Advancement of Colored People
NCL	National Consumers' League
NLRB	National Labor Relations Board
NRA	National Recovery Administration
NSL	National Student League

NWP	National Woman's Party
NYA	National Youth Administration
OCD	Office of Civilian Defense
OEO	Office of Economic Opportunity
OIT	Office of International Trade, Department of Commerce
OPA	Office of Price Administration
SISS	Senate Internal Security Subcommittee
SP	Socialist Party of the United States of America
SSB/SSA	Social Security Board (1935–46)/Social Security Administration (1946–)
UN	United Nations
UNESCO	United Nations Educational, Scientific, and Cultural Organization
UNRRA	United Nations Relief and Rehabilitation Administration
UPWA	United Public Workers of America
USHA	United States Housing Authority
USIA	United States Information Agency
WPA	Works Progress Administration

Selected Government Officials Investigated under the Federal Loyalty Program

BERNICE LOTWIN BERNSTEIN, regional director, Department of Health, Education, and Welfare

MARY McLEOD BETHUNE, director of Negro Affairs, National Youth Administration

THOMAS C. BLAISDELL JR., assistant secretary of commerce

ESTHER BRUNAUER, State Department liaison to UNESCO

RALPH BUNCHE, United Nations diplomat

JOHN CARMODY, Federal Works Agency administrator

WILBUR J. COHEN, Social Security official, later secretary of health, education, and welfare

MORDECAI EZEKIEL, New Deal economist and United Nations agricultural expert

ARTHUR "TEX" GOLDSCHMIDT, public power expert and United Nations development official

LEON KEYSERLING, President Truman's Council of Economic Advisers, chair

MARY DUBLIN KEYSERLING, Commerce Department official, later director of U.S. Women's Bureau

DAVID DEMAREST LLOYD, New Deal lawyer and Truman White House aide

FRIEDA S. MILLER, director of U.S. Women's Bureau

OLIVER A. PETERSON, State Department labor adviser and husband of Esther Peterson, later director of U.S. Women's Bureau and consumer adviser to Presidents Johnson and Carter

PAUL R. PORTER, Economic Cooperation Administration (Marshall Plan) official

CAROLINE F. WARE, consumer agency official, expert on community organization in Latin America

The Second Red Scare and
the Unmaking of the New Deal Left

The Second Red Scare stunted the development of the American welfare state. In the 1940s and 1950s, conservatives in and out of government used concerns about Soviet espionage to remove from public service many officials who advocated regulatory and redistributive policies intended to strengthen democracy. The crusade against "Communists in government" had even more casualties than we thought. In addition to its well-known violation of civil liberties and destruction of careers, the Second Red Scare curbed the social democratic potential of the New Deal through its impact on policymakers who sought to mitigate the antidemocratic tendencies of unregulated capitalism.

This book examines a cohort of women and men who entered government service during the 1930s and 1940s and then were investigated under the federal employee loyalty program. Created in the early 1940s and formalized in 1947, the loyalty program ostensibly sought to prevent government employment of Communists, but it also drove out noncommunist leftists, who were more numerous in the higher ranks of the civil service than has been recognized. During the crises of the Great Depression and Second World War, service in the dynamic Roosevelt administration offered the luster and cachet—although not the financial rewards—that in other eras would be found on Wall Street or in Silicon Valley, and the federal government hired some of the nation's most brilliant and ambitious talent. That high-powered group included some people who were inspired by the opportunity to forge policies they believed would prevent future depressions and wars by reducing inequalities—of class, race, and even gender—within the United States and abroad. Although a few of them were or had been members of the Communist Party, most never were. They did not dominate the policymaking arena, but their increasing influence provoked a powerful reaction from American conservatives. That reaction included exploiting Americans' fear of Soviet espionage to ensnare left-leaning officials in investigations that either marginalized them or forced them toward the political center.

Some of the prominent people whose hitherto secret or little-known loyalty cases this book explores are Leon Keyserling and Mary Dublin Keyserling, Arthur Goldschmidt and Elizabeth Wickenden, Wilbur Cohen, Catherine Bauer, Esther and Oliver Peterson, Frieda Miller, Caroline Ware, David Demarest Lloyd, Thomas Blaisdell, and Paul R. Porter.[1] The cumulative impact of their loyalty investigations and many others altered the general tone and content of the reform agenda and also affected specific policy fields, including labor and civil rights, consumer protection, national health insurance, public assistance, worker education, public works, public housing, Native American rights, and international aid.

The loyalty program's constricting effect on public policy thus was deeper and more direct than has been recognized. Until recently, the inaccessibility of government loyalty case records hampered scholarly inquiry, and the destruction of many files by the National Archives poses a permanent challenge.[2] A further complication stems from the reluctance of many loyalty defendants to publicize their experiences, at the time or later. The highly educated civil servants who are the subject of this study recognized the power of history, and many of them carefully documented their achievements for the historical record. As they did so, however, they tried to protect themselves, their survivors, and their causes by playing down their leftism, playing up their anticommunism, and omitting or minimizing the facts of their investigation. The loyalty program not only constrained policy development; it also produced distortions in the sources on which scholars have relied to write American history.

The federal employee loyalty program was a crucial instrument of the Red scare that gripped the nation after the Second World War, climaxing in the ascendance of Senator Joseph R. McCarthy (R-Wis.). Although that Red scare—longer and even more virulent than the one that followed the First World War—metastasized beyond government institutions and beyond the realm of employment, its momentum derived from claims that Communist spies in powerful government positions were manipulating U.S. policy to Soviet advantage. In response to conservative charges that the U.S. Civil Service Commission had been lax in screening federal workers, President Harry S. Truman institutionalized the loyalty program in 1947 by expanding existing procedures for weeding out employees deemed disloyal to the U.S. government. During the program's peak between 1947 and 1956, more than five million federal workers underwent loyalty screening, and at least 25,000 were subject to the stigmatizing "full field investigation" by the FBI. An estimated 2,700 federal employees were dismissed, and about 12,000 resigned.[3] Such numbers, however, cannot capture the program's broader effects on the civil service, on politics and public policy, and on historical memory.

Existing scholarship on the loyalty program suggests that it chiefly affected low-level government workers and Communist Party members. In fact, loyalty investigations truncated or redirected the careers of many mid-level and senior officials, who generally kept secret the fact that they had been investigated. Many of the accused were neither mainstream liberals, as early critics of the loyalty program maintained, nor Communist Party members (much less Soviet spies). Rather, they were a varied group of leftists who shared a commitment to building a comprehensive welfare state that blended central planning with grassroots democracy. Some called themselves social democrats, some belonged to the Socialist Party, and others resisted categorization, but they agreed that economic and technological development had created interdependences among people and among nations that rendered the ideologies of individualism and nationalism obsolete and even dangerous. As internationalists, they sought to use the social policies of other nations as models and to apply American resources to reduce inequalities and promote peace abroad. The power of these leftists was never uncontested, but their expertise, commitment, and connectedness gave them strength beyond their numbers. Before loyalty investigations pushed this cohort either out of government or toward the center of the political spectrum, the transformative potential of the New Deal was greater than is commonly understood.

Some loyalty defendants left public life, some moved to lower-profile jobs, and others reinvented themselves as Cold War liberals who celebrated American capitalism and advocated an aggressively anticommunist foreign policy. Several resurfaced as advisers to the Kennedy and Johnson administrations and framed their proposals in more centrist language than they had used before being investigated. They generally kept their distance from the new generation of radicals that emerged in the 1960s. For these New Deal veterans, the rightward drift of liberalism toward the "vital center" was at least in part a response to firsthand experience of political repression. It was not, as much scholarship suggests, a purely intellectual response to American economic performance, Soviet conduct, or other exogenous factors.[4] The loyalty program profoundly shaped not only individual careers but also U.S. politics and policy from the New Deal of the 1930s through the Great Society of the 1960s.

A striking number of professional-level loyalty defendants were women. Historians have noted the Second Red Scare's impact on women in voluntary associations, labor unions, and artistic circles, but women in government have received less attention.[5] Although women's opportunities in government were hardly equal to men's—women held fewer than 3 percent of federal policymaking positions in 1947—women had more options in government than they did in academia or the private sector. During the Roosevelt and Truman administrations, small numbers of professional women, especially lawyers, social workers, and economists, worked their way into positions of authority, most visibly in the temporary New Deal and war agencies, the Federal Security Agency, and the Labor and Commerce departments.[6] Anticommunists challenged the loyalty of high-ranking women with disproportionate frequency. Furthermore, male loyalty defendants often faced allegations about their wives' political activism. Conservatives' tactics and language in their crusade against "Communists in government" tapped popular hostility to powerful women and "effeminate" (or just egalitarian) men to rally support for hunting subversives and for rolling back liberal policies. In other words, government and private actors manipulated the fear of espionage toward ends that included shoring up social hierarchies that New Deal policies had helped destabilize. This exploration of the antifeminism of the Old Right suggests that the New Right that emerged in the 1970s was not in fact so new.

Scholarship on the federal loyalty program and the wider Red scare has ranged between two poles, one emphasizing the threat of Soviet espionage and the other emphasizing the dangers of political repression. Prior studies of the loyalty program per se were completed during the 1950s, when key government documents (such as the files of the Civil Service Commission, FBI, congressional investigative committees, and executive agencies) were closed to researchers. Limited to interviews and published materials, contemporary scholars nonetheless offered enduring critiques of the loyalty program. They identified flaws that invited injustice to employees: the program relied on vague and shifting standards of loyalty, on dubiously constructed lists of subversive organizations, and on the testimony of FBI informants whose anonymity denied defendants the right to confront their accusers. In addition to leaving many people jobless and stigmatized as unemployable, those early studies correctly concluded, the program undermined the morale and caliber of the civil service by discouraging original thinking and hindering recruitment. More generally, it contributed to an atmosphere that curtailed civil liberties, especially the freedoms of speech and association. The impact of these flaws was magnified as other employers imitated the federal program.[7] The next generation of scholarship debated the relative culpability of President Truman, congressional conservatives, and the FBI in creating and sustaining the loyalty program. Historians' observation that the loyalty program was ineffective at catching spies deepened the consensus that the program had been unnecessary as well as unfair.[8]

The tone changed in the 1990s, when newly declassified Soviet and U.S. intelligence sources indicated that a few Roosevelt and Truman officials, most notably Alger Hiss, indeed were Communist Party members or sympathizers who passed information to the Soviets—just as anticommunist conservatives from Congressman Martin Dies (D-Tex.) to Senator McCarthy had charged.[9] These findings reignited the disagreement between espionage scholars and those who emphasized the negative consequences of the Red scare. Each side accused the other of ignoring a grave threat to American democracy—espionage on the one hand, repression of political dissent on the other. The espionage historians have been very harsh, likening critics of the anticommunist crusade to Holocaust deniers, and castigating them as Stalin apologists bent on creating a left mythology of the "Lost Cause." In their view, focusing on the repressive aspects of anticommunism implies a moral equivalence between the Soviet dictatorship and the U.S. government.[10] Although the espionage scholars acknowledge that the drive to eliminate communism in the United States produced some injustices, they imply that it was relatively rare and incidental, when in fact the repression was widespread and resulted from a coordinated reaction against democratic challenges to the political and economic status quo.[11] Best-selling authors such as Ann Coulter have selectively appropriated the new espionage research to cast McCarthy as a martyred hero and his critics as traitors. The Texas Board of Education has revised its curriculum standards to require teaching that the most recent scholarship "basically vindicates" McCarthy.[12]

We can accept key findings of the new scholarship on espionage without minimizing the harm done by the repression. Soviet espionage was a legitimate worry for officials responsible for national security, and identifying and prosecuting spies was difficult. Although the people named by the ex-Communist informants Elizabeth Bentley and Whittaker Chambers had left government service by 1947, officials remained vigilant because they knew unidentified Communist cells had existed. Notwithstanding all the false accusations that were made, one should not dismiss out of hand the possibility that a loyalty defendant had been a Soviet agent.[13] Nevertheless, these facts do not preclude the obligation of scholars to mine newly accessible sources for insight into the objectives and consequences of the Red scare.

The threat of espionage was real, but no less so was repression in the name of catching spies. This book does not engage the ongoing debate over the extent to which espionage jeopardized U.S. security. It does demonstrate, however, that the Second Red Scare did even more damage than is generally known.[14] The campaign against "Communists in government" began before the Cold War and was driven by conservatives whose objectives were broader than the eradication of the Communist Party.[15]

Uncovering a significant leftist presence in the Roosevelt and Truman administrations does not vindicate those anticommunists who claimed that the government was riddled with subversives. I searched for but did not find evidence of espionage or other illegal conduct; the policymakers and administrators studied here were neither subversives nor spies. They hoped for a transition through constitutional methods to what they called social democracy or democratic socialism. While conservatives promoted limited government and the sanctity of property rights, left-leaning officials argued that the public interest was better served by an active government that, at the very least, regulated private interests to protect the public, provided opportunities and security for those that the private labor market did not, and further promoted political and economic democracy by prohibiting racial and sexual discrimination.

Many decades ago the preeminent historian Richard Hofstadter observed that the "real function" of the Second Red Scare was "not anything so simply rational as to turn up spies . . . but to discharge resentments and frustrations, to punish, to satisfy enmities whose roots lay elsewhere than in the Communist issue itself." Hofstadter argued that nativism, religious fundamentalism, and hatred of the welfare state and the United Nations were the "deeper historical sources of the Great Inquisition." In his view, these attitudes added up to an antimodern, reactionary populism.[16] Regional and local studies built on Hofstadter's insight by showing that Red scares were most virulent where rapid change threatened old regimes. Political fundamentalists everywhere feared the trend toward a "pluralistic order and a secular, bureaucratizing state." In Detroit, though, they defended class prerogatives above all, whereas in Boston religious conflict was key, and in Atlanta maintenance of white supremacy was paramount. In other words, the intensity of Red scare politics was not simply a function of the strength of the Communist threat. Red scares erupted at various places and moments in defense of class, religious, and racial hierarchies.[17]

These astute analyses of anticommunism do not address the conservative reaction to women's increasing sexual and economic independence. Meanwhile, historians interested in gender analysis have exposed the intersections between Cold War politics and restrictive constructions of masculinity and femininity, but without sufficient attention to anticommunist attacks on actual women, especially women in government. Domestic anticommunism indeed was fueled by anxiety about the perceived threats to American masculinity posed by totalitarianism, corporate hierarchy, and homosexuality. Congressional conservatives indeed used charges of homosexuality—chiefly male homosexuality—in government agencies for their own political purposes.[18] The flip side of the anticommunist right's hostility to insufficiently masculine men, however, was antipathy to powerful women. Scholars of the right in the 1920s and 1980s have shown that men and women who feared homosexuality, racial and religious pluralism, and state bureaucracy were not enthusiastic about feminism, either. Advocacy of the white, Christian, heterosexual, *patriarchal* family often was their driving concern.[19]

If one engine of the Second Red Scare was popular resistance to the rise of the government expert, as Hofstadter argued, that resistance was intensified by the fact that some of those experts were women. The crises of the Depression, war, and the nuclear threat expanded the federal bureaucracy and also shifted power from legislators to bureaucratic experts. These career civil servants typically were better educated and more cosmopolitan than legislators. Furthermore, the masculinity of male civil servants long had been suspect. Stereotypes about male bureaucrats and male homosexuals overlapped: both groups could be seen as non(re) productive, nonentrepreneurial men laboring in subordinate positions to other men. The fact that federal jobs were sexually integrated at a time when most workplaces were not created additional negative perceptions of both male and female government workers. In the 1920s, conservatives' belief that the state subverted patriarchal gender norms was apparent in their fear that newly enfranchised women would vote to expand state agencies protecting women and children, empowering state administrators—many of whom were female—at the expense of male heads of household.[20] During the 1930s, more professional women found employment in government because the creation of new agencies increased staffing needs, the expansion of the merit system made hiring procedures more objective, and some relatively feminist men were making hiring and promotion decisions. The result was a perceived feminization of the civil service that gave conservatives another reason to dislike the bureaucratic state.

Many of these same patterns and attitudes affected Jewish civil servants, male and female. The Roosevelt administration was more open to Jews than its predecessors had been, and as we shall see, many loyalty defendants were Jewish. Commentators at the time speculated about the likelihood of bias in loyalty charges against Jews, and scholars have long understood that the right's hostility to the New Deal was tinged with anti-Semitism.[21] By contrast, the loyalty program's impact on women, and on husbands of activist women, has not been appreciated.

The first chapter introduces a group of young radicals, male and female, who ascended with surprising rapidity in the Roosevelt administration. The women were not part of the better-known network of older female New Dealers, most of who had been born in the 1870s and 1880s. That older group, clustered in the female enclaves of the U.S. Women's and Children's Bureaus and the Women's Division of the Democratic Party, wielded significant influence over certain social policies and in party politics at the height of the New Deal. Their achievements were constrained by the limits of their own vision and by resistance from more powerful men.[22] Most of the women I describe were born in the first decade of the twentieth century, and they were further to the left than the older New Deal women. The left's stronger influence on the younger women contributed to several other differences. Many of the younger group advocated women's sexual emancipation and conducted their personal lives accordingly. Women in the younger cohort were less likely to make "maternalist" arguments that stressed women's innate differences from men, and they identified less exclusively with women-only organizations. They were more likely to marry and to have children than the previous generation. Although predominantly white and middle or upper class, the younger group was more culturally diverse in that it included atheists, Jews, and women who married across religious, ethnic, and national lines. The younger women also were more likely than their predecessors to actively oppose racial discrimination.

These women did not call themselves "left feminists," but the term usefully distinguishes them from nonfeminist leftists and from the "pure" feminists of the National Woman's Party, whose proposed equal rights amendment antagonized advocates of wage and hour laws for women. Other scholars have referred to activists of similar outlook as "labor feminists," but "left feminist" better captures the breadth of their commitments, which in addition to workplace activism included antiracist initiatives and consumerist campaigns to raise working-class living standards. Some years ago I tried to convey the sense of the left-liberal spectrum by calling these same people "Popular Front feminists," but many readers inferred that I meant primarily people who were in or close to the Communist Party. The people discussed here did move in circles that included Communists, especially in the 1930s and early 1940s, when the ideological lines were not so sharply drawn. But I have decided not to use a phrase that some will interpret as indicating Communist leadership. This book uses "left feminist" in an inclusive sense to refer to women and men who pursued a vision of women's emancipation that also insisted on class and racial justice.[23]

Left feminism was more vital in the 1930s and 1940s than one would guess from most studies of the left or of feminism. It is often argued that leftists focused primarily on class justice in the 1930s and were not attuned to racial and gender politics until the postwar period.[24] And until recently, the conventional wisdom held that feminism was dormant between the suffrage victory in 1920 and the 1960s, and that leftist women had little influence beyond insular radical circles.[25] In fact, the American left in the 1930s attracted women and men who saw that the values of "free enterprise" and "rugged individualism" protected prerogatives of gender and race as well as class. Furthermore, some of those people got jobs in government. Left feminism was closer to power than we have thought—although not as close as its enemies feared, or pretended to fear.

Not all women in government were left feminists. But those who were gained force from the fact that they often knew one another, through shared interests in labor, poverty, housing, public health and health insurance, consumer rights, and international peace—interdependent causes that in their vision had a feminist subtext. From their sometimes precarious positions in government, these women pushed for policies to raise the living standards of poor and working-class Americans, which they argued would strengthen both the economy and American democracy. They advocated raising wages through unionization and wage-hour laws; combating unemployment through planning, public works, and generous relief and social insurance policies; and further protecting purchasing power with national health insurance, public housing, and consumer rights. The historical gender division of labor encouraged them as women to be especially concerned with health, housing, and child welfare, and they understood how that division of labor made women particularly vulnerable to poverty and labor exploitation. These civil servants tackled barriers to the economic and political participation of women of all races, for example by lobbying against racial and sexual discrimination in employment, against the exclusion of female and minority-dominated occupations from the Fair Labor Standards and Social Security Acts, and against the poll taxes that disproportionately disfranchised minorities and women.

Those policy goals resounded across a left-liberal spectrum that was quite fluid before the rising tide of anticommunism produced more self-conscious political identification and inhibited coalition building. Leftists of varying stripes had already begun cooperating when the Communist Party USA announced its Popular Front strategy in 1935. Most scholarship on the Popular Front has been dominated by the "Communist issue," the long-standing debate about the relative importance of Moscow's influence over the Communist Party USA leadership, on one hand, and American Communists' significant contributions to the labor and civil rights movements, on the other. That debate is unlikely to end soon. In any case, it has diverted attention from the independent leftists who outnumbered the Communists and by no means depended on them for direction.[26] Notwithstanding their ideological differences, participants in the Popular Front pursued a social democratic electoral politics that attracted broad public support: a 1942 poll reported that 25 percent of Americans favored socialism and another 35 percent "had an open mind about it."[27] Popular Fronters shared the social democratic objective of extending "the democratic principle of equality from the civil and political spheres to the entire society and the economy."[28] Together social democrats, Socialists, and Communists tried to push the New Deal to the left, urging interventions in the market to redistribute wealth and increase public control. Although Communist doctrine opposed reforms that might hinder the development of class consciousness, in practice many party members cooperated with those who believed progress toward the ideal of socialism would come through constitutional, gradual reform rather than through revolution. Social democracy, with its emphasis on evolutionary change and the growing interdependence of classes, was especially attractive to middle-class people who sought a constructive role in reform. A related feature of social democratic theory was the prominent role it accorded to consumers as arbiters of the public interest. Because consumers often were construed as female, social democracy had special resonance for progressive middle-class women, including some who found opportunities in the federal civil service.[29]

The story of these ambitious, left-leaning women in government would be incomplete without attention to the men who were their allies, colleagues, lovers, and sometimes their codefendants. Long before the days of the Clintons and the Obamas, there were many "power couples" in Washington's left-liberal circles. In addition to Eleanor and Franklin Roosevelt, prominent dual-career couples in and around government in the 1930s and 1940s included Caroline Ware and Gardiner Means, Leon Keyserling and Mary Dublin Keyserling, Charlotte Tuttle and David Demarest Lloyd, Lucy Kramer and Felix Cohen, Abe Fortas and Carol Agger Fortas, Lucille and Mordecai Ezekiel, Wilbur Cohen and Eloise Bittel Cohen, and Elizabeth Wickenden and Tex Goldschmidt, to name just a few whose achievements and struggles I explore. The wives played key roles in fostering the dense heterosocial networks that characterized New Deal Washington. The husbands, like New Deal men more generally, were not immune to sexism. Some Roosevelt administration policies in fact reinforced gender (and other) inequalities, and female New Dealers sometimes chafed at the insufficient enlightenment of the men who were their purported allies.[30] These were significant limitations, but they should not obscure the substantial differences in gender ideology between left-liberal men and their conservative counterparts during the midcentury decades.

More than historians have, the right noticed the influx of left-feminist women and men into government and began attacking them well before the federal loyalty program's formal creation in 1947. Chapter 2 introduces key figures in the emerging anticommunist network and analyzes two early episodes: the Smith Committee attack on the National Labor Relations Board and its allies, and the Dies Committee attack on the consumer movement, especially the League of Women Shoppers and the Office of Price Administration. The power of the labor movement in stimulating the reaction against the New Deal is well known, but the consumer movement should be recognized as another major trigger. Women were important in the ascendance of both industrial unionism and organized consumerism, and conservatives highlighted women's role in an effort to undermine public confidence in those movements and their allied government agencies.

Chapter 3 documents the antifeminism of key instigators of the Second Red Scare: staff members of congressional investigative committees and the conservative journalists with whom they cooperated. Their public statements and private correspondence indicate that they associated communism with men's loss of control over women's labor and sexual conduct. For them, the need to stabilize white male supremacy was one reason to oppose communism. Antifeminism, an objective in and of itself, also was a means to other objectives. Leading anticommunists deployed antifeminism, just as they did homophobia, to generate popular enthusiasm for their attacks on the Roosevelt and Truman administrations.[31]

From 1940 through the mid-1960s, Mary Dublin Keyserling and Leon Keyserling were particularly prominent targets for the anticommunist right. His first claim to fame was drafting the National Labor Relations Act, and her career began as a consumer activist, so they aptly represent the movements whose successes mobilized anticommunist crusaders. The Keyserlings were "purchasing-power progressives" who argued that raising working-class living standards was essential for a healthy economy and a healthy democracy.[32] During the Truman administration, Leon provided intellectual leadership for the Fair Deal from his position on the Council of Economic Advisers, while Mary analyzed international aid and trade statistics for the Department of Commerce. As chapter 4 reveals, they both experienced long, bruising loyalty investigations. They resigned in 1953 during the transition to the Eisenhower administration. Leon reemerged as an economic adviser to the Democratic National Committee and the AFL-CIO in the late 1950s and then as an ally of the centrist Democrat Hubert Humphrey. In 1964, President Lyndon Johnson appointed Mary head of the U.S. Women's Bureau, over the objections of congressional conservatives who revived the old disloyalty allegations. The Keyserlings are remembered as Cold War liberals who supported the Vietnam War and celebrated capitalism's ability to eliminate poverty through growth, rather than redistribution. But in the 1930s, as chapter 5 reveals, both had been leftists. Under the pressure of recurring investigations, both of them moderated their goals and language, and they elided radicalism from their autobiographical narratives.

We have known little about the experience of being under investigation because so few loyalty defendants, especially high-ranking ones, were willing to talk about it. In the 1950s and 1960s, scholars tried to document those stories and gave up. Chapter 6 uses private letters and other unpublished sources about defendants other than the Keyserlings to recapture the subjective experience of being investigated, not as an exercise in voyeurism but to explain why the effects were so profound. It reviews the grave consequences of dismissal in order to re-create the context in which defendants made painful choices about what tone and tactics to adopt during their inquisitions. It then discusses the range of strategies used by defendants, with particular attention to how those strategies often played on and in turn reinforced conservative gender prescriptions.

Judges and politicians began to rein in the loyalty program in the late 1950s. An anti-McCarthyite network convinced the public that the loyalty program was crushing civil liberties, wasting money on harmless low-level people, discriminating against racial and ethnic minorities, and being exploited as a tool of partisan politics. In the process of documenting these real problems and achieving these necessary reforms, however, critics deflected attention from the ways in which the loyalty program reinforced male supremacy and also repressed what had been a substantial social democratic influence in policy circles.

Some loyalty defendants left government or left public life altogether, reducing the range of policy debate by their marginalization or absence. Others stayed in public service, but they reflexively hedged against the threat of further investigation by softening their critiques of capitalism and couching their reform proposals in anticommunist terms. Loyalty defendants frequently destroyed or withheld from archival collections those sources that documented their early leftism and their investigations. In interviews and memoirs, they typically took every opportunity to stress their anticommunism while downplaying their sympathy with the noncommunist left. The silences and distortions produced by loyalty investigations have been reproduced in the historiography of twentieth-century American politics. More important, as chapter 7 demonstrates through examples from many fields, "the American inquisition" faced by federal officials in the 1940s and 1950s constricted public policymaking and forestalled the extension of social democracy in the United States.

Many forces combined with the loyalty inquisition to push American liberalism toward the political center in the 1940s and 1950s, away from the regulatory and redistributive approach of the New Deal—sometimes called "social Keynesianism"—and toward the growth-oriented, fiscal Keynesianism of the Fair Deal and Great Society. The disappointing "Roosevelt recession" of 1937, combined with the dramatic economic growth of the war years, persuaded some policymakers that stimulating economic expansion, rather than trying to reslice the existing pie, was the most effective way of raising American living standards. Liberal Democratic administrations' dependence on cooperation from congressional conservatives on national defense—from World War II to Korea to Vietnam—made less interventionist economic policies politically expedient. The labor movement narrowed its objectives after the CIO's southern drive failed and in response to accusations of Communist infiltration. The confidence and unity of the American left were shattered by disillusionment with the brutality of Stalin's regime and the undemocratic methods of the Communist Party USA. A nascent conservative moment led by business ideologues relentlessly denounced regulatory and redistributive economic policies. The list could continue.[33]

Thus the federal employee loyalty program was hardly the sole or determinative cause of the transformation of American liberalism from the 1930s to the 1960s. But disloyalty charges were a hitherto hidden factor that, often in interaction with the other developments, had a significant political impact. Historians simply have not known how many senior officials had direct and protracted encounters with the loyalty machinery. It is impossible to prove that the loyalty program was *the* decisive force that altered these people's trajectories. The ideas and priorities of individuals change for many reasons, and isolating a single one is difficult. Furthermore, generalization is perilous because loyalty defendants faced diverse circumstances and responded in diverse ways. But the timing and nature of repositioning on the part of one public servant after another make it hard to dismiss the loyalty program's influence.

The evidence available for each case varies, but I draw my conclusions from the following kinds of sources (and from their juxtaposition): Civil Service Commission case files, papers that loyalty defendants deposited in archives, papers they withheld from archives, public statements over the course of many years, and autobiographical representations in memoirs and interviews. In cases where it is possible to map the chronology of an employee's investigation in relation to his or her evolving policy prescriptions, a correlation often is apparent. Leon Keyserling's evolution from a champion of labor rights and economic planning to a leading proponent of economic growth and of militarizing the Cold War transpired, it turns out, against a backdrop of potentially career-ending investigations that included interrogation about his views of capitalism and his wife's political associations. The change in tune of public housing advocate Catherine Bauer, as another example, is less puzzling in light of the discovery that allegations of her radicalism were crippling her husband's career by denying his firm government contracts. As we will see in chapter 6, some defendants explicitly acknowledged the traumatizing impact of being accused of disloyalty, either in private correspondence to friends or behind the doors of closed hearings.

Sometimes I draw inferences from the absence of sources. After reading the voluminous documentation in Civil Service Commission case files—which include materials of which defendants would have had copies—the lack of any such records in those individuals' archival collections stands out. Similar gaps are apparent in many loyalty defendants' memoirs and interviews. In some instances, materials surfaced in the possession of relatives after a defendant's death. These newly discovered sources are illuminating in and of themselves, revealing, for example, that some individuals once were further to the left than we have known. But the very fact that loyalty defendants withheld these materials from the archives further attests to the deep impression made by the investigations. The government anthropologist Lucy Kramer withheld papers from the Beinecke Library that document her socialism and that of her husband, the Indian law expert Felix S. Cohen. The FBI file of social welfare expert Wilbur Cohen turned up in his attic after he died; his embrace during the 1950s of antipoverty policies that addressed the failures of individuals rather than of the labor market takes on a new coloration in light of the persistent investigation he and his wife faced.

The accumulated evidence from these and many other cases makes it fair to conclude that loyalty investigations induced influential government figures to move toward the political center and sometimes to obscure earlier leftist activism, thereby affecting both policy and historical sources. Those loyalty defendants whose objectives and tone did not change found their career options and influence truncated. Future researchers may wish to analyze specific cases more closely to assess the relative importance of being investigated to a particular individual's ideological and career trajectories. The intent here is to identify a broad pattern and invite further exploration of the questions it raises.

Uncovering and interpreting these stories has been a tricky and sometimes uncomfortable process. With difficulty, I located and gained access to a group of surviving loyalty case files, some of which include hearing transcripts and FBI reports (see appendix 1). Occasionally I was able to locate relatives who shared materials that loyalty defendants had not expected to become public. Sifting through these hitherto confidential and private sources, I experienced the unpleasant sensation of retracing the footsteps of the Red-hunters. These public servants understandably did not wish their distinguished careers to be defined by their demeaning encounters with McCarthyism. In trying to interpret the often contradictory or fragmentary evidence—poring over transcripts for inconsistent statements, decoding acronyms from appointment books, evaluating the words of hundreds of witnesses and informants—it was easy to slip into the narrow mentality of the investigators and take on their obsession with delineating each defendant's relationship, if any, to the Communist Party. But focusing only on the question of Communist Party membership neglects the dynamism and complexity of the American left in the 1930s and 1940s.[34] Preoccupation with the Communist question also oversimplifies the motives of the right. The fuller portrait of these civil servants' political views and networks that emerges here is valuable not for reductive ideological categorizing but rather for demonstrating that, for a brief historical moment, left feminists were positioned to shape American policymaking.

To focus on the noncommunist left is not to suggest that the repression of Communists was unproblematic. But for various reasons, by the time the loyalty program went into full gear in 1947, very few people holding significant government jobs belonged to the Communist Party.[35] That noncommunist officials were subjected to excruciating, often protracted loyalty investigations underscores that it was not communism that the right most feared.

The social scientist Caroline Ware was neither a Communist nor a spy, and loyalty officials never seriously believed she was. She nonetheless was dragged into the machinery of the loyalty program by accusations that she was a dangerous subversive. Over the course of a long career as a scholar, civil servant, and activist, Ware promoted what she called "the fuller participation as active and responsible members of their communities and nation of more and more kinds of people who, through past centuries, furnished the passive base for the wealth and culture they did not share." She saw empowering ordinary people to participate in democratic government as the crucial challenge of the twentieth century.[36] For Ware and others on the left wing of the New Deal, the proper role of government in a democracy was not to solve all problems but rather to ensure the basic levels of economic security, education, and legal protection that would enable groups to organize to solve their problems collectively—as workers, as consumers, as women, as members of oppressed racial or ethnic groups, or as colonial subjects. By reducing the influence of people like Caroline Ware, the campaign against "Communists in government" did not protect American democracy but rather impeded the solution of problems that continue to imperil it.

CHAPTER 1

When the Old Left Was Young ... and Went to Washington

In a famous description of the changes that Franklin Roosevelt's New Deal wrought in the nation's capital, one veteran civil servant grumbled that "a plague of young lawyers settled on Washington. They all claimed to be friends of somebody or other and mostly of Felix Frankfurter and Jerome Frank." In another classic portrayal, the historian Arthur M. Schlesinger Jr. explained that the Great Depression, by reducing private employment options, "made men of intellectual ability available as never before; and the government had never been so eager to hire them. . . . With each prominent New Dealer acting as his own employment agency, Washington was deluged with an endless stream of bright young men." Schlesinger described their ideological orientations as ranging from fiscal orthodoxy to Wilsonian liberalism to Theodore Rooseveltian progressivism. They were passionate about ideas and worked long hours, but that did not prevent them from drinking, dancing, and arguing much of the night, transforming stuffy, sleepy Washington into a lively, sophisticated city. "The memories would not soon fade—the interminable meetings, the litter of cigarette stubs . . . the call from the White House, the postponed dinner, the neglected wife, the office lights burning into the night, the lilacs hanging in fragrance above Georgetown gardens while men rebuilt the nation."[1]

Schlesinger's evocative portrait omitted a cohort of leftist women and men whose presence was crucial to Washington's transformation and to the design and implementation of many hallmark New Deal policies. It is widely known that capitalism's crisis shifted the American political spectrum to the left in the 1930s, and also that the decade's protest movements included one comprising radical students on college campuses around the nation.[2] Less recognized is the fact that after graduation many of those young radicals—economists, social workers, and yes, lawyers, foremost among them—took jobs in the federal government. The high unemployment rate did make government jobs more attractive to men, but the civil service was especially attractive to a growing pool of professional women, who had trouble obtaining corporate and academic positions regardless of the state of the economy.

The influx of leftists and women (not exclusive categories) into government made it easier for conservative critics of the New Deal to paint it "pink." When Schlesinger published his paean in 1958, the postwar Red scare was dissipating but still emitting noxious fumes. It is not surprising that Schlesinger, a liberal activist as well as a historian, did not highlight the leftist or female presence in Washington's corridors and lilac-scented gardens. Deliberate or not, Schlesinger's omissions—compounded by the reticence of many former civil servants—contributed to misunderstandings that subsequent scholarship has not dispelled.[3]

"HOPE THAT THE PRESENT GOVERNMENT IS SOMETHING MORE THAN A CONSCIOUS AGENT OF VESTED INTERESTS"

Many of the young professionals who came to Washington had been deeply influenced by socialism, and their initial expectations of the Roosevelt administration were low. They were attracted more by the promise of a job than by the promise of a New Deal. However, in agencies such as the Federal Emergency Relief Administration, the Department of the Interior, the National Labor Relations Board, the Social Security Administration, the Works Progress Administration, and later the Office of Price Administration, these pragmatic leftists found unexpected opportunities to advance their convictions, as well as their careers. They came to believe that it might be possible in the United States to realize the social democratic vision of a mixed economy in which a vital public sector balanced the power of the private sector. In view of capitalism's demonstrated, structural tendency to create an economically and educationally impoverished class, they argued that democracy could be sustained under capitalism only with government action to mitigate economic and social inequalities.

Arthur "Tex" Goldschmidt is a good example of a young radical who initially had little faith in the New Deal. In his eighties, he explained:

> I call myself an early New Dealer because it seems so from this perspective. But you would be wrong to assume immediately that I was one of those idealistic young people who flocked to Washington in 1933 to help Roosevelt's program save the country. It was not quite like that. Sure, I was young and idealistic. Sure, I went to Washington at the first job offer. But neither I nor anyone I knew had much confidence in the new administration or even thought it had a program.[4]

The son of freethinking German immigrants to San Antonio, Texas, Goldschmidt worked his way through Columbia University, where he studied economics and government with the left-leaning professors Rexford Tugwell and Joseph McGoldrick. As a founder of the Social Problems Club, which became the Columbia chapter of the National Student League, Goldschmidt helped organize some of the student movement's formative events, including a pilgrimage in support of striking Kentucky coal miners in the spring of 1932, followed by a protest of Columbia's expulsion of the student newspaper editor Reed Harris. Newspaper coverage of both events foregrounded Goldschmidt and his friends Rob Hall and Howard Westwood. Hall soon joined the Communist Party and left school to organize sharecroppers in his native Alabama.[5] Goldschmidt and Westwood continued their studies and then took jobs in Washington—as did the young radicals they married.

During the fall of 1932, Goldschmidt fell in love with a woman who shared his disdain for Franklin Roosevelt's campaign platform. Raised in a prosperous Ohio family, Elizabeth Wickenden had graduated in 1931 from Vassar College, where her professors included Caroline Ware, and where she wrote her senior essay on the "still taboo subject" of federal relief for unemployed workers. An aspiring writer, she then spent a year in Europe, including a month in the Soviet Union that produced a series of articles published by the *Cleveland Plain Dealer*. She decided to try her luck in New York City, where she rented a studio apartment on the top floor of a five-story walk-up on Twelfth Street. Unable to find paid employment, she volunteered at the Emergency Exchange Association, a nonprofit experiment in organizing the production of goods and services among the unemployed. One of her fellow volunteers was Tex Goldschmidt. They shared lunches at the local Automat, where they discussed the "need for more radical approaches" than anything they were hearing in the presidential campaign. Tex recalled that "as it became clear that Hoover would surely lose, most thoughtful people sought to express their dissatisfaction with the Tweedledum-Tweedledee likenesses of the two major parties and debated whether a vote for Norman Thomas or William Z. Foster would best serve to do so." Goldschmidt did not record which way he and Wickenden voted. But he did note that she soon bought him "a toothbrush to hang alongside hers" in that Twelfth Street studio.[6]

Despite their agreement that Roosevelt's victory was "politically meaningless" and that Washington was "a sluggish southern backwater," when a friend from the Emergency Exchange Association offered Wickenden and Goldschmidt jobs in the new Federal Emergency Relief Administration, it was hard to say no. Freshly married and with "a nest egg of $125 to start out staring winter in the face," they took the jobs, promising each other to stay no more than six months in Washington. They stayed for eighteen years—and departed then only because Goldschmidt's move to the United Nations required them to live in New York. Between them, they became experts on public assistance, social insurance, public works, and public power, and they advised such prominent figures as Harry Hopkins, Harold Ickes, Wilbur Cohen, and Lyndon Johnson. They became Democratic Party members, but they never stopped trying to push that party to the left. Goldschmidt later claimed, "Neither my wife nor I were motivated by planned goals for ourselves but kept restlessly seeking ways to nudge for changes that might yield progress in the evolution of our society. My own work was rarely boring. My role was almost always a yeasty one—critical, doubtful, experimental; on the cutting edge—or the left fringe, if you prefer."[7]

Meanwhile, Goldschmidt's fellow Columbia radical Howard Westwood married Charlotte Tuttle, like Westwood a star at Columbia Law School (and also, it happened, Wickenden's former classmate at Vassar). Westwood clerked for Supreme Court Justice Harlan Stone before going into private practice.[8] Tuttle, the daughter of a U.S. Attorney and former Republican candidate for governor of New York, had drawn headlines at the age of nineteen by declaring herself a socialist after an undercover stint as a factory girl, and then by defending the rights of students arrested while trying to organize female garment workers.[9] She became one of six women in the class of 1934 at Columbia Law School and one of two women who made the *Columbia Law Review*. Her father paid her tuition despite his certainty that no law firm would hire a woman. The federal government, however, proved eager to hire her. Even before she had passed the bar exam in 1934, Tuttle was recruited into the Interior Department solicitor's office by Felix S. Cohen, who had known Tuttle through the socialist League for Industrial Democracy (LID) as well as at Columbia Law. Tuttle helped Cohen shape New Deal policy on Native American rights. She traveled to reservations to help tribes draft constitutions under the Indian Reorganization Act, and she contributed to Cohen's classic *Handbook of Federal Indian Law* (1941). After Westwood divorced her in 1939, Tuttle married David Demarest Lloyd, a New Deal lawyer whose radical forebears included the muckraking journalist Henry Demarest Lloyd. From 1945 to 1948 she was assistant general counsel for the United Nations Relief and Rehabilitation Administration in Washington and London. When David Lloyd became an aide to President Truman in 1948, Charlotte suspended her career and focused on raising their two children. Later, Charlotte Tuttle Lloyd became the first woman assistant general counsel in the Treasury Department (1965–73).[10]

Young leftists joined the Roosevelt administration because it was the best employment available to them, not because they had much faith in its potential to fulfill their social justice ideals. Once on the job, their skepti-

Figure 1.1. Elizabeth Wickenden and Tex Goldschmidt, Lake George, N.Y., July 1933. Wickenden kept this photo, taken shortly after they married, on her desk for many decades. Courtesy of Ann Goldschmidt Richardson and Arthur Goldschmidt Jr.

cism softened. Goldschmidt was impressed by Harry Hopkins's penetrating critique of the existing relief system. Present at what he later called the Federal Emergency Relief Administration's "Big Bang" in September 1933, Goldschmidt helped conceive and administer the Civil Works Administration, which created several million jobs during the harsh winter of 1933–34. After Wickenden wrote a perceptive report on the problem of transients—who did not meet states' residency requirements for aid— she found herself in charge, at age twenty-five, of a pioneering federal relief program affecting about 350,000 people around the country.[11] By

Figure 1.2. As a lawyer in the Interior Department, Charlotte Tuttle Westwood helped administer the Indian Reorganization Act of 1934. In 1940 she married David Demarest Lloyd, whom she met at a hearing on the exploitation of migrant agricultural workers. Courtesy of Louisa Lloyd Hurley.

1938 she had concluded that "democracy can be made to work within the framework of modern capitalist organization"—*if*, through "public taxing and regulatory power," democratic government could "reconcile conflicting economic interests in order that all people may have reasonable security, an adequate standard of living, and an opportunity to participate in the solution of common problems through political or other action." She spent the rest of her career trying to change that *if* to *when*.[12]

Felix Cohen was another person who found himself unexpectedly impressed by the possibilities under the Roosevelt administration. After a few weeks as assistant solicitor in the Interior Department, Cohen wrote to his mentor, the Socialist Party leader Norman Thomas, that his early impressions supported "the hope that the present government is something more than a conscious agent of vested interests, and that a political seizure of power by a party that appeals to the masses will not face the threat of sabotage from within the civil service, though it will undoubtedly face that threat from Big Business."[13] The son of the distinguished philosopher Morris Raphael Cohen was named after Felix Frankfurter, and he excelled in both those men's fields, earning a Ph.D. in philosophy at Harvard in 1929 and a law degree from Columbia in 1931. As an undergraduate at the City College of New York, he had been active in the Socialist Party and the League for Industrial Democracy well before the Depression swelled their ranks. In 1925 Felix used his position as editor of the campus newspaper to protest mandatory military training in the form of Reserve Officers' Training Corps courses. The college administration prohibited the newspaper from discussing the topic further, and the ensuing battle mobilized pacifists and civil libertarians across the nation. It also resulted in Felix's temporary exclusion from City College's Phi Beta Kappa chapter.[14] The experience only deepened Cohen's convictions. On a date in 1927 with his future wife, the anthropologist Lucy Kramer, they attended an execution-day vigil for the anarchists Sacco and Vanzetti in Union Square, where Felix shared the platform with Norman Thomas.[15]

Despite Cohen's radical commitments, when the new Interior Department Solicitor Nathan Margold offered Felix a job in 1933, he quickly accepted.[16] Describing to Norman Thomas "the position that one Socialist finds himself in within the framework of a capitalist government," he explained that he had "no illusions about the efficacy of boring from within" but would have "a good deal of leeway" in his new job. Cohen reminded Thomas that, during a 1926 LID conference, Thomas had advised young Socialists to avoid getting married or having children and to get "strategic positions in civil service." Married but childless when the government hired him, Cohen joked that "67% would be a passing mark."[17] Thomas reassured Cohen that he did not blame him for taking the job: "You are young and as yet your name does not imply Socialist approval of the administration. . . . We simply must have workers so trained if we are to build successfully in the future."[18] Cohen soon discovered that both Margold and Interior Secretary Harold Ickes were serious about the rights of minorities, whether Native Americans or African Americans or Jews.[19] Cohen stayed at Interior until 1947, acquiring a reputation as a passionate advocate for Native Americans—and also as someone who hired smart women like Charlotte Tuttle.[20]

A New Deal for Women

Tuttle was not the only woman in that "plague of young lawyers" descending on Washington in the 1930s, and Felix Cohen was not the only man hiring them. The top law schools had begun opening their doors to white women, but they gave alumnae little help in finding jobs. Private law firms, if they hired women at all, relegated them to departments like trusts and estates, "where all the clients were dead and no one would see you," explained one Columbia Law alumna.[21] By contrast, high scorers on the government's civil service exams were hard to reject based on their sex, and some of the men doing the hiring were relatively egalitarian. The National Labor Relations Board (NLRB), created in 1935 to enforce the Wagner Act's guarantee of workers' right to form unions, had a particularly impressive record of hiring women. Led by Thomas I. Emerson, the agency's Review Division hired enough women so that by 1939 women comprised 11 percent of its attorneys, when women were only 2 percent of all lawyers.[22]

Emerson is a good example of a consummate New Dealer whose commitments to the left, including women's emancipation, have been insufficiently appreciated. The first in his class at Yale Law School in 1931, Emerson turned down offers from the top law firms in order to specialize in civil liberties cases. His first assignment was to assist in defending the "Scottsboro boys," nine black Alabama teenagers sentenced to death for allegedly raping two white women. The case became an international cause célèbre and produced a landmark Supreme Court decision. Initially skeptical of Franklin Roosevelt, when Emerson saw that "the government was actually attempting some regulation of the economic structure," he went to Washington and was immediately hired by the brand-new and rapidly growing National Recovery Administration (NRA).[23] Emerson was so busy that he slept on couches for his first ten days in Washington. Within a few months, he was sharing what became one of the most famous "bachelor houses" of the New Deal. His roommates, all lawyers, were Leon Keyserling, then secretary to Senator Robert F. Wagner, Ambrose Doskow and Howard Westwood, both clerks to Supreme Court justices, and NRA employee James Allen. When Westwood left to marry Charlotte Tuttle, his room was filled by Abe Fortas, the future Supreme Court justice who began his career in the Agricultural Adjustment Administration.

While participating in the losing battle to enforce the NRA codes, Emerson discussed the development of the separate labor relations statute that became the Wagner Act over meals with its chief drafter, his roommate Leon Keyserling. In 1934 Emerson left the NRA to join the first National Labor Relations Board; by 1940 he would be the agency's associate general counsel.[24] In 1934 Emerson married Bertha Paret, a former officer of the Women's Trade Union League who herself worked for a series of New Deal agencies. Reflecting their shared passion for left causes, they spent their honeymoon in Scottsboro—and were almost run out of town by local whites who remembered his role in the trial. In his choice of spouse as well as in his hiring practices, Emerson favored smart, politically engaged women.[25]

Three such women who made the most of the opportunity to prove themselves at the NLRB were Ida Klaus, Margaret Bennett Porter, and Carol Agger. Ida Klaus was in the first class of women admitted to Columbia Law School in 1928 (she had been rejected based on her sex a few years earlier, but she persisted). Klaus had decided to be a lawyer while watching her mother fight the court system over her husband's estate. While working her way through college as a waitress, Klaus unionized her coworkers. At Columbia Law, she recalled, most of the male students were hostile, sometimes stomping their feet in class so that female students could not be heard (her classmate Felix Cohen was an exception, she noted). Klaus was hired at the NLRB in 1937, and in 1948 she became the agency's solicitor, which made her the highest-ranking female lawyer in the federal government.[26] Margaret Bennett Porter joined the NLRB on the recommendations of Jerome Frank and the former NLRB chair Francis Biddle, who described her as "unusually able with a liberal point of view, I should say, turned left." Back in 1929, she had been one of the students whose arrest for organizing New York garment workers was protested by Charlotte Tuttle. (The world of left feminists was not small, but their wide-ranging activism produced many points of intersection.) Bennett Porter graduated from Columbia Law School in 1932 and soon after that secretly joined the Communist Party.[27] Not as far to the left was Carol Agger, whom the NLRB hired straight out of Yale Law School in 1938. It may have helped her that Tom Emerson had roomed with her new husband, Abe Fortas, but Agger was highly qualified. Before finishing second in her class at Yale Law, she had earned a master's degree in economics from Wisconsin and high praise at the Resettlement Administration.[28] Klaus, Bennett Porter, and Agger all married other New Dealers. Apparently when those "bright young men" of the New Deal stayed up dancing, drinking, and debating, their partners were often bright young women with government jobs themselves.

Social insurance and public welfare, like labor relations, were fields with a large supply of credentialed and job-hungry women at a moment when new agencies were being created at a rapid pace. Like the NLRB, the Social Security Board earned a reputation for hospitality to professional women. In 1932, when Bernice Lotwin became one of the first women to graduate from the University of Wisconsin Law School, the state governor Philip La Follette advised her to go into government because private practice was "too tough" for a "girl" to get into. After growing up in her town's only Jewish family and graduating at the top of her undergraduate class at the state university, Lotwin made the *Wisconsin Law Review*, despite the hostility of professors who refused to call on her and male students who excluded her from study groups. Wisconsin was among the states with merit systems in place, and her high score on the civil service exam required the state to offer her a position. She became executive assistant to the commissioner of markets and advised Governor La Follette on consumer protection, until one of her former law professors recruited her to Washington for the National Recovery Administration. In 1935 she joined the legal staff of the Social Security Board (SSB), aided by her Wisconsin connections to Edwin Witte and Arthur Altmeyer. She helped draft the model state unemployment insurance bill and then traveled widely to promote federal-state cooperation in unemployment insurance. On those trips, employers often challenged her on the ground that a young woman could not understand business, but she found that the top-level men of the SSB and its legal division were "very supportive and impartial."[29] In 1942, Lotwin became associate general counsel to the War Manpower Commission, and in 1947, after her husband left the Treasury Department to practice law in New York, she became the Federal Security Administration's head attorney for the New York region, a job she held while raising three daughters.[30] Another woman who entered government service through the Social Security Board was Eleanor L. Dulles, an economist trained at Bryn Mawr, the London School of Economics, and Harvard. Hired in 1936 as the SSB's director of financial research, in 1942 she moved to the State Department, where she survived for twenty years as a career diplomat in spite of, rather than because of, the ascendance of her brothers Foster and Allen in the Eisenhower administration.[31]

As the example of Dulles indicates, not all the talented women who headed for Washington were lawyers. Dorothy Bailey of Minnesota did graduate work in social economy as a scholarship student at Bryn Mawr and then got a clerical job with the U.S. Employment Service (USES) in 1933. When the USES came under the merit system in 1934, she earned the second-highest score in her district, forcing the USES to promote her. Bailey held positions of increasing importance in the personnel training section until 1948, when her union activism sparked allegations of Communist sympathies that led to her suspension.[32] Pennsylvania native Mary Taylor did graduate work in economics at the University of Wisconsin and London School of Economics before joining the U.S. Department of Agriculture's Office of the Consumer Counsel. Taylor arrived in 1933 as assistant to the division chief, Frederic Howe, an older reformer who had fought for woman suffrage on the grounds that it would free men as well as women; not incidentally his wife, Marie Jenney Howe, was a founder of Heterodoxy, the Greenwich Village feminist group. Mary Taylor was a socialist and pacifist active in many left causes. When Donald Montgomery became Agriculture's consumer counsel, she worked closely with him on several controversial initiatives; they married in 1943, after he had left government to serve as an adviser to Walter Reuther at the United Auto Workers.[33] Then there was Eloise Bittel, who grew up in the Texas hill country, did graduate work at the University of Chicago, and got a job in 1936 under Jane Hoey at the new Bureau of Public Assistance in the Social Security Administration, where she met her husband Wilbur Cohen. Active in left initiatives such as the American League for Peace and Democracy and poll-tax repeal, Bittel Cohen also briefly worked for a Washington public housing agency.[34]

Many New Dealers did not hold permanent government jobs but took short-term consulting assignments, and women were prominent among them. Often they were academics, albeit in positions less secure than those of their male counterparts. The English-born socialist Eveline Burns earned her Ph.D. at the London School of Economics and in 1928 became the first woman appointed to Columbia University's graduate economics faculty. One of the many brains behind the nation's social insurance system, she was a consultant to the Committee on Economic Security and its successor the Social Security Board. After Columbia's Economics Department refused to tenure her, because her husband also was on the faculty or perhaps simply because she was a woman, she took full-time work with the National Resources Planning Board (1940–43) as chief of the Economic Security and Health Section, from which position she wrote an influential and controversial report proposing to expand the American welfare state.[35] Caroline Ware, a professor at Vassar, Sarah Lawrence, American University, and Howard University in succession (at least two other universities refused to hire her because of her sex), served on a series of consumer advisory committees with the National Recovery Administration, the Office of Price Administration, and the Council of Economic Advisers.[36]

Women whose husbands also worked for the federal government were likely to work on a temporary basis in order to get around a federal policy, in effect from 1932 through 1937, that prevented the government from employing both halves of a married couple. In practice the policy penalized married women, and feminists demanded its repeal. On the dubious ground that married women were not primary breadwinners, many private employers refused to hire them during the Great Depression. Thus the federal policy did not decrease the relative attractiveness of government jobs to women, but the rule could make their situation tenuous and often resulted in their being underpaid. Caroline Ware, whose husband was the government economist Gardiner Means, worried that if she tried to move from her temporary NRA position to a permanent one, it would make her "likely at any moment to be closed out under the rule against husband and wife both working. I had that experience with the Labor department [last] fall."[37] Lucy Kramer worked without pay for the Interior Department for several years under the supervision of her husband, Felix Cohen, and her anthropological expertise was essential to achievements for which he received the primary credit.[38]

Some administrators ignored the rule against employing couples but reduced their individual salaries. At the Federal Emergency Relief Administration, Harry Hopkins promoted both Elizabeth Wickenden and Tex Goldschmidt but without giving them raises, on the grounds that their combined salaries were sufficient. Goldschmidt recalled that "when Wicky or I was being suggested for promotion . . . we would get the title but were never paid commensurately. We were subjected to an informal 'means test' by Hopkins who kept adding our salaries together. . . . At times each of us would be directing staff that included individuals with double our own salary."[39]

White women broke into professional government jobs in larger numbers than black men, who in turn outnumbered black women. The most prestigious law schools rarely accepted black women until the 1940s, but social work schools did train some in the 1930s.[40] Those few black women who could secure top credentials had even more difficulty than white women in obtaining positions commensurate with their qualifications. Older black leaders like Mary McLeod Bethune, director of the Division of Negro Affairs in the National Youth Administration from 1936 to 1944, along with liberal whites like Harold Ickes and Clark Foreman at the Interior Department, worked hard to integrate New Deal agencies. Most of the beneficiaries were men, like the Harvard-educated lawyers William Hastie and Robert Weaver, but a few black women participated in the breakthrough, and most of them were decidedly to the left of center. Some agencies offered educated black women access to government jobs outside Washington: future feminist civil rights leaders Pauli Murray and Ella Baker, for example, both worked for the Workers Education Project (WEP) of the Works Progress Administration in New York City.[41] An initiative of the labor education pioneer Hilda Worthington Smith, the WEP hired unemployed teachers, many of whom hoped that education would encourage workers to join unions. Ella Baker and Pauli Murray concentrated on WEP outreach to black workers, and Baker became assistant supervisor of the Harlem office. Frances Harriet Williams, a Mt. Holyoke graduate with a master's degree from the New York School of Social Work and work experience with the Young Women's Christian Association, was the adviser on race relations for the Office of Price Administration (OPA) from 1940 to 1946. She and her white ally Caroline Ware claimed credit for the fact that 14 percent of OPA employees were black, compared with fewer than 1 percent on average at other agencies.[42]

As the example of the OPA suggests, professional women's opportunities in government did not disappear with the shift from welfare state to warfare state, nor did that shift immediately eliminate the attractiveness of government service to leftists. Women's policy influence decreased during World War II, a diminution that some of them commented on bitterly, but still, female professionals were better represented in government than historians' inattention to them might suggest.[43] The war mobilization produced new agencies that required expertise in labor relations and migration, housing, and price control, all fields with a large supply of female experts who leaned leftward. Particularly after the Hitler-Stalin pact of August 1939, many noncommunist leftists concluded that fighting fascism required them to drop their pacifism, and some of them joined the government in defense-related jobs.

Mary Dublin is a good example. In 1940 she left her position as head of a women's labor reform organization and moved to Washington to marry Leon Keyserling, the aide to Senator Robert Wagner whom she had met while lobbying to defend the Wagner Labor Relations Act. A socialist who had done graduate work in economics at Columbia and the London School of Economics, Dublin Keyserling served as hearings coordinator for the House Committee on National Defense Migration, chief of research and statistics at the Office of Civilian Defense, and chief of the Liberated Areas Division of the Foreign Economic Administration. In 1945 she was one of two women in the twenty-five-member U.S. delegation to the United Nations Relief and Rehabilitation Administration. After the war she became head of the International Economic Analysis Division of the Commerce Department's Office of International Trade. In 1964, after a period out of government service, Dublin Keyserling was appointed head of the U.S. Women's Bureau.[44]

Thus, the Depression and World War II years offered women unprecedented opportunities in government. In 1930, only about 15 percent of all federal employees were women, but by 1947 women comprised 24 percent of federal employees nationwide and 45 percent of federal employees in Washington. Most were clerical workers, but professional women found that the government was more likely than other employers to hire them.[45] Credentialed women found it easier to get a foot in the government's door because the creation of emergency agencies increased demand and the merit system made the hiring process more objective. In 1944, a woman who had joined the Treasury Department after a dozen years in private industry reported, "not only did I find the Government does not discriminate. It actually bends over backwards to give [women] opportunity . . . even in the traditionally male professions. It isn't a wartime conversion to womanpower either, as has been the case to date in industry, since I find it has been going on steadily for the past decade."[46]

The gender egalitarianism in federal agencies should not be overstated. Washington in the Roosevelt and Truman years was no feminist paradise. Goldschmidt recalled that Harry Hopkins "expressed concern that I might suffer from Wicky's increasingly conspicuous rise in the hierarchy." Hopkins's worry that Wickenden's rapid ascent would hurt her husband is a reminder that New Dealers did not always escape the assumption that marriage was a hierarchical relationship—in which the husband should be on top. Jacob Baker, who had brought Goldschmidt and Wickenden to Washington, later remarked to an FBI agent that Wickenden was the "dominant member of the family."[47] Even at the NLRB, Ida Klaus recalled, "the women got the little jobs and on promotions they didn't fare so well."[48] Subordinates, male and female, often resented female supervisors. Eleanor Dulles declared that to be a woman in government "you have to work ten times as hard—and even then it takes much skill to paddle around the various taboos. But it is fun to see how far you can get in spite of being a woman."[49] Some liberal men were unabashedly sexist. Tom Corcoran, the Frankfurter protégé who became one of the New Deal's inner circle, liked to brag that he had never recommended a woman for a position above the rank of secretary. Corcoran's boast suggests, however, that he saw himself holding the line against the general trend. Furthermore, as Elizabeth Wickenden was pleased to point out, his claim was false because he once recommended her for a job.[50] Leon Keyserling theoretically supported women's equality but did not always practice what he preached. He was unenthusiastic about admitting women to Washington's Cosmos Club, for example (ironically, not long after his death, his wife was among the first women admitted to the club).[51]

New Deal women met resistance, not only from male peers, but also from male and female administrators who valued women's abilities but thought giving them top positions was too expensive politically. Roosevelt's appointment of Frances Perkins as secretary of labor in 1933 provoked outrage from the right and from the American Federation of Labor. Labor Department official Isador Lubin believed that the reason Roosevelt did not put Perkins in charge of the new social security program in 1935 was that sexists in Congress did not like her. Perkins herself did not dare appoint Clara Beyer to head the Labor Department's Division of Labor Standards, so Beyer effectively ran it from behind the scenes for several decades. Josephine Roche, former assistant secretary to the Treasury, had widespread backing in 1939 to head the new Federal Security Agency, but Eleanor Roosevelt agreed with her husband that "it should be a man."[52] That same year, Elizabeth Wickenden was crushed when Aubrey Williams, her boss at the National Youth Administration, reneged on his promise to promote her to deputy administrator, on the grounds that the position could not go to a woman.[53]

Despite these real and painful limitations on women's ability to advance to the very top, the fact remains that many New Dealers departed from the old guard in their recognition of female talent and willingness to use it, at least in the middle ranks, where women would not be too visible. Just as a few white administrators were particularly courageous in hiring African Americans, so did the open-mindedness of certain male administrators enable some female professionals to flourish and prove their abilities, in the process inspiring other women and converting other men. "It was a New Deal for women, really," Charlotte Tuttle Lloyd Walkup recalled.[54]

THE MAKING OF THE NEW DEAL'S "LEFT FRINGE"

Not all leftists who entered government in the 1930s and early 1940s were feminists, and not all the women who fought sexual discrimination to secure professional degrees and government careers were leftists. But the overlap was substantial. Many of these young intellectuals shared a set of experiences that encouraged them to question all kinds of orthodoxy, including traditional assumptions about "woman's place." They came of age during the 1920s, when the pre–World War I sexual radicalism of the Greenwich Village bohemians spread more widely through the urban middle class, albeit with some blunting of its feminist edge. Indeed, several of the young leftists who became New Dealers were the children of the radicals of the 1910s, for whom "questions of sexuality and sex roles merged with those of class equality."[55] Val Lorwin, a socialist who worked in the Labor and State departments, was the son of the distinguished economist Lewis Lorwin and Rose Strunsky, a socialist-feminist writer like her better-known sister, Anna Strunsky Walling. Nathaniel Weyl, who briefly worked in the Agricultural Adjustment Administration while a member of the Communist Party, was the son of Bertha Poole, a socialist labor organizer and writer, and Walter Weyl, a founding editor of the *New Republic*. Others had fathers who were prominent progressive academics or mothers who were settlement house workers, or both.[56]

Most of the mothers and many of the fathers were interested in feminism, including but not limited to supporting woman suffrage. As one historian explains, "throughout the left intelligentsia, the emancipated woman stood at the symbolic center of a program for cultural regeneration. . . . freedom of thought and action and 'the removal of barriers between the sexes' went hand in hand."[57] There were exceptions. Lucy Kramer observed that her father-in-law, Morris Raphael Cohen, was certainly not the source of the feminism of her husband, Felix Cohen. Charlotte Tuttle recalled that her father was still "late Victorian in his view of women," even though he advocated civil rights for blacks and Jews. Charles Tuttle was no antifeminist, however. His wife persuaded him to vote for woman suffrage, and he supported his daughter's wish to attend law school.[58] One thing that many young leftists who joined the New Deal had in common, then, was having been raised in families in which radical views, including ones about gender relations, were at least debated, if not always fully embraced.

Some of the leftists streaming into the civil service in the 1930s had been influenced by their professors, although that factor may not have been as important as family background.[59] Many of the female undergraduates were exposed to progressive ideas at selective women's colleges such as Vassar, Barnard, Bryn Mawr, and Smith, which all had small but vital left-feminist presences on the faculty. At Vassar, students could find role models in Caroline Ware in economic history, her friend Helen Lockwood in English, and Hallie Flanagan in experimental theater. The writer Mary McCarthy later described Lockwood's renowned course in critical reading of the contemporary press as "the scene, almost like a camp meeting, of many a compulsory transformation, as hitherto dutiful Republican daughters turned into Socialists and went forth to spread the gospel." (McCarthy admitted she had never taken the course.)[60]

But even women who had excelled at the best women's colleges had to fight for admission to the most prestigious graduate programs, and not only in the field of law. In one advanced mathematics course at Harvard, the future anthropologist Ruth Benedict, who had studied under Franz Boas at Barnard, "had to sit in a closet with the door open so as not to contaminate the [male] undergraduates."[61] Perhaps Harvard was right to worry about contamination, because when women were admitted to those stellar graduate schools, their very presence stirred debate over women's status on and off campus. Many future New Dealers attended graduate school at Columbia, Harvard, Wisconsin, and the London School of Economics, each of which had a few leftist instructors. Some, like Rexford Tugwell, Eveline Burns, and Thomas Blaisdell of Columbia, were hired by New Deal agencies and in turn hired former students. Occasionally the direction was reversed; Vassar's Hallie Flanagan became director of the Federal Theater Project because her former student Wickenden, by then an assistant to Harry Hopkins, recommended her for the job.[62] Relations between students and faculty thus could nurture radical ideas and create networks that spread into government.

Contrary to recurring suggestions that leftist faculty dominated college campuses, they were in the minority everywhere. Many would have sympathized with Caroline Ware's complaint that the Vassar administration was hiring conventional thinkers and "steering the college firmly down the path of the genteel tradition, aided and abetted by the old guard." She also was exasperated that her interdisciplinary interests were constantly thwarted by "the Chinese wall around the economics department."[63] Ware moved to Sarah Lawrence, where she befriended the new economics instructor Mary Dublin, and later to a permanent position at Howard University, where she became a mentor to Pauli Murray. Wherever Ware taught, she made an impression. Elizabeth Wickenden and Charlotte Tuttle, both Vassar class of 1931, cited Ware and her "sociological method" as an inspiration.[64]

Dynamic leftist professors like Ware exercised an influence disproportionate to their numbers in the 1930s because the Great Depression seemed to bear out their teaching. Serious-minded students gravitated to those who could help explain "the crisis of the old order."[65] Ware's Harvard dissertation on the history of cotton textile manufacturing in New England had won a major prize for its innovative methods and acute insights. By the time the dissertation was published in 1931, it seemed that prescience was another of its virtues. Ware's study examined not only the evolution of management but also the lives of women and men of the changing working class. She showed how structural forces such as competition and the availability of immigrant labor led to the formation over time of an exploited, relatively permanent working class. As the historian Ellen Fitzpatrick explains, Ware's study concluded that

> industrial development had produced "a new alignment of classes and a wider gulf between rich and poor than America before had known." New corporate organizations and unprecedented forms of wealth "made of the capitalist a giant in the community whom others served and feared." In Ware's view, these economic arrangements had profound political implications. "Could political democracy encompass industrial autocracy, could it harbor a working class and a moneyed class and survive?" The answer to such questions, Ware concluded in the late 1920s, "still lies in the future."[66]

In the 1930s, Ware's students were fascinated by her invitation to write working-class history. A pioneering social historian, she taught students to mine unconventional sources such as payroll, company store, and census records for insight into the lives of non-elite Americans.[67] Ware's scholarship convinced her, and many of her students, that ordinary citizens would need to act collectively in order to sustain democracy in a capitalist economy. As an instructor at various schools for workers, Ware taught about the benefits of unionization, and later she encouraged housewives to organize as consumers.

The Great Depression was ultimately the most important factor in the emergence of a cohort of young radicals on college campuses and then in New Deal agencies. Often at the top of their classes at highly competitive institutions, these students concluded, with or without the assistance of instructors like Ware, that old orthodoxies did not fit the evidence before their eyes.[68] Sometimes students' personal experiences—of material deprivation or of some form of discrimination—informed their critique of the status quo. Even those who occupied relatively privileged positions, however, became attuned to the imperfections of the American economic, political, and social systems. Searching for explanations of capitalism's international crisis, they studied economics, history, and sociology and concluded that free-market doctrines were to blame. Any of them could have written the piece in which Mary Dublin enumerated the "dismal inadequacies" of laissez-faire economics. In attacking government spending and taxation without acknowledging the market's failures, she argued, orthodox economists offered "excuses for inaction rather than preparation to help stave off the troubles of the modern world."[69] These confident young people believed that they could and should help remedy those troubles. They undertook research on government policies such as minimum wage, public works, public housing, and social insurance for the unemployed, elderly, and sick, often through comparative analysis of other countries' approaches.[70]

In the context of the economic crisis and resurgent threats of war, a vocal and growing segment of students across the nation came to see the dominant values espoused on campus as foolish or worse. Long before the better-known protest campaigns of the 1960s, a student movement swept the United States in the 1930s, and a striking number of its alumni ended up in government service. Student radicals criticized the influence of fraternities, football, and mandatory military training, as well as college efforts to regulate sexual behavior. Campus newspaper editors voiced controversial opinions, not only on campus policies, but also on national and international events. College administrators added fuel to the fire by censoring student editors, as in the case of Felix Cohen's campaign against military training at the City College of New York. Mary Dublin upset Barnard College officials in 1929 with editorials condemning police raids on birth control offices and criticizing the suppression of a novel about lesbianism.[71]

Several future New Dealers participated in a widely publicized free speech conflict in the spring of 1932, when Columbia University expelled the campus newspaper editor, Reed Harris, for a series of controversial articles, including one that challenged the privileged position of college athletics. Tex Goldschmidt and his allies in the Social Problems Club called a strike to demand Harris's reinstatement. On a warm spring day, in front of several thousand people, Goldschmidt tried to tie a black crepe gag on the statue of Alma Mater to symbolize the university's repression of free speech. A riot broke out, in which Goldschmidt was egged and then dragged down by a "flying wedge of be-sweathered and noticeably husky gentlemen." In the ensuing tug-of-war over the strip of black cloth, the athletes prevailed after dragging Howard Westwood a few hundred feet. Press accounts played up Reed Harris's attack on "King Football" and the rowdy reaction it elicited from the campus "athletic crowd," but Harris's pro-labor views, and his right to express them, also were at issue. Harris had criticized the university for paying low wages to student cafeteria workers, and he had supported a student delegation to assist striking coal miners in Harlan County, Kentucky. After the campus strike, the Columbia administration reinstated Harris in exchange for his promise to resign from the editor's post. The administration also agreed to investigate conditions in the cafeteria. This small victory demonstrated to the students, as well as to surprised elders on the left, that middle-class young people were capable of effective political action. Long after the eggs were washed off Columbia's Alma Mater, many of the protesters remained activists, and some of them entered government service. Reed Harris himself became assistant director of the Federal Writers Project and later director of the Voice of America program.[72]

The student movement began in New York City, but after the spring of 1932 it spread rapidly to campuses across the nation, even in the more conservative South.[73] In Texas that summer, Goldschmidt spoke about "the New Student Movement" from the University of Texas radio station: "The idea of keeping students away from the world, of cloistering them like medieval monks, of teaching them abstractions, has kept this vast force dammed. . . . But we are beginning to see leaks in the dam and students' awakening to the fact that football and fraternities are secondary . . . and to a consciousness of their power."[74] The National Student League (NSL) departed from the League for Industrial Democracy, the group founded in 1921 for student socialists, in putting political action ahead of study groups. NSL leader Rob Hall also recognized that organizing around civil liberties violations (on and off campus) was a way to mobilize students who might not be drawn in by anticapitalist rhetoric. Although Communists like Hall provided key leadership, the NSL was not a "Communist front" group: the Communist Party did not dominate it and in the early years ignored it. Communists, Socialists, and unaffiliated students cooperated in the NSL, for a time avoiding the sectarianism of the adult left. The NSL's formation also revitalized the LID, which adopted a more activist approach in the face of competition from the NSL. In 1935 the NSL and LID merged into the American Student Union. The student movement had adopted a coalition-based approach well before Communist Party leaders called for a "Popular Front against fascism" in 1935.[75]

As student activists, many women and men who ended up in the Roosevelt administration participated in events that can be seen as rites of passage for a generation of left intellectuals. Actions in support of the labor movement were common. Some students joined in organizing workers, as suggested by the 1929 arrest of Margaret Bennett Porter and others for distributing pro-union leaflets to garment workers, and by Charlotte Tuttle's protest of those arrests at a garment workers' rally. While Tex Goldschmidt went to Kentucky with eighty men and women from various northeastern campuses, others, like the future Commerce Department economist Mary Dublin, expressed their solidarity in writing. To her, the events in Harlan County—the "domination by employers of all branches of local government as well as the production of knowledge by media and educational institutions"—suggested that capitalism readily yielded to fascism. Like the ten famous writers who had visited a few months earlier, the eighty-member student delegation was greeted with violence. The students were harassed by police deputies and angry crowds, taunted with anti-Semitic slurs (whether or not they were Jewish), threatened at gunpoint, and beaten up on their buses as they were escorted out of state. Although they were prevented from delivering material aid, the students won political support for the strikers by generating media coverage and by sending delegations to Kentucky and Tennessee officials and to Congress. The treatment they had received, they argued, was part of the same "reign of terror" that oppressed the coal miners.[76] Back in New York, Mary Dublin wrote that company towns such as Harlan County's were "a vacuum jar for capitalist institutions," in which one could analyze "the supposed distinction between business and government . . . and the concept of free individual choice, which is commonly assigned a central place in our economic system."[77] The Harlan expedition inspired other student initiatives around the country. Wilbur Cohen, a University of Wisconsin student and future social security expert, filled a truck with donated food, picked up a friend at the University of Chicago, and tried to deliver the supplies to striking coal miners in southern Illinois.[78]

Another left rite of passage in the late 1920s and the 1930s was visiting the Soviet Union to see the socialist experiment firsthand. Thousands of Americans toured the Soviet Union, through American travel groups such as the Open Road, which coordinated with Intourist, the Soviet tourism agency.[79] Those whose impressions are on record were not uncritical. They admired some Soviet achievements or objectives, but they also recognized—increasingly so over the course of the 1930s—that they were seeing only what their guides wanted them to see, and that the Bolshevik Revolution had eliminated neither poverty nor repression.[80] The authoritarianism that James and Nancy Fraenkel Wechsler saw during their 1937 visit to the Soviet Union hastened their departure from the Communist Party. "Jimmy" had been politicized as a freshman journalist covering the Columbia student strike over Reed Harris's expulsion, and he succeeded Harris as editor of the campus newspaper. He met Nancy at an anti-Nazi rally in 1933; together they joined and then quit the Communist Party. The daughter of a famous civil liberties lawyer, Nancy became a top-notch government lawyer, working for the OPA and other agencies before serving as counsel for Truman's Committee on Civil Rights in 1946 and 1947. Jimmy spent over thirty years as editor of the then-liberal *New York Post*.[81] Anticommunists would later ridicule the American tourists to Russia as fanatical propagandists or starry-eyed dupes, but to people interested in economic planning and social reform, the desire to see for oneself how the experiment was coming along was reasonable and did not indicate wholesale approval of Soviet communism.[82]

Part of the fascination with the Soviet Union was that it was perceived to have achieved a revolution in gender relations as well as in class relations. Young left feminists believed, too optimistically, that in the process of granting women's political and economic equality, the Russian Revolution also had abolished the moral double standard for the sexes that protected male property rights in women. After spending a month in the Soviet Union in 1931, Elizabeth Wickenden reported that Russians thought American attitudes toward sex were "absurd," and they were mystified by Americans' fears of the "nationalization of women" under Bolshevism. In Russia, Wickenden wrote, "women are the equal in every respect of men. Birth control is legal. A pregnant woman receives four months' vacation from her work with full pay and a nursing mother is allowed time from her work to feed her child. No distinction is made between legitimate and illegitimate children." Wickenden associated Russia's disruption of patriarchal sexual control with its other feminist public policies. She reported that women and men received comparable pay rates, and that worker housing featured communal kitchens and "large, airy nurseries" staffed by trained attendants. Wickenden concluded that the Russian Revolution, despite its failings, seemed "the ideal way in which to achieve equality of opportunity and status for men and women."[83]

SEXUAL AND RACIAL MODERNISM ON THE LEFT FRINGE

As in the 1910s, members of the left intelligentsia of the 1930s were thinking about more than economic relations. They debated how economic hierarchies produced, and in turn were buttressed by, racial and sexual hierarchies. The Socialist Party had supported woman suffrage and black suffrage when the mainstream parties did not, and in the 1910s and 1920s it attracted many women and some black activists. The Communists promoted absolute equality of the races and sexes. Though their practice did not always live up to their tenets, the egalitarianism attracted many members and was admired by others who did not join.[84] Young people especially were inspired by the left's egalitarianism. The NSL's 1932 program included a demand for the abolition of racial and sexual discrimination on campus. The student movement did not prioritize feminist demands, but it did offer women leadership opportunities. Women outnumbered men, for example, as LID officers in the New York region.[85]

Men as well as women responded to the left critique of female subordination and the lack of sexual autonomy that went with it. As a student at Columbia in November 1929, Tex Goldschmidt had an epistolary argument with his father back in Texas about the moral double standard for the sexes. His father criticized him for having sexual intercourse with a woman "of his own set," suggesting that he had harmed the girl and her family. Goldschmidt disagreed: "the almost intrinsic value heretofore placed upon virginity crashed as fast as the market. . . . I would defend my position . . . before anyone—believing it to be—with almost fanatical zeal—the only true, good, healthy, normal and decent position possible." He elaborated that "in olden days when daughters had a real commercial value (wore their chastity belts, etc.) such an act as mine might have been considered thievery . . . but a girl of [his lover's] age is certainly giving what is hers—and if there is another claim to it something is radically wrong here." Goldschmidt's father responded by predicting that in five years Goldschmidt would refuse to marry a woman who had had sexual relations with someone else.[86] When Goldschmidt married Elizabeth Wickenden in 1933, he almost certainly defied his father's prediction. Wickenden had written of enjoying "the same social rights as my male contemporaries," which included "bachelor quarters" and "traveling about the world at will." She also had protested the "man-made conception that the unmarried woman must remain inviolate as a nun."[87] Goldschmidt was smitten.

Goldschmidt was attracted to Wickenden's independence and intellect, not just to her sexual radicalism. Before they met, she negatively reviewed an article called "Spinster Factories." That article lamented the low marriage rate of college alumnae and proposed revising the college curriculum for women to make them more marriageable. In her review, Wickenden retorted that the fault lay "not with the education of women but with the attitude . . . of the men they must marry." Most men, she wrote, still prefer the "clinging vine. . . . Even today it is a rare young man who will admit in practice as well as in theory the equality of women." Until men adapt, "It is natural indeed that young women who enjoy a useful, independent life doing the work they like and are trained to do should hesitate to marry a man who feels, even vaguely, that a woman's work is home-making and that he as the superior creature should watch over and protect her."[88]

Wickenden found one such "rare young man" in Goldschmidt. On the day of their marriage he wrote to her parents, "Wick knows, perhaps better than most of us her age, just what she wants; and she wants to remain an individual, a person in her own right; and I do and always shall admire and respect that desire. Both of us want to do things, and we feel that the other can help each to do them. . . ." Wickenden modified the wedding vows to make them identical for bride and groom and to omit references to God. She also kept her own name. When she hesitated to have children, Goldschmidt promised to do at least his share of child rearing, and their son recalls that he did so, taking him and his two sisters out on the weekends so his mother could write. The marriage lasted sixty-seven years, until Goldschmidt's death in 2000.[89]

The Wickenden-Goldschmidt relationship illustrates how young left-ists who would influence the New Deal saw themselves as challenging all kinds of orthodoxy, not just an economic system. They defied the taboo on premarital sex; they rejected the usual wedding conventions. Wicken-den and Goldschmidt eschewed the spectacle of the father handing his daughter over to her husband by getting married in the office of a Tam-many Hall judge. Lucy Kramer wanted a black wedding dress.[90] Many leftists—and not just the men—had several lovers before they married. Divorces and remarriages were common, indicating high expectations of marriage as well as lack of deference to the institution itself.[91] The social-ist journalist Mary Taylor took lovers across Europe and had intended never to marry, until she met the Scripps-Howard columnist Rodney Dutcher, who divorced in order to marry her. (Lawrence Todd, the cor-respondent for the Soviet news agency Tass, said of Taylor, "no female in the Eastern United States can match her for sexual allure.") After Dutcher died, Taylor married her Agriculture Department colleague Don Mont-gomery, who himself was divorced from a Communist first wife. As those examples suggest, these sex radicals were heterosexual, although they were more tolerant of homosexuals than the general public.[92]

The intertwined relationship histories of Leon Keyserling, Catherine Bauer, and Mary Dublin further illuminate the gender egalitarianism and heterosociality of left circles in and around New Deal agencies. As a Harvard student, Keyserling had complained to his father of the dif-ficulty of finding a woman who had both beauty and brains; after he moved Washington to work for Senator Wagner, however, he had better luck. He dated Bernice Lotwin, and they remained lifelong friends after she married the progressive government lawyer Bernard Bernstein and he married Mary Dublin.[93] In the interval between Lotwin and Dublin, Keyserling had a long, intense relationship with the public housing expert Catherine Bauer. Widely regarded as the quintessential "New Woman," Bauer was an outdoorswoman who drank, smoked, and wore her hair short. After she graduated from Vassar in 1926, she scandalized her middle-class New Jersey parents by living alone on the Left Bank of Paris, associating with a bohemian intellectual crowd, and having affairs with men of diverse nationalities. Relocating to Greenwich Village, she joined a circle of radical writers and social critics and turned her interest in city planning into a career, with the help of her married lover Lewis Mum-ford. Her 1934 book *Modern Housing*, which contrasted European poli-cies with the United States' failure to provide high-quality housing for the working class, made her an international star and became the bible of the U.S. public housing movement. Working with labor groups, she helped build demand for a federal housing program, and then she helped draft it and get it through Congress. As an employee of the resulting U.S.

Figure 1.3. By the time this photo was taken in the 1940s, Catherine Bauer was a leading advocate of high-quality public housing. Courtesy of the Bancroft Library, University of California, Berkeley.

Housing Authority from 1937 to 1940, Bauer also helped to implement it. Her close colleague, the socialist labor leader John Edelman, offers this description: "With the profile of a hawk, she was not a conventional beauty, but she had an enormous amount of sex appeal—which she was perfectly willing to use on susceptible senators. She had a lucid, sparkling mind coupled with almost inexhaustible energy that enabled her to work sixteen hours a day, day after day, and she had unswervable drive."[94]

Bauer met Keyserling during the push to get housing legislation through Congress in 1936, and they began a close friendship that lasted, despite occasional policy disagreements, until her death in 1964. Well over one hundred letters from him survive in her papers, and a smaller number of her letters to him recently were added to his family's archival collection. In addition to a behind-the-scenes view of U.S. housing policy, the letters convey the intense physical and political passions shared by Bauer and Keyserling. During the early, intimate phase of their relationship, they briefly lived in the same boardinghouse, and for a time they talked about marriage. When Bauer went to Scandinavia on a Guggenheim Fellowship to study housing in 1936, she wrote longingly from her ship: "Just when I knew I loved you more than anything . . . why had I gone away? . . . Your physical presence haunted me like a ghost."[95] Three years later, as she headed off to the Soviet Union for research, Keyserling urged "Kitten" to avoid her tendency to overwork and to "come back looking like the filling of an Elizabeth Hawes ensemble." Hawes was an avant-garde fashion designer and emerging left-feminist writer; Keyserling's reference is another example of male New Dealers' attraction to women of the left.[96]

Keyserling's letters to Bauer show him striving to take a modern view of sex and courtship, in which jealousy was considered unenlightened. Their romance continued on and off even as they dated others, until both married other people in 1940.[97] If Keyserling's new wife Mary Dublin resented his relationship with Bauer, it is not apparent in her warm letters to the latter. Dublin may have known Bauer already, because the women had two other "beaux" in common. The wealthy environmentalist Robert Marshall wooed Dublin in 1931, and he was courting Bauer not long before his sudden early death in 1939. Bauer and Dublin each had a romance with the architect and public housing advocate Oscar Stonorov, and they remained friends with him after he married a third woman.[98] Meanwhile, before and after meeting Keyserling, Dublin dated several prominent men besides Marshall and Stonorov, including the socialist labor journalist Paul R. Porter and the left-liberal lawyer Ambrose Doskow, who happened to be Keyserling's housemate.[99] Close platonic friendships between former lovers, and spousal tolerance of those friendships, were part of the sexually modern code on the New Deal's left fringe.

Related to their willingness to question the sanctity of marriage, or at least the convention that a woman should have only one sexual partner in her life, many left feminists were skeptical of organized religion. They thought that religion functioned historically as a tool for maintaining social order, including inequality. In addition to eliminating references to God from her wedding vows, Wickenden would later write "A Plea for Tolerance," which lamented that atheism was being equated with political subversion. Goldschmidt, too, was an atheist, which he attributed to his mother's influence.[100] Another freethinking couple was Thomas C. Blaisdell and Catherine Maltby Blaisdell, who married in 1921. He was a socialist instructor of economics at Columbia before serving at several New Deal agencies. She was active in the leftist League of Women Shoppers, and during the 1940s she worked for the Office of Civilian Defense and then the United Nations Relief and Rehabilitation Administration.[101] In 1931 Catherine convinced a publisher to omit a picture of children saying bedtime prayers from a forthcoming children's book, explaining that "a great many children today are brought up without ever hearing of God and religion. Mine are among them. To introduce a small child to the idea of an omnipotent Father may easily rob him of his self-dependence. He may form the habit of leaning on some person or power instead of growing up in the belief that he alone must meet and solve his problems as they arise."[102] When ultraconservatives complained that leftists were godless and sexually depraved, they were exaggerating, but they were responding to what historian Robert Cohen calls the left's relatively "open, meritocratic, and cosmopolitan vision." Even the many leftists whose politics were infused by religiosity—whether as Quakers, Unitarians, Lutherans, Catholics, or Jews—socialized and sometimes married across religious lines.[103]

Conservatives also were onto something, although again they went too far, when they warned that leftists were trying to remake the country by promoting interracial sex.[104] Sex across the color line, especially when it paired white women with men of color, challenged white male supremacy at its core. Few white radicals who ended up in government service are known to have had interracial liaisons, but they did push to integrate government workplaces and social functions, which required confronting the assumption that black men should never supervise or even be in proximity to white women. Federal antilynching legislation was a top priority for black civil rights organizations, and white leftists and liberals joined in the unsuccessful effort to convince Roosevelt to push such a measure. Progressive whites increasingly recognized that southern hyperbole about black rapists helped keep white women, as well as all blacks, in their places, and that it also inhibited poorer whites from challenging the southern elite. Palmer Weber, the campus newspaper editor at the University of Virginia in the mid-1930s, wrote editorials challenging the myth of the black rapist and urging the university to admit blacks. Weber joined the New Deal in 1940, serving on the staff of several liberal congressmen before being forced out of government because of his former membership in the Communist Party.[105]

Within the Roosevelt administration, small but vocal groups of blacks, radicals, and southern liberals worked against race discrimination, in the federal bureaucracy and in the national polity and economy. Clark Foreman and Tex Goldschmidt, both white southerners, helped write an influential 1938 report arguing that the South was the nation's "number one economic problem." The published report was mild compared with early drafts, which took a class analysis of race to argue that white supremacy held down both black and white wages in the South, in turn depressing wages and undermining unionization efforts nationwide. By then, even liberals who were not passionate about racial justice had come to recognize they would have to "buck the Bourbons" who ran the South in order to take control of the Democratic Party. White liberals thus for a time joined with black and white leftists in and out of government in an attempt to democratize the South by eliminating poll taxes (which reduced voting by women and poor whites as well as blacks), supporting the organization of sharecroppers and other southern workers, and pressing for a national minimum wage to raise southern wages.[106]

Figure 1.4. Lucy Kramer (center, in regalia) with members of the Oglala Sioux at Pine Ridge Reservation, S.D., probably August 1935. Courtesy of the Felix S. and Lucy Kramer Cohen Photograph Collection.

The antiracism of some leftists developed out of an orientation toward the U.S. West. Intellectual interest in indigenous cultures expanded during and after the 1920s, partly because of the influence of the anthropologist Franz Boas and his female students at Barnard. A radical pacifist who believed in the "inherent equality of all peoples," Boas inspired in left feminists such as Ruth Benedict, Gene Weltfish, and Lucy Kramer an appreciation of Native American cultures and a commitment to showing that racism was not supported by good science. Boas's books would be burned in Nazi Germany, and after his death in 1942 Benedict and Weltfish would take up the mantle of discrediting Nazi science, writing an

Figure 1.5. Felix S. Cohen, Lucy Kramer, and their daughter Gene on her third birthday, 1942. Courtesy of the Felix S. and Lucy Kramer Cohen Photograph Collection.

important antiracist pamphlet for use in training the U.S. armed forces.[107] During the New Deal, Lucy Kramer and Felix Cohen tried to make U.S. policy more respectful of Native American cultures. They named their first daughter Gene, for Weltfish, and they carried her on an Oglala Sioux cradle board.[108]

Felix Cohen's boss at Interior, Harold Ickes, came to his racial liberalism after observing the treatment of Native Americans in New Mexico. Other western-oriented antiracists were concerned, like their southern counterparts, with how agricultural interests exploited labor, whether white, Filipino, or Mexican. The lawyer and writer Carey McWilliams worked for the National Labor Relations Board before publishing a best seller on the exploitation of migrant farmworkers in California.[109] The photographer Dorothea Lange and her husband, the agricultural economist Paul S. Taylor, worked for several government agencies over the course of careers oriented toward improving the lives of farmworkers and small farmers of all races.[110]

The left and right thus clashed along several axes during the 1930s. Leftists opposed exploitation of workers, of course, but they also criticized male domination of women, white domination of other races, and the use of repressive tactics to support those and other hierarchies. Many leftists lumped those oppressions together under the umbrella term "fascism." As early as 1932, student activists Mary Dublin and Joseph Lash were describing the U.S. South as fascist. After California authorities violently suppressed strikers in 1934 and collaborated with the Hearst press in blocking Upton Sinclair's gubernatorial bid, Caroline Ware asked a friend whether she was ready to "watch California go fascist."[111] Many leftists, including some in government, joined the antifascist American League for Peace and Democracy or groups that supported the Spanish resistance to fascism. But fascism was a term that resonated with injustice at home, as well as abroad. As the historian Daniel Geary observes, antifascism from the early 1930s through the war was a "political sensibility . . . focused on domestic events as well as international ones; it cannot be reduced to a cover for the Communist party line . . . it bridged gaps between Communists, New Dealers, and independent radicals." Questioning the standard interpretation that the left was primarily focused on class in the 1930s and only later mobilized around race issues, Geary shows that antifascism "constituted an early version of multiculturalism, that is, an antiracist sensibility focused on Mexican Americans, Asian Americans, and Native Americans as well as African Americans."[112]

That advance in understanding the antifascist left of the 1930s and 1940s should be extended even further to include recognition of its feminism. Opposition to fascism reflected alarm over its policies toward women as well as toward minorities and labor. Especially after Hitler declared in 1934 that the German woman's world should be *Kinder, Küche, und Kirche* (children, kitchen, and church), American feminists often tried to delegitimize discriminatory policies by calling them fascist. In 1935, when the University of Wyoming broke an employment contract with Caroline Ware after learning that she was married, Ware waged a national campaign for married women's employment rights. She gave the press a copy of her blistering response to the university's policy against hiring married women: "This measure is, in reality, a move to relegate women to the position to which Hitler has openly consigned them in Germany and to which American Hitlers are pushing them, under cover of 'emergency' action." To the university's claim that its rule was intended to "spread employment," she retorted that the university was an educational institution, "not a work-relief organization." Because its responsibility was to the students and not to the unemployed of Wyoming, it was obligated to select faculty strictly on a basis of teaching capacity. With respect to the university's female students, Ware asked, "are you condemning these girls to celibacy, or are you wasting the State's money training them for positions from which your actions are designed to exclude them?" Ware accused the university's trustees of lining up "the once progressive state of Wyoming with the dictators of the old world who are deliberately seeking to reestablish a mediaeval society. . . . assigning to women the role of bearing soldiers for new wars." Ware did not in the end sue the university, but she did generate nationwide newspaper coverage, and many others would follow her lead in linking sexual discrimination with "Hitlerism."[113]

As Ware's example suggests, although the leftist women in and around the Roosevelt administration were not primarily identified with a women's movement, they were feminists.[114] More often than not, they kept their own names after marriage. Ware described her decision to keep her own name by saying that when she married Gardiner Means in 1927, she had more of a reputation than he did and she did not want to lose it by taking his name. "Then he got more reputation than I, and I didn't want to ride on his coattails. And then we were about fifty-fifty and it didn't matter."[115] Left feminists took it as a given that women should enjoy the same political rights and educational and professional opportunities as men. They opposed sex-based wage differentials and restrictions on married women's employment. In outlining a public works program in 1935, Elizabeth Wickenden insisted that "women should not be discriminated against on any projects."[116] They believed, however, that equal rights with men of their own group would not solve the problems of the majority of women who were poor or working class.

This left variant of feminism avoided positions that might be perceived as prioritizing gender equality above class justice. Left feminists of the 1930s through 1950s were repelled by "equal rights" feminism as they understood it. The word "feminist" was then associated with the National Woman's Party (NWP), which after helping win woman suffrage in 1920 had devoted itself single-mindedly to promoting an equal rights amendment (ERA). By the 1930s the NWP's professed neutrality on all issues other than sexual discrimination put it in the same camp as anti-labor forces. Women on the left did not call themselves "feminists" or support the ERA, because they rejected the individualistic implications of the NWP brand of feminism.[117]

Young women on the left also worried about the stereotypical association between feminism and man-hating. Calling for a new word to describe "the present-day aspirations of women," Elizabeth Wickenden wrote that "there was a tendency on the part of the early pioneering feminists to assume that they were wresting certain rights and privileges from their rivals and enemies, the male sex." She suggested wryly that younger women "weaned on Freud" were unwilling to help their egos at the expense of their libidos, and she urged women to shatter stereotypes by proving that they could be both smart and charming to men.[118] She also asserted the value of "passive feminism" for women "whose talents lie along other lines than reform and protest." By excelling in some chosen activity, women would "prove their worth and equality not only to men, but also lead the way for the more conservative of their own sex."[119]

The focus of these young female New Dealers on demonstrating their competence and getting along with men was a deliberate strategy that they believed was suited to their moment. This strategy had its pitfalls, because the effort to avoid confronting men could undermine the women's goal of proving their abilities. Cultivating one's appearance and tiptoeing around male egos took a lot of energy. Bernice Lotwin Bernstein recalled, "certain men had great difficulty taking supervision and direction from a woman. . . . I tried to be very sensitive and understanding in my relationship with them."[120] Most of these women prided themselves on being "team workers" who did not "look for glory" and were content to have influence behind the scenes. They believed that the hypercompetitive style they found more common in men got in the way of problem solving. That self-effacing approach sometimes prevented women from getting full credit for their accomplishments, hindering the objective of proving their capabilities.[121]

That these women did not always make direct confrontation of sexism their highest priority did not make them lesser feminists. In the context of the mass deprivation of the 1930s, the reluctance to foreground sexual discrimination reflected rather these women's consciousness of their relatively privileged position as white professionals, as well as their optimism that by supporting the left they would sweep away all kinds of oppression, including that based on gender. As Wickenden put it in 1933, "Where women, because of their sex, suffer special economic injustice during the depression it is only fair that we should consider their plight specifically, but this is obviously secondary to . . . the terrible plight of all working people."[122]

These young left feminists called not for war between the sexes but for war between the forces of progress and reaction, which they cast in generational rather than gendered terms. During World War II, Wickenden would observe that "women, in their hunger to have their men back home, are in no mood to wage a war between the sexes." She begged women instead to take up the mantle of youth. "Young people are the driving force of progress," she claimed, and most young men were away in uniform. This was a "revolutionary war" between "the forces making for social progress, that is, for a better life for the greater number, and the forces intent on maintaining the status quo of personal [sexual], racial, class, and national privilege." To Wickenden, the forces of conservatism seemed to be gaining an upper hand, thanks in part to the decline in young people's political power that resulted from men's enlistment. She urged young women to "enter the rough and tumble competitive struggle for the places where they can furnish leadership as well as mass support for the principles of change and progress. They must . . . hold jobs at the policy making level, they must run for office, they must . . . keep alive the shouting voice of youth." As Wickenden saw it, the women would not step aside when the men came home. Rather, the men and women would carry their generation's banner "forward together in the kind of partnership meant for men and women in a peaceful world."[123] If in hindsight the hope that young men and women marching together would emancipate women seems naïve, Wickenden's cohort was not the first or last group of radical women to be disappointed.[124]

It was not so foolish, actually, for these young female New Dealers to have high expectations of their male counterparts, because they knew men who were quite enlightened on the "woman question." Seeing themselves as pioneers shaking up the old-line Washington bureaucracy, some New Deal men were willing to hire women with stellar credentials and progressive views like their own. They also were willing to marry them. New Deal agencies produced countless romances and marriages, and not all the men were marrying their secretaries (as Tom Corcoran did). Some worked in separate policy fields from their spouses, but others were partners in work as well as in love. Mary and Leon Keyserling edited each other's work and coauthored some publications, as did Lucy Kramer and Felix Cohen. Donald and Mary Taylor Montgomery worked together on consumer policy. Catherine Bauer influenced her lover Leon Keyserling and later her husband William Wurster on housing policy.

A few other examples suggest New Deal men's relatively progressive views on gender roles. Abe Fortas met Carol Agger, a divorced, cigar-smoking economist and future lawyer reputed to be at least as smart as he was, when they both worked in the Agricultural Adjustment Administration. Agger was hard-driving and confident. Her style is captured in an anecdote about a dinner party she and Abe hosted circa 1938. As Tex Goldschmidt recalled it, when Abe opened the door for Lyndon and Ladybird Johnson, "they beheld a roomful of guests in formal dress watching Carol, a tomboy as well as a lawyer and blue-stocking, who had just felled me in a wrestling game and was triumphantly sitting on my chest."[125] Abe Fortas is not known as a feminist, but an antifeminist would have been unlikely to marry a divorced economist known for her brilliance and her wrestling skills.

Esther Peterson, the labor activist and later head of the U.S. Women's Bureau, said that the feminism of her husband, the government economist Oliver Peterson, was key to her success. The son of Norwegian immigrants to North Dakota, Oliver was "a handsome farmboy" and the first of his family to attend college, where he became a socialist and also president of the Lutheran Student Association of the United States. He met Esther Eggertsen when both were graduate students at Columbia, and he proposed to her on the steps of an old church in Greenwich Village on New Year's Eve, 1931. Esther claimed that her conversion to labor activism began when she heard how a union had helped Oliver's family survive after his stepfather was injured on the job. Oliver held jobs in the Works Progress Administration and Office of Price Administration before spending the bulk of his career as a labor attaché with the State Department. Esther worked as a labor organizer and lobbyist, raised four children, and then as head of the U.S. Women's Bureau inspired the creation of the President's Commission on the Status of Women. Oliver's support was essential. After the first of her four children was born in 1938, she recalled, "I felt depressed. Is motherhood all I want? Oliver, a man liberated long before it became fashionable, encouraged me to work outside the home. He said that I could be both a mother and worker. He knew work was good for my mental health. . . . He made me feel as though I had ability. I think Oliver loved me so much he wanted me to be my own person. He was secure enough in his manliness that he didn't mind having a working wife."[126] Esther Peterson believed there was a correlation between how men treated women at home and how they treated women at work. "Throughout my life I've had more trouble with men who didn't have professional wives. Men who appreciated their wives and valued what they did with their time outside the home were much easier to work for."[127]

Thus, many male New Dealers fell in love with women who had careers of their own, as professionals or as unpaid activists. Those men did not always place as high a priority on feminist issues as their wives did, and some did not always fulfill their egalitarian principles in practice. In most cases the wife earned less, relocated when her husband's career required it, and assumed responsibility for overseeing the household staff that made it possible for them to combine demanding jobs with parenthood. On balance, however, the husbands were supportive and proud of their wives' careers.[128] Indeed, right-wing critics would insinuate that Roosevelt and Truman officials were *too* supportive of their wives' careers—in other words, that the wives got government jobs only because of their husbands' influence.[129] These women were making their marks before they married, however; their success was a cause, not a result, of their attractiveness to New Deal men.

The presence of a crop of talented and ambitious women in government was a critical factor in the development of the dense social networks that furthered the characteristic movement of people and ideas from one New

Deal agency to another. Wickenden later recollected that the functioning of the executive branch was facilitated by "the fact that most young New Dealers knew each other socially. Young bachelors took big houses and lived together until one by one they hived off into marriage."[130] The bachelor houses were important, but women's connections—to other women, and to men—also forged many links. Not only did the young left feminists typically date a succession of people who shared their outlooks, but the couples and former couples all knew one another. The Fortases and Wickenden-Goldschmidts were close for decades, in ways more enduring than wrestling matches between Carol and Tex. The Fortases also were close to the Keyserlings, who themselves socialized often with the Blaisdells and the Ware-Meanses, as well as with the Felix Cohens, who separately saw a great deal of the Lloyds. Catherine Bauer stayed in touch with the Keyserlings and with the Wickenden-Goldschmidts, who in turn were close to the Wilbur Cohens. Everyone was friends with Paul R. Porter and with Tommy and "Bert" Emerson and with Helen Gahagan Douglas . . . and so forth. At the frequent social gatherings, they all debated politics and policy.

Historically, women often turned their exclusion from male institutions into a weapon and formed gender-segregated networks that were essential to whatever they achieved. Indeed, same-sex networks and friendships remained politically important to women in government during 1930s and 1940s. They did not abandon women's groups. Many were active in the American Association of University Women, the National Consumers' League, and the League of Women Shoppers, for example. And not all female civil servants were in heterosexual couples or circles; some had lesbian partners, and some were single women whose orientation is not known to scholars but whose social lives revolved around other women. The historical invisibility or even devaluation of women's same-sex relationships has prompted feminist scholars to emphasize them.[131] Particularly for the generation that came of age during the 1920s and early 1930s, however, heterosocial relations too were significant. And the distinction between public and private life is blurry. Heterosocial relationships and networks shaped New Dealers' vision and helped them move toward it.

Reconstructing a sexually modernist, relatively feminist left-liberal scene in Washington changes our image of the left and of the New Deal, and it also helps explain the reaction against the latter. Contrary to the stereotype of grim doctrinaire types isolated in Communist cell meetings in New York City, young leftists attained positions of some authority in the federal bureaucracy.[132] Their presence also qualifies the image of New Deal Washington as "a world overwhelmingly dominated by middle-class white men, most of whom were insulated—by position or temperament or both—from many of the pressures and claims of popular politics and social movements."[133] To the contrary, many of the women and men who became New Dealers brought the ideas and spirit of Popular Front social movements with them. Most Roosevelt administration policies did not turn out to be as leftist, or as feminist, as they would have liked. The influence of left feminists in some New Deal agencies—contested as it always was—nonetheless confirmed the right's stereotypes and stimulated a powerful reaction.

CHAPTER 2

Allegations of Disloyalty at Labor and Consumer Agencies, 1939–43

In May 1939, a front-page story in the *Chicago Tribune* warned that a "communist united front organization" called the League of Women Shoppers (LWS) was conducting an "ingenious campaign" to intimidate employers by threatening to boycott companies that backed pending amendments to the National Labor Relations (Wagner) Act. Many LWS officers were married to prominent New Dealers, and the *Tribune* implied that New Dealers were leaking information to their wives in order to suppress criticism of the Wagner Act and generate the appearance of grassroots support. Furthermore, LWS members and by implication their husbands in government were "fellow travelers of the communist party."[1] The article did not mention that the LWS also was backing a bitter CIO strike against Hearst Corporation newspapers, a strike that would culminate in an injunction against Hearst.[2] A few weeks later, the daughter-in-law of Interior Secretary Harold Ickes told the woman sitting next to her at a luncheon that the LWS was "the fashionable thing to belong to in Washington now." Unbeknownst to Mrs. Ickes, her lunch companion was an undercover investigator, whose report on the LWS soon reached the Special House Committee for the Investigation of Un-American Activities (the Dies Committee).[3]

Long before the formal creation of the federal employee loyalty program in 1947, conservatives began accusing New Deal agencies of harboring subversives. Two examples in the 1939–43 period involved charges that the Wagner Act's administrative agency, the National Labor Relations Board (NLRB), and the Office of Price Administration (OPA) had ties to Communist-dominated elements in the labor and consumer movements. Women were important in those movements and in the government agencies they helped create, and conservatives highlighted and even exaggerated women's influence in an effort to undermine public confidence in the agencies. The role of the NLRB's perceived sympathy for the CIO in stimulating the reaction against the New Deal is well known, but the consumer movement also should be recognized as a trigger of the campaign against "Communists in government."

The *Chicago Tribune* article that labeled LWS officers and their New Deal husbands "fellow travelers" was only the public face of a much broader effort. Although the anticommunist right in the late 1930s was not the mighty force it would become in the Cold War era, it commanded enough leverage to put left-leaning New Dealers on the defensive and to thwart their proposals for redistributing economic and political power. Employers in labor-intensive industries resented New Deal initiatives to raise wages by recognizing union rights and curtailing employment discrimination. Some industries resented the New Deal's sporadic anti-trust efforts as intrusions on private pricing prerogatives. Also hostile to the Roosevelt administration were the so-called "press lords," including William Randolph Hearst, Robert McCormick, Frank Gannett, and Roy Howard, whose media empires dominated major markets.[4] Joining forces with congressional conservatives, these media and manufacturing employers used the close associations between certain government agencies and labor and consumer groups to allege the existence of a Communist conspiracy.

The anticommunist attack on the New Deal, often understood as a response to the rise of mass-production unionism, also was a reaction against the emergence of a consumer movement that was pro-labor, antiracist, and feminist. Indeed it was the very conjunction of these movements—sit-down strikers demanding higher wages at the same moment that housewives demanded lower prices and higher quality— that alarmed American conservatives. The movements were not rivals so much as they were two sides of a coin, with much overlap in personnel. The League of Women Shoppers was at the nexus of both movements: it formed as a vehicle for non-wage-earning women to support strikers, but soon it also advocated regulation of the price and quality of consumer goods. The burgeoning labor and consumer movements were allied aspects of the left-liberal coalition of the New Deal era, but far more attention has been paid to the labor aspect.[5]

Scholars have begun to redress that neglect. They have shown that beginning in the 1910s, liberal businessmen, labor leaders, and reformers argued that increasing "mass purchasing power" was vital to the nation's economic and political health. Raising the living standard of the working-class majority, they believed, was not only a matter of social justice—it was good economics. The Great Depression illustrated the U.S. economy's vulnerability to "underconsumption" and brought purchasing-power progressives into office in Washington. They declared workers' legal right to organize, and they implemented public works, minimum wage laws, social insurance, and public assistance to get money into the hands of the people. They also encouraged consumer involvement in policymaking and implementation, to stimulate grassroots civic engagement and to ensure that employer concessions to labor unions did not come at the public's expense in the form of high prices or poor quality. An alliance of organized labor, consumers, and sympathetic policymakers challenged business prerogatives during the New Deal and World War II years, working through government bodies such as the National Recovery Administration, National Labor Relations Board, and Office of Price Administration, among others.[6]

Aided by an enormous budget and staff, the OPA was particularly novel in its enlistment of the participation of ordinary citizens as volunteers. By mobilizing consumers to enforce price controls and rationing, it melded technocratic planning with participatory democracy, producing a model of a powerful interventionist state that was as alarming to the right as it was inspiring to the left. After the war, conservatives took advantage of inflation to divide organized labor and consumers against each other, facilitating the OPA's demise and the weakening of the National Labor Relations Act with the Taft-Hartley Act of 1947. The right also used the fear of communism to taint policies that aimed at structural reform. Thanks to a barrage of charges of un-Americanism from the late 1930s through the early 1960s, the objectives of the labor and consumer movements became less redistributive, and were expressed in terms of promoting the interests of specific groups rather than the general public welfare. Despite these important insights, the existing scholarship overlooks the consumer movement's linkages with the labor left, and the role of left consumerists in the making of New Deal policy and the reaction against it.[7]

LEFT FEMINISTS AND THE LABOR MOVEMENT

Although Franklin Roosevelt was lukewarm in his enthusiasm for labor's right to organize, he deferred to the argument that unions would help the economy by raising "mass purchasing power," and he recognized the political advantages of enlarging the labor vote and cementing its allegiance to the Democratic Party. Well before May 1935, when the U.S. Supreme Court struck down the 1933 act that had created the National Recovery Administration, New Dealers recognized the need for a separate labor relations statute to put teeth into the NRA's Section 7(a) asserting workers' right to form unions. Senator Robert Wagner (D-N.Y.) set his aide, Leon Keyserling, to drafting an enforceable bill. After earning his law degree from Harvard in 1931, Keyserling did graduate work in economics at Columbia, and that dual background helped him draft the bill that was passed in July 1935 as the National Labor Relations (Wagner) Act, which recognized employees' right to form unions and required employers to bargain collectively with those unions. Keyserling's former roommate

Tom Emerson, who helped administer the Wagner Act and defend its constitutionality, recalled it as "one of the best-drafted pieces of New Deal legislation." The statute was flexible but also precise enough to withstand formidable attack—for a time.[8]

Major employers proceeded to ignore the Wagner Act because they assumed the Supreme Court would strike it down as the Court had the NRA. Employers were encouraged in that expectation by a brief circulated by the American Liberty League, a group of anti–New Deal corporate leaders and their lawyers. The NLRB staff strategized to bring the most promising test cases before the Supreme Court quickly in order to end the legal limbo that hindered enforcement.[9]

One early case to come before the NLRB had little to do with its test case strategy but is noteworthy here because it showcases the consumer-labor alliance and also because it embittered one individual who later would be in a position to do much damage to leftists in and out of government. A strike began just weeks after the Wagner Act's passage in 1935, when a company called Consumers' Research (CR) fired three white-collar employees who had helped organize a union. After the company reneged on an agreement to reinstate the fired workers, forty-one of its seventy employees went on strike. The company called in replacement workers and armed guards, and the daily picketing began to include fights and arrests. The strike attracted a disproportionate amount of publicity because CR had been a darling of progressives and a "thorn in the side of business" since its founding in 1929. Consumers' Research tested advertisers' claims and shared the results with its 55,000 subscribers. By 1935 CR principals included Stuart Chase, F. J. Schlink, and J. B. Matthews, who by his own later description was an ardent "fellow traveler" of the Communist Party.[10] The perceived irony of a left-wing group engaging in unfair labor practices attracted much comment from both left and right.

The CR strike turned into the first victory for the fledging League of Women Shoppers. Founded in May 1935, just three months before the CR strike, the LWS mobilized middle- and upper-class women to "use their buying power for social justice, so that the fair price which they pay as consumers will also include an American standard of living for those who make and market the goods they buy." In that mission the LWS resembled an older group, the National Consumers' League, but the latter focused on wage and hour legislation, whereas the LWS prioritized union rights. The LWS originated at a meeting in the New York apartment of Aline Davis Hays to discuss a strike at a neighborhood department store and how the women present, as patrons of the store, might contribute to its resolution. Hays, an artist married to the civil liberties lawyer Arthur Garfield Hays, became the first LWS president. The organization's initial directors and sponsors consisted of about fifty left and liberal women, most of them prominent in their own right—as writers, artists, lawyers, and other professionals—and some of them married to prominent left and liberal men.[11] When the CR strike began, its former counsel Dorothy Kenyon, an LWS member, offered to arbitrate, but the CR board refused. The CR board declined to meet with LWS delegations, which included well-known reformers such as Cornelia Bryce (Mrs. Gifford) Pinchot and Mary Phillips (Mrs. Jacob) Riis. The LWS investigated the circumstances surrounding the strike, found the CR board at fault, and organized direct actions. It urged its members to request the CR board to submit to arbitration; join the picket line; attend a mock trial dramatizing the events; and donate funds to the strikers, directly or by attending a benefit performance, which was based on a proletarian novel by Grace Lumpkin.[12] At the crowded theatrical spectacle of the mock trial, the leftist New York congressman Vito Marcantonio played the prosecutor, LWS members formed the jury, and the judge was played by the radical writer Heywood Broun. The CR management declined to attend. A distinguished independent committee chaired by the socialist theologian Reinhold Niebuhr investigated both sides of the strike and confirmed the LWS finding that CR's management was at fault.[13]

In early 1936 the National Labor Relations Board reached the same conclusion and ordered that the fired workers be reinstated with back pay. By this time, CR's intransigence had cost it many subscribers. Its further decline was ensured when a group of strikers formed a rival organization, Consumers' Union, rather than accept reinstatement at CR. To highlight its pro-labor orientation, Consumers' Union recruited an interracial advisory committee of labor leaders. CR founder Stuart Chase moved to Consumers' Union, whose subscribers soon far outnumbered CR's.[14] Consumers' Union shared some personnel with the LWS, whose visibility the strike enhanced. The labor expertise of the LWS was acknowledged by the NLRB, which in its understaffed early years asked the LWS for help in mediating disputes and monitoring union elections. LWS members also were appointed to the state boards that implemented state minimum wage laws for women. By 1939 the LWS had fourteen chapters around the country; the Washington D.C. chapter counted many female New Dealers, and wives of New Dealers, among its members. The league soon broadened its scope to include cost-of-living issues, and during the war it mobilized volunteers to help enforce price control legislation.[15]

For the CR leaders Schlink and Matthews, this humiliating defeat was the catalyst for a sharp swing from left to right. In early 1938, they wrote an article urging Congress to repeal the Wagner, Social Security, and Soil Conservation Acts, to shelve the fair labor standards bill, and to abolish the Works Progress Administration. In August, Matthews testified before the newly created Dies Committee that Communist influence over the

NLRB was producing biased rulings. The CR case was his major example, and he labeled the LWS and Consumers' Union Communist fronts.[16] Congressman Martin Dies (D-Tex.) promptly hired Matthews to be his committee's chief investigator, from which position Matthews waged an ongoing vendetta against the NLRB, LWS, and Consumers' Union, among others. He would continue that campaign after joining Senator Joseph McCarthy's staff in 1953. J. B. Matthews became the "unofficial éminence grise of American anticommunism," foremost among the handful of former leftists who obtained powerful positions on congressional investigating committees.[17] Although the consumer-labor alliance defeated Matthews in the 1930s, later he would gain the upper hand.

Employers much more powerful than CR likewise ignored the Wagner Act at first. In May 1936 another Supreme Court decision encouraged the expectation that the statute would be found unconstitutional.[18] Labor strategists decided to work on public opinion by persuading the Senate to authorize the La Follette Civil Liberties Committee to investigate employer tactics in resisting unions. Initially staffed in part by NLRB employees who had little to do while the Wagner Act's constitutionality was in question, the La Follette Committee documented employer brutality against workers who tried to organize unions. In a series of hearings and reports from 1936 through 1941, the committee revealed the widespread use of industrial espionage, private police forces, strikebreaking services, and stockpiles of machine guns and tear gas to break strikes or prevent workers from exercising their legal right to form unions. Two particularly shocking inquiries in 1937 publicized employer violence against Kentucky coal miners and against South Chicago strikers and their families at the "Memorial Day massacre" outside Republic Steel's plant.[19] Even people who considered themselves informed about labor conditions were appalled. Leon Keyserling wrote to his father: "the films of the Chicago Massacre of two weeks ago, subpoenaed by the La Follette Committee, are a revelation. They show close-ups of the police firing machine guns into the backs of retreating and unarmed men, women and children." Keyserling fumed that the Little Steel companies had "banded together to circumvent the law, openly, secretly, legalistically, terroristically, and in every other way open to hired lawyers, editorialists, police, thugs and agents provocateurs."[20]

When the Supreme Court stunned labor's friends and foes alike by upholding the Wagner Act in April 1937, the NLRB went into high gear. The Court's shift was widely believed to reflect the pressure of public opinion as manifested in Roosevelt's landslide reelection, in the surge of workers into unions, and popular support for Roosevelt's dubious proposal to expand the number of justices on the Supreme Court, effectively diluting the influence of sitting conservatives.[21] Emboldened by its perceived

Figure 2.1. Rep. Martin Dies (D-Tex.) on April 3, 1937, shortly after he introduced a resolution for a congressional inquiry into the CIO's sit-down strike. Dies was a leading opponent of the Wagner Act before he became the first chair of the Special Committee to Investigate Un-American Activities. Harris & Ewing Collection, Library of Congress.

Figure 2.2. Testifying before the new Dies Committee on August 22, 1938, J. B. Matthews said the immediate objectives of President Roosevelt's administration were identical to those of the Communist Party. Matthews soon joined the Dies Committee staff. Harris & Ewing Collection, Library of Congress.

mandate from the Court and a sympathetic public, the NLRB within weeks was holding hearings all over the country, and by the end of the year it had "tackled the Big Boys in every industry." Under the chairmanship of J. Warren Madden, the board "chose to make a record of vigorous enforcement . . . unmatched in the history of administrative agencies."[22] The Madden Board issued an astonishing number of decisions, which were generally fair and legally well crafted. Of the sixteen decisions that were appealed to the Supreme Court in the year ended June 30, 1938, for example, none were overturned. According to Tom Emerson, who headed the NLRB Review Division in this period, "the Supreme Court rather quickly began to have confidence in the board's work in contrast to some of the other agencies."[23]

The NLRB's early record won the admiration of legal experts and labor advocates, but it also made some bitter enemies. As historian James Gross observes, "no administrative agency could handle these powerful employers the way the NLRB was handling them without being subjected to intense political pressure." From 1938 into 1941, the NLRB would be under constant attack from employers and their associations, congressional conservatives, much of the press, and, startlingly, the American Federation of Labor (AFL).[24]

After the Supreme Court sustained the Wagner Act, its opponents turned to Congress. In 1939, employers and the AFL introduced amendments that NLRB lawyers believed would have undercut the act. The employers' proposed amendments reflected their complaints that the Wagner Act was "one-sided," giving rights to employees but not to employers, and that it gave the NLRB an unprecedented and dangerous amount of authority with no provision for appeal. Meanwhile, AFL proposals sought to limit the NLRB's power to determine the bargaining unit in a given workplace, because that power enabled the board to invalidate union contracts that it found did not represent the free choice of a majority of workers. The AFL leadership complained that NLRB rulings in jurisdictional disputes between the AFL and its chief rival organization, the CIO, favored the CIO.

Most NLRB employees indeed were pro-CIO, believing it served the interests of most workers better than the AFL. Even NLRB lawyers who were considered relatively conservative, such as Ida Klaus, Estelle Frankfurter, and Robert Watts, thought the CIO was more democratic and progressive than the AFL. According to Chairman Madden, employers feared the CIO because "their leaders were scrupulously honest. . . . They weren't people that you could do business with . . . like the heads of some of the old craft unions where what the employers did was to pay off the head of the union instead of paying the working people very much." Tom Emerson recalled being "astonished by the incompetence, narrowness, and stupidity of the AFL traditionalists. The CIO group was incomparably more alert, intelligent, and aggressive." NLRB critics took such views as evidence of pro-CIO bias, but the NLRB's favoritism was based on substantial evidence of AFL shortcomings.[25]

The Wagner Act took as its constitutional basis the "tangible public interest in the stabilization of the wages, hours, and working conditions of the labor force at large." This was a departure from common-law precedent and from the AFL view of collective bargaining as a private activity between unions and employers. The NLRB's responsibility was not primarily to protect *union* rights, but the *public interest* in the welfare and purchasing power of *individual* employees. Many AFL leaders were horrified as the implications of this dawned on them.[26] Advocates of unskilled or unorganized workers saw it differently. They welcomed the shift toward the "public interest" as a means of countering union discrimination against certain groups of workers.[27] They believed that without federal government support, unions would be unable to overcome massive business opposition. Advocates for southern workers were especially likely to believe federal intervention would be more a help than a hindrance to the labor movement.[28] It is true that the Wagner Act increased the labor movement's dependence on the federal government and encroached on the autonomy of unions as well as of employers. But the law's drafters were more interested in worker self-organization and living standards than in maximizing productivity.[29] In its early years, the NLRB defended union rights so energetically that it won the loyalty of labor radicals. Not until later, after sustained attack by conservatives, would the NLRB begin to prioritize stability and seek to curb rank-and-file activity.[30]

The enthusiasm that advocates of black or female workers displayed in defending the Wagner Act from amendment in 1939 indicates their appreciation of the NLRB's early efforts. Groups who testified against amendment included the LWS, the National Consumers' League, the Washington Women's Trade Union League, the Church League for Industrial Democracy, and the National Negro Congress. These groups also wrote editorials for their local papers and urged members to write their representatives opposing amendment.[31] In 1935, the National Negro Congress had protested that the Wagner Act did not include a clause prohibiting racial discrimination by unions, but by 1939 its leaders were impressed with NLRB efforts against exclusionary practices. Leon Keyserling claimed that the original bill he drafted had prohibited discrimination by unions but that the AFL "fought bitterly to eliminate this clause and much against his will Senator Wagner had to consent to the elimination in order to prevent scuttling of the entire bill."[32] The CIO established itself as eager to organize black workers, and although its record on racial issues was not perfect, it was better than the AFL's.

Mary Dublin, a top official of both the National Consumers' League and the New York League of Women Shoppers, played an important role in the drive to block amendments. Working behind the scenes with Senator Wagner's office, Dublin contacted potential witnesses to testify against the amendments. She collected signatures from 1,500 "prominent citizens" who opposed the amendments and had them entered into the *Congressional Record*. She wrote a pamphlet analyzing the proposed amendments and distributed twenty thousand of them around the country through local chapters of allied voluntary associations. In that pamphlet and in her own testimony before the House and Senate labor committees, Dublin rebutted various criticisms of the NLRB. She offered data showing that the NLRB had not favored the CIO over the AFL. In reply to the AFL, she defended the NLRB's power to invalidate certain union contracts, arguing that unions needed "merely to turn to their own membership to seek democratically the strength which will give their contracts validity before the law." Restricting that NLRB power, she claimed, would "make for collusion between employers and minority representatives and deal a powerful blow to the cause of industrial democracy." Certain workers were especially likely to be victims of such collusion with employers, as Dublin was well aware. She denied that the Wagner Act had increased strikes, but she also defended workers' right to strike: "We consumers want peace based on the dignity of working men and women, and recognition of their essential rights, not the shotgun peace that comes from acquiescence in the suppression of those rights."[33]

Dublin's testimony was effective in helping to block amendments to the Wagner Act, but it also put her in the spotlight, for better and for worse. Leon Keyserling was dazzled, and he married her the following year. Her testimony was so impressive, apparently, that one congressman had difficulty believing she had written it herself. He was taken aback when she described herself as an economist, and he asked whether she was married and whether she earned a salary. LWS officer Nina Collier's testimony met with the same gendered condescension.[34] The right, meanwhile, expressed outrage at organized women's defense of the Wagner Act. The *Chicago Tribune*'s response was to label the LWS a Communist front group. With respect to Dublin's efforts, one columnist warned that "an organization styling itself as the National Consumers' League is flooding the mails with propaganda in opposition to any amendments of the national labor relations act, and in support of its position makes appeals as specious and absurd as ever came from the 'minister of propaganda and enlightenment' in Nazi Germany." That writer also claimed, erroneously, that after the Wagner Act was upheld came "the period of the sit-down strike and the statement from *the Perkins woman* that the illegality of such a strike had never been established."[35]

The support of the NLRB by pro-labor women's groups was part of a broader effort to push the New Deal toward social democracy, an effort in which activists inside and outside the government cooperated. In addition to helping defend the Wagner Act, the National Consumers' League and LWS lobbied less successfully to cut appropriations for the Dies Committee and to renew appropriations for the La Follette Committee, whose reports on unfair labor practices aided the NLRB's work.[36] LWS petitions and leaflets circulated regularly through NLRB offices, and prominent officials attended LWS and Consumers' League events.[37] With a stronger presence in Washington than the NCL, the LWS was especially active on the heterosocial left wing of the New Deal. Parties, dances, and conventions held by the Washington branch of the LWS routinely attracted four hundred or five hundred people. Not stopping at formal lobbying against the Dies Committee, LWS members publicly mocked it. At an elaborate LWS fund-raiser in 1940, New Dealers acted in skits that lampooned their opposition; one skit featured a southern congressman named "Martin Pies." Dies Committee staffers were not amused, recording the names of participants as "derogatory information." In 1940 left feminists in and out of government were not yet terribly worried about being accused of Communist leanings, but that would change. Anticommunist investigators characterized the ties between social movement organizations and government agencies as evidence of a Communist-directed conspiracy, and data they gathered in this early period would haunt federal employees later.[38]

PAINTING THE NLRB PINK

After all amendments to the Wagner Act were blocked in 1939, congressional conservatives tried a tactic that proved to be more successful: they created a special House committee to investigate the NLRB. Named for its chairman, Howard Smith (D-Va.), and dominated by anti–New Dealers, the Smith Committee conducted a lopsided investigation that was designed to undermine public support for the NLRB. It succeeded, not least because of the ample coverage provided by the "press lords." In effect the Smith Committee continued the campaign begun by the American Liberty League, the Du Pont–backed conservative group, against the Wagner Act and the wider New Deal.

In June 1940, amendments proposed by the Smith Committee passed by a large margin in the House, thanks in part to the committee's startling alliance with the AFL. New Dealers in the Senate managed to delay further action until after the 1940 elections, when the amendments were rejected. However, the Smith Committee achieved its objective. The pressure on the Roosevelt administration from the AFL-conservative alliance resulted in personnel and policy changes that weakened both the letter and the spirit of NLRB enforcement of worker rights. The Smith Committee also popularized the idea that Communists controlled the NLRB. Some NLRB employees in fact were Communists, but the Smith Committee was less interested in identifying them than in damaging the image of the entire agency.[39]

One tool in the Smith Committee's kit for discrediting the NLRB was to exaggerate women's influence in the agency. The NLRB in its early years hired many female lawyers and economists, although professional women remained a small minority. The Smith Committee called most of those women to testify, creating a false impression that women dominated the agency. Three of the NLRB's twenty-two regional directors in 1939 were women, and the Smith Committee summoned two of them. Dorothea de Schweinitz, a Smith College graduate with advanced training in economics, was director of the St. Louis NLRB from 1938 until 1942. Elinore Herrick was director of the NLRB's largest regional headquarters, in New York, from 1934 until 1942. A divorced mother of two, Herrick was close to Senator Wagner and Labor Secretary Perkins, which along with her hard-driving, chain-smoking style, made her a person to be reckoned with. Much of her testimony criticized NLRB personnel and policies rather than defending them, but her prominence in the hearings contributed to the feminization of the agency in the eyes of the public.[40]

More dramatically, the first six Review Division attorneys summoned by the Smith Committee's general counsel were women, creating an impression of female predominance that was misleading given that only 11 of 105 review attorneys were women. Every day for a week in January 1940, the front page of the *New York Times* featured a smiling portrait of one of the women lawyers, who, like their male counterparts at the NLRB, averaged about thirty years of age. Under the aggressive questioning of counsel Edmund Toland, the witnesses sometimes hesitated or contradicted themselves. Headlines included "Inexperience Laid to Aides of NLRB" and "Lawyer of NLRB Changed Her Mind." NLRB personnel were at a great disadvantage because the Smith Committee had all their files. The witnesses did not know which cases they would be questioned on, and they had no opportunity to refresh their memories. Comparably experienced men would have done little better under Toland's questioning. Although Toland bullied all witnesses, he treated female and male witnesses differently. He shouted at the women to speak up and to give more "responsive" answers. He interspersed personal questions with queries about intricate details of NLRB cases. In questioning women, Toland emphasized their youth and their sex. He brought out that several of the women had been hired even before their admission to the bar—insinuating that they were not qualified. In fact it was typical for the top graduates of the best law schools to be snapped up before passing the bar, and the pattern actually indicated the strong credentials of these recruits. According to Tom Emerson, the head of the Review Division, "women professionals were looked upon with considerable skepticism by Congress and perhaps the general public. [Toland] exploited that negative attitude." Toland did not call any of the top officials who would have been able to represent the Review Division more effectively. Emerson recalled, "the net effect was not favorable to the Review Division."[41]

In addition to casting the female Review attorneys as inexperienced and incompetent, Toland undermined public sympathy for them by revealing that some were married to men who also worked for the federal government. Carol Agger's husband Abe Fortas was counsel to the Interior Department's bituminous coal division, Ann Landy's husband Mortimer Wolf was in the NLRB's litigation division, and Margaret Bennett Porter's husband John Porter was in the Justice Department. Toland asked each woman to state her salary and that of her husband. This revealed that the women earned substantially less than their husbands, but gender inequity was not Toland's point. He expected to tap the widespread resentment of wage-earning married women, a resentment that became still more potent in the case of government couples because it fused with taxpayer indignation. His tactics were so heavy-handed that, according to the *New York Times*, "members of several women's organizations" began attending the Smith Committee hearings because they were concerned over reports of "sex discrimination by Mr. Toland."[42] Particularly offensive was one committee member's insult to the female attorneys' sexual respectability, in the form of a joke about "professional ladies" that equated them with prostitutes.[43]

The Smith Committee's tactics were calculated to generate titillating media coverage, but the more fundamental objective was to undermine the NLRB. With the help of Toland (who, not incidentally, had represented the steel company in the case that challenged the Wagner Act's constitutionality[44]), the Smith Committee made the NLRB the subject of ridicule. The conservative congressman Clare Hoffman (R-Mich.) told his colleagues that if they would

> take a look at the reviewing attorneys you will understand why there has been so much trouble. Those girls who are acting as reviewing attorneys for the Board are fine young ladies. They are good looking; they are intelligent appearing; they are just as wonderful, I imagine, to visit with, to talk with, and to look at as any like number of young ladies anywhere in the country, but the chances are 99 out of 100 that none of them ever changed a diaper, hung a washing, or baked a loaf of bread.[45]

These NLRB lawyers were not successful as women, according to Hoffman's rating system, but their neglect of the domestic arts did not mean that they were competent lawyers either: "None of them has had any judicial or industrial experience to qualify her for the job they are trying to do, and yet here they are . . . good looking, intelligent appearing as they may be, and well groomed all of them, writing opinions on which the jobs of hundreds of thousands of *men* depend and upon which the success or failure of an industrial enterprise may depend and we stand for it."[46] Hoffman and his ilk used these young women as a symbol of government incompetence.

Showcasing the women lawyers also was a way of insinuating that the NLRB was dominated by Communists and their sympathizers. The Smith Committee portrayed the agency as staffed by young women who not only were ignorant of political and economic realities but also were enamored of idealistic social policies and malleable enough to be controlled by Communists. Several weeks earlier, the Dies Committee had published a list of more than five hundred government employees whose names appeared on membership lists of the anti-fascist American League for Peace and Democracy (ALPD), which Dies alleged was a Communist front. The NLRB had a relatively high proportion of ALPD members, and in turn a high proportion of those were women.[47] Three of the six female Review attorneys called by Toland, for example, belonged to the ALPD. Stereotypes about women's innate pacifism and instinctive sympathy for the weak, as well as their irrationality and gullibility, fed into an assumption that women were especially susceptible to communism. The Smith Committee lost no opportunity to point in that direction. The Hungarian-born Ann Landy Wolf was asked about her accent and date of naturalization. Questions about the circumstances of each woman's hiring by the NLRB revealed that two of them had worked at the left-leaning Resettlement Administration. Much was made of the fact that Margaret Bennett Porter was recommended to the NLRB by Jerome Frank, whose group had been "purged" from the Agricultural Adjustment Administration in 1935 after angering powerful southern growers.[48]

Margaret Bennett Porter indeed was a member of the Communist Party. She and her husband had joined by the time she arrived at the NLRB in 1935. In 1955 her former colleague Herbert Fuchs testified that he, Bennett Porter, and fifteen others had been part of a Communist Party cell in the agency. In 1950, former CIO counsel Lee Pressman confirmed what had been widely suspected since 1939 by admitting that he and board member Nathan Witt had been party members.[49]

The NLRB mission attracted talent from across the left-liberal spectrum, including some who secretly—more or less so, depending on the individual—belonged to the Communist Party. "The Labor Board was the place to go if you were concerned about justice in the workplace," recalled the NLRB lawyer Ida Klaus.[50] Tom Emerson remembered his five years with the agency as the high point of a long and distinguished career: "I felt a sense of mission, a sense of active struggle against the opposition, and a sense of accomplishment. . . . By establishing the power of labor to organize into associations, the [Wagner] act was creating an institutional force . . . the most significant organized force in support of the New Deal and in support of the change—in the social, political, and economic structure of the country—which I thought was necessary."[51]

The noncommunists knew that some colleagues were probably Communists, but their theoretical differences did not seem to affect job performance. As Emerson explained, the NLRB board and staff "thought that issues of communism were relatively unimportant and should not be permitted to distract attention from the merits of the issues involved." Board members Warren Madden and Edwin Smith held it to be "relatively immaterial" if a lawyer or stenographer who was doing a competent job happened to be a Communist Party member. Howard Smith's committee used that tolerance to suggest that top NLRB officials were either dupes or conspirators with the Communists who worked there.[52]

They were not. At the NLRB, Nathan Witt was in a position to coordinate with his fellow party member Lee Pressman at the CIO, but there is little evidence that their strategizing yielded actions substantially different from those that their noncommunist colleagues would have taken. There was little policy difference between Communists and other labor advocates with respect to the Wagner Act: everyone at the NLRB wanted to enforce the act aggressively, believed the labor movement would promote industrial and political democracy, and believed the CIO better served most workers than the AFL. Herbert Fuchs testified that he and his Communist colleagues believed that being a good Communist meant doing the best possible legal work for the board; their approaches to cases were not guided by any party line. Fuchs's impression that the Communist presence did not significantly affect NLRB policy is confirmed by Tom Emerson. After Nathan Witt's party membership was revealed, Emerson tried to recall incidents in which Witt's political views might have improperly influenced his work—they had worked together closely—but in the end Emerson remained convinced that Witt had done "an exceedingly competent and reliable job."[53]

Communists in government jobs did not get there as part of any systematic plan for infiltration. Nathan Witt hired Herbert Fuchs without knowing he was a party member; Witt had nothing to do with party member Bennett Porter's hiring, whereas he did hire the noncommunist Ida Klaus. As one historian puts it, "not all of the movement of party members from agency to agency was the design of hidden operators, and perhaps rather little of it. . . . There was a motion and life in the government service that was quite independent of any contrivance, responding to the restlessness of people interested in promotions . . . more challenging responsibilities, more interesting jobs."[54] Although the consensus remains that Communist employees had little impact on NLRB policy and decisions, the Communist issue did produce factionalism that destroyed the agency's early cohesiveness. That Nathan Witt was widely and accurately believed to be a CP member, for example, meant that routine bureaucratic conflicts took on a different coloration, when colleagues who disliked his policies, like Elinore Herrick, associated them with his communism. Some blame the resulting divisiveness on the Communist Party's secrecy. Others blame it on the cynics who knowingly exaggerated the Communist threat in order to achieve their own objectives. Communist infiltration of the NLRB was the major theme of the Smith Committee's final report of December 1940, but the committee's indiscriminate attacks on noncommunist leftists and civil libertarians such as Warren Madden, Tom Emerson, and Shad Polier indicated that it was chiefly concerned with swaying public opinion.[55]

The changes that resulted from the campaigns by the Dies and Smith Committees "marked the final curtain on any aggressive New Dealism" at the NLRB, in the words of Tom Emerson. When Chairman Madden's term expired in late 1940, political considerations persuaded FDR not to reappoint him, even though the president believed Madden was competent and honest. Madden's forced exit increased the power of board member William Leiserson, who in the view of many NLRB employees destroyed the agency's *esprit de corps*. Many talented employees resigned. The early NLRB survived only as "a legend among government lawyers. As young lawyers arrived in Washington, they would hear tales of an agency that was characterized by tremendous courage, great ability to resist pressure, and great tenacity for its positions."[56] The Smith Committee hearings of 1939 and 1940 transformed the NLRB into "a conservative, insecure, politically sensitive agency preoccupied with its own survival and reduced to deciding essentially marginal issues using legal tools of analysis exclusively."[57] By 1941, the radicals—Communist and otherwise—had left.

Implicit in the NLRB's transformation was its decreased openness to professional women who had brought training in economics, sociology, and social work as well as activist perspectives to their legal careers. By 1942 few of the female lawyers who had been called before the Smith Committee remained at the NLRB, and they were not replaced by women. When the U.S. Women's Bureau surveyed the status of professional women in the civil service just after the war, the NLRB no longer stood out as a beacon of opportunity; in fact, it had fewer high-ranking women than most agencies.[58]

The Consumer Movement

After the NLRB was reined in and the La Follette Committee was discontinued, left-feminist government employees looked elsewhere for fulfilling work. Quite a few of them ended up at the National Defense Advisory Commission and its successor, the Office of Price Administration (OPA). Not long after Tom Emerson resigned from the NLRB in protest of Roosevelt's refusal to reappoint Chairman Madden, he was hired as the OPA's associate general counsel. Similarly, after four years as the assistant general counsel to the La Follette Committee, David Demarest Lloyd became chief attorney for a branch of the OPA's rationing division.[59]

The migration of radicals from the NLRB to other agencies was reflected in the choice of targets by congressional conservatives. After 1941 the Dies Committee virtually ignored the NLRB and instead attacked agencies such as the OPA and the Office of Civilian Defense. In 1943 a second Smith Committee formed, and it focused most of its criticism on the OPA. Dies, Smith, and their peers might have said they were simply following the Communists, but it would be more accurate to say that after manipulating the Communist issue in order to tame the NLRB, conservatives turned their sights on new challengers to corporate prerogatives.[60]

The radical consumer movement of the 1930s sought to support the labor movement and also to mobilize groups not directly represented by organized labor, such as non-wage-earning women and the unemployed. A long view of the tradition of consumer activism would include American colonists' dumping of British tea, abolitionist boycotts of slave-made goods, and working-class women's boycotts of price increases for staples such as bread and meat. In the early twentieth century, campaigns on cost-of-living issues waged by labor groups as well as upper-class women stimulated intellectual interest in the role of the consumer in the emerging mass-production economy. During the 1920s, a handful of reformers began to argue that raising the purchasing power of poor and working-class Americans was essential to the health of the economy, as well as to the health of those groups.[61]

As the Great Depression gave the "underconsumptionist" view wider currency, diverse activists came to believe that consumer organization would complement labor organization in securing a larger share of the fruits of economic production for workers and consumers, as opposed to managers and investors. Not long after beginning his job at the Department of the Interior in late 1933, Felix Cohen reported to Norman Thomas, the Socialist Party leader, that many New Dealers thought "the consumer is getting a raw deal and that any sort of organized consumer pressure would be pretty effective." Cohen thought this represented a strategic opening: "If the Socialist Party or individual Socialists could take the lead in organizing such pressure and pressing forward the social-ist implications of price-fixing (which has so far benefited only capital-ists), I think much would be accomplished toward the political education of the masses. I think we have the opportunity of a lifetime to build the popular feeling that . . . capitalism has faults."[62]

The Socialist Party did not formally act on Cohen's suggestion, but socialists were among those who encouraged and were encouraged by the surge of grassroots consumer activism in the 1930s. Embracing as-cendant ideas about the importance of "mass purchasing power" to a healthy industrial economy, left-leaning New Dealers argued that a redis-tribution of wealth was imperative not just for humanitarian reasons but for economic stability, and therefore for political stability. "The economy of our time, unregulated and unsupported by government spending, has a tendency to restrict its own market and so to destroy itself," stated Eliz-abeth Wickenden.[63] The lopsided distribution of wealth that restricted the mass market in turn threatened the survival of democracy. "Politi-cal democracy depends on the achievement of industrial democracy, and this is still far away from us," Mary Dublin asserted, citing statistics on economic inequality and the obstacles to informed political participation by the poor.[64]

Such ideas encouraged the organization of new voluntary associations to mobilize and represent consumers, and some government agencies cre-ated consumer-oriented divisions staffed by purchasing-power progres-sives. During the New Deal, these agencies included the Consumers' Ad-visory Board of the National Recovery Administration, the Office of the Consumer Counsel in the Department of Agriculture, and the Temporary National Economic Committee. During World War II, those initiatives were sustained through the Office of Civilian Defense and, especially, the OPA. Later, the Consumers' Advisory Committee to the President's Council of Economic Advisers and similar committees under Presidents Kennedy and Johnson tried to keep the consumer's interest on the agenda. Those agencies relied on mutually supportive relationships with a succes-sion of voluntary associations, including the League of Women Shoppers (1935–49), Consumers' Union (1935–present), and Consumers' National Federation (1937–41) and its successor, the National Association of Con-sumers (1946–54).

A remarkably constant core of thinkers, activists, and policymakers sustained this series of consumer initiatives from the 1930s through the 1960s. Recent scholarship implies that men—well-known economists such as Gardiner Means, Paul Douglas, and Leon Henderson—did the consumer movement's thinking while housewives did the agitating. In fact, women were predominant among both the leaders and the rank and file of the movement. Persia Campbell, Caroline Ware, Mary Dublin Keyserling, and Esther Peterson were among its earliest and most dedicated strategists. Strikingly, many of them married left-consumerist men.[65] Right-wingers recognized women's centrality at all levels of the consumer movement. When they investigated the consumer movement on the grounds that it was dominated by Communists, female activists came under especially close scrutiny—sometimes with ramifications for their husbands.

The Consumers' National Federation (CNF) and LWS are less well-known than the Consumers' Union, but all three groups forged the ties between consumer groups and government officials that were a key source of strength before the Red scare but a liability thereafter. The LWS also stands out for its distinctly feminine direct action tactics and for the antifeminist response it provoked. These organizations should be included along with the better-known labor, antifascist, and civil rights causes as associations in which membership later became the kiss of death for government employees facing allegations of disloyalty.

Founded in 1937, the CNF was an umbrella group for progressive consumer organizations that served as a two-way communication medium between ordinary consumers and government officials. On one hand it developed educational materials for housewives (on the cost of living, prices, quality standards, and cooperatives, for example), and on the other it offered expert representation of "the consumer point of view" in government councils. Ultimately, the CNF wanted consumer agencies in local, state, and national governments, but its leaders recognized that vocal grassroots support was critical to creating and sustaining such agencies. As CNF leader Helen Hall put it, the group tried to create a "widespread expression of a buyers' demand to which administrators can refer. . . . this is not to disparage administrative leadership itself. But these agencies can function best when the groups they are set up to serve are articulate." So the CNF tried to stimulate in cities across the nation a "conscious, educated . . . consumer movement as a decentralized force in American democracy."[66] CNF objectives also included distinguishing "bona fide" consumer organizations from business fronts. Opposing the campaign of "captive" consumer groups to blame high prices on union-driven wage increases, the CNF yoked consumer and labor interests together in a march against unchecked corporate profit-seeking.[67]

The Consumers' National Federation enjoyed easy access to New Deal officials, a fact unnoticed by historians but not by conservatives at the time. After meetings with President Roosevelt and Secretary of Agriculture Henry Wallace in 1938, Persia Campbell reported, "'CNF' is an 'open sesame' in Washington. I never have the least difficulty in making appointments in or out of the government."[68] The CNF took partial credit for the creation of the Temporary National Economic Committee, a key platform for purchasing-power progressives.[69] In the spring of 1939, the CNF did at least two things that antagonized powerful conservatives, at the very moment that its member organization, the LWS, was provoking them with its pro-CIO activism. Testifying before the Temporary National Economic Committee, CNF executive Persia Campbell warned that representatives of various industries were setting up bogus consumer groups in an effort to co-opt the "widespread consumer impulse to organize independently."[70] Second, the CNF filed a complaint against *Good Housekeeping* magazine that led the Federal Trade Commission to cite its owner, Hearst Magazines, for running fraudulent advertising. Hearst promptly hired an undercover agent to investigate Campbell. Lengthy reports on her career and personal life soon reached Dies Committee files. Hearst probably was also behind the simultaneous investigation of the Chicago League of Women Shoppers, which was supporting a strike against Hearst newspapers. Notes on Chicago LWS meetings, along with its bank statements and the arrest records of its officers, reached the Dies Committee around the same time as the CNF report.[71]

The Dies Committee used this material for a sensational report charging that most of the consumer groups that had burst onto the political scene since 1935—including the League of Women Shoppers, Consumers' National Federation, Consumers' Union, and several others—were controlled by Communists. In a highly irregular proceeding, Dies Committee researcher J. B. Matthews testified before a subcommittee consisting solely of Martin Dies, and then Dies released his report to the press before other committee members saw it.[72] Matthews charged that the Communist Party was exploiting consumer protests against "real or fancied abuses" in order to discredit "free enterprise in the United States." Headlines all over the nation publicized his claim that the Communist Party USA had decided to use the consumer movement as a "Trojan horse" for winning middle-class support. According to Matthews, the Communist Party leader Earl Browder himself had told the Dies Committee that the LWS, CNF, and other consumer groups were Communist "transmission belts."[73]

Matthews tipped his hand by claiming that the advertising industry was Communists' primary target. "Advertising performs an indispensable function" in the "capitalist system of free enterprise," he asserted. "The current government procedures against advertising and advertising media have been instigated and are being aided by these consumer organizations which are under the control of communists." His lead example was the cooperation between CNF and the Department of Agriculture's consumer counsel, Donald Montgomery, in the complaint against Hearst's *Good Housekeeping*. Only with additional funding, Matthews concluded, could the Dies Committee undertake the thorough investigation of Communist infiltration of the government that this incident indicated was urgently required.[74]

This Dies report provoked a storm of protest. Consumer movement leaders did not deny that Communists participated, but they emphatically denied that Communists controlled their organizations. Eleanor Roosevelt announced that she had been a member of the League of Women Shoppers, President Roosevelt scolded Martin Dies, and angry letters from distinguished citizens poured in to the Dies Committee. Many suspected a brazen scheme to increase the committee's funding. Journalists also uncovered Matthews's personal grudge against the LWS and Consumers' Union, which dated back to the Consumers' Research strike in 1935. Next it came out that only days before his subcommittee appearance, Matthews had met with top advertising and corporate executives at the home of George Sokolsky, a Hearst columnist and paid lobbyist for the National Association of Manufacturers. (It was later learned that the official copy of Matthews's report had been stenciled at Hearst Magazines.) Consumer activists who already had been calling for abolition of the Dies Committee intensified their efforts. Matthews took a drubbing in the press and before the full membership of the Dies Committee. It seemed he and Dies had made fools of themselves.[75]

This was only the opening skirmish, however, in a thirty-year war against the consumer movement, waged in the name of anticommunism by conservative business interests and their allies in government. The anticommunist campaign did eventually damage the movement by undercutting its grassroots support and pressuring its leaders to moderate their objectives. Consumers' Union, which once had supported fair labor standards and strong regulatory action on behalf of consumers, narrowed its agenda to product testing.[76] Because consumer activists had the ears of federal policymakers and sometimes obtained jobs in federal agencies, right-wing hostility to these consumer advocates was an important source of the crusade against "Communists in government," which in turn produced the federal employee loyalty program.

J. B. Matthews was wrong that the consumers' movement was a Communist plot, but he was right that it was ambitious, influential, and innovative in its tactics. The consumer movement attracted the most prominent left and liberal women of the era, as well as thousands of less famous ones. They included New Deal Democrats, independent leftists, and Communists. A 1936 list of prospective CNF members illustrates its inclusive impulse. The list featured mainstream women's clubs; liberal groups such as the Women's Trade Union League, the Amalgamated Clothing Workers, and the National Association for the Advancement of Colored People; and Communist-affiliated groups such as the International

Workers' Order, National Negro Congress, and Progressive Women's Council. Contrary to Matthews's suggestion, the original executive council of the CNF was not Communist dominated. One or perhaps two of seventeen members were Communists.[77]

Of CNF members, the LWS arguably pulled in the greatest star power. By 1939 the organization claimed twenty-five thousand members in fourteen chapters across the country. The LWS conceived its agenda broadly: "We work for high wages, low prices, fair profits, progressive taxation, adequate health protection and housing for all and the ending of racial, religious, or sex discrimination in employment." The league produced frequent digests of pending legislation in all those areas.[78]

In the late 1930s and early 1940s that agenda attracted big names, whose presence generated abundant newspaper coverage for the LWS, particularly in Washington. "Mrs. Dean Acheson entertained the League of Women Shoppers at a membership tea at her home, with nearly 100 attending," was the caption for a typical *Washington Post* photograph of three elegantly dressed LWS officers holding teacups. The District of Columbia chapter quickly grew to about five hundred members, including female legislators, government officials, and journalists, as well as wives of men in those occupations. The Washington newspapers covered its activities regularly, on and off the women's pages.[79] In another typical event, Lillian Hellman, national league vice president, addressed league members at the home of Cornelia Bryce Pinchot, the prominent feminist and wife of the former governor of Pennsylvania. Also present was the star of Hellman's play *Little Foxes*, Tallulah Bankhead (daughter of the Speaker of the House). Those who took turns pouring tea included two female judges, a congresswoman, peace activist Dorothy Detzer, and several New Dealers' wives.[80]

For these women, the consumer movement's goal of raising the living standards and political participation of ordinary people had a feminist dimension. They demanded women's rights in the workplace, but they also recognized that women, whether wage earners or housewives, usually did the shopping and often worried as much about the price and quality of household goods as about wage rates. The CNF sought to "make the pay envelope, whatever it is, count for more" by fighting inflated prices and shoddy goods on many policy fronts. Helen Hall believed the movement had added "some understanding and some dignity to the job of the low-income housewife." Not only living standards but political democracy was enhanced.[81] Professional women too were taken more seriously when they spoke as "consumers" than when they spoke as representatives of labor or business. By the 1930s the political discourse increasingly cast "consumers" as the working-class masses, eroding the Progressive-era association between upper-class women and consumption. Still, although consumers were no longer *only* women, they clearly *included* women—more indisputably than "workers" or "employers" did.[82]

The consumer movement challenged white supremacy as well as male supremacy. LWS chapters demonstrated against stores that refused to hire African Americans. The Washington chapter surveyed six hundred women about the wages and hours of their household employees and then arranged for a domestic worker, laundry worker, and hotel waitress, all African American women, to address the group. When a House committee refused to consider extending Social Security coverage to household workers, the LWS protested the racially discriminatory impact of their exclusion.[83] The wider consumer movement shared the LWS's convictions. African American groups joined CNF. The civil rights feminist Ella Baker was an active member of the Consumers' Advisory Committee to the OPA and later to the President's Council of Economic Advisers, and she also was a founding officer of the postwar National Association of Consumers.[84] This racial egalitarianism only deepened anticommunists' suspicion of the consumer activists.

The consumer movement used gendered styles to get results. Members of the Councils against the High Cost of Living projected a working-class feminine image, presenting themselves as simple housewives on tight budgets.[85] By contrast, the LWS deliberately took advantage of its members' class and gender status as "ladies." Its fund-raising and publicity stunts included a mink coat raffle and a silk-free fashion show in support of a controversial boycott of Japanese silk. Newspaper coverage of the Washington chapter's fashion show, attended by six hundred in January 1938, featured close-ups of the cotton-stockinged legs of the city's socialites.[86] Cornelia Bryce Pinchot assured members that picketing was not "unladylike." Lucille Ezekiel, local league president and wife of a prominent New Deal economist, led a delegation in evening gowns to picket the Harrington Hotel for dismissing sixteen waitresses.[87] Another stunt that generated newspaper photographs was picketing on roller skates, as Washington LWS members did in June 1939, bearing placards that read "we used to be patrons, now we're pickets."[88] A few years later, when Capitol Hill police interfered with a women's delegation to present legislators with pro–price control petitions, LWS officers traded on their femininity by protesting the rough handling, which they claimed had sent a pregnant woman into shock.[89]

Conservatives highlighted and deprecated the presence of upper-class women in the consumer movement. An article titled "Halfway to Communism with the League of Women Shoppers," published in the bulletin of J. B. Matthews' old group, ridiculed women who went from a tea party to picketing: "Truly, this sets a new style in teas . . . we may expect to see worthy matrons cut short their bridge parties and teas to dash off

Figure 2.3. "We used to be patrons, now we are pickets," reads the sign held by Lucille Ezekiel, president of the Washington D.C. League of Women Shoppers, shown with other LWS members and members of the International Association of Mechanics (AFL), June 21, 1939, *Washington Star*. Reprinted with permission of the D.C. Public Library, Star Collection, © Washington Post.

to some strike headquarters." The author suggested that women were as fickle in politics as they were in shopping: "The fashion forecasters, however, predict . . . it will in time be fashionable to be a lady once again."[90] After a sarcastic editorial in the *Pittsburgh Press* made fun of lady picketers, the local league's executive retorted that there was nothing illogical about a group of fortunate women "opposing the unwise and anti-social activities of others in similar position who oppose the legitimate objectives of organized labor." In fact, she continued, "women who can afford to lunch at the Mayflower Hotel" should be "commended for not being impervious to the needs and welfare of waitresses and chambermaids."[91]

Critics were wrong that the LWS was a fad, an indulgence of bored ladies who joined for the parties and publicity. No doubt the group acquired a certain cachet, which helps explain why hundreds of prominent people turned out for its events. But many of the big names on its letterheads were dedicated activists, and they did not melt away at the first sign of a shift in political climate. The Washington chapter and its supporters initially were not intimidated by the Dies Committee allegations. Four hundred people showed up for an LWS benefit party held in May 1940 on the roof of the Washington Hotel. Staged as a country fair, the event included satirical skits in which New Dealers played each other and sometimes their antagonists. An Interior Department official cast as Leon Henderson of the Temporary National Economic Committee struggled to tame three lions representing three intransigent industries; one of the "lions" was David Demarest Lloyd of the La Follette Committee. Another sketch mocked Congressman Dies, and its star was the local league president Lucille Ezekiel, whose husband was the economic adviser to Secretary of Agriculture Henry Wallace.[92]

The LWS also was adept at more conventional, less glamorous tactics. Many of the "fur-coated New Deal wives" knew a lot about social policy and legislative politics, and they were hard workers. At the Washington chapter, nine committees (living standards, legislation, education, collective bargaining, etc.) churned out savvy legislative digests, letters to editors, and press releases. In 1940 and 1941, the work of the Washington LWS included creating a thirteen-part radio series on consumer and labor issues; boycotting a Disney film in support of striking cartoonists; organizing conferences on household employment, housing, and defense issues; lobbying on national and district legislation; and investigating the dismissal of a woman from the War Department. Despite the Dies allegations, female New Dealers like Caroline Ware, Eveline Burns, and Josephine Roche remained members, and New Dealers' wives continued as active officers. Between 1943 and 1946, the Washington chapter followed the national organization in focusing primarily on price control, earning recognition from the Office of Civilian Defense and the OPA for its advisory and educational efforts. That focus on price control did not mean a shift away from labor interests to consumer interests, because the LWS understood these as the flip side of the same coin, living standards for the poor and working class.[93]

J. B. Matthews and the Dies Committee did not go away, however. In fact, they intensified their attack. The League of Women Shoppers, after being cited as a Communist front group several more times, eventually did begin to lose its most distinguished members, increasing the influence of lesser-known women, some of whom were Communists.[94] As government employees began to be screened for loyalty in 1941 and 1942, they grew more circumspect about their affiliations, and so did their spouses. This affected all LWS branches, as federal workers were scattered around the country, but it was devastating for the District of Columbia branch. The expansion of the federal loyalty program in 1947 prompted more resignations, and the national LWS dissolved in 1949. The Consumers'

National Federation had folded in 1941, and its postwar successor, the National Association of Consumers, never generated as much support.[95] Conservative anticommunists had bigger fish to fry than the consumer movement, however. Far from being chastened, they took New Dealers' indignant defense of the consumer movement in December 1939 and their close ties to its member groups as evidence of a Communist conspiracy.

Allegations of Subversion at the Office of Price Administration

In 1940 the prospect of war and the likely need for rationing and price control moved consumer issues to the center of the domestic political agenda. In May of that year, Roosevelt created the National Defense Advisory Commission, whose responsibilities included price stabilization.[96] Consumer advocates saw a chance to win at last the permanent consumer agency they long had wanted. They did not get it. From inception, the price control initiative met with predictable resistance from industry and agricultural interests within and without the government. New Dealers divided over how far to accommodate that resistance. The consumer advocates won some victories, but those produced a backlash that included charges of un-Americanism.

In September 1941 Dies declared in an open letter to President Roosevelt that Communists had infiltrated the price control agency, now the Office of Price Administration. Four of the five OPA employees named by Dies worked in the agency's Consumer Division.[97] Like the Dies and Smith Committee attacks on the NLRB, the charges against the OPA were viewed by the Roosevelt administration as without merit but dangerous in their impact on public opinion. Two months later, the Consumer Division was effectively demoted, and much of its staff resigned, an early casualty of antisubversive campaigns.

The OPA Consumer Division was run by women experienced in using the consumer cause to promote social reform. It was headed by Harriet Elliott, a political scientist and Democratic Party worker who had organized women to fight inflation during World War I. Elliott immediately hired as her deputy the formidably talented social scientist Caroline Ware. By all accounts Ware was the real force at the Consumer Division.[98] She had served on the Consumer Advisory Board to the National Recovery Administration (1933–35) and run the consumer program of the American Association of University Women; she belonged to the LWS and National Consumers' League.

Ware strategized with Elliott on how to ensure that the war mobilization strengthened consumers' new foothold in the federal government rather than destroying it. "We have a great opportunity to make a major

Figure 2.4. Caroline Ware, Consumer Division, Office of Price Administration, on right, with research assistant Helen Barnard, 1941. Office of War Information Collection, Library of Congress.

contribution in re-orientation of our producer-oriented economy toward a consumer-centered one," she observed.[99] The Consumer Division immediately butted heads with business representatives who, war or no war, did not want to weaken their company's position by expanding production too quickly. The Consumer Division was adamant that military production should come from expansion rather than from cuts in civilian production, because unemployment remained high and because cutting civilian production would drive prices upward. As Ware recalled, "the Division came into conflict continually with the Industrial Division of the Defense Commission and subsequently with all the representatives of industry groups who saw in industrial expansion a threat to their economic position." Other progressives at OPA, including its top administrator Leon Henderson and the young Harvard economist J. Kenneth Galbraith, agreed with the Consumer Division on the urgent need for industrial expansion.[100]

The Consumer Division received less internal support, however, for its vision of public participation in OPA's implementation. The division believed the defense program "required the active, democratic, understanding participation of the public, and that the Division had a responsibility for mobilizing that participation." Toward that end, Elliott and Ware enlisted a team of consultants that included Mary Dublin of the National Consumers' League, the African American YWCA worker Frances Harriet Williams, the Texas women's leader Minnie Fisher Cunningham, and the labor leader and public housing expert John Edelman, among others. This group embarked on an ambitious program to inform and mobilize various groups of consumers. It soon became clear that other OPA divisions, particularly the Information Division, "heartily distrusted the public." According to Ware, too many OPA officials "took the attitude that people were likely to do the wrong thing if they were told too much."[101] This skepticism of the capacities of ordinary consumers was gendered, because women did most of the buying for households. Even some of the more leftist men at OPA shared the skepticism: Galbraith promised businessmen in 1942 that no "Gestapo of volunteer housewives" would be empowered to check prices.[102]

Some of the Consumer Division's difficulties, internal and external, resulted from the fact that it was run by women. "Because the Consumer Commissioner was a woman, and no other special provision had been made for considering the role of women in the defense program, the Consumer Division was continually being called upon to advise on something involving women."[103] That perception persisted even though Elliott repeatedly emphasized that she was responsible for the consumer function, not women. Being a woman also made it more difficult to get cooperation from other agencies. When Elliott tried to implement Roosevelt's request to coordinate health and national defense, for example, the surgeon general told her bluntly that "medical people would not work under the direction of lay people, especially a woman, and that he would wait until the President had a better idea."[104] Within the agency, the slights may have been less deliberate but they were no more subtle. While the other OPA division heads ate in the "stag" (men only) executive dining room, Elliott ate alone. Ware urged her to bring it up, but Elliott declined.[105] According to OPA lawyer Tom Emerson, "Harriet Elliott was quite outclassed" by the rest of Henderson's staff. "She was a pleasant, mild person," he recalled, but "she and her staff took a less compromising point of view than Henderson, less willing to accept reality." Elliott may not have been as high powered as someone like Galbraith, but her staff was stellar. Emerson's condescension suggests what women were up against even in dealing with relatively feminist men on their own team.[106]

Another distinctive effort of the Consumer Division was its successful drive to racially integrate its offices. Ware supported Frances Williams, who had long experience as a national YWCA staff member in charge of black colleges, in a series of guerrilla actions. Williams told Ware, "It's a step backward to ask for a black secretary, but in order to get black secretaries on our staff, I've got to be the one to ask for them." (By "step backward," Williams probably meant that some might think she was conceding that white secretaries should not work for black women.) When the personnel office claimed it could not find a black secretary, Williams went out and found one, who performed well. Soon the personnel office hired a second black secretary. Her work was terrible, so Williams concluded she had been hired because she was so light-skinned she could pass for white. Williams trained her so that her poor work would not discredit other African Americans. She did the same thing with the messengers and with mailroom personnel, retraining inefficient workers and ensuring that talented, reliable ones were promoted. When the Consumer Division was folded into the wider OPA, Ware and Elliott held out for the entire agency's stenographic pool be integrated. After this and many other incidents, Williams was made race relations adviser to the OPA, and the agency achieved an unusually good record on hiring African Americans.[107]

The Consumer Division quickly attracted the disapproving attention of anticommunist investigators. Dies Committee staffers tracked Elliott's and Ware's appointments from the start, immediately flagging the names of Mary Dublin and Frances Williams.[108] Significantly, a few weeks before Dies charged the OPA with harboring subversives, the FBI began an investigation of Caroline Ware herself. According to her FBI file, that investigation was precipitated by "a review of the indices of the Washington Field Office" that revealed her association with the League of Women Shoppers, among other suspect groups. The Dies Committee must have prompted the FBI to check with its Washington field office on Ware, and she no doubt was one of those Dies referred to when he announced on September 7 that fifty unnamed subversives worked for OPA.[109]

In October, Dies turned up the pressure on the Roosevelt administration by telling the press he had sent the attorney general a list of over one thousand alleged subversives in federal positions, over a quarter of them in high-ranking positions. Dies declared, "the retention on the Federal payroll of several thousand persons who, to put the matter mildly, have strong leanings toward Moscow will confirm the widely held suspicion that a large and influential sector of official Washington is utilizing the national emergency for undermining the American system of democratic government."[110] Even though the Roosevelt administration generally adopted the position that Dies was a fanatic best ignored, the new allegations increased the pressure on OPA head Leon Henderson to demonstrate that he was serious about eliminating subversives.[111]

In November 1941, Henderson reduced the Consumer Division's function to communicating OPA directives to the public. Elliott resigned in protest. In early December, Ware declined Henderson's invitation to resign, and she urged him to retain people named by Dies. But on December 19, a Civil Service Commission field examiner interviewed her about "derogatory information" on her record. At about the same time, two people whom she had hired and defended, Robert Brady and Mildred Edie Brady, became the only OPA employees publicly dismissed in response to Dies's charges. In January Ware resigned after all. She gave her reason as "agency reorganization," but the ongoing investigation must have influenced her decision.[112]

Gutting the Consumer Division was Henderson's attempt to appease congressional conservatives, even as he publicly maintained a defiant attitude toward them. Frances Williams remarked cryptically years later that "they had Mr. Leon Henderson eat her [Harriet Elliott] up."[113] Contemporary observers described the fate of the Consumer Division as the triumph of "businessmen and hard-headed economists," who prioritized production, over "sociologists and social workers," who thought the purpose of price control was to raise living standards.[114] That is correct, but it is not the whole story.

In response to the Dies Committee allegations, the Civil Service Commission (CSC) created a loyalty board, which proceeded to review employees whom Dies had called subversive. When many of those employees were retained, the Dies Committee attacked the CSC, going so far as to subpoena its case files. Many of the disputed cases involved OPA employees. Dies charged that Leon Henderson had pressured the CSC loyalty board to reverse negative decisions on certain OPA cases. One of those cases was Tom Emerson's, and the "derogatory information" against him included his wife's activism in the League of Women Shoppers. That Henderson himself was married to an LWS activist summed up the whole problem, in the view of Dies Committee investigators.[115] In 1942, the CSC expressly forbade inquiry into membership in the LWS (or the American Civil Liberties Union, the Socialist Party, and several others) in order to avoid catching liberals and noncommunist leftists in a net officially intended for Communists. The Dies Committee took those rules as further evidence that the CSC was far too tolerant. Professing outrage that CSC standards were even looser than those of the employing agencies, the Dies Committee began to shift its attention from the OPA to the Civil Service Commission. Dies's hitherto little-noticed attack on the OPA, which originated from conservative hostility to the consumer movement, was critical to the prehistory of the federal employee loyalty program that President Truman would create in 1947.[116]

But even as Dies turned his attention elsewhere, other conservatives kept charges of un-Americanism at OPA before the public. After the Democrats' disappointing results in the 1942 midterm elections were blamed on the OPA's unpopularity, Henderson decided the best thing for the agency and for the Democratic Party would be for him to resign.[117]

Not placated, Congressman Howard Smith formed a new subcommittee that proceeded to treat the OPA much as his earlier committee had treated the NLRB. It charged the OPA with "controlling business profits," as if that were proof of its un-Americanism, when price control by definition necessitated profit control. Congressional committees, Emerson recalled, "were a constant thorn in our side, occupying not only our time, but undoubtedly having a substantial effect on public opinion."[118] Galbraith, who effectively headed the OPA for a time after Henderson left, recalled that in the early months of 1943, "I arrived at the office each morning to ascertain what committee was investigating me that day." Meanwhile the Scripps-Howard newspapers, the *Chicago Tribune*, and various trade journals carried more or less permanent headlines to the effect that "Galbraith Must Go." Roosevelt dismissed him in May 1943.[119] Chester Bowles, a public relations man who was appointed to head the OPA in the fall, estimated that he spent one-third to one-half of his time before congressional committees.[120]

That Tom Emerson's résumé included both the NLRB and the OPA made him an especially juicy target. In mid-1944, Representative Fred E. Busbey (R-Ill.) said the OPA was being run by "subversives," naming Tom Emerson and two others. Busbey, whom Emerson later described as a "product" of the *Chicago Tribune*, told an anecdote about a local OPA employee who could not do his job because everything he did had to be approved by "some one of the long-haired professors or the palace guard."[121] The next OPA appropriations bill contained an "antiprofessor" amendment to discourage the agency's employment of university faculty; it was unconstitutional, so purely symbolic.[122] After Emerson left the OPA in April 1945 for a position at the Office of Economic Stabilization, he had to fight rumors that the OPA had fired him. Those rumors followed him out of government service to Yale Law School, where he became a professor in 1946. Throughout the 1950s, he contended with organized campaigns to persuade Yale to dismiss him, but since he was a tenured, prolific scholar, and a brilliant teacher described even by conservative students as scrupulously fair, his position was secure.[123]

As Busbey's reference to "long-haired professors" suggests, conservatives charged intellectuals with subverting the nation's gender norms as well as its political economy. Another congressman referred in 1946 to social scientists as "short-haired women and long-haired men."[124] That same year, the right-wing radio journalist Fulton Lewis Jr. challenged the claim of Caroline Ware—a short-haired social scientist—to represent twenty-three organizations in testifying before a Senate committee on behalf of extending price control.

Ware's detailed analysis warned that eliminating price control too quickly would unleash inflation on "the great mass of the American

Figure 2.5. Caroline Ware appeared before the Senate Banking and Currency Committee in April 1946 to testify on the extension of the OPA and wartime price controls. The right-wing journalist Fulton Lewis attacked her after this testimony. © Bettmann/Corbis.

people." Lewis's response was to question whether she truly spoke for the millions who belonged to those twenty-three organizations, which were predominantly women's organizations. After referring pointedly to "*Miss Ware*," Lewis addressed his listeners: "you know something about the

Parent-Teachers Association yourself, probably, if you have any children as I do." The implication was that Ware, as a woman without children, did not really represent the Parent-Teachers Association, or American women more generally. Lewis also told listeners that Eleanor Roosevelt and the Communist Party were the chief advocates of continuing price control. Over the course of several months, Lewis claimed that without the OPA's meddling, prices actually would fall, and he challenged listeners to "show them what some letter writing is." The resulting flood tipped the balance of congressional mail from pro- to anti-OPA. With legislators nervous about the impending midterm elections, OPA soon was dead. When inflation immediately surged as price control advocates had predicted, Lewis first denied that prices were rising, then insisted that the spike was only temporary. After those illusions became untenable, he joined with other conservatives in arguing that organized labor's wage increases were to blame for the inflation.[125]

One of the OPA's notable successes was in fostering "state-building from the bottom up," through the mobilization of volunteers to aid in enforcement. This exercise in participatory democracy had to be forced on top OPA officials, however, by the women of the Consumer Division.[126] Although Emerson described the Consumer Division staff as too uncompromising and "less willing to accept reality," in fact the ones unwilling to accept reality were those OPA officials who initially resisted using volunteers. The OPA's enforcement budget was tiny; congressional conservatives proved to be no more enthusiastic about paid OPA inspectors than they were about volunteer housewives. Tight budgets and escalating prices forced the OPA to concede the necessity of involving unpaid consumers in enforcement, and by 1944 a massive volunteer program was in operation. The OPA historian Imogene Putnam hailed that program's success in building "at the grassroots, non-bureaucratic administration of bureaucratic controls" as OPA's great achievement—one that would have succeeded further had it embraced community participation from the outset.[127]

Ironically, given that she had been forced out with the gutting of the Consumer Division back in late 1941, Caroline Ware was foremost among those who implemented the volunteer program beginning in late 1943. The newly appointed OPA head Chester Bowles recognized the need for consumer participation and asked Ware to chair the executive committee of a Consumer Advisory Committee. This was an unpaid position, so it was not subject to loyalty review procedures. Ware did an enormous amount of crucial work for the OPA without getting paid for it. Her committee's work in explaining price control to citizens and involving them in its administration generated much grassroots support for the agency. It was that popularity that Lewis and other conservatives sought to dispel by casting OPA volunteers as the naïve instruments of long-haired men and short-haired women.[128]

After a few more years of right-wing alarms about Communists in government—which contributed to the Republican Party's success in the 1946 congressional elections—in 1947 Truman authorized a sweeping program requiring all federal workers to pass loyalty tests. Many of the people most prominent in the consumer movement of the 1930s and 1940s, as well as others who had only minor associations with it, would be investigated under the auspices of the federal employee loyalty program. Priscilla Hiss's membership in the LWS was one of the initial bases for investigating Alger Hiss. Dean Acheson came under fire not only for defending Hiss but because his own wife was in the LWS too.[129] For other federal employees the albatross was a connection to the Consumers' Union or Consumers' National Federation. Many of these investigations lasted for years and forced their subjects out of government service, at least for a time. Other federal employees resigned rather than undergo investigation.[130] Affiliation with these groups also made it harder to get government employment in the first place. Helen Hall, the executive of CNF and its successor, the National Association of Consumers, was nominated for a regional loyalty board but was rejected on grounds that included her LWS affiliation.[131] As word of the investigations spread, others who had been affiliated with "subversive" consumer groups may not have bothered to apply for government jobs.

The investigation of federal employees associated with consumer groups continued long after most of those groups had faded away. The FBI kept tabs on Caroline Ware into the 1960s. After she resigned from the OPA in early 1942, she joined the faculty of Howard University, where she taught until 1961. She later credited Howard for shielding her from the worst of McCarthyism. After serving the OPA on a volunteer basis, Ware began applying for government consulting positions, chiefly to promote community organization among women, under the auspices of the Pan American Union of the Organization of American States. These were short-term assignments, and each time she started a new one she had to get loyalty clearance again. The FBI investigated her repeatedly from 1951 to 1955, which cost her some jobs and delayed others. "My efforts to get out of the country are surely jinxed," she confided to her friend Pauli Murray in January 1953. "I've still been unable to get cleared to be sent on any U.S. assignment." She was formally cleared in 1955, but the FBI continued to track her activities. In 1960 the FBI warned that she was on the Coordinating Committee for Enforcement of D.C. Anti-Discrimination Laws; in 1962, the FBI reported that she had visited the pro-labor, antiracist Highlander Folk School.[132]

As these details suggest, associations with the consumer movement were only part of the case against Caroline Ware. Also suspect were her use of her maiden name, her commitment to African American civil rights, her membership in a government workers' union, her work in labor education, her attendance at the Socialist Party convention in 1940, her failure to conduct loyalty checks on others, and her "tendency to empathize with downtrodden of other nations" (a reference to her extensive development work in Latin America). In 1951, the FBI expended significant resources pursuing the assertion of a "reliable informant" that Ware was secretly the daughter of Ella Reeves Bloor, "a.k.a. Mother Bloor, America's leading woman Communist" (Ware was the surname of Bloor's first husband). Disappointingly for the FBI, perhaps, Ware in fact was the daughter of a well-known Boston lawyer.[133] In spite of the allegations that never died, Ware led an intensely busy and productive life. Her activities in the 1960s and 1970s included service on national and international commissions on the status of women, participation in consumer advisory councils to two U.S. presidents, community organizing in Latin America, and employment with UNESCO and the Inter-American Development Bank. But the investigations made it impossible for her to hold long-term government positions during her forties and fifties and complicated the process of obtaining even short-term assignments.

Thus in the 1930s and early 1940s, left feminists obtained positions in consumer- and labor-related government agencies, often after participating as activists in the dynamic consumer and labor movements. Aided by media allies, congressional conservatives publicized the influence of leftists, and especially of women, in an effort to discredit the NLRB and then the OPA. Left-feminist women in government, and their husbands and male mentors (long-haired professors or otherwise), were early targets of the charge that the New Deal harbored subversives, charges that were made, and felt, long before the postwar Red scare. The federal employee loyalty program originated from a conservative campaign against the New Deal that was underway well before the Cold War elevated fears of Soviet espionage.

CHAPTER 3

"Pinks in Minks": The Antifeminism of the Old Right

In 1951 Jack Lait and Lee Mortimer published *Washington Confidential*, a racy, sensationalistic account of life in the nation's capital that within weeks topped the *New York Times* best-seller list. The two Hearst tabloid journalists characterized Washington as a "femmocracy" of self-supporting women, whose alleged unhappiness proved that "the emancipation of women is baloney." The home of the federal bureaucracy, they further claimed, was an incubator of sexual depravity and communism. Women outnumbered men by one hundred thousand, and "g-girls" (government girls) slept their way to the top, sometimes with the help of older female bureaucrats who procured ambitious prospects from the heartland for the few government men who were not "eunuchs" or "pansies." Communists allegedly took advantage of the situation, using suave male Reds to recruit "sex-starved government gals," "white girls" to recruit the many "colored men" in government jobs, and "trained good-lookers" to recruit "meek male clerks in soporific jobs at standardized sustenance-pay." Often cited as an example of McCarthy-era homophobia, *Washington Confidential* also was profoundly misogynistic, not to mention racist. The book generated such a buzz that the Civil Service Commission launched a publicity campaign to improve the image of federal employees.[1]

The Hearst columnists who wrote *Washington Confidential* belonged to a network of conservatives whose influence in the media and government stoked the Second Red Scare. The politicians, investigators, and journalists who drove the "Communists-in-government" crusade were intensely antifeminist, and they used popular antifeminism as a tool in their battle against leftists and liberals. The differences in gender ideology between liberals and conservatives were especially apparent in the press. Although journalists of all political stripes sometimes relied on gender stereotypes that after the 1960s would be considered demeaning toward women, conservative journalists distinguished themselves with their negative portrayals of those women whose words, actions, or achievements challenged male superiority—in other words, feminists.

During the Depression and World War II, the rapid expansion of the federal government combined with the merit system and a growing pool of women with professional degrees to increase women's presence in government, and not only at the lower levels, as we have seen. Many New Dealers were influenced by the left's theoretical commitment to gender and race equality, and relative to the right, they were quite egalitarian. Some liberals shared conservatives' anxiety about a decline in masculinity in postwar America, but they did not blame the perceived decline on women. Arthur M. Schlesinger Jr., for example, worried about mass society's smothering of the individual (male) self, but he ridiculed the right's shrill alarms about the decline of male supremacy.[2] That many New Deal men married highly educated and accomplished women has drawn little notice from scholars, whose general assumption has been that "feminism was not yet on the table" and that the main players of midcentury liberalism "traveled in a white man's world."[3]

Contemporary conservatives, by contrast, certainly noticed the prominence of women in and around the Roosevelt and Truman administrations, as their gripes about femmocracy suggest. In the 1930s and 1940s, the novelty of having women in positions of authority gave them a visibility beyond their numbers. The legions of g-girls in nonsupervisory positions endured sexist treatment and patronizing commentary from across the political spectrum, but it was high-ranking women with policy influence who most obviously subverted male dominance, and the right focused on them. In 1949, George Dixon of the conservative *Washington Times-Herald* wrote a column on Mary Dublin Keyserling, then a section chief in the Commerce Department's Office of International Trade, that illuminates right-wing perceptions of liberal Washington. Dixon wrote, "A pretty woman in her thirties, who looks as if she didn't know a trade balance from a trade last, is currently up to her unruffled eyebrows in one of the most complicated problems of higher economics ever tackled by a member of her sex." He predicted that Dublin Keyserling, whose job was identifying ways to increase imports, would produce "a nice expensive report that no one will read." The report was sure to be "erudite," because "despite her creamy complexion and quiet charm, the lady trade balancer is a heavy thinker." Rather than exploring her heavy thinking, the rest of the column described how her husband, Truman's chief economic adviser, had fallen for "the slim ex-schoolmarm with the blue-green eyes." According to Dixon, a power couple was setting Truman's economic policy. "The President listens avidly to practically everything Leon Keyserling tells him," and soon Truman would "be listening as carefully to his chief economist's missus." Dixon's column managed to imply both that the Truman administration was opening its doors to high-powered women and that it was making exceptions for attractive wives of senior officials. Neither implication was intended to endear readers to Truman's Fair Deal.[4]

SEEING PINK LADIES

Conservatives who charged that the civil service was riddled with Communists devoted much attention to high-ranking women. In 1938, one of the first efforts of the newly created Dies Committee was to try to have Secretary of Labor Frances Perkins impeached for her refusal to deport the alleged Communist and labor activist Harry Bridges. She survived, but the allegations generated enough hostile, often sexist letters from the public to convince the president not to give her a prominent wartime role, and her agency was bypassed in the mobilization process. Next the Dies Committee grilled Hallie Flanagan and her supervisor Ellen Sullivan Woodward about communism in the Federal Theatre Project, which soon was terminated as a result. (With characteristic audacity, Flanagan invited Martin Dies to a Federal Theatre Project production of *Pinocchio*, intimating that Dies could learn something from the tale.) Workers' education expert Hilda Worthington Smith of the Works Project Administration came under fire, as did Eleanor Roosevelt, who was accused of using her influence to "starve" the Dies Committee of funding. In 1943, congressional critics of the National Resources Planning Board labeled the economist Eveline Burns, who had drafted that board's blueprint for a generous welfare state, a prime example of the New Deal's harboring of Communists. In 1950, Senator McCarthy's nine lead examples of subversion in the State Department included the former New York judge Dorothy Kenyon and the international affairs expert Esther Brunauer. Mary Dublin Keyserling would experience a loyalty investigation that was only briefly in the public eye but featured most of the big players in the anticommunist network. Behind the scenes, Frieda Miller, who headed the U.S. Women's Bureau under Truman, faced allegations that eventually restricted her access to government jobs, as did Caroline Ware, Pauli Murray, and Esther Peterson, not to mention many less familiar figures.[5] In electoral politics, allegations that they were "pink" contributed to the defeats of the Democratic congresswomen Emily Taft Douglas of Illinois in 1946, Helen Douglas Mankin of Georgia in 1948, and Helen Gahagan Douglas of California in 1950.[6] These women were all, to varying degrees and in varying ways, left feminists. They were forced to confront gender inequality in pursuing their own careers, and their goals included expanding opportunities for all women, especially the most disadvantaged ones.

Loyalty charges against women in government had antifeminist sources, as well as antifeminist outcomes. Proving such intent on the part of those who accused female officials of disloyalty is, however, a tricky business. After all, many left-liberal men were accused as well. One approach is to investigate whether women were accused out of proportion to their numbers in government. Fragmentary evidence does suggest that women were overrepresented among defendants in federal employee loyalty cases. Women made up only about 3 percent of high-level employees but seem to have comprised about 18 percent of high-level cases. Furthermore, the agencies that bore the brunt of subversion charges also were notable for the high status or recently improved status of women. Commerce and State, favorite targets of anticommunists, were the departments in which women as a proportion of employees had grown the most between 1923 and 1947. The Commerce Department stood out for having many high-level women as well as an unusual number of loyalty cases involving high-level employees.[7] These patterns are suggestive. However, even if one could prove conclusively that women were overrepresented among the accused, it could be argued that women were more likely to be leftists, or to have "suspect" associations, than men in government.

Indeed, the simplest explanation for why so many female government officials were accused is that anticommunists believed they were Communists. Most of the female loyalty defendants in fact were on the leftmost edge of the New Deal and Fair Deal. The formal charges against them were similar to those against left-liberal men, typically based on associations with alleged Communist fronts (usually labor, consumer, antifascist, and civil rights causes, many of which had a feminist aspect that made them especially attractive to women). But formal charges were only part of the story. The loyalty program's standards of "loyalty" were vague, and investigations turned on highly subjective assessments of the subject's character and "tendencies."[8] Evidence from loyalty hearings, FBI reports, and public and private statements by leading anticommunists reveals that women were judged by different standards and attacked in different ways from their male counterparts.

First of all, investigators scrutinized women's challenges to male supremacy, reading even small feminist gestures as evidence of Communist inclinations. Because the Communist Party theoretically supported women's equality, investigators reasoned that feminists might well be Communists. The association was widespread. The authors of the 1947 best seller *Modern Woman: The Lost Sex* warned that "agents of the Kremlin abroad continue to beat the feminist drums in full awareness of its disruptive influence" on the Soviets' enemies. (Jews and African Americans in the civil service faced an analogous problem: because the Communist Party championed racial equality and denounced fascism, investigators assumed that minorities were predisposed to communism.)[9] Dorothy Kenyon was on the United Nations Commission on the Status of Women when Senator McCarthy attacked her in 1950 as one of the State Department's subversives. In defending herself, Kenyon stressed that she had challenged Russian claims that communism emancipated women. FBI agents reported a 1944 comment by the African American New Dealer Mary McLeod Bethune to the effect that the United Sates could learn from Russia when it came to women's rights and minority rights. In Mary Dublin Keyserling's case, one piece of "derogatory" evidence was that she had said Russian women enjoyed more rights after the Bolshevik Revolution than before.[10] A loyalty official noted that Caroline Ware "uses single name yet has been married for several years. Known to defy conventions." He recommended further investigation. Similarly, an FBI agent reported a coworker's comment that Dublin Keyserling was "a queer woman [who] used her maiden name and didn't want to be blamed for her husband's mistakes."[11] Helen Hill Miller of the Labor Department was investigated after she questioned the agency's promotion policies, and Dorothy Bailey's challenges to racial and sexual discrimination by her employer, the U.S. Employment Service, were an issue in her loyalty case.[12]

Some accused women and their lawyers were certain that their sex affected their loyalty cases. Two formal allegations against Dublin Keyserling came from people whose work she had found wanting, and other coworkers interviewed by the FBI clearly disliked having a female boss. Her lawyer told the loyalty board: "She was a very young woman in very, very important positions. It is hard enough for an older woman to run an organization without incurring animosity. It is exceedingly difficult for a young woman to run an organization and to hire and fire and be responsible for promoting and demoting people without incurring a certain amount of hostility." Female and male civil servants alike were less tolerant of a coworker's forcefulness or ambition when that coworker was a woman.[13] Esther Brunauer also believed her sex worked against her. After she failed to convince her all-male loyalty board that she could be trusted not to share sensitive information with her husband (who in his youth had briefly belonged to a Communist group), Brunauer concluded, "their opinion of the reliability of women in professional positions is very low."[14]

THE RIGHT'S REPRESENTATION OF GENDER ROLES UNDER COMMUNISM

Conservative anticommunists, unlike liberal ones, believed an essential feature of communism was its totalitarian repression of what they assumed to be natural and proper gender roles. This view was shared not just by private individuals and groups on the far right but also by key congressional committee staffers and their influential media allies. This was especially true of J. B. Matthews, whom one scholar has dubbed "the spiritual leader of the Far Right in America," and his friend Ben Mandel, the two self-proclaimed experts on communism who spent years in key positions on the Dies Committee, its successor the House Un-American Activities Committee (HUAC), the Senate Internal Security Subcommittee (SISS), and McCarthy's Senate subcommittee.[15] Allied with Matthews, Mandel, and certain conservative politicians were the journalists Westbrook Pegler, George Sokolsky, Fulton Lewis Jr., Jack Lait, and Lee Mortimer of the Hearst empire, and Walter Trohan and George Dixon, who wrote for Robert McCormick's newspapers.

The power of conservative media magnates Hearst and McCormick was such that they were dubbed "the press lords." Some thirty million Americans read Hearst papers each day, while McCormick's *Chicago Tribune* boasted a million readers by the late 1930s. McCormick's *Washington Times-Herald*, the capital's leading daily, secretly shared its dossiers on individuals with intelligence agencies. The press lords had more influence over their columnists' political writing than most readers realized, and from the 1930s until the ascendance of television in the 1950s, syndicated columnists enjoyed unprecedented influence on public opinion. Government aides and newspapermen worked together to instigate and sustain the hunt for "Communists in government."[16]

In speeches and news stories, these men represented Communist women either as devoid of femininity or as exploiting their femininity in order to serve the Soviet cause. Unfeminine Communist women appeared as "mannish" lesbians, as robotic workers who competed with men at work rather than taking care of men at home, as bad mothers whose sons became dancers (i.e., homosexuals), and as domineering, even murderous wives. Right-wingers cast Julius Rosenberg and Earl Browder as "henpecked," while the women they alleged to be Communists, from Ethel Rosenberg to Eleanor Roosevelt, were portrayed as unloving mothers.[17]

If some Communist women were dumpy and overbearing, others appeared as treacherously ultrafeminine. They allegedly exploited their perceived religiosity, motherliness, physical weakness, and political innocence for subversive purposes. The middle-aged black clerk Annie Lee Moss was accused of using her Bible as a shield against charges of communism. Younger women, especially white ones, often were suspected of deploying their sexual attractiveness. When the ex-Communist informant Paul Crouch claimed he had known Dublin Keyserling to be a Communist in her youth, he played up her beauty. "She was brilliant but didn't look it," he told the FBI, as if being both smart and beautiful made her inherently deceitful. He and J. B. Matthews portrayed Dublin Keyserling as an attractive, romantic rich girl seduced by—and perhaps willing to seduce for—radical causes.[18] This testimony resonated with the right's

Figure 3.1. This 1952 cartoon used gender stereotypes to cast Communist organizations as seductresses who ensnared the gullible. Clipping from *Washington Times-Herald*, in "Communists in Government" scrapbook of the Senate Internal Security Subcommittee, Record Group 46, National Archives.

stereotype of Communist women as promiscuous seductresses who were loyal to no man, only to party discipline. That stereotype coexisted awkwardly with the image of Communist women as dowdy fanatics. The underlying commonality was that both types, the domineering asexual (or lesbian) and the irresistible seductress, served the Soviet state instead of their husbands.[19]

Since the 1920s, anticommunist experts had argued that the Bolshevik Revolution "nationalized" women, making their sexuality and labor subject to state control. The Communist Party allegedly arranged and broke up marriages; trained women to use sex for recruitment, espionage, and sabotage; and fostered miscegenation, rape, homosexuality, and general sexual chaos. Conservative anticommunists projected an apocalyptic vision of a world in which men's proper control over wives and daughters was disrupted—particularly their prerogative to control with whom their wives and daughters had sexual relations. The scenario may have aroused their audience in more ways than one. Indeed, Jack Lait and Lee Mortimer provided readers of *Washington Confidential* with phone numbers of gay bars and "call girls," even as they purported to deplore the depravity of the allegedly Red-infested city. It seems that envy and lust mingled with fear in the right's fantasy of a sexualized Communist underworld.[20]

In Lait and Mortimer's portrait, life in a city dominated by the federal bureaucracy offered a taste of what life would be like under communism. Furthermore, their belief that the federal government stifled individual initiative was saturated with assumptions about race and gender hierarchies. Conservatives and progressives held opposing views of the civil service's merit system, under which an applicant's performance on a standardized test was a key hiring criterion. Progressives viewed the merit system as helping ensure that employment was based on qualifications rather than on prejudices—whether in favor of a political supporter or against a certain demographic group. Conservatives, by contrast, associated lack of discrimination with mediocrity. In the conservative view, the bureaucracy was filled with rejects from the private sector who sought lifetime security on the government's "perennial payroll." In the civil service, according to Lait and Mortimer, "in the mediocrity and virtual anonymity of commonplace tasks, the sexes—*all four of them*—are equal in the robot requirements and qualifications. *There is no color line, no social selectivity* . . . once the precious appointment is filed in a machine *which knows no discrimination*, there it stays for life."[21]

That image of the government as run by minimally competent robots of indeterminate sex and commingled races was unusual only for the vividness with which it expressed conservatives' distaste for egalitarianism. Lait and Mortimer described Washington as "Negro Heaven," where employers could not fire blacks for fear of antagonizing Eleanor Roosevelt, and where the "rich" NAACP deliberately kept its headquarters in a poor area in order to bring visitors through its "stage-managed slave-quarters area." Like some other conservatives, Lait and Mortimer claimed to oppose Jim Crow, but their prejudices were evident: "under Negro occupancy, some of the best dwellings in Washington . . . now look like the slums the Fair Dealers decry."[22]

The discomfort with blacks' boundary crossing in Washington workplaces and neighborhoods was inextricable from the fear of sexual relations between white women and black men, a fear compounded by the autonomy of white "government gals." To right-wingers, the government's practice of paying men and women the same for equal work meant that "the income is high for females," which enabled them to be sexually aggressive. Lait and Mortimer claimed they personally had disappointed some "young ladies" by insisting on paying for the whole group's drinks, foiling the women's attempt to buy sexual favors. They claimed that government girls "hunted" servicemen, who "seldom were allowed to pick up checks," and also sought out "colored men, especially jazz band musicians." Seven white women who worked for the Social Security Administration supposedly had been caught paying a "colored janitor" to sleep with each of them a different night of the week.[23] Such anecdotes, probably apocryphal, both titillated and alarmed readers with the suggestion that in Washington, large numbers of economically independent single white women were on the prowl for sex with whomever they could seduce, be they white men, black men—or other women.

"Lesbianism is scandalously rampant" in Washington, claimed Lait and Mortimer. Government girls "are a hard, efficient lot, doing men's work, thinking like men and sometimes driven to take the place of men—in the proscribed zones of desperate flings at love and sex." Lesbians were harder to count than "fairies" because lesbians were more discreet, Lait and Mortimer explained, but experts reportedly believed there were "at least twice as many Sapphic lovers as fairies," which by Lait and Mortimer's calculations implied about twelve thousand lesbians and six thousand gay men in the government service.[24]

For the right, the connection between lesbians and communism was somewhat less direct than it was for male homosexuals and communism. Male homosexuals allegedly wanted to be dominated and thereby were especially tolerant of party discipline. Also, male homosexuals' alleged proclivity for debauchery supposedly was readily exploited by trained Communist agents who staged opulent parties, filmed the participants, and used the films to obtain whatever they sought by blackmail. The right connected lesbians to communism through more general associations, for example between communism and women's employment (and therefore independence from a male breadwinner). Male homosexuals and lesbians both were labeled "deviants," however, unrestrained by religion's moral discipline and indifferent to all kinds of taboos. There may have been some truth to Lait and Mortimer's observation that "there is free crossing of racial lines among fairies and lesbians," but the authors' portrayal was a grossly exaggerated caricature. They cast Washington as an endless round of "interracial, inter-middle-sex mélanges" and "yachting parties" of black drag queens.[25]

In the view of right-wing journalists, these sexually and racially variegated government bureaucrats would not be satisfied until ordinary Americans had been forced to join in their moral depravity. In a postmortem attack on New Dealer Harry Hopkins, the columnist Westbrook Pegler alleged that Hopkins had been a Communist who favored "drafting both men and women for enforced labor at fixed wages." To Pegler, this meant Hopkins had wanted to separate husbands and wives and to compel "a genteel, moral woman in a religious American home . . . to keep boarding-house for any riff-raff that might be billeted upon her." Pegler was intimating that rape, possibly interracial rape, would be the result of leftist social policies. Matthews too hinted at the threat of rape under left-liberal regimes. In 1950 he spearheaded a campaign to discredit Dorothy Kenyon, whose spirited response to Senator McCarthy's charges was making her a hero among liberals. Matthews told radio listeners that Kenyon was going into "hysterics" in an effort to "smear" McCarthy. He cited her alleged associations with Communist front groups as proof that "this Kenyon woman" was "unfit to hold a high position on the State Department's payroll." In defense of "guilt by association" as a legitimate criterion for termination of employment, Matthews suggested that if liberals had their way, "a girls' school could not discharge a male teacher who had a record of several arrests on charges of rape but had never been convicted."[26]

In addition to depriving women of protection from rape, Communists allegedly also encouraged white women to offer themselves to black men. The ex-Communist informant Sylvia Crouch, a white former millworker from North Carolina, told a legislative committee that "white girls were instructed to have close relations with Negro boys" to attract black men to the Communist Party.[27] In 1948, Ben Mandel, then HUAC's research director, gave a radio talk on how Communists recruited American youth. He offered cautionary tales of "young men and women who left happy and comfortable homes to follow the Communist will-o-the-wisp, with tragic results." His example of tragedy for a young man was the loss of his career as a doctor. By contrast, "a brilliant young woman Communist, a graduate of a New York college, was induced to run off with an elderly Negro."[28]

Did these leading anticommunist instigators believe what they were saying, or were they just trying to scare their audiences into supporting the Red hunt? Apparently a bit of both. Their private correspondence suggests that their gender and race fears were genuine rather than adopted purely as tools for swaying public opinion. When Pegler was looking for damaging information on two leftists who had been married to the same woman, he asked Matthews to confirm whether "that common wife of theirs spent some of her spare time sleeping with a coon." Matthews's reply was more circumspect in wording but indicates a similar disapproval of interracial relationships.[29] Other correspondence suggests Matthews really believed that Communists had infiltrated mainstream women's groups such as the League of Women Voters and the General Federation of Women's Clubs.[30]

The questions that congressmen and loyalty board officials asked behind closed doors further demonstrate anticommunists' worry that female independence would lead to both communism and interracial liaisons. In quizzing a white female administrator about her staff, her loyalty board was interested in whether and how her staff was "mixed"; when she said she had supervised a "colored man" at one time, she was asked whether he was a professional or clerical employee. The board seemed to think that hiring an educated black man to work alongside white women indicated subversive tendencies on the supervisor's part.[31] The Senate Internal Security Subcommittee queried law professor Tom Emerson about why he had posted bond for a white woman who was arrested for "lascivious carriage" with a black man in her New Haven apartment. Emerson explained that her civil liberties had been violated because she would not have been arrested had she not attended a May Day parade from which police followed her home. SISS members were incredulous that Emerson had defended her without concern for her "lewd" conduct or her likely Communist sympathies. The exchange deepened their suspicion of Emerson himself.[32]

Although conservative anticommunists sincerely believed the Communist threat had worrisome gender and sexual dimensions, they were not above deliberately sensationalizing and exaggerating them. In 1951, Matthews made a dramatic speech, titled "Operation Women," to a New York patriotic society. He claimed to be drawing on U.S. Army sources and "important government reports," when in fact he was borrowing heavily from an informal memo by Sylvia Crouch. Not only did Communists intend to destroy the American family, Matthews warned, but also they planned to take advantage of loyal Americans' chivalrous assumptions about women in order to achieve their goal of world conquest. "The Communist utilization of women on a wholesale scale for revolutionary purposes" was evidence of "the diabolical cunning of the Communist conspiracy." Matthews claimed the army had learned of Communist plans to deploy women as spies and saboteurs in defense industries. Invoking the specter of women pushing men out of defense jobs because of women's "special aptitudes" for "delicate precision operations" in areas such as electronics, Matthews warned that Communists intended to exploit this feminization of production. "The Party proceeds on a very interesting and probably correct assumption, namely, that a reasonably good-looking female is much less suspect as a subversionist than a husky male, and would therefore be subjected to less rigid screening tests." Also, he declared mysteriously, "once inside a plant the woman saboteur is more difficult to detect than her male counterpart." Communist women allegedly would use their sexual allure to obtain jobs in transportation and civil defense, where they could serve as couriers, spies, and saboteurs. Sylvia Crouch's original memo claimed, "Communists have never hesitated to exploit sex for their objectives. Girls will be assigned to become sweethearts of as many soldiers as possible," so that each one could gather information on "perhaps a dozen" different military units. Matthews reported that American soldiers had dated Korean "girls" who turned out to be "highly trained Communist intelligence agents." Other Korean women had smuggled weapons in their babies' blankets.[33]

In other words, a woman who appeared to be an innocent worker, a pretty date, or a loving mother might in fact be a Communist agent. She also might be a killer: Matthews closed with the dramatic observation that of the twelve Americans involved in the plot to assassinate Leon Trotsky, nine had been women.[34] Matthews's warning against underestimating women may have had a feminist ring, but his emphasis of women's particular talents for deception had antifeminist implications for the small but important group of professional women in government.

RICH FEMINISTS AS COMMUNIST DUPES

Not only did investigators believe that women were more likely than men to be attracted to the Communist Party (because it espoused women's emancipation); they also believed that the party had a particular interest in recruiting women—especially wealthy ones. To finance their operations, Communists allegedly targeted rich women, who were perceived to be susceptible because they were prone to idealism and felt guilty about their wealth. Rich women supposedly also were more susceptible than working-class women because they were bored and because they had been exposed to college professors—then as now characterized by the right as integral to a leftist conspiracy.[35] According to Matthews, wealthy feminist reformers were the most effective weapons in Communists' propaganda campaign. Calling International Women's Day (March 8) a "holiday of the Communist world movement," Matthews listed prominent American women who "wittingly or unwittingly cast themselves in the role of stooges for this Communist holiday." He named Eleanor Roosevelt, Dorothy Kenyon, Helen Keller, Mary McLeod Bethune, and Virginia Gildersleeve, the Barnard College dean whom President Roosevelt had appointed to help draft the United Nations charter. Matthews also named wives of liberal men whom he had reason to embarrass. These included Mrs. Chester Nimitz, whose husband Truman had appointed to head the new Commission on Internal Security and Individual Rights, and Mrs. Joseph Davies, wife of the former U.S. ambassador to Russia.[36] Rich feminists were a favorite target too for the authors Lait and Mortimer, who mocked Cornelia Pinchot, the prominent activist and former suffragist, as an "elderly hostess" of interracial gatherings of Reds who were "making hay" with her name.[37]

It is well established that McCarthyism was fueled by class resentment of the East Coast establishment—resentment of that "silver spoon" old boys' network formed in exclusive prep schools and Ivy League colleges and sustained in various New Deal agencies, especially the State Department. Furthermore, this class tension between the likes of Sumner Welles, Alger Hiss, Dean Acheson, and Charles Bohlen, on the one hand, and conservative legislators Kenneth Wherry (R-Neb.), Joseph McCarthy (R-Wis.), and Richard Nixon (R-Calif.), on the other, also was a clash of rival masculinities. The "patrician manhood script," to use the historian Robert Dean's phrase, stressed loyalty to a brotherhood forged in the sex-segregated elite institutions of the Northeast, heroic volunteer service to the state in military and public life, and cosmopolitan cultivation. On the other side were men infuriated by the patricians' dismissal of nonmembers as provincial primitives. They interpreted the brotherhood's loyalty to its members as evidence of a homoerotic "conspiracy of the gentlemen"; the patricians' government service as inability to compete as entrepreneurs; their urbane intellectualism as "fancy-pants" effeteness; and their internationalism as lack of patriotism. Questioning the masculinity of the "imperial brotherhood" became one tactic by which ultraconservatives tried to gain control over U.S. foreign policy.[38]

But anticommunist conservatives also resented the "old girls' network," an attitude that seems to have resonated deeply with certain voters. As right-wingers pointed out, female New Dealers and wives of New Dealers often knew each other through a dense web of ties with elite women's colleges and voluntary associations. Conservatives resented liberalism's activist college women as much as its "effete" intellectual men, casting the women as naïve, pampered do-gooders and busybodies with too much time on their hands. If the men of the State Department were "striped-pants diplomats," the corresponding stereotype for affluent female activists and administrators was "pinks in minks," as one headline put it.[39] Conservatives ridiculed members of the Washington League of Women Shoppers who picketed with striking chambermaids.[40] In 1942, Pegler called Eleanor Roosevelt a "meddler in many matters which are very improper business for the wife of the President," who was "quietly salting around her personal friends in the Government employ" and trying to install a "petticoat government." In 1951 Lait and Mortimer still hammered on the same theme, claiming that Eleanor Roosevelt's "kitchen cabinet continues to rule the nation" (not least, they alleged, by forcing federal agencies to hire black women and retain them even though they were incompetent).[41]

Westbrook Pegler was skeptical of all women's political intelligence, but he was particularly scathing toward elite women. One of his regular columns was "George Spelvin, American," an immensely popular satire about the life of an ordinary family man. In "Never Argue Politics with a Woman," Mr. Spelvin tells his wife it was crazy to let women vote, because they just choose the handsome guy. Mrs. Spelvin's retort clinches her husband's point: she declares her intention to prove him wrong by voting for Eisenhower, because he is bald. Mrs. Spelvin might have been foolish, but compared to professional or activist women, she was the salt of the earth. Another Pegler column pitted Mrs. Spelvin, the inarticulate but hardworking housewife, against a "shrill" lady columnist who did not do her own dishes or spend time with her children. In Pegler's writing, jabs at women who hired others to do their domestic work were as common as the attacks on union bosses for which he is better known. Pegler's readers "frequently wrote that they considered him the last great defender of the common man," and many of them apparently empathized with George Spelvin, the sexist "regular guy" of his day.[42]

Anticommunist accusations against female and male New Dealers differed. Conservatives challenged women's job qualifications by questioning their high salaries, naming their ties to influential men, and stressing their femininity, or lack thereof. These sorts of attacks often were made in the public arena by conservative politicians and their media allies, apparently in an effort to undercut public support for liberal administrations. Senator McCarthy opened his attack on the lawyer and former judge Dorothy Kenyon with the observation that "this lady" received an annual salary of $12,000 from the State Department, as if that alone warranted outrage. In trying to discredit Kenyon's counterattack on McCarthy, Matthews and his friend the Hearst columnist George Sokolsky always mentioned the $12,000 salary, even though that figure was extrapolated from the fraction of that amount that she actually earned as a part-time consultant. Matthews also asserted that Kenyon had no "legal competence."[43] When Truman nominated the highly accomplished Kathryn McHale, head of the American Association of University Women, to the Subversive Activities Control Board, Pegler wrote that she had no qualifications for the job except that her brother was an important Democrat. Meanwhile, behind the scenes, Senator McCarran, the anticommunist Democrat who headed SISS, tried to block McHale's appointment by suggesting she was a lesbian.[44]

WHO WEARS THE PANTS? REPRESENTATIONS OF DUAL-CAREER COUPLES

While high-earning single women could be cast as lesbians, high-earning married women were seen as taking jobs they did not need (because their husbands should be supporting them), selfishly indulging material desires or unwomanly ambitions. If their husbands also worked for the government, then the wife probably had been hired because of the husband's influence. Pegler attacked Ida Klaus, a Truman appointee to the National Labor Relations Board, by stressing that she was married to a man who had been "on the Washington payroll since 1934." Sam Klaus had "bounced from the Treasury to the Foreign Economic Administration, a Bubblehead Wallace enterprise, to State, and now we find his wife running the Labor Relations Board." Pegler also insinuated that Truman had appointed Klaus because he wanted her to sabotage the antiunion Taft-Hartley Act, which Congress had passed over his veto in 1947. Pegler interpreted Klaus's long experience as an NLRB lawyer and with the International Labor Organization as evidence not that she was qualified for the job but that she was a socialist (which she was not). Pegler ignored her demonstrated abilities and instead linked socialism, pro-labor views, and deviation from the ideal of female domesticity.[45]

Conservatives took every opportunity to call Washington's numerous high-earning couples to public attention. Senator Robert Taft (R-Ohio) attempted to discredit a major government proposal to expand the welfare system by calling its chief author, Eveline Burns, a Communist and observing that she and her husband both earned large government salaries.[46] In 1942, a conservative journalist lambasted "Miss Mary Dublin" for accepting a $5,600 salary at the Office of Civilian Defense when "in private life she is Mrs. Leon H. Keyserling." Leon Keyserling then was second in command at the U.S. Housing Authority. "The women who are working without thought of compensation," the columnist warned, would figure out who Dublin really was and wonder why it was necessary to pay so much to the wife of a well-paid official.[47] Dublin Keyserling herself probably wondered why she earned so much less than her husband. A decade later, word was leaked to the media that the Commerce Department had suspended Dublin Keyserling pending the results of a loyalty investigation. One beneficiary of the leak, Walter Trohan, the Washington bureau chief of the *Chicago Tribune*, told radio listeners that Dublin Keyserling's $10,000 salary reflected less her own performance than the influence of her husband, "one of the most powerful men in the government." The "spectacle of husband and wife on the federal payroll is not uncommon in Washington," he lamented. With combined government salaries of about $25,000 a year, Trohan claimed, the couple was living the high life at taxpayer expense. The reason the Keyserlings had no children was that they had "been too busy gathering dollars to gather children." Only after establishing the Keyserlings' high income and deviation from the all-American family model did this early radio shock jock describe the substance of the loyalty allegations.[48]

Those publicly expressed sentiments about dual-career couples reflected and reinforced private ones, and both could weigh subtly on the course of a loyalty investigation. One administrator who called Dublin Keyserling "radical" also complained to an investigator that she and her husband together made five times his salary.[49] Hostility to the many dual-career couples in Democratic Party circles derived not just from economic envy, however, but also from disapproval of, or perhaps inability to imagine, egalitarian couples. In 1951, the Senate Internal Security Subcommittee questioned Leon Keyserling closely about his wife's affiliations. When Leon said he was uncertain whether Mary had sponsored a particular dinner event in 1941, the committee expressed surprise that he did not exercise closer control over his wife.[50] Walter Trohan similarly had definite ideas about wives' role. In 1970 he praised Bess Truman for having been a "great woman" because "she believed her job was to be a wife and not going around to beautify America or to make speeches or to campaign or anything else." Trohan was making a disparaging reference to former First Lady Ladybird Johnson's work on highway beautification.[51]

Conservatives assumed that in a normal marriage the husband would control the wife, and therefore, if he were disloyal, she would be his puppet or spy. If their relationship was abnormal, as was assumed to be more likely for Communist marriages, she would control him. Right-wingers' apparent inability to envision a marriage in which neither spouse dominated had ominous implications for individuals who married leftists. If one spouse inevitably "wore the pants," then how could the other exercise independent political views? If one spouse was a Communist, then the other must be too. Ben Mandel claimed that Communist Party policy explicitly forbade members to marry "known enemies of the party." In 1946 Mandel selectively quoted the bylaws of the Communist Party USA to that effect and highlighted Dublin Keyserling's suspect associations in an attempt to block her husband's appointment to the Council of Economic Advisers.[52]

Under the federal employee loyalty program, allegations against a spouse were potentially as damaging as allegations against the employee. When both spouses worked for the government, the opportunities for suspicion multiplied and could be fueled by the resentment of dual-career couples. Loyalty and security standards varied by agency and over time, but "sympathetic association" with known Communists was always grounds for investigation. After June 1950 in certain agencies, and in all agencies after Eisenhower's Executive Order 10450 in 1953, a person could be cleared on *loyalty* grounds but dismissed as a *security* risk. Many more government workers were dismissed on security grounds than on loyalty grounds. There were several categories of "security risk," including alcoholics, homosexuals and others deemed immoral, and relatives of people who had been declared loyalty risks. The distinction between security risk and loyalty risk was that in the former case, the employees' personal circumstances—regardless of their own political views—impaired their judgment or made them vulnerable to blackmail or coercion. Civil servants typically illustrated the security risk idea with the example of alcoholics, but conservative congressmen reaped political hay by noisily pursuing homosexuals.[53]

Many people dismissed as security risks were homosexuals, but relatives of people who had been labeled loyalty risks comprised a larger group of security dismissals. Officials assumed spouses held more influence than other relatives. Certain agencies treated husband and wife as one, as Esther Brunauer learned in 1952 when the State Department dismissed her as a security risk. After McCarthy named her in 1950 as an example of the agency's laxity, State cleared her on loyalty grounds. However, when her husband, a Hungarian-born chemist who had belonged to the Young Workers' League in the 1920s, resigned from the navy, her case was reopened, and he appeared before her loyalty board. The hearing was supposed to be about her loyalty, but the board quizzed him in detail about his own case. Although he had already explained inaccurate rumors about his efforts to observe the Bikini Island bomb tests to the satisfaction of the navy, the State Department loyalty board decided that he was a loyalty risk and therefore his wife must be a security risk.[54]

That the loyalty program often treated husband and wife as one did not play out symmetrically for men and women. Because about 97 percent of high-ranking civil servants were men, allegations about spouses of senior officials usually were allegations about wives. In one sample, at least 10 percent of the cases involving male defendants featured allegations about wives' activism, whether in women's organizations such as the League of Women Shoppers and Women's International League for Peace and Freedom or in mixed-sex groups such as the National Lawyers' Guild and the American League for Peace and Democracy.[55] As a result, not only did civil servants become more circumspect about their own affiliations, but their spouses did as well. The federal loyalty program was a major factor in the demise or contraction of women's reform organizations, particularly but not only in the Washington area, as women resigned to protect their husbands' careers.[56] The tribulations of those New Deal men who married left-liberal activists may have influenced the next cohort of ambitious men to marry women who were less politically outspoken.

An activist wife could be a real liability for a government official in the late 1940s and 1950s, and many men's careers suffered as a result. However, men sometimes could convince loyalty boards that they were not influenced by their wives' politics, whereas loyalty boards usually assumed a female government employee would be unable to resist a suspect husband's pressure. Esther Brunauer was dismissed, for example, but economist Mordecai Ezekiel was not. Ezekiel had been a member of the New Deal "brain trust" before joining the United Nations Food and Agriculture Organization in 1946. He faced loyalty boards in 1954 and 1955, chiefly because his wife Lucille had headed the Washington LWS and had a sister who lived with the prominent Communist Marion Bachrach. Ezekiel told loyalty investigators his wife was bored by "long economic discussions" and also that she had cut off contact with her sister at his request.[57] Loyalty officials who perceived a male defendant as sufficiently in control of his wife sometimes dismissed the wife's political views as less threatening to national security than the views of a female official's leftist husband would be. That perception did not stop partisans from digging for dirt on officials' wives. But male officials were more likely than female officials to be able to neutralize charges about their spouses.[58] Furthermore, female professionals who were dismissed as security risks had fewer alternatives in academia and private practice than their male counterparts. Brunauer, whose expertise had made her in 1946 the third American woman to reach the diplomatic rank of minister and a U.S. delegate to UNESCO, wound up editing textbooks in Evanston, Illinois, where she died of heart trouble at age fifty-eight.[59]

Male loyalty defendants tried to show that they were "normal" men, and female defendants tried to show that they were "normal" women, but these analogous burdens weighed more heavily on women. Conservative anticommunists presumed "normal" women to be more susceptible to communism, and less suited to policymaking, than "normal" men. FBI agents, informants, and loyalty hearing witnesses often assessed a subject's femininity when evaluating her loyalty. People who suspected Dublin Keyserling was a Communist portrayed her as "power mad," "domineering," "ambitious," and "out for herself." Her defenders, by contrast, emphasized that "she conducted herself like a lady" and was "reticent," "refined," and "charming." The defense attorney took pains to deny Matthews's assertion that Dublin Keyserling had a "dominant personality," and he disagreed with another witness that she could have "ever used the word 'hell.'" Dublin Keyserling's lawyer apparently recognized that loyalty boards might interpret female assertiveness as evidence of Communist tendencies.[60] References to Dublin Keyserling as "aggressive" and a "self-serving opportunist" could have reflected anti-Semitism rather than sexism, but nearly identical language was used against the Boston Brahmin Caroline Ware.

Male supporters downplayed the political views of female defendants and played up their normative femininity. Asked to explain Dublin Keyserling's presence at a leftist conference in Mexico, her friend Nathaniel Weyl said she had seemed more interested in shopping than in the conference. Oliver Peterson explained that his wife Esther was friendly with the alleged Communist Mildred Kramer because both had had difficulty becoming pregnant, and that the two women chiefly talked about their children. Mordecai Ezekiel said his wife Lucille was not interested in politics (a claim belied by her extensive work for the League of Women Shoppers) and that she and her sister's Communist roommate talked mainly about cooking and gardening. Presumably female defendants' interests in shopping, children, and other domestic pursuits were expected to make them seem more like typical women and less like Communists.[61]

Female civil servants and their defenders walked a tightrope, however, because being seen as too feminine also was risky. Although "reticence" and "charm" allegedly were uncharacteristic of Communist women, other normatively female traits—emotionalism, idealism, malleability—supposedly made women susceptible to Communist influence. One sympathetic witness tried to counter these stereotypes by telling investigators that Dublin Keyserling was "sober," "sensible," and "cynical about isms."[62]

Anticommunists used gendered language to attack men as well as women. Walter Trohan's October 1952 radio broadcast impugned Leon Keyserling's masculinity by pointing to his Ivy League background, lack of war service, lack of employment outside government, and his childless marriage to a professional woman. Fulton Lewis Jr. quoted Leon's criticism of the values promoted by college football as evidence that he had rejected "the American way of life." Leon had written in 1934 that football's celebration of competitive individualism made it a training ground for business elites. Conservative journalists often mentioned left liberals' disdain for college sports, presumably to make them seem less manly and more elitist.[63] During the 1952 presidential campaign, the *New York Daily News* ridiculed the Democrat Adlai Stevenson as "Adelaide," who used "teacup words" in a "fruity" voice. Stevenson's wit and eloquence became disadvantages rather than virtues, making him look like an "egghead" in comparison to his opponent, the plainspoken former football player and army general Dwight Eisenhower. After the State Department's 1950 admission that it had dismissed ninety-one homosexuals, ultraconservatives charged the Democrats with nurturing an aristocratic clique of "sexual misfits" in the diplomatic service.[64]

That gender was the basis for attacks on men as well as women does not undercut the claim that attacks on women had antifeminist intent.

First, the attacks on men arguably also had antifeminist intent: men were being chastised for not manifesting values and behaviors on which male dominance rested: martial valor, physical and entrepreneurial competitiveness, sole breadwinning, heterosexual virility. Second, men who had a sufficiently "masculine" record or personal style could inoculate themselves against such attacks. Female officials, by contrast, faced a nearly irresoluble double bind because normative constructions of femininity were incompatible with the wielding of power and expertise. Men were constrained to demonstrate their masculinity, but women faced a paradox: being unfeminine, or being too feminine, could indicate susceptibility to subversion.

Occasionally, conservatives found a female civil servant they could admire. In 1953, the *Times-Herald* columnist George Dixon favorably contrasted the new head of the U.S. Women's Bureau, Alice Leopold, with Roosevelt and Truman appointees to that post. "The holy state of matrimony has been given a boost by the Eisenhower administration," he wrote approvingly. The new head of the Women's Bureau, "a tall, very good-looking party," was married and the "mother of two teen-age sons"—unlike her predecessors Mary Anderson and Frieda Miller, whom Dixon described as "childless spinsters." In fact Frieda Miller was neither childless nor single; she and her partner Pauline Newman had raised a daughter. Whether Dixon knew it or not, Miller had been plagued by loyalty allegations. Her successor Alice Leopold would lead the Women's Bureau away from the pro-union, pro–civil rights feminism that Miller had promoted. George Dixon's approval of Leopold was the exception that proved the rule: professional women were not to be trusted, unless perhaps they were *married* mothers of *grown* children (heaven forbid they work while the children were young), whose personal circumstances, along with their views, affirmed the status quo.[65]

In sum, women's growing presence in the high ranks of the federal civil service in the 1930s and 1940s gave conservatives another reason to dislike the bureaucratic state. Conservatives perceived correctly that men in liberal Democratic administrations had promoted professional women and in some cases even married them. Right-wingers associated communism with men's loss of control over wives and daughters. The sketchy available statistics suggest that conservative anticommunists singled out women for disloyalty charges. Certainly they judged women by different standards, and their language in accusing women reflected and reinforced antifeminist assumptions. Men too suffered gendered attacks, but female officials were more vulnerable because "proper" femininity was more difficult to reconcile with wielding authority than was "proper" masculinity.

Conservative anticommunists had many goals. Certainly they wanted to get the Democrats out of power, roll back the welfare state and internationalist foreign policies, halt the labor and civil rights movements, and contain a perceived surge in homosexuality. But key players on the right also feared that communism—and the liberalism they viewed as a slippery slope to it—would erode men's control of women's sexuality and labor. Furthermore, they found that tapping into popular antifeminism was an effective way of increasing the breadth and depth of public support for their other objectives. Antifeminism was both an end and a convenient instrument of the right. Scholars widely recognize U.S. political elites' historical playing of the "race card," but we have paid insufficient attention to the "gender card" that often was part of the same hand. It also bears emphasizing that the gender card had more than one face. The flip side of the era's well-documented anxieties about masculinity and homosexuality was fear of female independence.

CHAPTER 4

The Loyalty Investigations of Mary Dublin Keyserling and Leon Keyserling

In June 1940, the Dies Committee researcher Benjamin Mandel sent a cryptic postcard to the anticommunist journalist Benjamin Stolberg: "You should look into Consumers' League: NY local now headed by Mary Dublin (CP)."[1] Mandel did not have his facts quite right. Mary Dublin headed the National Consumers' League, not its New York branch, and she was not a member of the Communist Party. She was, however, an officer of the New York chapter of the League of Women Shoppers, which the Dies Committee claimed was a Communist front group. A few months after Mandel wrote Stolberg about her, Dublin married Leon Keyserling, who as Senator Robert Wagner's legislative aide was the chief draftsman of the National Labor Relations Act of 1935 and the U.S. Housing Act of 1937. As people associated with the progressive consumer and labor movements, the Keyserlings aptly represent both prongs of the movement to raise "mass purchasing power" that so antagonized American conservatives. During the 1940s, the Keyserlings held increasingly important government jobs. Mary became an international economist in the Department of Commerce. Leon drafted the 1946 Employment Act that created the Council of Economic Advisers, to which he was appointed, and in 1950 he became its chairman.

For decades after Mandel sent that postcard in 1940, the Keyserlings were prime targets of the anticommunist right. They underwent protracted loyalty investigations that took place behind closed doors until 1952, when leaks to the press briefly generated headlines. At the time and throughout their long subsequent careers, the Keyserlings publicly dismissed their experiences as fleeting manifestations of Red scare hysteria. In fact, they endured recurring, elaborate investigations that were rigged against them by a combination of forces with diverse interests.

The commitment to social change that attracted loyalty investigators' attention to Mary Dublin Keyserling was manifested long before she entered government service. Born in 1910 in New York City to Russian Jewish immigrants, she was profoundly influenced by the example of her parents. Her father, Louis Dublin, was a famous public health expert and statistician; Augusta Salik Dublin was a settlement movement activist for housing reform. At her mother's alma mater, Barnard College, Mary's professors included the economist Wesley Clair Mitchell, an early proponent of the economic importance of mass consumption, and the future New Dealer Raymond Moley. On a summer fellowship at the Geneva School of International Studies in 1929, Mary studied with John Maynard Keynes, another rising star of underconsumptionist theory. Her lifelong interest in women's employment emerged in her senior honors thesis, which examined the industrial revolution's impact on New England women. After graduating in 1930, Dublin researched national health insurance proposals for the Committee on the Costs of Medical Care and then did graduate work at the London School of Economics, where she was inspired by the socialist political scientist Harold Laski, and Columbia University. From 1933 to 1938, she taught at Sarah Lawrence College, where she required privileged young women to survey slum housing conditions and design family budgets for varying incomes. During those years she lived in Greenwich Village and taught adult education classes nearby at the famous Henry Street Settlement. In 1938 she was recruited to lead the National Consumers' League (NCL), the venerable women's organization that promoted legislation to regulate labor conditions, hours, and wages. Dublin coordinated successful NCL campaigns for the Fair Labor Standards Act of 1938, which established the first permanent national standards for a minimum wage and maximum hours, and against weakening the National Labor Relations Act. She also pushed the NCL into bold initiatives on behalf of labor standards for domestic workers, national health insurance, and a labor-consumer political alliance. Her forceful leadership style drew both admirers and critics at the NCL, but all agreed she was brilliant. Late in 1940 she moved to Washington to marry Leon Keyserling and to begin the career in government that would lead to her loyalty investigation.[2]

Leon was raised in Beaufort, South Carolina, but otherwise he and Mary had much in common. Both were the children of progressive, upwardly mobile Jews whose parents hailed from Lithuania or Russia. Both their families were secular, highly educated, and assimilated; they honored their heritage by valuing tolerance and civil liberties rather than by observing Jewish religious traditions. Leon's mother Jennie Hyman, a native New Yorker, had known Mary's mother Augusta Salik at Barnard. In 1906 Jennie married William Keyserling, who was prospering as a farmer and merchant in Beaufort and who shared her intellectual and reform interests; in the 1920s William made local headlines for his denunciations of the Ku Klux Klan. Leon, the first of William and Jennie's four children, was born in 1907. He earned his B.A. in economics in 1928 from Columbia, where he was advised by the future brain truster Rexford

Tugwell (himself a student of Simon Patten, another early theorist of underconsumption). After earning his law degree at Harvard in 1931, Leon did graduate work in economics back at Columbia with Tugwell, who hired him into the Department of Agriculture in 1933. Leon soon became Senator Wagner's legislative assistant, from which position he drafted key New Deal legislation: Section 7a of the National Industrial Recovery Act (1933), its successor the National Labor Relations Act, and the U.S. Housing Act of 1937. From 1937 to 1946 he worked for the U.S. Housing Authority, first as general counsel and eventually as acting administrator. He also helped write the Democratic Party platforms of 1936, 1940, and 1944 for Wagner, who served on the platform committee.[3]

Meanwhile, Leon married Mary. Shared political views and ambitions were foundational to their marriage, which was sparked and occasionally strained by intellectual sparring and rivalry. They had met in 1934, but she was not interested in marriage then, at least not to him. In 1939, when Mary was NCL general secretary, NCL board member William H. Davis suggested that she get Leon's comments on a draft of her statement to Congress against amendments to the Wagner Act. Leon first said he was too busy, but eventually they reviewed her testimony over breakfast at the Hay-Adams hotel. He declared her statement perfect and insisted on taking her to lunch. "The funny part is," she later recounted, "he wasn't too busy at all from then on, and seemed to have more free time than I did."[4] After they married in 1940, the couple discovered they were unable to have children, a disappointment that they coped with by intensifying their focus on work.[5]

Some observers—including Mary—credited her with influencing Leon's thinking. She herself had planned to write the essay on full employment that led to creation of the Council of Economic Advisers (CEA), but two days before the essay submission deadline in 1944, she injured her wrist and prevailed on Leon to write it instead. The resulting essay won second prize in a competition sponsored by the Pabst Brewing Company and eventually led to Leon's appointment to the CEA.[6] Years later, the powerful congressman Wilbur Mills (D-Ark.), who had been friends with Leon since they were at Harvard Law School together, commented to President John F. Kennedy that Leon's wife was "a brilliant economist. . . . I assume he's learned what he knows from her . . . because he was a lawyer." It is uncertain whether Leon would have agreed with that assessment; he did have some economics training himself. In any case, Mary and Leon had very similar views on politics and economics, and they collaborated on many projects over the decades.[7]

The substance and outcome of federal loyalty cases varied widely, but most followed the same general timeline (see appendix 2), and the Keyserling cases fit the pattern. Screening of federal workers began well before the formal creation of the federal loyalty program in 1947. The 1939 Hatch Act, passed partly in response to Dies Committee charges that Communists had infiltrated the government, prohibited federal employees from belonging to any "political party or organization which advocates the overthrow of the existing constitutional form of government."[8] Employees had to swear they did not belong to any such group, and employing agencies requested background checks from the FBI. The FBI checked the databases of other agencies, including the Dies Committee. If any red flags popped up, the FBI conducted its own investigation, which often culminated in a transcribed interview in which the employee was invited to explain any derogatory associations. The FBI reported its findings to the employing agency and also to the Civil Service Commission. To the displeasure of the Dies Committee, the CSC loyalty examiners distinguished between leftism and Communist Party membership, and they also tended to forgive Communist associations that predated the Hitler-Stalin pact of August 1939. Although wartime loyalty-security measures evolved hastily and with little public scrutiny, they were often fairer to employees than what was to follow.

Soviet conduct immediately after the war, combined with publicity about the Canadian spy ring revealed by Russian defector Igor Gouzenko, made the American public more receptive than before to alarms about Communist infiltration of the U.S. government.[9] The Republicans' dramatic gains in the 1946 elections were widely credited to their hammering of Truman on the "Communists in government" issue. Hoping to undercut charges that his administration harbored subversives, Truman instituted a sweeping employee loyalty program in March 1947.[10] Under Executive Order 9835, each executive department established a loyalty board, whose proceedings were to be strictly confidential. Employees for whom "reasonable grounds for belief in disloyalty" could be established were to be dismissed. As critics then and since have shown, the program's flaws included the anonymity of confidential informants, the vague definition of "derogatory" information, reliance on arbitrary and inconsistent lists of subversive organizations, and the double jeopardy problem: employees were investigated repeatedly for the same charges, because every promotion or job change required a new loyalty check and because loyalty standards changed several times.[11]

Truman's hope that the loyalty program would short-circuit the campaign against Communists in government was thwarted by a combination of world events and partisan opportunism. In the two years after Truman's narrow election victory in 1948, the political terrain shifted profoundly, undercutting his administration's ability to control the anticommunist fervor it had fanned. The Soviets ended the U.S. monopoly on the atomic bomb; Communists took control of China; Justice

Department employee Judith Coplon was caught meeting with a Russian while carrying FBI documents in her purse; Alger Hiss and Julius and Ethel Rosenberg were convicted; the Korean War broke out. Congress passed Public Law 733, which gave the heads of certain agencies wide latitude to dismiss employees deemed to be security risks, as opposed to loyalty risks. The credibility of hard-line anticommunists surged among the American public, as demonstrated in the ascendance of Senator Joseph McCarthy and the 1950 election returns. The new Senate Internal Security Subcommittee joined the House Un-American Activities Committee in charging that the Truman administration was soft on Communists in government. Under terrific partisan pressure, in April 1951 Truman issued Executive Order 10241, which broadened the grounds for employee dismissal. Of the more than 9,300 employees who had been cleared after full investigation under the 1947 standard, at least 2,756 found their cases reopened as a result of the new standard.[12]

It was not unusual for a career civil servant to be investigated under the Hatch Act during the war, then again under Executive Order (EO) 9835 (1947), and again under EO 10241 (1951). Such was the case for both Keyserlings. Employees who survived those investigations as well as the transition to the Eisenhower administration—no simple feat, since incoming Republicans tried to evict holdovers from the Roosevelt and Truman administrations[13]—had to clear an even higher hurdle. In April 1953, Eisenhower's Executive Order 10450 extended the "security risk" standard to all agencies, expanded the list of suspect behaviors, and eliminated certain procedural protections for employees.[14] Under EO 10450, Mary Dublin Keyserling almost certainly would have been labeled a security risk, and Leon, as her spouse, would have been, too. Had they not left government when Eisenhower took office, they probably would have been forced out on security grounds.

EARLY SUSPICIONS

The Keyserlings knew from 1942 on that they were under scrutiny. Most of the pressure initially was on Mary. Notwithstanding a few early allegations against Leon, until 1951 investigations of him stemmed primarily from questions about his wife. The professional anticommunists J. B. Matthews and Ben Mandel had their eyes on Mary Dublin from the moment she entered government service in 1940. Only a short time before she did so, she had testified before the Dies Committee to protest its December 1939 attack on the consumer movement, and she had campaigned to eliminate the committee's appropriations. If Matthews had not noticed her before, he did then.[15]

So did Matthews's new colleague Ben Mandel. A former New York City schoolteacher, Mandel had been expelled from the Communist Party with Jay Lovestone's faction in 1929. Beginning in 1939 Mandel worked for the Dies Committee and its successor HUAC on and off for seven years before joining the staff of the Senate Internal Security Subcommittee. Matthews and Mandel were the most important of the former Communists and "fellow travelers" who were so vital to the anticommunist network.[16] It was probably Matthews or Mandel who underlined Dublin's name in a June 1940 newspaper announcement of appointments to the Consumer Division of the National Defense Advisory Commission.[17] That agency asked the FBI to check on her. The FBI reported back that Dublin was a member of the American Council on Soviet Relations, was possibly an associate of the alleged Communist Mary van Kleeck, and had sent greetings to the Emergency Peace Mobilization Committee, a Communist-sponsored group.[18] In May 1941 Ben Mandel included Dublin in a list of fifty-three "big shots" in government whom he suspected were Communists. Mandel did not know that Dublin had married Leon Keyserling, but he would soon discover that fact and put it to use.[19]

Leon apparently had no expectation that his new wife's associations would become a liability. When he was questioned in late 1941 about his own distant connection to a Communist front group, he included Mary in a list of associates whose respectability he assumed was beyond question and therefore evidence of his own good character.[20] In early 1942, he must have recognized his mistake. In February, citing the Dies Committee as their source, congressional conservatives read a list of Mary Dublin's suspect associations into the *Congressional Record*. She recently had become chief of the Research and Statistics Division at the Office of Civilian Defense (OCD) at the invitation of Eleanor Roosevelt, whose role at that agency was under fire. Leon was by this time deputy administrator and general counsel of the U.S. Housing Authority, which was no more popular with conservatives than the OCD. Anti–New Dealers now made the connection between Leon and Mary. Representative John Taber (R-N.Y.) included them in a list of people he called "parasites on the federal payroll" because of their high salaries, subversive associations, and advocacy of programs he judged to be boondoggles. That both spouses earned federal salaries enabled Taber to imply that the Keyserlings were especially parasitic. Legislation prohibiting federal employment of married couples had been repealed in 1937, but hostility to the practice lingered. The conservative press was soon castigating "Miss Dublin" for accepting any salary when her husband was a high-paid official, warning that "out on Main Street of America the folks are going to become embittered at the spectacle of the government handing out fancy salaries to political favorites or the wives of political favorites for doing a little work in civilian defense." Stung by the suggestion that the use of her maiden name was deceptive, she began using the name Mary Dublin Keyserling.[21]

The FBI questioned Leon about rumored connections with Communist groups in April 1942; after Leon swore he had never belonged to the Communist Party or any organization he had reason to believe was controlled by Communists, he was not investigated further until 1948.[22] Mary, however, remained under close scrutiny throughout the war years, notwithstanding her similar denials under oath. Her initial investigation turned up more "derogatory" information than Leon's did, and each time she changed jobs—which, like many talented, ambitious people, she did several times during the war—investigators continued digging.

The vast majority of the dozens of witnesses interviewed in this phase of Dublin Keyserling's investigation described her as "loyal" and not a Communist. However, a few people who had clashed with her ascribed the conflict to her leftism. In particular, some older National Consumers' League officers who disapproved of Dublin Keyserling's leadership vented their grievances to the FBI. Board member Florence Whitney claimed that Dublin Keyserling had tried to replace veteran staff members with Communist friends. Another NCL officer, Elinore Herrick of the National Labor Relations Board, commented casually that Dublin Keyserling was the kind of person who fell for new ideas and might be used by Communist front groups. When Herrick was reinterviewed later—after the loyalty program had demonstrated what impact such comments might have—she chose her words more carefully and stated that Dublin Keyserling was definitely loyal and not a Communist. Over the full course of Dublin Keyserling's investigation, ten NCL officers, all quite distinguished, dismissed Whitney's story as the irresponsible accusation of a disgruntled, ill-informed individual. Whitney herself could not be questioned more closely because she died in 1942. Her words lived on, however. They got carried forward from one report to the next, while exculpatory testimony got buried.[23]

In 1945, by which time Dublin Keyserling was an economic analyst for the Foreign Economic Administration, CSC examiners recommended calling her in for questioning. However, more senior officials decided that "while recognizing the borderline elements in this case," further interrogation was "not necessary or desirable." The CSC loyalty board concluded that although she probably had been a socialist and might still be, there was no evidence of Communist Party membership, and testimony as to her loyalty had been "predominantly favorable." This wartime board rejected the report of its overzealous examiners, who used "liberal," "radical," and "fellow traveler" interchangeably, made factual errors (such as confusing the Consumers' Union and the National Consumers' League), and chose the most sinister possible reading of FBI reports.[24] Although

Dublin was rated eligible for the time being, the wartime investigations generated much of the information that would be held against her later, after the political climate changed and loyalty standards tightened.

The CSC's clearance of Dublin Keyserling did not satisfy professional anticommunists and their congressional allies, who kept up the drumbeat. Soon the press was identifying Dublin Keyserling as "a favorite target of Representative John Taber (R-N.Y.)."[25] In 1946, HUAC staffer Ben Mandel tried to prevent the Senate from approving Leon Keyserling's appointment to the Council of Economic Advisers, stressing the potential from that office for "economic espionage and sabotage in behalf of a foreign power." Mandel cited a rumor that Leon's appointment was backed by a former leader of the United Federal Workers union, which had some Communist officers. Mandel placed greater emphasis, however, on Mary, about whom he offered eight allegations—all old ones or as flimsy as the new one about Leon. According to Mandel, the American Communist Party's constitution forbade members to have personal relationships with "known enemies of the party." If a Communist could only marry someone who was friendly to the party, and if Mary was a Communist, then Leon must be at least a sympathizer.[26] But in 1946, such tenuous charges did not get much traction.

On the Left Edge of the Truman Administration, 1945–48

These early investigations and accusations may have caused the Keyserlings to be more careful about the people and organizations with whom they casually associated, but the couple did not avoid controversy in the immediate postwar years. Far from lying low, the Keyserlings took leading roles on behalf of policies that were at the top of conservatives' most-hated list, including price control, high wages, strong protection of union rights, and the European Recovery Plan, better known as the Marshall Plan. Mary's work in this period centered on foreign aid and trade policy while Leon focused on domestic policy, but both argued that a healthy economy required raising "mass purchasing power," at home and abroad, by directing more of productivity's gains to wages rather than to profits and by encouraging economic expansion and full employment.

Leon was widely identified as one of Truman's most pro-labor advisers and the most liberal member of the new Council of Economic Advisers. After the Republicans' sweeping gains in the 1946 elections, a group of Truman officials including Keyserling, Clark Clifford, Charles Murphy, and others began meeting weekly at the Wardman Park apartment of Oscar Ewing, who headed the Federal Security Administration and also was vice-chairman of the Democratic National Committee. This group functioned behind the scenes as a rival to the relatively conservative cabinet. Its members orchestrated the shift to the left that enabled Truman to eke out a reelection victory in 1948, when high turnout by organized labor offset the defections from the Democrats by the Dixiecrats to the right and by the Progressive Party to the left. Truman's largely symbolic veto in 1947 of the antiunion Taft-Hartley bill (which Congress overrode) was key to this strategy, and Keyserling helped draft the veto message. Another key to Truman's 1948 strategy was blaming the surging cost of living on the Republican-dominated Congress's termination of the OPA. Unlike Truman's cabinet, Keyserling recommended a return to price controls, insisting that inflation was caused not by high wages, as industry groups argued, but by high profits and business reluctance to expand. Outraged conservatives denounced the CEA's 1947 annual report as a plot conceived by the "ghost of Harry Hopkins" to "steal votes from Wallace," the Progressive Party candidate.[27] In December 1947, *Newsweek* described Keyserling as "one New Dealer whose influence is actually growing."[28] Keyserling's access to Truman through the Wardman Park group and his blending of party politics with economic analysis antagonized his CEA superior, Chairman Edwin Nourse. Nourse came from the ranks of more orthodox academic economists who believed that Keyserling's high-wage, expansionist vision was dangerously inflationary.[29] In early 1949, Keyserling endorsed a controversial move to pressure the steel industry by threatening to build government-run mills if the industry did not expand its capacity. Nourse disagreed. When Nourse later resigned, congressional conservatives circulated his bitter words as evidence of Keyserling's leftist influence on the administration's economic policy.[30]

Mary Dublin Keyserling too was a prominent advocate in these years of policies that were anathema to conservatives. Now an economist in the Commerce Department, she continued her long-standing support of national health insurance and stronger, more inclusive labor laws and unions. Meanwhile, like many left liberals in the late 1940s, she increasingly prioritized poll-tax repeal and permanent legislation against employment discrimination, recognizing those steps as prerequisites for the advancement of minority men and all women. In 1946 Dublin Keyserling was the Washington organizer for the Conference on Unfinished Business in Social Legislation, a project of Helen Hall, her friend from the Henry Street Settlement. This major conference criticized congressional conservatives for blocking progress toward a comprehensive, nondiscriminatory welfare state. The conference resolutions reflected a feminist perspective by opposing the linkage of social benefits to military service and demanding universal benefits instead. The war had been won by women and men, in and out of uniform, the delegates emphasized. Dublin Keyserling summed up the conference by urging a renewed fight to ensure

Figure 4.1. Leon Keyserling drafted the bill that led to the creation of the Council of Economic Advisers. Left to right: Keyserling, chairman Edwin Nourse, and John Clark, Council of Economic Advisers, with President Truman after they were sworn in, August 9, 1946. Courtesy of Jewish Heritage Collection, College of Charleston.

that "the efforts of small, selfish groups do not triumph over the interests of the majority of our people."[31]

To help wage that fight, Dublin Keyserling joined with Helen Hall, Caroline Ware, and Ella Baker to form the National Association of Consumers. That group was the successor to the Consumer Advisory Committee of the Office of Price Administration, on which Hall, Ware, and Baker had served, and to the prewar Consumers' National Federation, the umbrella group involving many of the same people.[32] In a May 1948 speech to the consumer group, Dublin Keyserling warned that prices would continue to rise unless Congress authorized standby price control. The organization adopted price control as one of its key planks, along with rationing, reciprocal trade agreements, rent control, and more public housing. Thus, at the same time that her husband was drawing fire for recommending price control through the CEA, Dublin Keyserling was cooperating publicly with nongovernmental activists for price control.[33]

Amid popular outcry over surging prices in 1947 and 1948, conservatives and left liberals offered rival explanations. In an effort to drive a wedge between the unionized working class and those who lived on salaries or fixed incomes, the right blamed inflation on, above all, the high wages won by unions.[34] Conservatives also blamed inflation on the European Recovery Plan, better known as the Marshall Plan, to rebuild war-ravaged Europe. Dublin Keyserling was among the many government economists who had a hand in designing the Marshall Plan, and when conservatives blamed it for draining resources and fueling price rises, she gave speeches laden with data that suggested otherwise.[35] If Dublin Keyserling initially attracted conservatives' ire for her consumer and labor activism, she did not endear herself further when she became a proponent of generous foreign aid programs.

Since joining the Foreign Economic Administration in 1943, Dublin Keyserling had been applying to international aid and trade policy the philosophy that saving the economy, and thus democracy, required redistributing purchasing power. In 1945, as one of two women in the twenty-five-member U.S. delegation to the United Nations Relief and Rehabilitation Administration, she worked on estimating the foreign aid needs of smaller European countries devastated by the war. From 1946 to 1949, as chief of the Special Programs Branch, Areas Division, Office of International Trade (OIT), Department of Commerce, she recommended increasing imports from European nations to help them become self-sufficient and to keep peace. Toward that end she advised and wrote speeches for Secretary of Commerce Averell Harriman and OIT director Thomas Blaisdell, in addition to making speeches herself to civic groups and in training sessions for U.S. Foreign Service officers.[36] One way to increase imports was to eliminate protective tariffs, and in urging that approach Dublin Keyserling and her department antagonized American manufacturers who relied on tariffs to maintain their share of the domestic market.[37] Like other left internationalists, she saw foreign trade and aid policies as tools for eliminating the roots of war. Believing World War II had originated from the punitive settlement of World War I, she argued it was in Americans' long-term interest to be generous in foreign aid in order to prevent desperate people from "turning to a Hitler." In 1947 the Commerce Department made her its representative in drafting the Krug report, which undertook to demonstrate that the United States could afford a massive aid package for Europe. She was among the handful of people who during the hot summer of 1947 actually produced the influential report.[38] In the spring of 1948, she wrote articles on the European Recovery Plan for publication under her superiors' names, and she herself promoted the plan among civic groups.[39]

Dublin Keyserling's work on the Marshall Plan gave the professional anticommunists another opportunity to remove her from government—and to discredit Leon Keyserling and, ultimately, President Truman. In March 1948, even as conservatives were still fuming that the CEA's 1947 annual report contained "unadulterated Marxist doctrine,"[40] they launched an unsuccessful campaign against the Marshall Plan. In addition to arguing that the plan would ruin the U.S. economy, they called it "largely a scheme through which socialism will be subsidized in Europe." Congressional conservatives in both Houses demanded lists of personnel involved in the Marshall Plan and then highlighted the role of alleged leftists. On a copy of the Krug committee personnel list that ended up in investigators' files, Dublin Keyserling's name was among those marked as suspect.[41]

THE 1948 INVESTIGATION

On March 16, 1948, the FBI received a tip from a journalist at the *Washington Times-Herald* that Dublin Keyserling worked at OIT "under the supervision of one of the drafters of the original Marshall Plan," Lewis Lorwin. Lorwin was emerging as exhibit A for conservatives' claim that the Marshall Plan was a leftist plot. The journalist gave the FBI a 1944 letter in which Lorwin recommended Dublin Keyserling for a Foreign Economic Administration position in Poland. "While it would be rather unusual to appoint a woman as a special representative," Lorwin had written, "I think Mrs. Keyserling is an exception for which it is worth while to break the custom."[42] FBI director J. Edgar Hoover immediately ordered his most experienced agents to expedite a full investigation of her. On March 29, the conservative congressman E. E. Cox (D-Ga.) publicized the names of eight "Communist sympathizers, socialists, and collectivists" who had helped design the Marshall Plan.[43] Four of the eight men Cox named were people with whom Dublin Keyserling had worked closely: Lewis Lorwin, Thomas Blaisdell (who succeeded Lorwin as Director of OIT), OIT Areas Division head Herbert Parisius (who had hired Dublin Keyserling), and Tex Goldschmidt from the Department of the Interior. A fifth was Dublin Keyserling's close friend Felix S. Cohen, who had just left the government after many years as associate solicitor for Interior. All those named by Cox soon were under investigation. Parisius would resign in May; Lorwin and Blaisdell would be forced out later.[44]

Given the developments in counterespionage and electoral politics in 1948, it is not surprising that FBI director Hoover took a "personal interest" in Dublin Keyserling's investigation and soon requested a full field investigation of her husband as well. An enormous volume of telegram correspondence among FBI offices around the nation and internal memos annotated with terse orders by Hoover himself indicate his sense of urgency.[45] In late 1945, the FBI had been stunned to discover the extent of Soviet espionage through the defector Igor Gouzenko and the American ex-Communist Elizabeth Bentley. The professional anticommunists on HUAC belittled the FBI's wartime performance, and Hoover was determined not to be caught off guard again.[46] Anticommunists were especially suspicious of the Commerce Department because the left-leaning former vice president Henry Wallace had headed it. His successor, Averell Harriman, left Wallace loyalists in their jobs and refused to turn Commerce loyalty board files over to HUAC. (The executive branch's denial of congressional access to CSC and FBI case files was an ongoing source of conflict between the Truman administration and Congress.)[47] Now it appeared that OIT might be full of subversives. The investigation of OIT's William Remington, named by Bentley as a Communist who had passed information to her during the war, was already underway when Representative Cox charged that Lorwin, Blaisdell, and Parisius had Communist associations.[48] In this context, it is small wonder that Hoover took seriously the tip about Dublin Keyserling.

Hoover's excitement no doubt increased when he recognized that Dublin Keyserling's brother-in-law George Marshall was a prominent, wealthy leftist (and not to be confused with the general and Secretary of State George C. Marshall). The son of the distinguished New York lawyer Louis Marshall, he had married Mary's sister Elisabeth in 1930. When his brother, the environmentalist Robert Marshall, died in 1939, George became executor of the Robert Marshall Foundation and used it to fund many left-wing causes. George Marshall was a leader of the National Federation for Constitutional Liberties (one of the "front" groups Mary was charged with joining) and its successor, the Civil Rights Congress. He was active in Soviet-American friendship groups, and he made substantial donations to Communist-influenced organizations such the Southern Negro Youth Congress. In 1944, Hoover put Marshall on the FBI's Security Index, a list of people to be kept under surveillance so they could be detained in the event of a security crisis. In 1946 HUAC cited Marshall for contempt because he refused to produce the membership records of the National Federation for Constitutional Liberties.[49]

The FBI's spring 1948 full field investigation yielded a vast trove of inconclusive data and contradictory impressions from dozens of Dublin Keyserling's past and present associates. There was disagreement about how far to the left she might have been in the 1930s. Some people believed she was "opportunistic" or "immature" and so might be used by Communists, but they offered few compelling specifics. One OIT employee claimed that Dublin Keyserling's advocacy of price control indicated she followed Communist doctrine, and that she belonged to a radical clique in Commerce. By contrast, several distinguished people cited evidence that certainly by 1946 she was anticommunist, whatever her earlier views had been. One reported that as a board member for the Committee on the Nation's Health, Dublin Keyserling had argued that the committee should not share information or cooperate in any way with Communist front groups. Another informant had heard she was associating with Communist sympathizers when she came to Washington in 1940, but he believed she subsequently had "matured in her political thinking." He explained that at the 1946 Conference on Unfinished Business in Social Legislation she had voted against affiliating with a group she had been advised was Communist infiltrated. Helen Hall observed that Dublin Keyserling had resisted Communist efforts to take over consumer groups.[50]

When questioned about Dublin Keyserling's relationship to George Marshall, Helen Hall stated that Mary had nothing to with his activities and in fact had been turned down when she solicited funding from his foundation for a consumer group. Hall's view was undermined by the FBI's discovery of two instances in which Dublin Keyserling and George Marshall had supported the same cause. That Mary's brother-in-law was a prominent supporter of Communist causes might have been read as evidence that she was *not* a secret Communist. Anticommunist experts knew by this time that if Dublin Keyserling were an underground Communist assigned to work her way up in the government or marry a powerful government official, she would have long since severed contact with George Marshall, and the party might even have instructed Marshall himself to lie low. But most loyalty board officials, and the general public, were unfamiliar with the Communist policy of forbidding underground members to associate with other Communists or radical causes, and so they interpreted the Marshall connection as a red flag about the Keyserlings.[51]

While the Commerce Department loyalty board tried to sort through this jumble of information in the summer of 1948, HUAC was preparing to launch its espionage hearings. On July 21, newspapers introduced the public to Elizabeth Bentley's story with headlines such as "Red Ring Bared by Its Blond Queen."[52] With the election approaching and the right pounding away on the Communists-in-government issue, the Commerce loyalty board decided to take no chances. On July 30 the board sent Dublin Keyserling an interrogatory asking her to respond to eight allegations of disloyalty. She was charged with being among the signatories to the "Open Letter to American Liberals" published in *Soviet Russia Today* in March 1937; receiving Communist mail from Mexico in 1937; joining or associating in the 1938–40 period with four organizations on the Attorney General's List of Subversive Organizations; in 1947 lending "the only copy of a Department of Commerce publication to a person known to be connected with the Washington Committee for Democratic Action," also on the attorney general's list; and, more generally, associating with "Communists and persons sympathetic to the Communist Party."[53] By the time Dublin Keyserling received the charges, the nation was spellbound by the sensational HUAC testimony of Whittaker Chambers and Elizabeth Bentley about secret cells of Communists in government.

With the assistance of her lawyer and old friend Abe Fortas, who was now in private practice, Dublin Keyserling emphatically denied that she ever had been a Communist or Communist sympathizer, knowingly associated with such persons, or knowingly joined or associated with any Communist-dominated group. In her written reply to the loyalty board and in two days of hearings, she offered standard examples of her divergence from the "Communist line": she had favored U.S. aid to England and France during the Hitler-Stalin Non-Aggression Pact (August 1939–June 1941) when the Communist Party opposed American war preparations; she had opposed the so-called Morgenthau plan to deindustrialize Germany; and she had helped develop and win passage of the Marshall Plan, which the Communist Party opposed.[54]

Dublin Keyserling placed the most emphasis on responding to the charges that she had signed the March 1937 "Open Letter to American Liberals" and associated with Communists or their sympathizers. She correctly assumed that the latter charge reflected the fact that George Marshall was her brother-in-law. She avoided labeling Marshall a Communist, but she took pains to distance herself from him. She stated that she had never agreed with his politics and that she saw him only a few times a year at large family gatherings, where they did not discuss politics or foreign policy because of "our recognized and strong conflicts of opinion."[55]

Having avidly denied any political sympathy with George Marshall proved awkward when it came to explaining her signing of the "Open Letter to American Liberals," because George and Elisabeth both had signed it, and George was an editor of *Soviet Russia Today*, which published the letter. Dublin Keyserling claimed to have no recollection of how she came to sign the letter but also (rather illogically) denied it had come to her from George or Elisabeth. This letter attacked the American Committee for the Defense of Leon Trotsky, which formed to investigate the Moscow show trials and was nominally headed by the distinguished progressive educator John Dewey. The "Open Letter" called the Dewey Committee investigation a gesture of "hostile intent" toward the Soviet government, which was "improving conditions for all its people, whether or not one agrees with all the means whereby this is brought about." The signers applauded the "progressive movement undertaken by the Soviet Union under the five-year plan and the Soviet foreign policy of peace."

Claiming that "the reactionary sections of the press and public" in the United States were seizing on "the anti-Soviet attacks of Trotsky . . . to further their own aims," the letter concluded sternly, "we feel sure that you do not wish to be counted an ally of these forces." The eighty-eight signers included radicals such as Corliss Lamont and Lillian Hellman and progressives such as the social worker Lillian Wald and the Columbia sociologist Robert Lynd.[56]

At the loyalty hearings, Dublin Keyserling called the letter "dreadful" and regretted signing. She guessed that she had done so casually and, in hindsight, naïvely. "Had that letter come to me a little later, I should never have signed it." She reminded the loyalty board that in early 1937 the Soviet Union recently had joined the League of Nations and professed to renounce the doctrine of world revolution, and many American officials sought to promote friendly relations with Russia. In reconstructing her own motives, Keyserling said she must have meant to warn liberals against endorsing "Trotsky's world revolutionary doctrines" and against driving the Soviet Union into an alliance with Hitler. Fortas, her lawyer, asked the board whether it was such a sin to have been anti-Trotsky and argued that her act was foolish but understandable at the time. He might also have pointed out that it was not until later in 1937 that the full horror of the Moscow trials became known in the United States. Still, Dublin Keyserling was disingenuous when she denied that the letter implied approval of the Soviet Union.[57]

Dublin Keyserling's strategy no doubt reflected the advice of her counsel, whose firm Arnold, Fortas & Porter was rising to prominence as one of the few willing to defend those brought before loyalty boards.[58] Dublin Keyserling and Fortas not only had been friends since the 1930s; they had much in common. Both were born in 1910 to Russian and Lithuanian Jewish parents. During the 1930s Fortas shared a house in Washington with Leon Keyserling, and Fortas's wife, Carolyn Agger, had overlapped with Mary at Barnard. Fortas's opposition to the loyalty program probably reflected his personal experiences, as well as his professional objections to the program's lack of due process. He himself had been questioned about association with alleged Communist fronts while in government service in the early 1940s.[59]

The friendly tone of the 1948 hearings may have been set in large part by Fortas. He and Dublin Keyserling took every opportunity to be conciliatory. She applauded the Commerce loyalty board's work as vigorously as she asserted her innocence. Communists and their sympathizers were "unfit for Government employment," she declared, agreeing that reviews were necessary to "weed out" such persons. Innocent people such as herself would suffer from having their innocence questioned, but she willingly bore such suffering in order to protect "the interests of our nation."

For his part, Fortas controlled his frustration with the loyalty board for sporadically introducing new allegations from undisclosed sources during the hearings. The officials treated Dublin Keyserling cordially, and all parties seemed to regret the unpleasant necessity that had brought them together.[60]

Dublin Keyserling was cleared in 1948, but not without a suspenseful delay. Although her hearing had seemed to end with a unanimous sigh of relief, the Commerce Department loyalty board took more than two months to decide that there were no reasonable grounds to believe she was disloyal. By this time growing differences of opinion divided loyalty investigators and higher-level Truman officials. Although the board's report cleared Dublin Keyserling on loyalty grounds, it recommended further review on security grounds because she "had taken a very deep interest in the affairs of the Communist Party." Secretary of Commerce Charles Sawyer rejected this recommendation, however, and ordered that Dublin Keyserling be given the necessary security clearances immediately.[61] Meanwhile, the investigation of Leon had turned up nothing new other than a rumor that he had dated a Communist coworker at the U.S. Housing Authority, in addition to complaints that he and Mary were "aggressive," "opportunistic, and "interested only in self-advancement." In December, the central Loyalty Review Board that audited agency board decisions notified Hoover that Leon and Mary both had been retained by their agencies.[62]

The Keyserlings' relief at this outcome could not have lasted long. Although neither of them was investigated formally again until 1951, the campaign against "Communists in government" gathered momentum during 1949 and 1950, aided by international events. At home, several developments set the stage for a fresh attempt to discredit the Keyserlings. Senior officials at the Commerce Department infuriated hard-core anticommunists by reversing the agency loyalty board's negative decisions in the cases of OIT employees William Remington and Michael Lee.[63] The subsequent perjury convictions of former State Department official Alger Hiss (January 1950) and Remington (February and October 1951) were widely perceived as proof that they had spied. In February 1950, Senator McCarthy entered the spotlight with his now-infamous declaration that the State Department was "infested" with Communists. The partisan rancor intensified still further after Congress overrode Truman's September 1950 veto of the Internal Security Act, which required Communist organizations to register with the U.S. attorney general and created the Subversive Activities Control Board. Although the fireworks at the State Department got the most publicity, OIT remained under intense scrutiny. The press soon reported that OIT director Thomas Blaisdell was under investigation on the grounds that he had defended Remington and that his wife and father had been the witnesses to Robert Marshall's will, which created the foundation that funded Remington's legal defense. That foundation was headed by the Keyserlings' brother-in-law George Marshall, who by this time was in serious trouble. He was known to have furnished the $23,000 bail for Soviet agent Gerhardt Eisler, who promptly fled the country. In the summer of 1950, Marshall spent three months in prison after the Supreme Court declined to hear his appeal of the contempt citation by HUAC.[64] Finally, and most ominously for the Keyserlings, an ex-Communist named Paul Crouch became an FBI informant and eventually connected with the Keyserlings' nemesis Benjamin Mandel. In March 1951, Mandel joined the staff of the new Senate Internal Security Subcommittee. With help from Crouch, Mandel would try to put SISS on the map—at the Keyserlings' expense.[65]

A Conspiracy So Immense? Setting Up the Keyserlings, 1951–52

Paul Crouch had joined the Communist Party while in the U.S. Army in 1925 and soon was discharged and sentenced to forty years in prison for subversive activities. In 1928 President Calvin Coolidge pardoned him for reasons that are unclear. After a stint in the Soviet Union, in 1929 Crouch went to Gastonia, North Carolina, to organize Loray Mill textile workers for what became a famously violent strike. There he met Sylvia McMahan, who had worked at Loray since she was twelve. They married and worked together for the party in several southern and western states. According to the Crouches, by 1941 they had become disillusioned. Both Paul and their son developed serious health problems, which they used as an excuse to leave the party. They later claimed they would have been "liquidated" for quitting had they not been so well known that their murder would have damaged party morale. A different version of the Crouches' departure from the Communist Party holds that he was demoted for erratic behavior and incompetent leadership. In any case, it was only a matter of time before he emerged publicly as the "West Coast Whittaker Chambers."[66]

In 1947, Paul Crouch began giving names of party members and their associates to the FBI. In 1949, in the context of listing about one hundred Communists with access to important government officials, he alleged that one Gilbert L. Parks was a Communist and a friend of Leon Keyserling. Like Keyserling, Parks came from the Beaufort, South Carolina, vicinity, had ties to Harvard, and had worked for the government in the 1930s. Unlike Keyserling, Parks was a founder of *Nudist* magazine and in the mid-1930s ran a nudist-friendly resort on his family farm near Port Royal, South Carolina. In 1937 the Communist Party reportedly

Figure 4.2. Leon Keyserling and Mary Dublin Keyserling, circa 1950, between rounds of investigation. Courtesy of Thomas Dublin.

sent Paul Crouch to Parks's resort to convalesce from an illness. Crouch later alleged that during that period Parks, his wife, and both Crouches belonged to a Communist cell that met on the property. (Crouch also characterized the nudist movement as pro-Soviet, antireligious, and bent on undermining marriage.) In 1949, Crouch told a Miami FBI agent that Parks had introduced him to Keyserling in late 1937 when the latter, then an aide to Senator Wagner, was visiting his father in Beaufort. That information drew little notice at first, but when the FBI upset Crouch by declining to use him as a witness in a Smith Act trial, Crouch contacted HUAC, explaining later that he "wanted to get the truth to the American people." In mid-1949 HUAC called Crouch to testify in closed hearings, during which he mentioned the alleged connection between Parks and Keyserling. At that time Crouch said that he was not questioning Keyserling's loyalty; rather he was merely pointing out that Communists like Parks had a lot of influence. The timing of when Crouch said what about Leon Keyserling became important later.[67]

HUAC staff member Ben Mandel must have found Crouch's report extremely interesting, but he did not show his hand yet. First, it had to be established that Parks was indeed a Communist. In October 1949, the FBI interviewed Parks. He said he never joined the Communist Party, although, he conceded, some people might label him as a fellow traveler in the 1930s because he had shared some Communist objectives. Not satisfied, the FBI asked the Office of the Attorney General to consider trying Parks for perjury. In the meantime, the FBI completed a full field investigation of Gilbert's wife Gertrude Parks, who as a clerk with the Veterans Administration was subject to the federal employee loyalty program. In April 1950, the Fourth Regional Loyalty Board heard her case. More than half of Gertrude's hearing was devoted to questioning Gilbert, who appeared as a witness. He denied that either of them ever belonged to the Communist Party, although he had been friendly with many people he knew to be Communists, including the Crouches. Surprised by a newspaper clipping describing Crouch's allegations about him, including a passing mention of his friendship with Keyserling, Gilbert expressed indignation that "they'd try through me to smear Leon Keyserling." He said he had no recollection of introducing Crouch to Keyserling. He said he knew Leon only slightly, but he was friendly with Leon's father. Indeed, the senior Mr. Keyserling had provided an affidavit attesting to the Parkses' loyalty.[68]

In June 1950 the loyalty board voted two-to-one to dismiss Gertrude Parks. One board member explained that he would rate her husband ineligible, and "while the record is not so strong against her, I can't conclude from all the evidence how she could be eligible and he not."[69] The dissenting vote came from a woman (whose sex made her a rarity among loyalty officials). In urging that Gertrude Parks be rated eligible, she argued that Gertrude was a hard-working, tolerant wife stuck with a problem husband who was "long on ability to expound theories, but short on the knack of keeping a job." This official stressed that the Crouches were the only witnesses against the Parkses and that their story, even if true, pertained only to the period before 1938. This alternative interpretation of the Parkses' marriage did not prevail, however, and in August 1950 the Veterans Administration dismissed Gertrude Parks.[70] Meanwhile, the Crouches had attracted national attention by testifying that the atomic scientist J. Robert Oppenheimer had held a Communist Party meeting in his home in 1941.[71] The implications for Leon Keyserling, whom Truman had just made chairman of the CEA, were not good, but the danger was not yet fully apparent.

During the next few months, Congress overrode Truman's veto of the McCarran Internal Security Act and created the Senate Internal Security Subcommittee to monitor its administration. The powerful senator Pat McCarran (D-Nev.) appointed himself head of the subcommittee and assembled an "all-star team of anti-subversives" for its staff, including Ben Mandel from HUAC and five ex-FBI agents.[72] Mandel did not officially join the SISS staff until March 1951, but in the interim he did the groundwork for the new committee to investigate the Keyserlings. It was most likely Mandel who created the December 1950 chart that ended up in SISS's file on Leon. The chart traced the connections among the Keyserlings, Blaisdells, and Marshalls. Blaisdell was Mary Dublin Keyserling's boss; Blaisdell's wife and father witnessed Robert Marshall's will, of which George Marshall was executor; and George was married to Mary's sister. Leon was at the top of the chart, and at its center was a list of George Marshall's twenty-four subversive associations. Still, Leon was separated by two degrees of marriage from George Marshall. Crouch's story about Gilbert Parks yielded more direct evidence against Leon. With Parks's subversive tendencies apparently confirmed by his wife's dismissal from government employment, Mandel asked Crouch to provide more information on the alleged meeting with Keyserling and Parks in Beaufort.[73]

Crouch obliged with a memo claiming that in late 1937 Keyserling was "friendly to the [Communist] party," despite his "mild criticism of the party line." Crouch described in detail how Parks took him to the Keyserling home and introduced Crouch as a Communist Party leader for the southern region. Crouch claimed that the three of them—with no other witnesses—spent an afternoon talking politics and then toured the Keyserling cotton ginning operation. According to Crouch, Leon criticized the Communist Party program on "minor points," calling it "too dogmatic about the inevitability of armed revolution as the only way to power in the United States." Leon supposedly opined that Communists did not fully appreciate how the "New Deal was starting a chain of events and releasing forces that would take on increasing momentum until the economic and social structure of the country was completely revolutionized." It was possible, Crouch's memo to Mandel charitably observed, that Keyserling was among the many "left-liberals" who turned against the party after the Hitler-Stalin pact of 1939. But at the time of their meeting, "Keyserling certainly was 'close to the party' and could properly be called a 'party sympathizer.' This does not NECESSARILY mean he remains friendly to the party and the Soviet Union in 1951." That same month, Crouch sent Senator McCarthy a similarly dramatic memo, which concluded: "If Parks remains in the party and if his friendship with Mr. Keyserling continues, the Communist Party has a direct pipeline to the White House." In his cover letter to Mandel Crouch mentioned that he was unemployed and needed money for his hospitalized son. Later, the Keyserlings would suspect a plot against them. This correspondence is part of the evidence they were correct.[74]

Although Mandel and Crouch had been working together for several months with the Keyserlings as their primary target, they took care to make it appear that they were chiefly interested in Gilbert Parks. In a new memo to SISS, Crouch claimed he had heard that Parks applied for a job on the SISS staff and so felt impelled to warn SISS about Parks, "one of the most capable Communists in the country" and a personal friend of Eleanor Roosevelt, Justice Frankfurter, and Leon Keyserling. It is very unlikely that Parks actually applied for a job with SISS as Crouch claimed; Parks's wife had been barred from government employment, and he would have known he would not be hired. Saying Parks tried to get on the SISS payroll probably was an effort to hide the real motive for pursuing him, which was to get Keyserling. Crouch urged SISS to call Parks and Keyserling in for questioning.[75] Within a few weeks, both Crouch and Parks testified under oath before SISS. Parks denied he had been a Communist and that he had ever spent an afternoon with Crouch and Keyserling. Parks's denial produced a two-pronged response from the countersubversives. First, they redoubled their effort to confirm Crouch's story about Parks. The FBI went to such lengths as sending agents to the schools attended by the Parks children in the late 1930s to determine who had signed the children's report cards, in order to track the parents' movements. But the intensive effort did not produce any smoking guns. The former Communists who Crouch said could confirm his story all told the FBI that they did not know Parks or that they did not know whether he was a Communist.[76]

While the additional investigation of Parks was under way, a second strategy emerged: Crouch claimed he was fairly certain that Leon's wife had in 1929 been a secret member of the Communist Party. The timing of Crouch's announcement was suspicious, as the Keyserling defense team would point out. Crouch later would say that he had told the FBI about a Communist named "Mary" in 1948, that the Pittsburgh FBI questioned him about Mary Dublin in April 1951, and that only during the SISS hearings about Parks in May 1951 did he become aware that Mary Dublin had married Leon Keyserling. The first two claims were certainly false, as a later FBI report confirms.[77] The third very likely was false as well, given that Crouch had been corresponding with Ben Mandel about Leon since before January 1951 and that Mandel had been trying to use Leon's marriage to Mary against him since at least 1946. Most likely Crouch and Mandel spoke about Mary early in the spring. In any case, Crouch spent several days in May with J. B. Matthews preparing testimony on Leon and Mary to present before SISS in June.[78] Someone, probably Crouch, shared the story with Senator McCarthy, who made inquiries but did not act on it until the following year.[79] On June 6, 1951, Ben Mandel got the OK from a member of SISS to gather witnesses against Mary.[80]

On June 8 Crouch gave a statement about her to the FBI. He claimed that in 1928 or 1929 he had met a girl named Mary, age about nineteen, at meetings of the Communist Party and Young Communist League at the home of Julius Heiman in Yonkers. He recalled that her father was chief statistician of the Metropolitan Life Insurance Company and that she did not want him to find out about her Communist activities. (Dublin Keyserling was born in 1910, and her father was Met Life's chief statistician.) According to Crouch, this Mary was a close friend of Julius Heiman's daughter Beatrice, whom Paul Crouch dated, while Mary dated his friend and fellow Communist George Pershing. Crouch reportedly introduced Mary to Communist Party official Jack Stachel, who had asked for someone who would appear to be above suspicion for confidential fieldwork. (Both Pershing and both Heimans remained Communists in 1951, Crouch explained, so they would be unlikely to corroborate his story.) Beatrice Heiman was well known to investigators as a former secretary to the Russian ambassador and employee of the Tass news agency whose name had been found in the address book of Soviet spy Judith Coplon. The possibility that she had been associated with Mary Dublin Keyserling must have been exciting news to countersubversives.[81] Crouch speculated in notes for his SISS appearance, "Mary might be out of party now and potential witness of great value to government—or she may still be top leader in CP underground." This was a melodramatic flourish, given that Crouch's allegations, even if true, hardly indicated that "Mary" had been a "top leader in CP underground."[82]

SISS subpoenaed Leon Keyserling on June 12, and he appeared before the committee the next day. The subpoena did not specify why he was being called, and he apparently believed the committee was after Gilbert Parks. The aggressive questioning by Senator Homer Ferguson (R-Mich.) caught Keyserling off guard. A former prosecutor with presidential ambitions, Ferguson was among the most partisan of Republicans. He had accused Roosevelt of allowing the Japanese to attack Pearl Harbor, and he wanted to impeach Truman for denying Congress access to federal employee loyalty files.[83] Ferguson brought Crouch in to repeat the story about his afternoon discussing politics with Leon Keyserling and Gilbert Parks. Crouch now elaborated that Keyserling had agreed on the need to move from a capitalist to socialist system of production but argued that it would occur without a revolution. As Crouch recalled it, Keyserling had said New Deal reforms would produce a chain reaction, in that "the more you give people the more they'll demand . . . and through this chain reaction the power of capitalism is going to be weakened." Keyserling also had disagreed with the Communist Party's advocacy of a "separate Negro republic" as a solution to American racism, and because of these differences Crouch had decided Keyserling was not "ready" to join the party. Overall, however, his impression in 1937 had been that Keyserling was friendly to the Communist program.[84] Keyserling replied indignantly that such a conversation could never have taken place and that *he did not remember* meeting Crouch—a qualification that some interpreted as self-protection against perjury charges in the event that a witness to their meeting could be found.[85] Through several days of hearings, Ferguson kept Keyserling on the defensive by abruptly changing topics and disrupting his efforts to present exculpatory information.

Things got even stickier when Ferguson, after disarmingly pretending to be uncertain whether Keyserling was married, brought up the old allegations about his wife's subversive associations. When Dublin Keyserling appeared the next day to defend herself, SISS produced Crouch again, who stunned both Keyserlings by testifying that she appeared to be the same person as *"a girl whom I recollected by the name of Mary"* who was a Communist in the late 1920s.[86] The Keyserlings listened in shock as Crouch told the story he had given the FBI about Mary, Beatrice Heiman, and George Pershing. He added a new detail: the girl had told him she had a sister who also was a Communist. SISS staffer Ben Mandel proceeded to show Crouch a series of photos from Mary's passport applications in 1928 and 1929. He declared his certainty that she was the girl he had known. Mary protested that she had never once met Crouch or Pershing, and that although she had known Beatrice Heiman at Barnard, she had disapproved of Beatrice's leftist politics and never was at her house. Crouch must be confusing her with her sister Elisabeth, who never was a Communist but had been a good friend of Beatrice. Crouch now backed off and said that the girl he had known might have had lighter hair than Dublin Keyserling. Indeed, Crouch had described to the FBI "a rather blond young lady of medium or very slightly above medium height, perhaps five feet, seven or eight, very good-looking." Mary Dublin Keyserling had dark brown hair, her sister Elisabeth had light brown hair, and both stood five feet three inches tall.[87]

Over the course of further SISS hearings throughout the summer—seven days of testimony in all—the Keyserlings demonstrated that

Crouch had confused Dublin Keyserling with her sister, leaving it to the committee to judge "whether this was mere confusion or a deliberate action done with intent to injure and abuse."[88] Elisabeth Dublin Marshall made a dramatic appearance in which she greeted Crouch with remarks on how his appearance had changed and described how George Pershing had proposed to her. She said she had attended meetings at the Heiman home at which Communists were present, although she never joined the party herself. She insisted she could not have told Crouch that her sister was a Communist because Mary had always been violently anticommunist.[89] Crouch wavered but did not give up, saying the girl he knew went to Europe in the summer of 1929 (which Mary did, as he might have deduced from the passport applications shown to him at the hearings), the girl he knew did not wear glasses (which Mary did not and Elisabeth did, ditto), and the girl he knew had a "well-modulated voice." Mary did have a "soft, deep voice," but Crouch had heard her speak at the hearing before he mentioned that detail. Investigators explored at length whether the sisters had plotted to create confusion: had either of them ever colored their hair, or taken the other's name? Of course not, they replied.[90]

It seems clear that Crouch deliberately confused Dublin Keyserling and her sister, presumably reasoning that, at the very least, the Marshalls' record would taint the Keyserlings. It also seems clear that Crouch stretched his story about meeting Leon Keyserling in 1937, although Leon might possibly have met him and expressed some of the views Crouch later attributed to him. The Keyserlings were correct in suspecting that Crouch was part of a conspiracy to discredit them. However, in their efforts at self-defense, the Keyserlings themselves were less than fully honest.

Both Mary and Leon portrayed themselves to SISS as more conservative politically than their records indicated. Their lawyers may have advised them to take this approach, but it was a tactical error because they undermined their credibility. Mary, when questioned about trips she made to the Soviet Union in 1932 and 1936, lamented that "our elders" had made it so easy for the Russians to get American students to come visit. She inaccurately claimed that she had been an outspoken antiradical at Barnard and that she had brought only zealous anticommunists onto the board of the National Consumers' League.[91]

Leon's self-representation was even less convincing. He suggested that he had been apolitical in his youth, focused on his studies and trying to make the junior varsity football squad at Columbia (student radicals including Leon had denounced college football in the 1930s, so this was his effort to sound like a traditionalist). He said that he "might even have been a Republican" when he started to work for the government in 1933. Then, as he recalled it, his views became "just a little to the Right of what is commonly understood to be the New Deal." The main draftsman of the National Labor Relations Act, U.S. Housing Act, and Employment Act told SISS in 1951 that he did not think "the programs of the New Deal ought to be pursued or pushed now." He claimed he always had opposed some aspects of the New Deal, such as "pinning the reprehensible label on the business community as a whole," and substituting "regulation for an effort to help business in doing its job." He submitted excerpts from his speeches and articles since the late 1940s that highlighted his emphasis on growth rather than redistribution. Under close questioning, Keyserling denied advocating government-run steel plants. He had left the National Lawyers' Guild when it began "following the Commie line." Put on the defensive about his membership in Americans for Democratic Action, Leon said he did not agree with everything liberal Democrats wanted, offering as an example that he did not support "some aspects of the civil rights program." The latter remark may have been for the benefit of SISS member Senator Willis Smith of North Carolina.[92]

If the hearing transcripts had been made public, both Keyserlings would have been embarrassed by their retreat from principle, and their later silence on the subject of the investigations may have reflected shame at how they had handled the charges more than shame at having been charged. At the time, the Keyserlings disclosed what had happened before SISS to as few people as possible and claimed that they had routed their accusers. In a letter outlining the SISS hearings for President Truman, Leon expressed confidence that none of the senators present "could have been moved in the slightest by Mr. Crouch's fantastic story." Asserting his hatred of Communism and loyalty to his country, Leon invited the president to request a full investigation of him.[93] As Leon probably knew, that investigation was going to happen whether he invited it or not. Although the Keyserlings hoped they had disposed of the Crouch stories, the SISS hearings were just the beginning of a new round of investigation, one far more exhaustive than anything they had faced so far, and one that would not end until Truman left office and the Keyserlings resigned.

Combined with Truman's April 1951 executive order tightening loyalty standards, the June 1951 SISS hearings gave the White House and Commerce loyalty boards little choice but to reopen the investigations of Leon and Mary, respectively. In August Hoover formally authorized another full field investigation on each of them. "Imperative investigation be completely thorough . . . handle with extreme discretion," he instructed in dozens of urgent telegrams. FBI agents interviewed hundreds of people around the nation and abroad, including associates from every phase of the Keyserlings' educational and professional careers, as well as former and current neighbors, landlords, and friends. The FBI checked credit, arrest, and voter registration records. Long lists of ex-Communist informants were asked whether they had known the subjects to be Communists (they had not). For Leon's case, agents interviewed seemingly every resident of Beaufort, South Carolina, none of whom had observed a connection between Leon and Gilbert Parks. FBI agents covertly obtained photographs of the inside of the house where Crouch claimed to have met Leon, trying to resolve their dispute over the size of the room and to confirm rumors about Russian books. They also labored to determine when the Keyserling cotton gin had ceased operation, another point on which Leon disputed Crouch's story. Agents noted that Leon's name was in the address book of the former NLRB and OPA official Thomas Emerson, who had published articles critical of FBI wiretapping and of the loyalty program in general. Much interest was stirred by a report that Leon had hired Bertram Gross at the CEA even after being warned of Gross's reputation as a Communist. Rumors that Leon had dated Communists at the U.S. Housing Authority could not be confirmed, nor could other guests at a 1945 dinner party confirm a report that Leon had called Truman a reactionary. Dozens of distinguished people, including some who disliked Leon, said they were certain he never was a Communist. However, testimony by witnesses friendly to the subject often was followed in FBI reports by recitation of the witness's own suspect associations. The housing expert Catherine Bauer vouched for Leon's loyalty and offered detailed examples of his anticommunism, but the report's next paragraphs cast Bauer herself as subversive.[94] The White House loyalty board sifted this mountain of mixed data, issued Leon an interrogatory, and rated him "eligible." The Loyalty Review Board confirmed that decision on February 8, 1952.[95]

After all that effort, allegations about Mary remained the strongest point in investigators' case against Leon. Her case dragged on for much longer and was never resolved clearly. In October 1951 the Commerce loyalty board sent Dublin Keyserling a new interrogatory listing eleven allegations against her. The board recycled most of the 1948 charges and added new ones based on Crouch's claims, including, most seriously, that she herself had been affiliated with the Communist Party and the Young Communist League. Mary's alarm must have intensified the following week when her boss and friend, OIT head Thomas Blaisdell, resigned in the midst of his own loyalty investigation; a few days after that, former OIT employee William Remington, for whom Blaisdell had vouched, was indicted for perjury. Mary sent a detailed reply to charges and followed her lawyers' advice to request an opportunity to clear her name in a hearing. Little could she have guessed that her hearings before Commerce loyalty and appeals boards would drag on for over a year, totaling fifteen days and about two thousand transcribed pages of testimony taken in three cities. Additional charges were added as new witnesses emerged with recollections of seeing Mary in Communist company. The intrigue and innuendo got very thick, and the tone was far less polite than in 1948.[96]

In late 1951 the Keyserling cases took on new importance for the professional anticommunists, because they turned into a referendum on the veracity of Paul Crouch. In November an ex-FBI agent who was a security officer for the Commerce Department leaked word back to Hoover that Abe Fortas had announced his intention to present evidence that would demolish Crouch's credibility. This news worried FBI officials because Crouch was a key witness in the Remington case and was being considered for use in pending Smith Act cases. "From past experience in the Hiss case," they predicted, defense counsel might bring out Crouch's criminal record and try to show "mental aberration."[97] The FBI stepped up its efforts to corroborate Crouch's claims about Mary and Leon and to try Gilbert Parks on perjury charges. As tempting a target as the Keyserlings were in their own right, the stakes were higher than their reputations alone.

Mary's views and associations during the late 1920s and 1930s, when she was very young, did not work in government, and was not married to Leon, now became the major focus of the investigation. Crouch testified before the Commerce loyalty board and identified the same photographs he had before SISS. Mary again claimed he had confused her with her sister. The FBI ran down every lead. It obtained photos of the sisters from Barnard College yearbooks (their selected quotations, "the welfare of the people is the supreme law" [Mary] and "give me liberty or give me death" [Elisabeth], drew no comment). Agents interviewed Barnard classmates and teachers as well as the uncooperative Beatrice Heiman and George Pershing. They searched unsuccessfully for passenger lists that might show Heiman on the same ship to Europe with a Dublin sister in 1929. Meanwhile, the defense produced witnesses who had known the sisters during their college years, who testified to remembering dinner-table arguments between the moderate, sensible Mary and the radical, impulsive Elisabeth. As she had before SISS, Elisabeth vouched for this scenario of the loving but politically divided sisters. According to Elisabeth, "she was conservative and I was radical"; when Elisabeth herself started to become disillusioned with the Soviet Union in about 1936, Mary was "much relieved," saying "I told you so."[98]

Evidence emerged during the Commerce loyalty hearings to indicate that although Mary might have been more conservative than her sister, she had agreed with at least some tenets of socialism. The ensuing questioning about the extent and timing of her sympathy for socialism weakened Dublin Keyserling's credibility. A discussion of her editing of pamphlets for the socialist League for Industrial Democracy led the board to ask whether she ever had advocated socialism or "an economic system of production for use and not for profit." She said she had not. Told that informants had described her as "an advocate of Norman Thomas's

Figure 4.3. During Mary Dublin Keyserling's loyalty investigation, the FBI obtained old photographs of Mary (right) and her sister Elisabeth (left) from their Barnard College senior yearbooks and passport applications. Investigators asked informant Paul Crouch to identify the woman he recalled as a Communist in 1929. Crouch initially selected a photograph of Mary but then wavered. Reprinted from *Mortarboard* 1929, 1930. Courtesy of Barnard College Archives.

theory of economics," Dublin Keyserling backpedaled. Although she had been "very conservative at college," in the early Depression years she was one of many "socially-minded young people" who "found many of the things that Thomas said appealing." She had voted for Norman Thomas in 1932, she volunteered, but that had been merely a protest vote, reflecting her impatience with the major parties. She had agreed with Thomas about the need for public power projects, and health, old age, and unemployment insurance. But she "wouldn't have gone along with him on everything by any means." By 1936, she told the board, she regretted her 1932 vote and was an ardent supporter of Franklin Roosevelt. Dublin Keyserling and her lawyers did not know the FBI had checked her voter registration history. According to one report, she registered for the Socialist Party in 1932, 1934, and 1936, and for the American Labor Party in 1937 and 1939. The loyalty board probably found Dublin Keyserling's description of her political loyalties in the 1930s, and especially in 1936, to be disingenuous.[99]

Dublin Keyserling's understatement of her commitment to socialism disinclined loyalty officials to give her the benefit of the doubt as they waded through the contradictory data in the FBI reports and hearings transcripts to discern her relationship, if any, to the Communist Party.

Based on the evidence before the board, in addition to evidence the board did not have, it seems clear that Dublin Keyserling never joined the party.[100] During her investigation, politically sophisticated people of diverse ideological stripes stated that she was not a Communist. Norman Thomas, Harry Laidler, and James Carey, all prominent socialists or former socialists, so testified, stressing that they were qualified to distinguish among leftists because they had been alert to the Communist threat well before most liberals. Those three delicately avoided labeling Dublin Keyserling a socialist, but others did not. A Milwaukee union official told the FBI he had known Mary Dublin to be a prominent and active member of the Socialist Party from 1931 to 1934. The party then had three factions, he explained, the old guard, a middle group led by Norman Thomas, and a left-wing group led by J. B. Matthews. Mary had been in the Norman Thomas camp, he said, and had opposed collaboration with the Communists. A former colleague at Sarah Lawrence College similarly described Dublin Keyserling as a noncommunist socialist.[101] That information would have been helpful to her if the countersubversive agenda had been limited to its formal mandate of eliminating Communists from government, but for a government official in the 1950s to be labeled a socialist, even an anticommunist one, was almost as damaging as being labeled a Communist.

One ex-Communist witness, Nathaniel Weyl, had been cooperating with the FBI and had known Dublin Keyserling and her family for many years, so one might expect that his testimony that she never was a Communist would have carried considerable weight. In 1951 a newspaper publisher named William Loeb told the FBI that he had seen Mary in 1937 at numerous meetings at Weyl's apartment of the American Boycott Association against Japanese Aggression, a group with Communist sympathies. Loeb's story led investigators to Nathaniel and Sylvia Weyl.[102] Both Weyls had quit the Communist Party in 1939. In about 1943 Nathaniel falsely told the Dies Committee he never had been a party member, but in 1950 both Weyls went to the FBI as confidential informants, deciding that the intensifying Cold War obligated them to aid in counterespionage. In early 1952 Nathaniel went public, testifying he had known Alger Hiss to be a Communist. Some investigators held it against the Weyls, however, that they had not come forward sooner.[103] Paul Crouch, probably perceiving their potential to undermine him, claimed the Weyls' anticommunism was halfhearted.[104]

Nathaniel Weyl told Dublin Keyserling's loyalty board in June 1952 that she never was close to the Communist Party. His testimony was not as powerful as it might have been, however, because in his effort to help her, and to protect her from damage by association with him, Weyl portrayed her as apolitical and claimed he had been friends with her sister but not Mary. The board was not convinced, aware that Mary had been an active socialist. The board also may have known that Weyl had told the FBI that between 1931 and 1937 he had had a "close association" with Mary.[105] In 2003 Weyl reaffirmed his certainty that Dublin Keyserling was never a Communist.[106] Other prominent ex-Communists concurred with Weyl's assessment or at least did not contradict it. Some knew her and thought she was a noncommunist socialist (Jay Lovestone); others knew her but did not know her political views (Max Yergan); others did not know her at all (Elizabeth Bentley).[107]

However, Dublin Keyserling's denial that she had been a socialist, combined with the fact that she had some enemies who told investigators they questioned her political loyalty, created enough murkiness that the loyalty board felt unable to decide her case without more information.[108] Throughout 1952 the board asked the FBI to follow up one lead after another. Most of the key players in the anticommunist network helped keep the picture murky—for long enough that the case remained unresolved as the fall elections drew near. J. B. Matthews and the ex-Communist witness Louis Budenz claimed Mary was a Communist, although when pressed both admitted that they based their opinion on the positions she took rather than on firsthand knowledge.[109] Senator McCarthy, SISS, journalists, and zealous amateur anticommunists all did their part in ratcheting up the pressure on the Commerce loyalty board.

On February 9, 1952, speaking at a Lincoln's Day dinner in Wheeling, West Virginia, where two years earlier to the day he had seized the limelight by charging that the State Department was infested with Communists, Senator McCarthy blew the lid of confidentiality right off the Keyserling cases. Calling both Keyserlings Communist sympathizers, he gave a distorted summary of the Crouch stories and revealed that Mary remained under investigation. "That is the picture . . . of the man who is determining the economic policies followed by the President." McCarthy claimed that Leon's inflationary policies would lead to nationalization of all American industries. McCarthy may have been cooperating with his fellow Republican senator Homer Ferguson of SISS.[110] J. B. Matthews later testified that he had seen Don Surine of McCarthy's staff with the confidential SISS transcripts.[111]

The Keyserlings dismissed McCarthy's charge as "utter nonsense." In statements to reporters, Leon characterized the allegations as stemming entirely from an "ex-convict, ex-Communist" (Paul Crouch) who was "eking out a living as a third-rate informer." He and Mary both were "bitterly opposed" to communism, he insisted, and neither had ever joined any organization sympathetic to it.[112] Liberal newspapers scoffed at McCarthy's tale. "Ho Hum," commented a *Washington Post* editorial, adding that Keyserling would have been better off ignoring the ridiculous charges.[113] A few days before McCarthy's speech, the Loyalty Review Board had confirmed Leon's clearance, and Mary's lawyers had made what they thought was the closing summation before the Commerce loyalty board.[114]

Behind the scenes, however, the case was anything but closed. The anti-Crouch offensive by the Keyserlings and their counsel now was public. The professional anticommunists redoubled their efforts to shore up Crouch's reputation. By late April, the FBI had learned that aspects of Crouch's story about the Keyserlings were questionable, but in order to avoid damage to other cases in which he was a witness, the FBI kept its doubts to itself and told the Commerce loyalty board that it judged Crouch to be reliable.[115]

The pressure on the loyalty board mounted further when, during the intense controversy over Truman's takeover of the steel industry, McCarthy reopened fire on the Keyserlings from the Senate floor, where he was immune from libel charges. Steelworkers and industrialists were at an impasse, and to force employers to the table Truman ordered Secretary of Commerce Sawyer to keep the mills running, citing his obligation to supply the Korean War effort. Fairly or not, some commentators attributed the seizure of the steel industry—which the Supreme Court soon declared unconstitutional—to Leon Keyserling's advice. Privately, Keyserling disavowed responsibility for the steel seizure, but he could not do so publicly for fear of embarrassing the administration. McCarthy accused Keyserling of assuring Truman that steel could afford to pay higher wages. McCarthy claimed that cutting "investor wages" by raising union wages would bring a crash "worse than 1929." The Democrats cared only about votes, he averred, and union members outnumbered investors.[116]

McCarthy's charges generated hostile press about the Keyserlings and brought more witnesses out of the woodwork to complain about one or the other half of the couple. The California businessman Alfred Kohlberg, a prominent member of the conservative China lobby (which opposed U.S. recognition of the Communist People's Republic of China), found a college classmate of Mary's who offered to give McCarthy an affidavit about Mary's "enthusiasm for the Russian experiment." The archconservative radio journalist Fulton Lewis Jr. ran a scathing four-part series on them in May (with research assistance from J. B. Matthews, it later came out).[117]

Amid this flurry of media interest, the Commerce loyalty board took no chances. Mary's hearings dragged on through the summer of 1952 as new details were uncovered. A coworker of Mary's complained that Mary had suppressed publication of his anti-Soviet articles in Commerce Department reports, but Secretary of Commerce Sawyer decisively refuted that claim.[118] The FBI learned that Mary had planned a 1934 trip

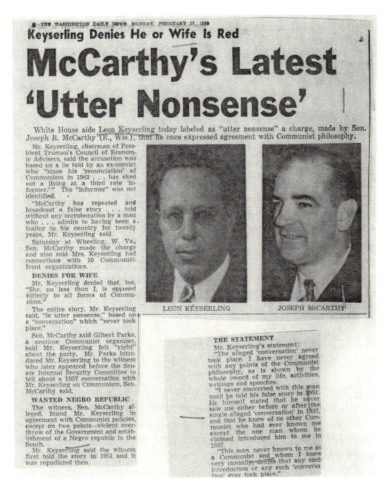

Figure 4.4. Clipping from the *Washington Daily News*, February 11, 1952, in Mary Dublin Keyserling file, SISS Records, National Archives.

to Russia in addition to the 1932 and 1936 trips she already had been questioned about. She had intended to lead a group of college students to study in Moscow under the auspices of the Soviet agency Intourist, but illness prevented her from making the trip. The FBI tracked down the curriculum her group would have pursued and noted its pro-Soviet orientation. Finally, the board's desire to hear the publisher William Loeb in person caused a long delay and yielded nothing beyond what he had told the FBI a year earlier. The Keyserling defense team suspected a deliberate effort by Loeb and allied forces to stall until the elections were imminent.[119]

ELECTION EVE 1952: DUBLIN KEYSERLING'S SUSPENSION AND APPEAL

The FBI was still gathering information when, in late August, the Commerce loyalty board ruled Mary Dublin Keyserling ineligible for government employment. Secretary Sawyer approved her suspension without pay—despite White House pressure, some claimed—effective September 7, 1952. Fulton Lewis Jr. promptly got wind of Commerce's action and alluded to it in a broadcast. Arnold, Fortas & Porter protested the leak to the press and appealed the board's decision.[120] The defense team prepared a comprehensive brief arguing that the Keyserlings were the victims of a politically motivated conspiracy. They had not laid this out in their August summation because they did not want to seem to criticize the loyalty board. Now that the case had moved up to the appeals board, there was no reason to hold back. The defense presented what evidence it had been able to piece together about collusion among Crouch, McCarthy, Matthews, and the journalists Loeb and Lewis. The defense also elaborated on earlier claims that Paul Crouch had changed his story over time, quoting from FBI reports to show the inconsistencies.[121]

These developments created a furor behind the scenes both within the Truman administration and among the professional anticommunists. White House officials had been nervously monitoring the case since McCarthy's February attack.[122] Now they had a new problem. The Commerce loyalty board was upset that the Keyserlings' lawyers had apparently obtained access to their clients' FBI files. Commerce Secretary Sawyer learned that the FBI had given reports on both Keyserlings to the White House loyalty board, which must have shared them with Leon. This put the White House in an embarrassing position, because one of Truman's own directives prohibited loyalty defendants from seeing their files. One member of the Commerce loyalty board, South Trimble Jr., long had complained that pressure from above was negating his board's decisions. Now Trimble had evidence of impropriety, which he shared with the FBI, among other parties. Secretary Sawyer met with President Truman, who responded testily that he had not requested any FBI reports on the Keyserlings and had no interest in the topic. While the appeal proceeded, Sawyer "clamped a complete lid on the case," reportedly threatening to dismiss any Commerce employee who leaked information about it.[123] As Election Day approached, the pressure was felt at the highest levels of the Truman administration.

On September 30, Arnold, Fortas & Palmer submitted their brief on appeal, which argued that the charges against Mary Dublin Keyserling represented a partisan conspiracy to embarrass the Democrats by discrediting Truman's chief economic adviser.[124] The very next day, tabloid headlines stunned the Keyserlings but confirmed their analysis, by indicating another leak. "Wife of Truman Aide Probed" was the unpleasant phrase sprawled all the way across the front page of the *Washington Daily News*.[125] That was only the beginning. Conservative newspaper and radio journalists spent the next two weeks fulminating over the unconfirmed report that Sawyer had suspended Dublin Keyserling. Mary was not quoted in the press, but Leon issued a series of denials and challenges to Paul Crouch's veracity.[126]

The Keyserlings and their lawyers believed that their chief opponents were Paul Crouch, J. B. Matthews, and Senator McCarthy. Although those parties did work against them, it appears that the real culprits were over at SISS. SISS staffer Don Connors had urged Senator McCarran to publicize the Keyserling case despite Sawyer's effort to keep it quiet: "This is, of course, a terrific story on the eve of the Presidential election, and it is difficult to see how Leon Keyserling can retain his position if Mary Dublin Keyserling's suspension is upheld." McCarran told Connors to "do nothing," saying he wanted to "play it Sawyer's way."[127] But SISS member Homer Ferguson proved willing to act on Connors's suggestion. Ferguson was in the hard-core anticommunists' inner circle; Attorney General Tom Clark later complained that Ferguson received FBI reports before he did. It was Ferguson who gave the SISS transcripts on the Keyserling case to the press, or to someone who spoke to the press.[128]

Having created a media frenzy, Ferguson then subpoenaed Leon to appear before SISS on Saturday, October 18. No other members of the committee were present; they had been told about the hearing only the preceding day. Apparently trying to trap Keyserling into committing perjury, or perhaps trying to scare him into revealing something damaging, Ferguson badgered the forty-four-year-old economic adviser over his statements to the press, his access to FBI reports, and his discussion of prior SISS hearings with various White House officials, including the president. Leon nervously declared that he was entitled to be heard by a larger segment of the committee, but Ferguson disagreed: "I have the authority to hold this hearing and I am a quorum." Ferguson acted insulted by Keyserling's (accurate) suggestion that SISS had leaked to the press, but he also declared that the public was entitled to know that Dublin Keyserling had been suspended. Ferguson called the White House's refusal to allow Congress access to employee loyalty files the "Iron Curtain of America." Leon wanted to present his evidence of Crouch's unreliability, but Ferguson did not let him. Instead the discussion bogged down on the subject of the League for Industrial Democracy, the socialist group to whose publications Mary had contributed in the 1930s. When Leon asserted the group's respectability by listing others who had been associated with it, Ferguson seized on one name Leon mentioned: Paul R. Porter, then the European director of the Mutual Security Agency (MSA), the

Marshall Plan successor. Keyserling had not meant to create trouble for Porter. He tried to change the subject back to Crouch's falsehoods, but Ferguson would not be diverted. Did Leon think a socialist should hold an important job with the MSA? No, said Leon, but he doubted Porter was still a socialist. Ferguson ended the hearing before Leon could present his material.[129]

Three days later, Ferguson issued a press release demanding Paul R. Porter's recall from Europe. In Porter, Ferguson had found a new target to use in telling voters that the Truman administration harbored leftists. Porter had been a prominent leader of the Socialist Party until 1941, when he quit over the party's foreign policy stance and went on to hold a succession of significant economic advisory posts in Europe. Letters defending Porter poured in to editors and politicians; CIO leader James Carey accused Ferguson of orchestrating an election eve stunt. Ferguson did not relent. He told radio listeners in Michigan that the cases of Porter and the Keyserlings were proof that Democrats appointed subversives to high office. "My friends, we are not talking about inconspicuous clerks in the wildlife service. . . . We can get rid of [these subversive top officials] by electing a Republican administration."[130]

Ferguson did not mention that Dublin Keyserling had dated Porter, but the columnist Westbrook Pegler had no such compunctions. A week before the election, he gave millions of Scripps-Howard newspaper readers details of the Porter and Keyserling cases that came from the supposedly confidential SISS transcripts. Calling Porter a "big, sedentary slob of the Roosevelt-Truman bureaucracy," who along with "a whole army of parasitic unemployable misfits" had been "living high on the hog at our expense" in Europe, Pegler remarked that Dublin Keyserling's onetime engagement to him "might give you a clue to the things that you could surmise about the character of both of them." Ad hominem remarks coupled with sexual innuendo were Pegler's trademark.[131]

It is impossible to measure precisely how much the coordinated attack on the Keyserlings and Paul R. Porter, among other high-ranking government employees, contributed to the Democrats' defeat on November 4, 1952. The election was not close, and Eisenhower was so popular that he might have won in any case. But certainly the lesson that many on the right had drawn from the 1948 election was that the Republican candidate Thomas Dewey failed to hit Truman hard enough on the "Communists in government" theme. Ferguson's enthusiasm for exposing key Truman appointees as erstwhile leftists indicates that he was among those Republicans who were determined not to let their party make the same mistake in 1952 that they believed it had in 1948.[132]

Although it furthered the objectives of Ferguson and other conservative Republicans, the election of Dwight D. Eisenhower did not resolve ongoing loyalty cases. As Leon told SISS, "there is a saying that when a

Loyalty Investigation starts, it never ends."[133] Paul R. Porter was forced to resign in June 1953. The Keyserlings resigned even sooner, after Mary's appeal resulted in less than full satisfaction. While Fortas was working on a new brief, the FBI found information that would be used during the appeal hearing to put Mary back on the defensive. Old data in Mary's file linking her to the social scientist and alleged Communist Mary van Kleeck took on new life when the FBI contacted an ex-Communist informant who said she had seen van Kleeck with Mary Dublin in the 1930s and so inferred Dublin had sympathized with communism. Although that informant advised "not to put too much stock" in her impression, the FBI hastened to locate van Kleeck in Europe. Van Kleeck told the FBI that she had known Dublin to be a "free independent thinker who leaned toward socialism but opposed some aspects of it." Rather than emphasizing this exonerating assessment, the FBI and Commerce loyalty officials focused on the fact that van Kleeck and Dublin Keyserling offered different accounts of the extent of their acquaintance in the 1930s. Mary's appeal hearing on November 4—Election Day—concluded sourly, amid debate over the phrase "quasi-professional association" as it applied to her relationship with van Kleeck.[134]

On January 5, 1953, the appeals board overturned the lower board's decision and cleared Dublin Keyserling on loyalty grounds. The Keyserlings claimed that Mary had been fully vindicated. That was not quite true. The FBI's man in the Commerce security office reported that the appeals board, despite finding her loyal, had recommended rating her undesirable on *security* grounds. Secretary Sawyer reportedly concurred, prohibited her from handling classified information, and expected her to resign. On January 19, both Keyserlings did resign. Their publicly stated reason was that a Republican administration was taking power, but in fact Mary had been denied security clearance. In April 1953 President Eisenhower's EO 10450 would make security requirements even more stringent, and had Mary not resigned in January she probably would have been dismissed under EO 10450. Her dismissal on security grounds in turn would have made it impossible for Leon to work in government, on or off the Council of Economic Advisers. As it was, because she resigned before the Loyalty Review Board completed its "post-audit" of her loyalty clearance, her name was "flagged," which meant that if she tried to reenter government service she would be reinvestigated on loyalty as well as security grounds.[135]

THE FALL OF PAUL CROUCH AND JOSEPH MCCARTHY

Even the Keyserlings' departure from government employment did not bring closure, because the battle over Crouch's reputation, and over the legitimacy of the campaign against Communists in government, did not abate. On the heels of the Keyserling resignations, Joseph and Stewart Alsop of the *Washington Post* called for an investigation of "hired informers," beginning with Paul Crouch. The Alsops' information clearly came from the Keyserlings. Later in 1953 Leon located early testimony by Paul Crouch that contradicted his later allegations by characterizing Leon as a Keynesian who believed in "the capitalist system of production." Crouch was a liar, but in discussing the case Leon and the Alsops did simplify the evidence against Mary, and they overstated the extent of her vindication.[136] Meanwhile, hard-core anticommunists like Alfred Kohlberg rallied to defend Crouch against journalists' "libelous" attacks. In mobilizing supporters, Crouch grossly distorted the facts of the case. He claimed that he had never questioned Leon's loyalty and that his testimony about Mary was an insignificant aspect of her case.[137]

Both sides knew that the other side made misrepresentations, and so both sides nurtured a righteous indignation that did not fade quickly. J. Edgar Hoover tried to have Dublin Keyserling prosecuted for perjury. When an assistant attorney general rejected that plan, Hoover was so incensed that he checked that official's loyalty record.[138] In July 1953 SISS gave Dublin Keyserling's name to the Immigration and Naturalization Service as a subversive who might be deported or denaturalized; the INS determined that she was a native-born American and therefore not subject to such action.[139] The public battle over Crouch's reputation resumed in the spring of 1954. Influential columnist Drew Pearson joined the Alsops in calling Crouch a fraud. After more examples of inconsistent testimony and new evidence of fabricated claims came to light, the Department of Justice stopped using Crouch.[140] By that time, McCarthy's charges against the U.S. Army had provoked a serious counteroffensive, and the tide was shifting against the professional anticommunists. Crouch soon was widely discredited, and McCarthy was on his way down as well. In 1954 McCarthy tried to use the Keyserling case to forestall investigation of how he had obtained an FBI document on the army cases. McCarthy warned that if an issue were made of it, he would publicly ask why no one had been prosecuted when Leon Keyserling obtained FBI reports. The Senate did censure McCarthy, but the matter of his improper access to FBI documents apparently was dropped.[141]

The Keyserlings and their lawyers were correct that there was a conspiracy against them, but that conspiracy began earlier and involved more players than they ever knew. Ben Mandel had been suspicious of Mary Dublin since 1940 and kept tabs on her as he moved from the Dies Committee to HUAC to SISS. Congressional conservatives such as John Taber had criticized the Keyserlings individually and as a couple since 1942, and Mandel used Mary's record to try to block Leon's appointment to the CEA in 1946. It was probably Mandel who made the December 1950 chart mapping the Keyserlings' ties to George Marshall. When Mandel learned that Crouch had said Gilbert Parks knew Leon Keyserling, he asked for more information; Crouch complied with the January 1951 memo that was much more damaging to Leon than anything Crouch had said earlier. That memo is just one piece of evidence contradicting Crouch's later explanation that it was through his testimony on the Parks case in May 1951 that he came to testify against Leon and that he only later learned the identity of Leon's wife. Additional evidence comes from Mary's FBI file, which shows that Crouch lied when he said that the Pittsburgh FBI had questioned him about a Mary Dublin in April 1951 in connection with Beatrice Heiman. Although the FBI searched diligently, it could not find evidence that Crouch had ever mentioned a "Mary" to an FBI agent before June 1951. Dublin Keyserling's FBI file indicates that before Crouch gave his June 1951 statement, the FBI had not associated Dublin Keyserling with Heiman and so would not have asked Crouch about Mary in connection with her. The FBI did not share its discovery that Crouch's explanation did not square with its records, not least because the FBI wanted to preserve Crouch's credibility as a witness in other cases. The FBI thus was complicit in the plot against the Keyserlings as well.

What most likely happened is that after Mandel received Crouch's January 1951 memo linking Leon Keyserling and Gilbert Parks, Mandel asked Crouch whether he knew anything about Leon's wife Mary Dublin, and Crouch then realized that Leon had married the sister of the leftist Elisabeth Dublin, whom Crouch actually had known. It is unclear whose idea it was for Crouch to pretend to confuse the two Dublin sisters, but Crouch's careful phrasing about "the girl whom he recollected by the name of Mary" suggests that the mistake was not innocent and that he was wary of perjury charges. It also is unclear who thought of pretending that SISS stumbled onto the Keyserlings in the process of investigating Gilbert Parks, but in any case Senator Ferguson pursued the Keyserlings relentlessly from June 1951 through the 1952 election. The staffs of SISS and McCarthy cooperated on the case, as did at least one member of the Commerce loyalty board. Various members of the anticommunist network got the word out to sympathetic journalists: someone spoke with William Loeb in 1951, J. B. Matthews gave information to Fulton Lewis Jr. in May 1952, and Ferguson leaked information that made its way to reporters including Andrew Tully, Walter Trohan, and Westbrook Pegler.

Abe Fortas called Mary Dublin Keyserling's case the most exhaustive loyalty investigation he had experienced, which was saying a lot, given his position as one of the leading lawyers for loyalty defendants.[142] It is hardly surprising that the Keyserlings had many enemies. Both were prominent in causes that were anathema to the right. Mary was associated with the consumer movement in the 1930s and then with the United Nations, Marshall Plan, and reduced import tariffs. Leon helped draft key labor, public housing, and full employment legislation, and then as chair of the CEA was identified with Truman's seizure of the steel industry and with an expansionist orientation that many believed was inflationary. It is not possible to link each actor in the campaign to discredit the Keyserlings directly to an interest group that was threatened by their policy prescriptions, but there are plenty of arrows pointing to the right. With Hearst's backing, J. B. Matthews went after the League of Women Shoppers, which brought Dublin to his attention, and Mandel first learned of her through Matthews. Mandel, Matthews, and Crouch all earned their livings from the anticommunist cause. For Mandel in 1951, there was the additional incentive of making a name for SISS and taking the limelight back from McCarthy.[143] These self-interested professional anticommunists worked with congressional conservatives, including Martin Dies, John Taber, Joe McCarthy, and Homer Ferguson, who had their own reasons for pursuing the Keyserlings. The politicians' interests ranged from publicity, to persuading voters that the Democrats were soft on communism, to pleasing powerful constituents—such as media or real estate interests, protectionist producers, and antiunion employers.

These forces did not give up easily, and their bitterness ran deep. In the late 1950s J. B. Matthews still was fuming that the Keyserlings had not been indicted for perjury. "In a manner reminiscent of Alger Hiss circling around Whitaker Chambers examining his teeth, etc., Leon Keyserling refused to swear he had never met with Crouch or Parks," he complained.[144] In 1963, with the Democrats back in power and the Keyserlings reemerging as vocal members of that party, Mandel reminded his SISS colleagues about Mary's case. "Government files must be full of such cases which have never been disclosed," he told SISS counsel Jay Sourwine, who agreed they should discuss it.[145] When Lyndon Johnson nominated Dublin Keyserling to head the U.S. Women's Bureau in 1964, Mandel tried unsuccessfully to prevent her appointment by disseminating memos about her loyalty case. Congressional conservatives did resurrect the old allegations. They also complained that she represented "the old programs of the 1930s and 1940s which have failed so miserably." But Abe Fortas was now a confidant to President Johnson, and he backed Dublin Keyserling for the Women's Bureau position by declaring the earlier charges against her "one of the more outrageous instances of accusation on account of consanguinity," meaning her family tie to Elisabeth and George Marshall.[146] By 1964, many were recalling the McCarthy-era hunt for Communists in government as an embarrassing episode of mass hysteria. The legacy of that crusade would not dissipate so quickly.

CHAPTER 5

Secrets and Self-Reinvention: The Making of Cold War Liberalism

It is hard to forgive the professional anticommunists for their self-serving partisanship, disregard of civil liberties, and multitudinous dirty tricks. Their vindictiveness, however, was intensified by their accurate perception that the Keyserlings were hiding something. That something was not Communist Party membership or anything remotely resembling treason, but the Keyserlings were not honest about their political histories. Over the long course of their loyalty investigations, they portrayed themselves as having been political centrists during the 1930s, when in fact they had been decidedly on the left.

The Keyserlings are remembered as loyal Johnson Democrats who favored Cold War military spending, backed U.S. policy in Vietnam, and argued that poverty could be eliminated through economic growth rather than redistribution.[1] Before coming under investigation, however, they were socialists. Faced with a relentless stream of disloyalty allegations that began in the 1940s and climaxed in 1952, they were forced to modify their political rhetoric and moderate their policy proposals. They also denied they ever had held leftist views. Conservatives may have lost the battle to exclude the Keyserlings from public influence, but by narrowing the range of permissible debate, they won the war.

"THE TYRANNY OF LABELS"

There was a lot about the young Mary Dublin that investigators did not uncover, for all their national security apparatus. A cache of her annual appointment books, found by relatives in a metal box in her bedroom during her final years, offers a tantalizing glimpse into the world of a dedicated young left feminist. The record is incomplete because, for some of the years that became most sensitive in her investigation, books are missing or sections have been torn out. Dublin Keyserling apparently destroyed material she thought incriminating.[2] On the surviving pages, tiny notations in faded ink outline a packed schedule of political and social engagements. These books demonstrate the inaccuracy of Dublin

Keyserling's later representations to loyalty investigators on certain specific points, and it seems unlikely that a faulty memory was to blame, because she had the appointment books. Taken cumulatively, the events that filled Dublin Keyserling's calendar suggest a more leftist political orientation than she later felt free to acknowledge, but she does not seem to have been concealing illegal activity. Rather, she appears to have hidden legitimate associations because doing so was necessary as she faced the "American inquisition."

In addition to downplaying her commitment to the Socialist Party during the 1930s, Dublin Keyserling misled loyalty investigators about her relationships with a few individuals and understated her involvement in the 1930s with two groups that included Communists, the League of Women Shoppers and the Teachers' Union. Although Mary told investigators she never had a "social" relationship with her allegedly Communist brother-in-law, her appointment books show that she was very close to both Elisabeth and George Marshall. She hosted parties for them, attended political and social events with them, and frequently spent weekends at their home into the early 1940s. The books similarly reveal that she had an enduring friendship with Nathaniel Weyl. A Communist from 1933 through 1939, in 1952 Weyl appeared before the Commerce loyalty board to support Mary's claim that he had been friends with Elisabeth but not Mary. Although Weyl may have been closer to Elisabeth, with whom he was active in the Social Problems Club at Columbia, he and Mary also were good friends. He first appears in her appointment books as a theater companion in 1929. When they both were at the London School of Economics in the spring of 1932, they dined together regularly, and they continued to socialize when both were back in New York City later that year, until he left for a job in Washington. There he soon joined the Communist Party. In 1935 Nathaniel married the Communist activist Sylvia Castleton, and they moved to Texas, where she was in charge of party organizing for Texas and Oklahoma. In 1938 the Weyls were back in New York, where they saw Mary on many occasions, often dinner parties at the Marshalls' apartment. The Weyls by this time had become disillusioned with the party, because of the Moscow show trials and also because of their experiences with Communists in Mexico, where they spent a year coauthoring a book on the Cárdenas government. After the Hitler-Stalin pact of August 1939, the Weyls officially left the party. They saw a great deal of Mary in New York City in 1940 and of Mary and Leon together in Washington before and after Weyl served in the military. In 1946 Mary helped Nathaniel get two writing assignments in government agencies. In other words, Mary and Nathaniel were friends before, during, and after his Communist phase, but during Mary's loyalty hearing she and Weyl deemed it wise to downplay their relationship. Leon too knew Weyl, at first independently of Mary and then later when the two couples met to play bridge and talk politics, but Weyl's friendship with Leon never came up in the hearings.[3]

Weyl's testimony before the Commerce loyalty board opened up a line of questioning that produced another discrepancy between Mary's testimony and her appointment books. When Weyl casually mentioned he had seen Mary at a 1938 Industrial Relations Institute conference in Mexico, loyalty officials took notice. In 1948 and again in 1951, the board had asked Dublin Keyserling to explain why the Communist Party's *Daily Worker* listed her as a delegate to that conference, which was held in conjunction with two Communist-affiliated conventions, the Latin American Labor Congress and the World Labor Congress against War and Fascism. Dublin Keyserling said she vaguely recalled stopping by a large meeting held in Spanish while vacationing in Mexico, but that she could not have been a delegate as she had not known about the conference before she left the United States. After Weyl's testimony, the board questioned Dublin Keyserling on the topic once again. She insisted she had "bumped into" the Weyls in Mexico. Her 1938 appointment book indicates, however, that she spent a weekend at the Weyls' home in Woodstock, New York, just a month before they all were in Mexico. She and the Weyls most likely planned in advance to attend the conference. A conference registration list indicates that it involved a few dozen American social scientists and lawyers—not a large meeting held in Spanish. Dublin Keyserling was on the list, along with many people she knew: the lawyer Ambrose Doskow, the economist Otto Nathan, the CIO lawyer Joseph Kovner, Fred and Shoshona Krivonos of the National Labor Relations Board, and Dorothy Douglas of Smith College. Also present was the NLRB's Edwin Smith, who like Dorothy Douglas and Mary van Kleeck was close to the Communist Party. Dublin Keyserling is discernible, barely, in a photograph from the event. Edwin Smith's allegedly anti-American speeches at one of these Mexico conferences had been the subject of extensive inquiry in January 1940 during the Smith Committee's probe of the NLRB, so Dublin Keyserling's effort to minimize her participation is not surprising.[4]

Dublin Keyserling's presence at the Mexico conference was suspicious to investigators on its own, but it caused further difficulties because it led the loyalty board to probe Dublin Keyserling's relationship with the conference organizer, Mary van Kleeck. Dublin denied that she ever had had a personal conversation or an arranged meeting with van Kleeck. In late 1952, van Kleeck told the FBI that Dublin Keyserling had visited her office five or six times during the 1930s to discuss social policy. Dublin Keyserling's appointment books indicate that van Kleeck's account is more accurate. Mary's friendships with the Marshalls and Nathaniel Weyl and her half-dozen lunch meetings with Mary van Kleeck during the 1930s hardly made her a threat to national security. During the Red scare, however, it would have been risky to acknowledge those relationships.[5]

The need to distance herself from George Marshall may partially explain one final point of dissemblance by Dublin Keyserling. She denied to investigators that she ever had a particular interest in Russian affairs. However, the appointment books document, more fully than the FBI did, a long-standing concern that ranged across time from a "Russia benefit" in 1927 to a "Russian Relief dinner" in February 1946. During the 1930s she shared the fascination of many American progressive intellectuals with the Soviet experiment, and she traveled there in 1932 and 1936; she also planned trips there in 1934 and 1939, but those were canceled. She was not very active in the Soviet-American friendship societies that proliferated in the 1930s, but her brother-in-law was, and Dublin Keyserling's calendars indicate that she occasionally attended their meetings, sometimes with the Marshalls. She chaired a planning session of the American Russian Institute in 1938, made note of an American Council on Soviet Relations meeting in 1940 and a "Soviet reception" in 1941, and was taking Russian lessons in 1945. These activities were not evidence of Communist views, nor did they contradict the official U.S. stance toward the Soviet Union, which after all was a U.S. ally from 1941 to 1945. Given her profession and her ancestry—her mother especially cherished her Russian heritage—Dublin Keyserling's interest in the Soviet Union is not surprising. During the loyalty investigation, however, she felt compelled to conceal it.[6]

Although Keyserling's appointment books can be used to detect some misrepresentations she made in later years, they are perhaps more interesting for their vivid clues about the daily life, networks, and program of left feminists in the 1930s and 1940s. Dublin Keyserling and her associates were remarkably energetic and well-connected people. Dublin Keyserling typically had several engagements per day, and classifying them can be difficult because her professional, political, and social lives were deeply interwoven. The people with whom she worked on a particular cause—whether organizing a faculty union, researching a social problem, drafting a bill, or mobilizing public opinion—were the same people with whom she attended cultural events, spent weekends, and enjoyed frequent cocktail and dinner gatherings. Her social life centered on celebrating and supporting left causes. It also reflected the interpenetration of Popular Front politics and culture. She attended the hit Broadway review *Pins and Needles*, produced and performed by members of the International Ladies Garment Workers Union, not long after it opened in 1937. Twice in 1940 she and her friends attended performances by the African American Communist Paul Robeson. (A thespian herself in her student years, at the London School of Economics in 1932 she produced

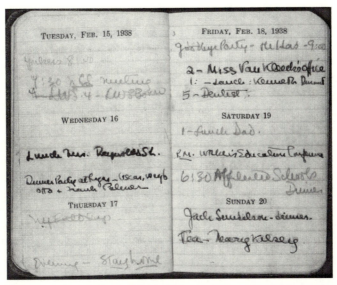

Figure 5.1. A page from Mary Dublin's 1938 appointment book hints at a more leftist political orientation than she later acknowledged to loyalty boards. Investigators would have been suspicious of the LWS meeting, the dinner party hosted by her sister and attended by the Weyls, the appointment with Mary van Kleeck, and the lunch with Kenneth Durant of Tass, the Soviet news bureau. Courtesy of the Schlesinger Library, Radcliffe Institute, Harvard University.

and acted in a George Bernard Shaw play with the social theorist T. H. Marshall.) She hosted or attended parties for left luminaries including the expatriate Russian socialist Angelica Balabanoff (with whom she also went to the movies) in 1936, the British Fabian writer H. G. Wells that same year, the British feminist and Labour Party welfare expert Margaret Bondfield in 1938 and 1939, the director Orson Welles in 1943, the labor journalist Mary Heaton Vorse in 1945, and the political scientist Harold Laski in 1946. Her 1938 calendar included a "party for Spain" and a *Nation* party for sharecroppers. An "evening at home—reading" was rare enough for Dublin Keyserling to note it in her engagement book.[7] These activists not only were confident of their ability to change the world for the better, or at least sentient of an obligation to try; they also had a lot of fun, and often found romance, in the undertaking.[8]

Although cemented by shared passions for social transformation and intellectual debate, Dublin Keyserling's political community was hardly monolithic, insular, or marginal. Her networks included diverse leftists and liberals and extended across reform, labor, academic, and government circles. Her mentors included socialists and social democrats such as the economists Eveline and Arthur Burns, the sociologists Robert and Helen Lynd, and Helen Hall of the Henry Street Settlement. She lunched with the socialist author Ruth Shallcross in 1934, made note of a *New Masses* meeting and a Socialist Party rally in 1936, met the Marxist economist Paul Sweezy several times in 1938, went to the opera with Sweezy's leftist Harvard colleague Ray Walsh in 1939, hosted the CIO lawyer and Communist Party member Lee Pressman and his wife for dinner in 1939 and 1941, and socialized with Corliss and Margaret Lamont, prominent Friends of the Soviet Union, in 1939 and 1940. But her good friends in these same years also included the New Dealers Abe and Carol Fortas, Herb and Elsie Wechsler, and Caroline Ware. Dublin Keyserling had access to powerful people in government, if sometimes only through their wives: she hosted Senator Wagner for cocktails in 1940, met with Eleanor Roosevelt on consumer affairs that same year, took tea with Alice (Mrs. Dean) Acheson in 1941, and lunched with Congresswoman Helen Gahagan Douglas in 1945 and 1946.[9]

Dublin Keyserling was not living two lives, one in a left-wing underworld and the other in the New Deal mainstream. Rather, before and after she entered government service in 1940, she belonged to a dynamic network of women and men in voluntary associations, academia, labor unions, and government who, notwithstanding ideological variations, agreed on the need for state policies to improve the living standards and political participation of poor and working-class Americans. In addition to documenting the vital presence of women in every circuit of that network, Dublin Keyserling's appointment books capture the fluidity of the left-liberal political spectrum in the 1930s and early 1940s. In those years, there was a grain of truth to the right's warning that "a liberal is only a hop, skip, and a jump from a Communist."[10] But leftists like Dublin Keyserling sought to influence policy not through conspiratorial secret cells, brainwashing, or blackmail but rather through the power of their ideas expressed in open debate.

Dublin Keyserling's engagement books convey a sense of the broad range of causes that interested her and of the variety of forums through which she pursued them. Her activity in the Sarah Lawrence chapter of the Teacher's Union suggests her commitment to organizing the middle class, while her teaching at the Henry Street Settlement, her engagements at Brookwood Labor College, and a series of events related to sharecroppers and domestic workers attest to her interest in mobilizing the working class—and not just its white male industrial workers. Her left-labor vision was international: she lectured at women's colleges on "labor's stake in world peace," for example, and in the summers of 1937 and 1938 she taught seminars on "economic factors behind world unrest" at student peace institutes under Quaker auspices. Before the Hitler-Stalin pact of 1939, she promoted nonmilitary responses to fascism abroad. For example, she supported the League of Women Shoppers' boycott of exports from fascist nations, whose policies, she stressed, exploited their own workers, especially women and ethnic minorities, in addition to promoting militarism.[11]

Dublin Keyserling's appointment books may tell us who she knew and where she went, but they cannot tell us what she thought. Recently discovered letters from Mary to her parents—letters she probably thought had been destroyed—illuminate her political views in her youth.[12] Most of the letters date from Mary's 1929 summer at the Geneva School of International Studies and her 1931–32 year at the London School of Economics. Although Dublin Keyserling later would claim she never had embraced socialism and always had opposed communism, the letters make clear that, from age nineteen to twenty-two at least, she identified herself to her parents as a socialist and that she was at least briefly attracted to communism. When read in conjunction with her parents' letters to her, Mary's letters from this period indicate that she was very close to both Augusta and Louis Dublin and that her parents welcomed political debate with their children. Mary's openness with her parents, as well as the economic insecurity that was a recurring theme in their correspondence, demonstrate, once again, that Paul Crouch fabricated his story about the Dublin sisters. Crouch later claimed that "Mary" was terrified in 1929 that her wealthy, bitterly anticommunist father would find out about her Communist activities. In fact, the Dublins were financially pinched during the Depression years, and Louis Dublin adored scrapping over politics with his favorite child, with whom his ideological differences were not so vast in any case.[13] Although Mary's mother never was mentioned during Mary's investigation, the family correspondence also indicates that Augusta viewed herself as a socialist and encouraged Mary in that direction.

The tone of Mary's youthful letters from abroad is exemplified by her description of a 1929 incident at the Geneva School: "All of us with socialistic inclinations, or even bents, 22 of us in fact . . . had a cafe meeting. Each of us gave a riotous speech on the doings of socialism in our own countries (ten of them I believe). . . . Of course we sang the Internationale and sent all the bourgeoisie of the various countries to their respective Hells." In London in 1931 and 1932, she canvassed and lectured for the Independent Labour Party, which she described as "the left wing of the Socialist Party." That party's defeat at the polls, combined with her experiences in London slums gathering data for her thesis on maternal mortality rates, moved her further to the left. By July 1932 she told her parents, "many of us have come round to an acceptance of the major elements of Communism—altho I think we or I shall work thru the Socialist

Party for a while until we can build up a better party on the further left. Even the young militants, as the more active bunch in the S.P. so romantically call themselves, are not beginning to be thoroughgoing enough to please me." A week later, Mary elaborated that she had become "sympathetic" to Communism, "not only as a Russian idea but as a feasible program when modified for many other countries." (In 1951 she would insist that she "expressed vigorous opposition to Communism as early as my undergraduate days and during all my adult life.") In the summer of 1932 Mary spent several weeks in the Soviet Union with a group from the London School, determined to see the Soviet experiment for herself. She told her parents she was tired of "having to shriek about Russia and then confess I haven't been there."[14]

Louis and Augusta Dublin were delighted by Mary's letters. Louis Dublin was a prominent public health reformer who encouraged his children's social justice impulses, although he favored incremental approaches and was constrained to protect his reputation as Metropolitan Life's statistical expert. He sent draft manuscripts to both daughters and took their radical critiques in stride. Soliciting Mary's opinion of an address on health insurance, Louis wrote, "you may find it innocuous, but I feel it is miles ahead in my own thinking and the company's." For his upcoming speech on abortion, Elisabeth urged her father to endorse legalized abortion and contraception on women's rights grounds. She argued that high unemployment, a function of "this last decadent stage of capitalism," was to blame for the falling birthrate, not birth control. "If you're for a rising birth rate work for Socialism," she declared, before signing off teasingly, "yours for the revolution, Elisabeth. G [George Marshall] says I should have written this in Red."[15] Louis was unperturbed by his daughters' revolutionary passion, which he may have indulged as a youthful phase (he predicted to Mary that an English friend would "outgrow his Communism"). In response to one of Mary's more radical letters, he told her how proud he was that she and her sister were "well-launched along lines that should prove very useful to the next generation." Louis also contrasted Mary's situation favorably with Elisabeth's: "you have all of the ardor plus a well-balanced intellectual equipment. I am not afraid of your going off on a wild goose chase."[16] Both parents encouraged Mary to visit Russia, and Augusta lamented that she could not afford to join her daughter on the trip.[17]

Augusta Salik Dublin was never as well known as her husband, having given up a career in the settlement house movement to raise two daughters and two sons. But Augusta kept abreast of developments in the social welfare field, particularly housing policy, and she had strong political views. In the spring of 1932, Augusta's work on housing reform was radicalizing her just at the same moment that Mary was moving left-ward in London: "I am waiting for you to come back and reorganize the Socialist Party. Perhaps we can start a real people's party with eventual government ownership of land and public utilities as the main plank and Norman Thomas the first successful mayor on that ticket in New York." Augusta frequently told Mary that young people were the ones to take up the fight against the concentration of wealth and the injustices she believed it produced.[18] The end of the Depression did not shift Augusta markedly rightward. In 1948, she sent Mary praise for a recent article by Leon: "While it is too much middle of the road for me I agree that that is the only way you can engage the interest of the large mass of the peo-ple. . . . It is a well worthwhile attempt to get some oxygen in the lungs of our very sick capitalistic system. . . . Am I too radical? I, too, am still hop-ing that private enterprise with the cooperation of the government will be equal to the task of intelligent planning. . . . But where is the intelligent government and where are the willing enterprises?"[19] Thereafter, Augusta ceased making leftist comments in letters to Mary, but that silence seems to have reflected a desire not to get her daughter in trouble rather than a change in Augusta's views.

The Dublins belonged to a distinguished circle that illustrates how often the young leftists of the 1930s were the children of the Progressives of the 1910s. Louis and Augusta Salik Dublin, Walter and Bertha Poole Weyl, William and Anna Strunsky Walling, Morris and Mary Cohen, and Louis and Florence Marshall were prominent New York reformers who knew one another and whose children knew one another. The older gen-eration nurtured not only their own but also their friends' children. Many of the younger generation gathered for conversational evenings with the renowned philosopher Morris Raphael Cohen, father of Felix. Mary Dublin dined with the senior Weyls in London, in the same period that Louis and Augusta Dublin entertained Mary's friends and suitors in New York. Members of the younger generation became best friends through their shared political passions, and Mary's appointment books testify to the endurance of their networks in the 1930s and 1940s. Not only were the Dublin sisters close to Nathaniel Weyl, but Mary roomed with Ro-samond Walling in London and remained close to her for decades; Mary had a lifelong friendship with Felix and Lucy Kramer Cohen; Elisabeth married George Marshall, whose brother wooed Mary—and so on.[20] In 1931, the young socialist leader Paul R. Porter listed Nathaniel Weyl, Elisabeth Dublin, and George Marshall among the brightest "young mili-tants" in the New York City Socialist Party.[21] In late 1931 Mary reported happily to Elisabeth and George that in London she had fallen in with a group that "closely resembles the Felix [Cohen] gang in New York.

Intellectual and largely Jewish and wide awake."[22] For these young people, radical activism was not a rebellion against parental expectations; for the most part, they were fulfilling a familial tradition.

Feminism was part of the radical legacy inherited by women of Mary's generation and deepened through their own experiences in the 1930s. Augusta's letters to Mary reveal that she bitterly regretted giving up her career and chafed at the ensuing loss of economic independence and intellectual stimulation. She cautioned her daughters not to follow her example and worried when Elisabeth did so anyway. "Stay-at-home housewives do not have many chances for change and relaxation, especially when money is tight," she grumbled in 1929. Two years later, when her husband said he could not afford for her to join him on a trip, she threatened to "emancipate herself from this situation" by getting a job. The frustrations of managing a household, and the longing for a broader field in which to exercise her talents, were constant themes across three decades of letters from Augusta to Mary.[23] Elisabeth, although she may have worried her mother by depending on her husband's income, was nonetheless an ardent feminist whose commitment to women's reproductive rights was intensified by firsthand experience with unwanted pregnancy.[24]

The feminism that Mary expressed to her parents in letters from London reflected the lessons she drew from her mother's and sister's personal experiences, but it also reflected her exposure to socialist theory. Indeed, Mary's articulation of feminist views deepened in tandem with her commitment to socialism during the year in London. Describing her stay with some English nobility, she analyzed "that strange object known as the English gentleman. . . . It regards women as a lower order of the species. . . . As a socialist it is the very group one is most critical of." After speaking to an Independent Labour Party women's meeting, Mary reported her disappointment that working-class English women, like middle-class ones, were less "emancipated and independent" than their American counterparts. "Their education has been very much inferior to their husbands, they are much less able to express themselves—and the household drudgery has taken out the fire from them." She continued, "I am still as upset as ever about this 'woman question'—and we have a long way to go before we shall have liberated one half of the human race from the outworn traditions which grew up when her economic functions were entirely different."[25]

Back in New York, Mary Dublin would pursue her left version of feminism through activism on behalf of wage-earning women with the National Consumers' League and the League of Women Shoppers. Those groups advocated wage-hour and collective bargaining laws for all workers and regulations to protect all consumers, but their activism was inspired by the exploitation of women as wage earners and as house-wives. The NCL and LWS emphasized women's lower wages, narrower job opportunities, extra burden of unpaid household labor, and difficulty in stretching family budgets to provide decent food, clothing, housing, and health care.[26] In addition to pursuing woman-friendly social policies, Dublin Keyserling asserted women's right to influence policy. She rallied female activists in 1940 by accusing businessmen of telling them to "go home to your knitting and leave us free to starve those whom we will."[27] Like most left feminists, she opposed the equal rights amendment on the grounds that it would benefit professional women at the expense of more modestly employed women, because it would invalidate a significant body of state labor legislation that applied only to women.[28] But empowering women of all classes was an underlying theme throughout her career.

Mary Dublin Keyserling remained a feminist for the rest of her life, but how long did she remain a socialist? We do not know. In 1932 she told her parents she planned to resume socialist activism on her return from London: "Nate Weyl has just sent me an amazingly interesting letter on the socialist situation at home and I long to get in the thick of those things again." Describing Chicago to her mother in 1933, she wrote, "Nowhere have I so deeply felt the buccaneer, plundering, brutal and stupid face of capitalism." Later letters from Mary to her parents have not survived, nor have her letters to close friends or her sister Elisabeth.[29] An incomplete set of Dublin Keyserling's teaching notes and public addresses and articles for the 1934–48 period indicates her sustained commitment to a democratic regulatory and redistributive state but does not generate a precise ideological classification. Was she a Communist sympathizer, an anticommunist socialist, or a liberal—or some or all of these in succession? It may be a futile question, and not only because of a lack of evidence. The preoccupation with political labels seems unproductive because people's ideas evolve with world events and their own life experiences, because people's ideas do not always add up to a coherent ideology, and because in the Depression decade the political spectrum was especially fluid. During a loyalty hearing in 1948, one prominent defense attorney warned the board against "falling into the error of 'the tyranny of labels,'" by which he meant the futility of categorizing individuals according to whether they were "left, right, or center of the Communist Party lines" on various issues.[30] As left economist Paul Sweezy recalled decades later, the New Deal produced many "radicals who didn't proclaim any strong theoretical positions," many of whom worked happily enough with "the capitalism savers." It was the Red scare that forced people to adopt tidy labels, he suggested: "[there were] a lot of inconsistencies in that whole period. They were all straightened out later on, by the other side."[31] One result of that "straightening out" was the loss of historical sources, as leftists and former leftists destroyed records and avoided discussing their intellectual histories. That loss led to others by obliterating much nuance and context from discussions of left history.

Leon, too, had a political orientation in the 1930s that was different from what he claimed to investigators in the 1950s and for the rest of his life. Unlike Mary, he did not join organizations later labeled "Communist fronts," and he left fewer public traces of his youthful radicalism than she did. Mary was a nongovernmental activist throughout the 1930s, whereas Leon was in government from 1933 onward and probably felt less free to take public stands. However, recently discovered letters from Leon to his father reveal that Leon was a socialist in the 1930s, even as he drafted key legislation of the New Deal.

In 1951, Leon Keyserling tried unsuccessfully to convince the Senate Internal Security Subcommittee that he "might even have been a Republican" when he came to Washington in 1933, and that thereafter he was "halfway between the liberal New Deal and conservatives."[32] Senator Ferguson and his staff found this preposterous given Leon's public record as legislative aide to Senator Wagner, general counsel of the U.S. Housing Authority, and member and chair of the CEA. They also were suspicious because the list of writings he submitted to them omitted a 1934 anthology he had coedited with Rexford Tugwell. Leon's contribution to that volume was hardly a call to revolution, but it urged breaking away from the individualistic values of "the business man's civilization."[33] Investigators may have been correct in suspecting that Leon's refusal to swear he had not met Crouch indicated that they had met, even if Crouch distorted aspects of the incident in the retelling. But Mandel and the rest were unable to prove that Leon had ever been to the left of Franklin Delano Roosevelt.

Fortunately for Leon, when FBI agents were covertly taking pictures inside his father's residence they did not find Leon's letters home. Leon was the eldest and most successful of four children, and he and his father corresponded regularly from the late 1920s until William died in 1951. Especially after Leon's mother died in 1935, following protracted struggles with cancer and depression, Leon was William's chief confidant on topics from public affairs to intrafamily relations. In turn Leon proudly described his latest achievements, ambitions, and ideas. Their correspondence, hitherto unknown to scholars, was recently donated to a South Carolina archive that holds the papers of the extended family. The correspondence provides a window on Leon's views from his first exposure to Karl Marx at Columbia, through his progress into the inner circles of the Roosevelt and Truman administrations, to a final phase when, unbeknownst to William, the pressure on Leon of being under investigation was mounting and he wrote as if the FBI might be reading over his shoulder.

A child prodigy with a photographic memory, Leon amazed his teachers and mentors with his analytical and writing talents. He was keenly aware of his brilliance, and throughout his life his abrasiveness and vanity alienated many people. He believed Rexford Tugwell envied his superior intellect, and he claimed to have written many speeches and publications for which Tugwell and his next boss, Senator Wagner, received credit. Leon's critical faculties prevented him from embracing any doctrine without argument. From Columbia in 1926, he explained Marx's *Das Kapital* and proceeded to critique it. "In general theory, Marx is fairly correct," he told his father, adding that capital's contradictory impulses to extend and limit markets helped explain "what is wrong in the Industrial (Mfg) world today." But, Leon argued, Marx neglected the productive role of the capitalist as a manager and was wrong that labor created all wealth. Always career-minded, as a student at Harvard Law School in 1929 Leon told his father that his political party affiliation would depend on what line of law he went into, but that he was learning toward labor law, in which case he could follow his inclinations and join the Socialist Party. Still, he was skeptical of all "panaceas": "Economically, socialism is probably sound; but we must know a great deal more about psychology before being able to say whether the incentives to progress would be as great . . . under a collectivistic organization." Leon then articulated an idea that he did not formulate himself but that he would embed in New Deal labor policy. Under capitalism, he explained, the substance and the implementation of the law favored the ruling classes, and that needed to change. "As a matter of fact, the rich and the poor *should not* be 'equal' before the law. The law should help the weaker party." [34]

As the Great Depression deepened, Leon's commitment to socialism solidified. He reassured his father that his "socialistic views" had protected him from the stock market crash because "socialists know that the Stock Market is the place where the big fish swallow the small." During the 1932 election campaign Leon casually suggested he might vote for the Communist William Z. Foster, but then he voted for the Socialist, Norman Thomas: "I predict that he will poll close to 2 [million] votes, which will mark in the future the definite turn toward socialism in this country." [35] Even as Leon worked night and day to draft the labor provisions of the National Industrial Recovery Act, he told his father that it would be but a limited step. His explanation is worth quoting at length:

The setting up of schemes of control merely transfers the social struggle to another field. . . . Under a capitalistic society, the same people who profited by the anarchy are likely to work most of the controls, and in the same stupidly selfish and self-destructive manner. Without revolution which transfers power to the workers and sets up a socialized state, little will be gained. But the establishment of controls and the centralization of authority make the revolution more likely, because the excesses of the capitalists will become so great and their abuses so violent that the reaction will be terrific. . . . the next quarter century, if it does not culminate in a war which will destroy most of civilization (which seems most likely), will witness changes everywhere more complete than those which began in 1790.

Leon was correct in anticipating the limits of industry self-regulation under the NRA codes—a problem that later economists would label "regulatory capture," in which agencies created to serve the public interest were dominated or "captured" by the industry they were supposed to regulate. His prediction that regulatory measures would hasten revolution proved less accurate. In any case, Leon was making intellectual observations, not rushing to the barricades himself. "I find the work I am doing intensely interesting, and if our present society lasts, it is work most likely to bring opportunities for the sort of notoriety and success that present society values."[36]

Leon's expressed hopes for revolution were the strongest in 1934, a year that violent strikes swept the nation. Chafing at the bitter opposition to the labor disputes bill that he had drafted and that Senator Wagner was trying to get out of committee, Leon wrote his father: "I am very much afraid that the country is recovering too rapidly. A few more years of depression would have promoted violence, and without violence fundamental reform is unlikely." He concluded, with callous sarcasm, "However, I see considerable hope in the certainty of even more serious depressions in the near future."[37] When Leon's father asked why he was not more interested in farmers' problems, Leon responded impatiently that "there is no chance for lasting gains to either farmer or laborer save by revolution, and the only materials for revolt are the industrial workers. The farmers in this country show not the slightest sign of class consciousness or the collective spirit. They are all individualists. Even in Russia (which was predominantly agrarian while we are predominantly industrial) the revolution was engineered by the proletariat, and after two decades has not won over the farmers."[38]

Was this the bravado of a rising star in his midtwenties, trying to startle his provincial father? Did Leon use his father as a sounding board for things he could not say at the office? William was progressive himself and relished debating politics with his son. It seems likely that if Leon had expressed such views widely during the 1930s, more informants would have said so later. Leon's revolutionary words were not matched in his daily actions. Leon told his father that revolution was necessary for justice at home and peace abroad. He claimed to believe that revolution would come only if industrial workers became "sufficiently angry." Meanwhile, however, Leon burned the candle at both ends to draft legislation that could not certainly be predicted to make workers more angry rather than less.

However serious he was about the likelihood of revolution, Leon never wanted to be part of it. Investigators never discovered it, but Leon briefly lived with Nathaniel Weyl in 1933 or early 1934. Weyl invited Leon to join his clandestine Communist group in Washington, but Leon was not interested. Weyl speculated that he must have perceived Leon as "closer to the CP than Mary," because he invited Leon to join but "never considered approaching Mary" even though he knew her very well.[39] Whatever the extent of Leon's sympathy with the Communist Party in the early 1930s, he was too dedicated to fulfilling his career ambitions and his father's dreams, and to alleviating the financial difficulties of his siblings, to risk entering the fray himself.[40]

Over the next few years Leon came to identify more closely with the New Deal, even as he grumbled about its limitations. He fumed over the administration's "swing to the Right" that forced the lawyer Jerome Frank and his group out of the Agricultural Adjustment Administration after Frank angered the "big Chicago packers."[41] In 1936, Leon probably voted for Roosevelt, although we do not know for certain. To his lover Catherine Bauer, who was in Scandinavia studying housing policy, Leon wrote cynical descriptions of the American presidential campaign. The man who had just drafted the National Labor Relations Act complained that the Democrats had not gone further: "The amazing thing is that, with the Democrats having done so little that is real, the class divisions with respect to the election are becoming so pronounced." A few days later he added, "That's the whole trouble over here: Landon and the Republicans are such jackasses that they make the Donkey look like a cantering roan, and everyone wants to get in the saddle."[42] But Leon had helped draft the Democratic platform, and he told his father that he did "not see how anyone with progressive or humanitarian views could fail to favor Roosevelt over the Republicans and what they stand for— namely the greed of entrenched wealth."[43]

Leon still spoke the language of class conflict during Roosevelt's second term, but his heroes were progressives such as Senators Wagner and La Follette in alliance with the CIO, not revolutionaries. Leon supported FDR's controversial court-packing plan of early 1937, which failed but had the desired effect on the Supreme Court. When the Court sustained the Wagner Act in 1937, Leon rejoiced on the grounds that "a powerful labor movement is the only thing that can save us from Fascism" (at that moment, fascists had taken power, or were trying to, in Italy, Germany, and Spain, destroying independent labor unions and trying to eliminate targeted ethnic minorities). Leon Keyserling and his father agreed that Jews had a special obligation to fight racial discrimination everywhere. Both were horrified by the Ku Klux Klan and lynching. Leon drafted Wagner's speeches for an antilynching bill and chafed that southern Democrats like South Carolina senator Ed Smith "and his mental peers" blocked it.[44] Leon continued to argue that "monopoly capital" was farmers' and workers' "common enemy," and he regretted that the farmers could not see it.[45] Leon favored Roosevelt's effort to "purge" conservative Democrats in 1938, disagreeing with his father's view that Roosevelt was becoming dictatorial. By that time Leon believed Roosevelt was "a leader about whom could be rallied in time the sinews of democracy."[46] It is conceivable that in 1937 Leon actually did say something along the lines that Paul Crouch claimed: that revolution was unnecessary because "the more you give people the more they are going to demand and . . . through this chain reaction the power of capitalism is going to be weakened to the point of extinction."[47] By 1937, Leon's letters to his father were no longer predicting a revolution.

Leon's intellectual insights did not mesh neatly with his personal ambitions. He cheered on the CIO against the American Federation of Labor, but in the next breath, thinking ahead about his career options, he exulted that his new work with the Senate Banking and Currency Committee would offer "more lucrative avenues for departure from the Capitol than did the labor work."[48] Leon occasionally acknowledged the irony of his position. Noting that his elevation to general counsel of the U.S. Housing Authority made him the youngest general counsel in Washington, he mused that, like a businessman's, his success did not "arise from greater personal productivity, but from achieving a strategic position where one can draw a percentage of the credit for the work of a large army of people in subordinate positions."[49] Over the ensuing years Leon's letters became less reflective and more focused on his siblings' difficulties and his father's business. In 1945 Leon reported that he had met with the new president and was optimistic that Truman would continue the New Deal. Soon he was insisting that the postwar strike wave was justified.[50] On the whole, however, politics moved to the margins of Leon's letters to his father in the 1938–48 period. Those letters seem to have been written not by a hotheaded radical but by an extremely busy person who believed in left-liberal causes but chiefly focused on his own career advancement and family problems.

Around 1949, Leon's letters home began sounding a new note that almost certainly reflected growing nervousness about his vulnerability to

Red-baiting. He never told his father about the first major round of loyalty investigations in 1948. After his clearance and Truman's unexpected
win in November, he perceived his career opportunities to be unlimited
("It would be perfectly senseless for me to leave just when the great liberal victory and my part in it open the way to doing much more than ever
before").[51] But Leon's euphoria did not last long. When his father asked
for portraits to send to surviving relatives in Russia, Leon replied sharply
that it was out of the question for William to send his photo "overseas."
Corresponding with relatives "behind the Iron Curtain" was by then
risky for any government employee, and as a high-ranking official Leon
would not have wanted his portrait found on display in a Soviet home.[52]
In 1950, Leon denied that he had meant to discourage his father from
sharing his views in letters: "my only possible reservation would be that
you not say anything indiscreet in some of your rather idealistic flights of
fancy about the good intentions of the whole world." He went on to criticize the Soviet Union much more strongly than he ever had before in their
correspondence: "I have been telling you for a number of years that the
Soviet dictatorship is the greatest threat to the peace and security of the
world."[53] Apparently Leon feared that investigators would read his mail
and associate him with his father's view that the United States and Britain were exaggerating the Soviet threat.[54] Leon further distanced himself
from his father's views by assuring his father he respected his opinions
even though he did not agree with them. Indeed, it was his respect for
dissent, Leon explained, that convinced him that "Soviet Communism,
as practiced, is such a tyranny and there is no hope for man in it."[55] The
following year, having gotten the hint, William cited those words back to
Leon and added, in a reference to the Spanish Inquisition, "Torquemada
should be satisfied with that."[56]

Although it appears that Leon was playing up his anti-Soviet views in
case his mail was read (or to create a paper trail that he could use later),
my point is not that Leon secretly worshipped the Soviet Union. None
of the Keyserlings were blind Russophiles. During the Hitler-Stalin pact,
William castigated Roosevelt for not doing more to aid Britain.[57] In late
1945 and early 1946, William and Leon seem to have been in general
agreement that the United States was being unnecessarily antagonistic
toward the Soviets. As William put it, he was not for appeasement, but he
did not favor provocation or bullying either.[58] By 1947, Leon and his father had begun to disagree. Leon told his father it was "nonsense" to say
the Soviets "are justifiably afraid of us": "The Russians believe too much
in pressure and force. . . . It is they who wrap themselves in the secrecy
and censorship which breed suspicion elsewhere."[59] Leon's view of the
Soviets was becoming more negative before he personally felt the heat of
investigation. It is noteworthy, however, that he first articulated harshly

anti-Soviet views in 1950, when his brother-in-law George Marshall was in jail, McCarthy was ascendant, and pressure was mounting on Truman to ratchet up the loyalty program.

In short, Leon was a socialist for much of the 1930s and then a left-liberal. The transformation from socialist to New Dealer was not an uncommon one during the Depression decade, but Leon refused to explain his past that way. When he was summoned before SISS in 1951, one senator asked whether Leon "had any contrary views when you were in college or during that period of the 1930s when we were having so much trouble and when so many men now say that they became infected with some of these ideas from Communism because of the terrible conditions we were in and didn't see any hope in the free enterprise system." Leon admitted nothing: "I had quite the same ideas then [as now], but I can't document it in writing because as a minor employee at that time I didn't make speeches or write articles." Leon seems to have underestimated SISS and its staff, who correctly disbelieved him on both points (his views, and his inability to document them).[60] Under the pressure of loyalty investigations, Leon Keyserling denied he had ever been to the left of the New Deal, much less a socialist, thereby convincing investigators that he was hiding something—and confusing future scholars to boot.

SUFFERING IN SILENCE

The Keyserlings, like many loyalty defendants, kept their investigations as secret as possible, not only during those investigations but for decades thereafter. They almost succeeded in taking their secret to their graves. Leon had died and Mary was suffering from Alzheimer's disease by the time I stumbled on complaints about Mary's 1930s radicalism in the papers of a Massachusetts reformer.[61]

Surviving relatives did not know how extensive Leon's and Mary's loyalty investigations had been. Anyone who had read the newspapers in 1952 knew that McCarthy attacked Mary and Leon and that the Commerce Department suspended her briefly, but those headlines faded away quickly, and McCarthy's attacks had been so indiscriminate that few people not on the hard-core anticommunist right remembered the specifics. Leon's sister-in-law was unaware that he had experienced anything beyond what most Democrats did in the early 1950s.[62] Dublin Keyserling's nephew Thomas Dublin and his wife Kathryn Kish Sklar, professional historians who had taken some interest in Mary's career, were under the impression, nurtured by Mary, that she was always a centrist Democrat, and they believed the same of Leon.[63] Mary's brother Thomas D. Dublin knew there had been some difficulty at the Commerce Department, but Mary had declined to discuss it. He recalled Mary telling him something like, "I don't like to talk about it, and I don't like other people to talk about it." He was amazed to learn that she had faced numerous hearings, some featuring appearances by his other sister Elisabeth and her husband George Marshall. An epidemiologist with the U.S. Public Health Service, Thomas D. Dublin himself had been confronted with an interrogatory asking him to explain his membership in the Washington Bookshop cooperative and a 1936 visit to Russia. Later, for reasons probably related to Mary's case, he was excluded from a scientific delegation to Russia.[64] Mary's sister Elisabeth urged their brother Thomas to destroy any letters from her or Mary that he might find in their father's papers. George Marshall declined a request to discuss his sister-in-law's case.[65]

Mary's parents seem to have been unaware of the investigations until the newspapers reported them. "We have been concerned but not worried knowing how absurd the whole situation was I hope," Augusta wrote nervously to Mary after McCarthy's first public attack in February 1952. "We do want to know whether it is all cleared up by now."[66] After the next ripple of publicity in October revealed the gravity of Mary's situation, Augusta tried to bolster her daughter: "There is little doubt in my mind that some of this, at least, stems from the jealousy of people who resent your rapid advancement and success in your job." Augusta railed against unprincipled politicians who were "crucifying" the nation's brightest servants in order to seize power. "Do stay calm in the assurance that you are among the most devoted and loyal citizens in the country," Mary's mother wrote. She added cryptically, "We shall both heed what Leon urged." Leon probably had warned the senior Dublins to be careful what they put in writing. Obligingly, Louis was discreet a few weeks later when he wrote Mary from Geneva: "I hope you will have good news for me soon." He reminded his daughter that it was Geneva where she had first developed her "deep interest in social problems," and he wished that Washington D.C. had "such a spirit as Geneva." That was Louis's only written reference to Dublin Keyserling's investigation.[67]

The trauma of being under a potentially career-ending investigation was compounded in Leon's case by the fact that his father died in the midst of it, quite possibly as a result of stress over his own inadvertent part in the case against his son. In July 1951, Leon first wrote to his father that he was under investigation. His father soon reported that he had canceled his subscription to "the paper we discussed" (even as he regretted that "we cannot breathe the free air for fear that somebody who entertains different political views might have contaminated it"). The subscription that William canceled at Leon's request was the *Daily Compass*, a successor to the leftist periodical *PM*.[68] In September, William wrote Leon to describe a strange and worrisome incident. Out of the blue, Gilbert Parks had arrived "like an apparition" on William's doorstep to tell him that two FBI agents had just taken him by surprise and questioned him about Leon. Parks told William the gist of Crouch's story about Leon. Although William had no memory of Crouch, he wrote Leon, he feared that he himself might have spent an afternoon with Crouch and Parks and expressed sentiments that Crouch years later would seize on and attribute to Leon by "association or environment." Throughout the 1930s, Leon had repeatedly warned his father not to boast about or otherwise discuss Leon's work, a temptation William had not always been able to resist. It may have been William who discussed politics with Paul Crouch in 1937, perhaps even touching on Leon's views. William must have felt terrible about the possibility he had jeopardized his son's stellar career, and he tried to assure Leon the whole thing would blow over. William was worried, however. He correctly perceived Senator McCarran's Senate Internal Security Subcommittee to be more dangerous than HUAC: "judging by McCarran's inhumanity to the Indians, by his deal with Franco, by his position on Immigration, I believe him capable of selling the bodies of his next of kin for the price of their shrouds."[69] A few weeks later, William headed north intending to visit his son after making a speech in New York. In his appointment book, he wrote, "discuss with Leon . . . Parks affair. FBI. *Daily Compass*."[70] But William and Leon never had that discussion. William died of heart failure at the podium in New York, four days before he was scheduled to arrive at his son's house in Washington.[71]

The Keyserlings' silence is not surprising, given how stigmatizing and exhausting their investigations were. In offering to obtain affidavits from college acquaintances to refute Paul Crouch's story, Dublin Keyserling commented, "I trust the Committee [SISS] will appreciate why I have not thus far sought such testimonials. I have suffered intensely because of the hearing. I have been put to acute embarrassment to have had my passport photographs and civil service papers requisitioned. To go to my friends and former faculty and to tell this story would be very humiliating. But if there is doubt in the mind of the Committee, I shall assume this burden."[72] Even in her own appointment diaries, Mary did not name her investigation: she marked dates for her hearings simply "xxx."[73] When SISS asked Leon to explain why he had waited three months to tell the press he had found new evidence of Crouch's perjury, Leon answered that "a man who has gone through what I have, and who has had this thing over his head for all this time, was perfectly glad to see the matter quiescent."[74]

Many loyalty defendants devoted enormous amounts of time and energy to clearing their reputations. When Dublin Keyserling first received a letter of charges, she went to the Library of Congress to research the named groups and events in old newspapers. She and Leon were frantically energetic in their own defense, generating chronologies, background memos on hostile witnesses, and suggested lines of questioning for their lawyers. In December 1952, while the Keyserlings were waiting for the ruling of the Commerce Department appeals board (and after the Republican victory had lightened Leon's workload), Leon sent SISS a supplemental statement that brimmed with resentment. After poring over the transcripts of his various appearances before SISS, he also filed seven pages of corrections for the record. He was still steaming a year later, when he sent Abe Fortas fresh evidence of Crouch's dishonest statements about him.[75] For people as ambitious as the Keyserlings, the bitterness ran deep. They believed they had made sacrifices—in their family lives and in their pay levels—by choosing careers in public service, and now instead of appreciation they faced insults and suspicion.

Another emotion with which many loyalty defendants grappled was shame, not necessarily for what one had done to be investigated but for compromises one had made in trying to save oneself. Mary and Leon would not have been proud of their lack of candor in closed hearings. Distancing herself from George Marshall, whom she, her parents, and her siblings all adored (more than some of them liked the egotistical Leon), probably was painful for Mary. For Leon, pretending to disapprove of Truman's civil rights policy would have been especially embarrassing. Marshall and other people they admired took defiant stands against political repression when they were attacked. As high-ranking government officials, the Keyserlings were in a different position, but they must have hoped that their hearing transcripts would never see the light of day.

Scarred survivors of loyalty investigations may have reached out to support others who faced similar troubles, but they often did so very tentatively and without putting much in writing. When Leon's old friend Catherine Bauer asked for advice about an upcoming hearing, Leon wrote obliquely: "with respect to the matter of August 26th, the whole thing is appalling, and it is even more appalling that we have arrived at a point where people feel unable to make useful suggestions. . . . How can one be rational about the irrational?" Leon scoured Bauer's early writings for quotations showing she was not subversive, and he helped her secure the services of Abe Fortas, but he remained behind the scenes. Mary added, "What is so frustrating at this end is that there is so little we can do to help." Mary empathized with Bauer, especially because they both had caused trouble for their husbands' careers. William Wurster's architecture firm lost its federal contracts because of Bauer's associations. Mary wrote to Bauer that she understood "the unbelievably nightmarish experience" of finding something "that you haven't done" has been "distorted to injure others." None of the written correspondence referred directly to any loyalty investigation, so only readers with independent knowledge would understand the references.[76]

Loyalty investigations taxed personal relationships. The Keyserlings' marriage was under strain in the early 1950s, for example. They fought bitterly, and Mary considered leaving Leon. She suffered from stomach problems. He became very overweight. The loyalty investigations were at least a contributing factor to these marital and health difficulties.[77] The investigations strained other family relationships as well. Mary's mother often pressed Mary and Leon to join family gatherings with Elisabeth and George Marshall and was disappointed when they did not attend. After she understood the risks for Mary and Leon of association with the Marshalls, Augusta served as a go-between. Elisabeth "hesitates to call you," Augusta explained to Mary during George's 1950 stint in jail, before passing on Elisabeth's news. Leon sent a book he had borrowed from George to Augusta, asking her to return it for him.[78] Leon's sisters believed he and Mary were aloof and self-centered, which they may have been, but their desire to keep the investigations secret would have exacerbated those traits. Leon did not record his feelings about his father's death, but he must have been pained and angered when he found, in his own FBI file, photographs of the inside of his father's house that were taken by undercover agents just months before his father's death.[79] The Keyserlings' case illustrates how civil servants under investigation were forced to struggle with multiple, sometimes conflicting definitions of "loyalty" and frequently ended up isolated from the networks that once had sustained them.

Rightward Shift

Scholars hitherto have been unaware of Leon Keyserling's loyalty case, while the few to note that McCarthy accused Mary Dublin Keyserling interpret her appointment as head of the U.S. Women's Bureau in 1964 as a triumph over the injustices of the Second Red Scare.[80] That moral is too simple. Their "triumph" came at great cost to the causes they once had espoused, because under the pressure of investigation the Keyserlings adopted anticommunist rhetoric and edged away from causes associated with the left.

The repressive impact of loyalty procedures was felt well before the program was formalized in 1947. The Keyserlings were aware that they were under scrutiny by 1942, when both were interviewed by the FBI. Mary's appointment books indicate that they thereafter reduced their contact with the Marshalls and that Mary became more selective about the organizations with which she associated. At this point, however, the Keyserlings' experience with allegations of subversion had been no more intense than that faced by dozens of their friends and coworkers. In 1947 and early 1948, Leon felt secure enough to play point man in orchestrating Truman's appeal to the working class during the 1948 election campaign. Meanwhile Mary promoted the Marshall Plan, increased imports, and price control, as well as a broad range of "unfinished business in social legislation." Although their detractors continued to make allegations about the Keyserlings' suspect associations, there was little new development on their cases until the FBI opened full field investigations in March 1948.

That round of investigation, which ended relatively quickly with clearances for both of them by the end of 1948, nudged the Keyserlings to begin moving toward the political center. Mary reduced her extracurricular activism and stayed behind the scenes at the Commerce Department. Leon, his ambitions undiminished, continued to battle CEA chair Edwin Nourse until Nourse resigned in late 1949, complaining about the inflationary bias of Keyserling's expansionism. Leon's emphasis on economic growth irked fiscal conservatives, but it also laid the ground for a shift away from the left's call for redistribution. Leon recognized that significance. When he submitted quotations to SISS in 1951 to prove he was not an "extremist," he selected passages he had written in 1949 and 1950 that called for increasing production "instead of redistributing what we have" and for government cooperation with big business rather than hostility toward it.[81]

In 1949 Keyserling's pro-growth orientation began to include support for increasing the military budget. The following year, he was an important force behind the Truman administration's approval of the National Security Council Report 68 (NSC-68). In calling for a massive increase in the defense budget, NSC-68 signaled victory for advocates of a primarily military response to the Soviet Union. At several critical junctures in 1950, Keyserling won over skeptics, including the president himself, by asserting that the American economy could afford the military spending that NSC-68 proposed.[82] Keyserling's newly vocal support for increased military spending probably reflected his desire to bolster his anticommunist credentials in the wake of the investigations. If indeed the loyalty investigation put pressure on Leon to throw his influence behind the faction within the administration that favored heavy military spending to fight communism, then that investigation had a powerful impact on U.S. foreign policy, as well as on the domestic policy for which Leon is better known.

Truman's 1950 appointment of Leon as chairman of the Council on Economic Advisers brought a fresh wave of hostile attention from conservatives in Congress and the media at the very moment that Leon's brother-in-law George Marshall headed to jail for contempt of HUAC.[83] Several civil servants associated with one Keyserling or the other recently had been or were about to be dismissed, including William Remington,

Thomas Blaisdell, Lewis Lorwin, and Gertrude and Gilbert Parks. That was the context for Leon's adopting the language of a zealous Cold Warrior in a February 1951 article titled "We Can Have Butter and Guns." He called for strengthening "free peoples" against "aggression," and for focusing less on economic controls and more on economic expansion.[84] After Mary's loyalty case was reopened in October 1951, she too began calling for the "free world" to mobilize against "Communist aggression." By contrast, when she was promoting the Marshall Plan back in the spring of 1948, she did not mention communism.[85] Leon, in a November 1951 letter to President Truman, took pains to create a permanent record portraying himself as a passionate anticommunist. The economy could afford further defense spending even if Congress refused to raise taxes, he told the president: "Inflation is a bad thing and should not be underestimated. But it would seem to me highly dangerous to be concerned so exclusively with inflationary dangers as to underestimate Communist dangers. The Communist danger is the central, overwhelming danger which our economy faces. If that danger is not met, our economy and way of life may be destroyed." Leon dramatically annotated this letter "top secret," but it is in his papers at the Truman Library, and scholars have cited it as evidence of his intense anticommunism.[86] The letter reads differently when juxtaposed with the newly accessible SISS hearing transcripts, which show Leon trying to convince SISS that he was "to the right of the New Deal." It is difficult to avoid the conclusion that the Keyserlings adopted fervent anticommunist rhetoric in 1950 and 1951 in an effort to deflect questions about their loyalty. Leon took his new argument that Stalin was more dangerous than inflation into public forums such as the *Washington Post*.[87] The stratagem did not stop McCarthy and others from calling the Keyserlings Communist sympathizers, and it probably contributed to the press's perception that Leon was trying to be "all things to all men" and "telling Truman what he wanted to hear."[88] By the end of the Truman administration the CEA was reportedly under fire because of Leon's leadership, and Republicans in Congress were threatening to disband it. Scholars have assumed Republican hostility to the CEA stemmed from Leon's partisan style, but that hostility was likely reinforced by congressional awareness of Leon's loyalty investigation.[89]

After the investigations forced them out of government, Mary and Leon started a private consulting project, the Conference on Economic Progress (CEP), and kept a low profile. Funded chiefly by organized labor, the CEP was a nonprofit organization that published studies of national economic issues such as full employment, public housing, minimum wages, and fiscal policy. Mary conducted the research and supervised the small staff, while Leon took primary responsibility for the writing. CEP publications reflected the Keyserlings' long-standing commitment to increasing the purchasing power and raising the living standards of the nation's poor and working-class citizens. Gone, however, was the critique of inequality that had underpinned their earlier advocacy. Growth, not redistribution, was the answer, and Communism, not social injustice, was the enemy. Back in 1946, Leon had promoted a comprehensive housing bill by arguing that private enterprise was incapable of solving the housing shortage without government intervention to stop overbuilding for the luxury market and to stimulate construction of affordable housing. Back then, his question was, "shall we equitably distribute this abundance [generated by wartime technological advances] among all the people?" Also in 1946 Leon had made the case for social programs aiding not just veterans but all middle- and low-income Americans, including racial minorities.[90] To his father, Leon had raged against "entrenched wealth" and called congressional conservatives "menial servitors of privilege and pillage."[91] In the 1950s, however, Leon called for government-business cooperation, made respectful references to "free enterprise," and said those who called for redistribution were pessimists resigned to the economics of scarcity. In 1957 Mary wrote to Catherine Bauer to describe European labor's ambivalent reaction to one of Leon's speeches: "Our concepts of our capacity to work within the status quo for economic expansion in the benefits of which all can share is still a very strange one to those steeped in the Social Democratic tradition of Europe, and who still scrap over the share of a pie they continue to regard as fixed in size. . . . Leon's confidence in growth worries them."[92]

Over the course of the 1950s, both Keyserlings reemerged as Democratic loyalists who called for strengthening the nation against the Communist threat. Leon influenced the AFL-CIO and the Americans for Democratic Action (ADA) as well as the Democratic Party. It was Leon who persuaded George Meany and Walter Reuther to adopt the "guns as butter" strategy of pursuing full employment through major defense spending rather than fighting for broad social welfare programs, which Leon argued would invite charges of communism.[93] The Keyserlings had joined the ADA, the liberal anticommunist group, at about the same time as the first phase of their loyalty investigations in late 1948.[94] When a recession in early 1954 provided an opening for attacking the Eisenhower administration, the ADA published an essay collection that indicted Republican economic policy while disavowing the left's critique of capitalism. Leon's contribution argued that a full employment policy to increase consumption by middle- and low-income Americans would raise living standards, increase business profits, and make the free world more secure. For the rest of the decade, the ADA platform consisted of "undiluted Keyserling," supporting a range of liberal policies but stopping short of discussing guaranteed incomes or income redistribution.[95] By 1958, Leon was on the economic advisory subcommittee to the Democratic National Committee. In the run-up to the 1960 presidential election, he contributed to the Democrats' comeback—and also tried to engineer his own, it seems—by hitting the anticommunist note hard, attacking the Republicans' fiscal conservatism for jeopardizing U.S. competitiveness in the arms race. Americans needed massive military superiority over the Russians, not just equivalence, Keyserling argued in a series of editorials, and the bankers' fears of inflation were preventing the Eisenhower administration from spending what was necessary for military preparedness and for matching the Russians' economic growth rates.[96] This tack was not unique to Leon; he had the company of *Washington Post* columnist Joseph Alsop, who, not incidentally, had his own brush with loyalty charges in 1957. But it set Leon apart from other liberal Democrats, including John Kenneth Galbraith, who argued that some degree of unemployment was inevitable under capitalism, and who called for compensatory welfare programs. After about 1950, Leon was uncomfortable suggesting that capitalism had inherent weaknesses.[97]

Meanwhile, Mary was rising through the ranks of the Women's National Democratic Club, which she had joined in early 1949 after the first round of her loyalty investigation. By the late 1950s, outrage she earlier had directed at "the dominant class . . . that knows no responsibility save service of profit" now was directed at the Republican Party. "A vote for the Democratic Party is a vote for jobs," was her new motto; twenty years earlier, "independent political action by labor" had been an essential plank in her program. Dublin Keyserling elided the Socialist Party from her political biography, describing herself as a lifelong Democrat who as an undergraduate in 1928 had toured New York with a megaphone for Al Smith.[98] In 1960 she was the only woman member of the Democratic Platform Committee, and by 1963 she was president of the Women's National Democratic Club. Her appointment to the U.S. Women's Bureau in 1964 rewarded her effective campaign work as well as the support of Johnson adviser Abe Fortas. In that position Dublin Keyserling helped make the War on Poverty more responsive to women. She pressured the Office of Economic Opportunity to raise its quotas for female teenagers in the Jobs Corps, and she challenged the assumption, fostered by Assistant Secretary of Labor Daniel Patrick Moynihan, that discouraging black women's employment would increase their marriage rate and thereby stabilize black families. She also was a persistent advocate of minimum wages for domestic workers and of high-quality public day care programs. But she carefully avoided public criticism of Democratic administrations. Her refusal to allow a Women's Bureau meeting to serve as a venue for criticizing the Equal Employment Opportunity Commission, which was not cracking down on sexual discrimination, reportedly led to the formation in 1966 of the National Organization for Women.[99] Thus did an enthusiastic left feminist of the 1930s become a cautious, moderate feminist of the 1960s.

When disagreement over U.S. policy in Vietnam split the Democrats in 1968, both Keyserlings sided staunchly with Johnson and Hubert Humphrey. Leon was largely responsible for convincing the AFL-CIO to support the Vietnam War. After the ADA endorsed the antiwar candidate Eugene McCarthy, Leon noisily quit, taking the labor members out with him, and offered his services to Humphrey. A Humphrey win, which Leon believed would have occurred had Democrats united behind him earlier, would have put Leon back in the inner circle.[100]

It is conceivable that the Keyserlings' intellectual shift would have occurred even without the loyalty accusations—in response to their changing perceptions of communism, the Soviet Union, the American economy, or American political realities, for example—but the timing and all-consuming nature of the loyalty investigations makes it hard to discount their impact. The fact that we are left guessing is certainly attributable to the loyalty program, because it led the Keyserlings to obscure their intellectual evolution.

RESHAPING THE RECORD

Like other loyalty defendants, the Keyserlings tried to extend the silence about their loyalty investigations into the historical record. In organizing their papers for archives, they omitted reference to their investigations and also for the most part to the activities that triggered them. Leon's extensive papers, which he and Mary organized and she deposited at Georgetown University (with Robert Wagner's papers) and the Harry S. Truman Library, include none of the voluminous records of the loyalty investigation—no interrogatories, hearing transcripts, affidavits, or official clearances. A few letters about the case from Leon to Truman and his advisers can be found in those officials' collections, but not in Leon's. Leon's clippings files include only a few reports of McCarthy's charges against him and Mary, and those are from liberal papers that treated the story dismissively. Leon and Mary did not deposit any of his personal correspondence.[101]

Mary's papers, the organizing of which became "almost an obsession" for her in the 1980s, contain no clippings or other records of her investigation. In the papers that Mary gave to the Schlesinger Library, there is a six-year gap in her personal correspondence during the period of her investigation. She did not give the archives the appointment books that she used each year from the late 1920s into the 1980s. In her last years, Mary spent much of her time shredding papers, according to her housekeeper. Relatives attributed this compulsive behavior to her mental decline, but it may have been an echo of earlier, more deliberate behavior. Unaware that Mary might have withheld these materials deliberately and concerned that she would destroy them, they deposited the appointment books with the rest of her papers. When the letters from a young Mary to her parents were later found among her father's papers, those were sent to the Schlesinger Library as well.[102]

In interviews, too, the Keyserlings avoided the topic of loyalty accusations against them. For the rest of their lives they sustained the image they constructed in the 1950s of themselves as lifelong middle-of-the-roaders. In discussing their careers with historians for the Columbia Oral History Project, the Truman and Johnson presidential libraries, and the Schlesinger Library, neither mentioned the investigations, and both took every opportunity to emphasize their anticommunism. When asked about "some nastiness" over President Johnson's 1964 nomination of Dublin Keyserling to head the U.S. Women's Bureau, Leon replied dismissively that "Senator John Tower . . . referred to the fact that Senator McCarthy had dredged up the fact that Mrs. Keyserling had signed a statement for the protection of the foreign-born in the early 1930s, the other signers being Eleanor Roosevelt . . . that kind of thing. But it didn't amount to anything, and Tower was the only one of the ninety-six senators who opposed her."[103] That was an extreme understatement of what had happened.

In 1985 a biographer of Abe Fortas elicited the Keyserlings' most substantial discussion on record of Mary's loyalty investigation. In a joint interview with both Keyserlings, the historian Laura Kalman asked whether Dublin Keyserling had spoken to Fortas during the McCarthy era. Dublin Keyserling replied that "Abe was unbelievably generous to . . . a great many people who were attacked by McCarthy. McCarthy did attack me, and one of the major crimes was that . . . when I was executive director of the NCL, Mrs. Roosevelt had written me a letter and asked me to sign a statement. . . ." That was not a representative summary of the allegations. Mary continued, "of course I was totally exonerated in time, but it was a very painful thing. Abe was so kind, not only to me which I gather you know was a problem, but to others who were similarly just totally attacked." She added, "Literally everything that was down on the list from McCarthy could be answered, literally everything. And everything had to be totally dismissed." More convincing was her comment that it "was the most terrible experience of my life." Asked for more specifics about Fortas's role, Mary began to describe the Commerce Department hearings, but Leon broke in to change the subject. Later he came back to it, trying to make sure the last word stressed Mary's vindication: "May I say as a commentary upon this McCarthy thing, the McCarthy attacks were so damaging to even the people who were cleared that I don't know of any person except Mary after an attack by McCarthy who was appointed to a high position by an administration." That Leon himself had been investigated never came up in this or any other interview.[104]

After the Keyserlings died, it became possible to obtain their FBI and CSC files by Freedom of Information Act request, but that required someone to suspect the existence of such files. It is not surprising that the Keyserlings did not volunteer details on unflattering and painful incidents from their pasts. My point is not to tarnish their impressive careers or to moralize about their sometimes ignoble responses to unfair treatment. Rather, my point is that the Keyserlings' omissions produced distortions in scholarly interpretations of twentieth-century liberalism and of the modern women's movement. Working from biographical materials shaped by the Keyserlings, scholars have portrayed them (admiringly or otherwise) as lifelong moderates. Dublin Keyserling's biographer, unaware of the loyalty investigation, dismissed the "preposterous" allegations during her 1964 confirmation hearings as a partisan effort to paint President Johnson as an "ultra-liberal." Historians of feminist politics in the 1960s have sketched Dublin Keyserling as an incrementalist who resisted militant approaches to social change.[105] Those interpretations are not so much wrong as insufficient.

Meanwhile, scholarship on Leon assigns him a key role in the history of liberalism from the 1930s to the 1970s. Alonzo Hamby's influential work casts Leon as a pillar of "vital center" liberalism who articulated the Fair Deal critique of the New Deal and claimed that voluntarism and growth could mitigate group conflict.[106] Subsequent scholars have identified Leon as one of the key "purchasing-power progressives" of the New Deal; as one of the advisers who pushed Truman leftward in 1947 to secure his return to the White House in 1948; as a gung ho anticommunist who, through his influence on NSC-68, advocated military spending to achieve full employment and win the Cold War; and as a main contributor, through his influence on the AFL-CIO, to the split between organized labor and other liberals over the Vietnam War.[107] Nobody has covered the whole span of his life to explain the imperfect fit between some of those roles, although some have noticed that his ideas seemed "an odd mixture of liberalism and conservatism," and that he "assiduously avoided labels more specific than 'forward-looking' or 'the middle way.'" Truman scholars describe him as an insecure and bitter man who for the most part declined to cooperate with scholars.[108]

Leon Keyserling's insecurity and irascibility late in life were more than quirks of personality. They were the unhealed wounds from a long, mostly secret battle against charges that he and his wife once had been Communist sympathizers. Their years under scrutiny as disloyalty suspects may not have been the exclusive cause for the Keyserlings' rightward shift to the "vital center" in the 1950s, but it was a major factor. The transformation of these New Dealers into Cold War liberals was an adaptation to political repression, not a purely objective intellectual development; like other markets, the marketplace of ideas was not really a free one. Whatever weight one assigns the loyalty investigations in the Keyserlings' abandonment of the left, the investigations certainly caused them to attempt to erase their youthful socialism from the past. They were not unique; other high-ranking loyalty defendants similarly shifted to the center and then denied any such shift. Restoring the missing pieces is crucial, not just to explaining individual political histories, but also to recognizing that leftists were closer to power in New Deal–era Washington than anyone not on the far right has recognized.

Finally, the distortions and silences produced by accusations of communism obscured the Keyserlings' earlier commitments from the view of a younger generation of radicals, not just of historians. During the 1960s and 1970s, young activists fighting male supremacy, war, and inequality denounced centrist Democrats like the Keyserlings as the repressive liberal establishment, part of the problem rather than the solution. No wonder Leon seemed bitter.[109] The Keyserlings' disingenuity about their youthful politics and moderation of their political goals and style enabled them to salvage their careers after resigning from the Truman administration and to enjoy comebacks in the Johnson years. That victory over the right may have lost some of its sweetness, however, when it put them at odds with the New Left, which was capturing the imagination of a younger cohort of thinkers and activists.

CHAPTER 6

"A Soul-Searing Process": Trauma in the Civil Service

The experience of being under loyalty investigation produced a wide range of responses from individuals and had many long-lasting effects—on their economic security, mental and physical health, personal relationships, and civic participation. Many loyalty defendants preferred to remain silent about these humiliating experiences, but examining them is necessary to establish the context in which these people made difficult strategic and ethical decisions about how best to protect themselves.

Individual traumas eventually produced collective responses. During the latter half of the 1950s, critics of the loyalty program convinced many Americans that it needed a drastic overhaul. In the course of making their case, however, critics highlighted some of the program's injustices and obscured others. They showed how it was exploited as a tool of partisan politics and also how it persecuted low-level employees in nonsensitive positions. The exposés rarely featured high-ranking leftist defendants, presumably on the assumption that those were less sympathetic victims and also because those people were especially unwilling to discuss their cases. Prodded by organized minority groups, reformers rightly protested the loyalty program's discrimination against blacks, Jews, and gays. But its antifeminist bias went unexamined. The loyalty program encouraged obeisance to gender conventions on the part of accused individuals, discouraged female activism more generally, and linked female breadwinning with trauma and shame. In addition to damaging the careers of high-ranking government women, then, there were other, less direct ways in which the loyalty program acted as a hitherto unnoticed force in constructing the rigid gender roles associated with the 1950s. By 1959, a series of congressional committee reports and court decisions had led to the loyalty program's reform, but some of its most damaging effects remained hidden.

Few loyalty defendants were willing to talk about their cases, at the time or later. A handful of defendants who were cleared, typically low-level employees against whom the charges had been particularly specious, told journalists their stories. A few others protested rulings against them by appealing to the courts, sometimes all the way to the Supreme Court. And in late 1955, several dozen government employees contacted a Senate subcommittee headed by Olin Johnston (D-S.C.) to describe the injustices they believed the program had done them.[1] But the vast majority of defendants kept their tribulations as secret as possible.

There was good reason to do so. In 1954, the Ford Foundation's Fund for the Republic (FFR) invited more than one hundred lawyers to submit summaries of loyalty cases in which they had served as defense counsel. To protect defendants' privacy, FFR researchers interviewed counsel and reviewed transcripts without recording the employee's name. The FFR published summaries of fifty cases in 1955. The next year the newly formed Wright Commission on Government Security asked the FFR for the names of all the loyalty defendants it had identified.[2] The FFR contacted its cooperating attorneys and asked them to solicit the employees' permission to release their names to the Wright Commission. This request alarmed many of the lawyers, not least because one member of the Wright Commission, Representative Francis Walters (D-Pa.), also was chair of HUAC. One attorney expressed his concern "over the use that may be made by the Commission of the names that are revealed to it. . . . We would hate to have names released to the Commission staff and then have Mr. Walters subpoena the people to appear before the House Committee." Fewer than one-third of the 353 loyalty defendants whose cases the FFR had written up authorized release of their names. Their reluctance proved to have been justified, because in November 1956 HUAC indeed asked the FFR for the names. The FFR promptly destroyed any records that could be used to identify defendants who had denied permission for release of their names.[3]

Although loyalty defendants' silence was prudent, it posed a problem for scholars. In the early 1960s, the Princeton political scientist Paul Tillett launched a study of the "social costs" of the federal loyalty program, but he soon found that "people did not want to relive the experience." He received little response to the hundreds of queries he mailed to loyalty defendants whose names had appeared in newspapers. Finding government employees willing to talk became the "sticking point" in Tillett's research. After five years of work, he was forced to abandon the project, and his findings were never published.[4] Loyalty defendants' preference for anonymity, combined with the fact that government records were inaccessible, prevented other researchers from getting much further than Tillett did.

It seems that high-level employees were less willing than low-level ones to reveal they had faced questions about their loyalty. Among the cases submitted by defense counsel for the FFR study, only a few involved high-ranking civil servants, and fewer still consented to publication of anonymous descriptions of their cases. Summarizing cases that involved senior officials without providing clues to their identity was sometimes impossible, and career professionals feared further damage to their reputations. The law firm of Arnold, Fortas & Porter, which represented high-profile employees like the Keyserlings, did not participate in the FFR study. Thus the two published samples of large numbers of loyalty cases,—the printed hearings of the Johnston Committee and the Fund for the Republic book—understate the investigation of high-level employees.

Revealing that one had been investigated had other risks beyond the possibility of triggering further investigation. Jacob Fisher, a social security analyst at the Department of Health, Education, and Welfare, recalled that he and other loyalty defendants labored "to keep one's status a secret from neighbors, relations, fellow-employees" because they knew the stigma "lingered, long after the questions raised by the charges were resolved, favorably or unfavorably." After Fisher was suspended in 1954, he tried to hide the fact that he was not going to work by swearing the members of his car pool to secrecy. Among civil servants, "the agreed-on etiquette of the day . . . was . . . that it was indecent to talk about persons known or rumored to be Security Risks." Avoiding gossip was not just a matter of pride. Private employers were reluctant to hire someone who had resigned or been dismissed from government. Furthermore, the stigma spread easily to family members and friends. Fisher's coworkers began avoiding him. Even after he resigned and his family moved to a new town, they lived in fear that word of his resignation would leak out and jeopardize his wife's job as a social worker in the public schools.[5]

The secretiveness of loyalty defendants also prevented Fisher from knowing that some of his superiors, including Isidore Falk and Wilbur Cohen, faced loyalty charges themselves. That information might have softened Fisher's disappointment, which still rankled when he wrote his memoir thirty years later, that they did not make more effort to defend him. Senior officials were hardly uninterested in their employees' fate: when an obscure press published Fisher's memoir in 1986, Wilbur Cohen bought a copy and underlined his own name throughout the text. The program produced anxiety for supervisors as well as for defendants themselves.[6]

Cohen also went to the trouble of obtaining the 1982 oral history of his former colleague Bernice Lotwin Bernstein, a senior lawyer at the Department of Health, Education, and Welfare, but if he was looking for discussion of her own loyalty case he did not find it. Bernstein did her utmost to keep her case quiet. In 1954 she offered to resign rather than have the FBI proceed with a full field investigation that she believed stemmed from the fact that her husband's former coworkers at the

Treasury Department included some "rotten characters" named by Eliza-beth Bentley. An investigation would turn up nothing derogatory, she as-sured her agency's counsel, but it would inflict a "grievous hurt" on her three children. To have FBI agents questioning her neighbors would "give rise to talk of a most undesirable sort" in her Long Island suburb, where she knew from experience that schoolchildren and adults alike assumed that someone who was being investigated must have done something wrong. She also worried that rumors about her investigation would dam-age voluntary organizations in which she was prominent, such as the Na-tional Council of Jewish Women. Bernstein begged her supervisors to sus-pend the FBI investigation and review the materials she had submitted, at which point if they were not convinced of her loyalty she would resign. "I have built my entire professional career in the government service," she explained. "This matter is eating at my heart . . . my conscience and that of my husband are absolutely clear." Bernstein's supervisors rejected her proposal out of hand, pointing out that they could hardly diverge from standard procedures just for her.[7] The FBI investigated, and she was suspended. In gathering affidavits to present at her hearing, Bernstein pleaded with her supporters to keep her request strictly confidential.[8] She described the subsequent hearing as "an exhausting and soul-searing process. . . . I don't think anything in my whole life has hit me as hard as has this proceeding." Only after many months and much strategizing was she finally cleared.[9]

Esther Peterson and her husband disagreed over whether to publicize the 1952 charges against him. "I didn't want to keep quiet or lie about what was going on; I didn't want to accept any feeling of shame. I wanted to go public and fight it out in the open right then, but Oliver wanted to keep it quiet. Oliver felt that people wouldn't believe him. 'Esther,' people will say, 'Where there's smoke, there's fire.'" Even years later Peterson disliked discussing the experience, but in 1989 she admitted: "We went through hell. It was one of the things that killed Oliver. He could not stand it. . . . He wouldn't let me talk about it, I couldn't tell the children about it because 'they'll say there's something about Dad.' . . . And how can you explain."[10]

Caroline Ware told only her husband, her employer, and her two best friends that she had been required to answer an interrogatory. She kept the story quiet to protect not only herself but also the reputations of her associates. She did not want to "contribute to the sense of insecurity of the people associated with me, especially my new executive secretary of the Washington Urban League." She also dreaded having to ask for affidavits from "people who may find themselves in difficulties because they stood up for me." She explained, "one of the suspicious characters that I am accused of associating with is on the list, I am sure, solely because he stood up for somebody else." When Ware was cleared in 1955 after a yearlong delay, she rejoiced that it was done without "a hearing and the attendant publicity."[11] Defending someone accused of disloyalty was indeed a good way of getting oneself on the suspect list. After the American Association of University Women (AAUW) executive Kathryn McHale defended Dorothy Kenyon and Esther Brunauer from Senator McCarthy's allegations, her own appointment to the Subversive Activities Control Board was delayed by loyalty questions, and the AAUW was labeled "pink."[12] So another reason for loyalty defendants to keep friends and associates in the dark was to prevent them from trying to help.

People who had been accused also worried that they would do more harm than good if they tried to defend others. By making it dangerous to vouch for one's associates, loyalty investigations damaged not just individuals but also ties among individuals. The fraying of networks and coalitions on the "left fringe" in turn made it difficult to organize politically. Ware recalled that "I could not do anything to help my friends, for since I, too, was under suspicion, I could only give them the kiss of death if I made any effort to support them."[13] For Ware, the shock of receiving a list of allegations against her was softened by knowing how many of her friends were also under suspicion, but she soon realized that the practical impact was that none of them could safely help each other or anyone else. Eminent persons whose loyalty was above challenge found themselves inundated with requests for affidavits and had to be careful not to dilute the value of their support by extending it indiscriminately. Loyalty defendants were eternally grateful to those who used up chips for them. After the American Legion called for Tex Goldschmidt's dismissal from government service in 1948, Goldschmidt thanked the powerful Texas Democrat Alvin Wirtz for "going to bat" for him, adding ruefully, "all the rest of your friends are in about the same fix."[14]

Loyalty defendants often were at a loss to figure out the source of charges against them, because loyalty board interrogatories did not identify the source or precise nature of the derogatory information. The anonymity of the loyalty program encouraged people to ventilate ill-informed suspicions and personal grievances. Caroline Ware seems never to have guessed that two young women who worked for her at the OPA reported her to be a Communist. When questioned more than a decade later about her association with them, Ware described the two women as efficient, harmless subordinates she barely knew.[15] Not all informants were malicious. Some inadvertently damned their associates with offhand assessment. Unbeknownst to Tex Goldschmidt, for example, his early mentor Jacob Baker told investigators in 1943 that although Goldschmidt was a good public servant, was not a Communist, and was not by intention a fellow traveler: "he talks too much and has a lot of very close associates who are definitely Left Wing and some Communist Party members." That murky assessment took on a life of its own in subsequent reports. Goldschmidt apparently never knew what trouble Baker's comments caused him, and when he was under investigation again in 1954, Goldschmidt asked Baker to vouch for him (Baker provided an affidavit that was entirely positive about Goldschmidt's loyalty).[16] More often, however, not knowing the source of allegations disrupted trust in colleagues and friends, further disorienting and isolating loyalty defendants.

Some people were not surprised to receive interrogatories from their agency loyalty board. Civil servants whose colleagues included someone named by Whitaker Chambers or Elizabeth Bentley knew they would be under extra scrutiny. The espionage charges against Alger Hiss, to give the most famous example, meant trouble for anyone who had ever worked with him, and that was a lot of people, given the amount of personnel movement as New Deal and war agencies proliferated. Tex Goldschmidt had to explain his relationship to the Hisses because he and they had once lived on the same street in Georgetown. Fortunately for Goldschmidt, he could state that he had been in the Hisses' home only once, and only as far as the foyer while trick-or-treating with his children (more pumpkin imagery). The economist Mordecai Ezekiel was questioned after a babysitter reported that Ezekiel's son said Hiss was not guilty. Ezekiel and also Edwin Witte, the Wisconsin social security expert, faced repeated difficulties because Hiss's office at the State Department had included them in lists of recommended candidates for UN jobs.[17]

Government employees with a close relative who was widely known or perceived to be a member of the Communist Party also were not surprised to receive an interrogatory, but that did not make their position any less painful. Economist Jean Flexner was forced to disavow absolutely her Communist sister, Eleanor Flexner, a pioneering feminist historian. Like Mary Dublin Keyserling, Jean Flexner had a prominent Jewish progressive father and a sister who was well known in left circles. Also like Dublin Keyserling, Jean Flexner studied under Harold Laski in London, married a government employee, had no children, and distinguished herself as a government economist. Jean stressed that her sister was nine years younger and that she and Eleanor had not lived in the same city since 1925. Their views had diverged especially sharply after 1938, she said, to the point that they now avoided political topics even as they maintained "affectionate sisterly relations."[18] Flexner was asked whether, if she were hiring people responsible for handling secret materials while "we were at war with Russia . . . would you employ your sister Eleanor?" She answered, "No, I would not, but I would not employ her in a lot of things short of war with Russia, either." Back when Jean Flexner first received the interrogatory, she asked her agency loyalty board to dismiss the charges on the grounds that they were vague and, even if true, not prejudicial to her loyalty. But in the end, to keep her job she had to distance herself from her sister and label her a loyalty risk. Jean's supporters did the same. Her former supervisor Clara Beyer commented that Eleanor was "a thorn in the flesh" of the Flexner family, adding that Jean had been active in reporting disloyal activity in the agency. Jean Flexner faced successive rounds of investigation, which always featured questions about Eleanor, before her eventual clearance in 1955.[19]

Absent such a "red flag" association, being accused of disloyalty often came as a severe shock. Pauli Murray was stunned in 1952 when Cornell University asked her to withdraw her application for a position sponsored by the State Department because of her radical associations in the 1930s. Murray mobilized distinguished supporters to protest Cornell's action, but to no avail. "One feels frightened, insecure, exposed. One thinks of all the personal errors, the deep secrets of one's life, unrelated to political activities. One is apprehensive that all the details of one's intimate life will be spread on the record to be read, sifted, weighed, evaluated, and judged by strangers."[20]

Murray, who was tormented by doubts about her sexual identity, suffered the special fear that must have been felt by anyone with personal secrets, especially but not only gays and lesbians. The State Department rated the diplomat Esther Brunauer loyal but dismissed her on security grounds because her husband had belonged to a Communist organization in the 1920s and also faced "moral turpitude" allegations. Stephen Brunauer, a Hungarian-born chemist for the navy, had at least two affairs while married to Esther. Desperate to save their careers, Esther argued that her husband's infidelity was a private matter and irrelevant to his employment qualifications. She stated that her husband's lovers were "fine young women" who did not reflect poorly on his professional judgment (in other words, he was not susceptible to seduction by Communist spies). These painful disclosures did not prevent the cruelly ironic ruling by the State Department loyalty board that Esther was a security risk—because she was married to an adulterer.[21] That was not the final humiliation. After she obtained a job with the Library of Congress, congressional conservatives attacked the library for employing her, which led the library's newsletter to publish a notice that Brunauer would not have access to sensitive materials. Mortified, she left Washington, ending up in a mundane job at a privately endowed organization in the Midwest. She died a few years later at the age of fifty-seven.[22]

Brunauer's story illustrates the gravity of a loyalty investigation's potential consequences. Damage to one's pride and career aspirations were significant, but the blunt economic threat of dismissal should not be overlooked. Most government employees, even high-ranking ones, could not afford to be unemployed for long. Financial worries were an ongoing theme in their correspondence.[23] Once someone was flagged as a loyalty risk, it was impossible for that person to keep any government job. Even employees who had been cleared after having undergone full field investigation by the FBI were more vulnerable than others to dismissal.[24] Dismissal from the federal government made employment with state and local governments unlikely because they quickly followed the federal example in implementing loyalty procedures. And private employers who received government contracts were required to adopt "industrial security" programs. Pauli Murray, whose race made it especially hard to obtain private-sector jobs suited to her training as a lawyer, was desperate when Cornell denied her the project funded by the State Department.[25] Loyalty troubles also followed government employees into seemingly more independent sectors, as Thomas Emerson learned when right-wing alumni campaigned for his dismissal from the Yale Law School. Other academics were less successful than Emerson in retaining their positions.[26] Not surprisingly, when employers could choose among candidates, they avoided hiring those who might invite controversy, even when the employers did not themselves doubt candidates' loyalty.

Devastating as it was, loss of employment was only one of the clubs that investigators wielded. The FBI often urged the Justice Department to prosecute loyalty defendants on perjury charges. A federal grand jury indicted Val Lorwin even though the State Department loyalty board had cleared him. It took Lorwin two years to get the indictment thrown out on the grounds that Justice's attorney had misrepresented the evidence to the jury.[27] Foreign-born civil servants were subject to deportation. Loyalty defendants often faced passport restrictions that curbed their international travel, which could be a serious professional problem. Thomas Emerson and Charlotte Towle, academics who had been in government, won prestigious international grants but had difficulty obtaining passports to use them.[28] Academics also stood to lose government research grants, which meant, as John Peters put it, "complete extinction of all my investigative activities and those of the youngsters who have been associated with me."[29] People who were dismissed as loyalty risks or who resigned before final clearance also risked losing their pensions. When Paul R. Porter applied for federal retirement benefits in 1970, examiners reviewed his record to see whether it contained evidence of perjury that could be grounds for denial of benefits (they concluded it did not).[30]

Harassment and surveillance were facts of life for suspect civil servants—and their relatives. They widely believed their phone lines were tapped; accurate or not, the perception heightened their anxiety.[31] The FBI obtained suspects' address books, sometimes by illegal means. The FBI "found" Tom Emerson's 1939 address book, supposedly in an apartment he had vacated.[32] Aubrey Williams's teenage son was held in jail by the District of Columbia police in 1958 after leaving his father's car parked in a bus stop. Not only was the punishment disproportionate to the offense, but when the dust settled, Williams's address book was missing from the car's glove compartment. Williams claimed the police admitted they were acting on orders from the FBI. He took the story to the press, pointing out that the damage was not just to him and his son but to the hundreds of people in his address book who would now find themselves under suspicion.[33] The long list of unpleasant consequences intensified loyalty defendants' desperation to impress loyalty officials favorably.

DEFENSE STRATEGIES

Loyalty defendants and their lawyers developed a wide range of tactics for convincing officials to rate them eligible. They all struggled to find a balance between saying what they guessed loyalty officials wanted to hear, on the one hand, and upholding their own principles, on the other. The form and effectiveness of their tactics were conditioned by gender prescriptions.

The obvious priority for every loyalty defendant was demonstrating that one had never been sympathetic to communism or, if need be, explaining that one had been briefly interested but had long since become hostile to the Communist Party. Active members of the Communist Party, of course, had to either leave government or lie; it is impossible to know how many chose the latter, but it was probably a small number. A larger number may have succeeded in concealing *past* membership in the party.[34] In the early years of loyalty screenings, former party members who could document their resignation sometimes won clearance. The lawyer Nancy Fraenkel Wechsler was retained by several agencies during the war and then served as counsel to the President's Committee on Civil Rights despite the fact that she and her husband, the journalist James Wechsler, had belonged to the Young Communist League from about 1933 to 1937. It probably helped that her husband had written publicly about the couples' disillusionment with Soviet communism, but Nancy Wechsler nonetheless was careful to present herself to examiners as "now apolitical." When the loyalty program became more stringent in 1947, she went into private practice. Her civil service file was "flagged" in case she tried to return, which it appears she did not.[35]

In distancing themselves from communism, defendants displayed a broad spectrum of attitudes toward the CP and toward the loyalty program itself. Neutrality was not an option. With any derogatory information in the record, it was insufficient to show one had not been *pro*-Communist; one had to convince officials that one had been *anti*-Communist. Some defendants avoided criticizing Communists even as they explained their own differences with them. Some commended loyalty officials for their hard work in rooting out Communists in government and sympathized with the difficulty of their task. Others boldly declared that the effort to label political subversives was repressive and counterproductive. Some combined those approaches. Esther Brunauer condemned Communists and said they should be disqualified from government jobs, but she also indicted the loyalty program. Because the loyalty program held that the individual counts for nothing and the interest of the state is paramount, she argued, "the system is built purely along Russian lines."[36]

For the many civil servants who faced allegations about their associations with alleged "fronts" such as the National Lawyers' Guild, the United Public Workers union, and the League of Women Shoppers, one of the most effective defenses was to produce evidence of one's resignation at some date before or soon after Communist control of the group increased. Also helpful was documentation (from one's writings, or in the form of affidavits or testimony from witnesses) of one's divergence from the CP line: criticism of the Soviet invasion of Finland, advocacy of aid to Britain during the Hitler-Stalin pact, opposition to the Morgenthau Plan to pastoralize Germany, support for the Marshall Plan, or opposition to Henry Wallace's Progressive Party in 1948. Many left liberals offered their membership in the Americans for Democratic Action as proof of their anticommunism. In fact, so many civil servants cited their ADA membership as evidence of loyalty that one might wonder whether providing shelter for noncommunist leftists was a major reason for the ADA's founding in 1947, the same year that the loyalty program was formally established. Public health expert John Peters's unusual refusal to join the ADA seems to confirm the point: "My reason for being uninterested is that I do not share your fears that Communists and Communism are hidden under every bed, in fact I am one of those that don't have time to look under the bed."[37]

Defendants who could not muster documentary proof of having opposed communism often tried to persuade officials that they simply were not the type of person to be a Communist. Some defendants listed examples that proved their commitment to democracy and insisted they could never have been Communist because they abhorred Communists' undemocratic methods. But defense attorneys and their clients learned not to count on loyalty boards' appreciation for the distinctions between radical democracy and communism. The process for selecting loyalty board members (of whom there were about 2,000 on boards of first jurisdiction, 200 on regional boards, and 26 on the Loyalty Review Board) favored people who had not been involved in controversy. Liberals and intellectuals were rarely appointed, apparently on the theory that they were naïve. The results demonstrated, as Eleanor Bontecou drily observed after perusing loyalty hearing transcripts, that "naiveté is not the monopoly of any one class of persons." Bontecou concluded that the Civil Service Commission's decision to appoint solid citizens who inspired public confidence and to avoid anyone who might have "tilted at windmills in the days of their youth" often yielded boards whose members were well-meaning but uninformed about "the many varied and complex social movements in the United States."[38] Rather than relying on loyalty officials' appreciation for nuance, defendants tried to appeal to them by stressing their independence of thought, insisting they were not "joiners," and reciting their all-American lineage.

Arguing that a loyalty defendant was too independent to submit to the Communist Party's rigid discipline was a tactic that seems to have worked better for men than for women. In two cases that reached the Supreme Court, former U.S. Employment Service supervisor Dorothy Bailey and U.S. Public Health Service consultant John Peters faced similar charges and had the same counsel. In both cases the defense argued that their client was "too independent a thinker to follow the Commie line." Bailey and Peters were equally prickly toward loyalty officials: they challenged vague questions, corrected poor assumptions, and refused to say that Communists were a grave threat to national security. Bailey was dismissed in 1951; Peters was reinstated in 1955. Timing may help explain the differing outcomes. By the time the Supreme Court heard the Peters case, Senator McCarthy had been disgraced and cries to reform the loyalty program were at last gaining traction. Gender seems to have been another factor, however, in officials' contrasting reactions to Dorothy Bailey and John Peters.

Bailey was anything but deferential. She infuriated her first loyalty board by refusing to declare that her local of the United Public Workers union included a Communist clique. The fact that a few union members decided to call themselves "the right-wing group," she observed, did not prove the existence of a "left-wing" counterpart. She claimed to be an independent who was attacked by the right-wing faction because she refused to join in calling the others Communists. She also refused to state that a Communist Party member could not be loyal to the United States. The loyalty board ruled against her. Bailey told her appeals board they were being used as a "goon squad" in an internecine union conflict. Then, when asked to define a Communist, she asked the examiner what his own definition would be. "Please don't ask me questions. I am supposed to ask you," he snapped, adding that he knew what a Communist was even if he was not a "Bryn Mawr graduate or a Phi Beta Kappa" like the defendant.[39]

By contrast, male loyalty defendants could get away with a defiant attitude. The Yale medical professor John Peters was downright rude. "I presume your letter follows a stereotyped form for which you are not responsible," he wrote to the chairman of his agency loyalty board. "I have read it carefully repeatedly and submitted it to several intelligent friends for interpretation to no avail. . . . My own impression is that Lewis Carroll missed a perfect gem for 'Through the Looking Glass.'" Peters mocked the board's request that he bring evidence to his hearing to defend himself when he had not been told the specific substance and sources of the charges. He was left "to conjure from my imagination what sinister acts I may have unconsciously performed. . . . Limited time and a sense of humor have saved me from keeping a diary."[40] At his appeal hearing, Peters likened Communist Party activity to secret boys' clubs and said that repressing it was ridiculous. Since his previous hearing, Peters had publicly petitioned for repeal of the McCarran Internal Security Act. A man who would do that, his counsel argued, "would never accept the discipline" of the Communist Party. The Loyalty Review Board rejected Peters's appeal, but the Supreme Court did not, and Peters was reinstated. Dorothy Bailey remained barred from government employment and ended up a clerical worker for her defense attorney at Arnold, Fortas & Porter.[41] The Interior Department's Ralph Russell was cleared in 1955 despite associations with the same union leaders who had been held against Bailey. Russell's loyalty board concluded that his association with union and civil rights causes simply reflected Russell's "Yankee conscience" and "pugnacious" personality. Such allowances rarely were made for female defendants. Loyalty officials seem to have judged independent thinking a good sign in a man but worrisome in a woman.[42]

The case of Dorothy Kenyon publicized the dangers of having been a "joiner" in the 1930s. Kenyon was the first person named by Senator McCarthy when he appeared before the Tydings Committee in March 1950 to support his charges against the State Department. Kenyon had distinguished herself as a lawyer in New York City since 1917 and was appointed a municipal court judge by Mayor Fiorello La Guardia in 1939. In 1947 President Truman named her U.S. delegate to the United Nations Commission on the Status of Women. That appointment was under State Department auspices, and McCarthy thought he could use her to embarrass that agency and Truman. McCarthy claimed that Kenyon had been affiliated with "at least twenty-eight" Communist front organizations. Kenyon responded to McCarthy with a defiance that became legendary. Kenyon told the press, "He's a low-down worm and although it ought to be beneath my dignity to answer him, I'm mad enough to say that he's a liar and he can go to hell." By the time of McCarthy's accusation, Kenyon's UN commission had expired, which put her beyond the loyalty program's reach for the moment. Banner headlines described Kenyon as "flaying" and "blasting" McCarthy. She called him an "unmitigated liar" and a "coward to take shelter in the cloak of Congressional immunity." She might have lent her name to groups that later turned out to include Communists, she said, but she had never been a Communist or a sympathizer.[43] (Key people on the right knew McCarthy was wrong about Kenyon, but they kept this knowledge to themselves.)[44]

Supporters cheered Kenyon's "spirited reply," but in the long run her bravado may have harmed more than it helped.[45] Molly Dewson, the Democratic Party women's leader, wrote to ask, "Well, how is the unhung old witch yet?" Kenyon replied, "The old witch isn't hung yet . . . . but the truth never does catch up with the lie and there will always be people who will think me a Red."[46] Indeed, Kenyon never received another public appointment. The Johnson White House considered her for a position in 1964 but decided against it.[47] In 1971, Kenyon reflected that she had been lucky "in being the first on the list and therefore *relatively* fearless." If she had had any idea how much damage the "unmitigated liar" and his allies were about to do, she might have been more circumspect.[48]

Loyalty defendants and their lawyers learned from headline cases such as Kenyon's that it could be effective to demonstrate that one had never joined many organizations. By the early 1950s, "joiners" were caricatured as easy marks. Leon Keyserling claimed a "temperamental aversion" to organized activity. UNESCO official Isador Lubin assured the Loyalty Review Board he had been too busy and too cautious to join groups or even to socialize widely when he worked on sensitive war-related projects.[49]

Professional women had more difficulty than men showing they had not been "joiners." For one thing, women may have been more likely in fact to be "joiners." Their more limited career opportunities and the social approval for women's volunteer activities made it especially common for women to participate in many clubs and organizations. Furthermore, many Popular Front causes had feminist appeal: women had particular reason to oppose fascism and militarism, to favor poll-tax repeal, to admire the CIO, and so forth. Women like Dorothy Kenyon and Mary Dublin Keyserling did have associations with many left-led groups. When a female loyalty defendant did not have such associations, she and her lawyer highlighted that point. Abe Fortas said of his client Rhea Radin, a public health policy analyst, "she has not been, I'm glad to say, a joiner." A sympathetic witness told the FBI that Jane Hoey, director of the Bureau of Public Assistance, was not "the type of person" to join organizations.[50]

Another strategy for defendants was to create a patriotic narrative describing their all-American lineage. Pauli Murray went so far as to write a family memoir in reaction to accusations of disloyalty. The book's title, *Proud Shoes: The Story of an American Family* (1956), takes on new meaning in light of attacks on her as "un-American."[51] Another defendant, Murray's mentor and friend Caroline Ware, enumerated the achievements of her distinguished New England ancestors, from her paternal grandfather's work on behalf of freedpersons during Reconstruction, to her great-grandfather, a Harvard theology professor who shared a pulpit with Ralph Waldo Emerson, to her maternal grandfather's friendship with Abraham Lincoln. Ware argued that the heritage she cherished was "utterly incompatible" with communism's "regimentation of thought and rule by fear."[52] Similarly, NLRB regional director Dorothea de Schweinitz informed loyalty officials that her mother's family had been in North America since the 1600s and her paternal great-great-grandfather, a minister, had arrived in 1770.[53] Mordecai Ezekiel noted that his Portuguese-Jewish ancestors had been in the United States since before the Revolution, "so we are Americans from a long way back."[54]

Loyalty defendants whose ancestors were recent arrivals to the United States tried to show that their families did not fit nativist stereotypes. Isador Lubin began his loyalty hearing by explaining that his father, a clothing merchant born in Russia, had voted Republican, and that there were no "no radical ideas in [his] family." His own trip to Russia in 1929 had convinced him, he explained, that its people lived in fear and poverty.[55] Jewish civil servants who were not part of the mass exodus from Eastern Europe made sure to point this out, since those Jews were assumed to be predisposed toward communism.

Another common defense tactic under the pressure of investigation was to stress one's conventionality—whether in taste, religion, or aspirations. This approach seems to have been effective even though it did not mesh smoothly with assertions of independent-mindedness. The defense attorney Joseph Fanelli, who handled about two hundred loyalty cases, found it necessary to "expose [the defendant's] innermost life," such as his or her taste in books, theater, music, clothing, and art. Loyalty officials often talked about trying to get a picture of "the whole man," and some of them were quick to see a red flag in such attributes as atheism, attraction to experimental art and literature, or passion for Russian music.[56] The lawyer Bernice Lotwin Bernstein assured her loyalty board that she disliked modern art and music and that her children attended traditional schools.[57]

Because many anticommunists were suspicious of both atheists and Jews, Protestant and Catholic defendants frequently highlighted their religiosity. Indeed the loyalty program may have induced a surge in overt displays of Christian faith on the part of civil servants. In the same year that David Demarest Lloyd was drafting the ADA constitution and waiting for a loyalty clearance from the State Department, he became superintendent of the Sunday school at his Episcopal church and with his wife founded a church lecture series. He highlighted those activities in a biographical statement he submitted to loyalty officials in 1952.[58] Harold Ickes began his defense of Tex Goldschmidt by describing him as "of German-Lutheran stock." Goldschmidt later explained, "he wanted to say I was not Jewish, Jews and Communists being often equated in that era."[59] Goldschmidt claimed he had worried more about explaining his atheism at hearings than about how to represent his views on capitalism.[60]

To convince investigators that they were not subversive, loyalty defendants and their lawyers frequently played up their obeisance to conventional expectations about the roles of women and men. For women, this could mean highlighting their interests in children, cooking, or shopping. Deference to conventions of femininity also could mean emphasizing one's selflessness rather than one's rights. Bernice Bernstein's lawyer brought her husband to the hearing and had him explain why she was working when they did not need her salary. Rather than asserting Bernice's rights, Bernard Bernstein argued it would be best for the government to keep her services, and best for their children and for his own career that she be cleared and retained. In Lucy Kramer Cohen's case, friendly informants stressed that she needed employment because she had been widowed with two young daughters; they also mentioned her "charm" and domesticity.[61] Married women who used their maiden names had to explain their practice, and they rarely did so in feminist terms. Mary Taylor said that she kept her maiden name so that her pacifism would not embarrass her first husband, the journalist Rodney Dutcher. For good measure she noted that her pacifism was based on her religious views and her father was a minister.[62]

For men, deference to gender conventions could mean stressing their control over wives. Joseph Churchill Murray, an economist employed by the U.S. Army after the war to strengthen the noncommunist wing of the Japanese labor movement, was asked why his wife did not accompany him to Japan. Esther Murray had made headlines in 1948 by insisting on a civil rights plank in the Democratic Party platform and had been the Democratic nominee in a tight California congressional race in 1950. She lost, just before her husband's loyalty hearing. After speculating that the wife's electoral battle had led to the charges against her husband, the defendant's counsel took pains to normalize the couple's relationship. He brought out that they had a "very mutual relationship," that the husband supported her decision to run for office, and that she faithfully performed such wifely duties as arranging his poker games.[63] Catherine Bauer, in trying to clear her name to save her husband's career, stressed to the Army-Navy-Air Force Personnel Security Board that she had followed her husband wherever his work took them. Before her marriage, Bauer was well known as an archetypical "New Woman": she smoked, drank, and took many lovers as she traveled the world.[64] Similarly, in refuting allegations against his wife, Wilbur Cohen highlighted her volunteer work as a Cub Scout den mother and explained that it was her Baptist upbringing that motivated her to fight for poll-tax repeal.[65]

The gender expectations of loyalty officials sometimes surfaced when they tried to assess an employee's susceptibility to influence by a relative. Many loyalty defendants faced allegations involving relatives other than spouses, and they faced a tricky task as they tried to disassociate themselves from an allegedly Communist sibling or parent without getting that person into deeper trouble. Loyalty boards wanted to hear that the defendant thoroughly disapproved of the relative in question and was in no way under that person's influence. Husbands had greater success than wives in convincing boards that a radical spouse did not influence them. Similarly, officials seem to have been more able to perceive men as independent from leftist female relatives than vice versa. Eugene Landy, whose mother belonged to the CP, was cleared, but in three other cases daughters with allegedly CP fathers were dismissed.[66]

Choosing among and implementing strategies for convincing officials of one's "loyalty" took an enormous amount of time and money and drained defendants' mental and physical energies. Given how many employees were forced to spend weeks researching charges, replying to interrogatories, gathering affidavits, preparing for hearings, correcting hearing transcripts, and waiting for rulings, it is surprising that the government kept functioning at all. Civil servants also spent hours on their colleagues' cases—answering questions from FBI agents, writing affidavits, appearing at hearings—a burden that was heavier for those in supervisory positions. Critics of the loyalty program tried to appeal to taxpayers by pointing out how expensive the program was, in terms of hours diverted from normal operations as well as in direct administrative costs. After receiving an interrogatory, employees dropped everything in order to get legal advice and complete the research and writing in time to respond within the allotted ten days. One woman attorney who acted as her own counsel spent three hundred hours of work and vacation time preparing her reply to interrogatory, which came to nineteen thousand words plus nineteen exhibits, and for the subsequent hearing.[67] The president of Amherst College told Walter Gellhorn he was shocked that "a person like you should have to waste so much energy on such foolishness."[68] Cynics wondered whether the loyalty program was chiefly a tool by which conservatives prevented civil servants from getting anything done—thereby making a self-fulfilling prophecy of the mantra that government bureaucracy wasted taxpayer money.[69]

But the financial burden of the loyalty program fell more heavily on loyalty defendants than on taxpayers. The threat of unemployment was the greatest financial worry, but the legal fees alone could be overwhelming, even for high-ranking officials and even though defense attorneys often reduced their rates in loyalty cases.[70] Esther Peterson recalled that during Oliver's investigation in the 1950s, her four children helped finance their college educations by picking fruit in Utah, just as she had done in the 1920s.[71] Government employees earned relatively low salaries for their education levels and experience, and for those who faced loyalty investigations, financial worry was a constant theme. Suspension without pay was common, and employees had no way to predict how long it would take for their case to be resolved. It could be a matter of a few months, but yearlong waits were not uncommon. Esther Brunauer was suspended in April 1951, had hearings in July, waited nine months before a negative ruling, and then went through the appeals process before being dismissed in July 1952. Even at half rate, her legal fees were $2,500, a sum that probably represented at least a quarter of her annual salary.[72] One's career suffered from the long uncertainty even when one was cleared. Mordecai Ezekiel, the former brain truster and advocate of agricultural planning, replied to the interrogatory of his loyalty board in December 1953 and was not cleared until April 1955. By then based in Rome as a top official at the UN Food and Agriculture Organization, he struggled to gather dozens of affidavits from abroad, and he faced two hearings. He eventually was made the agency's assistant director general, but the proceedings held up his promotion.[73]

Such experiences imposed psychological costs. One was the burden of living with the strategic choices one had made in the high-stakes game of trying to win clearance. Defendants had to decide, sometimes on the spot, which views, organizations, friends, and relatives to disavow and which to stand by. No doubt some people regretted their choices. In trying to establish their anticommunist credentials, some people created a distorted self-portrait that they then had to live with. Defendants often likened their loyalty trials to a trip with Alice in Wonderland, or to looking into a fun house mirror at Coney Island.[74] After their inquisition, some loyalty defendants may have been ashamed of what they saw in the regular mirror. Reinventing oneself could be unhealthy. Marriages suffered. Leon Keyserling ended up grossly overweight, bitter, and estranged from his wife. Mary Dublin Keyserling spent her last years shredding papers, a behavior that relatives attributed to Alzheimer's disease but that may have been a manifestation of earlier actual or symbolic destructions.[75]

The number of the accused who died at a young age is striking. Esther Peterson believed that the years of stress aggravated her husband's cancer and left him a "broken spirit." McCarthyism "killed my man," she concluded bitterly.[76] Mary Taylor was diagnosed with a brain tumor not long after an extended investigation resulted in her clearance in 1951; she continued working, was cleared again in 1955, and died in 1957 at age fifty-seven. Her husband Donald Montgomery, the former government consumer advocate and United Auto Workers official, committed suicide weeks later; his associations had been an issue in his wife's case.[77] Former Truman aide David Lloyd died at fifty-one of an aneurysm, which his widow attributed to his having been a smoker, but the strain of McCarthy's attacks could not have helped.[78] As noted already, Esther Brunauer died of heart failure at fifty-seven. Kathryn McHale, a Truman appointee to the Subversive Activities Control Board, died suddenly of unknown causes in 1956, at a moment when the FBI was pursuing rumors that she was a lesbian with a drinking problem.[79] High-powered jobs and health problems might have done these people in even without loyalty trials, but the stress of being investigated was probably a contributing factor.

COLLECTIVE RESPONSES

With the help of a few defendants like Dorothy Bailey, John Peters, and Esther Brunauer, who challenged the loyalty program head-on, an anti-McCarthyite network did emerge. These critics—lawyers, academics, journalists, foundations—succeeded in exposing some of the most egregious aspects of the loyalty program and bringing about reforms. They were cautious, though. They kept their distance from left critics of the loyalty program. And even as they challenged some forms of discrimination in the operation of the program, they ignored others. They performed invaluable service by documenting racial and ethnic discrimination and the decline of civic participation, but they overlooked certain gendered corollaries, such as the curtailment of wives' activism and of women's demands for workplace rights. Some of their assumptions and tactics in fact reinforced barriers to women's advancement: for example, when loyalty charges left husbands unemployed, program critics portrayed family dependence on wives' earnings as a tragedy.

Leftist journalists and government employee unions protested the loyalty program from the start, but their critiques had little impact on public opinion, particularly in the 1947–52 period, when international events and party politics contributed to a climate that favored the hard-core crusaders against Communists in government. The United Public Workers of America (UPWA) vociferously protested the loyalty program on many grounds. The UPWA officer Alfred Bernstein, who eventually served as defense counsel in over four hundred cases involving UPWA members, prepared an early analysis stating that the loyalty program had become "an instrument to intimidate all Americans who oppose racial discrimination, who want to join unions of their choice, who want to think, and who want to speak their minds on any issue." Observing that laws were already in place for removing disloyal employees, Bernstein concluded that the loyalty program's true function was "thought control."[80]

Among those to whom UPWA sent its report was Yale Law School professor Thomas Emerson, who had just published a study of the loyalty program. Back when he held important positions at the NLRB and then the OPA, Emerson himself had been at the vortex of congressional allegations that those agencies employed Communist sympathizers. His own experience was an unacknowledged source for his analysis of the procedural deficiencies of the program. After assessing the threat of Communists in government, he enumerated the negative impacts of the loyalty program and compared it to its counterparts in other countries. Emerson recommended reforming loyalty procedures and restricting their application to security-sensitive positions. He concluded that the loyalty program was crippling the effectiveness of democratic government.[81]

Emerson's indictment of the loyalty program made him a hero to leftists and civil libertarians, but it also put him back in the crosshairs of countersubversives. Because the essay lambasted the FBI for illegal wiretapping, J. Edgar Hoover issued a formal rebuttal. Hoover's agents also stepped up their surveillance of Emerson. He would find himself denied a passport in 1952, called before SISS in 1953, and the subject of successive campaigns to get Yale to dismiss him; association with him also led to investigation of some of his students.[82]

Assisted by financial support from private foundations, several other scholars undertook studies of the loyalty program, and like Emerson some of them found their own loyalty questioned. With a grant from the Rockefeller Foundation, the Cornell University Press published a series that included two monographs by Columbia Law's Walter Gellhorn and one by civil rights lawyer Eleanor Bontecou. Published between 1950 and 1953, these studies remain the standard overviews of government loyalty-security measures.[83] In 1954, the Ford Foundation's Fund for the Republic hired the young lawyer Adam Yarmolinsky to study personnel loyalty cases. In publicizing the resulting study, Yarmolinsky positioned himself as an objective observer. He explained that for security reasons the government's side of each case was unavailable and therefore unrepresented. In radio talks, press releases, and cover letters distributing ten thousand copies of the published study, he avoided making recommendations, instead simply listing six questions that the cases raised about the program. The official response was nonetheless chilly. The Office of the

Attorney General called it a "subjective one-sided presentation" based on unrepresentative cases. The FFR's point had not been that its sample was representative but rather that it indicated serious flaws in the program.[84]

Scholars of the loyalty program and the foundations that funded them were accused of Communist sympathies. In 1954 a House committee launched an investigation of un-American activities at the major philanthropic organizations, including the Ford, Rockefeller, and Guggenheim foundations. The two-year investigation did not find evidence of wrongdoing by the foundations, and the studies they funded, along with the work of journalists, began to undermine the loyalty program's credibility. Nonetheless, in 1959 the Fund for the Republic dropped its plan to publish additional loyalty cases.[85] Even after it became safer to criticize the loyalty program, its early critics found themselves hampered by the taint of subversiveness they had acquired by challenging the program during its heyday. Gellhorn, Bontecou, and Yarmolinsky all found themselves locked out of government service, ostensibly because of other associations but in fact because their dissent had triggered hostile scrutiny.[86]

As examples of injustice to government employees continued to emerge in the press and from academic studies—and after McCarthy's censure in 1954 and the admission by ex-Communist informant Harvey Matusow that he and other government witnesses had lied—the balance of public opinion on the subject of "Communists in government" began to shift in favor of those who sought to reform the loyalty program. During the run-up to the 1956 elections, some Democrats abandoned their defensive crouch and tried to make Republican abuse of the loyalty-security program a campaign issue. Back during the 1954 congressional campaigns, Vice President Richard Nixon had credited the Eisenhower administration with ousting some eight thousand Truman appointees as loyalty or security risks. Senator Olin Johnston, chair of the Post Office and Civil Service Committee, won authorization of a subcommittee charged with investigating what Democrats called the "Nixon numbers game." Research by Johnston's staff demonstrated that Nixon's numbers indeed had been grossly distorted: under Eisenhower, very few dismissals were on loyalty-security grounds, and many of those dismissed had been hired by the Eisenhower administration, not Truman.[87]

The subcommittee also achieved something that Eleanor Bontecou and others had been trying to do for several years: it put the spotlight on executive agency security officers, who wielded power with little oversight. Johnston's staff turned the tables by investigating the hiring and conduct of security officers, and what it found was not pretty. As a result, the State Department's notorious security officer Scott McLeod, a former FBI agent, was chastised, as was his counterpart at the Department of Agriculture. Most sensationally, Johnston Committee investigators discovered that the security officer of the Small Business Administration, George V. McDavitt, was involved in a fascist group that was on the Attorney General's List of Subversive Organizations. McDavitt ran his office like a tyrant, and several members of his staff were happy to explain to the subcommittee how McDavitt manipulated the security clearance process, for example by rewriting reports to include only derogatory information and by demanding personal favors in exchange for clearance. The subcommittee also discovered that McDavitt, who had zealously denied clearances for "immoral conduct," himself had an adulterous affair with a German woman, battered and divorced his wife, and then brought the German "Miss X" to the United States. He also allegedly favored gay men and lesbians on his staff. McDavitt denied it all and had the temerity—given his conduct in investigating others—to complain that his privacy rights were being violated. The evidence was incontrovertible, however, and he was dismissed. For leftists and liberals, the irony was delicious. The Eisenhower administration boasted that its revamped security program had thrown hundreds of Truman-appointed Communists out of government, when in fact it had put civil servants and the administrative capacity of the U.S. government in the hands of failed FBI agents (which is what many agency security officers were) and even a Nazi sympathizer.[88]

In addition to the efforts of individual government employees and concerned lawyers, academics, and journalists, another factor that tarnished the image of the loyalty program and pressured politicians to reform it was organized protest from groups who correctly perceived that the program discriminated against them. In varying ways, homosexuals, Jews, and African Americans responded collectively to the loyalty program. By contrast, women made little explicit protest of the particular discrimination they faced.

The purge of homosexuals from the federal government was a major stimulus to the emergence of a gay and lesbian movement. Lawyers who handled loyalty cases observed that homosexuals were getting "at the very least an extremely raw deal," and they sometimes challenged the assumption that homosexuals were automatically security risks because of their presumed susceptibility to blackmail. Joseph Fanelli pointed out, for example, that if a homosexual could be manipulated by his fear of disclosure, then a married man could be manipulated by threats against his family.[89] The nation's first formal homosexual organization, the Mattachine Society, emerged during the "lavender scare" of the early 1950s, and its Washington branch formed in direct response to the crusade to get gays out of government jobs. In the late 1950s and early 1960s Mattachine publications protesting the loyalty program mainly reached gay readers, but by the mid-1960s gay organizations were pressuring the

Civil Service Commission to stop discriminating against homosexuals, and they secured victory with a 1969 court ruling. Ironically, "policies meant to counter the power and influence of gay civil servants actually fostered the creation of an effective and influential political gay pressure group."[90]

Commentators at the time and since noted the prominence of racial and ethnic minorities among the victims of loyalty investigations. Whites who were vocal in opposing racial discrimination were frequent targets, too.[91] When twenty-six Jewish and black postal workers charged discrimination in a suit that eventually reached the Supreme Court, public awareness of the problem increased, even though the Court was not persuaded (*Washington v. McGrath*, 1951). In the Fort Monmouth army cases publicized by Senator McCarthy, thirty-three of the thirty-five defendants were Jewish. Their lawyers argued that the security officers who initiated the cases were "in part motivated by flagrant anti-Semitism."[92] The American Jewish Committee issued press releases denouncing anti-Semitic comments by loyalty officials, and it wrote to the Johnston Committee with suggestions for reforming the program.[93] Other minorities benefited from the increased scrutiny of bias in the loyalty program. When a Chinese American was suspended in 1955 from his job inspecting electrical equipment for a defense contract manufacturer on the grounds that he had relatives living in Communist China, the American Civil Liberties Union paid his legal fees, and he was cleared.[94]

Like Jewish groups, black organizations such as the NAACP were quick to point out the loyalty program's bias against minority employees. African American groups did not submit complaints or proposals to the Johnston Committee, perhaps because Senator Johnston, although liberal in some respects, was an avowed white supremacist, but a white attorney did inform the committee that in his experience many loyalty defendants were "Negroes" in low-level, nonsensitive jobs against whom there was little substantial evidence.[95] White liberals focused on the high number of blacks among the "little people" hurt by the loyalty program, but black activists were especially concerned about its impact on the relatively small number of high-ranking blacks. From the beginning, when the Dies Committee began issuing lists of alleged subversives in government, black journalists protested its disproportionate attention to prominent African Americans such as William Pickens, Mary McLeod Bethune, Ralph Bunche, and E. Franklin Frazier. Pickens was a Yale-educated sociologist who was director of branches for the NAACP from 1930 to 1941 and then took a position in the Treasury Department. Bethune was an educator who founded the National Council for Negro Women in 1935 and then, as an official of the National Youth Administration, became a close friend of Eleanor Roosevelt and the unofficial leader of the administration's "Black Cabinet." Bunche, a political scientist who specialized in colonial territories and influenced the formation of the United Nations, won the Nobel Peace Prize in 1950 for his diplomatic efforts in the Middle East. Frazier was a prolific and distinguished sociologist at Howard University who worked for UNESCO in Paris, Africa, and the Middle East. In the process of fighting for black civil rights, all four had been associated with Communists. All could document their own early anticommunism, but the associations nonetheless hindered them for the rest of their careers.[96]

The obviousness of racial bias in the loyalty program paradoxically gave African Americans a degree of protection that grew stronger with time, as black protest and diplomatic imperatives eroded the respectability of overt racism. An early illustration occurred during one of the Dies Committee's salvos against "Communists in government." In 1943, the House amended an appropriations bill to deny salaries to employees named by Martin Dies as "crackpot radicals." For technical reasons, the bill forced the dismissal of only one employee, William Pickens, who was also one of the only two African Americans on Dies's list of thirty-eight civil servants (the other was Mary McLeod Bethune). This result apparently was unintentional, but the ensuing criticism from the lone black congressman (William L. Dawson, D-Ill.) and the black press strained the bipartisan conservative coalition. Worried about the northern black vote, Republicans distanced themselves from Dies and other southern Democrats, whom they suspected of setting them up by concealing Pickens's race. Pickens was reinstated.[97] In the years after the loyalty program was formalized in 1947, many observers commented on investigators' tendency to associate advocacy of racial equality with Communism.[98] By the mid-1950s, loyalty officials had recognized that it was unreasonable to expect black employees not to have been active on behalf of racial justice.

Ralph Bunche's case had a demonstrable effect on his loyalty board. Back in the 1930s Bunche had been active in Communist-influenced groups such as the National Negro Congress. In 1953 Bunche, then a top UN official, was called before SISS, which claimed the UN had become a refuge for American Communists. Under pressure from congressional conservatives, the president extended the loyalty program to American employees of the United Nations and other international organizations. The new International Organizations Employee Loyalty Board (IOELB) soon took up Bunche's case. At his May 1954 hearings, white and black witnesses supported Bunche's claim that he had been a forceful anticommunist at least since 1940. An account of the hearing was leaked to the press, and the NAACP called the inquiry a "farce." After twelve hours of hearings in which two paid ex-Communist witnesses were shown to be lying, the IOELB departed from its usual secrecy by issuing a public and unanimous clearance.[99]

Publicly embarrassed by the Bunche case, the IOELB subsequently was more tolerant of civil rights activism by black officials, even if it had led to contact with Communists. In 1961, when Bunche's Howard University colleague E. Franklin Frazier applied for a position with UNESCO, one IOELB member urged his fellow board members to take a lenient view of Frazier's past associations with Communist "fronts." In view of "present world tensions, race difficulties, our past experience with some accusing witnesses, [and] the experience in the Bunche case . . . we must take a realistic look at this file. We must not rush into possible error nor incur judicial or individual *or group wrath* over a palpable error on our part." That official worried about the political fallout at home and abroad if the board appeared to be unfair to a distinguished African American. His sensitivity did not help Frazier himself, who died before replying to the interrogatory, but it indicates that loyalty officials could be influenced by the threat of "group wrath."[100]

Few women of any race challenged the loyalty program's association between feminism, or even gender nonconformity, and political subversion. Neither politicians nor loyalty officials showed any concern about incurring the "group wrath" of women, and the loyalty program's gendered biases were never recognized, unlike its discrimination against homosexuals and racial and ethnic minorities. The one organization that called itself feminist during the 1950s was the National Woman's Party, and its Republican-leaning leadership did not speak out against McCarthyism.[101] Women were prominent in the resistance to Red scare politics—from Dorothy Kenyon to Kathryn McHale to Eleanor Bontecou—but they rarely articulated their grievances in feminist terms. Although women were among those loyalty defendants who contacted the Johnston Committee in 1955, none suggested that gender prejudice had been a factor in their dismissal.[102] Individual women perceived that their sex worked against them, but they rarely made that a public issue. Racism was on the defensive by the mid-1950s in ways that sexism was not, so this may have been a practical strategy, but it accommodated the status quo.

A good example of how women buried feminist complaints within more general principles is a *Washington Post* column by Malvina Lindsay. She hinted that McCarthy's "reckless charges of communism" against Dorothy Kenyon and Esther Brunauer were really a reaction against those women's stepping out of their prescribed roles. Observing that Kenyon had been criticized for her work with the Women's Committee for Lasting Peace, she commented that "such direct action was unheard of from a group of women." The group would have been wiser, she added, to call itself "the Genteel Females' Poetry Circle." Lindsay also mocked McCarthy's suspicion of Brunauer's "consumer activities" at the American Association of University Women. But then she dropped her gender analysis and complained of the suppression of civic participation by "Americans" in general. Thanks to McCarthy, more and more "Americans" would "play it safe," she predicted. "They will belong to nothing, contribute to nothing. They will say nothing, do nothing, even think nothing that might conceivably put them in line of an ideological mudslinger." Despite her acuity in noticing the reaction against female activism, the journalist's challenge to the antifeminist aspects of McCarthyism was muted.[103]

In sum, although the loyalty program operated in ways that disadvantaged gays, Jews, blacks, and women, the asymmetrical positions of those groups produced divergent collective responses. The loyalty program stimulated the emergence of a gay rights movement, and civil rights groups effectively protested racial and ethnic discrimination, but organized women did not articulate a feminist critique of the loyalty program.

The lawyers, academics, and journalists most prominent in the anti-McCarthyite network lamented above all the program's curbing of civic participation by government employees—and thus by their relatives, by prospective government employees, and so forth, rippling outward through the whole society. As we have seen, loyalty defendants hastened to assure security officials that they were not "joiners." Some agencies developed guidelines advising employees to avoid suspicion by "seeking wise and mature counsel prior to association with persons or organizations of any political or civic nature, no matter what their apparent motives may be."[104] Defense attorney Joseph Fanelli observed that the loyalty program devastated Washington's civic and social life. If government employees were invited to a social gathering, for example, no one whose views or associations might be controversial could be invited.[105] Fanelli was one of several attorneys to propose in 1960 that government employees be disqualified from grand or petit juries on matters relating to communism. Federal employees, he argued, were "a thoroughly frightened group who in fear of possible security prejudice to themselves are incapable of impartial judgment" in cases involving communism.[106] The political scientist Paul Tillett concluded that the loyalty program hindered freedom of political expression and in the process "enhanced pressures toward a privatized, personalized existence."[107]

This dampening of civic participation had a gendered corollary that critics at the time did not notice. The loyalty program may have encouraged professional men to avoid activist wives. It also taught women to avoid the feminist label if they wanted to advance their careers—or to marry an ambitious man. Commerce Department consultant Curtis

Warren believed that a colleague's loyalty troubles derived from the "ill-advised utterances of his wife who is a super-intellectual and goes off half-cocked."[108] At least 10 percent of the cases collected by the Fund for the Republic featured men who faced allegations about their wives' activities. Other men in that sample faced allegations about their mothers' political activities.[109] Men could not choose their mothers, but they could choose their wives.

Contemporary critics of the loyalty program constructed representations of the program that inadvertently reinforced its antifeminist tendencies. With the help of liberals seeking to influence popular opinion, the trope of the broken man "supported in ill-health by his wife's laundry earnings" after dismissal on loyalty grounds became one of the horror stories associated with McCarthyism. Harry Magdoff's son stressed how hard his mother worked when loyalty accusations hindered Magdoff's employment. Tillett's 1965 draft report presented wifely employment as part of the costs of McCarthyism.[110] Scholars have demonstrated that in the 1950s female breadwinning was associated with crisis, because the Great Depression and the war drew married women into paid employment.[111] Loyalty-security dismissals were yet another reason that the next generation associated wives' earning with trauma.

By the late 1950s many observers had become convinced that the loyalty program served partisan purposes, operating first to shake the Democrats' grip on power and then, after Eisenhower took office, to get rid of the Truman administration "holdovers." Vice President Nixon's inflated election-year claim about dismissals of subversive Truman appointees is an example. Television journalist Ed Murrow believed that the Republicans put up with McCarthy as long as they did because his crusade opened up civil service jobs for Republicans. Walter Salant of the Council of Economic Advisers believed that a 1953 attack by Representative John Taber (R-N.Y.) on alleged subversives at the council was a ploy to clear out Democrats.[112] There was much truth to this charge, and the injustice of it lent further impetus to reform. However, the emphasis on the damage to liberal Democrats has obscured the devastating effect of the loyalty program on socialists.

Like women, Socialist Party members rarely protested the program's bias against them. Few loyalty defendants admitted to socialist views and asserted their right to them. The most common response was to obscure one's socialism from investigators or, if that was impossible, to call it a thing of the past, a product of a bygone era since rendered obsolete by world events. Another tactic was to remind investigators that the Socialist Party had been among the earliest critics of the Communist Party. Some defendants brought in respected socialists like Norman Thomas or former socialists like James Carey of the CIO or Representative Andrew Biemiller (D-Wis.) to make this point. But few if any defendants defended socialism as a legitimate political viewpoint, much less as good public policy. Lucy Kramer Cohen's reply to her interrogatory defended her membership in the socialist League for Industrial Democracy without using the word "socialist."[113] When Norman Thomas wrote to the Johnston Committee in 1955 to offer suggestions for reforming the program, he focused on general civil liberties principles and did not mention the right of socialists to hold public office.[114]

Thus, the anti-McCarthyite network that emerged in the early 1950s and began to gain the upper hand in the late 1950s succeeded by dramatizing how the loyalty program punished harmless "little people" in nonsensitive positions, discriminated against Jews and blacks (and gays, they added later), discouraged civic involvement, and served as a partisan tool for replacing Democrats with Republicans. However, the anti-anticommunists ignored the program's shoring up of the gender hierarchy and its stigmatizing of socialist views. The loyalty program was a powerful force in the suppression of a left-feminist perspective that had been widespread among a talented cohort of idealistic women and men who entered government service in the 1930s and early 1940s.

A LONG SHADOW

Several developments after 1954 contributed to changes that curtailed the worst abuses of the loyalty program. The end of the Korean War and the censure of Senator McCarthy made it easier to challenge Red-baiters, and the composition of the Supreme Court changed as four conservative justices were replaced between 1953 and 1957. In 1955 and 1956, the Supreme Court ruled that the loyalty program's jurisdiction was limited to government employees in sensitive positions. In two cases decided in 1959, the Court restricted the use of anonymous informants, providing defendants with the right to confront their accusers.[115]

By the early 1960s, lawyers and security officials widely agreed that the loyalty program had been reined in. One official estimated in 1962 that 90 percent of the people who had been dismissed on loyalty grounds back in the early 1950s would have been cleared under the same circumstances in 1962. However, the damage took a long time to reverse. The civil service suffered a sharp and enduring decline in the applicant pool.[116] Perhaps even more significant, however, was the damage done to those who had been marked indelibly during the program's heyday.

It cannot be stressed enough that once charged, it was virtually impossible for a defendant to put the matter to rest permanently.[117] "You can never get cleared," an economist told the Johnston Committee in 1955.

Esther Brunauer put it best: "Under such a system of jurisprudence no one is ever acquitted. To be sure, some employees are cleared and return to their jobs, but they know full well that the sword of Damocles hangs over them. They are out on parole but . . . the suspension notice will come, and the whole tragic farce will be started over again. And the farce is conducted with all the trappings of legality."[118]

The defendants' fears that their cases would never be closed were not paranoid. The ideologues and opportunists on the right watched and waited for their chance to revive old allegations. During the Kennedy administration, SISS staff member Benjamin Mandel tried to stir up renewed interest in the cases against Health, Education, and Welfare official Wilbur Cohen and Mary Dublin Keyserling, among others.[119] The loyalty program expert Adam Yarmolinsky became an adviser to President Johnson, helped draft legislation authorizing the War on Poverty, and was expected to become Sargent Shriver's deputy in administering the program. But Johnson dropped Yarmolinsky after southern Democrats protested that he was a subversive.[120]

The stakes in the contest over the public memory of former loyalty defendants were high. In 1958, three years after the death of Mary McLeod Bethune, FBI agents attended a play about her, presumably to look for Communist influence in the play or in the audience. In 1960 FBI officials considered sabotaging an effort to create a memorial to Bethune. Cooler heads decided not to interfere, pointing out that, after all, "she was not a Communist and she is dead."[121] The absurdity of such efforts was no joke, however, to loyalty defendants trying to sustain or resurrect careers.

By the time that the loyalty program had been curbed, publishers had no interest in manuscripts on its human costs. Eleanor Bontecou drafted a book that featured a dozen compelling cases, but she could not find a publisher. One editor told her the book's "commercial possibilities seem severely limited," while another said "the time has gone by for a book on this subject."[122] Jacob Fisher was told that his book manuscript "said too much, too late."[123] For those few willing to talk, it seemed there was no one who wanted to listen. Most former loyalty defendants preferred to try to forget.

CHAPTER 7

Loyalty Investigations and the "End of Reform"

Although many loyalty defendants were forced out of government, others sustained or later resurrected government careers, and some did so by repositioning themselves rightward on the political spectrum. They remained committed to social reform, but they tried to protect themselves by avoiding criticism of capitalism and reframing their proposals in the language of anticommunism.

Those shifts were subtle, but they were not merely rhetorical; they had policy consequences. Discussions of the loyalty program's policy impact have centered on the legacy of the purge of the State Department's "China hands" or on the defeat of national health insurance.[1] But other policies similarly were blocked or narrowed after loyalty allegations undermined their leading advocates inside government. Direct repression of progressive policymakers was hardly the only force that stifled and stigmatized social democracy in the United States. The accumulated evidence from many cases across many fields, however, indicates that the loyalty program had pervasive effects.

Untold numbers of top and midlevel officials found their influence reduced by allegations of disloyalty, and we will never know all their names because most of the case files have been destroyed (see appendix 1). To demonstrate the general pattern, this chapter presents a succession of examples from diverse policy areas: Paul R. Porter, Thomas Blaisdell, and Lewis Lorwin, economists whose international aid and planning expertise influenced the Marshall Plan; Felix Cohen, Lucy Kramer, and Charlotte Tuttle Westwood Lloyd, who helped design and implement the "Indian New Deal"; David Demarest Lloyd, a lawyer for several New Deal agencies and then a Democratic Party speechwriter and aide to President Truman; Frieda Miller, Esther Peterson, Caroline Ware, and Pauli Murray, all advocates of workplace democracy, including equal opportunity for women and minorities; Catherine Bauer in public housing; Bernice Lotwin Bernstein, Wilbur Cohen, and Elizabeth Wickenden in social insurance and public assistance; and John Carmody and Tex Goldschmidt in public works and power.

By forcing these and many other leftists either out of the policymaking arena or toward the political center, the loyalty program silenced discussion of the antidemocratic tendencies of capitalism, thereby forestalling the development of policies to mitigate those tendencies. Left-leaning New Dealers had advocated measures designed to expand political democracy by regulating the economy, which they understood to require an integrated system of policies for maintaining mass purchasing power against the structural pressure to increase profits by raising prices or reducing labor costs. Sensitive to how industrialization had increased the interdependence not only of individuals but also of nations, some of these civil servants tried to implement similar policies on an international scale, through multilateral organizations and generous U.S. aid programs. But that coherent set of policies never emerged. The reforms achieved during the postwar decades were limited and piecemeal. The right used disloyalty charges not simply to discredit Democratic administrations as soft on communism and espionage—although that was a major objective, especially in election years—but also to block policy initiatives that impinged on American business prerogatives at home and abroad.

The connection between disloyalty charges and the shift toward the political center, or out of government service, by many public officials has been difficult to discern because of the silence that loyalty defendants maintained, even many years later. As they organized papers, gave interviews, and drafted memoirs, they typically avoided disclosing that they had been investigated and downplayed the leftism that had put them in the line of fire. Leon and Mary Dublin Keyserling were not the only former loyalty defendants to offer accounts that were distorted by an accumulation of omissions. They are not to blame for trying to protect themselves and their associates from further persecution. The point of documenting their omissions is not to expose or condemn them but rather to substantiate the existence of a pattern that has warped the historical record. In addition to impeding progressive reform, policymakers' traumatic encounters with the federal employee loyalty program impoverished the primary sources on which scholars have relied to understand mid-twentieth-century American politics.

"A World New Deal"

The years from about 1944 to 1950 saw a terrific struggle within the United States between competing visions of the postwar world. The fragile U.S.-Soviet alliance crumbled, and the structures of imperial domination were disintegrating. At this critical juncture, a group of left-internationalist civil servants strove to translate into U.S. foreign policy the social democratic vision they had tried to implement through the New Deal. "All of the best people are rapidly deserting the home front for foreign fields," Caroline Ware observed to a friend in late 1943. "Those of us who are still battling for life, liberty, and democracy at home are getting lonely. It's a great temptation to join the throng. For all the effect any of my efforts yield, I think I might just as well!"[2] Many of these experts who moved from New Deal planning, labor, and social welfare agencies to programs for international relief and reconstruction had undertaken comparative research and attended conferences abroad, and their cosmopolitan perspective helped equip them for working in international groups.[3] They argued that, in the long run, democracy would be served best by promoting international economic planning and development aid for projects such as public power, public health, and even women's emancipation. Critical of both capitalism and communism, these American civil servants tried to strengthen the international prospects for social democracy through initiatives in Europe and in less-developed countries. The battle over foreign aid and collective security policy during the Truman administration often is described as a clash between liberal international capitalists and conservative nationalist ones. However, the internationalist camp usually celebrated by liberal scholars and criticized by New Left historians included many leftists, until they were forced out or toward the right under pressure of investigation.[4]

The repression that truncated these left internationalists' careers and delegitimized their policy proposals coincided with the militarization of the Cold War—indeed, Leon Keyserling seems to have tried to save himself by supporting that militarization—soon followed by the triumph under President Eisenhower of the "Trade Not Aid" approach. The pressure of competition with the Soviet Union for the loyalties of Third World countries soon persuaded Eisenhower to abandon his resistance to providing foreign aid. The intensely anticommunist focus of the resulting U.S. aid programs, however, made them too narrow to be very effective in promoting economic development or democracy.[5] A decade earlier, some influential public servants had hoped for a different outcome.

During the Second World War, as the prospects for Allied victory improved, American leftists had high hopes for the U.S. role in the postwar reconstruction of Europe. They did not advertise them, though, because they did not want to add fuel to the right's nationalistic fires. Felix Cohen, the associate solicitor for the Department of the Interior, wrote privately in 1943 that postwar planning could advance socialist objectives, but only if it were couched in terms of American economic self-interest: "I am firmly convinced that we shall have to justify beneficent works in Europe by applying bad names to the work we shall be doing." Leftists would succeed politically, he continued, only if they could "clear good deeds of the taint of altruism and charity"—for example, by casting aid to Europe as a way to beat Britain to world markets.[6] Cohen would have found backward the New Left interpretation that the drive for markets was the hidden motivation behind the window dressing of idealistic rhetoric about saving democracy.[7] If Cohen's brand of internationalism was no capitalist plot, it also was not a Communist one. An influential Socialist Party member, Cohen was an early critic of the Communist Party. Whereas conservatives believed, or pretended to believe, that strengthening socialist governments in Europe would serve Communist objectives, the left-leaning policymakers they were denouncing believed that democratic socialism would be the strongest bulwark against Communist domination of Europe.

The ideological disagreement over the proper American role in the postwar world manifested itself early in debates over the United Nations Relief and Rehabilitation Administration (UNRRA). In 1943, before the United Nations itself was formed, forty-four countries approved the creation of UNRRA to provide relief to areas liberated from Axis powers. Senator Arthur Vandenberg (R-Mich.) complained that the original draft of the UNRRA agreement "pledged our total resources to whatever illimitable schemes for relief and rehabilitation all around the world our New Deal crystal gazers might desire to pursue." UNRRA indeed represented a transfer of responsibility for relief from the private to the public sector and as such "marked a further internationalization of New Deal–style problem-solving."[8]

UNRRA's concern with refugees and other victims of war attracted social scientists experienced in administering domestic programs directed at groups such as migrant agricultural workers, relocated war workers, Native Americans, and the unemployed. Many of these experts were leftists who a few years later would be called subversives. In addition to Mary Dublin Keyserling, examples include Lewis Lorwin, Charlotte Tuttle Lloyd, Catherine Maltby Blaisdell, and the labor journalist Mary Heaton Vorse.[9] Two Hearst journalists would charge, with typical hyperbole, that UNRRA was "a principal Communist apparatus" whose "Red membership was moved almost en masse to the payroll of the United Nations secretariat."[10]

There indeed was significant continuity in intention and personnel between UNRRA, the United Nations, and the early Marshall Plan, so conservatives were not entirely imagining things when they detected leftist fingerprints on all those initiatives. A cluster of progressive economists, many of whom had worked together in New Deal and wartime economic planning agencies, were involved in early plans for the United Nations and also helped design or implement the European Recovery Plan. The most important of these were Lewis Lorwin, Thomas Blaisdell, and Paul

R. Porter. Born in 1883, Lorwin was the oldest, and he contributed chiefly as an intellectual influence, authoring numerous books on labor and on international economic planning while employed by the Brookings Institution, the International Labor Office, and various U.S. agencies. Blaisdell worked for a long list of the New Deal's most innovative agencies before serving as chief of the Mission for Economic Affairs in wartime London and then assistant secretary of the Department of Commerce, from which position he helped design the Marshall Plan. Paul R. Porter was a labor advocate before he became Blaisdell's right-hand man in London, eventually succeeding him as chief of the Mission for Economic Affairs. Porter next was chief U.S. delegate to the Economic Commission for Europe and then a high-ranking administrator of the Marshall Plan, first in Greece and then Europewide. Despite their varying ages and backgrounds, these three men had much in common. All were serious intellectuals whose studies had led them to socialism. All were feminists, as evidenced by the causes they supported and the women they chose as wives, allies, and protégées. In the early 1950s, all were unfairly forced out of government by accusations of disloyalty. Finally, they all tried to bury the record of that painful experience. Their stories follow, along with those of two secondary examples, the agricultural economist Walter Packard and the international affairs specialist Rowena Rommel.

The eventual success and popularity of the European Recovery Plan, also called the Marshall Plan after Secretary of State George C. Marshall, makes it easy to forget how controversial it was in its day. Over four years beginning in April 1948, the program provided about $13 billion to participating European countries for use in rebuilding their economies, to be administered jointly by American officials and each cooperating government. From beginning to end, conservatives attacked the Marshall Plan as a burden on the U.S. economy and a boon to European socialism. The Communist Party opposed the Marshall Plan after the Soviets declined to participate, correctly discerning that one of its unstated objectives was to discourage Soviet expansion.[11] But the noncommunist left supported the Marshall Plan, and the right tried to discredit the whole program by blurring the distinction between Communists and other leftists. In March 1948 Congressman E. E. Cox (D-Ga.) charged that the European Recovery Plan had been conceived by individuals who "are or were Soviet sympathizers . . . were affiliated with Communist front organizations . . . are or were Socialists . . . [or] are or were believers in collectivism and a classless society." He named eight examples, including Lewis Lorwin and Thomas Blaisdell from the Commerce Department's Office of International Trade, and Tex Goldschmidt and Felix Cohen from the Department of the Interior. (Cox did not name Mary Dublin Keyserling, but investigators had already flagged her participation on one Marshall Plan committee as suspicious.) After charging the named individuals with a hodgepodge of allegedly subversive associations, Cox demanded an amendment limiting Marshall Plan executive personnel to "Americans who believe in our economic and political system and who always have believed in it."[12]

Lorwin became a focal point for congressional conservatives' resistance to the European Recovery Plan. Born in Kiev in 1883 and brought to the United States as a child, he had a varied career as a scholar and foreign correspondent before entering government service. In the 1930s and 1940s Lorwin emerged as a leading authority on international economic planning. In 1931 he was the principal speaker at the World Social and Economic Congress, convened in Amsterdam by Mary van Kleeck, an expert on women's employment and an advocate of planning as a solution to the Great Depression. Lorwin later claimed that his address, published as "A Five-Year Plan for the World," "outlined concrete suggestions for policies which two decades later were developed in the United Nations."[13] In 1934 he was a founder of the National Planning Association, and over the next dozen years he wrote several influential books while working as a consultant to many U.S. and UN agencies.[14]

Congressional opponents of the Marshall Plan tried to discredit it by linking it with Lorwin and in turn linking him with Russia and Mary van Kleeck, who in 1948 remained unapologetically sympathetic to the Soviet Union (association with the distinguished van Kleeck was used against dozens of civil servants who did not share her close ties to the Communist Party, as we saw in Dublin Keyserling's case). In December 1947, congressional staffers reported that an unnamed government official had "let it slip out that Lorwin was connected with the Marshall Plan." Investigators confirmed the tip by having a "white Russian . . . pretending to be a 'comrade'" telephone Lorwin, who "admitted" he helped draft the Marshall Plan.[15] Checking Lorwin's publications led congressional aides to his "Five-Year Plan for the World," which had proposed a system of world planning boards. In his March 1948 statement to the House, Congressman Cox quoted selectively from that article, in which Lorwin had stated: "Such planful control would undoubtedly have to limit the powers of individuals and corporations, and subject the making of profits to social ends." The congressman omitted the end of Lorwin's sentence: ". . . but such control would not eliminate individual and group initiative on a private basis."[16] Cox had been warned that "Lorwin's defense would likely be that he is a Socialist and not a Communist and he would rely on this explanation to try to make a member of Congress look foolish," so Cox tried to tie Lorwin to communism by stressing that he had been born in Russia as "Louis Levitski Levine." Cox thereafter referred to him as "Levine-Lorwin," not only conveying that he was Jewish but also insinuating that the name change was deceitful.[17]

Conservatives were not wrong about Lorwin's intellectual importance to the development of international planning, although they exaggerated his direct influence over the Marshall Plan. Lorwin's *Economic Consequences of the Second World War*, the last chapter of which was titled "A World New Deal," was called one of the five most important books of 1941.[18] Lorwin's critics were incorrect, however, to suggest there was anything antidemocratic about his proposals or his tactics. As a young man he had decided that Marxism's usefulness was limited by its historical determinism, and he was dismayed by Soviet authoritarianism. His investigation file held no compelling evidence of disloyalty even by the program's own nebulous standards.[19]

Congress approved the Marshall Plan, of course, albeit with an amendment stipulating that the administering agency, the Economic Cooperation Administration, could not employ anyone who had belonged to a Communist or Communist front organization.[20] Congressman Cox's attack on Lorwin and other drafters was chiefly a tactic by which conservatives gained some leverage over the Marshall Plan's details and fortified their portrayal of the Democrats as soft on communism. But for Lorwin and the others, the momentum of Cox's public allegations continued building long after the spotlight had moved on.[21] Herbert Parisius, another Office of International Trade official named by Cox, resigned in 1948. Lorwin "resigned after unfavorable agency action" in December 1951. Both insisted on their loyalty but said they were tired of fighting. When Lorwin was notified that the Commerce loyalty board had found "reasonable doubt" of his loyalty, he immediately appealed: "The Board is grievously in error. . . . The derogatory information in the case which has been made known to me is absurdly insubstantial." The next day, however, Lorwin dropped the appeal and resigned. "If only for the benefit of others who may be later similarly situated, I would prefer to continue to fight the case," he explained. "However, after fifteen months of effort, I no longer have the strength nor will I have the financial resources to carry on."[22]

Lorwin's forced exit cost the civil service a feminist, as well as a distinguished economist. Lorwin was married to Rose Strunsky, a feminist writer whose activities some informants had characterized as subversive. When questioned, Lorwin acknowledged his wife's "socialist views." Over the course of his career Lorwin had promoted women like the economist Jean Flexner, who wrote books with him at Brookings before joining the U.S. Bureau of Labor Standards, and Mary Dublin Keyserling, whom he recommended as special representative to Poland for the Foreign Economic Administration in 1944.[23] Not only did these women lose an ally, but investigators used Lorwin's resignation to cast doubt on his protégées. Lorwin's loyalty case also had repercussions for his son Val, a socialist historian who worked for the Departments of Labor and then State, and who served on various Marshall Plan committees.[24]

Lorwin wanted recognition for his contribution to the acceptance of international economic planning but not for his battle against charges of disloyalty. His voluminous archival papers contain nothing about his investigation except his resignation letter, and he tore off portions of some documents that identify them as part of his case file.[25] In 1961 Lorwin completed an oral history that ends without covering his postwar career. Only someone with independent knowledge of his loyalty case would find it significant that he read to his oral-history interviewer a passage from a 1933 newspaper clipping that described him addressing radicals who had marched on the White House: "last night the young men and women heard Lewis Lorwin of the Brookings Institution warn them against being too hasty about trying to stage revolutions."[26] Lorwin wanted to emphasize for the historical record that he was never a revolutionary. In 1967, he wrote a thoughtful memoir of sorts in the form of a long letter to a grandson who had asked about his "philosophy of life." After summarizing the evolution of his belief that democratic social-economic planning was the best means to achieve "adequate living conditions for all, racial and political cooperation, and international good-will and peace," Lorwin predicted that progress would come not from the "utopian" New Left but from the "pragmatic idealists" among America's youth.[27] If Lorwin had not borne scars from his associations with the Old Left, would he have felt the need to warn his grandson away from the New Left? Lorwin's silence about his loyalty trials compounds the difficulty of the question.

Thomas Blaisdell, dubbed the Marshall Plan's "earliest prophet" by his junior colleague Paul Porter, like Lorwin was forced to resign as a result of disloyalty allegations and like Lorwin did not leave records of that experience.[28] Born in Pennsylvania in 1895, Blaisdell was more experienced than many of the other, better-known New Dealers recruited from academia. After college he taught history and studied land reform in India, wrote a master's thesis on British housing legislation, and taught social work and economics in Peking, where he also produced studies of child labor and trade unions in China. In 1932 he celebrated the completion of his Columbia economics dissertation on the Federal Trade Commission by touring the Soviet Union with his wife Catherine Maltby Blaisdell.[29]

Blaisdell's wide-ranging expertise made him a significant player at a succession of New Deal agencies. Brought into the Agricultural Adjustment Administration in 1933 by his Columbia professor Rexford Tugwell, Blaisdell soon was deemed "the most respected economic mind" at the agency.[30] He was an early ally of the consumer movement, first from Agriculture's Office of the Consumer Counsel and then from the Consumers' Advisory Board of the National Recovery Administration, in which capacity he forged lifelong friendships with Caroline Ware and her husband Gardiner Means (with whom Blaisdell shared a house before Ware moved to Washington). Blaisdell's other close colleagues included Mordecai Ezekiel, Leon Henderson, Jerome Frank, and Isador Lubin, all of whom too would face allegations of disloyalty triggered by conflicts with powerful private interests. Blaisdell directed statistical research for the Social Security Board, analyzed the problem of monopoly for the Securities and Exchange Commission and the Temporary National Economic Committee, and headed the research division of the National Resources Planning Board, where he hired Eveline Burns to author the controversial proposal for an expanded welfare state that became known as the "American Beveridge Plan." After distinguishing himself at the War Production Board and the Office of War Mobilization and Reconversion, Blaisdell was dispatched to London as the chief of Mission for Economic Affairs, responsible for administering the Lend-Lease agreement with Great Britain and for representing the United States on a long list of international organizations including UNRRA. Returning to Washington as director of the Office of International Trade in Averell Harriman's Department of Commerce, Blaisdell was one of the key thinkers behind the development and promotion of the Marshall Plan, assisted by a staff that included Lewis Lorwin and Mary Dublin Keyserling.[31]

At the Office of International Trade Blaisdell also was responsible for export control, and in that role he made enemies. At least one of them charged that Blaisdell's administration of controls "worked to the advantage of world-wide communism" (Blaisdell later claimed he had "maintained those controls in the face of sharp criticism when they were the only hindrance to the shipment of strategic materials to the Iron Curtain countries").[32] It did not help Blaisdell that his wife had been active in the League of Women Shoppers and worked for two agencies loathed by the right, the Office of Civilian Defense and UNRRA. She also was a witness to the will of the environmentalist Robert Marshall, who had rented a room from the Blaisdells in the mid-1930s and whose fortune, administered by his brother George Marshall, funded many leftist causes. Rated eligible after investigation in 1943 and 1948, Blaisdell found his case reopened after he defended two controversial subordinates: William Remington, named as a spy by Elizabeth Bentley, and Michael Lee, a Manchurian-born economist under fire for his handling of export licenses to China. Further rousing the suspicion of investigators were his wife's associations as well as his own relationships with Lorwin, Dublin Keyserling, and Caroline Ware. Although no witnesses called him a Communist and many witnesses attested to his dislike of the Communist Party, examiners remained unconvinced of his loyalty to the United States. Blaisdell resigned in October 1951 before his case was resolved, which meant that his name was flagged in case he tried to return to government service later. When Blaisdell applied for a United Nations job in 1955, he faced an interrogatory about the same allegations. After a long wait, he withdrew the application and finished his career in academia.[33]

It appears that investigators never discovered that Blaisdell was active in the Socialist Party while an economics instructor at Columbia in the early 1930s. Unsurprisingly, he did not volunteer that information.[34] When Blaisdell deposited his papers at the Truman Library, he did not include materials about his investigation or about his youthful socialism, and his 1971 oral history also is silent on those subjects.[35] For thirty years after the Truman Library Institute was created in 1957, Blaisdell served on its board of directors, which suggests both his loyalty to the legacy of the president who had defended him and his awareness of the importance of the historical records—qualities that may have ended up at odds.

Paul R. Porter probably would be more widely known had loyalty allegations not forced him out of government at the height of his career. Not only did he himself drop out of public sight, but also the sources that he shaped are silent on the circumstances leading to his resignation. Born in 1908 in Missouri, Porter was a member of the Socialist Party from 1928 until 1941, during which period he served as field secretary of the League for Industrial Democracy, editor of a labor newspaper in Wisconsin, and member of the SP Executive Committee. After briefly dating Mary Dublin, in 1933 he married labor activist Eleanor Nelson at a wedding presided over by the prominent socialist author Upton Sinclair. Porter and Nelson became estranged after she joined the Communist Party, and in 1940 Porter remarried, to Hilda Roberts, a Wisconsin native who worked for the CIO. His printing plant published *The Call*, the SP's official newspaper, and he was a close adviser to SP leader Norman Thomas despite their growing disagreement over whether U.S. aid to the Allies would advance or retard the cause of international socialism. Both Porter and Thomas were intensely anticommunist by 1940, but Thomas feared that U.S. aid would strengthen imperialism abroad and foster militarism and hysteria at home. Porter argued that a fascist takeover of Europe would be even more crushing to the left than Allied imperialism. The conflict led to Porter's public resignation from the SP in early 1941. He soon entered government service as a labor adviser to a succession of war production agencies.[36]

After the Dies Committee called him a "Red" in 1943, Porter told Civil Service Commission examiners that he was a socialist. Because of the common misunderstanding of the term, he explained, he preferred to call himself "a Social Democrat, or at least a Democratic Socialist, to distinguish from the Russian variety. I hold these views because I consider them to be sound public policy." In 1943 a civil servant might still offer an affirmative defense of socialism. Porter likened his views to those of the British deputy prime minister Clement Attlee and the governments of Sweden, New Zealand, and Australia. He also argued that the United States already was socialist in some respects, in that it had enlarged the area of public enterprise to include schools, roads, and—he added pointedly—investigation of potential subversives. The CSC cleared Porter, on the grounds that his anticommunism was well established and his socialism was "irrelevant." After all, the examiner commented, it was "entirely legal to advocate a change in government through constitutional methods."[37]

Over the next decade Porter remained an anticommunist socialist as he distinguished himself at the War Production Board and then in the postwar reconstruction of Europe. As Blaisdell's deputy at the U.S. Mission for Economic Affairs in London, Porter was an early advocate of generous U.S. aid to Europe, cooperating behind the scenes with the State Department to overcome congressional resistance. Blaisdell reportedly gave Porter "free rein," and Porter took over as mission chief.[38] From London, Porter corresponded with American SP leaders about the prospects of European labor and socialist parties. In 1946 he wrote, "It is too early to state when and how the LSI [Labor and Socialist International] will be revived. . . . I have a feeling that the [British] Labour Party . . . is prepared to give a vigorous lead to rebuilding social democracy on the Continent." In admiring the British foreign secretary Ernest Bevin, the anticommunist Labour Party leader, Porter noted with satisfaction that "some of the people who have thought that it would be possible to collaborate with the Russians have had quite a jolt in the last several months."[39]

An opponent of deindustrializing Germany, Porter believed that political democracy in Europe depended on economic recovery, which in turn would require integration of European economies. Reporting on a London visit by the leader of the German Social Democrats, Porter applauded him for reaching out to the British and for "discarding a considerable amount of Marxist baggage and . . . laying much greater emphasis on the humanist side of their program." Porter continued, "whether or not they will be able to succeed will depend in large measure upon whether or not the U.S. occupation authorities will permit socialization."[40] Porter remained a socialist but began to focus more on the need for Europewide economic planning than on increasing the degree of public ownership within individual countries. "I have not changed the basic philosophy I acquired in the LID," he explained to Thomas in 1947, but he thought

socialists needed more appreciation of the dangers of economic nationalism and of the need for planning on a continental scale.[41]

Porter had a significant but underappreciated role in the creation of
the Marshall Plan. Undersecretary of State Will Clayton has been called
the plan's "intellectual architect," but Clayton relied heavily on Porter, the
"star economist" in Clayton's Economic Affairs group. A Houston cotton broker, Clayton is credited with promoting European economic integration through reduced tariffs.[42] From a different place on the political
spectrum, however, Porter long had advocated economic integration—
meaning not just free trade but coordinated planning—as the only way
by which European labor and social democratic governments could pros-
per and prevent Russian domination of Eastern Europe. As Porter later
described it, Clayton was much more interested in the General Agreement on Tariffs and Trade negotiations than in the Economic Commission for Europe, so he gave Porter "a free hand" in the latter arena. Like
Thomas Blaisdell, Porter believed the Marshall Plan should have been
implemented at least a year earlier and regretted the delay imposed by
congressional conservatives.[43]

Thus, the Marshall Plan initially was a vehicle for the hopes of noncommunist leftists, among others.[44] That changed after the Korean War
began in mid-1950. "In retrospect more than at the time it happened, I
recognize how profoundly the Korean War changed the goals and the
character of the ECA [Economic Cooperation Administration]," Paul
Porter recalled. "We were like a peacetime factory converted to defense
production."[45] It has been argued that the Marshall Plan "employed U.S.
capital and a free-market ideology to prop up socialist regimes, in the
name of saving them from Communism."[46] But not all the U.S. policymakers who pushed for a generous European Recovery Plan saw aiding
European socialism merely as a distasteful and temporary necessity to
block communism; some sought to improve the outlook for democratic
socialism in the United States. Congressman Cox and other conservatives
were not entirely wrong when they complained that the Marshall Plan
might become "largely a scheme through which socialism will be subsidized in Europe. . . . Such a situation could easily develop if American Socialists were placed in charge."[47] But conservatives were unfair to ignore
the anticommunism of many leftists and to claim that their internationalist projects were products of a Communist conspiracy.

In 1949, while chief U.S. delegate, Economic Commission for Europe,
Porter was investigated by the State Department loyalty board. By the
time he was cleared, he had been appointed chief of the ECA Mission to
Greece. He left State to take the new job before the central Loyalty Review Board had "post-audited" his clearance, which meant that his case
was "flagged" as unresolved: he would not be able to return to a U.S.

agency without reinvestigation. In 1950, the ex-Communist informant Paul Crouch began trying to get the attention of congressional anticommunists by naming Porter, along with the Keyserlings and J. Robert Oppenheimer, as important government officials to whom Communists had access. In October 1952, as discussed in chapter 4, Leon Keyserling mentioned in a closed SISS hearing that Porter, by then the European director for the Mutual Security Agency (MSA), was a member of the LID. Keyserling's testimony gave Senator Homer Ferguson an excuse to embarrass Truman on the eve of the election by airing Porter's socialist record and demanding his resignation. In an MSA press release, Porter responded by stressing his work against communism in Europe and explaining that he had left the Socialist Party in 1941. "In due course I ceased to hold socialist views," he added vaguely. Despite an outpouring of support from distinguished labor and business representatives, Porter was forced to resign in June 1953. Publicly he claimed he had resigned for personal reasons, such as that his government salary would not put four children through school, but allegations of leftism clearly were a factor in his exit.[48]

That chapter was not the final one. Porter started his own international business but sold it in 1967 after suffering a stroke. In 1968, he applied for the position of special assistant to the director of the Bureau of International Commerce, which required an update to his investigation file. The Commerce Department rated him eligible after sympathetic witnesses explained that Porter was no longer at all radical and that he strongly supported U.S. policy in Vietnam. Porter did not become conservative. He maintained his contacts with the League for Industrial Democracy and wrote a book recommending a Marshall Plan for American inner cities. However, being Red-baited out of government intensified Porter's need to prove his anticommunism, cutting him off from the young leftists who opposed U.S. policy in Vietnam.[49]

Given this protracted experience, it is not surprising that in a 1971 interview Porter declined to discuss his loyalty troubles. Then and in a later essay about his role in the Marshall Plan, Porter repeatedly downplayed his conflicts with American businessmen and congressional conservatives. Instead he foregrounded his own anticommunism. There is no doubt that Porter was an early and vociferous critic of Soviet communism; the point is that after he was attacked as a subversive, Porter retroactively made anticommunism the sole theme of his career.[50]

Porter's handling of his private papers underscores that point. In the 1970s and 1980s, he organized his papers into six series for the Truman Library but deposited only three series.[51] The arrangement of those three groups of papers highlights his anticommunist efforts in Europe: his work to revive free trade unions to prevent Communist control of the labor movement; his contribution in Greece to programs that undercut

Communist guerrillas; and his opposition to the Morgenthau proposal to disable German industry. Porter deposited no materials related to his socialist career or his loyalty investigations. The biographical profile that accompanies his archival collection omits his first marriage to the Communist activist Eleanor Nelson, as well as his work for the League for Industrial Democracy and Socialist Party. Porter probably would not have made these omissions had he not been scarred by successive accusations that culminated in his exit from a stellar government career at the age of forty-five.[52]

Walter Packard, a colleague of Porter's at the ECA in Greece, was another leftist who after facing loyalty charges felt the need to present himself first and foremost as an anticommunist. An Iowa-bred agricultural expert on irrigation and public power who studied and then taught at the University of California at Berkeley, Packard worked for a succession of progressive New Deal agencies, including the Resettlement Administration and the Farm Security Agency. Then and later, he joined forces with women such as Helen Gahagan Douglas, Catherine Bauer, and the labor reformer and state relief administrator Florence Wyckoff, all of whom shared his interest in challenging California's powerful growers on issues from water use to housing to labor.[53] From 1945 to 1948 Packard continued to advance the interests of small farmers as a land consultant to Rexford Tugwell, who was then governor of Puerto Rico. Next he went to Greece, first as irrigation specialist for the American Mission for Aid to Greece, and then as chief of land reclamation for the ECA.

In Greece, Packard angered American utility companies by blocking certain lucrative private contracts. He soon was confronted with loyalty charges, and he believed the timing was no coincidence.[54] He fought off the attack in 1949, but apparently that was not the end of it. After he resigned in 1954, the State Department restricted his passport. Packard was furious, but he chose to keep the matter quiet. In June 1955 he appeared on Ed Murrow's *See It Now* TV program. Packard emphasized to Murrow that his successful public power project in Greece represented an advance for democracy because it alleviated the poverty that caused people to turn to communism. Viewers unaware of the context—Packard's defensiveness after being attacked for promoting public power—would have come away with the impression that preventing communism was the sole objective of ECA policy. People like Porter and Packard did want to prevent the spread of communism, but above all they sought to promote social democracy, not free-market capitalism. Packard's counsel Abe Fortas wrote him after seeing the program: "Perhaps the rest of the story ought to be made public: the outrageous experience to which you have been subjected, and the absurd action of the State Department in giving you a limited passport." Despite Fortas's urging, Packard never did tell the story. No government file on his case has survived, so the specifics may never be known.[55]

After the Marshall Plan's success enhanced its popularity with American voters, the United Nations became a softer target for conservative resentment. The fact that American employees of the United Nations initially were exempt from the federal employee loyalty program enabled the right to charge that UN agencies were a safe haven for subversives. The UN Charter technically prevented the secretary-general from receiving instructions from any government, and successive secretaries-general publicly protested American interference. Privately, however, they assented to U.S. screening of American applicants for UN jobs. In 1949, Senator McCarran launched a campaign to convince Americans that Communists had infiltrated the United Nations. In 1951 a New York grand jury began investigating; in 1952 SISS undertook its own investigation. Under pressure, UN secretary-general Trygve Lie dismissed about forty-five employees, most of them Americans in professional jobs. Nineteen of them appealed to the UN Tribunal, which reinstated twelve with back pay. Outraged American legislators threatened to cut off UN appropriations, which would have eliminated about 40 percent of the UN budget. In 1953, Presidents Truman and Eisenhower responded to this pressure by closing the perceived escape hatch for leftist civil servants. The resulting International Organizations Employee Loyalty Board was to investigate all current professional-level American employees as well as new applicants. The IOELB technically did not have the power to dismiss, but most UN agencies abided by its advisory opinions. By the end of 1954, after holding hearings in Rome and Paris, the IOELB had investigated almost four thousand American employees of international organizations.[56]

Of the more than forty UN agencies, the United Nations Educational, Scientific and Cultural Organization (UNESCO) came under the closest scrutiny. Founded in 1945, UNESCO sought to promote world peace by fostering intellectual and cultural exchanges among participating nations. UNESCO's origin in a commission of the League of Nations did not endear it to American isolationists. Neither did its bold statements against racism, nor its employment of many professional women. One of McCarthy's lead examples in his opening gambit in 1950, as we have seen, was State Department employee Esther Brunauer, who had helped create UNESCO and represented the United States at many of its conferences.[57] In 1954, the IOELB issued adverse opinions on eight employees (five of them women, and some of whom had been Communist Party members). Most of them refused to appear for their IOELB hearings in Paris, on the principle that the IOELB violated the UN Charter. The American head of UNESCO dismissed some but said he lacked the authority to fire others. Far from mollified by the IOELB's efforts, SISS held its feet to the fire for not somehow forcing UNESCO to follow its dismissal recommendations.[58]

Rowena Rommel was another McCarthy target who moved from State to UNESCO. Hailed back in 1944 as an example of talented women climbing the ranks of the civil service, Rommel became an international affairs analyst "because of firm convictions on her part for peace and a sincere conviction that the United States does not follow or approve the theory of colonization." Her competence and work ethic won applause from her colleagues at the State Department, but apparently she also made an enemy, who in turn made a connection on Capitol Hill. In 1948 Congressman Fred Busbey (R-Ill.) portrayed Rommel as "one of the cleverest, most sinister figures in the entire State Department set-up," allegedly responsible for inflating State's budget, reorganizing its administrative functions, and stacking its personnel with "Russia-firsters."[59] The State loyalty board cleared her after hearings in 1948 and 1950, but before the central loyalty board approved the latter clearance, Rommel took a position with UNESCO in Paris. In 1953 she appeared twice before the IOELB, which finally rated her eligible; SISS staffers later grilled the IOELB chair for having made that decision.[60]

There was no evidence of subversive activity by Rommel. The "derogatory information" related to her workplace associations with alleged spies Robert T. Miller, Alger Hiss, and Owen Lattimore, and she explained them fully. Rommel's file suggests that charges against her stemmed from an internal rival's resentment of her ability and progressive views, combined with politicians' recognition of an opportunity to embarrass the State Department by implying that a woman was in charge. (In grumbling that Rommel "had no particular skill" and yet made a high salary, Congressman Busbey typified conservatives' appeal to prejudice against women in high places.) State Department officials described Rommel to the FBI as someone with "complete integrity," who demonstrated "tremendous enthusiasm and leadership in working out the early Point Four programs." Some hinted at why she might have detractors: one colleague explained that Rommel had "antagonized some high officials because of her boldly stated convictions" against colonization. Another former supervisor explained that Rommel favored "the improvement of race relations" as well as "a broad construction of Point Four which would include an interest in improving the health of the people of foreign lands as well as their industry." Then there was Rommel's assumption of gender equality; she was appalled when her UNESCO boss resisted appointing women to the highest ranks. Finally, Rommel had the audacity to question the loyalty program. She protested the summary dismissal of colleagues on loyalty charges, and she joined the leftist Washington

Bookshop cooperative expressly to protest its inclusion on the Attorney General's List of Subversive Organizations. Rommel was a left feminist—and, incidentally, divorced and Ivy-League educated—but she was not a spy. The FBI's ex-Communist informants had never heard of her, and the dearth of derogatory evidence gave the IOELB little choice but to clear her.[61] To congressional conservatives, however, the defiant Rommel represented all that was wrong with the State Department, and with the civil service in general.

The congressional anger and media publicity surrounding UN employees' resistance to U.S. loyalty screening put enormous pressure on the IOELB, which responded by intensifying its scrutiny of American applicants to the United Nations. Many senior-level former New Dealers were affected. Between late 1953 and early 1955, among the hundreds who prepared replies to interrogatories, in some cases traveled to hearings, and waited months for an IOELB ruling were the social security expert Wilbur Cohen, women's labor expert Frieda Miller, social scientist Caroline Ware, and public power advocate Tex Goldschmidt. Another was Mordecai Ezekiel, who had been a top agricultural policy adviser to President Roosevelt before he joined the United Nations' Food and Agriculture Organization. Investigators had been watching him and his wife closely since 1942, and the expansion of the loyalty program in 1947 may have contributed to his move to the United Nations. Ezekiel was cleared in 1955, but only after an agonizing and disruptive sixteen-month wait.[62]

In short, some American leftists played a significant role in developing and implementing postwar reconstruction plans in Europe; conservatives responded by attacking them and their policies as friendly to communism, which they were not. As Isador Lubin, who was involved with the Marshall Plan and the United Nations and who had his own run-in with the loyalty program, commented in 1957: "In this international business, if you attempt to do anything which may be interpreted in any way as hurting anybody in the business field, your life isn't worth anything. They will just crucify you."[63] Scarred by accusations of disloyalty, a cohort of social democratic internationalists edged away from the left. They often also avoided documenting their earlier views and the resulting investigations, thereby impeding comprehension of their policy objectives—and of the weapons that defeated them.

NATIVE AMERICAN AFFAIRS

Felix Cohen and his wife Lucy Kramer had a significant impact on policy affecting Native Americans during and after the New Deal, and their left feminism informed their dedication to the Native American cause.

Despite his early criticism of the Communist Party, congressional conservatives Red-baited Felix, and loyalty charges kept Lucy on the defensive and for a time out of government. The accusations were so traumatic for her that, after his death in 1953, she elided their decades of Socialist Party activism from the record. As a result scholars have underestimated the influence of socialist ideas on federal Indian policy and also how loyalty charges weakened some dedicated advocates of Native American rights.

In the early 1930s, Cohen and Kramer moved in the same circle of young LID socialists as Paul Porter, Tom Blaisdell, Mary Dublin, and Charlotte Tuttle.[64] After distinguishing himself at Columbia Law School, Cohen joined the Department of the Interior in 1933. Over the next fourteen years, as assistant and then associate solicitor, he worked on diverse issues whose common theme was group rights to self-determination. He drafted proposals and bills on the settlement of Jewish refugees in Alaska, the governance of Puerto Rico and other territories, and employment discrimination, for example.[65] He also represented the Department of the Interior on a Marshall Plan drafting committee, in which capacity Congressman Cox named him as evidence of that plan's un-American intentions, as we have seen. Cohen hardly saw himself as un-American; he argued that the ideals of the American Revolution and the legal order created by the Constitution justified and provided the means for a democratic transition from capitalism to socialism.[66]

Cohen is best known for his contributions to the Indian New Deal. He knew little about Native American policy when he entered government service, but his wife was an anthropologist who had studied Native American cultures. With her assistance, Cohen drafted an early version of the Indian Reorganization Act of 1934 (IRA). When Congress weakened the bill's provisions for Native American cultural development and self-determination, Cohen threatened to resign. Despite its flaws, the IRA reversed the direction of federal policy, which since the 1880s had sought to forcibly assimilate Indians by privatizing land ownership and reducing tribal authority. Not all Native communities voted to adopt the IRA, but that they were able to choose was itself a remarkable departure from precedent.[67] Another major project of Cohen's employed a large team, including his wife, to survey treaties, statutes, and court rulings related to Indian law over the course of the centuries. The resulting six-volume *Handbook of Federal Indian Law* (1941) antagonized the Justice Department by strengthening Native American land claims. Cohen then helped establish the Indian Claims Commission, which created a process by which tribes could obtain compensation for broken federal treaties.[68]

Cohen's attraction to democratic socialism reflected his prioritization of the rights of minorities, whether Jews, African Americans, or Native Americans. With respect to the latter, he wrote to Norman Thomas in

1933 that "the central problem today in the administration of Indian affairs [is] whether capitalist individualism is to be forced on the Indians, through the allotment of tribal property to individual Indians and through the inculcation of the capitalist psychology, or whether a communal economy is to be protected and encouraged."[69] In subsequent years, his support of the latter objective put Cohen in bitter conflict with the Justice Department and with congressional conservatives. He never yielded, insisting that the American Indian "is to America what the Jew was to the Russian czars and Hitler's Germany. For us the Indian tribe is the miners' canary, and when it flutters and droops we know that the poison gasses of intolerance threaten all other minorities in our land."[70]

The views of Felix Cohen and Lucy Kramer brought them into conflict with American Communists, too. In 1940 Cohen resigned from the National Executive Board of the National Lawyers' Guild because of a disagreement over Communist influence in the organization. He explained that he had "long believed that communism and fascism are united [in the belief that] the ends justify the means," even including lying and assassination. He argued that the means are more important than the ends, because social change is a process and "we are living the means, not the end." That same year, the couple founded the Institute for Living Law to study and recommend solutions for diverse social problems. In a statement unusual at the time for its explicit feminism, the institute declared its opposition to "all theories of race, religion, or sex which attempt to bar any group in law-making, law reform and effective legal criticism."[71] Meanwhile, Cohen and Kramer remained leading members of the Washington D.C. chapter of the Socialist Party until 1947, and Cohen drafted bills for the national SP on the condition that his contribution would remain anonymous. After Cohen was appointed to Interior's new loyalty appeals board in 1947, he resigned from the SP, but he remained a small s socialist.[72]

In December 1947 Cohen abruptly resigned from government service. He had many reasons for doing so—he was fighting an uphill battle on Indian rights, and he was bitter not to have been promoted to solicitor (despite Felix Frankfurter's intercession on his behalf) when Nathan Margold retired. But Felix Cohen's socialism, and that of his wife, contributed to his conflicts with Congress and to his superiors' decision not to promote him. Although the loyalty program did not directly force Cohen out of government, the declining tolerance for socialism that the loyalty program facilitated did undermine his efficacy and foster his departure.[73]

In his subsequent work as a private attorney representing certain Indian tribes in their claims against the government, Cohen sustained the battles he had waged as an insider. In 1950, Truman appointed Dillon Myer as commissioner of Indian affairs; Myer proceeded to replace

"Indian New Deal" veterans with his own former staff from the War Relocation Authority, which had overseen the internment of Japanese Americans. Cohen lost a series of vituperative skirmishes with Myer, whom he publicly compared to Hitler and Stalin. Myer in turn had the FBI investigate Cohen on the grounds that he had encouraged civil disobedience by the Blackfeet and also had profited personally from Indian claims. Cohen was exonerated, but the Indian New Deal was dead. In October 1953, so was Felix Cohen, killed by cancer at age forty-six.[74]

In addition to assisting her husband's work on Indian policy, Lucy Kramer pursued her own career in a series of government agencies from Interior to the War Labor Board to the Department of Labor. Kramer was gifted in statistics as well as anthropology. Her research assignments ranged from the diet of African American children to cost-of-living adjustments on collective bargaining agreements for the United Auto Workers. She also worked for Congresswoman Helen Gahagan Douglas (D-Calif.) and would have become the first female administrative assistant to a U.S. senator had Douglas defeated Richard Nixon in the 1950 election. Kramer was behind the dramatic 1947 speech in which Douglas wheeled a grocery cart onto the floor of the House and explained that as a result of conservatives' termination of price control, the cart's contents cost a third more than they had eight months earlier. Kramer was active in the League of Women Shoppers, and she convened the Capitol City Forum, a racially integrated group of Norman Thomas socialists who met weekly for lectures and discussion.[75]

Lucy Kramer's socialism, combined with her husband's prominence, drew the scrutiny of loyalty investigators. The Civil Service Commission required a full field investigation by the FBI before rating her eligible in 1946. After another full field investigation in 1950, she was required to answer an interrogatory. She was cleared yet again in 1952, but the next year, a few months before Felix's death, she was dismissed on reduction-in-force grounds. Kramer tried but was unable to obtain government work until 1958, when the Public Health Service hired her. She now was a widow supporting two children, and during those five years her search for employment grew increasingly desperate. Throughout the rounds of investigation, the allegations remained the same, chiefly involving membership in the LWS and LID as well as association with the allegedly Communist anthropologist Gene Weltfish.[76]

Kramer was a former loyalty defendant struggling to find government work during the very years that she was writing biographical sketches about her distinguished husband, organizing his papers for the archives, and selecting articles for a published volume of his writings. Her family's economic survival, as well as Felix Cohen's legacy, was at stake. In that context, it is understandable that she did not mention Cohen's decades of SP and LID involvement in the short biography that she wrote about him, and that she withheld from the archives several cartons of materials documenting the couple's engagement with leftist political and artistic circles from the late 1920s into the mid-1940s.[77] Like so many others, Kramer also kept secret that fact that she had been investigated. Two decades later, in an interview about Helen Gahagan Douglas, Kramer described how Douglas had helped Val Lorwin fight disloyalty charges, but she never mentioned that she herself had faced such charges and received support from Douglas. Even Kramer's daughters were unaware of her encounters with the loyalty program.[78]

For similar reasons, the Kramer-Cohens' dear friend Charlotte Lloyd too retroactively downplayed Felix's socialism. Interviewed in 2006 about her work with him at the Interior Department, she firmly denied that socialist thought had influenced the Indian New Deal.[79] It is not surprising that Charlotte Lloyd was protective of Cohen's legacy. At Columbia Law School he had been one of the few men who respected female classmates, and it was he who recruited her to Interior. Twenty years later he hired her to work in his private practice, and Charlotte was with Lucy at Felix's bedside when he died.[80]

FROM THE NEW DEAL TO THE TRUMAN WHITE HOUSE: CHARLOTTE AND DAVID DEMAREST LLOYD

Like Lucy Kramer, Charlotte Lloyd had her own concerns about the loyalty program, because much of her career was spent in government service. The activist-turned-author Joe Lash interviewed her about Felix Cohen in 1965, when she was a lawyer for the Treasury Department. Lash found her "so careful and remote that it was really a profitless affair. . . . But Lucy told me later that [Charlotte] had had difficulties with Treasury because of past activities and that was why she is so cautious."[81] Back in 1941, Lloyd received notice from the Department of the Interior that the FBI had investigated her and found nothing damaging. For the sake of her husband's career, she left government in 1948 and did not return until 1961, when she was hired by the Treasury Department and rapidly promoted to assistant general counsel. It does not appear that she faced any difficulty obtaining clearance at that point, but she would have known the FBI was interviewing her associates to update her file. No wonder she was careful when speaking with Joe Lash in 1965. In her early career she had worked on Indian welfare and then for UNRRA, but after her return to government in the 1960s, she wrote opinions on excise taxes and other less overtly charged topics.

If Charlotte Lloyd's encounter with the loyalty program was relatively minor, the experience of her second husband, David Demarest Lloyd, who became an administrative assistant to President Truman, was not. Both Lloyds were dedicated to labor and consumer causes. Charlotte had been interested in the challenges faced by wage-earning women since her undercover stint as a teenager in a Chicago factory. After her first marriage to student radical Howard Westwood ended in divorce, she married David, like herself a brilliant lawyer from a distinguished family. They met when Charlotte was vacationing in California and dropped in on a hearing on agricultural labor held by the La Follette Civil Liberties Committee, for which David was the assistant chief counsel. The zeal for social justice that had led Charlotte to spend her vacation at a labor hearing presumably was among the qualities that impressed David.[82]

Unlike his wife, David Lloyd never joined the Socialist Party, but his efforts to push the Roosevelt and Truman administrations leftward made him anathema to conservatives. David Lloyd's pro-labor work on the La Follette Committee, combined with his public support of left-feminist groups such as the League of Women Shoppers, earned him top billing on early lists of suspected subversives. He continued to irritate various corporate interests during stints with the Federal Communications Commission and the Office of Price Administration.[83] Between 1943 and 1946, he joined other left-leaning New Dealers at the Foreign Economic Administration and the Mission for Economic Affairs in London. From 1948 through early 1953, David Lloyd served on the White House staff, and in later years he remained an important adviser to the Democratic National Committee.

After loyalty procedures began to tighten in 1941, each time David Lloyd moved from one agency to another he faced questions about his own activities and those of his wife. Loyalty concerns apparently prevented him from obtaining a U.S. Navy Reserve commission in 1943 and then an UNRRA job under State Department auspices. Loyalty clearance difficulties may have influenced his 1947 decision to leave government to become director of research and legislation at the fledgling Americans for Democratic Action. The ADA sought to strengthen liberal forces within the Democratic Party while deflecting charges of "fellow-travelerism" by trumpeting its anticommunism. Lloyd drafted the ADA constitution, including the clause that barred Communists from membership. During the 1948 presidential campaign, Lloyd deployed his talents as a Democratic Party speechwriter and strategist. After Truman's surprise victory David Lloyd became one of his key White House aides—and, notwithstanding Lloyd's vocal anticommunism, a juicy target for right-wingers.[84]

With David now in the limelight, and given the questions raised about Charlotte during his prior loyalty screenings, the Lloyds decided it would be wise for her to play a less visible, more traditional role.[85] She left the workforce and concentrated her attention on their two children. Charlotte's departure from government did not succeed, however, in shielding her husband from attack. In February 1950, Senator McCarthy included David Lloyd in the short list of cases that he offered as proof that the Truman administration harbored subversives. Among McCarthy's charges were that Charlotte had belonged to Communist front groups and that David had criticized the prosecution of Alger Hiss. After seven months of further investigation, the White House loyalty board cleared David. Truman promptly promoted him, in a gesture of support that earned Truman the Lloyds' undying loyalty. However, the cycle soon repeated itself. In early 1952, McCarthy assailed the Lloyds again, at the same moment that he told the press Leon and Mary Dublin Keyserling were under investigation. After another scramble, the White House loyalty board once more cleared David Lloyd, but that was not the end of it. For months the case continued to occupy White House staff.[86]

After these attacks, the Lloyds de-emphasized Charlotte's former socialism and shifted their policy interests into less controversial fields. In 1943, David had volunteered to navy investigators that Charlotte once belonged to the Socialist Party and the League for Industrial Democracy, but in 1952 the biographical statement he submitted in self-defense omitted reference to those affiliations.[87] David Lloyd left government when Truman did and became director of the Research and Education Committee for a Free World, which studied problems such as water desalination and population control. Those problems were politically safe compared with the labor and consumer rights for which he had battled as a lawyer for the La Follette Committee, the Federal Communications Commission, and the OPA. David Lloyd also led the fund-raising campaign for the Harry S. Truman Library, and he was vice president of the Truman Library Institute from its creation in 1957 to his death in 1962. When Lloyd donated his papers to that library, he did not deposit materials on his own investigation. Only a few scattered memoranda in White House files survive to permit reconstruction of Lloyd's case.[88] The silence surrounding the Lloyds' trials has prevented scholars from appreciating how the loyalty program forced two left-leaning lawyers, one of whom had significant influence as an aide to President Truman, away from pro-labor and pro-consumer activism and toward the political center.

THE OPENING OF THE AMERICAN WORKPLACE

A similar pattern emerges for the U.S. Women's Bureau at the Department of Labor, historically a voice for wage-earning women of all races.[89] The Women's Bureau anchored an interracial labor feminist network that from the 1940s to the 1970s achieved major progress in areas such as hiring and promotion, pay, sexual harassment, and child care.

Those victories become even more impressive in light of the revelation that, hitherto unbeknownst to scholars, three directors of the Women's Bureau—Frieda Miller (1944–53), Esther Peterson (1961–64), and Mary Dublin Keyserling (1964–69)—battled recurring loyalty investigations prompted by their early associations with the left.[90] Those investigations helped produce the moderate liberalism that scholars have ascribed to that agency in the postwar period. Historian Annelise Orleck observes that Frieda Miller and other labor feminists became more politically centrist over time, but she attributes that moderation to the achievement of "insider" status. Jennifer Mittelstadt characterizes Esther Peterson and her Presidential Commission on the Status of Women as "maternalists" who prioritized women's family obligations and de-emphasized the problems of women on public assistance. Kathleen Laughlin notes the postwar bureau's emphasis on economic growth rather than redistribution. She also points out that Peterson and Keyserling did not publicly criticize the indifference of the new Equal Employment Opportunity Commission (EEOC) to sexual discrimination and were ambivalent toward the fledgling National Organization for Women.[91]

Those findings are not incorrect, but they are illuminated by the discovery that such propensities and policy changes at the Women's Bureau were defensive reactions by successive administrators to challenges to their eligibility for government service. According to one scholar, the government economist Mary Dublin Keyserling "had little in common with social movement feminists like [Betty] Friedan."[92] In fact, the opposite is true: Dublin Keyserling had a great deal in common with Friedan. Both had been active in left-feminist social movements in the 1930s and early 1940s, and both later tried to hide that activism. Unlike Friedan, neither Dublin Keyserling nor Miller nor Peterson ever belonged to the Communist Party, but all three were more radical than has been understood. Like Dublin Keyserling, Miller and Peterson supported Popular Front causes, chose socialist partners, and registered with the American Labor Party in the late 1930s.[93] All were committed advocates of women's economic and sexual independence, but after the loyalty investigations they modified their styles and agendas in ways that have invited misinterpretation.

It would be unfair to say that Frieda Miller hid the fact that she underwent a loyalty investigation, because her papers hold her 1955 "Reply to Interrogatory" and the resulting letter of clearance. She died in 1973, before many historians were interested in women's history, without leaving any oral histories. Still, few people at the time or since have known that Miller was under investigation when she resigned her position as head of the U.S. Women's Bureau. As with Dublin Keyserling's departure from government, Miller's friends and associates assumed she left government because a Republican administration took office. Miller's biographical entry in *Notable American Women* claims that she resigned in 1952 "at the request of the incoming Republican administration."[94] In fact, Miller did not resign her post until December 1953, prior to a loyalty decision by the State Department on her application for an international position under its auspices. President Eisenhower would have appointed a Republican to head the Women's Bureau in any case, but without the loyalty investigation Miller might have moved readily to a different government job. Instead, she was unemployed for over a year before finally receiving clearance for a short-term job with the International Labor Organization (ILO).[95] Rightly celebrated by scholars for her early exposition of a feminism that was sensitive to the priorities of wage-earning women, Miller paid a heretofore invisible price for her principles.

Miller's loyalty case and FBI files reveal that she was cleared in 1949, after an investigation triggered by her associations with the LWS and American Society for the Protection of the Foreign-Born back in the years before those groups were labeled Communist fronts. In 1950 an ex-Communist union member reported that Miller had been close to Ruth Young of the Communist-led United Electrical Workers, and this charge seems to have been what gave the State Department pause in 1953. Miller's subsequent application for an assignment with the ILO produced the 1955 interrogatory from the International Organizations Employee Loyalty Board, which eventually cleared her. Each time Miller pursued a new ILO assignment, however, the FBI checked for new "derogatory" information, sometimes turning up something that delayed her clearance.[96] The prevailing impression that Miller left government because she was a Democrat is not entirely wrong. However, to understand the loyalty program's full power as a partisan tool, one must appreciate how many high-ranking civil servants were forced out by the threat of constant reinvestigation, and not just by a routine change of administration.

Esther Peterson was part of another left-feminist couple that, like the Keyserlings, Kramer-Cohens, and Lloyds, played down difficult encounters with loyalty charges. An inspiring figure, Peterson survived to become a key government ally of the feminist and consumer movements of the 1960s. Her husband Oliver was a government labor expert from 1941 through 1962. In the 1990s, with the Cold War safely over, Peterson acknowledged that she and her husband had been "very radical, no doubt about it."[97] Even then, however, she avoided talking about the loyalty investigation that she believed had destroyed Oliver—and which had relied heavily on allegations about her. "I try not to think about it because I get very emotional about it because it hurt my husband. It hurt me. It hurt my children. I can't talk about it, and Oliver wanted me not to talk about it."[98] Peterson's 1995 memoir and her papers at Schlesinger Library understate the complexity and longevity of the couple's loyalty troubles, and Oliver's papers at the Truman Library are silent on the subject.[99]

Oliver and Esther Peterson married in 1932 after meeting in graduate school at Columbia. He was a Minnesota-bred socialist before he became a Roosevelt Democrat, and she became "radical" after she met him, breaking with her Utah Republican upbringing. She held a variety of jobs serving the labor movement, particularly in workers' education, before joining the staff of the Amalgamated Clothing Workers in 1939. Meanwhile, they moved to Washington, and Oliver took a job with the Office of Price Administration. Loyalty officials rated Oliver eligible for the OPA in 1946, but things got sticky after Elizabeth Bentley named former associates of the Petersons as secret Communists. By that time Oliver was a labor adviser for the State Department. Esther's memoir suggests that Oliver's investigation exploded suddenly in December 1952 and was resolved quickly. In fact, the State Department loyalty board had issued Oliver an interrogatory in 1949, and after his case was reopened in mid-1952, he was not cleared until a year later. That was not the end of it.[100] In 1954, Susan B. Anthony III (Mrs. Henry Collins Jr.) left the Communist Party and told the FBI that Oliver Peterson was the missing man they had been seeking from the "Ware group" of underground Communists who met in Washington in 1934 and 1935. Anthony's claims were disproven, and Oliver was cleared again in 1955. The shadow hovered, however: he was reinvestigated in 1960 and not cleared until 1962. He then retired, in very poor health. Disloyalty charges hung over Oliver's head from 1949 through the end of his career—not just for a brief period in late 1952.[101] Although Esther later compressed the time frame of the investigation, she did not minimize its impact on Oliver. She believed that the cancer that killed him took hold while he endured "this time of stress." She added bitterly: "They used me. I was used against my husband definitely."[102]

Differences between draft and published versions of Peterson's 1995 memoir indicate that she considered acknowledging her socialism but decided against it. The published memoir explains that "many of my peers in the labor movement who were members of the Communist Party tried to recruit me," but J.B.S. Hardman, a Socialist official of the Amalgamated Clothing Workers union, convinced her that Communism was going to be "worse than the czars." It concludes, "In the end, both Oliver and I rejected communism." In a draft version donated to the archives after Esther's death, that sentence was longer: "Both Esther and Oliver reject Communism and define themselves as socialists." A question mark is penciled into the margin next to the latter part of the sentence, which disappeared from the published version.[103]

Although Peterson in the 1990s still was uncomfortable publicly identifying herself as a socialist (former or otherwise), she was willing to say that American Communists had never been a real danger. Distancing herself from both Communists and Red-baiters, she explained that she had known a "great many Communists" in the labor movement in the 1930s and 1940s, and they "were no threat to the stability of the United States government; in most cases they were simply idealistic—if impractical—activists."[104] Back when Oliver was under investigation, however, Esther tried to disarm their conservative attackers by joining a campaign against communism in European trade unions. After appearing before the IOELB in mid-January 1953, Oliver rejoined his family in Brussels to await the verdict. Their friends were "concerned on McCarthy," Esther reported cryptically in her diary. In particular, "Vic" Reuther was worried about the outlook for Oliver's case. A few days later, according to the diary, Esther "decided to volunteer with ICFTU."[105]

The International Confederation of Free Trade Unions (ICFTU) had formed in 1949 as a rival to the Communist-dominated World Federation of Trade Unions (WFTU). Esther Peterson was soon at work on a pamphlet urging European trade union women to fight communism. Printed in several languages, the pamphlet warned trade union women not to be fooled by the WFTU claim that communist countries treated women better than capitalist countries did. "Women workers in the free world bitterly resent this phony campaign by communists who take up the posture of defenders of women's rights." The pamphlet acknowledged that women workers in "free" countries faced discrimination and the double burden of paid and unpaid work, but it argued that the solution was free trade unions, not communism.[106] Esther's anticommunism was sincere, but if Oliver had not been in the crosshairs of loyalty investigators, she would not have been under such pressure to beef up her anticommunist credentials.

The loyalty questions affected Esther Peterson's career as well as her husband's. In 1961 President Kennedy named her assistant secretary of labor and director of the U.S. Women's Bureau, and in 1964 President Johnson made her his special adviser for consumer affairs. Apparently neither president was impressed by the allegations against the Petersons. Some of the same old hands were still running the loyalty machinery, however. In 1964 an FBI report intimated that the Petersons had been and still were part of the Communist underground. Reviewing the Petersons' association with several people named by Whittaker Chambers and Elizabeth Bentley, the report concluded that because "the Communists have not given up their goal of world domination . . . we must presume they are still busily at work at their task of subversion and betrayal" of the U.S. government.[107]

That FBI report fell into the hands of private-sector conservatives who disliked Esther Peterson's advocacy of regulatory policies to protect consumers. One of her nemeses was the Advertising Federation of America, which resented her success in winning the Fair Packaging and Labeling Act of 1966. The group had the ear of President Johnson's adviser Jack Valenti, a former ad agency head. Another opponent was the American Retail Federation, whose representatives followed her from conference to conference and tape-recorded everything she said. "They watched my every move, looking for a misstep." When Peterson was Johnson's consumer adviser in the mid-1960s, her opponents circulated a series of reports asserting Communist control of the consumer movement. Those reports gave her a lead role and asked how she had passed loyalty checks. At some point Peterson obtained copies of these reports and filed them without comment among her papers.[108]

Peterson's later writings discuss the fierce opposition she faced from some business interests, but she never explained that they held the charge of Communist sympathizer over her head. She positioned herself as a centrist: "I really caught hell from both sides. Industry attacked me as a threat to the American free enterprise system; some consumer advocates charged me with being too soft." The criticism Peterson took from the left was mild, however, compared with the virulent Red-baiting from the right. In 1967, it was the right's attacks that led her to resign her post as special adviser to the president on consumer affairs.[109]

Peterson had to fight forces inside the White House as well as without, and the lingering disloyalty rumors must have weakened her in those battles. "I was kicked out of the White House because I was too much of a zealot. I was pushed out; I was made so uncomfortable that I quit. . . . the stress was more than I could take." The Johnson advisers Jack Valenti and Joe Califano did everything they could to keep Peterson "a political instrument rather than a real instrument for consumer action."[110] They hoped her appointment as consumer advocate would win votes for Johnson, but they undermined her efforts at substantive reform, underfunding her office and blocking her access to the president. As a former advertising man, Valenti would have been familiar with the story of Peterson's alleged Communist associations. Even though President Johnson himself discounted that story, the old charges survived as a potential political liability that reduced her leverage.

Not just the top officials of the Women's Bureau but also many of its professional staff and long-term allies found their influence and employment options limited by the loyalty program.[111] In Dorothy Kenyon's case, being branded a fellow traveler while she was a member of the UN Commission on the Status of Women precluded further judgeships or other forays into government service. Kenyon's case was very public, thanks to Senator McCarthy. Others kept quiet about their investigations. One example is Caroline Ware, who like Peterson and Dublin Keyserling was on the Presidential Commission on the Status of Women. Waiting for clearances repeatedly hampered Ware's work for the Pan-American Union, which wanted her to foster community development and women's leadership in Latin America. She told no one but her husband and her two closest friends about the IOELB interrogatory she faced in 1954, and her papers include nothing related to her recurring investigation except for a few references deep within a stack of handwritten letters.[112]

Another example is Pauli Murray, the antidiscrimination lawyer who was very close to both Kenyon and Ware. Murray's memoir omitted the major reason for Cornell's 1952 refusal to hire her for a State Department–sponsored project, which was that she had briefly belonged to Jay Lovestone's faction of Communist dissenters. Murray's record from the 1930s barred her from government even in the late 1960s, because officials feared the political fallout for a liberal administration of appointing her.[113]

During the successful struggle to include the word "sex" in Title VII of the 1964 Civil Rights Act, Murray swayed many legislators with a memorandum arguing that without the word "sex," the bill would include "only one half of the Negroes." Murray long had advocated fighting racial and sexual discrimination together, rather than treating them as distinct or, worse still, competing causes. "As a Negro woman," she observed, "I knew that it was difficult to determine whether I was being discriminated against because of race or sex."[114] In 1966 Murray moved to Washington as a consultant to the EEOC, which was supposed to enforce Title VII. Soon the EEOC chairman asked the White House about making Murray the agency's general counsel. Word came back that she could not be appointed, because she once had been a Communist and appointing her would bolster segregationists' claim that workplace integration was a Communist plot. Murray was crushed to miss out on her "dream job" and to learn that "any thought of a government career" was "finished." Murray's formidable intellect and complex vision as an African American woman lawyer could have made a significant impact at the EEOC, which at that moment was ignoring its mandate to punish sexual discrimination.[115]

It is difficult to map precisely how public policy was affected by the fact that influential left feminists of the 1930s and 1940s either were marginalized or felt so vulnerable to loyalty accusations that they eschewed positions that might be construed as anticapitalist. By narrowing the range of debate through direct pressure on key individuals, though, loyalty investigations did shape both history and the writing of history. Dublin Keyserling, Miller, Peterson, and to some extent Ware and Murray have been known chiefly for their contributions as "liberal" feminists in the 1960s. In scholarship on the women's movement, they are the foil to

Figure 7.1. Pauli Murray (left), with Esther Peterson (right), All-Women Conference, New York City, October 11, 1962. Courtesy of the Schlesinger Library, Radcliffe Institute, Harvard University.

the women's liberationists, which rejected the older group's perceived allegiances to capitalism, the labor movement, and the Democratic Party.[116] In fact, those liberals had been left feminists until the anticommunist crusade pushed them to the sidelines or into adopting the language of the ideological center. When one considers that similar dynamics affected not just isolated individuals but clusters of individuals associated with certain causes or agencies, the loyalty program emerges as a weighty but hitherto hidden factor defining the contours of postwar social movements and public policy.

PUBLIC HOUSING

Public housing is another policy arena in which the range of debate was narrowed because some of its strongest advocates were forced away from the left by the pressure of investigation. Leon Keyserling's old ally Catherine Bauer was another "houser" who modified her tone and proposals in order to disarm loyalty charges. A brilliant researcher, writer, and advocate for public housing, she became an international star with her 1934 book *Modern Housing*, which helped her win a Guggenheim Fellowship to study housing in Russia and Scandinavia. As the executive secretary for the Labor Housing Conference from 1934 to 1937, Bauer became a key figure in the radical camp of the housing movement. She and her union allies pushed for non-means-tested public housing that would be attractive to the working class as well as to the poor and, through provision of day care, to working women as well as working men. In order to overcome opposition from real estate groups, who were not interested in housing the unprofitable poor but did not want competition in the working-class market, Bauer's group sought to link federal planning with grassroots participation (much as the consumer movement did through the Office of Price Administration). She cooperated with Keyserling to pass the U.S. Housing Act of 1937 and then worked for the resulting U.S. Housing Authority (USHA). Bauer proclaimed the 1937 legislation "a radical piece of legislation—perhaps the most clear-cut and uncompromising adopted under the New Deal."[117] In 1940 Bauer married William Wurster, an architect on the faculty at University of California at Berkeley. Under Bauer's influence, Wurster designed various award-winning public housing projects in California.[118]

Bauer left her USHA job around the time of her marriage, but thereafter she served as a paid consultant to various government housing agencies. She continued to press for making public housing accessible to employed Americans, which she believed was the only way to eliminate the "social-work-crime-and-disease smell" and thereby increase popular support. That stance placed her in direct conflict with real estate interests and their congressional supporters—by now including Senator Joseph McCarthy—who were adamant that only welfare clients should receive public housing. After the war, real estate groups undertook a major campaign to link Bauer's vision of public housing with communism. They argued that attractive public housing would weaken democracy by diminishing "the urge to buy one's own home."[119] California's Un-American Activities Committee, known as the Tenney Committee, claimed in its 1947 and 1948 reports that Bauer had been associated with Communist front groups. She ignored those reports until 1953, when her husband's architectural firm abruptly found its defense contracts canceled. It became apparent that the main reason Wurster's security clearance had been revoked was that he was married to Bauer. She spent the better part of a year trying to clear her name in order to save her husband's career. After months of research and preparation, she made a twenty-page presentation before the Army-Navy-Air Force Personnel Security Board in August 1953. The board restored Wurster's clearance.[120]

In the immediate aftermath of that hearing, Bauer submitted a memorandum to President Eisenhower's Advisory Committee on Housing that seems to have been an attempt to distance herself from her radical reputation. Most public housing advocates were disgusted with the Eisenhower committee (Leon Keyserling called its first report "execrable"). But Bauer took a conciliatory tone and stressed the need to go slowly on public housing until experts gained more experience. Keyserling commented on her December 1953 memo, "I like it far less than anything else you have ever written." He scolded her for "throwing yourself into [the new administration's] arms."[121] In the following years, Bauer became less a lobbyist for public housing and more an academic, teaching at various universities.

In 1957 Bauer shocked and angered her old allies by publishing a critique of the public housing movement at a moment when it was under heavy pressure from the right. Her article, "The Dreary Deadlock of Public Housing," which appeared in the May 1957 issue of *Architectural Forum*, castigated U.S. public housing policy as "ossified." Federal programs were administered by cautious, unimaginative bureaucrats, she complained. They had produced ugly collectivist high-rises where few American families wanted to live. She chastised U.S. housing officials for rigidly promoting the "beehive type of community life," and she recommended less centralized policies that would accommodate "traditional American ideas" about living arrangements. Her readers would not have known about her encounter with the loyalty program. In light of Bauer's grueling struggle to win back her husband's security clearance, it is hard not to read her 1957 piece as an effort to protect herself and her husband from further allegations.[122] That effort was not fully successful: notwithstanding Wurster's restored clearance, his firm never received another government contract. In 1962, Bauer's clearance to attend a White House conference on public housing was delayed until a sympathetic administrator interceded. Allegations of disloyalty, once in the file, never disappeared even if repeatedly disproven.[123] The constricting effect on former loyalty defendants' willingness to criticize capitalism therefore tended to be permanent.

Social Insurance and Public Assistance

Another arena in which loyalty investigations of key officials had a significant policy effect was in the broad field of social insurance (old age, unemployment, health) and public assistance ("welfare"). It is well established that the Red scare stigmatized advocates of national health insurance, marginalized radical social workers, and weakened those elements of the labor movement that advocated a comprehensive welfare system.[124] But it has not been understood that loyalty investigations put key figures such as Isidore Falk, Wilbur Cohen, Elizabeth Wickenden, and Bernice Lotwin Bernstein, among others, on the defensive. Scholars of the "social security apparatus" have noticed that its policy goals became less ambitious from the 1940s to the 1960s, but they have attributed this shift from redistributive to rehabilitative solutions to general historical conditions such as intensified congressional conservatism, the impressive performance of the capitalist economy, and social workers' growing interest in psychological approaches.[125] Because the affected officials rarely discussed or archived materials about their loyalty investigations, scholars have not recognized that the pressure of disloyalty allegations contributed to shifts in policymakers' rhetoric and goals.

The story of the Red-baiting of national health insurance advocates has been told before, but without appreciation of its lasting impact on high-level government officials. During the run-up to the 1948 election, Marjorie Shearon, a former employee of the Social Security Administration (SSA), got the attention of the National Industrial Conference Board, the American Medical Association, and certain Republican congressmen by charging that Truman's campaign for "socialized medicine" was being driven by bureaucrats with Communist sympathies. Senators Robert Taft (R-Ohio) and Forrest Donnell (R-Mo.) relied on Shearon during hearings on insurance bills from 1946 to 1948 (they later distanced themselves from her when it became clear she was mentally unbalanced). Shearon's primary initial target was her former boss Isidore Falk, a medical economist who headed the SSA's Bureau of Research and Statistics. Her "House of Falk" diagram tied him to a plot by the International Labor

Organization, which she called a "powerful, worldwide Socialist organization," to foist nationalized medicine on the unsuspecting American public. Falk and his assistant Wilbur Cohen devoted a large portion of their time to preparing rebuttals and testifying before Taft's subcommittee.[126]

Meanwhile, a House subcommittee headed by Forest Harness of Indiana (who faced an uphill reelection battle in 1948) launched an inquiry into alleged propagandizing on behalf of nationalized medicine by SSA employees. Harness latched onto Jacob Fisher, a policy analyst on Falk's staff who had belonged to many leftist groups and had been editor of the radical *Social Work Today*. "By sheer luck," Fisher wrote decades later, Harness "hit a gusher" in his record, which the congressman used to go after "bigger game." "A chance discovery that one member of the staff of one of its bureaus had a HUAC record had ballooned into a tale of Communist sympathizers and fellow travelers in the Social Security Administration as a whole, numerous enough to warrant the term 'hotbed.'"[127] The SSA was located in the Federal Security Agency (FSA), and the FSA loyalty board cleared Fisher in 1948. Shearon promptly accused FSA head Oscar Ewing of a whitewash. The continued publicity led to further investigation before Fisher was cleared again. Although Falk and Fisher were vindicated for the moment, the House Committee on Appropriations cut the budget of the Bureau of Research and Statistics by half for fiscal 1949; the bureau's functions were reduced, and it ran on a shoestring budget until 1961. Staffers became more circumspect in cooperating with the labor movement and more cautious in their proposals. Falk abandoned the ambitious approach he had taken in the controversial Wagner-Murray-Dingell health insurance bills and proposed a more limited measure, which became the prototype for the 1965 Medicare Act.[128]

The right-wing effort to paint Truman as a promoter of socialism at home also affected the FSA's Bureau of Public Assistance (BPA). At the same moment that the Bureau of Research and Statistics was under fire, the American Medical Association attacked BPA head Jane Hoey for commissioning and publishing social worker Charlotte Towle's *Common Human Needs* (1945). Towle's book included the following sentence: "Social security and public assistance programs are a basic essential for the attainment of the socialized state envisioned in democratic ideology, a way of life which so far has been realized only in slight measure." The controversy persuaded the Government Printing Office to withdraw the book from circulation. The American Medical Association kept up the clamor until FSA head Ewing in 1951 ordered the printing plates destroyed. Towle's job at the University of Chicago's School of Social Service Administration was secure, but she lost the possibility of consulting work for the government, and she was denied a passport in 1954. Jane

Hoey was cleared in 1949, but her defense of accused staff members reportedly was a factor in the decision to ease her out in 1953.[129]

As Towle's passport denial suggests, the machinery set in motion by disloyalty allegations continued to operate long after the accusers had moved on to fresh targets. Isidore Falk left the Social Security Administration in 1953, tired of continued accusations and frustrated at the lack of progress on even less ambitious health insurance bills. Falk landed on his feet with a series of private consulting jobs and then a faculty position at Yale, but the less prominent and more leftist Jacob Fisher was not so fortunate.[130] In 1954 Fisher was suspended from the FSA, and he resigned soon thereafter. Unable to find another job for several years, he turned to self-employment and opened a plant nursery.[131]

Decades later Fisher disclosed that, contrary to what he told his superiors and loyalty boards, he had belonged to the Communist Party from 1934 to 1940. He had lied on his civil service application forms in the early 1940s, he explained, because he did not interpret belonging to the CP as advocating violent overthrow of the government. He also did not want to cooperate with what he saw as a repressive system. He had served the government faithfully and saw no reason to offer himself to the "inquisition." In 1954, when his situation became graver, Fisher feared he would face perjury charges if he now changed gears and told the truth. By the 1980s, Fisher regretted his former admiration of the CP, but he remained adamant that the loyalty program had done him and all government employees a grave injustice.[132]

Fisher did not know it, but at the time of his suspension in 1954 his supervisor, Wilbur Cohen, too was under investigation. Jacob Fisher and Charlotte Towle were small fry compared to Cohen, but unlike theirs, the story of Cohen's encounter with the loyalty program has been left untold. A protégé of the Wisconsin social insurance experts Edwin Witte and Arthur Altmeyer, by 1954 Cohen had been the Social Security Administration's chief liaison to Congress for almost twenty years. He left government for an academic position in 1956 but in 1961 returned to the Department of Health, Education, and Welfare. President Johnson appointed him undersecretary in 1965 and then secretary in 1968. From the New Deal through the War on Poverty, Cohen wielded enormous influence over legislation on old age, survivors', and disability insurance, public assistance, and Medicare. Significantly, when he returned to government in the 1960s, his approach to social welfare became more conservative, treating unemployment and poverty as evidence of the failings of individuals more than of the labor market.[133]

Scholars have noted that as he grew more prominent, Cohen became a target of Marjorie Shearon's attacks on advocates of "socialized medicine," but they have been unaware of the extent of his encounters with the loyalty program. In the 1950s Shearon began publishing reports and newsletters accusing Cohen of left-wing sympathies, culminating in her 1967 book.[134] Shearon was a headache for Cohen over the years, but she was not the only source of allegations against him. Loyalty troubles plagued him from 1947 through 1955 and almost certainly influenced his decision to leave government in 1956. The charges were insubstantial, but they jeopardized his career. They also indicate that Cohen may have been further to the left than has been appreciated and that his wife certainly was.

Cohen's first major round with the loyalty program was no doubt intensified by conservatives' aforementioned effort to paint Truman's national health agenda as un-American. After interviewing Cohen in late 1947, the FBI went ahead with a full field investigation. The FSA loyalty board reviewed the results and rated him eligible in fall 1948. The central Loyalty Review Board disagreed, however, and remanded the case to the lower board with instructions to obtain a reply to interrogatory from Cohen. After reviewing Cohen's reply, the FSA again rated him eligible, in May 1949. The FBI continued generating reports on him, however, and in December 1950 the Justice Department discussed prosecuting him for perjury. His loyalty board rated him eligible yet again in 1951 and 1953. In 1953 Eisenhower named Oveta Culp Hobby as secretary of a new agency that subsumed the FSA, the Department of Health, Education, and Welfare (HEW). Hobby soon forced out top officials at the agency, including Arthur Altmeyer, Isidore Falk, Jane Hoey, and Ellen Woodward. Fearing he might be next, Cohen applied for a position as head of the United Nations pension fund. That application led to an interrogatory from the IOELB, which arrived in April 1954 (the same month that Cohen suspended Jacob Fisher). Cohen spent the next month composing a detailed reply. In October he had a hearing before the IOELB, which was under pressure from the right's charges that UN agencies were a refuge for American leftists. Not until June 1955 was the United Nations notified of the IOELB's favorable determination in Cohen's case.[135]

In other words, over a period of eight years Cohen was more often than not either under active FBI investigation (word of which would have reached him), responding to charges, or waiting for rulings. The care he took with his 1954 reply to interrogatory indicates that he perceived himself to be fighting to save his career. Cohen's private correspondence with Elizabeth Wickenden suggests that he was not confident about his options outside government.[136] Those options would have been sharply reduced by an unfavorable loyalty decision. His wife had given up her government career so as not to hamper his. Thus his family's livelihood, as well as his professional reputation, depended on his ability to continue obtaining clearances under a loyalty program whose standards were vague and in flux.

Wilbur Cohen's case indicates yet again that a leftist spouse was a serious liability for a government official, especially after the expansion of the "security" risk category (as opposed to "loyalty" risk) in 1953.[137] Wilbur Cohen's own associations with "Communist fronts" such as the American League for Peace and Democracy, the American Youth Congress, and the Washington Bookshop were fleeting, but for loyalty boards they took on greater significance in light of his wife's record. Raised in a German-American Baptist family in the Texas hill country, Eloise Bittel studied at the University of Chicago's School of Social Service Administration and then headed for Washington. She had hoped to work for the new National Labor Relations Board but landed instead in 1936 at the Bureau of Public Assistance in the Social Security Administration, where she met Cohen. After further training in social work, she took a supervisory position at a D.C. housing agency, the Alley Dwelling Authority. By the time she left government in late 1941, hostile coworkers considered her a "Communist sympathizer." An outspoken supporter of labor and consumer rights, she was in the D.C. Cooperative League, and she belonged to the Washington Bookshop until it was put on the Attorney General's List of Subversive Organizations in 1947. She also had worked as a volunteer for the American League for Peace and Democracy. Those associations were among the main topics of Wilbur's 1948 interrogatory. In 1954 those items were revisited along with new allegations stemming from Eloise's activism on behalf of political and social equality for African Americans. FBI informants were suspicious of her involvement with the Southern Conference for Human Welfare and other groups working to abolish the poll tax. Informants also cast her as an aggressive integrationist who was friends with the black radicals Paul and Eslanda Robeson, and who hosted an office party of "white and Negro members" where interracial dancing occurred. To loyalty investigators, those associations added up to the profile of a possible Communist. Over the years, Wilbur Cohen repeatedly had to deny that his wife was a Communist who had invited him to join the party.[138]

Also at issue in 1954 was Wilbur Cohen's friendship with the alleged Communist Michael T. Wermel. A Columbia-educated statistician, Wermel oversaw the postwar reconstruction of Germany's social security system and worked at the Department of Labor from 1948 until he resigned while under investigation in December 1952. Cohen had lived with Wermel in 1937 and recommended him for government positions; their wives became good friends. This mélange of supposedly derogatory information, when combined with right-wing charges that Cohen's policy recommendations were subversive, was enough to give loyalty boards pause.[139]

Notwithstanding Wilbur Cohen's clearance by the IOELB in mid-1955, the sword of Damocles still hovered above his head. When he was offered a job at the University of Michigan's School of Social Work, he accepted. By the time President Kennedy summoned him back to HEW in 1961, legal and political shifts had reined in the loyalty program. Still, Ben Mandel of SISS tried to stir up the old allegations about Cohen. Mandel did not succeed, but the effort warned Cohen that he remained under scrutiny.[140]

Cohen drafted fragments of a memoir that minimized his loyalty troubles. He suggested that the unstable Marjorie Shearon was the lone source of allegations. He said that his wife insisted that they move to Ann Arbor even after a new secretary of HEW invited him to stay: "I am not quite sure what the reasons were in my wife's mind that made her take such a strong position," he wrote.[141] As he well knew, Eloise Bittel Cohen had good reason to want to escape Washington. Her activities in the years up to 1941 had been the source of endless scrutiny and questioning, and although Wilbur had been cleared again in 1955, more of the same could be expected. Eloise may have decided she had had enough surveillance and suspense. Cohen did not deposit records related to his loyalty investigation with his papers at the State Historical Society of Wisconsin.[142]

Because Wilbur Cohen left little record of his loyalty case, scholars have been unaware of it and how it might have altered his policy prescriptions. Cohen's biographer portrays him as an incrementalist whose "own views seemed to be malleable" and who prided himself on his ability to get along with legislators on both sides of the aisle. As a result, Cohen "came to favor incremental over innovative policies." In the 1950s, Cohen reportedly acquired an enduring faith in the American economy and then was influenced by the Michigan School of Social Work, where he absorbed its confidence "in the therapeutic power of social services." By the time he returned to government in 1961, Cohen had "adjusted his views on welfare so that he advocated it as more than a pension to shield people from the stresses of the labor market. . . . [Welfare programs should] facilitate participation in rather than disengagement from the world of work." When Cohen returned to lead HEW in the 1960s, he backed welfare reforms that stressed interventionist training and rehabilitation rather than cash assistance, ushering in the transition to "workfare."[143]

Cohen's shift put him at odds with his former mentor Arthur Altmeyer, and Cohen's biographer takes their differences as emblematic of the generational difference between New Dealers and their successors. "Unlike Altmeyer, Cohen accepted the prevailing reality of prosperity and learned how to adopt [sic] his policy proposals to suit this reality. In so doing, he made the transition between the New Deal and the New Frontier." The discovery that loyalty investigators were breathing down his neck for

Figure 7.2. Wilbur Cohen (left) and President Lyndon Johnson, circa 1968. LBJ Library photo by Yoichi Okamoto.

almost a decade puts Cohen's transition in fresh perspective. Perhaps he was impressed by the performance of the U.S. economy, but he also must have been scarred by the frequent threats of dismissal. Similarly, Cohen's noted lack of engagement with the civil rights movement of the 1960s may have reflected the fact that Eloise's civil rights activism had given Red-baiters an excuse to attack him in the 1950s.[144]

Another high-ranking case at HEW involved the lawyer Bernice Lotwin Bernstein, like Wilbur Cohen a Wisconsin protégé of Witte and Altmeyer (and an old friend of the Keyserlings). She joined the Social Security Board's legal staff in 1935, drafted the agency's model state unemployment insurance bill, and then traveled widely to encourage states to adopt the bill. She continued to distinguish herself at the War Manpower Commission and then the Labor Department while raising three daughters. In 1947, her husband left the Treasury Department to go into private practice in New York, and the FSA recruited her to the position of New York regional attorney. In 1963, she won the distinguished service award for her agency (now HEW), and in 1966 she became its New York director. She held that position until 1977, supervising and evaluating the administration of about 350 different programs affecting about 30 million people.[145]

What one would not know from the oral histories left by Bernice and Bernard Bernstein is that loyalty allegations nearly derailed her impressive career. As in Wilbur Cohen's case, many of the charges stemmed from her spouse's associations and activities. Bernard had worked at the Treasury Department with colleagues accused by Elizabeth Bentley, and he had criticized Winston Churchill's "iron curtain" metaphor in an International Women's Day address to the radical Congress of American Women. Bernice was suspended for over four months before winning clearance in February 1955. The potential damage to her work and her children terrified her. In presenting herself to the loyalty board, she emphasized how conventional she was in every respect, including her tastes in art and child rearing as well as politics. She did not know that the FBI had reported her American Labor Party voting registration to the loyalty board, which therefore doubted her claim to be a lifelong moderate Democrat. The experience would have made her more cautious about antagonizing business interests in the course of supervising HEW program administration.[146]

The chief author of the Social Security Act, Edwin Witte, himself was "flagged" in 1953 by the Loyalty Review Board as a case of "unresolved question of loyalty (pro-Communist)." The charges against the distinguished Wisconsin economist were even more tenuous than those against his disciples Wilbur Cohen and Bernice Lotwin Bernstein, but the charges weakened his ability to help them during their own battles. Witte's flagging was a technicality based on the fact that his consulting job to the Wage Stabilization Board had ended before that agency's loyalty board decided his case.[147] If he had tried to return to government service, however, there would have been a delay, at the very least, while he was reinvestigated. Even the most eminent policymakers got caught up in the loyalty program machinery.

Up and down the chain of command, then, social security administrators faced the direct, career-threatening pressure of loyalty investigation. In the words of the welfare expert Elizabeth Wickenden, charges of Communist sympathies "became a kind of miasma that hung over all of government and particularly the New Deal agencies where there were more liberals."[148] That miasma hung heavily over HEW and its predecessors and subagencies, discouraging discussion of controversial measures in direct and immediate ways.

Elizabeth Wickenden knew of what she spoke. Not only had many of her close colleagues in the social welfare arena struggled with the loyalty program, but so had her husband, the public power expert Tex Goldschmidt. The loyalty program also was the chief reason that she herself was not in government service after the early 1940s. The Wickenden-Goldschmidts offer yet another example of a couple who entered government as outspoken left feminists in the 1930s but maintained lower profiles after facing loyalty accusations. Wickenden left government in

1942 for a variety of reasons, and not necessarily as a result of allegations against her.[149] However, had she tried to return to government after the loyalty program's formalization in 1947, she might well have had trouble obtaining clearance, and she would have magnified her husband's difficulties, because some of the allegations in his case stemmed from her activities. These factors must have entered into her decision to influence social policy from outside rather than inside the government. Unlike most survivors of loyalty probes, Wickenden and Goldschmidt planned to write about their loyalty cases, according to outlines for their memoirs. Both of them died, however, before drafting those chapters, so there is no way to know how they would have told their stories.[150]

Wickenden has not received in-depth scholarly treatment in her own right, but she was a key player in the postwar "social security apparatus."[151] Wickenden would have become more prominent had she been a man. During the early New Deal years, after running a Federal Emergency Relief Administration (FERA) program providing relief to some 350,000 transients, Wickenden made herself indispensable to Aubrey Williams, Harry Hopkins's assistant at the Works Progress Administration (WPA)—notwithstanding Hopkins's concern that she was "too much to the left." Williams refused to sign authorizations until Wickenden vetted them, and he credited her for the low incidence of improper use of WPA funds.[152] When Williams became head of the National Youth Administration, he brought Wickenden with him, and she quickly became a "dominant influence" at the agency. He told her and others that he would name her deputy administrator (his second-in-command), but when the time came he said he could not do it because "another man is necessary."[153] He nonetheless continued to depend on her, so that she was "again, in that anomalous situation of doing the work but not getting the title."[154]

A few anecdotes illustrate the challenges facing Wickenden as a "brilliant and beautiful" young woman with an unusual amount of authority. Some people assumed she and Williams were lovers, which they were not. Loyalty investigators made similar insinuations.[155] Others joked about a woman acting like a man. When a Montana official complained to Civil Works administrator John Carmody that FERA's Transient Division was headed by "a fellow who squats to pee," Carmody reassured him that the division really was run by an assistant "who had no such disability." "But John, I do!" Wickenden retorted when Carmody shared the story with her over lunch.[156] When Lyndon Johnson became Texas state director of the National Youth Administration, he soon learned that Wickenden was "the key to getting anything done." It was she whom Johnson wanted to meet when Wickenden and Goldschmidt visited Austin in 1935. Years later, Johnson would "occasionally introduce Wicky as his first boss in

Washington."[157] He admired Wickenden's intellect and teased Gold-schmidt about her independence. As Goldschmidt recalled,

> Even after Wicky left the WPA . . . Johnson was always respectful of her opinions. Among his many ways of teasing me was his claim that I had "outmarried myself." . . . Wicky's autonomy was the basis of an expression of resignation that Johnson, our mutual mentor, Alvin Wirtz, and I shared for many years. . . . I had complained to Wirtz and Johnson that Wicky kept on working through her second pregnancy as she had during her first. Wirtz said testily "Why don't you put your foot down?" When I answered: "And then what?" there was a moment of silence and an explosion of laughter. . . . "And then what?" became our private short-hand euphemism for impractical advice.[158]

Fortunately for the marriage, Goldschmidt was a feminist in practice as well as in principle. Self-confident and very much in love with Wicken-den, he was proud not to control her.

Wickenden subsequently became a confidante and adviser to Wilbur Cohen. Like Aubrey Williams, Cohen would disappoint her in the end. Wickenden and Cohen met in 1935 across a row of filing cabinets that separated her FERA staff from his work group, the Committee on Eco-nomic Security. In the 1940s and 1950s they collaborated on many social welfare measures, becoming so close that Goldschmidt joked she and Cohen had a "bedroom relationship"—in the form of late-night phone discussions from their respective beds. It was Wickenden who introduced Cohen to Lyndon Johnson.[159] In the 1940s, as the Washington representa-tive of the American Public Welfare Association (APWA), an organization of state welfare administrators, Wickenden focused primarily on joint federal-state programs. However, she also became expert in the (federal) social insurance arena and avoided the widespread tendency to pit the two types of programs against each other. She grasped the "grand de-sign" of the Social Security Act: although her priority was winning more generous public assistance programs, she also worked for better social insurance in hopes of reducing the need for public assistance. In addition to drafting APWA's influential *Statement of Principles*, Wickenden was the chief convener of the "social security crowd," both for small strategy discussions among key players and for public forums involving organized women, African Americans, and other civic constituencies. Particularly important was her role in bridging the split in the labor movement. She worked closely with the CIO's Kitty Ellickson (also a Vassar alumna) and the AFL's Nelson Cruikshank and brought them together with Wilbur Cohen from the executive branch and Fedele Fauri from Congress.[160]

Wickenden influenced legislation before and after leaving Washington in 1951 (when her husband took a job with the United Nations). In 1950,

Figure 7.3. Elizabeth Wickenden, circa 1951.
Courtesy of Ann Goldschmidt Richardson and
Arthur Goldschmidt Jr.

for example, while still APWA's Washington representative, she successfully represented the states' viewpoint in a confrontation that culminated
in the Social Security Amendments of 1950. Those amendments quashed
an initiative—led by Representative Carl Curtis (R-Neb.) with the backing by the U.S. Chamber of Commerce—to convert the retirement program from a contributions-based insurance principle to a flat, low-level
pension program. Wilbur Cohen continued to rely on Wickenden's advice
when she was based in New York and working as a consultant to various
social work and welfare groups. "You will be happy to know," he wrote
her in 1953, "that [labor lobbyists] Paul Sifton and John Edelman have
been bemoaning your absence from the Washington scene. There's just
nobody—just nobody—who is filling Wicky's place."[161]

From afar, Wickenden helped win the 1956 extension of the old age
insurance program to include disability. The proposal had passed the
House but was being blocked in the Senate Finance Committee by Robert
Kerr (D-Okla.). Wickenden sent a memo to Kerr's friend Lyndon Johnson, then the Senate majority leader, arguing that passing the disability
insurance bill would boost the Democrats in the 1956 elections by securing the labor vote and making Republicans the anti-social-security party.
Shortly thereafter, Senator Kerr not only reversed his position, enabling
the bill to pass, but he began his keynote address to the Democratic National Convention by boasting that "this is the party that has brought
security to millions of disabled people." Wickenden was a shrewd political tactician, as well as a policy expert. She later learned that her memo
to Johnson indeed had done the trick with Kerr. "In sixty years of advocacy," she recalled, "this is the one case of such a proven direct cause and
effect relationship."[162] In 1960, when President-elect John Kennedy asked

Wilbur Cohen to chair a Task Force on Health and Social Security, Cohen put Wickenden on it; in addition to her substantive policy contribution, she served as a bridge between the Kennedy and Johnson camps, a function whose importance increased after Kennedy's assassination.[163]

Had the loyalty program and her husband's UN career not forced Wickenden to operate at a remove from power, welfare recipients might have fared better in the 1960s. When Wilbur Cohen returned to lead HEW after his stint in academia, Wickenden was furious with her old friend's rightward drift. In 1961 she lambasted him for compromising Aid to Families with Dependent Children (AFDC): "The opportunity for a major look in new terms at public welfare policy in 1962 which you and I worked so hard to create has been sacrificed to the non-controversial minor repair jobs on which the oddly assorted group you have called together can agree. As you well know I have always been willing to go along with the strategy of small advance . . . when strategic considerations require but I do not think this can be done effectively unless the larger vision is kept constantly before people as a goal." Her bitterness was personal: "I shall not say any of these things publicly but what none of my adversaries was able to achieve has now been effectively accomplished by my friends."[164]

The context for their conflict was a powerful attack on public assistance from the right. Conservatives had never liked public welfare, but in the 1950s and 1960s African Americans and other racial minorities began gaining access to programs that since inception chiefly had served whites, notwithstanding minorities' disproportionate poverty. As the visibility of minorities on the rolls increased, white voters became more susceptible to conservative arguments that welfare recipients were undeserving. Because African American communities historically were more tolerant of unwed motherhood and the mothers less likely to put those babies up for adoption, the increased numbers of blacks on welfare also meant an increase in unwed mothers (although unwed motherhood was on the rise among whites as well). These demographic shifts made some whites receptive to the claim that welfare programs were a mechanism for liberal politicians to win votes through handouts to lazy, immoral individuals—handouts funded by hardworking taxpayers.[165]

The right's momentum was apparent first at the state and local levels, most clearly in Louisiana in 1960 and Newburgh, New York, in 1961. Louisiana instituted a punitive "suitable home" requirement that succeeded in its clear intent to push black mothers off welfare. In Newburgh, City Manager Joseph Mitchell became a national hero to conservative spokesmen like Senator Barry Goldwater and William F. Buckley Jr. by instituting measures such as providing vouchers instead of cash and cutting off benefits to unwed mothers who bore additional children. The New York Supreme Court voided most of Newburgh's restrictive policies, but their spirit would soon be embedded in federal policy in the Social Security Amendments of 1962.[166] One of the big players in those amendments was HEW assistant secretary Wilbur Cohen, and Wickenden believed he compromised more than was politically necessary.[167]

Wickenden thought the right's fallacies could be exposed and neutralized through a head-on challenge. In a January 1962 speech, "Social Welfare and the Radical Right," she argued that Goldwater, Buckley, and other "extreme conservatives" were fundamentally hostile to the social security program but that social security's popularity required them to attack it indirectly by using misinformation to confuse voters. She gave three examples of false claims about social security by the radical right: that the old age insurance program was financially unsound; that national health insurance would be a step toward communism; and that "people needing relief are not really 'needy' but are exploiting community goodwill to compensate for some willful failure or inadequacy of their own or the group to which they belong." That last phrase was a reference to race and gender stereotypes. She tried to rally resistance by exposing the right's worldview as an obsolete one biased in favor of the few:

> Right wing radicals are characterized in my observation by a virtually fanatical distaste for all popular institutions of mutual support (from labor unions to the United Nations) and a temperamental nostalgia for an imagined lost society based on virtues of rugged individualism as they visualize them. This is justified by a type of social Darwinism, doctrine of self-regulating economic laissez-faire, and international isolationism which historical reality has long since relegated to fantasy. Social security is, by any functional definition, the pure prototype of institutionalized mutual support, resting on a general recognition of the essential interdependence of modern life. It is, therefore, a prime target for attack from the radical right.[168]

Wilbur Cohen infuriated Wickenden by trying to appease conservatives rather than confront them. In 1967, she boasted about a legislative victory over Cohen to their mutual friend Abe Fortas (then on the Supreme Court but still advising President Johnson). "I won an unbelievable victory: on a roll-call vote 41–38 the Senate voted a clear repudiation of a coercive policy toward AFDC mothers." At the hearing, she and "the labor people" had "produced such a showing of strength" that Cohen (now HEW undersecretary) and the conservative Senator Russell Long were caught by surprise. "[Wilbur] said it couldn't be done and privately tried to thwart me at every turn. Even though his pride and reputation were badly damaged, he made the public gesture of taking me aside (. . . he had not spoken to me since August when he told me I would be 'finished' if I fought these provisions) to ask what 'we' should advise the President to do next year. It has been a very strange battle—David and

Goliath—and I always assumed I was making a futile gesture."[169] Wickenden told Fortas that despite that victory she did not expect the final bill to be very strong, so she was plotting a new campaign to work through the courts. She had drafted the key document leading to the creation of Legal Services for the Poor,[170] and she may have been referring to mass action through groups like the National Welfare Rights Organization. But her husband was now the U.S. representative to the Economic and Social Council of the United Nations, and she had to be careful.

Ironically, younger activists in the 1960s saw Wickenden as part of the liberal establishment: Richard Cloward and others at the Office of Economic Opportunity (OEO), where Wickenden was a consultant, tried to bypass her and other older women like Hilda Worthington Smith. OEO officials may have resented the fact that Wickenden had advised President Johnson against the Community Action Program, which sought to empower the poor by providing federal funds to citizens who organized self-help projects. Wickenden correctly predicted that OEO's bypassing of local and state authorities would provoke a political backlash. "I should have listened to Wicky," Johnson later lamented. Wickenden's misgivings about Community Action reflected her political pragmatism, not any mistrust of social movements.[171] But having downplayed their radicalism to salvage careers in the 1950s—or to protect spouses' careers—leftist New Deal veterans found it hard to establish credibility with the young radicals of the 1960s.

Scholars, too, have misunderstood Wickenden and her cohort. One welfare policy historian concludes that "without feminist analytical tools, the post–World War II liberals [referring to Cohen and Wickenden] spoke in contradictions . . . blaming women for their circumstances even as they implored the public to continue supporting welfare."[172] Elizabeth Wickenden had the analytical tools, but she was not in a position to use them. As a left feminist married to an important public official, she could not work in government, and even outside government she had to watch what she said. Scholars are correct that in the late 1940s and 1950s many social welfare experts abandoned noncategorical public assistance programs for stingier, rehabilitative ones that assumed individual failings, not structural inequalities, caused poverty; those scholars have not known, however, how many officials were forced into that shift by allegations of disloyalty to the United States.

PUBLIC POWER, AT HOME AND ABROAD

While Wickenden was trying to broaden public assistance programs, her husband Tex Goldschmidt was a key figure in public power projects. Providing electricity to rural areas—which was not profitable enough to interest private utilities—and lowering rates for those who did have power were important goals for those concerned with improving the living standards of the poor. Consumer activists, antitrusters, and advocates of rural economic development all were moved by the image of farmwives working "like peasant women in the Middle Ages" to haul well water and wash clothes.[173] By the late 1920s, a few private holding companies controlled most of the country's hydroelectric power and had developed elaborate financial structures that raised rates and thwarted regulators. New Deal initiatives such as the Public Utilities Holding Company Act of 1935 and the big dams funded by the Interior Department challenged the utility interests head-on. One response of the private utilities was to link public power advocates with socialism, a label that tended to stick and disrupt careers even many years later. Because construction of the dams functioned as public works projects, there was substantial overlap in the administration of public power and public works. Those civil servants accordingly drew fire not only from the private utilities but also from employers worried that the availability of public employment would put upward pressure on private-sector wages. Goldschmidt started his career in public works and then moved into public power, where his tangles with private utilities led to charges of disloyalty.[174]

Goldschmidt's ascendance through New Deal public works agencies and then the Interior Department reflected not only his considerable ability but also the backing of Texans Alvin Wirtz and Lyndon Johnson, who wanted friendly public power advocates in Washington. In 1939, Wirtz wrote Goldschmidt: "I have taken the liberty of suggesting to Lyndon that he start a boom to have [the new Federal Works Agency administrator] John Carmody appoint you Head of the Power Division, or something else with lots of authority and a good salary, under the new Public Works Administration. What effect is the new set-up going to have on Abe Fortas . . . and to what extent is it going to delay us in carrying out our deals with the T.P. & L. [Texas Power & Light Co.]?"[175] Sure enough, Goldschmidt became assistant to the director of the PWA Power Division, and by 1942 he was director of the Power Division in the Department of the Interior, reporting to undersecretary Abe Fortas.[176] In addition to promoting public power, Goldschmidt joined the ferocious battle over use of the water that dam projects made available for irrigation. He supported the campaign of California reformers like Paul S. Taylor and Helen Gahagan Douglas to enforce limits on commercial growers' use of public water.[177]

It did not take long for right-wingers to get Goldschmidt in their sights. In February 1943, Martin Dies named him as one of thirty-eight "crackpot, radical bureaucrats" in the Roosevelt administration.[178] Dies's Special Committee on Un-American Activities was about to expire, and he was fighting to keep it alive. Goldschmidt was in California working on the Central Valley hydroelectric project when Dies made his speech to the House. In the middle of a luncheon with state officials, Goldschmidt was summoned to take a call from Washington. It was Fortas, who told him what Dies had done. From his friend's formal tone, Goldschmidt knew Fortas was worried. Returning to his luncheon, Goldschmidt "felt the jolt of fear and anger I had not expressed to Abe," but he had to hide it because he was meeting with California attorney general Earl Warren, known to him then as an opponent of public power, whom he feared might sympathize with Dies. After Goldschmidt returned to Washington, Fortas and others spent weeks drilling him on how to present himself before the Kerr Committee, the House subcommittee formed to investigate the people named by Dies. Sympathetic letters poured in from friends. "Dear Red," Alvin Wirtz wrote facetiously. It was no joking matter to Fortas, who impressed on Goldschmidt that he had better take it dead seriously because "not only my own job, but the future of the public power program, the Department of the Interior and the Democratic administration depended on my approval by the committee."[179] Fortas exaggerated, but the stakes indeed were high, and the real issue had little to do with whether Goldschmidt had donated a few dollars to left-wing antifascists in Spain. Walter Packard, whose own battles with loyalty screening lay in the future, opined to Goldschmidt that Dies's attack stemmed from propaganda by private utilities.[180]

Of Dies's alleged crackpot radicals, the Kerr Committee found three suspect, cleared three, and never got to the others (Goldschmidt, who was cleared, suspected a "Solomonic deal" at higher levels). Goldschmidt recalled that for years he carried copies of the Kerr Committee report certifying him as a hardworking patriot everywhere he went—in his briefcase, his glove compartment, in his pocket when he went to Capitol Hill. But the talisman lost its power with time. As he ruefully recalled, "the Hearst press and others tended to remember the charges rather than the verdict. I would be characterized by the adjective 'pink,' as in the headline, 'Pink Aide to Head Science Team,' announcing my appointment to chair preparations for the United Nations Scientific Conference on the Conservation and Utilization of Resources five years later. Moreover, causes that I espoused such as the Marshall Plan were often attacked because of my espousal and part in its [sic] formation."[181] In 1948, the American Legion called for Goldschmidt's dismissal from government service on the grounds that he belonged to the Communist Party. Fortas, now in private practice, served as Goldschmidt's lawyer and demanded a retraction. When it was not forthcoming, Goldschmidt threatened to sue the American Legion for libel but apparently never did.[182]

The recurring accusations convinced Goldschmidt to leave the U.S. civil service. Although the Civil Service Commission cleared him without difficulty in 1948, he concluded that he would never rise higher because Dies had branded him indelibly. When he was offered a permanent position at the United Nations in 1950, he took it. Oscar Chapman had become secretary of the interior in 1949 and had already promoted two of Goldschmidt's subordinates over him. As Goldschmidt recalled, "I knew damn well he wasn't likely to appoint me to the next vacancy. I was too controversial . . . I had been attacked by Martin Dies and was too vulnerable to further attack from the emerging right-wingers." When Chapman feigned dismay at Goldschmidt's departure, Goldschmidt told him he would come back if needed: "if one of these Assistant-Secretaryships opens up you could always call me. . . . Well, the call never came. And I really didn't expect it to come."[183]

Although the Truman administration did not want to elevate one of Dies's favorite targets, it apparently was willing to use some of Goldschmidt's ideas, which included "a Marshall Plan for the rest of the world." Goldschmidt's work on the Krug Committee for the Marshall Plan led to his designation as the U.S. member of the organizing committee for the UN Scientific Conference on the Conservation and Utilization of Resources. In that capacity he gave a talk before American Academy of Arts and Sciences on January 12, 1949, that was uncannily similar to a section of Truman's Inaugural Address on January 20. Truman proposed what came to be known as the Point Four Program, to provide aid for technical assistance to poor countries. Although Clark Clifford took credit for Point Four, many journalists and politicians, including Lyndon Johnson, recognized Goldschmidt's influence.[184] Perceiving himself to be at a dead end in the U.S. civil service, Goldschmidt moved to the United Nations, where he applied his long-standing interests in economic development through public power and other public works projects in less-developed nations all over the globe.

Goldschmidt's respite from Red scare politics ended in 1953 with the creation of the International Organizations Employee Loyalty Board. In 1954 the IOELB gave him an interrogatory (reportedly second in length only to that of Ralph Bunche, the African American UN diplomat).[185] Many of the questions addressed the same old allegations, but there were new ones. Why had his wife gone to the Soviet Union in 1931? Why had he obtained his UN position with help from David Weintraub, who recently had resigned under pressure of loyalty charges?[186] The Wickenden-Goldschmidts braced for the worst. Their financial situation was precarious, and Goldschmidt began making inquiries about other jobs in case the board ruled against him. Wickenden vented her outrage by writing a

Figure 7.4. Tex Goldschmidt, circa 1951. Courtesy of Ann Goldschmidt Richardson and Arthur Goldschmidt Jr.

satirical fable about McCarthyism. In submitting it for publication, she asked that her name be withheld because "in these guilt-by-association times" her husband might be held accountable for "an errant wife."[187]

The IOELB finally cleared Goldschmidt in February 1955, but like so many others Goldschmidt and Wickenden carried the scars for the rest of their careers. Not only did Goldschmidt feel permanently marked by allegations already made (even though they had been rebutted); he could not predict what other detail from his past might be brought up and held against him. That was true for any loyalty defendant, but Goldschmidt had been more radical in his student years than investigators discovered. Drafting his memoirs in the late 1990s, he mused that he had not joined the Communist Party in 1932 chiefly because he had not been brave enough. He described his friend Rob Hall's decision to drop out of Columbia and become a CP organizer in Alabama as "an act of incredible courage." In 1932 Goldschmidt shared many of the party's positions (especially for "complete integration of the races and the absolute equality of the sexes"), but he "wasn't willing to accept the discipline" and "felt a bit guilty for lacking the courage of my convictions." Goldschmidt was not ashamed of his radical youth, but he feared it might provide an inexhaustible supply of ammunition against him.[188]

Goldschmidt continued to hold various high-level UN positions until 1966, when President Johnson appointed him U.S. representative to the Economic and Social Council of the United Nations (ECOSOC).[189] That ambassador-rank appointment was contingent on clearance by the American civil service (as distinct from the IOELB) and confirmation by the Senate. Goldschmidt's consternation when Johnson offered him the position illustrates how loyalty proceedings haunted civil servants. The president called to offer the position in November 1966. Goldschmidt hesitated because he opposed his old friend's policy in Vietnam, but since his prospective superior, ambassador to the United Nations Arthur Goldberg, did too, he decided the issue was not a deal breaker.[190] Goldschmidt also worried about the pay cut involved in moving from the United Nations to the U.S. Mission to the United Nations, but Wickenden's earning power made it possible for him to accept. (His predecessor in the position had complained about the pay, but, as the civil service's top official reassured Goldschmidt, "Jimmy [Roosevelt] had five wives and they all cost him money—you've only got one wife and she can make some money."[191]) Rather reluctantly, Goldschmidt told Johnson he was willing to be nominated.

President Johnson stunned him by saying he would announce the nomination first thing the next day. Goldschmidt's old wounds began to ache. He protested that Johnson had to wait for the FBI check. As Goldschmidt recalled it, Johnson's response was, "'Oh, for Christ's sake you've been checked back and forth. You've certainly got clearance.'" Goldschmidt explained that he did not have clearance in the American civil service.

> "Oh-oh," he says. "Well, just don't say anything. And you'll hear from me later." And then there was the goddamnedest lot of hoopla. . . . I got calls from all kinds of people that the FBI had been around to see. . . . It all was done in twenty-four hours so the next day Lyndon Johnson could announce my appointment. And there wasn't any way that he or anybody else could have read all of the FBI reports—because they went to all the places I'd ever been to and asked questions. Foreign embassies. . . . it must have cost a pretty penny and it couldn't have been looked at by anyone [before Johnson] announced it the next day. He knew damn well it was bullshit.

Johnson wanted Goldschmidt to take an interim appointment until the Senate could confirm him, but Goldschmidt refused "because I was afraid I would be attacked as a pinko, as I usually was." He told Johnson, "I don't want to embarrass you by having an interim appointment and then finding out that you're going to have to back off." Goldschmidt worried particularly about Senator Karl Mundt (R-S.D.), a HUAC veteran and "terrific red-baiter." Johnson was persuaded, and Goldschmidt waited to begin the job until the Senate confirmed him in February.[192]

In the interim, the Fortases threw a party for Goldschmidt at which the Johnsons were surprise guests. "The President came in and he came up and shook my hand, and he said 'don't tell me what you think of Vietnam until after you're confirmed.' Those were his first words to me. It was one of the very few times Vietnam was mentioned. He knew damn well how most of us felt about it, I think."[193] Goldschmidt believed it futile to talk with Johnson about Vietnam, but Wickenden tried to get to the president through Fortas: "Vietnam has become like a jealous mistress, bleeding the family not only of resources but emotional support and solidarity. . . . I see disarray among the liberal forces and a McCarthy-like movement on the right taking advantage of the vacuum."[194] While many former loyalty defendants, like the Keyserlings and Paul Porter, supported Johnson's policy in Vietnam, Goldschmidt and Wickenden did not. Loyalty accusations nonetheless inhibited their ability to influence their old friend, not least because they felt indebted to him and were reluctant to embarrass him by taking positions that might rekindle allegations of their Communist sympathies.

Goldschmidt was just one public power official subjected to ongoing loyalty investigation. Others include the aforementioned Walter Packard, Leland Olds,[195] and Goldschmidt's old boss John Carmody. Carmody was an engineer whose résumé included the Civil Works Administration, National Labor Relations Board, and Rural Electrification Administration when President Roosevelt elevated him to head of the new Federal Works Agency in 1939. Carmody's "advanced views" on race, labor, and peace brought him under attack from the Dies Committee and almost certainly contributed to Roosevelt's decision to ease him out in December 1941. Not only did Carmody never hold such an important post again, but the status of public works programs deteriorated.[196]

Historians' unfamiliarity with the leftist views of key public works administrators like Carmody and Goldschmidt has led to some faulty interpretations. The historian Jason Scott Smith, for example, divorces economic development and social welfare in explicating the New Deal agenda. Smith rightly argues that public works projects, prominently including the big power dams, represent one of the most important legacies of the New Deal, despite their limitations in ending unemployment or race and gender discrimination. He is incorrect to claim, however, that those limitations reflect the fact that public works programs were never intended to achieve social reform goals. "By and large," he concludes, "the New Deal was a political project not centrally concerned with advancing racial equality, redistribution of wealth, or social democratic ideals. It was focused instead on the goals of administering and managing resources efficiently while preserving the social order."[197] That conclusion is an example of how the silences produced by the federal loyalty program have distorted historiography. John Carmody, a central figure in Smith's study, certainly was concerned with advancing social democratic ideals, as were many people at his agency, which is why the

Figure 7.5. From New Deal to Great Society: Tex Goldschmidt, Elizabeth Wicken-den, Lyndon and Ladybird Johnson, probably 1967. Courtesy Columbia Rare Book and Manscript Library, Ann Goldschmidt Richardson, and Arthur Goldschmidt Jr.

Federal Works Agency topped Dies's list of agencies with large numbers of "subversives." The same could be said of Elizabeth Wickenden, Aubrey Williams, Hilda Worthington Smith, and many other public works administrators.[198]

In looking back on his career, Tex Goldschmidt drew an analogy between what the New Deal had done for the South and what the United Nations tried to do for undeveloped countries. "Economic development is too important to leave to the blind play of economic forces; it can be hastened or hindered by the intervention of policies designed to increase production and promote welfare. . . . The rich nations of the world will have to do for the poor nations what the Federal Government of the U.S. did for the South."[199] Contemporaries noticed the continuity in personnel and program. In 1965, columnist Drew Pearson described President Johnson's enthusiasm for Goldschmidt's UN work building dams on Vietnam's Mekong River. Almost three decades earlier, Pearson reminded readers, Goldschmidt and Abe Fortas had helped Johnson get loans for dams in thirteen Texas counties. The UN projects were an outgrowth of that New Deal impulse, engineered by some of the same people.[200]

That impulse was always hemmed in by the power of the American right and was even more constrained after the Cold War gave anticommunist rhetoric unprecedented potency. Goldschmidt knew that "the

Cold War fueled the development work of the UN system" and that his work therefore was restricted by the rigid framework of fighting communism.[201] Rather than abandon reform as a hopeless task, however, he and many like him tried to maneuver within those constraints to create the conditions for long-term social change. For them, the purpose of "economic development"—in the U.S. South, in the Mekong Delta, and everywhere—was to strengthen democracy by reducing social inequalities.

The federal employee loyalty program thus constricted the flow of people and ideas in both domestic and international policy. In one field after another, government officials who hoped to advance economic and political democracy by empowering subordinated groups and setting limits on the pursuit of private profit found themselves under attack from powerful opponents. Those opponents cynically capitalized on public fears of Communist espionage by charging leftist civil servants with subversion. Accused officials soon discovered that, once the machinery of the loyalty program was set in motion, extricating oneself was difficult and required compromise. Some loyalty defendants were more severely maimed than others, but the overall effect was to mute their policy influence at the time and obscure them from view since. The "end of reform" was neither natural nor foreordained.

CONCLUSION

In a 2006 telephone interview, the ninety-six-year-old lawyer Charlotte Tuttle Lloyd Walkup graciously answered my questions about her government career. Then she asked some questions about my research. My answer indicated sympathy for leftist civil servants caught up in the loyalty program's machinery. After a pause, the New Deal veteran remarked evenly, "I hope you won't reinforce McCarthy and Dies."

I hope so, too. Lloyd Walkup's concern echoed sentiments expressed to me by several Red scare survivors. In McCarthyism's long shadow, only detractors have labeled government officials as leftists, thanks to the endurance of the inaccurate but powerful association, forged during successive Red scares, between socialism and disloyalty to American ideals. The civil servants described here saw themselves as defenders, not betrayers, of fundamental American values such as egalitarianism and democracy. Not only does acknowledging their presence in the Roosevelt and Truman administrations yield a more accurate history, but a broader understanding of how the right misrepresented and curtailed their influence may contribute to a more informed political discourse.

In an early critique of the federal employee loyalty program, the former New Deal lawyer Thomas Emerson concluded:

> The answer to the basic problem of our time—the development of national common control over the functioning of our economic system and at the same time the preservation and extension of individual freedoms—depends upon the evolution of new methods of government and the creation of an alert, flexible and tolerant staff of administrators. . . . The democracies, which cannot compete [with totalitarian governments] in terms of highly centralized discipline, must seek their strength in resourceful and imaginative administration. If this be true the loyalty program is fast dissipating one of our most precious assets.[1]

The "resourceful and imaginative" government administrators of the 1930s and 1940s included a cohort of pragmatic idealists whose ideology was shaped by their parents' progressivism, their rigorous educations, and their participation in the Popular Front movement, itself energized by the crisis of capitalism that produced the Great Depression. Recognizing the limits of "rugged individualism" for most people living in modern industrial society, these civil servants advocated government intervention to provide at least the minimal levels of economic independence and education that were prerequisites to civic participation. "Political democracy depends on the achievement of industrial democracy, and this is still far away from us," Mary Dublin (later Keyserling) asserted in 1938, citing statistics on economic inequality and the obstacles to informed political participation by the poor.[2] In 1967, as social movements challenged the status quo in the United States and around the world, Caroline Ware opined that the most promising trend of the twentieth century was "the revolution of rising participation" by groups that historically had provided "the passive base for the wealth and culture they did not share."[3] Left-leaning New Dealers like Mary Dublin Keyserling and Caroline Ware were not trying to destroy American democracy; they were trying to strengthen it by making it a reality for more people. But they were among those most heavily penalized by the loyalty program. As the lawyer Eleanor Bontecou observed, the loyalty tests were less effective in identifying Communists than they were in punishing "the persons who have not adhered to a closed system of thought but reach out for new answers to the problems of our time."[4]

For public servants on the New Deal's left fringe, the "problems of our time" included race and gender inequality as well as class exploitation. The many women among them were especially sensitive to how the family wage ideal—which prescribed male breadwinning and female dependence—had structured the labor market and social welfare policies in ways that disadvantaged women and also excluded most racial minorities. Broadly trained in history and economics, left-leaning New Dealers believed that race and gender inequality served employers by creating lower-status groups of workers who supposedly needed or deserved less, thereby applying downward pressure on all labor standards, including those of white men. They saw their mission as sweeping away beliefs and practices that were based on obsolete conditions but defended by those whose interests they continued to serve. As Elizabeth Wickenden understood it, she and her colleagues were participants in a historic struggle between "the forces making for social progress, that is, for a better life for the greater number, and the forces intent on maintaining the status quo of personal, racial, class, and national privilege."[5] That linkage of gender, race, and class justice helps explain the left's wide appeal in the 1930s and 1940s.

That linkage also helps explain why the right's reaction was so powerful. The responsiveness of some New Dealers to the decade's progressive labor and consumer movements—which incorporated antiracist and feminist elements—triggered an immediate response from conservative business interests and their allies in Congress and the media. In 1938, well before Soviet espionage became a national security concern, the Dies Committee launched the crusade against "Communists in government."

Congressman Dies had been among the Wagner Act's most vociferous critics, and he opposed the Fair Labor Standards Act on the grounds that "you cannot prescribe the same wages for the black man as for the white man."[6] Dies Committee backers included private interests such as the Hearst Corporation, which was facing pressure from the CIO as well as from organized consumers (typically represented as "housewives"). The Smith Committee soon joined the campaign to paint the New Deal pink, investigating the National Labor Relations Board and then the Office of Price Administration (with the assistance, not incidentally, of the lawyer who had represented the steel industry in its effort to overturn the National Labor Relations Act). These initiatives generated enough pressure to win personnel and organizational changes that made the NLRB and OPA less threatening to conservatives. Encouraged by such successes, the Dies Committee continued to mine the anticommunist vein, sowing doubts about agencies from the Works Progress Administration to the Federal Communications Commission to the Securities and Exchange Commission, and challenging the loyalty of the Civil Service Commission examiners then in charge of screening government employees. By the time the Cold War gave charges of Soviet infiltration more political traction, anti–New Deal forces had laid the groundwork for a full-blown Red scare by priming public opinion and by collecting information on public officials that later would make them "loyalty defendants."

A surprisingly high proportion of those officials were women, as we have seen, and others were men who promoted women's rights. The gender and sexual conservatism of the New Right that emerged in the 1970s often is understood as a departure from the more purely class-driven (or in the South, class- and race-driven) Old Right of the preceding period.[7] But closer examination reveals substantial continuity. For conservatives of the 1940s and 1950s, no less than their successors, antifeminism was an integral objective as well as a convenient tool in the struggle to turn voters against the "Washington femmocracy." Conservatives cast the civil service as a bureaucracy of short-haired women and long-haired men bent on replacing the traditional American family with a "womb-to-tomb" welfare state (forerunner of today's similarly feminized specter, the nanny state). Imperfect as they were, government measures such as public assistance and equal opportunity weakened the prerogatives not just of employers but also of men as heads of household, by reducing women's dependence on the family wage system. Conservatives tried to weaken public confidence in government regulatory and social welfare agencies by highlighting women's influence in them, and by linking feminism with un-Americanism.

It is difficult to specify what would have happened if repression had not narrowed the spectrum of the possible. Many forces contributed to the defeat of social democracy in the United States, and civil servants, even the highest-ranking ones, are rarely powerful enough to dictate policy outcomes. But in one field after another, the loyalty program guaranteed the defeat of more democratic policy alternatives by removing or crippling their government advocates. The subsequent careers of those who were not permanently excluded from government service bore the mark of their earlier traumas, as they constantly reiterated their anticommunism and stopped discussing the tensions between capitalism and democracy.

In foreign affairs, we have seen how social democrats like Paul R. Porter, Thomas Blaisdell, Rowena Rommel, and Tex Goldschmidt, who advocated international economic planning, aid, and development programs that prioritized reducing inequality over promoting American hegemony, were forced to leave government service or, in the cases of Rommel and Goldschmidt, to transfer to UN agencies—where investigations by the International Organizations Employee Loyalty Board continually reminded them of their vulnerability.

In the case of public housing, loyalty charges that threatened her husband's career forced Catherine Bauer, the New Deal era's most famous public housing advocate, to soften her critique of the real estate industry and drop her insistence on high-quality public housing as an option for working Americans, not just the indigent. The fate of Bauer and other public housing advocates resulted in federal policies that deepened inequality by isolating the poor in stigmatizing and unsafe public housing "projects." Similar constraints shackled advocates of strengthening the representation and rights of all workers and consumers. Barred from government service in the late 1960s, the African American lawyer Pauli Murray had to wait a decade before the Equal Employment Opportunity Commission finally got serious about employment discrimination against women (under the leadership of her protégée Eleanor Holmes Norton).[8] Mary Dublin Keyserling and Esther Peterson held on in government service but waged their policy battles on behalf of wage earners and consumers with the knowledge that the opposition was armed and ready to revive allegations of un-Americanism. In the field of social welfare, Wilbur Cohen survived repeated loyalty investigations to become secretary of health, education, and welfare, but in the process he revised his prescription for addressing poverty to stress individual rather than systemic failings. Cohen's shift dismayed his former ally Elizabeth Wickenden, whose efforts to resist welfare policies that stigmatized poor single mothers were hampered by the fact that the loyalty program effectively forced her to lobby from outside government.

Some loyalty defendants were identified less with a single policy than with the broad social democratic program. The radical New Deal lawyers Leon Keyserling and David Demarest Lloyd became key Democratic Party strategists and top officials in the Truman administration, responsible for some of its most progressive initiatives. Both were battered by years of investigation, as we have seen. Both adjusted their priorities and tactics, and those adjustments in turn contributed to liberalism's shift toward the "vital center." Thus the loyalty program affected not just particular policies but also the general tone and scope of the reform agenda.

These constricting effects were even more pervasive, moreover, than the limited number of stories told here can convey. More than two thousand other large case files await examination. There is no list of the roughly 1.8 million smaller case files that were destroyed, so we will never know precisely who was investigated beyond the initial screening.[9] Certainly the repressive impact on government employees was not limited to the estimated twenty-five thousand who underwent the dreaded full field investigation by the FBI. Every federal employee filled out a loyalty questionnaire with each job change. Investigators interviewed employees about their colleagues. The machinery did not operate quietly.

It also did not operate fairly. Agency security officers, the FBI, and congressional investigating committees leaked confidential information to each other and to their allies in the press. The FBI also withheld information from loyalty boards that would have exposed the dishonesty of some informants. The FBI knew Paul Crouch had misrepresented key points about the Keyserlings, for example, but because Crouch was crucial to other cases, the FBI told Mary Dublin Keyserling's loyalty board that it deemed Crouch reliable. HUAC staffer Benjamin Mandel knew that Senator McCarthy was incorrect in labeling Dorothy Kenyon a Communist sympathizer, but Mandel stayed quiet as his colleagues continued to challenge Kenyon's loyalty.[10]

Knowing that the security apparatus was rigged against them, some loyalty defendants hid things they should not have had to hide. Because they could not trust loyalty officials to distinguish between Communists and other leftists, defendants typically downplayed any evidence of leftist views or activism. As a result, we have not recognized that many government officials participated in the radical student movement of the 1930s, for example, or belonged to the Socialist Party. When it came time to give oral history interviews and draft memoirs, many loyalty defendants avoided disclosing that they had been investigated, as we have seen. Before depositing their papers in archives, many people removed materials about the disloyalty charges against them and about the activities that had triggered those charges. These officials' reluctance to relive painful memories or to have their careers defined by such attacks is understandable, but it has had many consequences beyond the obvious one of misleading historians. Loyalty defendants' silence meant that the biases of the loyalty program against noncommunist leftists—and against feminists—were not confronted at the time and have not been recognized since. By forcing these civil servants to alter or hide their convictions, the loyalty program also severed transmission between generations of leftists. Scarred survivors from Paul Porter to the Keyserlings kept their distance from the radicals of the late 1960s, who in turn saw their forebears as part of the problem rather than part of the solution. By forcing policymakers and administrators to leave government or reinvent themselves as centrists, the loyalty program not only curbed the influence of noncommunist leftists in government; it obscured the fact that they had existed. The invisibility of socialists and social democrats in government has led to an underestimation of the reform potential that existed at midcentury and also of the repression that crushed it. The constriction and eventual demise of the New Deal resulted from coordinated attacks by those whose power it threatened, not from any inherent limitation of its appeal to the American electorate.[11]

Correcting the historical record seems especially important now, in the early twenty-first century, when conservatives have returned to arguing that goals such as a more equitable distribution of wealth are alien to the American tradition and to demonizing any deviation from free-market economic policy as socialistic.[12] Again, efforts to address debilitating economic and political problems are handicapped by an elite-driven right that masquerades as a grassroots movement.[13] In order to undercut popular support for progressive policies, right-wing politicians and media figures label President Barack Obama a socialist, a foreign-born Muslim, or a pro-abortion intellectual with an aggressive wife.[14] Antifeminism, like racism, remains integral to the right's vision and to its strategy for recruiting voters whose economic interests are poorly served by its program of privatization, deregulation, and tax cuts. Progressives generally appreciate the historical significance of the race card; until they also recognize how powerful the gender card is and how skillfully conservatives play it, not only will women continue to enjoy fewer opportunities in public life than men, but the right's grip on political power will be difficult to loosen. And until American voters reject "nostalgia for an imagined lost society based on virtues of rugged individualism,"[15] inequality will continue to deepen, and diminishing numbers of Americans will have the education and hope required to sustain political democracy. We could do worse than to recover the vision of some public servants who defined the pursuit of democracy and equality as the essence of Americanism.

Loyalty Case Records and Selection

There is no comprehensive list of federal employees whose investigations continued beyond the initial screening. The vast majority of the U.S. Civil Service Commission case files were destroyed in 1984 after a National Archives and Records Service study concluded they were not of sufficient research value to retain. Only the largest files, about 2,400 files more than an inch thick (the "oversize" files, totaling 1,200 cubic feet), were preserved, as Record Group 478 (RG 478). An estimated 1.72 million case files that were less than an inch thick (totaling 18,600 cubic feet) were destroyed.[1] Few scholars have cited RG 478, the existence of which I discovered only after much communication with archivists. The record group does not include every case that generated a large volume of documentation; there is no file for Dorothy Bailey, for example, whose case reached the U.S. Supreme Court. Although the record group thus is of limited use for sampling purposes, it contains rich data on at least some (and probably most) of the cases that generated files more than an inch thick.

What made files "oversize" was either exhibits submitted by the defendant, typically their own publications, or hearing transcripts. Hearings took place after a defendant replied to an interrogatory from a loyalty board. Sometimes the defendant requested a hearing, and sometimes the board required one because it was not convinced by the reply to interrogatory. Because high-level people were more likely to have publications and more likely to request hearings to clear their reputations, the oversize files disproportionately pertain to high-ranking employees. Low-level workers were less able to afford appeals, and they may have been less optimistic about their chances of success. Similarly, cases involving Communist Party members and cases involving gays and lesbians seem underrepresented in RG 478, perhaps because those individuals were more likely to resign or to be dismissed before their files became thick. The case records of the "lavender scare" probably were among those 1.72 million "thin" files that were destroyed.[2]

When I began my research, National Archives policy prevented me from seeing the list of 2,400 surviving case files that constitute RG 478. I had to guess who might have been a loyalty defendant, obtain an obituary or other proof of death, file a Freedom of Information Act (FOIA) request for each individual, and wait, often for months, in order to receive permission to examine the file at the National Archives. Obtaining FBI files took substantially longer. When an individual's RG 478 file contained FBI reports, I did not request that person's FBI file unless I had a particular interest in the FBI's internal correspondence. I also obtained FBI files on some loyalty defendants whose Civil Service Commission files are not in RG 478.

To decide what FOIA requests to make, I compiled lists of allegedly subversive government employees from the files of government and private anticommunists, and I examined records of the U.S. Civil Service Commission and the Truman White House, in addition to lists of professional women in the federal government that were generated by the U.S. Women's Bureau. I also searched secondary sources and the Internet. Obtaining one RG 478 or FBI file led me to other cases because allegations of association with suspect coworkers were common. By this arduous method, I obtained RG 478 and FBI files for about twenty relatively high-level loyalty defendants.

The National Archives changed its policy in 2006 and allowed me access to the list of about 2,400 people whose Civil Service Commission files survive in RG 478. That list permitted me to calculate the gender breakdown of those cases, and it also identified as loyalty defendants some officials whose names I knew from other contexts. I soon expanded my collection of RG 478 and FBI files to include about fifty loyalty defendants. Having the RG 478 case list from the beginning would have saved me time, but it would not have produced substantially different results. Now that RG 478 is more accessible, future researchers exploring different questions may decide to examine a larger number of its files, bearing in mind that its provenance limits the meaningfulness of statistical analysis.

Not initially having access to the list of RG 478 files actually may have improved this study by forcing me to search far and wide for even fragmentary records on government employee loyalty cases. In 2003, the records of two major congressional investigating committees opened (House and Senate rules require sensitive records to remain closed for fifty years). The sprawling research files and executive session hearing transcripts of the House Un-American Activities Committee and the Senate Internal Security Subcommittee yielded valuable information. Some White House aides and cabinet officials kept files on loyalty cases under their jurisdiction. The records of a subcommittee headed by Senator Olin Johnston in 1955 and 1956 to study the loyalty program include materials submitted by employees who believed they had been treated unfairly. The Arnold & Porter law firm kindly allowed me to examine some transcripts and nonprivileged files involving cases that had already been made public. The Fund for the Republic Foundation records include anonymous summaries of 353 cases made for a study published in 1955. I also found cases in the papers of prior scholars of the loyalty program and in books by the journalists Carl Bernstein and Selma Williams.[3]

In all I examined about 600 loyalty cases. I selected the most fully documented cases I could find that involved high-ranking civil servants, and I looked for diaries, letters, memoirs, and oral histories to examine whether and how the defendants represented their experiences. After the list of RG 478 files became available, it was difficult to stop examining additional cases—until I recognized that the contents of each new file were fascinating but no longer surprising. I had reached the point of diminishing returns, from an analytical standpoint. I leave it to future scholars to continue mining this mesmerizing, if exasperating, collection.

A note of caution about working in these files, and particularly in the FBI reports they often contain: they do not offer an impartial or unmediated view of a loyalty defendant's life and career. FBI agents checked voter registrations, passport applications, and arrest and credit records, and they spoke with past and present employers, coworkers, teachers, landlords, and friends. Attempting to limit the interpretive role of its often inexperienced agents, the FBI trained them to report every detail from their interviews. The resulting reports are crowded with gossip and unsupported opinion, much of it ill informed or contradictory. The reports' cover-page summaries typically highlight only the most "derogatory" information, belying any commitment to objectivity. Evaluation is further complicated by the anonymity of the FBI's confidential informants, whose motives and reliability varied.[4] Fortunately, the case files also give voice to the defendants: we have their written replies to charges, supporting affidavits from dozens of witnesses, and the hearing transcripts. Even there, one must bear in mind that the defense counsel often shaped the tone and content of a defendant's statements.

Case Summaries

From several hundred loyalty cases, I selected these forty-two for their significance and for the completeness or richness of sources. Many of these cases are referred to in passing throughout the text. These cryptic summaries do not enumerate allegations and refutations, because doing so properly would require many pages for each case.

EXPLANATORY NOTES

LRB: Civil Service Commission Loyalty Review Board (reviewed decisions of lower loyalty boards, 1947–53).

"Flagged": An employee who resigned before the LRB completed its post-audit of the employing agency's decision was flagged, which meant a full reinvestigation would be required if that person tried to return to government service.

RIF: Reduction-in-force dismissal (theoretically without prejudice to employee).

IOELB: International Organizations Employee Loyalty Board, created 1953; because it technically did not have power to dismiss or retain, its decisions are listed as unfavorable/favorable.

Employment outside government is not listed, and generally only the highest or latest position held at an agency is listed.

Spouse/partner name is in **boldface** if there were allegations about him/her.

For archival abbreviations, see the list at the beginning of the endnotes.

BERNSTEIN, BERNICE LOTWIN (1908-1996)
Attorney; New York regional dir. HEW, retained 1955
BA philosophy 1930, LLB 1933, University of Wisconsin. NRA 1934; SSB 1935–42, asst. gen. counsel; War Manpower Commission 1942–45, asst. gen. counsel; Dept. of Labor 1946; FSA/HEW 1947–77, Region 2 dir. 1966–77. Married **Bernard Bernstein** (asst. gen. counsel, Treasury Dept.) 1938; three daughters born 1940, 1943, 1946. Jewish.

Investigation (incomplete data): Aug. 1954 FBI full field investigation; Oct. 1954 suspended from HEW; cleared Feb. 1955. See her FBI file and see Bernard Bernstein Papers, HSTL.

BETHUNE, MARY MCLEOD (1875–1955)
Educator, NYA administrator; resigned Dept. Agriculture 1951
Scotia Seminary 1888–94. Founder National Council of Negro Women 1935. National Youth Admin., dir., Negro Affairs, 1936–44; organizer Federal Council on Negro Affairs ("Black Cabinet"). Married Albertus Bethune in 1898. Presbyterian.

Dies accused her of membership in Communist fronts repeatedly Oct. 1941–Feb. 1943; after hearing before Kerr Committee, retained Aug. 1942 by Federal Works Agency (NYA parent). In 1943 she signed anti–Dies Committee letter but also distanced herself from perceived leftists. Hired in 1951 as consultant to Farmers Home Admin., triggering extensive FBI investigation; she resigned before decision. FBI continued to monitor her; after her death agents attended a play about her and considered disrupting a proposed memorial to her. See her FBI file.

BLAISDELL, THOMAS C., JR. (1895–1988)
Economist; resigned Dept. Commerce 1951, flagged
BA Penn. State 1916, MA social history 1922, PhD economics 1932, Columbia. AAA office of Consumers' Counsel, 1933; NRA Consumers' Advisory Board, 1934–35; Resettlement Admin. 1935–36; SSB 1936–37; National Resources Committee 1937–38; Securities and Exchange Commission 1938–39; National Resources Planning Board, 1939–43; War Production Board, 1942–45; Office of War Mobiliz. & Reconversion, 1945, chief, Planning & Statistics; chief of Mission for Economic Affairs with rank of minister, London, 1945–47; Dept. Commerce, dir. OIT, asst. secretary, 1947–51. Married **Catherine Maltby** 1921; one son.

Investigated 1943, rated eligible by CSC after hearing 1944; retained after hearing by Commerce 1948; investigated 1951 and resigned before final decision, file flagged as "unresolved question of loyalty, Pro-Communist." In 1954 UN Technical Assistance Admin. invited him to represent it in Pakistan, triggering another comprehensive investigation and interrogatory. In his reply Blaisdell said he had withdrawn his application because he no longer wanted the position; the flag on his file remained in place. See RG 478 file.

BRUNAUER, ESTHER (1901-1959)
International affairs expert; dismissed by State Dept. 1952
BA 1924 Mills, PhD history, Stanford 1927. AAUW educator and author on international problems, 1927–44; State Dept. 1944–1952, US rep. on Preparatory Commission to UNESCO at rank of minister, then policy liaison for State Dept. to UNESCO. Married **Stephen Brunauer**

(Hungarian-born chemist) 1931; three children born 1934, 1938, 1942. Protestant.

Representative Busbey called her subversive in 1947; retained by State Aug. 1948 after hearing. Named as one of McCarthy's first nine examples of subversion at State, Feb. 1950; Tydings Committee exonerated her. State suspended her Apr. 1951 on security (not loyalty) grounds because U.S. Navy had just suspended her husband. Hearings in July–Aug. 1951, 14 witnesses, 68 exhibits, 604-page transcript. State dismissed her Apr. 1952 as a security risk; appeal hearing focused on husband, who had not been found disloyal by navy but had resigned on his supervisor's advice because of morals charges about his adultery; appeal denied June 1952. Her work in nonsensitive job at Library of Congress led to right-wing attacks, so she left government. See RG 478 file; case 325, FFR Papers.

BUNCHE, RALPH (1904–1971)
Political scientist, UN diplomat; favorable ruling by IOELB 1954

BA international relations, UCLA 1927, PhD political science, Harvard 1936. Howard University political scientist who specialized in colonial territories. During World War II, Africa analyst for Office of Strategic Services, then assoc. chief (under Alger Hiss), Division of Dependent Area Affairs, State Dept. Won 1950 Nobel Peace Prize for his work as UN mediator in Palestine 1947–49. Finished career as UN undersecretary-general, 1968–70. Married Ruth Harris, 1930; three children born 1931, 1933, 1943.

Called before SISS March 1953. Replied to IOELB interrogatory Feb. 1954. Details of May 1954 IOELB hearing were leaked to press and NAACP declared proceedings a farce. IOELB issued public and unanimous clearance. See RG 478 file.

CARMODY, JOHN (1881–1963)
Coal executive, labor mediator; retained by Small Defense Plants Admin. 1952

Elmira Business College 1908; Columbia University night school 1926. NRA Labor Board, 1933; Civil Works Admin. 1933–34; NLRB 1935–36; Rural Elect. Admin. head, 1936–39; Federal Works Agency head, 1939–41; US Maritime Commission 1941–46; War Assets Admin. 1947–48; presidential commissions on materials, water resources 1950–51; ECA consultant, 1951; Small Defense Plants Admin. consultant, 1951–53. Married Margaret Cross, 1913; daughter born 1915. Irish Catholic.

Named by Dies Committee as member of ALPD, 1939; accused of employing Communist sympathizers at Rural Elect. Admin., Federal Works Agency; eased out of Federal Works Agency 1941. "Flagged" after RIF from War Assets Admin. in 1948, cleared 1950 but case remanded by LRB on post-audit; retained 1952. See RG 478 file.

COHEN, LUCY KRAMER: SEE KRAMER, LUCY

COHEN, WILBUR J. (1913–1987)
Social insurance and welfare expert; favorable ruling by IOELB 1955
BA economics, Wisconsin 1934. SSB 1935–55, chief liaison to Congress; HEW 1961–68, asst. sec. to secretary. Married **Eloise Bittel** (social worker) 1938; three sons. Jewish (Eloise: Baptist).

Rated eligible by FSA after FBI interview, 1942. Questioned by Senate subcommittee about subordinate Jacob Fisher in Jan. 1948, followed by FBI full field investigation. FSA loyalty board rated him eligible but LRB remanded case to agency. Cohen replied to interrogatory Dec. 1948, retained by FSA May 1949. Marjorie Shearon gave FBI an elaborate report alleging Cohen's CP ties, Oct. 1950. Attorney general considered prosecuting him for perjury Dec. 1950. Another round of FBI investigation, rated eligible again by FSA June 1951. Applied for UN job 1953; IOELB interrogatory Apr. 1954; hearing Oct. 1954; favorable decision by IOELB June 1955, but he went to academia. Summary of file sent to Kennedy White House May 1961. See RG 478 file.

DE SCHWEINITZ, DOROTHEA (1891–1980)
Social worker, labor economist; retained by Wage Stabilization Board 1952
BA Smith 1912, MA economics, Columbia 1929. US Employment Service 1933–36; NLRB regional dir., St. Louis 1937–43; War Production Board, chief of Committee on Standards, 1943–46; Wage Stabilization Board, supervisory economist, 1951–? Moravian Church (Protestant).

FBI interview 1943; Full field investigation 1946; another investigation when she returned to govt. in 1951; replied to interrogatory and rated eligible April 1952. See RG 478 file.

EMERSON, THOMAS I. (1907–1991)
Lawyer; left government service (OPA) 1945
BA Yale 1928, LLB Yale Law 1931. NRA 1933–34; NLRB 1934–36; SSB 1936–37; NRLB 1937–40, head of Review Division; OPA 1941–45, deputy administrator for enforcement; Office of Economic Stabilization 1945, gen. counsel; Office of War Mobiliz. & Reconversion 1945–46, gen. counsel; Yale Law professor 1946–76. Married **Betty Paret** (labor reformer, later govt. administrator) 1934; three children. After Paret's death, married Ruth Calvin. Protestant.

Accused of CP sympathies during Smith Committee investigation of NRLB in 1940. Ben Mandel's 1941 list of 53 government "big shots" with CP associations included Emerson and his wife Paret. In 1941 FBI obtained Emerson's 1939 address book. Dies Committee subpoenaed his CSC file to try to prove CSC protection of subversives at OPA. Called subversive by Congressman Busbey 1944, by Fulton Lewis Jr. 1945, by right-wing media and conservative Yale alumni into 1960s. See FBI file, copy in his papers at Yale.

EZEKIEL, MORDECAI (1899–1974)
Agricultural economist; favorable ruling by IOELB 1955

BS agriculture, Maryland 1918, MS Minnesota 1923, PhD economics, Brookings 1926. While working for the Federal Farm Board, 1930–32, Ezekiel conceived the Agricultural Adjustment Admin. Adviser to Sec. of Agriculture 1933–44; Bureau of Agricultural Economics, economic adviser 1944–47, resigned in lieu of RIF 1947. UN Food and Agriculture Org. 1947–62, special assistant to director general. U.S. Agency for International Development 1962–67, UN division chief. Married **Lucille Finsterwald** (teacher, activist, sister of CP dancer Maxine Finsterwald) 1927; three children. Jewish.

Ben Mandel's 1941 list of 53 government "big shots" with CP associations included Ezekiel. CSC examiner in Sept. 1942 said Ezekiel and his wife "should be watched closely," but his agency retained him. He resigned in 1947 rather than be RIFed, possibly anticipating loyalty charges. His file was "flagged" in case he tried to return to U.S. govt. IOELB took up his case mid-1953; after full FBI investigation, he replied to interrogatory Dec. 1953; hearings in Rome July 1954 and Washington Jan. 1955; rated favorable by a divided IOELB Apr. 1955. Further FBI reports 1956–58; Interior Dept. declined to hire him 1958; rated eligible for U.S. Agency for International Development 1962. See RG 478 file.

FALK, ISIDORE (1899–1984)
Public health expert; retained by Federal Security Agency 1950

PhD public health, Yale 1923. Committee on Economic Security, 1934–35; SSB 1936–53, dir. Bureau Research and Statistics. Married; two sons. Jewish.

Falk's work on national health insurance was investigated by two Senate subcommittees, 1947–48. Investigated by FBI 1948, retained by FSA 1950. Resigned HEW Dec. 1953, effective Oct. 1954. See Falk Papers, Yale.

FLEXNER, JEAN (1899–?)
Labor economist; retained by Bureau Labor Statistics 1955

BA economics, Bryn Mawr 1921, LSE 1922, PhD economics, Brookings 1929. US Children's Bureau 1932–35; Bureau of Labor Standards 1935–42; War Dept. 1943–45; Bureau of Labor Statistics 1945–? Married **Paul Lewinson** (later a govt. archivist) 1927. Jewish.

FBI full field investigation 1948, reply to interrogatory Oct. 1948, rated eligible after hearing Nov. 1948. Rated eligible again Dec. 1951, reinvestigated by FBI 1954 and retained Jan. 1955.

FRAZIER, E. FRANKLIN (1894–1962)
Sociologist; flagged by IOELB 1954

BA Howard 1916, PhD sociology, Chicago 1927. 1951–53 UNESCO, Paris div. chief. Married Marie Brown.

FBI full field investigation 1953 when his appointment at UNESCO was extended; IOELB planned to issue interrogatory, but his 90-day appointment ended so his file was "flagged." Summoned before SISS ("Communist Penetration of Education") in Mar. 1955. Applicant for UNESCO job 1961; IOELB again planned to issue interrogatory but he withdrew his application, citing health issues and impending surgery. See RG 478 file.

GELLHORN, WALTER (1906–1996)
Lawyer; left government service (War Labor Board) 1946

BA Amherst 1927, LLB Columbia 1931. Clerked for Assoc. Sup. Ct. justice Harlan Stone 1931–32; US Solicitor General's Office 1932–33. Columbia Law faculty 1933–75, with leaves for govt. service: SSB regional attorney 1936–38; OPA regional attorney 1942–43; Dept. Interior 1943–44; War Labor Board, chair Region II, 1944–46. Married **Kitty Minus** 1932; two daughters.

Dies named him among "crackpot radicals" in govt., Feb. 1943; FBI interviewed him Mar. 1943; testified before Dies Committee Apr. 1943. Retained by OPA Oct. 1943 over CSC examiner's recommendation to terminate and flag. Investigated 1945 and retained by War Labor Board after internal debate. Left govt. 1946 but remained target, particularly of J. B. Matthews, who attacked him 1948–49 to try to discredit Gellhorn's forthcoming study of Dies Committee. As applicant for HEW job 1955, was questioned about his own and his wife's associations; did not get job. FBI continued to monitor him, noted his 1961 call to abolish HUAC. See RG 478 file.

GOLDSCHMIDT, ARTHUR ("TEX") (1910–2000)
Public power expert, UN official; favorable ruling by IOELB 1955

BA economics, Columbia 1932. FERA–Civil Works Admin. 1933–36; Wheeler Committee on Interstate Commerce 1936–37; (CIO, legislative researcher 1937–38); Asst. to Consumer Counsel, Bituminous Coal Commission, 1938; Public Works Admin. Power Div. 1938–40; Interior Dept. Power Div. 1941–47, dir. Special asst. to secretary of interior, on loan to UN Scientific Conference on the Conservation and Utilization of

Resources, UNESCO, UN ECOSOC, 1947–50. UN Technical Assistance Admin., dir., Programme Div., 1951–58 (on leave 1957 as chief, UN Mission on Resources and Industry to Iran); UN ECOSOC 1958–66, div. dir.; U.S. Representative to ECOSOC with rank of ambassador, 1967–69; Consultant to UN agencies 1969–87. Married **Elizabeth Wickenden** (social welfare expert) in 1933; three children born 1938, 1942, 1945. Atheist of Lutheran heritage.

Dies named him among "crackpot radicals" in government Feb. 1943. Appeared before Kerr Committee Apr. 1943, exonerated May. Included by Gov. Bricker of Ohio in Oct. 1944 list of subversives in govt. FBI full field investigation 1947; retained by Interior Oct. 48. Replied to IOELB interrogatory May 1954; IOELB hearing Feb. 1955; favorable rating Apr. 1955. Remained under FBI surveillance, for example 1961 after a report that his mother had made a pro-CP remark at a dinner party. See RG 478 file.

HARRIS, REED (1909–1982)
Journalist; resigned Voice of America (State Dept.) 1953, reinstated 1962

BA Columbia 1932. WPA Federal Writers' Project 1934–38, asst. dir.; National Emergency Council 1939–40; Office of War Information 1941–49; State Dept. International Information Admin. (parent of Voice of America), deputy dir. 1950–53, resigned after McCarthy attacks. Reinstated as deputy dir. (now USIA) by Edward Murrow 1962. Married Martha Tellier 1931; three children. Methodist.

Investigated by CSC 1942, by State Dept. 1946, by FBI 1948, by State in 1952 (cleared); testified before McCarthy's Permanent Subcommittee on Investigations for three days in spring 1953, then resigned. Harris's defiant testimony was aired as part of Edward R. Murrow's *See It Now* program in Mar. 1954, a broadcast that helped turn public opinion against McCarthy. See RG 478 file.

HOEY, JANE (1892–1968)
Social worker, dir. Bureau Public Assistance; favorable ruling by IOELB 1954

BA Trinity College 1916, MA political science, Columbia 1916, diploma New York School of Philanthropy. After working in New York state agencies for many years, served as dir. of SSB's Bureau of Public Assistance, 1936–53. Catholic.

FBI investigated her 1949 and found nothing derogatory. One study claims she was fired in 1953 partly because she had defended staff accused of disloyalty. In 1953 she applied for a position with Voice of America but withdrew before the IOELB rated her favorably in Aug. 1954. See FBI file.

KENYON, DOROTHY (1888–1972)
Lawyer; UN Commission on the Status of Women (State Dept.), accused by
McCarthy 1950
BA economics and history, Smith 1908, LLB New York University 1917. New York City municipal court judge 1939–40; U.S. delegate to UN Commission on the Status of Women 1946–50. Protestant.

Senator McCarthy named her on his list of alleged subversives in State Dept., which selected delegates to UN Commission on the Status of Women. Her commission had expired by the time she was the first person to appear before the Tydings Committee, created to investigate McCarthy's charges. Her defiant rebuttal of McCarthy's allegations won her much public sympathy, but she never received another govt. appointment. FBI investigated her again 1964 when she was under White House consideration for some appointment, but she did not receive it. See FBI file.

KEYSERLING, LEON (1908–1987)
Lawyer, economist; retained by Council of Economic Advisers 1952
BA Columbia 1928, LLB Harvard 1931. Legislative aide to Senator Robert F. Wagner 1933–37; USHA gen. counsel 1937–41, acting admin. 1941–42; FHA gen. counsel 1942–46; Council of Economic Advisers 1946–53 (acting chair 1949, chair 1950–53). Married **Mary Dublin Keyserling** (see next case) 1940; no children. Jewish.

Interviewed by FBI 1942. FBI full field investigation 1948, cleared by LRB Dec. 1948. SISS testimony June–July 1951. FBI full field investigation 1951–53, ongoing. LRB rated him eligible Feb. 1952; McCarthy publicized case next day. In Sept. 1952 SISS staff urged publication of Keyserlings' SISS testimony: "a terrific story on the eve of the Presidential election, and it is difficult to see how Leon Keyserling can retain his position if his wife's suspension is upheld." Leon subpoenaed to appear before SISS Oct. 1952. Eisenhower elected president Nov. 1952. Both Keyserlings resigned Jan. 1953. See Dublin Keyserling RG 478 file.

KEYSERLING, MARY DUBLIN (1910–1997)
Economist; Commerce Dept., cleared on loyalty grounds 1952
BA economics and sociology, Barnard 1930, grad. studies London School of Economics, ABD economics, Columbia 1933. House Committee on National Defense Migration (Tolan Committee), OPA, OCD, 1940–43; Foreign Economic Admin., dir. Liberated Areas Div., 1943–46; Commerce Dept. OIT, chief International Economic Analysis Div. 1946–53. President's Commission on the Status of Women, member protective labor legislation committee, 1961–63; US Women's Bureau, dir.,

1964–69. Married **Leon Keyserling** (see preceding case) 1940; no children. Jewish.

Included on Ben Mandel's 1941 list of 53 government "big shots" with CP associations. Interviewed by FBI 1942; rated eligible by CSC 1945 after further investigation; FBI full field investigation 1948, Commerce loyalty board interrogatory July 1948, hearings Aug. 1948, cleared Nov. 1948. SISS testimony June–July 1951. FBI full field investigation 1951–53, ongoing. McCarthy publicized the case Feb. 1952. Commerce loyalty board hearings Nov. 1951–Aug. 1952, negative ruling Aug. 1952, appeals board hearings Sept.–Nov. 1952. Eisenhower elected president Nov. 1952. Commerce appeals board cleared her on loyalty but withheld security clearance Jan. 1953. Both Keyserlings resigned two weeks later. Allegations resurfaced but did not prevent her appointment in 1964 as dir. of U.S. Women's Bureau. See RG 478 and FBI files.

Kramer, Lucy M. (1907–2007)
Anthropologist, statistician; retained by US Public Health Service 1958

BA Barnard 1928, MA/ABD anthropology, Columbia 1923. Indian Bureau, Dept. Interior, 1935, researcher; Solicitior's Office, Interior, unpaid research asst. to husband 1933–38; Bureau of Home Economics, Dept. Ag., 1938–39, statistician; Solicitor's Office, Interior, researcher and editor, 1939–42; War Labor Board, wage analyst, 1944–46; Bureau of Labor Statistics 1946–47 until RIF; research assistant to Congresswoman Helen Gahagan Douglas, 1948–50; Dept. Labor, economist, 1951–53 until RIF; U.S. Public Health Service 1958–89 (on contract after 1977). Married **Felix S. Cohen** (later assoc. solicitor, Interior Dept.) 1931; two daughters born 1939, 1943. Jewish.

CSC investigation 1945, rated eligible 1946. Congressional conservatives listed husband among alleged subversives working on Marshall Plan 1948. After FBI full field investigation for Dept. Labor, she replied to interrogatory Sept. 1950 and was retained Oct. 1950. Reinvestigated and rated eligible again Aug. 52. FBI received anonymous info on her Jan. 1953; RIFed June 1953; widowed Oct. 1953. Reinvestigated 1957 after applied for USIA job through State Dept. (not hired). U.S. Public Health Service hired her in 1958 and CSC rated her eligible in May. See Lucy M. Kramer RG 478 file.

Lloyd, David Demarest (1911–1962)
Lawyer, political strategist; retained by White House 1952

BA history and literature, Harvard 1931, LLB Harvard Law 1935. Resettlement Admin. 1935–36; La Follette Civil Liberties Committee 1936–40, asst. chief counsel; FCC 1940–41; OPA 1942–43; asst. to Secretary of Navy Adlai Stevenson, Italy, 1944; Foreign Economic Admin. 1945, asst.

gen. counsel, on loan in 1946 as legal adviser to Mission for Economic Affairs in London. (ADA dir. research and legislation 1947–48.) White House asst. to presidential aide Charles Murphy 1948–51; admin. asst. to president 1951–52. Married **Charlotte Tuttle** (Interior Dept. lawyer) 1940; adopted two children 1944, 1947. Episcopalian.

Included on Ben Mandel's 1941 list of 53 government "big shots" with CP associations. Interviewed by FBI 1942 and retained by OPA. Investigated 1943 when trying unsuccessfully for navy commission. FBI investigated him 1947 at State Dept. request, but he left govt. for ADA. Rated eligible by White House loyalty board Nov. 1948. Called a subversive by McCarthy Feb. 1950, rated eligible again by White House loyalty board Sept. 1950. Case reopened under EO 10241's new standard Aug. 1951. McCarthy attacked him again, along with another White House aide, Philleo Nash (see below). White House loyalty board cleared him Feb. 1952; Gillette Committee demanded his and Nash's files. See FBI file.

LORWIN, LEWIS (1883–1970)
Economist; resigned Commerce Dept. 1951, flagged
PhD economics, Columbia 1912. Professor, journalist. Consultant to Temporary National Economic Committee, National Resources Planning Board, Board of Economic Warfare 1939–43; Foreign Economic Admin., economic adviser, 1943–45; Commerce Dept. OIT, adviser, 1945–51. Married **Rose Strunsky** (socialist-feminist writer, sister of Anna Strunsky Walling) 1920; three children including adopted son Val (see next case). Jewish.

CSC investigated 1943, rated eligible by Foreign Economic Admin. Nov. 1943. Attacked by congressional conservatives 1947–48. FBI investigation 1949, reply to interrogatory Aug. 1950, hearings Feb.–Mar. 1951, further FBI investigation, rated ineligible by Commerce loyalty board Nov. 1951, resigned, file flagged. See RG 478 file.

LORWIN, VAL (1907?–1982)
Economist and historian; retained by State Dept. 1952, indicted for perjury 1953
BA Cornell, MA Ohio State, PhD Cornell. Dept. Labor, ca. 1935–41; U.S. Army lieutenant in Office of Strategic Services; State Dept., Div. International Labor Affairs, 1946–52. Married **Madge Grossman** early 1930s; no children. Jewish.

FBI investigation for State Dept. 1948–49; recalled from France (where he had been assigned to write book on French labor movement) for State loyalty board hearing Dec. 1949. McCarthy named him (case 54 on the list of 81) as subversive at State in Feb. 1950. In Feb. 1951 State rated him eligible on loyalty but suspended him on security grounds. On appeal, cleared and reinstated with back pay, Mar. 1952. Vindicated, left govt. for academia. Indicted by federal grand jury for perjury Mar. 1953; indictment thrown out 1954 after Lorwin and his lawyers determined Justice Dept. prosecutor had lied about evidence to jury (Justice then fired the prosecutor). From scattered sources.

LUBIN, ISADOR (1896–1978)
Statistician; retained by State Dept. 1950

BA Clark 1916, PhD economics, Brookings 1926. War Industries Board statistician 1918, Commissioner of Labor Statistics 1933–46, special statistical asst. to president 1941–45; U.S. rep. to UNESCO Economic and Employment Commission 1946–49; special asst. to secretary of state 1949–50 (advising on Marshall Plan); American minister to UN ECO-SOC 1950–53. Married Alice Berliner 1923, one child; divorced 1928; married editor Ann Shumaker 1932, who died after childbirth 1935; married ILO labor expert Carol Riegelman 1952. Jewish.

Loyalty hearing before LRB Mar. 1950; apparently rated eligible. See "loyalty hearing" folder in Lubin Papers, FDRL.

McHALE, KATHRYN (1890–1956)
Educator; Subversive Activities Control Board, rated eligible 1951

BA 1919, PhD psychology, Columbia 1926. While head of AAUW 1929–50, served as occasional consultant to UNESCO and State Dept. Confirmed by Senate as member of new Subversive Activities Control Board Aug. 1951, LRB rated her eligible Dec. 1951. Reappointed Aug. 1952, remained on the board until her death in 1956. Catholic?

Nominated to Subversive Activities Control Board by Democratic Party women's leader India Edwards Sept. 1950. Washington D.C. police kept her under surveillance for nine weeks trying to prove rumors she was a lesbian. The FBI withheld this information from White House and CSC but Jay Sourwine of SISS staff learned of it and pressured FBI and White House not to appoint her. She was confirmed by Senate only after long delay. In 1954, Eisenhower admin. reopened her case, and FBI now shared the morals rumors with White House (EO 10450 in Apr. 1953 broadened morals criteria used in identifying "security risk"). Further surveillance failed to prove lesbianism but uncovered suggestions of alcoholism, as reported to White House May 1955. She was due for reappointment Aug. 1955 but remained in limbo into 1956. Found unconscious in her apartment and died of unknown causes Oct. 1956. See FBI file.

MILLER, FRIEDA (1889–1973)
Labor economist, dir. US Women's Bureau; favorable ruling by IOELB 1955

BA Milwaukee-Downer 1912, ABD economics and political science, Chicago 1915. New York Labor Dept. 1929–42; U.S. delegate to ILO

1936–?; special asst. on labor to John Winant, U.S. ambassador to Great Britain, 1942–44; U.S. Women's Bureau dir., 1944–53. Consultant to ILO and UN, 1950s and 1960s. Met lifelong partner **Pauline Newman** (garment union activist) 1917; one daughter, born to Miller 1923. Non-Jewish German heritage (Lutheran?); Newman Jewish.

FBI full field investigation 1948, rated eligible by White House loyalty board July 1949. FBI furnished additional allegations July 1950, LRB declined to pursue. Knowing Eisenhower would replace her as Women's Bureau dir., Miller applied to a job under State Dept. auspices Apr. 1953; FBI updated her file; her Women's Bureau replacement was appointed Nov. 1953 and she resigned from govt. Dec. 1953. Unemployed for a year, she pursued a short-term ILO assignment and replied to IOELB interrogatory Feb. 1955; in Apr. 1955 IOELB made favorable decision. When ILO extended her appointment, FBI investigated again, and IOELB again found in her favor. This process recurred through 1960 as she continued to take international assignments. See FBI and RG 478 files.

MONTGOMERY, MARY TAYLOR (1900–1957)
Writer, economist; retained by HEW 1955

BA Mt. Holyoke 1920, MA economics, Wisconsin 1922. After working as foreign correspondent for *Chicago Tribune*: Agriculture Dept., Office of Consumer Counsel, asst. chief, 1933–43; U.S. Children's Bureau, editor, 1943–57. Married journalist Rodney Dutcher 1935; widowed in 1938; married **Donald Montgomery** (Office of Consumer Counsel, then United Autoworkers Workers official) 1943; no children (Montgomery had three children by his first marriage to CP member Sarah Adamson). Presbyterian, of Irish parentage.

Prominent in 1940 FBI report on alleged CP influence in Consumer Counsel office of. Agriculture Dept. Mandel's 1941 list of high-ranking alleged subversives in govt. included husband Donald Montgomery. FBI interviewed her 1942. Full field investigation 1948, FSA rated her eligible Sept. 1948. LRB remanded her case back to FSA May 1950; after reply to interrogatory and hearing, FSA rated her eligible Sept. 1950, approved by LRB Nov. 1950. HEW requested her file Oct. 1953; she again was retained, per CSC memo Feb. 1955. She died of a brain tumor in Aug. 1957. See RG 478 file.

MURRAY, PAULI (1910–1985)
Lawyer; denied govt. contract work 1952; rejected for EEOC general counsel 1967

BA Hunter 1933, LLB Howard 1944. WPA remedial reading teacher 1935; WPA Workers Education Project 1936–39. Lawyer in private practice and researcher/writer on race and gender discrimination. Briefly married then divorced 1930s; no children. Episcopalian.

In 1952 Cornell declined to hire her for Liberian law study under contract for State Dept., on grounds that her 1936–38 membership in Lovestoneite opposition faction within CP would embarrass Cornell. In 1967 EEOC dropped her from consideration for gen. counsel for fear of lending credibility to segregationists' charges that EEOC was Communist plot. From scattered sources.

NASH, PHILLEO (1909–1987)

Anthropologist, race relations expert; retained by White House 1952

BA Wisconsin 1932, PhD anthropology, Chicago 1937. Office of War Information, special asst. to dir., White House Liaison, 1942–46; special asst. then admin. asst. to president 1946–53; Wisconsin lt. gov. 1959–61; commissioner, Bureau of Indian Affairs, 1961–66. Married **Edith Rosenfels** (poet, cofounder interracial Georgetown Day School) 1935; two daughters.

Cleared by CSC Feb. 1943. Rated eligible by White House loyalty board May 1950. McCarthy attacked him as ex-Communist Jan. 1952, days after Nash's sister published an anti-McCarthy ad in her hometown Wisconsin newspaper. Nash submitted 50-page statement to White House loyalty board and was rated eligible Feb. 1952, confirmed by LRB May 1952. See Nash Papers, HSTL.

OLDS, LELAND (1890–1960)

Statistician, public power expert; retained by Interior Dept. 1952, flagged 1953

BA math and history, Amherst 1912, grad. work at Union Theological Seminary, then in economics and sociology, Harvard, Columbia. National War Labor Board 1918; (AFL researcher, Federated Press journalist); New York State Power Commission exec. secretary 1931–39; Federal Power Commission 1939–49 (chair 1940–49). Reappointed but not confirmed 1949, owing to allegations of disloyalty made by Senator Lyndon Johnson and others from natural-gas-producing states. President's Water Resources Policy Commission 1950; Interior Dept. Boston Office, program analyst, 1951–53. Married Maud Spear (civil engineer, architect) 1924; four children. Protestant.

FBI investigated 1948; apparently Federal Power Commission retained him, but information leaked to interested congressmen. Senate voted 53-15 against confirming him based on his associations and writings in the 1919–29 period. Extensive further investigation for Interior Dept.; replied to Second Regional loyalty board interrogatory and was rated eligible Apr. 1952; reinvestigated in 1953 but RIFed before a decision on loyalty and thus flagged. See RG 478 file.

PACKARD, WALTER (1884–1966)

Agricultural engineer, public power expert; retained by ECA 1949

Bachelor of Scientific Agriculture, Iowa State 1907, MS University of California at Berkeley 1909. After academic and consulting jobs related to irrigation, worked for AAA 1933–34; Rural Resettlement Admin., national dir., 1935–38; land and irrigation consultant to Gov. Tugwell of Puerto Rico 1945–47; American Mission for Aid to Greece, then Economic Cooperation Admin. in Greece, chief of land reclamation 1948–54. Married Emma Leonard 1909; two daughters.

While in Greece 1949 he was shown telegram ordering his dismissal from ECA on grounds he had been associated with a subversive organization on attorney general's list (Calif. Labor School). He sent his lawyer Abe Fortas documentation supporting his claim he was being fired because he was pushing public power rather than approving contracts for U.S. companies to charge exorbitant rates in Greece; his superiors had overruled him to approve the contracts and now wanted him out. He gathered affidavits from California progressives like Helen Gahagan Douglas, Florence Wyckoff, and Catherine Bauer and apparently returned to Washington for a hearing. He retained his job in Greece until 1954, when he retired and returned to California, but his passport was restricted. He appeared June 1955 on Ed Murray's *See It Now* program but did not discuss loyalty charges against him, prompting Fortas to urge him to make "the rest of the story" public. See Packard Papers, Bancroft.

PETERS, JOHN PUNNETT (1887–1955)

Professor of medicine; reinstated to US Public Health Service (HEW) 1955

BA Yale 1908, MD Columbia 1913. Renowned professor of internal medicine at Yale; secretary of "Committee of 400" physicians who favored national health insurance. Researcher and consultant to U.S. Air Force and Army during World War II. Consultant to review grants applications for National Institute of Health in the Public Health Service, 1947–53. Married **Charlotte Hodge**; four children. Episcopalian.

Replied to FSA interrogatory Jan. 1949, rated eligible Feb. 1949; replied to FSA interrogatory Dec. 1951; hearing Mar. 1952. FSA loyalty board clearance overturned by LRB Apr. 1953. After an LRB appeal hearing May 1953 he was dismissed by HEW secretary Oveta Culp Hobby. Arnold, Fortas & Palmer took his case to the Supreme Court, which vindicated him in June 1955 (*Peters v. Hobby*, 349 US 331). See RG 478 file and Peters Papers, Yale.

PETERSON, OLIVER A. (1903–1979)
Labor educator, Foreign Service officer; retained by State Dept. 1962
BA North Dakota 1926, grad. study Harvard, Columbia. WPA regional supervisor 1936–41; OPA 1941–42, 44–46; Stimson Committee for Marshall Plan, field rep. 1947–48; State Dept: labor attaché American embassy in Stockholm (1948–52), Brussels (1952–57), Bureau African Affairs (1958–62). In 1932 married **Esther Eggertsen** (labor educator and lobbyist, later dir. U.S. Women's Bureau, consumer affairs adviser to presidents Johnson, Carter); four children. Lutheran (Esther, Mormon).

Rated eligible by OPA 1943, 1946; retained by State after FBI full field investigation 1948. New allegations led to interrogatory Apr. 1949; State board cleared with one dissenting member; LRB approved Sept. 1949. FBI full field investigation and interrogatory 1952, recalled from Sweden for hearing Jan. 1953, clearance confirmed by LRB July 1953. Reinvestigated and cleared again Oct. 1955, Feb. 1962. Retired 1962. See RG 478 file.

PICKENS, WILLIAM (1881–1954)
Classicist, civil rights activist; retained by Treasury 1950
BA Talladega 1902, BA classics, Yale 1904, MA Fisk. Left academia to work for NAACP 1930–41, field secretary and dir. of branches; also LID board member. Treasury Dept. Savings & Bond Div., dir. Interracial Div., 1941–50. Married Minnie Cooper McAlpine 1905; three children. Protestant?

Rated eligible by CSC 1941. FBI interviewed and investigated him 1942. Dies named him among "crackpot radicals" in govt. Feb. 1943. House of Reps. singled him out in amendment to Treasury Dept. appropriation bill, drawing protest from NAACP. Appeared before Kerr Committee Apr. 1943, exonerated May. FBI full field investigation 1948 and again 1950, retained by Treasury both times. Resigned Dec. 1950 at age 69. See RG 478 file.

PORTER, PAUL R. (1908–2002)
Labor economist; resigned Economic Cooperation Admin. 1953, flagged
BA journalism, Kansas 1928. Labor journalist and SP official until 1941. War Production Board 1942–45, chief, shipbuilding stabilization branch; Foreign Economic Admin., labor economist 1945–46; Mission for Economic Affairs, London, asst. to acting chief, 1946–47; U.S. rep. and mission chief, Economic Commission for Europe, 1947–49; chief, ECA Mission to Greece, 1949–50; ECA 1950–51; Mutual Security Admin., chief of European office, 1951–53. Consultant to Bureau of International Commerce, 1968–? Married **Eleanor Nelson** (later a CP labor organizer) 1933, divorced 1940; married **Hilda Roberts** (CIO staff) 1940; four children.

Interviewed 1942 by FBI about ex-wife Eleanor Nelson who then was in govt. service; he explained they had divorced because she joined CP. Dies named him among "crackpot radicals" in govt. Feb. 1943; after investigation CSC rated him eligible June 1943. FBI full field investigation 1949; State rated him eligible, but he transferred to ECA before LRB post-audit and thus was flagged. Ex-CP informant Paul Crouch made allegations about Porter to McCarthy in 1950 and then to SISS staff in 1951. In Oct. 1952 Leon Keyserling told SISS that Porter, now a top MSA administrator, was in League for Industrial Democracy, trying to defend Mary Dublin Keyserling's association with that group, but instead arousing SISS's interest in Porter. SISS member Ferguson on election eve called for Porter's recall from Europe; Porter resigned June 1953 citing "personal convenience." See RG 478 file; Paul Porter file, Homer Ferguson Papers, Bentley Historical Library.

RADIN, RHEA (1910–2000)
Social worker; rated ineligible, dismissed by HEW 1953
BA University of Calif., Berkeley, 1931, MA public welfare, Chicago 1937. San Francisco Emergency Relief Admin. 1934–35, 1937, social worker; Calif. State Relief Admin. 1939–41, case worker and consultant; FSA consultant, 1941–42; War Manpower Commission section chief, 1942–45; UNRRA, deputy dir. Displaced Persons Div., 1945–47; UN International Refugee Org. 1947, technical consultant; U.S. Public Health Service (FSA) health program analyst, 1950–53.

Extensive investigation 1941–44; CSC hearing Feb. 1942, rated eligible with dissenting vote; 1944 one CSC examiner recommended dismissal and "flagging" but was overruled. FBI full field investigation (111 people contacted); reply to interrogatory Nov. 1950, Fourth Regional loyalty board hearing Nov. 1950; rated eligible and retained by FSA Sept. 1951. Separated because of unfavorable report July 1953. See RG 478 file.

ROMMEL, ROWENA BELLOWS (1911–late 1980s)
International affairs administrator; favorable ruling by IOELB 1954
BA 1932, MA international relations, Brown 1933. SSB clerical, 1937–39; Bureau of Budget admin. analyst, 1939–42; War Manpower Commission exec. secretary, 1942–43; State Dept. 1943–50, analyst in various divisions. UNESCO, dep. head of Technical Assistance, 1950–? (1954, at least). Married Wilfred H. Rommel, divorced 1951.

Accused of CP associations by Representative Dondero (1946), Representative Busbey (1948), Senator McCarthy (1950, 1952). She was McCarthy's State Dept. case 51 in 1950. State loyalty board hearings July 1948 (retained Jan. 1949); Nov. 1950 (favorable ruling by State Dept.

board, but she resigned to go to UNESCO before LRB completed post-audit, therefore was "flagged"). IOELB hearings Sept. and Dec. 1953, favorable rating July 1954. Passport withheld for nine months 1953–54, preventing her from returning to UNESCO in Paris. See RG 478 file.

WARE, CAROLINE (1899–1990)

Economic historian, consumer affairs expert; favorable ruling by IOELB 1955

BA Vassar 1920, grad. work Oxford 1922–23, PhD history, Radcliffe 1925. NRA Consumer Advisory Board, 1934–35; NDAC/OPA, asst. to consumer commissioner, 1940–42; OPA Consumer Advisory Committee, 1943–46; Consumer Advisory Committee to CEA, chair, 1947–52; President's Commission on the Status of Women member, 1961–63; SSA consultant, 1961, 1965; President's Consumer Advisory Council member, 1962–64. International agency work included Pan-American Union (Org. of American States) 1951–59, writing for UNESCO, and extensive consulting in Latin America. Married **Gardiner Means** (prominent economist) 1927; no children. Unitarian.

FBI investigated her beginning Aug. 1941. Dies claimed to have list of 50 subversives employed by OPA and named five of them Sept. 1941. Interviewed by CSC examiners Dec. 1941. Resigned Jan. 1942. Applied for international development job under U.S. Army Dept. Jan. 1951 and either finished job or withdrew application before a decision on loyalty, so her file was flagged. Full field investigation 1953; replied to IOELB interrogatory Apr. 1954; after extensive additional investigation, IOELB made favorable determination Oct. 1955. HEW loyalty board was going to issue interrogatory in 1961, but she finished her consulting assignment before it did. Her file was "reviewed in connection with case of Gardiner Means, USIA" in Apr. 1961. See RG 478 and FBI files.

WECHSLER, NANCY FRAENKEL (1916–2009)

Lawyer, President's Committee on Civil Rights; flagged 1947

BA economics and sociology, Barnard 1937, LLB Columbia 1940. Board of Economic Warfare 1942–43; OPA assoc. attorney, 1943–45, 1947; President's Committee on Civil Rights, counsel, 1947–48; Labor Dept. Solicitor's Office, 1948. Rest of career in private practice (notably, wrote amicus briefs in Supreme Court cases legalizing contraceptives and abortion). Married **James Wechsler** (prominent journalist and later publicly ex-Communist) 1934; two children. Jewish.

Interviewed by FBI 1943, discussed her membership in the Young Communist League 1934–37, her disillusionment with communism, and claimed to be apolitical since 1937. In 1947 she left OPA before a decision on her loyalty, so her file was flagged. Her appointment to Committee on Civil Rights expired before her case was adjudicated. She was similarly still under investigation when she left the Labor Dept. in 1948; her file remained flagged, and she did not return to govt. service. See RG 478 file.

WITTE, EDWIN (1887–1966)
Economist, social security expert; flagged by LRB 1953

BA 1909, PhD economics 1916, Wisconsin. Committee on Economic Security, exec. dir., 1934–35; Social Security Advisory Council 1937–38; Federal Advisory Council on Economic Security 1939–42, 1949–52; War Labor Board 1943–45; Atomic Energy Commission, labor relations panel member, 1949–52; Economic Stabilization Agency, wage stabilization board consultant, 1950–1953. Married Florence Rimsneider.

Rated eligible by CSC 1941. FBI full field investigation canceled 1949 after White House communication. Cleared by Atomic Energy Commission Apr. 1951. FBI was updating his file when Economic Stabilization Agency was terminated Apr. 1953; LRB flagged his file. See RG 478 file.

WURSTER, CATHERINE BAUER (1905–1964)
Public housing expert; husband's security clearance restored 1953

BA Vassar 1926. US Housing Authority, dir. research and information, 1937–39; per diem consultant to Resettlement Admin., National Resources Planning Board, and Public Works Admin. in 1935–36, to Federal Works Agency in 1941, and to USHA and other national housing agencies, 1940–53. Married William Wurster (architect) 1940; one daughter.

Interviewed by FBI 1942. Reports of Joint Fact-Finding Committee to California Legislature on Un-American Activities (Tenney Committee), 1947 and 1948, listed her allegedly subversive associations. In Jan. 1953 Army-Navy-Air Force Personnel Security Board terminated contract with husband's firm, and her husband's security clearance was revoked because of her associations. Bauer prepared for months for a hearing before that board in Aug. 1953. Husband's security clearance was restored, but his firm never received another govt. contract. In 1962 her clearance to attend a White House housing conference was delayed. C. B. Wurster Papers, Bancroft; scattered sources.

Chronology of the Federal Loyalty-Security Program

August 2, 1939: Section 9-A of the Hatch Act prohibits federal employees from "membership in any political party or organization which advocates the overthrow of our constitutional form of government."

October 25, 1939: Dies Committee releases a list of 500 federal employees allegedly associated with the American League for Peace and Democracy, alleged to be a "Communist front" organization.

June 29, 1940: The Alien Registration (Smith) Act criminalizes advocacy of, or belonging to, an organization that advocates overthrow of the government.

1940: Smith Committee hearings and report on the National Labor Relations Board stress its employment of alleged Communists.

September 7, 1941: Dies Committee alleges that at least 50 Office of Price Administration employees (Dies names 5), including some top officials, have "links to Reds." Civil Service Commission establishes a three-member loyalty board (Cannon, Klein, Smith).

October 20, 1941: Dies charges that 1,124 federal employees (not including those in OPA and other new defense agencies) are Communist Party members or sympathizers. Dies does not make the list public, but he claims that about a quarter of the list are high-ranking officials. Attorney General Francis Biddle authorizes the FBI to investigate those on the list.

September 24, 1942: In response to the attorney general's report that investigating those named by Dies had been largely unnecessary (many of the 1,124 had left government, the allegations against most others were unsubstantiated, and 2 were dismissed), Dies names 19 federal officials alleged to have ties to Communist groups.

February 2, 1943: Dies denounces 38 federal employees as "crackpot and radical bureaucrats" with subversive associations. Many of them work for OPA or the Federal Communications Commission. The House authorizes the Kerr Committee to hold hearings; it recommends dismissal of 3 employees, clears 3 others, and never gets to the rest.

February 5, 1943: FDR creates an Interdepartmental Committee on Employee Investigations to process and make recommendations on loyalty cases (CSC's Cannon a member).

1943–44: Dies Committee charges that the CSC loyalty board is lax. Dies staffers believe CSC examiner Klein is "red," and they resent CSC guidelines prohibiting its examiners from asking about associations with the Socialist Party, League of Women Shoppers, and other groups. Dies Committee subpoenas the CSC files of over 100 employees whose cases CSC allegedly treated too leniently.

October 30, 1944: John Bricker, the Ohio governor and Republican nominee for vice president, claims that Communists run the New Deal, citing 7 officials previously named and cleared.

February 1946: The American public learns of the Igor Gouzenko espionage ring in Canada.

July 20, 1946: A subcommittee of the House Committee on the Civil Service reports its findings of inconsistency in loyalty standards and procedures among federal agencies, the Civil Service Commission, and the Interdepartmental Committee on Employee Investigations. The report recommends establishing a commission to create a unified program. According to one historian, "in a political sense, this would have been the time to act if there was to be any action at all."[1]

November 25, 1946: In response to sweeping Republican victories in the midterm elections, widely credited to Republican charges that the administration was harboring Communists, Truman appoints a Temporary Commission on Employee Loyalty. With Republicans in control of Congress, his staff feared that Congress would create something worse if the White House did not act.

March 12, 1947: Truman Doctrine speech declaring the need to fight communism around the globe, beginning with aid to Greece and Turkey.

March 21, 1947: Truman's Executive Order 9835 establishes loyalty boards for executive departments to evaluate any derogatory information submitted by CSC or FBI investigators, with a central Loyalty Review Board to coordinate procedures and review agency board decisions. Evidence of "reasonable grounds for belief" in disloyalty is the stated standard for the refusal of or removal from government employment.

April 1947: The Attorney General's List of Subversive Organizations is formalized and expanded for use by loyalty boards.

July 31, 1948: HUAC launches espionage hearings; Chambers, Bentley testify publicly.

November 1948: Truman unexpectedly wins the presidency.

June 30, 1949: A Washington D.C. jury convicts former Justice Department employee Judith Coplon of espionage (a New York jury would convict her on a related charge in March 1950).

August 29, 1949: Soviets test their first atomic bomb.

October 1, 1949: Communists declare victory in China.

February 9, 1950: From Wheeling, West Virginia, McCarthy seizes the spotlight by charging that the State Department employed 205 Communists.

June 25, 1950: Communist North Korea invades South Korea.

August 26, 1950: Public Law 733 authorizes heads of certain agencies (State, Commerce, Justice, Defense, and Treasury Departments; Atomic Energy Commission; U.S. Army, Navy, Air Force; National Security Resources Board; National Advisory Committee for Aeronautics) to suspend without pay and dismiss employees they believe to pose a *security risk* (as opposed to a loyalty risk). An employee could be judged loyal in views and actions but a security risk because of a demonstrated lack of judgment or personal circumstances that would make the employee vulnerable to blackmail or coercion. Alcoholics, homosexuals and others deemed immoral, and relatives of Communists would become the major categories of security risk. Many more people would be dismissed on security grounds than on loyalty grounds, especially after Eisenhower's EO 10450 (see below) extends PL 733 to all agencies.

September 23, 1950: Overriding Truman's veto, Congress passes the McCarran Internal Security Act, which requires Communist organizations to register with the U.S. attorney general and creates the Subversive Activities Control Board.

December 21, 1950: A Senate resolution creates the Senate Internal Security Subcommittee to study the operation of the McCarran Internal Security Act and to investigate subversive activities, broadly construed.

January 1951: After almost two years of pleas from liberals in and out of his administration, Truman appoints the bipartisan Commission on Internal Security and Individual Rights, headed by Chester Nimitz, to review the loyalty program for unfairness to employees. Conservatives attack the commission, which fizzles out, in part because of SISS stalling on approval of appointments.

January 21, 1951: Former State Department employee Alger Hiss is convicted of perjury.

March 29, 1951: Julius and Ethel Rosenberg are found guilty of conspiracy to commit espionage related to atomic secrets and sentenced to death.

April 28, 1951: After McCarthy charges that the Loyalty Review Board (LRB) clears too many employees on appeal from the agency boards, the LRB asks Truman for more stringent loyalty criteria. Executive Order 10241 lowers the standard of evidence required for dismissal by stating that employees can be dismissed on "reasonable doubt" of loyalty (EO

9835 had required "reasonable grounds for belief" in disloyalty). Pressure from congressional conservatives does not abate, and in 1952 the LRB would urge agency boards to increase their dismissal rates.

April 30, 1951: In *Bailey v. Richardson*, 341 U.S. 918, a 4-4 decision by U.S. Supreme Court effectively affirms a lower court's finding that the loyalty program is constitutional, on the premise that government employment is a privilege rather than a right. See also *Washington v. McGrath*, 341 U.S. 923 (1951).

October 25, 1951: Former Commerce Department employee William Remington is convicted of perjury, confirming a February verdict by a different jury.

1953: In response to charges (particularly by McCarran's Senate Internal Security Subcommittee) that the United Nations harbors American subversives, Truman's EO 10422 (Jan. 9) authorizes creation of the International Organizations Employee Loyalty Board (IOELB); Eisenhower's EO 10459 (May 27) sets up the machinery. The IOELB begins investigating professional-level American employees as well as new applicants. The IOELB does not have authority to dismiss, but most UN agencies abide by its advisory opinions.

April 27, 1953: Eisenhower's EO 10450 extends the *security risk* standard to every agency and type of job and also elevates the significance of "morals" tests, barring "habitual use of intoxicants to excess, drug addiction, or sexual perversion." EO 10450 permits an employee's security clearance to be revoked without formal charges, mandates suspension without pay if formal charges are brought, and eliminates the defendant's right to a hearing. It also abolishes the regional loyalty boards and the LRB. In October 1953, EO 10450 would be amended to require automatic dismissal of an employee who pleaded the Fifth Amendment before a congressional committee.

October 20, 1953: Ed Murrow's television program, *See It Now*, examines the loyalty case of Milo Radulovich, an air force lieutenant who was dismissed as a security risk because of the alleged views of his sister and Serbian-born father.

1954: *Washington Daily News* coverage of the case of Abraham Chasanow, suspended from the navy as a security risk, wins reporter Anthony Lewis a Pulitzer Prize in 1955.

December 2, 1954: U.S. Senate censures McCarthy.

February 1955: FBI informant Harvey Matusow recants, stating that McCarthy and others encouraged him to supply false information to identify people as subversives; he claims that ex-Communist witnesses Paul Crouch, Louis Budenz, and Elizabeth Bentley did the same.

August 1955: Congress authorizes creation of the Commission on Government Security to study the loyalty-security program. (By the time the commission report appeared in 1957, court decisions had made it obsolete.)

1955–56: Two Senate subcommittees hold hearings on abuses under the loyalty program, the Johnston Subcommittee of the Post Office and Civil Service Committee, and the Hennings Subcommittee on Constitutional Rights of the Senate Judiciary Committee.

1955: In *Peters v. Hobby*, 349 U.S. 331, the Court rules that the Loyalty Review Board cannot on its own motion reopen a case on which an agency loyalty board has decided favorably. As a result, about 19 employees are reinstated. In *Parker v. Lester*, F.2d 708, the Ninth Circuit Court of Appeals strikes down a different but related program, the port-security program (which screened longshoremen and sailors), for not giving defendants enough information to defend themselves.

1956: In *Cole v. Young*, 351 U.S. 536, the Court rules that people in nonsensitive positions cannot be dismissed as security risks. Over 100 people are reinstated, many of them Post Office employees, and proceedings are dropped against numerous others.

1959: The Supreme Court further reins in the loyalty-security program in *Vitarelli v. Seaton*, 359 U.S. 535, and *Greene v. McElroy*, 360 U.S. 474. In the latter, the Court finds that defendants have a right to cross-examine hostile witnesses; Chief Justice Earl Warren criticizes the use of "faceless informers" whose identity is unknown to the defendant.

Statistics of the Federal Loyalty-Security Program

Data on dismissal from or denial of federal employment on loyalty-security grounds is fragmentary and tricky to work with. The Civil Service Commission's Loyalty Review Board (LRB) published information on the disposition of *loyalty* cases under Executive Orders 9835 and 10241, but those reports do not reflect dismissals under Public Law 733 (June 1950), which enabled heads of certain agencies to remove employees they deemed *security* risks. In April 1953, Eisenhower's EO 10450 broadened the security risk category to all agencies and also terminated the LRB, so its reports ceased. Data thereafter became the subject of controversy as Vice President Nixon and others inflated and otherwise misrepresented the numbers of dismissals under Eisenhower's expanded loyalty-security program. Thus no reliable data exists on the number of *security* dismissals between 1950 and 1956. Data also is lacking on separate federal measures such as the port-security and industrial security programs, which screened certain categories of private employees. Finally, it is not possible to determine the reasons behind every dismissal and resignation. People had other reasons to change jobs, so not every resignation indicated loyalty or security troubles; on the other hand, supervisors sometimes encouraged resignation as a way to "ease out" suspect employees without stigmatizing them or the agency.

During World War II, the CSC barred about 1,300 from the federal service on loyalty grounds. Thus screening began well before 1947, and most Communist Party members had left before then.[1]

The following numbers pertain only to Truman's *loyalty* program from March 1947 to mid-1953 (thus excluding investigations of suspected *security* risks made at the request of agency heads). A total of 4,756,705 employees filled out loyalty forms to be checked. Loyalty boards received 26,236 cases, but 2,748 of those people left government before the FBI completed its full field investigation, leaving 23,488 cases with completed full field investigations received for adjudication by loyalty boards. At that stage, 3,634 resigned. Of the remaining 19,854 cases, 17,060 were adjudicated under the loyalty program (16,503 of those were rated eligible on loyalty and 557 were dismissed or denied employment), and the rest were still pending at the time of the LRB's last report in 1953. Loyalty boards issued 12,859 interrogatories and held 4,119 hearings.[2]

In making his estimate of 8,850 dismissals under all the federal programs, Ralph Brown took the 557 reported loyalty dismissals to mid-1953 and added an estimated 650 Public Law 733 dismissals to that date, plus an estimated 1,500 loyalty-security dismissals from 1953 through 1956 under EO 10450, for a total of about 2,700 federal civilian dismissals under the loyalty-security program from 1947 to 1956. For the same period, Brown estimated 750 military dismissals and 5,400 dismissals of private employees subject to federal programs (industrial security, port security, atomic energy, IOELB, etc.). Those numbers add up to 8,850.[3]

Most of those dismissed were low-ranking employees. Civil Service commissioner Frances Perkins admitted in 1952 that for all the time and expense, the program had caught very few "big fish." However, investigations, unlike dismissals, occurred across the ranks, and thus so did the program's repressive tendencies.[4]

The changing standards of the program meant that employees were investigated repeatedly on the same evidence. One study found that of all employees dismissed, about 40 percent had survived previous loyalty-security proceedings. That statistic underscores how protracted—and thus traumatizing and costly—the investigations often were.[5]

By one estimate, the CSC and FBI together spent $24.5 million to make the first round of checks on all incumbent employees. The CSC requested approximately $5.5 million per year thereafter, and the FBI spent an estimated $10 million per year. Truman had intended loyalty investigations to be handled primarily by the CSC. He requested twice as much funding for the CSC as for the FBI, but Congress reversed that ratio and gave the FBI most of the funding, expanding the FBI's power considerably. The FBI immediately hired 7,000 additional agents. Other substantial expenses incurred in administering the program included travel and other expenses of agency loyalty boards, which initially consisted of approximately 2,200 people.[6] Additional costs—difficult to quantify—include the lost productivity of loyalty defendants as well as time spent by the coworkers and supervisors who wrote affidavits, met with FBI agents, and appeared at hearings.

Acknowledgments

Many individuals and institutions assisted me in the long process of researching and writing this book. For fellowships, leaves from teaching, and travel grants I thank the American Council of Learned Societies, the Harry S. Truman Library Institute, and, at the University of Houston, the Department of History, Women's Studies Program and College of Liberal Arts and Social Sciences. Among the dozens of archivists without whom I would not have gotten far, I am especially grateful to Fred Romanski, Herb Rawlings-Milton, Ed Schamel, Rodney Ross, and Jessie Kratz at the National Archives; Dennis Bilger, Randy Sowell, David Clark, and Liz Safly at the Harry S. Truman Library; John White at the College of Charleston Library; David Kessler at the Bancroft Library, University of California; David Klaassen at the Social Welfare History Archive, University of Minnesota; and Harry Miller at the State Historical Society of Wisconsin. The Arnold & Porter law firm kindly permitted me to examine loyalty hearing transcripts and other nonprivileged files from the firm's archives. Lisa Hazirjian, Katarina Keane, and Mary Klatt provided excellent research services in remote archives. Scholars who sent me helpful documents include Svetlana Chervonnaya, Ruth Fairbanks, Paul Rosier, David Shreve, and Nancy Beck Young. John Earl Haynes graciously checked some names for me in his database on the Communist Party USA.

Relatives and acquaintances of former loyalty defendants provided documents, photographs, and insights. Arthur Goldschmidt Jr. and Ann Goldschmidt Richardson shared many details, in addition to photos and the electronic version of their father's draft memoirs. Gene Cohen Tweraser and Karen Cohen Holmes gave me many leads on their parents and also put me in touch with the late Charlotte Tuttle Lloyd Walkup, who kindly spoke with me about her experiences as a government lawyer and with the federal loyalty program. Nancy Kramer Bickel sent me photos that she gathered in the process of making a fine documentary about her aunt: *A Twentieth Century Woman: Lucy Kramer Cohen* (2011). Louisa Lloyd Hurley and Bruce Cohen also shared photographs. For perspectives on Leon and Mary Dublin Keyserling, I am deeply indebted to her brother the late Thomas D. Dublin, her nephew Thomas Dublin, Kathryn Kish Sklar, Sally Dublin Slenczka, and Harriet

Keyserling. I also thank Anne Firor Scott for sharing her memories of Caroline Ware.

I thank the following for permission to include material previously published in article form: *Feminist Studies* and the Johns Hopkins University Press, publisher of the *Journal of Women's History*. I also thank Oxford University Press for permission to publish a version of the following article I wrote for the *Journal of American History*: "Red Scare Politics and the Suppression of Popular Front Feminism: The Loyalty Investigation of Mary Dublin Keyserling," the *Journal of American History* (2003) 90(2): 491-524.

Dozens of scholars helped me sharpen my analysis and correct errors. For incisive comments on conference papers, article manuscripts, and chapter drafts, I thank Sue Cobble, Jacquelyn Dowd Hall, Susan Hartmann, Dan Horowitz, Laura Kalman, Jennifer Klein, Thomas McCormick, Laura McEnaney, Joanne Meyerowitz, Deirdre Moloney, Robyn Muncy, Beth Rose, and Kate Weigand. I will be eternally grateful to those who critiqued the whole manuscript at one point or another: William Chafe, Linda Gordon, Chuck Grench, Nelson Lichtenstein, Nancy MacLean, Charles T. Morrissey, Tyler Priest, and Ellen Schrecker. At Princeton University Press, Chuck Myers offered excellent advice in the final stages of revision, while Nathan Carr gracefully guided the manuscript through the production process and Will Hively's expert copyediting saved me from many mistakes and infelicities.

Some of the aforementioned people have had a larger influence on this project than can be adequately recognized here. Kitty Sklar and Tom Dublin were present at the creation, validating my tentative ideas and helping me unearth key sources. A 1998 conference paper by Jacquelyn Dowd Hall inspired me to see missing evidence as a form of evidence, and our subsequent conversations about gender, the left, and the "tyranny of labels" have enriched this book. Linda Gordon influenced my interpretation of Mary Dublin Keyserling back when the latter made an appearance in my dissertation; as one of the series editors at Princeton University Press, she made exacting comments that improved the final result immeasurably. My biggest debt is to Ty Priest, who has lived with this project for as long as I have. He made this a better book not only by offering astute readings of countless drafts but also by helping me find the time to finish it. Thanks, everybody.

Notes

MDK Papers	Mary Dublin Keyserling Papers, SL
NA	National Archives
NCL Papers	National Consumers' League Papers, LC
NLRB	National Labor Relations Board
NYPL	New York Public Library, New York, N.Y.
NYT	*New York Times*
RG 233	Record Group 233: Dies Committee and HUAC Records, Center for Legislative Archives, NA
RG 478	Record Group 478: Oversize Civil Service Commission Investigative Case Files, NA
SHSW	State Historical Society of Wisconsin, Madison, Wis.
SISS Records	Senate Internal Security Subcommittee Records, Record Group 46, Center for Legislative Archives, NA
SL	Schlesinger Library, Radcliffe Institute, Harvard University, Cambridge, Mass.
Smith	Sophia Smith Collection, Smith College Archives, Northampton, Mass.
Stolberg Papers	Benjamin Stolberg Papers, Columbia Rare Book and Manuscript Library, Columbia University, New York, N.Y.
SWHA	Social Welfare History Archives, University of Minnesota, Minneapolis, Minn.
Tillett Papers	Paul D. Tillett Jr. Papers, Seeley G. Mudd Manuscript Library, Princeton University, Princeton, N.J.
WFGP	Women in the Federal Government Project, SL
Wickenden Papers	Elizabeth Wickenden Papers, SL

NOTE: Where there are no archival box numbers in the notes, it is because the collection has not been processed yet, or has been reprocessed since I used it (rendering my box numbers obsolete).

INTRODUCTION

1. See appendix 2 for a fuller list.

2. See appendix 1.

3. See David Caute, *The Great Fear: The Anti-Communist Purge under Truman and Eisenhower* (London: Secker & Warburg, 1978), 275; Ralph S. Brown Jr., *Loyalty and Security: Employment Tests in the United States* (New Haven: Yale University Press, 1958), 487–88. Those numbers do not include employees who left government because they believed loyalty charges were imminent. There is no way to quantify how many people decided against even applying for government jobs because of the loyalty program. Later it was called the "loyalty-security program," but I generally use the term "loyalty program" for all periods. See appendixes 3 and 4.

4. See Arthur M. Schlesinger Jr., *The Vital Center: The Politics of Freedom* (Boston: Houghton Mifflin, 1949); Alonzo Hamby, "The Vital Center, the Fair Deal, and the Quest for a Liberal Political Economy," *American Historical Re-*

view 77 (1972); Steve Fraser and Gary Gerstle, eds., *The Rise and Fall of the New Deal Order* (Princeton: Princeton University Press, 1989); Alan Brinkley, *The End of Reform: New Deal Liberalism in Recession and War* (New York: Vintage, 1995); Steven Gillon, *Politics and Vision: The ADA and American Liberalism, 1947–1985* (New York: Oxford University Press, 1987).

5. It is by now a truism that the reality of American women's lives in the early Cold War years belied stereotypes of the suburban housewife. See Joanne Meyerowitz, ed., *Not June Cleaver: Women and Gender in Postwar America* (Philadelphia: Temple University Press, 1994). Many monographs discuss the impact of anticommunism on individual women or women's organizations; examples include Landon R. Y. Storrs, *Civilizing Capitalism: The National Consumers' League, Women's Activism, and Labor Standards in the New Deal Era* (Chapel Hill: University of North Carolina Press, 2000); Dorothy Sue Cobble, *The Other Women's Movement: Workplace Justice and Social Rights in Modern America* (Princeton: Princeton University Press, 2004); Jacquelyn Dowd Hall, "Women Writers, the 'Southern Front,' and the Dialectical Imagination," *Journal of Southern History* 69, no. 1 (2003); Linda Gordon, *Dorothea Lange: A Life beyond Limits* (New York: W. W. Norton, 2009).

6. U.S. Women's Bureau, *Women in the Federal Service, 1923–47* (Washington, D.C., 1949–50), part I, p. 9, part II, pp. 7–8, 34–39.

7. Eleanor Bontecou, *The Federal Loyalty-Security Program* (Ithaca: Cornell University Press, 1953). Many private employers, and state and local governments, imitated the federal loyalty program, with the result that an estimated 20 percent of the workforce in the 1950s had to pass loyalty tests to keep their jobs; Brown, *Loyalty and Security*, 181.

8. Earl Latham, *The Communist Controversy in Washington from the New Deal to McCarthy* (Cambridge: Harvard University Press, 1966); Alan D. Harper, *The Politics of Loyalty: The White House and the Communist Issue, 1946–1952* (Westport, Conn.: Greenwood, 1969); Athan Theoharis, "Escalation of the Loyalty Program," in *Politics and Policies of the Truman Administration*, ed. Barton J. Bernstein (Chicago: Quadrangle, 1970); Francis H. Thompson, *The Frustration of Politics: Truman, Congress, and the Loyalty Issue, 1945–1953* (Cranbury, N.J.: Associated University Presses, 1979). For a journalistic treatment of loyalty cases involving defendants who responded to the author's published query, see Selma R. Williams, *Red-Listed: Haunted by the Washington Witch Hunt* (Reading, Mass.: Addison-Wesley, 1993). For a comprehensive treatment of the Second Red Scare, see Ellen Schrecker, *Many Are the Crimes: McCarthyism in America* (Boston: Little, Brown, 1998).

9. Findings from the Venona project and Soviet sources have convinced most scholars that the government officials Alger Hiss, Nathan Gregory Silvermaster, and Laughlin Currie, for example, shared information with the Soviets, chiefly during the Second World War. About 350 Americans, most of them not government employees, are known to have engaged in espionage. Disagreement remains about how damaging their actions were to U.S. security. There is consensus that information from Julius Rosenberg and others associated with the Manhattan Project accelerated the Soviets' development of atomic weapons. For

a brief review of this debate, see Ellen Schrecker, "Soviet Espionage in America: An Oft-Told Tale," *Reviews in American History* 38 (June 2010): 355–61.

10. John Earl Haynes, *Red Scare or Red Menace? American Communism and Anticommunism in the Cold War Era* (Chicago: Ivan Dee, 1996); Eric Breindel and Herbert Romerstein, *The Venona Secrets: Exposing Soviet Espionage and America's Traitors* (Washington, D.C.: Regnery, 2000); John Earl Haynes and Harvey Klehr, *In Denial: Historians, Communism and Espionage* (San Francisco: Encounter Books, 2003), 50–51, 260n55; Haynes and Klehr, *Early Cold War Spies* (New York: Cambridge University Press, 2006). Also see Ronald Radosh, "Bohemian Rhapsody," *New Republic*, Mar. 12, 2007, and Haynes, Klehr, and Alexander Vassiliev, *Spies: The Rise and Fall of the KGB in America* (New Haven: Yale University Press, 2009). For an example of the opposing view, see Ellen Schrecker and Maurice Isserman, "The Right's Cold War Revision," *Nation*, July 24–31, 2000, pp. 22–24.

11. See Haynes and Klehr, *In Denial*, 231; Haynes and Klehr, *Early Cold War Spies*.

12. William F. Buckley, *Redhunter* (Boston: Little Brown, 1999); Ann H. Coulter, *Treason: Liberal Treachery from the Cold War to the War on Terrorism* (New York: Crown Forum, 2003); M. Stanton Evans, *Blacklisted by History: The Untold Story of Senator Joe McCarthy and His Fight against America's Enemies* (New York: Crown Forum, 2007). See also John Willingham, "The Texas State Board of Education and the Vindication of Joe McCarthy," History News Network, Mar. 8, 2010 (http://www.hnn.us/articles/124045.html); "Texas Conservatives Win Curriculum Change," *NYT*, Mar. 12, 2010.

13. Some members of the Communist Party underground denied for many decades that they were or had been Communists. The public often did not know how much evidence there was against the defendants: some evidence was inadmissible in court because it had been obtained illegally, and some was not publicized for fear of tipping off the Soviets about counterintelligence successes. In addition to weighing evidence in FBI and Civil Service Commission files, scholars can now check records from the Venona project, the papers of the Communist Party USA, and Alexander Vassiliev's notes from records of the KGB, the Soviet foreign intelligence service.

14. Many scholars have shown that Red scare politics devastated the most progressive sectors of the labor and civil rights movements and created a climate in which Americans in general hesitated to express nonconformist political views.

15. I disagree with Jennifer Delton's claim that liberals, not conservatives, were the driving force of anticommunism. "Most anticommunism—the anticommunism that mattered—was not hysterical and conservative, but, rather, a methodical and, in the end, successful attempt on the part of New Deal liberals to remove Communists from specific areas of American life. . . . Anticommunism did not subvert New Dealism, but rather preserved and expanded it"; Jennifer Delton, "Rethinking Post–World War II Anticommunism," *Journal of the Historical Society* 10, no. 1 (Mar. 2010): 1–41, quotations 2, 4. See also Richard Gid Powers, *Not without Honor: The History of American Anticommunism* (New Haven: Yale University Press, 1998).

16. Richard Hofstadter, *Anti-Intellectualism in American Life* (New York: Knopf, 1963), 41–42. On reactionary populism, see also Nancy MacLean, *Behind the Mask of Chivalry* (New York: Oxford University Press, 1994).

17. M. J. Heale, *McCarthy's Americans: Red Scare Politics in State and Nation, 1935–1965* (Athens: University of Georgia Press, 1998). See also Schrecker, *Many Are the Crimes.*

18. For the argument that the "containment" of communism abroad had a domestic corollary that prescribed rigid gender roles within the nuclear family, see Elaine Tyler May, *Homeward Bound: American Families in the Cold War Era* (New York: Basic Books, 1988). See also K. A. Cuordileone, "'Politics in an Age of Anxiety': Cold War Political Culture and the Crisis in American Masculinity, 1949–1960," *Journal of American History* 87, no. 2 (2000); Robert D. Dean, *Imperial Brotherhood: Gender and the Making of Cold War Foreign Policy* (Amherst: University of Massachusetts Press, 2001); and David K. Johnson, *The Lavender Scare: The Cold War Persecution of Gays and Lesbians in the Federal Government* (Chicago: University of Chicago Press, 2004). The latter provides useful data on a few loyalty cases involving lesbians in low-level jobs.

19. MacLean, *Behind the Mask of Chivalry*; Kim Nielsen, *Un-American Womanhood: Antiradicalism, Antifeminism, and the First Red Scare* (Columbus: Ohio State University Press, 2001); Rebecca Klatch, *Women of the New Right* (Philadelphia: Temple University Press, 1988).

20. Hofstadter, *Anti-Intellectualism*, 30–42; Johnson, *Lavender Scare*; Cindy Aron, *Ladies and Gentlemen of the Civil Service* (New York: Oxford University Press, 1987); Nielsen, *Un-American Womanhood.*

21. See, for example, Hofstadter, *Anti-Intellectualism.*

22. Susan Ware, *Beyond Suffrage: Women in the New Deal* (Cambridge: Harvard University Press, 1981); Judith Sealander, *As Minority Becomes Majority* (Westport, Conn.: Greenwood, 1983); Robyn Muncy, *Creating a Female Dominion in American Reform, 1910–1935* (New York: Oxford University Press, 1991); Linda Gordon, *Pitied but Not Entitled* (Cambridge: Harvard University Press, 1994); Blanche Wiesen Cook, *Eleanor Roosevelt, Volume 2: The Defining Years, 1933–1938* (New York: Penguin, 2000). For the postwar period, see Cynthia Harrison, *On Account of Sex: The Politics of Women's Issues, 1945–1968* (Berkeley: University of California Press, 1988); Kathleen Laughlin, *Women's Work and Public Policy: A History of the Women's Bureau, U.S. Department of Labor, 1945–1970* (Boston: Northeastern University Press, 2000).

23. Left feminists fused "a recognition of the systematic oppression of women with an appreciation of other structures of power underlying American society," to cite the definition offered by Ellen DuBois, "Eleanor Flexner and the History of American Feminism," *Gender and History* 3 (1991): 84. See also Landon R. Y. Storrs, "Red Scare Politics and the Suppression of Popular Front Feminism: The Loyalty Investigation of Mary Dublin Keyserling," *Journal of American History* 90, no. 2 (2003). On the limits of the older phrase "social feminist," see Nancy Cott, "What's in a Name? The Limits of 'Social Feminism,'" *Journal of American History* 76, no. 3 (1989). Dorothy Sue Cobble refers to some of the women studied here as "labor feminists"; Cobble, *Other Women's Movement.* On the

intrafeminist conflict over the equal rights amendment, see also Storrs, *Civilizing Capitalism.*

24. See Gary Gerstle, "The Protean Character of American Liberalism," *American Historical Review* 99 (1994); Jefferson Cowie and Nick Salvatore, "The Long Exception: Rethinking the Place of the New Deal in American History," *International Labor and Working-Class History* 74 (2008). Some describe that perceived shift as a devolution from class solidarity to divisive "identity politics."

25. Other works that have challenged the classic narratives include, in addition to those cited above, Daniel Horowitz, *Betty Friedan* (Amherst: University of Massachusetts Press, 1998); Jacquelyn Dowd Hall, "Open Secrets: Memory, Imagination, and the Refashioning of Southern Identity," *American Quarterly* 50, no. 1 (1998); Kate Weigand, *Red Feminism: American Communism and the Making of Women's Liberation* (Baltimore: Johns Hopkins University Press, 2001).

26. On the debate over the nature of the American Communist Party, see, for example, Haynes and Klehr, *In Denial,* 134–39; Michael Kazin, "The Agony and Romance of the American Left," *American Historical Review* 100, no. 5 (1995). In the Popular Front, diverse activists worked in "the tradition of radical democratic movements for social transformation," to use Michael Denning's definition of "left." But critics used the Popular Front's inclusiveness to characterize it as Communist-dominated, and the "front" in Popular Front took on the connotation of duplicity, as in "front group," rather than its intended connotation of solidarity; Michael Denning, *The Cultural Front* (New York: Verso, 1996), 3.

27. *Fortune* magazine poll from July 1942 cited by Denning, *The Cultural Front,* 4.

28. James T. Kloppenberg, *Uncertain Victory: Social Democracy and Progressivism in European and American Social Thought* (New York: Oxford University Press, 1986), 6. On the social democratic consensus along the Popular Front, see Ira Katznelson, "Was the Great Society a Lost Opportunity?" in *Rise and Fall of the New Deal Order,* ed. Fraser and Gerstle, 186; Denning, *The Cultural Front,* 158–66; Doug Rossinow, *Visions of Progress: The Left-Liberal Tradition in America* (Philadelphia: University of Pennsylvania Press, 2007).

29. Storrs, *Civilizing Capitalism,* 18.

30. Ware, *Beyond Suffrage*; Gordon, *Pitied but Not Entitled*; Alice Kessler-Harris, *In Pursuit of Equity* (New York: Oxford University Press, 2001).

31. Johnson, *Lavender Scare,* argues that the "lavender scare" was distinct from the Red scare, in that homosexual conduct alone, even without evidence of political leftism, could result in dismissal. By contrast, I stick with the phrase "Red scare" and describe its chief instigators as "anticommunists." I am not suggesting that homosexual, women, and racial minorities were secondary to the "real" target, communists. Rather, my point is that right-wingers understood communism to have sexual, gender, and racial implications as well as class and "political" ones, narrowly defined.

32. On purchasing power progressives, see Meg Jacobs, *Pocketbook Politics: Economic Citizenship in Twentieth-Century America* (Princeton: Princeton University Press, 2005).

33. In the standard account, the exigencies of war mobilization ended the New Deal by about 1938; see William E. Leuchtenburg, *Franklin D. Roosevelt and the New Deal* (New York: Harper and Row, 1963). New Left historians countered that the New Deal was conservative from the beginning, chiefly concerned with protecting capitalism at home and projecting it abroad; Barton J. Bernstein, "The New Deal: The Conservative Achievements of Liberal Reform," in *Towards a New Past: Dissenting Essays in American History*, ed. Bernstein (New York: Knopf, 1968). For an approving view of liberalism's moving "beyond" the New Deal and maturing in the 1940s, see Hamby, "Vital Center." For a negative view of the same developments, see Fraser and Gerstle, eds., *Rise and Fall of the New Deal Order*, particularly the essays by Alan Brinkley, Nelson Lichtenstein, and Ira Katznelson. See also Gillon, *Politics and Vision*; Kevin Mattson, *When America Was Great: The Fighting Faith of Postwar Liberalism* (New York: Routledge, 2004); Kazin, " Agony and Romance of the American Left"; Kim Phillips-Fein, *Invisible Hands: The Businessmen's Crusade against the New Deal* (New York: W. W. Norton, 2009). On social Keynesianism, see Margaret Weir and Theda Skocpol, "State Structures and the Possibilities for 'Keynesian' Responses to the Great Depression," in *Bringing the State Back In*, ed. Peter Evans, Dietrich Rueschemeyer, and Skocpol (New York: Cambridge University Press, 1985).

34. On the politics of "outing" former leftists, see Carl Bernstein, *Loyalties: A Son's Memoir* (New York: Simon and Schuster, 1989), 75–82, 259; Gerda Lerner, *Fireweed: A Political Autobiography* (Philadelphia: Temple University Press, 2002); Hall, "Open Secrets"; Weigand, *Red Feminism*, 8.

35. Some who had left the party tried to keep their government jobs by keeping their past membership secret, but few managed to do so for long. During World War II, certain U.S. intelligence agencies hired Communists because they were useful while the Soviet Union was an ally. With the end of that alliance, government service was less attractive to most party members, and vice versa. With respect to underground Communists engaged in espionage, after the defections of Elizabeth Bentley in 1945 and Igor Gouzenko in 1946 the Soviets dismantled their espionage operation in anticipation of exposure. They tried to reactivate some agents in the late 1940s, but internal Soviet correspondence demonstrates that effort to have been unsuccessful. See Schrecker, *Many Are the Crimes*; Haynes and Klehr, *Early Cold War Spies*. For one Soviet official's 1951 assessment, see Walter Schneir and Miriam Schneir, "Cables Coming in from the Cold," *Nation*, July 5, 1999.

36. Caroline Ware, Address to Radcliffe Alumnae Association, 1967, quoted by Anne F. Scott, ed., *Pauli Murray & Caroline Ware: Forty Years of Letters in Black and White* (Chapel Hill: University of North Carolina Press, 2006), 183.

CHAPTER 1

When the Old Left Was Young . . . and Went to Washington

1. Arthur M. Schlesinger Jr., *The Coming of the New Deal* (Boston: Houghton Mifflin, 1958), 16 (quoting George Peek), 19–20.

2. Robert Cohen, *When the Old Left Was Young: Student Radicals and America's First Mass Student Movement, 1929–1941* (New York: Oxford University Press, 1993), 46; Harvey Klehr, *Heyday of American Communism* (New York: Basic Books, 1984), chap. 16.

3. Schlesinger did note the group of secret Communist Party members in the Agricultural Adjustment Administration. My point is that the focus on Communist Party infiltration, and liberals' defensiveness about it, has obscured the importance of noncommunist leftists in government. Schlesinger Jr., *Coming of the New Deal*, 52–54.

4. Tex Goldschmidt, draft memoir, workrelief.doc, in author's possession. I thank his daughter Ann Richardson of London for sending me these electronic files (which are unpaginated). Subsequently I learned that an earlier, slightly different, version is in Goldschmidt Papers.

5. Robert Cohen states that Hall was from Mississippi, but Goldschmidt repeatedly identifies him as from Alabama. Cohen, *When the Old Left Was Young*, 46. Goldschmidt, draft memoir, work relief.doc.

6. "Still taboo subject" from prologue, Wickenden, draft memoir, box 1, Wickenden Papers M2001–090. "Tweedledee" from Goldschmidt, draft memoir, work relief.doc. Hallie Flanagan connection from Reminiscences of Arthur Goldschmidt, CCOH.

7. "Politically meaningless" from Wickenden, draft memoir, Introduction, 8; other quotations from Goldschmidt, draft memoir, work relief.doc.

8. Charlotte Tuttle Westwood Lloyd Walkup took the names of three husbands. For more on her first husband, see Charlotte Walkup interview with author, June 12, 2006; Howard Westwood obituary, *NYT*, Mar. 21, 1994.

9. Walkup interview with author, June 12, 2006; *NYT*, Nov. 13 and 14, 1929.

10. Walkup interview with author, June 12, 2006; her obituary, *Washington Post*, Aug. 26, 2008. David Lloyd was the grandson of Henry Demarest Lloyd's brother. Henry was disinherited after supporting the Haymarket anarchists and is best known for his critique of monopoly, *Wealth against Commonwealth* (1894). Henry's direct descendants included William Bross, a founder of the American Communist Party, and Jessie Lloyd O'Connor; being related to them would create difficulties for David, as we shall see.

11. Goldschmidt, draft memoir, work relief.doc; Wickenden, "Life in New Deal Washington," *Constitution* (Winter 1993): 27.

12. Wickenden, "The Philosophic and Economic Basis of the New Deal," c. 1938, file 13, box 2, Wickenden Papers M99–098.

13. Felix Cohen to Norman Thomas, Nov. 3, 1933, box 50, Joseph Lash Papers, FDRL.

14. Dalia Tsuk Mitchell, *Architect of Justice: Felix S. Cohen and the Founding of American Legal Pluralism* (Ithaca: Cornell University Press, 2007), 24–30.

15. Lucy Kramer Cohen interview with Joseph Lash, Mar. 6, 1965, box 50, Lash Papers, FDRL. On Thomas and Cohen sharing the platform, Mitchell, *Architect of Justice*, 43.

16. Margold was a former student of Felix's father, and Felix had impressed Margold the preceding year when they worked together on a City College student rights case. Mitchell, *Architect of Justice*, 289n3.

17. Felix Cohen to Norman Thomas, Nov. 3, 1933, box 50, Lash Papers, FDRL.

18. Norman Thomas to Felix Cohen, Nov. 14, 1933, box 50, Lash Papers, FDRL.

19. Margold had worked with the American Civil Liberties Union and the NAACP before joining Interior. It was probably Margold who hired the African American lawyer William Hastie in November 1933 to the same rank as Felix Cohen (assistant solicitor). Ickes hired the white southern liberal Clark Foreman, who in turn hired several black professionals.

20. Lawyer Ida Klaus recalled that Felix had been one of the few men at Columbia Law School who respected the female students. Charlotte Walkup too commented on his advocacy of women at Interior. Klaus interview with Joe Lash, June 5, 1965, box 50, Lash Papers, FDRL; Reminiscences of Charlotte T. L. Walkup, CCOH, and Walkup interview with author, June 12, 2006. Chapter 7 discusses Felix Cohen's role in the "Indian New Deal."

21. Edith I. Spivack, Columbia Law '32, from *Brief History of Women at Columbia Law School* (online). Most of Columbia Law's early female graduates ended up in government service.

22. Landon R. Y. Storrs, *Civilizing Capitalism: The National Consumers' League, Women's Activism, and Labor Standards in the New Deal Era* (Chapel Hill: University of North Carolina Press, 2000), 217. See also Thomas I. Emerson, *Young Lawyer for the New Deal* (Savage, Md.: Rowman & Littlefield, 1991), 294. Chapter 2 discusses the conservative attack on women lawyers at the NLRB.

23. Emerson, *Young Lawyer for the New Deal*, 4–7.

24. Ibid., 34–36. The first NLRB was created by Wagner's Public Resolution 44; the Wagner Act creating the permanent board was passed in 1935. Emerson's stint at the NLRB was interrupted by a year at the Social Security Board, 1936–37.

25. On the honeymoon, see ibid., 5. See also *NYT*, Jan. 1, 1934. "Bert" Paret's career included jobs at the WPA and the Labor Department's Wage and Hours Division. Emerson's feminism is further suggested by his role in winning a Supreme Court ruling that decriminalized contraceptives (*Griswold v. Connecticut*, 1965), and his service on the Pennsylvania Commission on the Status of Women; finding aid to Emerson Papers, Sterling Library, Yale.

26. Ida Klaus obituary, *NYT*, May 20, 1999; *NYT*, May 13, 1996; Ida Klaus interview, June 5, 1965, box 50, Lash Papers, FDRL; Joseph P. Lash, *Dealers and Dreamers* (New York: Doubleday, 1988), 432.

27. *NYT*, Jan. 10, 1940, quoting Feb. 21, 1935, memo by Francis Biddle; see also Emerson, *Young Lawyer for the New Deal*, 116. Bennett Porter had joined the CP by the time she went to the NLRB from the Resettlement Association in 1935; see Earl Latham, *The Communist Controversy in Washington from the New Deal to McCarthy* (Cambridge: Harvard University Press, 1966), 147.

28. Agger was Barnard class of 1931. Laura Kalman, *Abe Fortas: A Biography* (New Haven: Yale University Press, 1990), 43–45.

29. Bernice Lotwin Bernstein interview, 75–79, WFGP. She credited the agency for hiring Molly Dewson and Jane Hoey, who in turn helped keep the agency welcoming to women.

30. Bernice L. Bernstein, Affidavit of Respondent as to Her Life [1954], 9, folder 2, box 9, Bernard Bernstein Papers, HSTL; Bernice Bernstein interview, 36, 54, WFGP.

31. Foster Dulles tried to move Eleanor out of the State Department to protect himself from nepotism charges, to which he was vulnerable because he had helped his brother Allen become head of the CIA. Eleanor Dulles was not as clearly on the left as the others described here, but she was a feminist and later would be anti-McCarthy. She defended Esther Brunauer in 1950, and she was furious with Foster for sacrificing State Department employees to McCarthy. She reportedly told Foster in October 1952 that if Republicans did not repudiate McCarthy and his tactics, she was going to vote Democratic. Eleanor Dulles to Senator Millard Tydings, Mar. 22, 1950, Esther Brunauer file, RG 478; Leonard Mosley, *Dulles: A Biography of Eleanor, Allen, and John Foster Dulles* (New York: Dial Press, 1978), 299. See also Eleanor Lansing Dulles obituary, *NYT*, Nov. 4, 1996.

32. "The Story of Dorothy Bailey," *Washington Star*, Mar. 27, 1949. Contrary to some scholarly accounts, Bailey was white.

33. Before they married, Mary Taylor was a widow and Montgomery was divorced. Mary Taylor Montgomery file, RG 478. Hope Hale Davis, *Great Day Coming: A Memoir of the 1930s* (South Royalton, Vt.: Steerforth Press, 1994), 39. Marie Jenney Howe was a leading New York suffragist, a Unitarian minister, and the biographer of the French radical George Sand.

34. See FBI report, June 2, 1948, and statements by Wilbur J. Cohen, June 2, 11, 1954, Wilbur Cohen file, RG 478. Bittel had wanted to work for the NLRB but began as a secretary at the Bureau of Public Assistance, according to Edward Berkowitz, *Mr. Social Security: The Life of Wilbur J. Cohen* (Lawrence: University Press of Kansas, 1995), 44.

35. Burns, "My LSE"; Columbia tenure trouble from folder 2, box 7; Burns résumé in box 1, all in Burns Papers, SWHA. The refusal to tenure Burns was controversial because she was regarded as "the leading professor of economics at Columbia"; see Mary Dublin Keyserling interview with Katie Louchheim, 16, CCOH.

36. Biographical sketch, finding aid to Caroline Ware Papers, FDRL. The University of Wyoming refused to hire her in 1935 because she was married, and the University of Maryland did not hire women at all.

37. "Lina" to Helen, Feb. 18, 1935, file 3.6, Helen D. Lockwood Papers, Vassar College Library. On Section 213 of the National Economy Act of 1932 and its repeal, see Lois Scharf, *To Work and to Wed* (Westport, Conn.: Greenwood, 1980).

38. Kramer did research for Cohen's drafting of the Indian Reorganization Act, and data she gathered while working for Franz Boas at Barnard became two chapters of the *Handbook of Federal Indian Law*; see Lucy Kramer Cohen

interview with Fern Ingersoll, Helen Gahagan Douglas Project, Bancroft; Lucy Kramer Cohen obituary, *Washington Post*, Jan. 5, 2007; Memorandum from Fourth Regional loyalty board, Sept. 11, 1950, Lucy Kramer file, RG 478. Felix Cohen's protégé Charlotte Tuttle Westwood got paid, but because she was a married woman she was hired at $2,000 per year; a single man with similar qualifications was hired at the same rank in the same office at $3,000. She began work in November 1934 but was not made permanent until November 1935. Reminiscences of Charlotte T. L. Walkup, 22–23, CCOH.

39. Goldschmidt, draft memoir, work relief.doc; pol and bureaucrat.doc.

40. Not until the 1940s did Columbia Law begin admitting black women; *Brief History of Women at Columbia Law School* (online). Michigan Law first admitted a black woman in 1942. Harvard Law admitted black men decades before it admitted women; in 1944 Harvard Law rejected the African American Pauli Murray based on her sex. J. Clay Smith, *Rebels in Law: Voices in History of Black Women Lawyers* (Ann Arbor: University of Michigan Press, 2000).

41. Barbara Ransby, *Ella Baker and the Black Freedom Movement* (Chapel Hill: University of North Carolina Press, 2003), 91–97.

42. Frances Williams interview, Black Women Oral History Project, vol. 10, pp. 275–307, SL; also see Caroline Ware interview, WFGP. As assistant to Consumer Division chief Harriet Elliot, Ware hired Williams in 1940.

43. On declining opportunities for women "in the higher brackets" during the war, see Wickenden, "Women and the War," 4, Wickenden Papers M2001-090. On women's drive for government positions in the 1940s, see Cynthia Harrison, *On Account of Sex: The Politics of Women's Issues, 1945–1968* (Berkeley: University of California Press, 1988); Martha Swain, *Ellen S. Woodward: New Deal Advocate for Women* (Jackson: University Press of Mississippi, 1995).

44. Preliminary Inventory to Mary Dublin Keyserling Papers, SL; Willadee Wehmeyer, "Mary Dublin Keyserling: Economist and Social Activist" (Ph.D. diss., University of Missouri–Kansas City, 1995). Other leftists who came to Washington for war jobs were Rhea Radin, Nancy Fraenkel Wechsler, Esther Brunauer, Paul R. Porter, and Walter Gellhorn; see appendix 2.

45. Managerial and policymaking positions were defined as those paying more than $6,000 per year in 1947. High-salaried women were employed by, in order of largest numbers, the Federal Security Agency and the Departments of Labor, Commerce, Agriculture, Treasury, War, State, and Interior. U.S. Women's Bureau, *Women in the Federal Service* (Washington, D.C., 1949–50), *Part II*, pp. 7–8; *Part I*, pp. 7, 9, 16, vi.

46. Lolita Flanagan, "The Federal Diary," *Washington Post*, Aug. 11, 1944. She went on to list a dozen "Government Gals who have made the big time." On the use of merit systems and union recognition to fight discrimination in the civil service, see Margaret C. Rung, *Servants of the State: Managing Diversity and Democracy in the Federal Workforce, 1933–1953* (Athens: University of Georgia Press, 2002), 185.

47. Civil Service Commission report, May 8, 1943, Arthur Goldschmidt file, RG 478.

48. Klaus quoted in Lash, *Dealers and Dreamers*, 432.

49. Eleanor Lansing Dulles obituary, *NYT*, Nov. 4, 1996 (quotation from 1958).

50. On Corcoran, see Wickenden, "On Being a Woman," typescript [circa 1993], Wickenden Papers M2001–090.

51. Harriet Keyserling to author (in person, Charleston, S.C.), Dec. 2007. "Eighteen Women End Cosmos Club's 110-Year Male Era," *Washington Post*, Oct. 12, 1988.

52. Storrs, *Civilizing Capitalism*, 117, 201. Isador Lubin interview, 67, 162, CCOH. Robyn Muncy, "Women, Gender, and Politics in the New Deal Government: Josephine Roche and the Federal Security Agency," *Journal of Women's History* 21, no. 3: 60–83.

53. Wickenden diary entry, Jan. 15, 1940, Wickenden Papers M2001–090.

54. Charlotte Walkup interview with author, June 12, 2006.

55. Christine Stansell, *American Moderns* (New York: Metropolitan, 2000), 7. See also Linda Gordon, *Woman's Body, Woman's Right* (New York: Penguin, 1976), chap. 8.

56. Nathaniel Weyl left government service in 1935 because he was uncomfortable with the need to keep his party membership secret; he formally left the party in 1939 (see chapter 4). Other left New Dealers from distinguished progressive families included David Demarest Lloyd, Felix Cohen, Mary Dublin, Jean Flexner, and Rhea Radin. Others had parents who were not well known but had unorthodox views: Tex Goldschmidt and Leon Keyserling had freethinking mothers, and Esther Brunauer's father was a socialist electrician.

57. Stansell, *American Moderns*, 225.

58. Those whose mothers are known to have been active woman suffragists include Mary Dublin, Charlotte Tuttle, Esther Brunauer, Nathaniel Weyl, Walter Gellhorn, Tex Goldschmidt, Val Lorwin, and Leon Keyserling. In the 1910s, "participation in suffrage was pretty much de rigueur for male intellectuals on the bohemian left"; ibid., 229. On Morris Cohen, see Lucy Kramer Cohen interview, box 50, Lash Papers, FDRL; on Charles Tuttle, see Reminiscences of Charlotte T. L. Walkup, 3, CCOH.

59. In a study of the radical student movement of the 1930s, 40 percent of those interviewed cited family influence as a source of their leftism while only 20 percent cited professors. Robert Cohen, "Activist Impulses: Campus Radicalism in the 1930s," http://newdeal.feri.org/students/essay05.htm.

60. Mary McCarthy, *How I Grew* (San Diego: Harcourt Brace Jovanovich, 1987), 205. Other important left feminists at women's colleges were Dorothy Douglas of Smith and Amy Hewes at Mt. Holyoke. Future feminist leaders nurtured by Douglas include her student Betty Friedan as well as the young labor activists Esther Peterson and Mary Dublin.

61. Lucy Kramer Cohen interview, Helen Gahagan Douglas Project, Bancroft. Benedict's experience convinced Kramer not to continue her advanced studies in mathematics.

62. On Wickenden's suggestion of Flanagan, see Reminiscences of Arthur Goldschmidt, CCOH. Flanagan became one of Martin Dies's targets in 1938; see "Hallie Flanagan," *Notable American Women: The Modern Years* (Cambridge: Harvard University Press, 1980), vol. 4, pp. 237–39.

63. Ware to Lockwood, Feb. 18, 1935, Lockwood Papers, Vassar.

64. For Ware's influence, see Reminiscences of Charlotte T. L. Walkup, CCOH; Goldschmidt, draft memoir, work relief.doc.

65. *Crisis of the Old Order* is the title of the first volume of A. M. Schlesinger's classic Age of Roosevelt trilogy.

66. Ellen Fitzpatrick, "Caroline F. Ware and the Cultural Approach to History," *American Quarterly* 43, no. 2 (1991): 187–88. Ware's dissertation won the Hart, Schaffner and Marx Economics Prize in 1929 and was published as *The Early New England Cotton Manufacture* (Boston: Houghton Mifflin, 1931). Her other books include *Greenwich Village, 1920–1930* (1935); *The Modern Economy in Action*, (1936, coauthor with Gardiner C. Means); *The Cultural Approach to History* (1940, editor); *The Consumer Goes to War* (1942); *History of Mankind, vol. VI: The Twentieth Century* (editor and coauthor, 1966). She also wrote several books in Spanish on community organizing that were widely adopted in Latin America. Ware was trained by Vassar's Lucy Maynard Salmon, a pioneering historian of women, and the Harvard historian Frederick Jackson Turner, who early called for exploring history "from the bottom up." Ware also studied economics and anthropology, which helped her see the interdependence of political, economic, and cultural forces.

67. Fitzpatrick, "Caroline F. Ware and the Cultural Approach to History," 175–76. Ware's scholarship foreshadowed the so-called "social history revolution" that would transform the writing of American history several decades later.

68. Cohen notes that "the campus Left included some of the most intellectually gifted members of their college generation," but his examples do not include anyone who went into government; Robert Cohen, "Activist Impulses: Campus Radicalism in the 1930s," http://newdeal.feri.org/students/essay05.htm. Among those prodigies who did go into government were statisticians Lucy Kramer and Mary Dublin; lawyers who graduated at or very near the top of their class, such as Charlotte Tuttle, Carol Agger, Felix Cohen, Walter Gellhorn, Tom Emerson, Abe Fortas, Leon Keyserling, Nancy Fraenkel, all at Harvard, Yale, or Columbia Law Schools, and Bernice Lotwin at Wisconsin (who later was told she had the best record not only in her class but of anyone who had ever attended that law school). The professors of National Student League leader Palmer Weber called him the most brilliant student at the University of Virginia in the 1930s; Patricia Sullivan, *Days of Hope: Race and Democracy in the New Deal Era* (Chapel Hill: University of North Carolina Press, 1996), 73.

69. Mary Dublin, review of Harry Scherman, *The Promises Men Live By* (New York: Random House, 1938), copy in MDK Papers.

70. Examples include Wickenden's seminar paper "Federal Relief of Unemployment" (Vassar, 1931) and Dublin's senior thesis, "The Changing Status of Women in New England, 1790 to the Present" (Barnard, 1930). Dublin then did graduate research on maternal mortality rates and for a 1932 Committee on the Costs of Medical Care report advocating national health insurance. Dublin became interested in "social problems" when she spent the summer of 1929 studying with John Maynard Keynes and others in Geneva. Catherine Bauer and Eveline Burns, among others, did research in Europe on social policies there.

71. The issue of mandatory military training would flare again at CCNY in 1931 with a different cast of characters. The novel whose suppression Dublin

condemned was Radclyffe Hall's *Well of Loneliness* (1927); see "Te Deum," *Barnard Bulletin*, Apr. 23, 1929, MDK Papers.

72. For accounts of the Columbia free speech fight, see *New York Evening Post*, Apr, 7, 1932; E. B. White, "Alma Mater's Eggs," *New Yorker*, Apr. 16, 1932; Goldschmidt, draft memoir, work relief.doc; James A. Wechsler, *Age of Suspicion* (New York: Random House, 1953), 24–32; and Cohen, *When the Old Left Was Young*, 55–68. Reed Harris's campus editorials would derail his career in 1953; see appendix 2.

73. Cohen, *When the Old Left Was Young*, 22–25, 52, 355n2. The National Student League (NSL) was founded in New York in December 1931. Cohen primarily credits Harry Magdoff and others at CCNY, but Goldschmidt claims his Social Problems Group at Columbia drew in students from other New York colleges and eventually became the nucleus of the NSL; Goldschmidt, draft memoir, work relief.doc. On the South, see also Sullivan, *Days of Hope*, 70–84; Glenda Gilmore, *Defying Dixie: The Radical Roots of Civil Rights* (New York: W. W. Norton, 2008).

74. Goldschmidt, draft memoir, work relief.doc.

75. Cohen, *When the Old Left Was Young*, 22–41.

76. Ibid., 44–55. Goldschmidt, draft memoir, work relief.doc.

77. Dublin, "The Company Town," 1932, Writings 1928–40, Carton 5, MDK Papers 88-M189.

78. The 1932 effort of Wilbur Cohen and his friend Mel Pitzerle was thwarted when a sheriff turned them back; Berkowitz, *Mr. Social Security*, 15.

79. Future New Dealers who visited the Soviet Union include Hallie Flanagan (1926, 1930), William Pickens (1927), Isador Lubin (1929), Elizabeth Wickenden (1931), John Carmody (1931), Mordecai and Lucille Ezekiel (1931), Tom and Catherine Blaisdell (1932), Mary Dublin (1932, 1936), Dorothy Bailey (1937), Nancy Fraenkel Wechsler (1937), and Catherine Bauer (1939). Of the named individuals, only Pickens was African American. On African American students in the Soviet Union in these years, see Gilmore, *Defying Dixie*, 47–51.

80. Wickenden article series in *Cleveland Plain Dealer*, Jan. 1932, box 15, Wickenden Papers. See also articles by John Carmody in his RG 478 file; Mordecai Ezekiel, Reply to Interrogatory, Dec. 18, 1953, p. 29, Ezekiel file, RG 478; Isador Lubin's comments on his 1929 impressions of Russia during his Loyalty Review Board hearing, Mar. 16, 1950, box 64, Lubin Papers, FDRL.

81. Wechsler, *Age of Suspicion*, 110–18; the acknowledgments state that Nancy was "really the co-author" of the book. Her father was Osmond Fraenkel, a famous ACLU lawyer. See appendix 2; Nancy F. Wechsler file, RG 478. McCarthy attacked James Wechsler in 1953. For a recent study of anticommunist liberals that prominently features James Wechsler, see Kevin Mattson, *When America Was Great: The Fighting Faith of Postwar Liberalism* (New York: Routledge, 2004).

82. Eugene Lyons, *The Red Decade* (Indianapolis: Bobbs-Merrill, 1941), typifies the mockery of leftists and liberals who supposedly saw only what they wanted to see—a utopia—when they visited the Soviet Union. As a journalist in Moscow in the early 1930s, Lyons was more informed than short-term visitors

about the Stalin regime's brutality; not until the full story of the Moscow show trials began to circulate widely in mid-1937 did the nature of Stalinism become obvious to outsiders. For an introduction to the large literature, see Judy Kutulas, *The Long War: The Intellectual People's Front and Anti-Stalinism, 1930–1940* (Durham: Duke University Press, 1995).

83. Wickenden, "Russian Worker Has Few Worries," and "Family Life Goes on in Russia," *Cleveland Plain Dealer*, Jan. 14 and 15, 1932; Wickenden, "The New Feminism," unpublished typescript [New York City, 1933], 4, all box 15, Wickenden Papers.

84. See Kate Weigand, *Red Feminism: American Communism and the Making of Women's Liberation* (Baltimore: Johns Hopkins University Press, 2001). For admiration of the Communist Party's stands on racial and sexual equality, see Goldschmidt, draft memoir, work relief.doc.

85. Cohen, *When the Old Left Was Young*, 269–71. Some African Americans joined the NSL or LID; the professor and later NAACP official William Pickens was on the LID board, for example. Because many others have discussed the left's antiracism in the 1930s and 1940s, and because more white women than African Americans were able to get high-ranking government jobs, I focus on the left's gender radicalism more than on its race radicalism.

86. Goldschmidt, draft memoir, Billy.doc. Goldschmidt selected this correspondence to transcribe as he worked on his memoir in the 1990s.

87. Wickenden, "The New Feminism," 2–3; "Sauce for the Gander" [Paris, 1932], box 15, Wickenden Papers.

88. Wickenden, "Sauce for the Gander," box 15, Wickenden Papers. In a satirical vein, she doubted that the curriculum for men would be revised, although "it would be pleasant indeed if more men were adept at writing love letters, at giving presents, at making love, at taking care of furnaces, at remembering anniversaries, and at disciplining their sons." Wickenden maintained that the economic underpinnings of women's dependence were obsolete but that public opinion lagged behind; see "The New Feminism," box 15, Wickenden Papers. For a similar analysis from an African American perspective, see Pauli Murray, "Why Negro Girls Stay Single," *Negro Digest* 5 (July 1947), discussed in Nancy MacLean, *Freedom Is Not Enough: The Opening of the American Workplace* (Cambridge: Harvard University Press, 2006), 122.

89. Tex to Mr. and Mrs. Wickenden, May 24, 1933, box 2, Wickenden Papers M99–098. To his own parents, Goldschmidt praised Wickenden's "intriguing mind" and "masculine directness." By contrast he noted that Ellen S. Woodward, with whom he worked at the WPA, was limited by her southern middle-class woman's style of "dealing with men by wheedling and indirection." Goldschmidt, draft memoir, work relief.doc. On Wickenden's reluctance to have children and his child-rearing role, see Arthur Goldschmidt Jr. e-mail to author, May 31, 2006.

90. Goldschmidt, draft memoir, work relief.doc. Apparently in the end Kramer wore a cream-colored dress, but see Mrs. Auerbach interview, May 19, 1965, Lash Papers.

91. Heterosexually active women who never married include Dorothy Kenyon, Dorothy Bailey, and Rhea Radin. Women known to have had lovers other

than their eventual spouses include Mary Dublin, Catherine Bauer, and Mary Taylor. Those who divorced include Carol Agger Fortas, Rowena Rommel, Joseph Barnes, Betty Brown Field Barnes, Howard Westwood, Charlotte Tuttle, Stephen Brunauer, Rodney Dutcher, Donald Montgomery, and Paul R. Porter.

92. Davis, *Great Day Coming*, 41–42, 90. Mary Taylor Montgomery file, RG 478.

93. On Bernice Lotwin and Leon Keyserling, see Bernice L. Bernstein, Affidavit of Respondent as to Her Life [1954], 9, folder 2, box 9, Bernard Bernstein Papers, HSTL; Leon's autobiographical poem, and Mary Dublin Keyserling's correspondence with Bernice after Leon's death, both in Leon Keyserling Papers, College of Charleston.

94. John Edelman, *Labor Lobbyist* (New York: Bobbs-Merrill, 1974), 109–15, quotation 109. The labor journalist Matthew Josephson described Bauer as the epitome of the "New Woman," according to Mary Susan Cole, "Catherine Bauer and the Public Housing Movement, 1926–1937" (Ph.D. diss., George Washington University, 1975). Also see H. Peter Overlander and Eva Newbrun, *Houser: The Life and Work of Catherine Bauer* (Vancouver: University of British Columbia Press, 1999); Gail Radford, *Modern Housing for America: Policy Struggles in the New Deal Era* (Chicago: University of Chicago Press, 1996).

95. These letters reveal a dimension quite absent in scholarly accounts of Keyserling and in his own official papers at the Truman Library. Catherine to Leon, July 19, 1936, Keyserling Family Papers, unprocessed 2005 accession, College of Charleston. He replied, "I've been thinking of you about every day, particularly of how the hair on the back of your head under your abominable beret looked just when you had scampered madly to the top of the stairs . . . and were inserting the key in the door—with me slightly in arrears." Leon to Catherine, Sept. 10, 1936, box 26, Bauer Papers, Bancroft. On the rooming house and their discussion of marriage, see Overlander and Newbrun, *Houser*, 147–49.

96. Leon to "Kitten," June 26, 1939, box 26, Bauer Papers, Bancroft. Hawes's dress designs were the foremost expression of the "labor feminist aesthetic," and in 1940 she began writing for the new left-wing paper *PM*; Michael Denning, *The Cultural Front* (New York: Verso, 1996), 146.

97. See Leon to Catherine, Aug. 12, 1939, in which he refers to being available because Mary had left for Europe; Leon's valentine to Catherine, Feb. 14, 1940; and, after both had married, Leon to Kittenitis, to the effect that he had sent the wedding gift "not as a token of the new friendship between the Wursters and the Keyserlings but rather of the old friendship ever to endure between CKB and LHK"; Oct. 19, 1940; all box 26, Bauer Papers, Bancroft.

98. Bauer and Dublin met up in Europe, and Dublin wrote her a letter of introduction to the Reuters news correspondent in Moscow; Mary Dublin to Henry Shapiro, Aug. 19, 1939, box 26, Bauer Papers, Bancroft. Dublin's relationship history has been reconstructed from conversations with her brother Thomas D. Dublin, and from her diaries and her correspondence with her mother in MDK Papers. On Bauer, Marshall, and Stonorov, see Overlander and Newbrun, *Houser*. Stonorov later sculpted a bust of Bauer for the Housing and Urban Development Building in Washington.

99. On Dublin and Porter, see Augusta Dublin to Mary, 1931, MDK Papers; Mary Dublin Keyserling testimony, Senate Internal Security Subcommittee (SISS) executive session, June 15, 1951, RG 46. On Doskow, see Dublin appointment books, MDK Papers.

100. Wickenden, "A Plea for Tolerance" [circa 1952], Wickenden Papers M2001–090; Goldschmidt, draft memoir, Rochs.doc, Dies story.doc.

101. See Thomas Blaisdell file, RG 478; on Catherine's UNRRA job, Blaisdell interview, 8, HSTL. Chapter 2 discusses the League of Women Shoppers.

102. "Children's Prayers," *Time*, Oct. 26, 1931.

103. Cohen, *When the Old Left Was Young*, 272–73.

104. See chapter 3.

105. On women's fight against lynching, see Jacquelyn Dowd Hall, *Revolt against Chivalry* (New York: Columbia University Press, 1979). On Palmer Weber, see his obituary, *NYT*, Aug. 24, 1986; Sullivan, *Days of Hope*, 70–84.

106. On the New Deal thrust to reform the South and on the 1938 report, see Sullivan, *Days of Hope*, 70–84; Storrs, *Civilizing Capitalism*. Also see Peter Coclanis and David Carleton, *Confronting Southern Poverty in the Great Depression: The Report on Economic Conditions of the South* (New York: Bedford, 1996).

107. Ruth Benedict and Gene Weltfish, *The Races of Mankind* (Washington, D.C.: Public Affairs Committee, 1943); Nan Rothschild, *A Century of Barnard Anthropology*, http://beatl.barnard.columbia.edu/rothschild/cent_anth/. Weltfish taught anthropology at Columbia from 1936 until 1953, when she was fired because of her radical views. She headed the Congress of American Women and took the Fifth Amendment when asked whether she was a Communist. Another Boas student, Margaret Mead, became famous for her research on Samoan sexual norms.

108. Interviews by Joseph Lash with people who knew Felix Cohen and Lucy Kramer contain many references to the couple's emulation of Native American culture. The Kramer-Cohens' 1939 holiday greeting card featured Gene as an infant in her papoose; folder 4, box 51, Lash Papers, FDRL.

109. Carey McWilliams, *Factories in the Field: The Story of Migratory Farm Labor in California* (Boston: Little, Brown and Company, 1939). From 1938 to 1942, McWilliams headed California's Division of Immigration and Housing. During the war he defended Latinos in "zoot suit riots" and challenged the internment of Japanese Americans. Later he edited the *Nation* for twenty years. See Daniel Geary, "Carey McWilliams and Antifascism, 1934–1943," *Journal of American History* 90, no. 3 (2003).

110. Linda Gordon, *Dorothea Lange: A Life Beyond Limits* (New York: W. W. Norton, 2009). Given their shared interests, it is not surprising that Taylor became close to Tex Goldschmidt, Catherine Bauer, and Tom Blaisdell.

111. Dublin column on Harlan County, "The Company Town," cited above; Lash on Harlan, Sullivan, *Days of Hope*, 79. Ware to Helen Lockwood, Feb. 18, 1935, folder 3.6, Lockwood Papers, Vassar.

112. Geary, "Carey McWilliams," 915.

113. Ware to President Crane, June 26, 1935, and related clippings, box 150, Ware Papers, FDRL. The media treatment of the story exasperated Ware; even her friend Rodney Dutcher described her as a "brain truster's wife." University of Wyoming officials were unmoved, although one trustee's daughter wrote Ware confidentially expressing admiration and asking whether she could work for Ware.

114. I do not find them to be "post-feminists," a term applied to some New Deal women by Linda Gordon, *Pitied but Not Entitled* (Cambridge: Harvard University Press, 1994), 106–7. For a mistaken suggestion that Elizabeth Wickenden was not a feminist, see Jennifer Mittelstadt, *From Welfare to Workfare: The Unintended Consequences of Liberal Reform, 1945–65* (Chapel Hill: University of North Carolina Press, 2005), 136.

115. Caroline Ware interview, 39, WFGP. Means was one of the most influential economists of the early New Deal. Means, Mordecai Ezekiel, and Rexford Tugwell took a structural approach that was distinct from that of John Maynard Keynes, whose ascendance in the late New Deal displaced Means; see Theodore Rosenof, *Economics in the Long Run: New Deal Theorists and Their Legacies, 1933–1993* (Chapel Hill: University of North Carolina Press, 1997), 2, 15–16, 75.

116. Wickenden to Aubrey Williams, "The Future of the Works Program," circa 1935, Wickenden Papers M2001–090. Her recommendation that no special projects be created for women distinguishes her from older New Deal women like Ellen Sullivan Woodward. This disagreement reflected Wickenden's accurate prediction that women would be ghettoized into low-paid projects like sewing; Goldschmidt, draft memoir, work relief.doc.

117. On the conflict between labor feminists and the NWP, see Storrs, *Civilizing Capitalism*, 46–59, 76–90, 249. The American Socialist and Communist parties opposed the ERA on the grounds that it would invalidate labor laws for women.

118. Wickenden, "What Lies Ahead for Women," unpublished essay [circa 1943], Wickenden Papers M2001–090.

119. Wickenden, "The New Feminism," box 15, Wickenden Papers.

120. Bernice Bernstein interview, 128, WFGP.

121. Bernice Bernstein interview, 121, WFGP. Wickenden decided to remove herself "from the line of authority and competition and striving to get ahead and satisfy myself with being an influence"; Wickenden interview with Jean Bandler, 2, box 16, Wickenden Papers. Charlotte Walkup interview with author on "not looking for glory"; also, "I came across as cooperative and not antagonistic," Reminiscences of Charlotte T. L. Walkup, 65, CCOH.

122. Wickenden, "The New Feminism," box 15, Wickenden Papers.

123. Wickenden, "Women and the War," unpublished essay [circa 1943], Wickenden Papers M2001–090.

124. On women's rights activists' disappointment with their abolitionist former allies, see Ellen DuBois, *Feminism and Suffrage* (Ithaca: Cornell University Press, 1978); on the resistance in the 1960s of some New Left men to feminism, see Sara Evans, *Personal Politics* (New York: Knopf, 1979).

125. This was Lyndon Johnson's first introduction to Carol, and for years he teased Goldschmidt about getting pinned by her. It was Goldschmidt who intro-

duced his fellow Texan to Abe Fortas, initiating a long and influential political partnership. Goldschmidt, draft memoir 7 Me and LBJ.doc.

126. Esther Peterson, *Restless* (Washington, D.C.: Caring, 1995), 21, 48.

127. Ibid., 134–35.

128. See Bernice Bernstein interview, 129, WFGP, on how her husband, "like all men then," saw household obligations as the wife's job. On how the wife was usually the one to relocate, see Wickenden, "On Being a Woman," typescript [circa 1993], Wickenden Papers M2001–090.

129. See chapter 3.

130. Wickenden, "Life in New Deal Washington," *Constitution* (Winter 1993): 27.

131. Estelle Freedman, "Separatism as Strategy," *Feminist Studies* 5 (Fall 1979): 512–29; Blanche Wiesen Cook, "Female Support Networks," in *A Heritage of Her Own*, ed. Nancy Cott and Elizabeth Pleck (New York: Simon and Schuster, 1979); Susan Ware, *Partner and I* (New Haven: Yale University Press, 1987); Annelise Orleck, *Common Sense and a Little Fire: Women and Working-Class Politics in the United States, 1900–1965* (Chapel Hill: University of North Carolina Press, 1995).

132. On stereotypes of the left, see Kathleen A. Brown and Elizabeth Faue, "Social Bonds, Sexual Politics, and Political Community on the U.S. Left, 1920s–1940s," *Left History* 7, no. 1 (2001).

133. Alan Brinkley, *The End of Reform: New Deal Liberalism in Recession and War* (New York: Vintage, 1995), 13. He continues, "Women, minorities, and working-class people became part of their deliberations from time to time, but they rarely shaped the direction or tenor of the conversation decisively."

CHAPTER 2

Allegations of Disloyalty at Labor and Consumer Agencies, 1939–43

1. "Bare Campaign of Intimidation on Wagner Act: New Dealers Strive to Still Critics," *Chicago Tribune*, May 7, 1939, p. 1. The article named the following sponsors and officers of the LWS's Washington chapter: Mrs. Mordecai Ezekiel (wife of the economic adviser to Secretary of Agriculture Henry Wallace), Mrs. William O. Douglas (wife of the Supreme Court justice), Mrs. Leon Henderson (whose husband had just moved from the Temporary National Emergency Council to the Securities and Exchange Commission), Mrs. John Collier (wife of the commissioner of Indian affairs) and her daughter-in-law Nina P. Collier (whose husband worked in the Department of Agriculture), Mrs. Ernest Gruening (wife of an Interior Department official), Miss Josephine Roche (National Youth Administration), Representative Caroline O'Day, D-N.Y. ("great friend of Mrs. FDR"), Emily Newell Blair (formerly head of the Consumer Advisory Board to the National Recovery Administration), Mrs. Ernest Lindley (wife of the liberal journalist), and Mrs. Donald Richberg and Mrs. Dean Acheson, whose husbands were former New Deal officials.

2. On LWS support of the American Newspaper Guild strike, see House Special Committee on Un-American Activities, *Investigation of Un-American Propaganda Activities in the United States, Appendix IX* (Washington, D.C.: GPO, 1944), 1002–17. The *Chicago Tribune* was not a Hearst newspaper, but its owners similarly opposed unionization.

3. Report of Helene Abbott, May 23, 1939, exhibit to report of Thomas J. Nash, Aug. 31, 1939, LWS-Chicago file, F&R: Orgs, RG 233.

4. See David Witwer, "Westbrook Pegler and the Anti-Union Movement," *Journal of American History* 92, no. 2 (2005); Kim Phillips-Fein, *Invisible Hands: The Businessmen's Crusade against the New Deal* (New York: W. W. Norton, 2009).

5. We have countless studies of the labor movement and of specific unions and strikes, but only a few monographs on the consumer movement, and those have not been integrated into general syntheses on the New Deal or McCarthyism.

6. This overview draws on Steve Fraser and Gary Gerstle, eds., *The Rise and Fall of the New Deal Order* (Princeton: Princeton University Press, 1989); Landon R. Y. Storrs, *Civilizing Capitalism: The National Consumers' League, Women's Activism, and Labor Standards in the New Deal Era* (Chapel Hill: University of North Carolina Press, 2000); Lizabeth Cohen, *A Consumers' Republic: The Politics of Mass Consumption in Postwar America* (New York: Knopf, 2003), 57, 134; Meg Jacobs, *Pocketbook Politics: Economic Citizenship in Twentieth-Century America* (Princeton: Princeton University Press, 2005).

7. Jacobs, *Pocketbook Politics*; Cohen, *Consumers' Republic*. Historians have noted anticommunists' attack on the consumer movement, but without sufficient appreciation of how radical many of the movement's leaders were or how extensive their investigations were.

8. Thomas I. Emerson, *Young Lawyer for the New Deal* (Savage, Md.: Rowman & Littlefield, 1991), 34, 48, quotation 52. "The inequality of bargaining power between employees who do not possess full freedom of association or actual liberty of contract and employers who are organized in the corporate or other forms of ownership association substantially burdens and affects the flow of commerce, and tends to aggravate recurrent business depressions, by depressing wage rates and the purchasing power of wage earners in industry"; National Labor Relations Act, 29 U.S.C., Section 1 [§151]. See also Kenneth Casebeer, "Drafting Wagner's Act: Leon Keyserling and the Pre-Committee Drafts of the Labor Disputes Act and the National Labor Relations Act," *Industrial Relations Law Journal* 11 (1989); Donald K. Pickens, *Leon H. Keyserling: A Progressive Economist* (New York: Lexington Books, 2009).

9. NLRB lawyers who were sent out to set up regional offices and find test cases often got quite an education. Assigned to Atlanta, Tom Emerson found himself under surveillance and frequently thwarted by company informers planted among textile mill workers. Emerson, *Young Lawyer for the New Deal*, 57–69. In St. Louis, NLRB regional director Dorothea de Schweinitz too found most employers ignored the new law, and her efforts to enforce it generated complaints that later were used to suggest she was subversive. See FBI reports and other materials in Dorothea de Schweinitz file, RG 478.

10. From 1928 through 1932, Matthews made five trips to the Soviet Union, which at that time he portrayed as a utopia. In 1934 Matthews was suspended from the Socialist Party for his advocacy of violent revolution. Nelson L. Dawson, "From Fellow Traveler to Anticommunist: The Odyssey of J. B. Matthews," *Register of the Kentucky Historical Society* 84, no. 3 (1986).

11. Quotation from LWS, "Statement in response to Mr. J. B. Matthews' irrational attacks" [Dec. 1939], 2, LWS-DC Papers, SL. Initial directors and sponsors included the photographer Margaret Bourke-White, the writers Mary Beard, Katherine Dos Passos, Josephine Herbst, Genevieve Taggart, and Leanne Zugsmith, labor feminists Dorothy Douglas, Dorothy Kenyon, Frieda Miller, Cornelia Bryce Pinchot, and Mary Van Kleeck, and journalists Dorothy Day, Freda Kirchwey, and Suzanne La Follette.

12. LWS, "Investigation of Strike at Consumers' Research," Oct. 21, 1935, LWS file, F&R: Orgs., RG 233. Grace Lumpkin was close to the CP. The performance was probably an adaptation of *A Sign for Cain* (1935), whose protagonist was an African American sharecropper, or *To Make My Bread* (1932), which was about white southern textile workers.

13. For a description of the strike, see Lawrence Glickman, "The Strike in the Temple of Consumption: Consumer Activism and Twentieth-Century American Political Culture," *Journal of American History* 88, no. 1 (2001).

14. See ibid.; Norman Silber, *Test and Protest: The Influence of Consumers' Union* (New York: Holmes & Meier, 1983); Kathleen Donohue, *Freedom from Want: American Liberalism and the Idea of the Consumer* (Baltimore: Johns Hopkins University Press, 2003).

15. Landon R. Y. Storrs, "Left-Feminism, the Consumer Movement, and Red Scare Politics in the United States," *Journal of Women's History* 18, no. 3 (2006).

16. LWS, "Legislative Low-Down," Dec. 18, 139, LWS-DC Papers, SL. August Ogden, *The Dies Committee* (Washington, D.C.: Catholic University of America Press, 1945), 65, 87, 100; Walter Goodman, *The Committee: The Extraordinary Career of the House Committee on Un-American Activities* (New York: Farrar, Straus and Giroux, 1968); Dawson, "From Fellow Traveler to Anticommunist."

17. Dawson, "From Fellow Traveler to Anticommunist"; Ellen Schrecker, *Many Are the Crimes: McCarthyism in America* (Boston: Little, Brown, 1998), 44 (quotation).

18. In *Carter v. Carter Coal Company* (298 U.S. 238), the Court found the Coal Conservation Act unconstitutional. Even the NLRB's lawyers interpreted that decision to mean that the Court also would strike down the Wagner Act; Emerson, *Young Lawyer for the New Deal*, 77.

19. Jerold S. Auerbach, *Labor and Liberty: The LaFollette Committee and the New Deal* (Indianapolis: Bobbs-Merrill, 1966).

20. Leon to Father, June 22, 1937, file 6, box 5, Keyserling Family Papers, College of Charleston. In that incident and related strikes in Little Steel, eighteen "strikers" were killed and hundreds wounded. On NLRB investigators' shock at what they saw in the course of doing their jobs, see James A. Gross, *The Reshaping of the National Labor Relations Board* (Albany: State University of New York Press, 1982), vol. 2, pp. 10–16.

21. See Emerson, *Young Lawyer for the New Deal*, 86–87; William E. Leuchtenburg, *Franklin D. Roosevelt and the New Deal, 1932–1940* (New York: Harper and Row, 1963).

22. Gross, *Reshaping of the National Labor Relations Board*, 16. Powerful employers whose labor practices the NLRB immediately challenged included

steel, oil, and aircraft companies, the growers' and shippers' associations, Western Union, Consolidated Edison, Montgomery Ward, Goodyear, Chevrolet, Ford, and Remington Rand.

23. The NLRB heard 1,451 cases and issued 701 decisions in the year that ended June 30, 1938; ibid., 17. Emerson was not uncritical of the board, lamenting in particular the long delays before its decisions. In response to the frequent criticism that most NLRB decisions favored workers, Emerson explained that cases decided in favor of employers rarely reached a formal hearing. Emerson, *Young Lawyer for the New Deal*, 95.

24. One NLRB lawyer observed, "A literal enforcement of an expressed policy" was "something that politicians generally were not used to. . . . That's not the way things are or ever have been." Gross, *Reshaping of the National Labor Relations Board*, 23.

25. Gross, *Reshaping of the National Labor Relations Board*, 11; Emerson, *Young Lawyer for the New Deal*, 29.

26. Tomlins, *The State and the Unions*, 122, 102.

27. On AFL discrimination against women and African Americans, see Alice Kessler-Harris, *Out to Work* (New York: Oxford University Press, 1982); Herbert Hill, *Black Labor and the American Legal System* (Madison: University of Wisconsin Press, 1985).

28. Steve Fraser, *Labor Will Rule: Sidney Hillman and the Rise of American Labor* (New York: Free Press, 1991).

29. Christopher Tomlins challenges the conventional wisdom that New Deal labor policies increased the power of unions. He suggests the AFL rightly wanted to amend the Wagner Act in 1939 because the act had made the legitimacy of collective bargaining contingent on its capacity as a means to "higher productivity and efficient capital accumulation." Tomlins, *The State and the Unions*, 101, xiii.

30. In addition to Tomlins, see Michael Goldfield, "Worker Insurgency, Radical Organization, and New Deal Labor Legislation," *American Political Science Review* 83, no. 4 (1989). Goldfield interprets the Wagner Act as a corporate-liberal response to an upsurge in radical labor activism. My point is that some of the Wagner Act's drafters and supporters believed it would increase industrial democracy, not co-opt it.

31. See House Labor Committee, *Proposed Amendments to the NLRA*, vols. 4–5 (June–July 1939); "NLRB 1939 campaign" file and related files, reels 83–84, NCL Papers, LC. For a typical example of LWS action, see "Resume of Activities of Pittsburgh League of Women Shoppers, June 1938–June 1939," 5, LWS folder 2, Harold J. Ruttenberg Papers, Pennsylvania State University.

32. House Labor Committee, *Proposed Amendments to the NLRA*, vol. 4, pp. 1458–67 (testimony of John P. Davis). Keyserling quoted in Hill, *Black Labor*, 106. Hill's criticism of NLRB acquiescence in racial discrimination is based on the post-1944 period.

33. Storrs, *Civilizing Capitalism*, 211–15.

34. House Labor Committee, *Proposed Amendments to the NLRA*, vol. 5, Dublin testimony, 1604–6; House Labor Committee, *Proposed Amendments to the NLRA*, vol. 4, Collier testimony, 1301.

35. *Daily Republican* (Phoenixville, Penn.), Apr. 24, 1939, and other papers of same syndicate, reel 83, NCL Papers, LC; emphasis added. In some newspapers "the Perkins woman" was changed to "Mrs. Perkins." The Wagner Act was not upheld until April 1937; the sit-down strikes began in December 1936. Ironically, Perkins had reservations about the Wagner Act; see George Martin, *Madam Secretary* (Boston: Houghton Mifflin, 1976), 328, 381–86.

36. Within a short period in late 1939 and early 1940, Mary Dublin held meetings at her apartment to strategize on all those initiatives; appointment books, MDK Papers. The minutes and newsletters of the NCL and LWS attest to their campaigns against the Dies Committee and for the La Follette Committee.

37. On LWS flyers in NLRB offices, see Earl Latham, *The Communist Controversy in Washington from the New Deal to McCarthy* (Cambridge: Harvard University Press, 1966), 140. NLRB employees whose wives belonged to the LWS included Thomas Emerson, Alexander Hawes, and Edwin Smith.

38. "Skytop Fair Held by League of Shoppers," *Washington Post*, May 1, 1940, and related clippings, LWS-DC Papers, SL. Investigators later held participation in that event against Lucille and Mordecai Ezekiel, David Demarest Lloyd, and Leon Henderson, for example. On not being worried about Red-baiting until later, see Emerson, *Young Lawyer for the New Deal*, 134.

39. Emerson, *Young Lawyer for the New Deal*, 127; Tomlins, *The State and the Unions*.

40. Dorothea de Schweinitz file, RG 478. On Herrick and the female Review Division attorneys, see Gross, *Reshaping of the National Labor Relations Board*, 117–21, 81–83; Emerson, *Young Lawyer for the New Deal*, 116. A list of NLRB employees in 1939 is on reel 84, NCL Papers, LC; some names are gender-neutral, so a precise breakdown is not available.

41. *NYT*, Jan. 8–12, 1940; House Special Committee, *Hearings to Investigate the NLRB*, 1061, 1222, 1587, 1594; Emerson, *Young Lawyer for the New Deal*, 116; Gross, *Reshaping of the National Labor Relations Board*, 181–83. Additional information on Review Division attorneys can be found in file A-10, entry 23, and box 4, entry 25, NLRB Records, NA.

42. House Special Committee, *Hearings to Investigate the NLRB*, 1061, 1222, 1587, 1594; *NYT*, Jan. 12, 1940. It is unclear which women's groups went to the hearings.

43. This was Congressman Harry Routzohn (R-Ohio); Gross, *Reshaping of the National Labor Relations Board*, 183.

44. Toland had represented the company unions at Jones & Laughlin; Emerson, *Young Lawyer for the New Deal*, 73.

45. *Congressional Record*, House, 76th Cong., 2d sess., 1940, pt. I: 302.

46. Ibid., emphasis added.

47. "League for Peace List," *Washington Evening Star*, Oct. 25, 1939. Communists indeed were influential in the ALPD, but many ALPD members were not Communists. Dies was using ALPD mailing lists, not membership lists, so not all those named were even members. Furthermore, the CP discouraged its secret members from association with "front" groups, so public activity in many such

groups might just as well be interpreted to mean that a given employee probably was not in the CP.

48. House Special Committee, *Hearings to Investigate the NLRB*, 1061, 1222 (Bennett Porter), 1587, 1594.

49. Latham, *Communist Controversy in Washington*, 137–47. After the dismissal in February 1935 of Jerome Frank, Gardner Jackson, and others at the Agricultural Adjustment Administration, Bennett Porter, who had been part of Frank's group, moved to the new Resettlement Administration, where she impressed that agency's general counsel, Lee Pressman, and they both soon moved to the NLRB. In 1936 Pressman left government to work for the fledgling CIO.

50. Ida Klaus quoted in Joseph P. Lash, *Dealers and Dreamers* (New York: Doubleday, 1988), 432. See also her obituary, *NYT*, May 20, 1999.

51. Emerson, *Young Lawyer for the New Deal*, 131.

52. Ibid., 125.

53. Latham, *Communist Controversy in Washington*, 144; Gross, *Reshaping of the National Labor Relations Board*, 149; Emerson, *Young Lawyer for the New Deal*, 99. See also Margaret Fuchs Singer, *Legacy of a False Promise: A Daughter's Reckoning* (Tuscaloosa: University of Alabama Press, 2009).

54. Latham, *Communist Controversy in Washington*, 129 (quotation), 49; Gross, *Reshaping of the National Labor Relations Board*, 145.

55. For contrasting although not mutually exclusive interpretations of the Communist presence at the NLRB and the Smith Committee's treatment of it, see Emerson, *Young Lawyer for the New Deal*, 122–28; Latham, *Communist Controversy in Washington*, 124–50; Gross, *Reshaping of the National Labor Relations Board*, 140–50. The Smith Committee did not pay much attention to Nathan Witt, but it made much of NLRB member Edwin Smith's attendance at some Communist-sponsored conferences in Mexico. Smith's attendance may have been impolitic, but it was not evidence of disloyalty. Witt left government service in 1941.

56. See Emerson, *Young Lawyer for the New Deal*, 131 (quotation); 97–103.

57. Gross, *Reshaping of the National Labor Relations Board*, 4.

58. On the distribution of high-salaried women by agency, see "Women listed in the Official Register, May 1, 1947," compiled by U.S. Women's Bureau staff as background research for the bulletin *Women in the Federal Service, 1923–47, Part II*. A 1954 U.S. Women's Bureau report similarly shows the NLRB no longer stood out as an employer of professional women.

59. Emerson was hired in June 1941. In between his jobs with the La Follette Committee and OPA, Lloyd worked briefly for the Federal Communications Commission and the Board of Economic Warfare; David D. Lloyd FBI file. Others who worked for the NLRB and then OPA include Shad Polier, Aaron Warner, Ed Scheunemann (CP, per Fuchs), and Rose Eden. Labor activists who joined OPA include Tom Tippett and Oliver Peterson.

60. On early lists of subversives in government generated by the Dies Committee staff, employees of the NLRB and the Labor Department were overrepresented. See "League for Peace List," *Washington Evening Star*, Oct. 25, 1939; "Dies Charges 1,124 in Federal Posts Help Communists," ibid., Oct. 20, 1941; Ben Mandel to JB, May 20, 1941, "The Big Shots," list of government subver-

sives, box 692, Matthews Papers. By contrast, Dies staff lists of CSC case files to subpoena during the war show none from the NLRB, and no NLRB employees were on the list of people Dies named in February 1943.

61. Lawrence Glickman, *Buying Power: A History of Consumer Activism in America* (Chicago: University of Chicago Press, 2009). See also Storrs, *Civilizing Capitalism*, 93–97; Jacobs, *Pocketbook Politics*.

62. Felix S. Cohen to Norman Thomas, Nov. 14, 1933, Norman Thomas Papers, NYPL.

63. Wickenden, "The Philosophic and Economic Basis of the New Deal," circa 1938, file 13, box 2, Wickenden Papers M99–098.

64. Mary Dublin, Handwritten address to Consumers' League of Michigan, Dec. 30, 1938, MDK Papers.

65. Consumerist couples include Caroline Ware and Gardiner Means, the Keyserlings, the Ezekiels, Mary Taylor and Donald Montgomery, Helen Merrill and Robert Lynd, and Charlotte Tuttle and David Lloyd. Both of Paul Douglas's wives, Dorothy Douglas and Emily Taft Douglas, belonged to the League of Women Shoppers. Esther Peterson's husband Oliver was on the OPA labor advisory committee. Mrs. Leon Henderson was an active officer of the LWS during and after the period that her husband headed the OPA.

66. See first issue of CNF's *The Consumer*, June 2, 1937, folder 10, box 59, and Helen Hall, funding application to Marshall Field Foundation, Mar. 15, 1945, pp. 23, 19, box 60, both in Helen Hall Papers, SWHA.

67. The federation's membership criteria required dedication to protecting consumers "in the purchase of goods and services *and* in the conditions under which such goods and services are made, performed, and distributed." *The Consumer*, June 2, 1937, folder 10, box 59, Hall Papers (emphasis in original), SWHA.

68. Persia Campbell to Helen Hall, Oct. 16, 1938, folder 9, box 59, Hall Papers, SWHA.

69. For the claim that CNF helped create the Temporary National Economic Committee, see statement by Helen Hall and Robert Lynd [early 1940], 4, folder 5, box 60, Hall Papers, SWHA. On the committee's importance, see Alan Brinkley, *The End of Reform: New Deal Liberalism in Recession and War* (New York: Vintage, 1995); Jacobs, *Pocketbook Politics*.

70. Confidential statement by Persia Campbell to TNEC [Temporary National Economic Committee], May 11, 1939, folder 10, box 59, Hall Papers, SWHA.

71. Francis Gosling report, Oct. 5, 1939 (he was hired April 20), General Consumer Movement file, box 81, series 11, RG 233. Reports of Helene Abbott, May 1939, exhibits to report of Thomas J. Nash, Aug. 31, 1939, LWS-Chicago file, F&R: Orgs, RG 233.

72. Dies released the report on a Monday, an old trick designed to maximize coverage since Monday was a slow news day. See Morris Ernst to Dies, Dec. 21, 1939, folder 5, box 60, Hall Papers, SWHA.

73. "Dies Investigator says Reds Utilize Consumer Groups," *NYT*, Dec. 11, 1939, p. 1. Matthews distorted Browder's testimony. Browder had said the CP tried to use mass organizations to propagate its views just as Republicans,

Democrats, and Socialists did; see Browder to Roger Baldwin, Sept. 8, 1939, copy to Helen Hall, Nov. 2, 1939, folder 5, box 60, Hall Papers, SWHA. Matthews also labeled as front groups the Milk Consumers Protective Committee and United Conference against the High Cost of Living. He named Susan Jenkins, Arthur Kallet, and Meyer Parodneck as Communists (which they may have been) involved in many of the named groups.

74. Subcommittee of the Special Committee on Un-American Activities, *Un-American Propaganda Activities*, Dec. 3, 1939, pp. 7189–94. At the insistence of other members of the Dies Committee, this published version was watered down from what the newspapers first got; *New York Post*, Jan. 5, 1940.

75. For protest letters, see box 81, series 11, RG 233; also Morris Ernst for CNF to Dies, Dec. 21, 1939, folder 5, box 60, Hall Papers, SWHA; statement by Hall and Lynd, *NYT*, Dec. 11, 1939, p. 1. On the Nov. 30, 1939, meeting at Sokolsky's house, see "The Dies Plot, Detail," excerpt from *Space and Time, Newsletter of Advertising*, Dec. 18, 1939, folder 5, box 60, Hall Papers, SWHA. For additional evidence of the advertising industry's involvement in allegations against the consumer movement, see the untitled Jan. 1940 and 1967 reports in box 5, Esther Peterson Papers, SL. On the stenciling by Hearst, see Katharine Armitage to LWS local presidents, Apr. 3, 1947, LWS-DC Papers, SL. For the embarrassment of Matthews by Dies Committee Democrats, see "Dies Sleuth Failed to Produce a Single Red When Challenged," *New York Post*, Jan. 5, 1940.

76. Silber, *Test and Protest*; Cohen, *Consumers' Republic*.

77. See Dec. 28, 1936 list, folder 9, and *The Consumer*, June 2, 1937, folder 10, box 59, Hall Papers, SWHA.

78. "Statement to be used if . . . LWS is on Attorney General Tom Clark's Blacklist," Apr, 3, 1947, LWS-DC Papers, SL.

79. *Washington Post*, Jan. 19, 1938, Clippings file, LWS-DC Papers, SL. In the photograph were Mrs. Marquis Childs, Elizabeth Wheeler Colman, and Nina Collier. Marquis Childs was a prominent journalist; Colman's father Burton Wheeler was a U.S. senator; Nina Collier's husband was an official in the Department of Agriculture, and her father-in-law headed the U.S. Indian Bureau. Dean Acheson had been undersecretary of Treasury and soon would rise to fame as Truman's secretary of state.

80. *Washington Post*, Feb. 7, 1940.

81. Quotation from Helen Hall, CNF funding application, Mar. 15, 1945, folder 5, box 60, Hall Papers, SWHA; see also Helen Hall, *Unfinished Business in Neighborhood and Nation* (New York: Macmillan, 1971), 332.

82. Storrs, *Civilizing Capitalism*, 18–23, 211–19.

83. "League Deplores Low Servant Pay," *Washington Post*, Nov. 9, 1938; letter to editor by Nina Collier, *Washington Post*, Mar. 23, 1939.

84. On Baker, see Hall, *Unfinished Business*, 341. The 1936 list of prospective CNF members included Marion Cuthbert of the Harlem YWCA, Thyra Edwards of the National Negro Congress, Louise Thompson of the IWO, and Mary Ovington (white) of the NAACP. For a recent synthesis of scholarship on black boycott tactics in the 1930s, see Cohen, *Consumers' Republic*, 41–53.

85. See report of Alice Belester's testimony before the Temporary National Economic Committee, *NYT*, May 11, 1939; Annelise Orleck, "'We Are That

Mythical Thing Called the Public': Militant Housewives During the Great Depression," *Feminist Studies* 19 (1993).

86. Most articles on the LWS's D.C. chapter referred to members' class status, for example, as "fur-coated New Deal wives," *Washington Post*, Mar. 18, 1937. On the mink coat raffle, see New York LWS minutes, Nov. 1, 1937, LWS Papers, Smith. On the silk boycott, which divided labor groups, see Jan. 1938 clippings, LWS-DC Papers, SL.

87. Hotel management contended it had replaced the white waitresses with black men because it could not afford to comply with the D.C. minimum wage law for women; the waitresses charged the hotel with trying to break their union. *Washington Times*, June 16 and 23, 1938. On Pinchot's talk, see *Washington News*, Apr. 10, 1940.

88. *Washington Evening Star*, June 13, 1939.

89. "OPA Women say Capitol Cops Shoved 'Em Around like Nazis," *Washington Times Herald*, Apr. 14, 1946. Mrs. Leon Henderson, wife of the former OPA head, was among the protesters.

90. M. C. Phillips, "Half-Way to Communism with the League of Women Shoppers," *Consumers' Digest*, Apr. 1940. Phillips and her husband F. J. Schlink remained close allies of J. B. Matthews.

91. Katherine Ruttenberg, letter to the editor, *Pittsburgh Press* [May 1939], LWS-DC Papers, SL. For other examples of conservatives' gendered hostility to consumer activism, see Cohen, *Consumers' Republic*, 57, 134.

92. "Skytop Fair," *Washington Post*, May 1, 1940, and related clippings, LWS-DC Papers, SL. Other distinguished performers included Abe Fortas, Carol Agger Fortas, and the real Leon Henderson. U.S. Supreme Court justice William O. Douglas, whose wife was active in the LWS, awarded the raffle prizes.

93. LWS-DC annual report for 1940–41, in House Special Committee on Un-American Activities, *Investigation, Appendix IX*. Disney would testify against the LWS in 1947. Chester Bowles and Paul A. Porter, OPA, to Katharine Armatage, May 14, 1946, LWS-DC Papers, SL. On the Office of Civil Defense, see Armatage to local chapters, Apr. 3, 1947, LWS-DC Papers.

94. The LWS was cited by J. B. Matthews in 1938 and 1939, in the Dies Committee report of Mar. 29, 1944 (House Special Committee on Un-American Activities, *Investigation*, 121, 181), and in the latter's *Appendix IX*, 1004–17. CP members were involved in the LWS from the outset but were not dictating the agenda. Some chapters seem to have been more CP-influenced than others (Philadelphia and New York more than D.C., for example), and LWS records suggest an increase in CP influence over time. The Dies Committee stressed indications that the national LWS "followed the CP line" during the Hitler-Stalin pact (1939–41) and also that a card file obtained through surveillance of the Philadelphia CP listed three members of the local LWS as a CP "fraction."

95. See resignations of Laura Somers, Sept. 30, 1948, and Asho Ingersoll Craine, Dec. 3, 1948, folder 7, LWS-DC Papers, SL. Craine's husband worked in the Interior Department. Kitty Gellhorn, whose husband Walter held a series of government positions later including an OPA job, resigned in 1940. David Lloyd later claimed his wife Charlotte Tuttle Lloyd had resisted Communist influence in the D.C. branch. Some said they resigned not because of the group's CP association

but because they differed with the group's direction or thought it was no longer effective, but the increasing influence of Communists (the ironic result of the Red-baiting) certainly contributed to these internal rifts. See Caroline Ware, reply to interrogatory, Apr. 24, 1954, p. 7, Ware file, RG 478. The LWS claimed three thousand members in mid-1946, according to Ware, "Joint Statement in Support of Extension of the Emergency Price Control Act," box 35, Ware Papers, FDRL. The LWS folded into the Congress of American Women in about 1949, according to Glickman, "Strike in the Temple of Consumption," 125. On the move to the center by Consumers' Union, see also Silber, *Test and Protest*.

96. In April 1941 the National Defense Advisory Committee became the Office of Price Administration and Civilian Supply, which became simply OPA in August, when the responsibility for civilian supply was transferred to another agency. After Pearl Harbor, the Emergency Price Control Act established OPA as an independent agency. Imogene Putnam, *Historical Reports on War Administration, Office of Price Administration: Vol. 14: Volunteers in OPA* (Washington, D.C.: GPO, 1947), 33. For simplicity I will refer to the OPA's predecessors as the OPA.

97. "Henderson, Aides Accused by Dies of Links to Reds," *NYT*, Sept. 8, 1941. Dies named OPA head Leon Henderson in addition to Consumer Division employees Robert Brady, Mildred Edie Brady, Dewey Palmer, and Tom Tippett.

98. A hostile FBI informant described Ware as the one running the show at the Consumer Division; see report of Robert Welton, Sept. 1, 1953, Caroline Ware file, RG 478. That appears to have been the case; see boxes 27 and 44, Ware Papers, FDRL and Ware interview, 78, 91, WFGP.

99. Caroline Ware to Harriet Elliott, "Tactics We Should Now Follow," Jan. 17, 1941, box 27, Ware Papers, FDRL.

100. Especially pronounced were conflicts over aluminum, steel, rubber, and housing. On steel, Ware got the economists Galbraith, Thomas Blaisdell, and Gardiner Means (her husband) to back her up with a strong memo that Elliott took to the president, but FDR said that rather than coerce the industry he would let its leaders take the blame later for failing to expand. Caroline Ware, untitled article on the history of the Consumer Division, box 27, Ware Papers, FDRL. For a scathing assessment of business representatives in Washington during the war, see John Kenneth Galbraith, *A Life in Our Times* (Boston: Houghton Mifflin, 1981), 107–9, 148–49.

101. Ware, "Contacts with Public," in untitled article on the history of the Consumer Division, box 27, Ware Papers, FDRL. For an insider's assessment of consumer experts in and out of government, see the eleven-page list Ware put together the night Elliott was appointed, part of Memorandum to Harriett Elliott from Caroline F. Ware, May 29, 1940, box 30, ibid.

102. Quotation from *Washington Post*, June 5, 1942, cited by Putnam, *Volunteers in OPA*, 32.

103. Ware, "Office of the Consumer Commissioner," untitled article on the history of the Consumer Division, box 27, Ware Papers, FDRL.

104. Ware, "Health and Welfare Division," untitled article on the history of the Consumer Division, box 27, Ware Papers, FDRL.

105. Ware interview, 78, WFGP.

106. Emerson, *Young Lawyer for the New Deal*, 147.

107. On the fight to integrate OPA, see Ware interview, 94–99, WFGP, and Frances H. Williams interview, vol. 10, pp. 275–307, Black Women Oral History Project, SL.

108. See "Assigned to Staff of Defense Board," *NYT*, June 29, 1940, marked copy in box 82, series 11, RG 233.

109. As far as I can determine, Dies never named the fifty alleged subversives at OPA, beyond the five he initially identified; see "Henderson, Aides Accused by Dies of Links to Reds," *NYT*, Sept. 8, 1941; FBI report of Sept. 22, 1941, summarizing Aug. 19 investigation, Ware FBI file. FBI director Hoover soon notified the Attorney General's Office of Ware's affiliations; Hoover to Matthew McGuire, Assistant to the Attorney General, Sept. 15, 1941, ibid. Ware might have caught J. B. Matthews's eye when she wrote a letter protesting his report on the consumer movement; see Ware to Martin Dies, Dec. 11, 1939, box 81, series 11, RG 233.

110. "Dies Charges 1,124 in Federal Posts Help Communists," *NYT*, Oct. 20, 1941. That list did not include war agencies and thus did not include OPA employees, but Dies's accompanying letter to the attorney general pointedly referred to the OPA. By "several thousand" Dies presumably meant the 1,124 plus others in war agencies. Extensive efforts have not located the list of 1,124 names.

111. On the Roosevelt administration view of Dies as a fanatic, see Emerson, *Young Lawyer for the New Deal*, 134.

112. Ware probably was arguing with Henderson about whether he should dismiss the Bradys. Henderson wrote her, "Your choice in not tendering a formal resignation is, of course, a personal choice. . . . The responsibility for the Consumers Division is clearly mine . . . [and I will] make the best disposition as to personnel and policies as seem sound in my own judgment"; Henderson to Ware, Dec. 11, 1941, cited in US CSC investigations report, June 26, 1942, Caroline Ware FBI file. CSC investigators requested the Bradys' dismissal in late December 1941; see FBI Report of Sept. 1, 1953, p. 11, Caroline Ware file, RG 478. Ware told investigators that the OPA personnel director had advised her to give "agency reorganization" as the reason for leaving because it would look better on her record.

113. Putnam, *Volunteers in OPA*, 12, 34; Harvey Mansfield et al., *Historical Reports on War Administration, Office of Price Administration: Vol. 1, Beginnings of OPA* (Washington, D.C.: GPO, 1947), 37–38. Frances H. Williams interview, vol. 10, p. 292, Black Women Oral History Project, SL.

114. Mansfield et al., *Beginnings of OPA*, 37–38, and Harvey Mansfield et al., *Historical Reports on War Administration, Office of Price Administration: Vol. 15, A Short History of OPA* (Washington, D.C.: GPO, 1948), 16–17.

115. Emerson was suspect chiefly because he had been close to CP member Nathan Witt at the NLRB, but Betty Paret Emerson's LWS connection also was an issue; see Ben Mandel to J. B., May 20, 1941, box 692, Matthews Papers. Also see CSC loyalty investigations, boxes 188–91, series 11, RG 233.

116. Eleanor Bontecou, *The Federal Loyalty-Security Program* (Ithaca: Cornell University Press, 1953), 8–10, 15. Scholars have overlooked the conflict between the Dies Committee and the Civil Service Commission; Dies's attacks on OPA have been noted only in passing.

117. Galbraith believed Henderson was "never completely happy again. Divorced from public concerns, he did not wholly exist"; Galbraith, *A Life in Our Times*, 180; Emerson, *Young Lawyer for the New Deal*, 192.

118. Emerson, *Young Lawyer for the New Deal*, 218–22, quotation 222.

119. Galbraith, *A Life in Our Times*, 181–89, quotation 183.

120. Emerson, *Young Lawyer for the New Deal*, 212–15.

121. On Busbey, ibid., 223. Busbey quotation from *Congressional Record*, House, 78th Cong., 2d sess., June 13, 1944, p. 5963.

122. Galbraith, *A Life in Our Times*, 189.

123. Chester Bowles denied firing Emerson; see notes of Wesley A. Sturges, Dean of Yale Law School, Dec. 26, 1945, and other materials in file 78, box 79, Emerson Papers, Sterling Library, Yale.

124. Quoted by Richard Hofstadter, *Anti-Intellectualism in American Life* (New York: Knopf, 1963), 36.

125. Typescript of Fulton Lewis Jr. broadcast, May 17, 1946, box 35, Ware Papers, FDRL. For Ware's rebuttal, see "Statement by CFW, Mutual Broadcasting Company, WOL," May 24, 1946, ibid. The brouhaha produced internal inquiries at the OPA to clarify its connections with Ware; see George Dolgin to Richard Field, May 29, 1946, ibid. A later article about Lewis described how he had "turned his guns on women's groups" as part of his successful effort to kill the OPA; Charles Van Devander, "Radio's Golden Voice of Reaction," *New York Post*, Dec. 8, 1949.

126. Jacobs, *Pocketbook Politics*, and Cohen, *Consumers' Republic*, overlook this internal conflict at OPA. "State-building from the bottom up" is Jacobs's phrase.

127. Putnam, *Volunteers in OPA*, 32, and see also 4, 10–13.

128. In addition to chairing its executive committee, Ware was secretary of the larger OPA Consumer Advisory Committee, and its minutes suggest she was the key player; see box 103, Hall Papers, SWHA. Bowles's support of consumer organization may have been encouraged by his second wife, the dynamic social worker Dorothy Stebbins. Stebbins was a close friend of Betty Paret Emerson's, and Tom Emerson described Stebbins as a major influence on Bowles. See Emerson, *Young Lawyer for the New Deal*, 208, 215.

129. On the importance of Priscilla Hiss's LWS association in her husband's FBI file, see Jeffrey Kisseloff e-mail to author, Apr. 6, 2007. On Dean and Alice Acheson, see Walter Isaacson and Evan Thomas, *The Wise Men* (New York: Simon and Schuster, 1986), 494. Affiliation with the LWS (directly or through a wife) would come up in investigations of the following Truman administration employees: Thomas Blaisdell, Lucy Kramer Cohen, Thomas Emerson, Mordecai Ezekiel, Walter Gellhorn, Tex Goldschmidt, Leon and Mary Dublin Keyserling, Dorothy Kenyon, Charlotte Tuttle and David Demarest Lloyd, Frieda Miller, and Mary Taylor Montgomery. The LWS also appears as derogatory evidence in many of the anonymous cases collected by the Fund for the Republic; see FFR Papers.

130. Donald Montgomery was hired by the United Auto Workers in 1942, perhaps with a push from his agency. Colston Warne of Consumers' Union insisted on paying his own expenses as a government consultant rather than sign the

loyalty oath; *Washington Daily News*, Nov. 3, 1947; *Washington Post*, Nov. 14, 1947.

131. On Hall's disqualification, see "Reports of Investigation" file, box 5, Records of the Loyalty Review Board, Record Group 146, NA; Helen Hall file, F&R Name Files, RG 233.

132. See Caroline Ware FBI and RG 478 files. Quotation is from Ware to Pauli Murray, Jan. 21, 1953, reprinted in Anne F. Scott, ed., *Pauli Murray & Caroline Ware: Forty Years of Letters in Black and White* (Chapel Hill: University of North Carolina Press, 2006), 75–78; see also 81, 102.

133. See Caroline Ware FBI and RG 478 files. Other "derogatory" associations noted in Ware's FBI file: the Consumers' National Federation, the Conference against the High Cost of Living, hiring and befriending leftist couples at OPA, "entertaining negroes," Brookwood Labor College, "socialistic teaching," Southern Summer School, Federal Workers School, Southern Conference for Human Welfare, and the Washington Bookshop. On the Bloor goose chase, see FBI Washington Field Office memo to J. E. Hoover, Mar. 12, 1951, Ware FBI file.

CHAPTER 3

"Pinks in Minks": The Antifeminism of the Old Right

1. Jack Lait and Lee Mortimer, *Washington Confidential* (New York: Crown, 1951), 74, 78, 101–2. For the book's impact, see David K. Johnson, *The Lavender Scare: The Cold War Persecution of Gays and Lesbians in the Federal Government* (Chicago: University of Chicago Press, 2004), 91–92.

2. On Schlesinger, see K. A. Cuordileone, "'Politics in an Age of Anxiety': Cold War Political Culture and the Crisis in American Masculinity, 1949–1960," *Journal of American History* 87, no. 2 (2000): 524.

3. Kevin Mattson, *When America Was Great: The Fighting Faith of Postwar Liberalism* (New York: Routledge, 2004), 11. Mattson does note that Reinhold Niebuhr, John Kenneth Galbraith, and James Wechsler were married to "strong women" who were intellectuals and activists in their own right. Janeway comments that many "Rooseveltians married unusual women by the standards of the day," citing Abe and Carol Agger Fortas, among others. Michael Janeway, *The Fall of the House of Roosevelt: Brokers of Ideas and Power from FDR to LBJ* (New York: Columbia University Press, 2004), 24. See also Alan Brinkley, *The End of Reform: New Deal Liberalism in Recession and War* (New York: Vintage, 1995), 13.

4. George Dixon, "Washington Scene" [1949], "Important Clippings" file, MDK Papers.

5. George Martin, *Madam Secretary* (Boston: Houghton Mifflin, 1976), 410, 444, 545. Hallie Flanagan to Martin Dies, Dec. 19, 1938, box 89, Martin Dies Papers, Sam Houston Regional Library and Research Center, Texas State Library, Liberty, Tex.; Jane De Hart Mathews, *The Federal Theatre* (Princeton: Princeton University Press, 1967); Westbrook Pegler, "Mrs. Roosevelt's Public Life," *Washington Post*, Feb. 12, 1942. Most of these examples are discussed further in later chapters; see also appendix 2.

6. Roger Biles, *Crusading Liberal* (DeKalb: Northern Illinois University Press, 2002); Lorraine Spritzer, *The Belle of Ashby Street* (Athens: University of Georgia Press, 1982); Greg Mitchell, *Tricky Dick and the Pink Lady* (New York: Random House, 1998).

7. Good statistics are hard to generate because there is no comprehensive list of people investigated under the federal employee loyalty program (see appendix 1). Exhaustive efforts have yielded data including the following: in one group of about 2,400 loyalty cases, women comprised about 18 percent of defendants, and those cases appear to involve primarily professional-level employees; finding aid case list, RG 478. On a 1950 list made by HUAC staffer Ben Mandel of 105 high-paid government employees (presumably people he found subversive), 16 percent were women; box 689, Matthews Papers. On a 1941 Mandel list, women comprised 25 percent of the 53 government "big shots" suspected of disloyalty; box 692, ibid. For cases by agency, see Eleanor Bontecou, *The Federal Loyalty-Security Program* (Ithaca: Cornell University Press, 1953), 146; for gender data by agency, see U.S. Women's Bureau, *Bulletin 236*, pp. 7–8, and *Bulletin 230*, p. 29.

8. Bontecou, *Federal Loyalty-Security Program*; Ralph S. Brown Jr., *Loyalty and Security: Employment Tests in the United States* (New Haven: Yale University Press, 1958).

9. Very few Mexican-Americans had government jobs, but they would have faced the same bias, offset to some degree by the perception that Roman Catholics were less susceptible to Communism.

10. "Statement of Miss Dorothy Kenyon," Mar. 14, 1950, Tydings Foreign Relations Subcommittee hearings, 15–16, file 26, box 47, Kenyon Papers, Smith. FBI file of Mary McCleod Bethune. Commerce loyalty board hearing, Nov. 27, 1951, p. 376, Dublin Keyserling file, RG 478. In 1954 a woman attorney who had worked for the government since 1936 was asked to explain why she had commented in a public talk on the large number of women judges in Moscow; case 312, FFR Papers.

11. A. G. Perrett notation on Oct. 29, 1941, memo, Caroline Ware file, RG 478; Anthony Hauke, Report of Investigation, U.S. Civil Service Commission, Nov. 4, 1943, p. 4, Dublin Keyserling file, RG 478.

12. Margaret C. Rung, *Servants of the State: Managing Diversity and Democracy in the Federal Workforce, 1933–1953* (Athens: University of Georgia Press, 2002), 153–55. Frances Perkins dismissed Helen Miller in 1941. Bailey's case became the loyalty program's first test before the U.S. Supreme Court.

13. Fortas quoted from Commerce loyalty board hearing, Aug. 24, 1948, pp. 282–83, Dublin Keyserling file, RG 478. In another case, an economist responding to reports that his wife was in the leftist faction at the Office of War Information explained that she had been resented by a group of older Italian-American men who did not like working for a woman; Commerce loyalty hearing board, July 14, 1950, Warren Wilhelm file, RG 478. On the gender prescriptions enforced by human relations managers in the civil service in the 1940s, see Rung, *Servants of the State*, 147–55.

14. Brunauer to Friends, Dec. 8, 1952, cited by Patricia C. Walls, "Defending Their Liberties: Women's Organizations During the McCarthy Era" (Ph.D. diss.,

University of Maryland, 1994), 99, 290. Bernice L. Bernstein thought she would not have been put through a loyalty hearing had her husband not worked at the Treasury Department; notes for her Jan. 1955 loyalty hearing, 20, folder 4, box 7, Bernstein Papers, HSTL.

15. David Oshinsky, *A Conspiracy So Immense: The World of Joe McCarthy* (New York: Free Press, 1983), 318. Matthews was the lead researcher for the Dies Committee from 1938 until 1945. He subsequently testified often before investigating committees, worked for Senator McCarthy's subcommittee, and was a consultant to the Hearst Corporation. Nelson L. Dawson, "From Fellow Traveler to Anticommunist: The Odyssey of J. B. Matthews," *Register of the Kentucky Historical Society* 84, no. 3 (1986). Mandel was on the staff of HUAC, then SISS.

16. Pegler, one of the nation's most popular columnists, won a 1941 Pulitzer Prize for his exposé of union corruption and was a major force behind the Taft-Hartley Act of 1947; David Witwer, "Westbrook Pegler and the Anti-Union Movement," *Journal of American History* 92, no. 2 (2005). On Pegler's hatred of homosexuals, see Johnson, *Lavender Scare*, 35, 68. The private correspondence of Matthews, Mandel, Pegler, and Sokolsky indicates that they were close friends. Fulton Lewis Jr. married the daughter of a Republican Party leader. On the *Times-Herald*'s cooperation with the FBI and CIA, see Deborah Davis, *Katharine the Great: Katharine Graham and the Washington Post* (New York: Harcourt Brace Jovanovich, 1979), 184.

17. Ellen Schrecker, *Many Are the Crimes: McCarthyism in America* (Boston: Little, Brown, 1998), 146–69; Robert D. Dean, *Imperial Brotherhood: Gender and the Making of Cold War Foreign Policy* (Amherst: University of Massachusetts Press, 2001), 66–70; John McPartland, "Portrait of an American Communist," *Life*, Jan. 5, 1948. On Eleanor Roosevelt as a failed mother, see William Bradford Huie, "How Eleanor Roosevelt Let Our Generation Down," *Today's Woman*, July 1953. An attack on the Congress of American Women noted that member Muriel Draper raised a dancer son, and that a Romanian Communist Party leader turned in her husband to the secret police and laughed as they murdered him; *National Republic Lettergram No. 217*, box 40, Alfred Kohlberg Papers, Hoover Institution.

18. On Moss, see "Annie Was a Red," *U.S.A.*, Nov. 7, 1958, box 127, Kohlberg Papers, Hoover Institution; Andrea Friedman, "The Strange Career of Annie Lee Moss: Rethinking Race, Gender, and McCarthyism," *Journal of American History* 94, no. 2 (2007). On Dublin Keyserling, see Commerce loyalty board hearing, J. B. Matthews, May 27, 1952, pp. 835–72, and Paul Crouch, Nov. 15, 1951, p. 51, Dublin Keyserling file, RG 478.

19. Ellen Schrecker, "The Bride of Stalin: Gender and Anticommunism during the McCarthy Era," paper presented at the Berkshire Conference on Women's History, June 11, 1993, Poughkeepsie, N.Y.

20. On the Bolsheviks' alleged nationalization of women, see Kim Nielsen, *Un-American Womanhood: Antiradicalism, Antifeminism, and the First Red Scare* (Columbus: Ohio State University Press, 2001). On Communists' arranging and breaking up of marriages, see Paul Crouch, "Memo regarding Kitty Harris (formerly Mrs. Earl Browder)," box 45, Kohlberg Papers, Hoover Institution. On the right's sexualization of the Communist Party, see Veronica A. Wilson, "Red

Masquerades: Gender and Political Subversion During the Cold War" (Ph.D. diss., Rutgers University, 2002).

21. Lait and Mortimer, *Washington Confidential*, 91 (emphasis added).

22. Ibid., 39–41.

23. Ibid., 78, 39–40.

24. Ibid., 77, 94–95.

25. Ibid., 94.

26. Westbrook Pegler column, *New York Journal-American*, June 16, 1951. J. B. Matthews, address on WFUV-FM, Mar. 15, 1950, box 120, Kohlberg Papers, Hoover Institution.

27. Deposition of Sylvia Crouch before the Florida Legislative Investigating Committee, Jan. 7, 1958, p. 67, box 1, Paul Crouch Papers, Hoover Institution.

28. "Communism and the Youth of America," Mandel interview, ABC, Nov. 27, 1948, box 692, Matthews Papers. Radical white women having sex with black men is a recurring theme in Lait and Mortimer, *Washington Confidential*.

29. Peg to Doc, Mar. 12, 1948, box 675, Matthews Papers. Pegler was asking about Betty Brown, who married first Frederick Vanderbilt Field and then Joe Barnes. Matthews answered that it was Edith Field, Frederick's second wife, who was "*close* to the Negro, Max Yergan" (emphasis in original). JBM to Peg, Mar. 13, 1948, ibid. Witwer incorrectly claims Pegler was conservative on economics but not on race; Witwer, "Westbrook Pegler," 551.

30. Schlink to J. B. [ca. Feb. 1948], box 679, Matthews Papers.

31. United Public Workers of America, "Thought Control," case 14, Mar. 15, 1949, file 554, Emerson Papers, Sterling Library, Yale.

32. Emerson testimony, June 16, 1953, Executive Sessions, SISS Records. Another type of private worrying about sex by conservatives appeared in comments by informants to the FBI that alleged subversives believed in "free love." This was an issue in the cases of Gertrude and Gilbert Parks, Esther Brunauer, Joseph Barnes, and Walter Gellhorn, all of whom either had been involved in divorces or had unconventional living arrangements.

33. J. B. Matthews, "Operation Women," address before the American Coalition, New York City, Feb. 17, 1951, box 120, Kohlberg Papers, Hoover Institution; Sylvia Crouch, "Communist Use of Women," annotated "received from Mr. Mandel for files, Dec. 21, 1950," Organizations: Women, RG 233.

34. Matthews, "Operation Women."

35. "Communism and the Youth of America," Mandel interview, ABC, Nov. 27, 1948, box 692, Matthews Papers.

36. Matthews, "Operation Women."

37. Lait and Mortimer, *Washington Confidential*, 136.

38. Dean, *Imperial Brotherhood*, quotations 40, 73–74, and see 260n2 for a collective portrait of congressional countersubversives, who typically came from rural or small-town backgrounds, attended public schools and universities, and held jobs tied to the agricultural economy before entering politics.

39. Frederick Woltman, "Pinks in Minks: Left-Wing's Distaff Side Hears What to Wear While Passing the Lily Dache," Scripps-Howard newspapers, July 8, 1947, copy in box 437, Organizations: Women, RG 233. As a founding member of an anticommunist caucus of the New York chapter of the American Newspa-

per Guild, Woltman knew and sympathized with Westbrook Pegler; Oliver Pilat, *Pegler: Angry Man of the Press* (Boston: Beacon Press, 1963).

40. M. C. Phillips, "Half-Way to Communism with the League of Women Shoppers," *Consumers' Digest*, Apr. 1940.

41. Pegler, "Mrs. Roosevelt's Public Life," *Washington Post*, Feb. 12, 1942. Lait and Mortimer, *Washington Confidential*, 41.

42. Pegler, "George Spelvin, American," column, Sept. 14, 1952; Pegler, "Mrs. Spelvin Speaks Her Mind," reprinted in *George Spelvin, American and Fireside Chats* (New York: Scribner's, 1942), 151–55. Quotation on reader letters from the online finding aid to Westbrook Pegler Papers, Herbert Hoover Library, West Branch, Iowa. Pegler's column "Fair Enough" was syndicated in over 140 newspapers by Scripps-Howard (1933–43) and then Hearst's King Features (1943–62); King Features carried "George Spelvin" from 1947 to 1962.

43. Senator McCarthy statement to Tydings Foreign Relations Subcommittee, Mar. 8, 1950, file 1, box 47, Kenyon Papers. J. B. Matthews, address on WFUV-FM, Mar. 15, 1950, box 120, Kohlberg Papers, Hoover Institution. Lait and Mortimer similarly ridiculed the abilities of female lawyers and judges while labeling them as promiscuous; Lait and Mortimer, *Washington Confidential*, 106, 120, 167.

44. Pegler column carried in *Washington Times-Herald*, Nov. 1, 1950, per memo in McHale file, Subject Files: SACB, box 279, SISS Records. On McCarran and rumors of McHale's lesbianism, see Leila Rupp and Verta Taylor, *Survival in the Doldrums: The American Women's Rights Movement, 1945 to the 1960s* (Columbus: Ohio State University Press, 1990), 107. McHale denied that she was a lesbian, and she was confirmed in 1951; see chapter 6.

45. "As Pegler Sees It," *New York Journal-American*, Nov. 27, 1951. His source was Robert Denham, a disgruntled Republican lawyer who blamed Ida Klaus, the NLRB's general counsel, when Truman removed him from the Labor Relations Board.

46. *Congressional Record*, Senate, 78th Cong., 1st sess., May 27, 1943, p. 5042.

47. "Just a Little Tip from Main Street," unidentified newspaper clipping, Mar. 8, 1942, file 23, box 1, Leon Keyserling Papers, College of Charleston.

48. "Broadcast of Walter Trohan, WGN-Chicago, Oct. 11, 1952, Dublin Keyserling FBI file. Dublin Keyserling's case is the subject of the next chapter.

49. Anthony Hauke, Report of Investigation, U.S. Civil Service Commission, Nov. 4, 1943, p. 3, Dublin Keyserling file, RG 478.

50. Executive Session transcript, June 14, 1951, pp. 153–57, SISS Records.

51. Walter Trohan interview, 18, HSTL.

52. Mandel to Hon. Styles Bridges, U.S. Senate, July 30, 1946, Leon Keyserling file, SISS Records. The full wording of the bylaw suggests it was intended less to limit association with pro-capitalists than with the CP's leftist rivals: "No Party member shall have personal or political relationship with confirmed Trotskyites, Lovestoneites, or other known enemies of the Party" (1938, Section 14, per Mandel's notes).

53. Brown, *Loyalty and Security*, 32, 57; Bontecou, *Federal Loyalty-Security Program*, 48–51, 111; Johnson, *Lavender Scare*, 9. See appendix 3.

54. The Brunauers wrote up their cases for the Fund for the Republic study; see cases 325 and 326, FFR Papers. Bontecou, *Federal Loyalty-Security Program*,

49; Richard Fried, *Nightmare in Red* (New York: Oxford University Press, 1990), 23–27; William F. Buckley and L. Brent Bozell, *McCarthy and His Enemies* (Chicago: Henry Regnery, 1954), 125–35.

55. Calculated after examining all 353 case files, boxes 104–7, FFR Papers. See especially cases 5, 128, and 312.

56. Asho Ingersoll Craine resigned from the League of Women Shoppers in 1948 at least in part because her husband worked for the Interior Department; Asho Craine interview with author, Sept. 24, 2004.

57. IOELB hearing, July 2, 1954, pp. 81–86, Mordecai Ezekiel file, RG 478. On Bachrach, see her brother's memoir: John J. Abt with Michael Myerson, *Advocate and Activist: Memoirs of an American Communist Lawyer* (Urbana: University of Illinois Press, 1993).

58. This pattern still holds, apparently. See "When He's Not the Better Half," *NYT*, Aug. 21, 2005.

59. "Esther Brunauer," *Notable American Women* (Cambridge: Harvard University Press, 1980), vol. 4, pp. 114–16.

60. See FBI reports of July 25, 1952, May 22, 1941, Apr. 28, 1941, and May 29, 1944, and Commerce loyalty board hearing, Sept. 25, 1952, pp. 97–98, 209, all Dublin Keyserling file, RG 478.

61. Nathaniel Weyl testimony, Commerce loyalty board hearing, June 6, 1952, Dublin Keyserling file, RG 478; 1964 FBI report on Esther Peterson, excerpted in "Preliminary Report: Subject: The Consumer Movement" (author and date unidentified), 34, 38, box 4, Esther Peterson Papers, SL. Lucille's sister roomed with the Communist Party member Marion Bachrach. Mordecai Ezekiel, Reply to Interrogatory, Dec. 18, 1953, p. 10, and IOELB hearing, July 2, 1954, pp. 81–86, 196–98, Mordecai Ezekiel file, RG 478.

62. Herbert Wechsler testimony, Commerce loyalty board hearing, Jan. 28, 1952, p. 447, Dublin Keyserling file, RG 478.

63. Broadcast of Walter Trohan, WGN-Chicago, Oct. 11, 1952; on football, Fulton Lewis Jr. broadcast for King Features syndicate, May 30, 1952, copies in Dublin Keyserling FBI file. The right also complained about criticisms of college sports by Tom Emerson and U.S. Information Agency journalist Reed Harris.

64. Richard Hofstadter, *Anti-Intellectualism in American Life* (New York: Knopf, 1963), 226–27; Cuordileone, "Politics in an Age of Anxiety"; Dean, *Imperial Brotherhood*.

65. George Dixon column, *Washington Times-Herald*, Nov. 30, 1953, copy in Frieda Miller file, RG 478.

CHAPTER 4

The Loyalty Investigations of Mary Dublin Keyserling and Leon Keyserling

1. Mandel to Stolberg, June 6, 1940, box 6, Stolberg Papers. Mandel added that "Doc here" had more information, a reference to his colleague J. B. Matthews of the Dies Committee. Stolberg was an anti-Stalinist leftist then in the process of moving rightward; Alan Wald, *The New York Intellectuals* (Chapel Hill: University of North Carolina Press, 1987), 131.

2. This biographical portrait is compiled from Dublin Keyserling interview by Cheek; Landon R. Y. Storrs, *Civilizing Capitalism: The National Consumers' League, Women's Activism, and Labor Standards in the New Deal Era* (Chapel Hill: University of North Carolina Press, 2000), 191–96, 231–38; Willadee Wehmeyer, "Mary Dublin Keyserling: Economist and Social Activist" (Ph.D. diss., University of Missouri–Kansas City, 1995).

3. For biographical information on Leon Keyserling, see finding aids to his papers at HSTL and to the Keyserling Family Papers at the College of Charleston; W. Robert Brazelton, *Designing U.S. Economic Policy: An Analytical Biography of Leon H. Keyserling* (New York: Palgrave, 2001); Donald K. Pickens, *Leon H. Keyserling: A Progressive Economist* (New York: Lexington Books, 2009).

4. From Dublin Keyserling interview with Katie Louchheim, 28, CCOH; quotation from George Dixon, "Washington Scene," Dec. 8, 1949, "Important Clippings" folder, MDK Papers, latest accession.

5. Dublin Keyserling's appointment books for several years after she married in 1940 include notations tracking the couple's effort to conceive; see MDK Papers 96-M106. On their disappointment, Thomas D. Dublin interview with author, June 17, 2000.

6. One of forty-four thousand entries in the competition, for which leading economists served as judges, Keyserling's essay won him $10,000. Dublin Keyserling interview, 106, WFGP; Pickens, *Leon H. Keyserling*, 74.

7. Wilbur Mills to John F. Kennedy, Aug. 6, 1962, Kennedy Presidential Tapes, Presidential Recordings Program, Miller Center, University of Virginia, available online or in Timothy Naftali, ed., *Presidential Recordings: John F. Kennedy* (New York: W. W. Norton, 2001), vol. 1, 255–56 (thanks to David Shreve for this reference). Mills claimed he was the one who urged Roosevelt to appoint Leon head of the U.S. Housing Authority in 1942. Several FBI interviews in the 1940s and early 1950s described Mary as a major influence on Leon. In the 1950s, they had a consulting business together, for which she did the research and he did the writing; she quit, however, because she did not like "having a husband for a boss"; Dublin Keyserling interview, 166, WFGP.

8. The Hatch Act also was a response to conservative charges that WPA workers were being pressured to vote Democratic. On the Dies Committee, see Eleanor Bontecou, *The Federal Loyalty-Security Program* (Ithaca: Cornell University Press, 1953), 8–10. Hatch Act quotation from Stanley Kutler, *The American Inquisition: Justice and Injustice in the Cold War* (New York: Hill and Wang, 1982), 35.

9. Gouzenko's revelations were publicized in mid-1946; see John Earl Haynes and Harvey Klehr, *Early Cold War Spies* (New York: Cambridge University Press, 2006), 48–57.

10. A widely publicized July 1946 report from a subcommittee of the House Committee on the Civil Service criticized inconsistencies in loyalty procedures between the Civil Service Commission and the Interdepartmental Committee on Employee Investigations that Roosevelt had created in 1943. From a political perspective, if Truman was going to create a formal loyalty program, he should have done so immediately after that report came out and before the November elections; Francis H. Thompson, *The Frustration of Politics: Truman, Congress,*

and the Loyalty Issue, 1945–1953 (Cranbury, N.J.: Associated University Presses, 1979), 25.

11. These are just some of the weaknesses identified by Bontecou, *Federal Loyalty-Security Program*, and Kutler, *American Inquisition*.

12. See appendixes 3 and 4.

13. Walter Salant interview, 81–86, HSTL; David Caute, *The Great Fear: The Anti-Communist Purge under Truman and Eisenhower* (London: Secker & Warburg, 1978), 273–74.

14. See appendix 3.

15. Under Dublin Keyserling's leadership, the National Consumers' League passed a resolution criticizing the methods of the Dies Committee. She also organized a letter-writing campaign to Congress urging discontinuation of the committee. See Dies Committee folder, reel 50, NCL Papers, LC.

16. "Key Man Behind the Commie Exposé," *New York World-Telegram*, Dec. 30, 1953. Ellen Schrecker, *Many Are the Crimes: McCarthyism in America* (Boston: Little, Brown, 1998), 42–45.

17. "Assigned to Staff of Defense Board," *NYT*, June 29, 1940, marked copy in box 82, series 11, RG 233. Dublin's name was one of only two that the Dies Committee flagged from a long list of appointees.

18. NDAC [National Defense Advisory Commission] personnel office to J. Edgar Hoover, Oct. 29, 1940; Hoover to NDAC, Dec. 9, 1940, in Dublin Keyserling file, RG 478.

19. Some of those on his list, which he sent to Matthews, belonged or had belonged to the CP; others never did. Mandel to J. B., "The Big Shots," May 1941, box 692, Matthews Papers.

20. Leon Keyserling, Deputy Administrator and General Counsel, USHA, to John Carmody, Administrator, Federal Works Agency, Sept. 17, 1941, Leon Keyserling FBI file. The FBI had reported to Carmody that Leon's name was found in the "active indices" of the American Peace Mobilization (APM), a Communist front group that during the Hitler-Stalin pact opposed U.S. intervention on the side of the British. The FBI frequently obtained mailing lists of suspect groups and reported on anyone whose name appeared on those lists. Leon denied any connection to the APM and pointed out that he could not help it if an organization put him on a mailing list.

21. *Congressional Record*, House, 77th Cong., 2d sess., Feb. 6, 1942, and FBI Report of Sept. 11, 1942, Dublin Keyserling file, RG 478. Dublin Keyserling's allegedly derogatory associations, according to Representative Richard Wigglesworth (R-Mass.), were that she had spoken to the Consumers' Union, sponsored the Consumers' National Federation and the Conference on Constitutional Liberties in America, and signed two open letters also signed by Communists, one opposing mandatory registration of aliens and the other criticizing the Committee to Defend Leon Trotsky (more on these below). Unidentified newspaper clipping, Mar. 8, 1942, file 23, box 1, Leon Keyserling Papers, College of Charleston. On right-wing hostility to the U.S. Housing Authority, see, for example, "Taber Charges Commie Sought to Defraud U.S.," *Washington Times-Herald*, June 27, 1947.

22. The FBI questioned Leon about mailing list associations with the National Federation for Constitutional Liberties, American Peace Mobilization, and United Spanish Aid Committee. Leon Keyserling FBI file.

23. On the generational conflict between Dublin Keyserling and the NCL old guard, see Storrs, *Civilizing Capitalism*, 230–37. For FBI interviews with some NCL officers, and affidavits and hearing testimony of others, see Dublin Keyserling file, RG 478.

24. Ratings examiners to "Chairman, Loyalty Board," July 6, 1945, and attached response dated Aug. 28, 1945, Dublin Keyserling file, RG 478.

25. "Inside Washington," *Printer's Ink*, Oct. [date illegible], 1946, excerpt in file 7, box 74, Helen Hall Papers, SWHA.

26. Benjamin Mandel to Senator Styles Bridges (R-N.H.), July 30, 1946, Leon Keyserling file, SISS Records.

27. George Sokolsky column, *Washington Times-Herald*, Dec. 28, 1947, in Leon Keyserling file, SISS Records.

28. *Newsweek,* Dec. 15, 1947, excerpt in Leon Keyserling file, SISS Records.

29. On the Wardman Park group, whose existence was not publicized until years later, "Ode to Members of the Wardman Park Monday Night Steak Club After Twenty-Five Years," box 47, Keyserling Papers, HSTL, and Leon Keyserling interview, HSTL. Some newspapers reported that Keyserling drafted the veto, but he said he only contributed to it; see ibid. On Keyserling at the Council of Economic Advisers and the conflict with Nourse, see Walter Salant interview, 52–59, HSTL; Meg Jacobs, *Pocketbook Politics: Economic Citizenship in Twentieth-Century America* (Princeton: Princeton University Press, 2005); Robert Collins, *More: The Politics of Economic Growth in Postwar America* (New York: Oxford University Press, 2000).

30. For examples of conservative anger with Keyserling, see Henry Hazlitt column, Jan. 12, 1948, read into the *Congressional Record*, House, 80th Cong., 2d sess., Mar. 22, 1948, by Rep. Fred Busbey (R-Ill.), p. A1846; George Sokolsky column, *Washington Times-Herald*, Apr. 3, 1949; Nourse article read into *Congressional Record*, Senate, 81st Cong., 1st sess., by Sen. Kenneth Wherry (R-Neb.), Feb. 21, 1950; and other clippings in Leon Keyserling file, SISS Records.

31. Helen Hall, "We Organized Impatience," *Survey Graphic* 35 (June 1946): 221, and see Mary Dublin Keyserling, "Highlights," ibid., 217. Dublin Keyserling's appointment books attest to her involvement with the Southern Conference for Human Welfare and Highlander Folk School and her leadership role in the Committee on the Nation's Health.

32. See boxes 59 and 60, Hall Papers, SWHA.

33. "Price Rises Held Peril," *NYT*, May 14, 1948; "Consumers Lay Plans," *NYT*, May 15, 1948.

34. Jacobs, *Pocketbook Politics*.

35. Dublin Keyserling, "The European Recovery Plan and the American Consumer," address before the National Association of Consumers, May 13, 1948, MDK Papers.

36. Dublin Keyserling wrote, for W. Averell Harriman, "We Must Import to Live," *Saturday Evening Post,* May 17, 1947; Address for Thomas C. Blaisdell

before the Chamber of Commerce of Philadelphia, May 19, 1947; and many others on this topic, in carton 2, MDK Papers. In 1950 the Special Programs Branch was renamed the International Economic Analysis Division, with Dublin Keyserling as director.

37. For examples, see "Address written by MDK for Thomas Blaisdell, Asst. to Secretary of Commerce," May 19, 1947; Dublin Keyserling, "The European Recovery Plan and the American Consumer," May 13, 1948; clipping on Dublin Keyserling address, *Atlanta Journal*, June 13, 1950; all in carton 2, MDK Papers.

38. Truman asked Secretary of the Interior Julius Krug to head an Interdepartmental Committee on the Foreign Aid Program and National Resources. Krug put Tex Goldschmidt in charge of the working group that drafted the report; Goldschmidt, draft memoir, debt.doc, in author's possession, and "Memories of the Marshall Plan," May 10, 1997, box 11, Goldschmidt Papers. Also see W. Averell Harriman to Dublin Keyserling, Dec. 8, 1947, "Letters to Dublin Keyserling" file, carton 1, MDK Papers. "Turning to a Hitler" appears in Keyserling, "The European Recovery Plan and the American Consumer," address before the National Association of Consumers, May 13, 1948, carton 2, ibid.

39. Thomas C. Blaisdell Jr., "Our Foreign Trade Outlook," *Foreign Commerce Weekly*, Mar. 6, 1948, and see other examples in cartons 2 and 3, MDK Papers.

40. Phrase from Henry Hazlitt's Jan. 12, 1948, column in *Newsweek*, read into *Congressional Record*, House, 80th Cong., 2d sess., Mar. 22, 1948, by Rep. Fred Busbey, p. A1846.

41. *Congressional Record*, House, 80th Cong., 2d sess., Mar. 29, 1948, p. 3624 (quotation); ibid., Senate, 80th Cong., 2d sess., Mar. 11, p. 2528. For the flagging of Dublin Keyserling, see *Interim Aid for Europe: Hearings before the Committee on Foreign Relations of the U.S. Senate* (Nov. 1947), 228, marked copy in box 154, Subject Files, SISS Records.

42. Memo on Dublin Keyserling as special representative to Poland, date illegible, author and recipient names redacted, submitted by Jim Walter to FBI, Mar. 19, 1948, Dublin Keyserling FBI file. Walter's memo named Lewis Lorwin as Mary's supervisor. The tipster's source may have been the *Times-Herald* columnist George Sokolsky, who recently had written that Leon was a socialist, and who probably knew about Mary through his working relationship with HUAC's Ben Mandel. On Mandel's cultivation of Sokolsky, see Mandel to Stolberg, Feb. 25, 1946, box 6, Stolberg Papers. Mandel outlined the need for a Washington media outlet to expose Communists in government in "Memorandum on the *Washington Daily News*," Oct. 1, 1944, ibid.

43. *Congressional Record*, House, 80th Cong., 2d sess., Mar. 29, 1948, pp. 3624–25.

44. Parisius said he had nothing to hide but was tired of taking a beating for public service. *Washington Times-Herald*, May 15, 1948, cited in FBI Report of July 31, 1952, Dublin Keyserling FBI file. Chapter 7 discusses the cases of Lorwin, Blaisdell, Cohen, and Goldschmidt.

45. Laughlin memo to Ladd, Mar. 27, 1948, Dublin Keyserling FBI file; Hoover request for investigation of Leon Keyserling, Apr. 13, 1948, Leon Keyserling FBI file.

46. Mandel complained that "the FBI with its staff of naïve college men, to whom the Communist movement is all Greek, is committing the most unbelievable blunders in handling this problem"; Mandel to Ben Stolberg, June 18, 1941, box 6, Stolberg Papers. The feeling was mutual; Hoover distrusted J. B. Matthews for his injudicious leaks to the press. See Athan Theoharis, *Chasing Spies: How the FBI Failed in Counterintelligence but Promoted the Politics of McCarthyism in the Cold War Years* (Chicago: Ivan Dee, 2002), 207; Haynes and Klehr, *Early Cold War Spies*.

47. On Harriman's conflict with HUAC member Richard Nixon over the case of Commerce employee Edward Condon, see Rudy Abramson, *Spanning the Century: The Life of W. Averell Harriman, 1891–1986* (New York: William Morrow, 1992), 411–12.

48. Gary May, *Un-American Activities: The Trials of William Remington* (New York: Oxford University Press, 1994). In 1947 Remington had worked at the Council of Economic Advisers under Leon Keyserling, who claimed that Edwin Nourse had hired Remington; Leon Keyserling testimony, SISS executive session, June 13, 1951, SISS Records.

49. Marshall's relation to Dublin Keyserling had been noted in her FBI file back in 1941, but at that time he had not been labeled a security threat; investigators did not focus on their tie until 1948. See George Marshall obituary, *NYT*, June 18, 2000; George Marshall FBI file; and FBI Report of Henry Alston, Aug. 27, 1951, Dublin Keyserling file, RG 478. Also see Harvey Klehr and John Earl Haynes, *Venona* (New Haven: Yale University Press, 1999), 477, 480; Gerald Horne, *Communist Front? The Civil Rights Congress, 1946–1956* (Rutherford, N.J.: Fairleigh Dickinson University Press, 1988), 31. The Civil Rights Congress raised substantial funds for the defense of the twelve Communist leaders on trial under the Smith Act.

50. Quotations from FBI Reports of Eldred Cox and William Hyde, both dated Apr. 22, 1948, Dublin Keyserling file, RG 478.

51. CP rules for underground members are discussed in Hope Hale Davis, *Great Day Coming: A Memoir of the 1930s* (South Royalton, Vt.: Steerforth Press, 1994).

52. *New York World-Telegram*, July 21, 1948, p. 1.

53. She was charged with joining the American Council on Soviet Relations (in 1938), the American Committee for the Protection of the Foreign Born (in 1939), and the National Federation for Constitutional Liberties (in 1940) and with participating in a 1940 program sponsored by the American Peace Mobilization. The dates were considered important because the Hitler-Stalin pact of 1939 produced changes in CP policy that made Communists more visible to those who had been cooperating with them in Popular Front organizations. South Trimble, Jr., Chair, Commerce loyalty board, to Mary Dublin Keyserling, July 30, 1948, Dublin Keyserling file, RG 478. For context on these organizations, see Bontecou, *Federal Loyalty-Security Program*, 175–88, and Robert J. Goldstein, *American Blacklist: The Attorney General's List of Subversive Organizations* (Lawrence: University Press of Kansas, 2008).

54. Keyserling to Trimble, Aug. 6, 1948, Dublin Keyserling file, RG 478, and see Commerce loyalty board hearing, Aug. 24–25, 1948, ibid.

55. Keyserling to Trimble, Aug. 6, 1948, Dublin Keyserling file, RG 478, and see Commerce loyalty board hearing, Aug. 24–25, 1948, pp. 96–109, 257–63, ibid.

56. "Open Letter to American Liberals," *Soviet Russia Today* 6 (March 1937): 14–15. The letter was correct that Trotsky supporters manipulated the Dewey Committee, according to Judy Kutulas, *The Long War: The Intellectual People's Front and Anti-Stalinism, 1930–1940* (Durham: Duke University Press, 1995), 116–21. Eugene Lyons made this letter infamous in his anticommunist manifesto; see Eugene Lyons, *The Red Decade* (New York: Arlington House, 1941), 252–55.

57. Commerce loyalty board hearing, Aug. 24–25, 1948, pp. 136–40, 244, 267, Dublin Keyserling file, RG 478, and Keyserling to Trimble, Aug. 6, 1948, pp. 2–3, ibid.

58. Laura Kalman, *Abe Fortas: A Biography* (New Haven: Yale University Press, 1990), 125–51. Fortas's firm also handled the important Dorothy Bailey, Owen Lattimore, and John Peters cases. Fortas claimed he never represented anyone who had been a Communist; Schrecker, *Many Are the Crimes*, 303.

59. Kalman, *Abe Fortas*, 131.

60. Keyserling to Trimble, Aug. 6, 1948, p. 1, Dublin Keyserling file, RG 478, and see Commerce loyalty board hearing, Aug. 24–25, 1948, p. 144, ibid.

61. Trimble to Director of Personnel, Nov. 5, 1948, Dublin Keyserling file, RG 478; Bernard Gladieux for Secretary Sawyer to Director of Personnel, Nov. 29, 1948, ibid.

62. Seth Richardson to Hoover, Dec. 7 and 17, 1948, Dublin Keyserling and Leon Keyserling FBI files. As a senior member of the Council of Economic Advisers, Leon was not evaluated by the council's loyalty board but by the White House loyalty board, which did not issue him an interrogatory, so there was no hearing in his case at this stage.

63. South Trimble of the Commerce loyalty board believed that pressure from higher up was behind the overruling of his board's decisions by the Commerce appeals board and Secretary Charles Sawyer. Trimble's complaint had wider ramifications later. See Vivian Truman to Harry Truman, Feb. 1949, in loyalty program file, box 872, White House Official File, HSTL.

64. George Marshall FBI file.

65. SISS was established in December 1950 to study the operation of the McCarran Internal Security Act and other antisubversive laws.

66. Biographical sketches of Paul and Sylvia Crouch, box 1, Paul Crouch Papers, Hoover Institution; for his criminal record, see [name redacted] to A.H. Belmont, Nov. 28, 1951, Dublin Keyserling FBI file. After the Comintern decided to concentrate on the South, Paul Crouch surveyed textile workers and recommended starting at Loray Mills. He became editor of the *New South*, and Sylvia was its business manager; both were involved in the Communist "fraction" of the Southern Conference for Human Welfare; Paul Crouch, unpublished memoir, chap. 13, box 17, Crouch Papers. For a synthesis of claims that Crouch was unhinged and a failure within the party, and for speculation that he acted as a double agent in exchange for his 1928 pardon, see Kai Bird and Martin Sherwin, *American Prometheus: The Triumph and Tragedy of J. Robert Oppenheimer* (New York: Knopf, 2005), 439.

67. Quotation on why Crouch went to HUAC is from his unpublished memoir, chap. 23, box 17, Crouch Papers, Hoover Institution. For the elaboration on nudism, see Crouch, "The Charges against Paul Crouch and the Facts about Them" [1954], box 16, ibid.

68. Gertrude Parks file, RG 478. It is unclear whether the senior Keyserling told his son that he had written an affidavit for Parks. Additional information on Gilbert Parks is in Leon Keyserling FBI file.

69. Dunton Fatherly to George Norris, Fourth Regional loyalty board, June 27, 1950, Gertrude Parks file, RG 478.

70. Marion Wade Doyle memorandum on Gertrude Parks, June 19, 1950, ibid.

71. The Crouches testified about Oppenheimer before the California State Senate Un-American Activities Committee in May 1950; this is when they earned the "West Coast Whittaker Chambers" moniker. Like the story about meeting Keyserling, the Crouches' story about the Oppenheimers included enough accurate details—about the interior of the Oppenheimer home, for example—to seem credible, but it was untrue. See Bird and Sherwin, *American Prometheus*, 438–41.

72. Michael J. Ybarra, *Washington Gone Crazy: Senator Pat McCarran and the Great American Communist Hunt* (Hanover, N.H.: Steerforth Press, 2004), 538. For the other members of the subcommittee McCarran selected six extremely conservative senators, three from each party.

73. Chart, Dec. 1950, and Crouch to Mandel, Jan. 31, 1951, with enclosures, Leon Keyserling file, SISS Records.

74. Crouch to Mandel, Jan. 31, 1951, and enclosure, "Original sent to Senator Joseph McCarthy: Memo on Gilbert L. Parks and Leon H. Keyserling," Leon Keyserling file, SISS Records.

75. Paul Crouch, "Recent Activities of Important Undercover Communists," n.d., box 16, Crouch Papers, Hoover Institution. Crouch later claimed that Frank Schroeder, a former FBI agent who joined the SISS staff, had told him in April 1951 that Parks applied for a SISS job; see Crouch to Alfred Kohlberg, Jan. 23, 1953, Alsops file, box 5, Kohlberg Papers, Hoover Institution. Gilbert Parks said he would have liked to work on the Marshall Plan project but knew his past associations would disqualify him. Gilbert Parks testimony, Fourth Regional loyalty board hearing, Apr. 12, 1950, p. 107, Gertrude Parks file, RG 478. For additional evidence that SISS was gunning for Keyserling earlier than Crouch would admit, see a February 1951 memo on William Remington's employment in Leon's agency, Leon Keyserling file, SISS Records.

76. See FBI reports, Gertrude Parks file, RG 478. In November 1951 Crouch gave the FBI another list of people who could be queried about Parks, but few of them supported his story. On the report cards, see FBI Report of James Martin, Jan. 4, 1952, ibid.

77. See two FBI internal memos dated Apr. 23, 1952, in Dublin Keyserling FBI file. Crouch's deception is explained more fully below.

78. J. B. Matthews testimony, Commerce loyalty board hearing, May 27, 1952, Dublin Keyserling file, RG 478.

79. Senator McCarthy to Metropolitan Life Insurance Co., May 25, 1951, to confirm whether Louis I. Dublin was their chief statistician in 1929; referred to in

FBI internal memo of July 3, 1951 (in Dublin Keyserling's FBI file) and in Arnold, Fortas & Porter analysis of Sept. 1952, Dublin Keyserling file, RG 478. Crouch claimed it was the detail about her father that reminded him of Mary's last name. It is unclear why McCarthy waited until February 1952 to attack the Keyserlings publicly.

80. Mandel to SISS counsel J. Sourwine and Richard Arens, June 6, 1951, annotated by Sourwine, "Sen. says OK"; Leon Keyserling file, SISS Records.

81. Crouch statement, June 8, 1951, Dublin Keyserling FBI file. On the Heiman-Coplon connection, see internal FBI memo, names redacted, Aug. 9, 1951, ibid.

82. "Questions for Mary Dublin Keyserling" [June 1951], Keyserling file, SISS Records.

83. Ybarra, *Washington Gone Crazy*, 412, 420, 511. In 1954 a Ferguson bill inserted the words "under God" into the Pledge of Allegiance. See the finding aid to Ferguson's papers at Bentley Historical Library, University of Michigan.

84. Crouch testimony, SISS executive sessions, May 8 and June 13, 1951, SISS Records.

85. Leon Keyserling testimony, SISS executive session, June 13, 1951, pp. 88–94, SISS Records. The SISS transcripts were supposed to be confidential, but the FBI, Senator McCarthy, and J. B. Matthews obtained them.

86. Emphasis added. The Keyserling defense team argued later that the italicized phrase indicated Crouch's effort to avoid perjury charges by not making a definite identification.

87. Crouch statement to FBI, June 8, 1951, Dublin Keyserling FBI file; passport applications of Elisabeth and Mary Dublin Keyserling, Dublin Keyserling file, SISS Records.

88. Dublin Keyserling supplemental statement to SISS, July 1951, p. 4, Dublin Keyserling file, SISS Records.

89. Elisabeth Dublin Marshall testimony, SISS executive session, June 22, 1951, SISS Records.

90. SISS executive sessions, June 13–15, 22, July 3, 1951, SISS Records. To the FBI, Paul Crouch backed off, saying that after seeing both sisters it was impossible to say which was the one he had known years earlier; FBI internal memo, July 5, 1951, Dublin Keyserling FBI file. On travel to Europe, see Crouch supplemental statement to FBI, June 19, 1951, ibid.; on glasses, Crouch interviewed by FBI, Aug. 10, 1951, ibid. A Cincinnati newspaper clipping noted Mary's "soft, deep voice"; see 1958 speech file, MDK Papers.

91. Dublin Keyserling testimony, SISS executive sessions, June 15 (quotation 12), July 20, 1951, SISS Records.

92. Leon Keyserling testimony, SISS executive sessions, June 13–14, 1951, pp. 129–31, 153, 188, SISS Records.

93. Leon Keyserling to President Truman, June 27, 1951, Keyserling file, box 108, President's Secretary's Files, HSTL. Leon's own papers at HSTL do not include this letter, although he carefully preserved other correspondence with Truman in a special file.

94. The wide range of people who vouched for Leon included ex-Communist Lee Pressman, anticommunist socialist James Carey, Leon's Council of Economic

Advisers nemesis Edwin Nourse. See FBI Reports of William Hyde, May 19, 1948, Robert Horner, Aug. 1, 1951, and Alfred Goff, Sept. 13, 1951, Dublin Keyserling file, RG 478. One former high-level official said any tendencies toward "ultra-liberalism" on Leon's part were "probably the result of his wife's influence." The same person also said Mary was "very competent, ultra-liberal, but sincere not opportunistic"; FBI Report of Robert Horner, Aug. 1, 1951, ibid. On Bauer, see FBI Report of (agent's name redacted), Aug. 31, 1951, Leon Keyserling FBI file.

95. The interrogatory and Leon's reply are not in his papers at the Truman Library, and his loyalty case file is not in RG 478.

96. Commerce loyalty board to Mary Dublin Keyserling, Oct. 12, 1951, and Commerce loyalty board hearing transcripts, 1951–52, Dublin Keyserling file, RG 478.

97. [Name redacted] to A. H. Belmont, Nov. 28, 1951, Dublin Keyserling FBI file. The FBI had reason to worry because Crouch had a history of erratic behavior. During the trial of labor leader Harry Bridges the preceding year, defense lawyers had presented evidence that Crouch had perjured himself; Bird and Sherwin, *American Prometheus*, 665n440.

98. Commerce loyalty board hearing, testimony of Elisabeth Dublin Marshall, Nov. 15, 1951, quotations 125, 152, 154, Dublin Keyserling file, RG 478; George Marshall, May 26, 1952, p. 771; Nathaniel Weyl, June 5, 1952, pp. 946 ff.; Dublin Keyserling, Sept. 25–26, 1952, pp. 112–14, 171, all ibid.

99. Commerce loyalty board hearing, Nov. 27, 1951, pp. 385–90, Dublin Keyserling file, RG 478; FBI Report of M. C. Clements, Sept. 11, 1942, ibid. The American Labor Party was a vehicle for bringing New York socialists to support Roosevelt; during the war Communists assumed greater influence in it. Loyalty officials were not supposed to ask about party affiliation, but they had the FBI reports.

100. Recent scholarship on espionage demands consideration of the possibility that Dublin Keyserling was an underground Communist. The CP USA records at the Library of Congress yield no evidence that she was in or close to the party. Two experts kindly checked the databases they created from American and Soviet archives and did not find Dublin Keyserling's name: John Earl Haynes, in person at the Library of Congress, May 2003, and the Moscow-based Svetlana Chervonnaya, e-mail exchange with author, Apr. 2007.

101. Commerce loyalty board hearing testimony of anticommunist socialists including Norman Thomas (Feb. 4, 1952), Harry Laidler, and James Carey (both Jan. 28, 1952), Dublin Keyserling file, RG 478; FBI interview with Milwaukee union activist Francis Henson, Report of Walter Roethke, Apr. 9, 1952, ibid.; FBI interview with Jean Trepp McKelvey, Report of W. E. Meehan, Apr. 22, 1948, ibid.

102. Report of Kenneth West, Aug. 30, 1951, Dublin Keyserling file, RG 478. Loeb claimed Mary had been there along with Max Yergan, Margaret Lamont, and T. A. Bisson, all of whom were in or close to the CP. Loeb was the archconservative publisher of the *Manchester (N.H.) Union Leader*.

103. While an employee of the Agricultural Adjustment Administration Weyl belonged from 1933 to 1935 to the Ware cell, of which Hiss also was a member. Weyl identified members of the group for the FBI in 1950. Initially Weyl did not want his CP past to be public, but in February 1952 he testified before SISS, and

in January 1953 he published his story in the *U.S. News & World Report*. He did not come forward about Hiss earlier, he explained, because he had not observed espionage and had no information on the specific charges against Hiss. In 1954, the IOELB rated Sylvia Weyl ineligible for government employment because the Weyls waited so long after leaving the Party to cooperate with the government and because the board thought a longer probation period was required to remove all doubt about their loyalty. IOELB, "Memorandum of Findings" [1954], Sylvia Weyl file, RG 478.

104. Crouch told SISS in October 1952 that Nathaniel Weyl had not fully broken with the CP and that Weyl had called on him after Dublin Keyserling's loyalty hearing to find out what Crouch knew; "Suggested questions for interrogation" [Oct. 1952], Leon Keyserling file, SISS Records. Crouch tried to motivate SISS by reporting that Weyl's 1951 book, *The Battle Against Disloyalty*, disparaged SISS chairman McCarran as well as the informants Louis Budenz and J. B. Matthews; "Background of the Porter Brothers" [Fall 1952], box 16, Crouch Papers, Hoover Institution. Unlike Crouch, the Weyls did not need money. The FBI may have fanned the rivalries among informers; the FBI's Lambert Zander reportedly told the Weyls to stay away from Crouch because he was unreliable; Nathaniel Weyl interview with author, June 18, 2003.

105. The Weyls had told the FBI that they "could not conceive of Mary Dublin Keyserling ever being a Communist or associated in any CP activity"; memo from SAC [special agent in charge], WFO [Washington Field Office] to Director, FBI, Aug. 24, 1951, Dublin Keyserling FBI file. The Weyls had been assured that their information would not be disseminated outside the bureau, which may explain why Nathaniel was not more careful to avoid inconsistency when he testified before the Commerce loyalty board.

106. Nathaniel Weyl interview with author, June 18, 2003.

107. On Lovestone and Bentley, FBI Report of Henry Alston, Aug. 27, 1951, Dublin Keyserling file, RG 478; on Yergan, FBI Report of Marcellus Meyer, Oct. 13, 1952, ibid.

108. At both the National Consumers' League and Office of International Trade (OIT), Dublin Keyserling made enemies of some subordinates. It seems she was abrasive and exacting as a boss, but it also seems that her detractors, male and female, had difficulty accepting criticism from a female supervisor. See FBI interview with NCL board member Florence Whitney, Report of M. C. Clements, Sept. 11, 1942, and accounts of OIT employees Ruth Cannon (Marjorie Garff to Senator Bennett, July 25, 1951, Dublin Keyserling file, SISS Records), Georgenna Page (J. E. Hoover to Newman Smith, Security Officer, Commerce Dept., July 25, 1952, Dublin Keyserling file, RG 478), Max Wasserman, and Leon Herman (FBI Reports of Donald Morrell, July 18 and 31, 1952, ibid.). Cannon and Page had been dismissed on Dublin Keyserling's recommendation, and she had rejected articles by Wasserman and Herman.

109. Matthews emphasized her signing of the "Open Letter to American Liberals" as well as a comment she allegedly made to him after he gave a lecture at Bennington College in April 1935. She denied having been to Bennington College, but she did go there in April 1935; see Mary to Lucy, Apr. 1935 postcard, Lucy Kramer Cohen Papers, Beinecke.

110. McCarthy cited a recent complaint by Ferguson that "by devious means" the U.S. government had exported materials needed for home construction (a shot at the Commerce Department, where Mary worked). *NYT*, 1952: Feb. 10, p. 34, Feb. 11, p. 4, Apr. 22, p. 14; transcript of McCarthy speech, Feb. 9, 1952, copy in Leon Keyserling file, Arnold & Porter Papers, Washington, D.C.

111. J. B. Matthews testimony, Commerce loyalty board hearing, May 27, 1952, pp. 904–12, Dublin Keyserling file, RG 478.

112. *NYT*, Feb. 11, 1952, p. 4, April 22, 1952, p. 14.

113. "Ho Hum," editorial, *Washington Post*, Feb. 12, 1952.

114. The defense counsel gave the summation in Mary's case on February 4; Leon was cleared February 8; McCarthy's speech was February 9.

115. The FBI's exhaustive search of all central and regional office files failed to find verification of Crouch's claim that he had told the FBI about a "Mary" before seeing her at the SISS hearing on June 8, 1951 (he claimed to have done so at the FBI's Miami office in 1948 and in Pittsburgh in April 1951). The FBI also found that many people Crouch had said would confirm Gilbert Parks was a CP member could not do so. The FBI decided, after much discussion of wording, to answer the Commerce loyalty board's question by saying they found Crouch reliable. See Memo from [name redacted] to A. H. Belmont, Apr, 23, 1952, and J. E. Hoover to Security Control Officer, Department of Commerce, Apr, 23, 1952, Dublin Keyserling FBI file.

116. *Congressional Record*, Senate, 82nd Cong., 2d sess., Apr. 21, 1952, p. 4212; Apr. 22, 1952, clippings, box 73, Keyserling Papers, HSTL. For Leon's disavowal, see Keyserling to Commerce Secretary Charles Sawyer, May 14, 1952, box 11, Charles Sawyer Papers, HSTL; SISS executive session, Oct. 18, 1952, SISS Records. When the Supreme Court struck down Truman's takeover, the steelworkers did go on strike. Truman may have received bad advice, especially from Secretary of Defense Robert Lovett, who overestimated the need for steel in Korea, according to Maeva Marcus, *Truman and the Steel Seizure Case* (Durham, N.C.: Duke University Press, 1994), 74, 256.

117. Kohlberg to McCarthy, May 6, 1952, in box 123, Kohlberg Papers, Hoover Institution. Lewis's syndicated columns appeared May 27–30, 1952. J. B. Matthews testimony, Commerce loyalty board hearing, May 27, 1952, pp. 904–12, Dublin Keyserling file, RG 478.

118. Sawyer himself killed Leon Herman's report, he explained, because the country needed Russian manganese to make steel and so he did not want to antagonize the Soviets just then. FBI Report of Donald Morrell, July 31, 1952, Dublin Keyserling file, RG 478.

119. Arnold, Fortas & Porter, "Analysis of Record and Testimony on Appeal," Sept. 1952, ibid. The Keyserlings had reason to be suspicious, given Loeb's anti-Truman editorials and an odd telegram he sent to Truman gloating about McCarthy's attack on Keyserling; Loeb telegram to President Truman, Feb. 13, 1952, White House Official File 252-K, HSTL.

120. The Lewis broadcast was Sept. 5, 1952. Don Connors of SISS claimed Sawyer had suspended Dublin Keyserling despite opposition from the White House. Connors to McCarran, Sept. 20, 1952, Dublin Keyserling file, SISS Records.

121. Arnold, Fortas & Porter, "Analysis of Record and Testimony on Appeal," Sept. 1952, Dublin Keyserling file, RG 478.

122. Only smatterings of this concern can be traced in records at the HSTL (for example, see Donald Hansen to Charlie Murphy, May 2, 1952, "K" folder, box 10, Murphy Papers, HSTL), but see White House–FBI correspondence in the Keyserlings' FBI files.

123. Truman's diary for Sept. 10, 1952, does not shed light on his meeting with Sawyer, but the Commerce security officer relayed these developments to the FBI; see Commerce security officer memos to J. E. Hoover, Aug. 26 and Sept. 12, 1952, Dublin Keyserling FBI file. See also South Trimble to Charles Sawyer, Sept. 18, 1952; Trimble to FBI, Feb. 25, 1953, ibid.; and Vivian Truman's report that she had seen Trimble in Missouri and he had complained that Sawyer was not listening to him about the disloyalty of some employees; Vivian Truman to Harry Truman, Feb. 1949, White House Official File 252-K, HSTL. "Clamped lid" from Connors to McCarran, Sept. 20, 1952, Dublin Keyserling file, SISS Records. Leon denied that there had been any impropriety. He said the White House loyalty board had shown him the FBI reports in order to question him about the specifics. That his lawyers did not conceal their access to the reports could mean they saw no impropriety, or it could mean that they were trying to intimidate the Commerce loyalty board with their superior connections. Senator Ferguson thought the latter; SISS executive session, Oct. 18, 1952, SISS Records.

124. Arnold, Fortas & Porter, "Analysis of Record and Testimony on Appeal," Sept. 1952, Dublin Keyserling file, RG 478.

125. "Wife of Truman Aide Probed as Security Risk," *Washington News*, Oct. 1, 1952. The Scripps-Howard reporter who wrote the article, Andrew Tully, had called the FBI about the case on Sept. 26, and the FBI reportedly declined to confirm his information; L. B. Nichols to J. E. Hoover, Sept. 26, 1952, Dublin Keyserling FBI file.

126. See extensive clippings and radio broadcast transcripts in the Keyserlings' FBI files and in their files in SISS Records.

127. See Connors to McCarran, Sept. 20, 1952, with the handwritten annotation, "Don—Sen. says let this go—do nothing about it. He wants to play it Sawyer's way." Dublin Keyserling file, SISS Records.

128. Willis Smith (D-N.C.) to Pat McCarran (D-Nev.), Oct. 20, 1952, Leon Keyserling file, SISS Records. On Ferguson's access to FBI reports, see Ybarra, *Washington Gone Crazy*, 420.

129. Keyserling testimony, SISS executive session, Oct. 18, 1952, SISS Records. Endless confusion existed at the time and since because there were two important Paul Porters in Washington circles, and both of them were friendly with the Keyserlings. Paul A. Porter was administrator of the Office of Price Administration before becoming partner of Arnold, Fortas & Porter, in which capacity he helped Fortas represent the Keyserlings. Paul R. Porter was the Socialist labor activist who dated Mary in 1931 and later worked on the Marshall Plan.

130. Ferguson press release, Oct. 21, 1952, box 14, Ferguson Papers, Bentley Historical Library, University of Michigan. Porter said he had offered to resign in 1951, predicting that his past might be used in an election year to attack the

Mutual Security Agency, but his superiors had convinced him to stay; see press release by Mutual Security Agency, Oct. 21, 1952; Ferguson radio address, type-script, n.d.; Carey to Ferguson, Oct. 27, 1952; all ibid. See also FBI interview with Paul R. Porter, 1943, excerpted in FBI Report of Robert Fauntleroy, Feb. 2, 1949, Porter file, RG 478.

131. "As Pegler Sees It," Oct. 28, 1952, box 130, Pegler Papers (I thank Nancy Beck Young for this clipping).

132. See Ben Mandel to Ben Stolberg, Nov. 3, 1948, box 6, Stolberg Papers; Mandel to Alfred Kohlberg, Nov. 12, 1948, box 119, Kohlberg Papers, Hoover Institution; J. B. Matthews to Kohlberg, Dec. 3, 1953, ibid.

133. Keyserling testimony, SISS executive session, Oct. 18, 1952, p. 117, SISS Records. Chapter 7 discusses Porter's case.

134. See FBI Reports of Marcellus Meyer, Sept. 17, 1952, and John McCarthy, Jan. 13, 1953, among many others concerning Mary van Kleeck, and Commerce appeals board hearing, Nov. 4, 1952, pp. 260–63, all in Dublin Keyserling file, RG 478.

135. C. Dickerson Williams et al. to The Secretary, Dec. 1953 [1952?], Dublin Keyserling file, RG 478; Agency Reports on Closed Loyalty Case, Jan. 5 and 21, 1953, ibid.; Commerce security officer to A. H. Belmont, Jan. 8, 1953, Dublin Keyserling FBI file. On the Loyalty Review Board's placement of a "notice of bar or flag action" in her file, see George Norris to Newman Smith, Feb. 11, 1953, Dublin Keyserling file, RG 478. For the public version of events, see *NYT*, Jan. 10, 1953, p. 4, and Feb. 4, 1953, p. 4, as well as Dublin Keyserling's obituary, *Washington Post*, June 13, 1997, and Dublin Keyserling interview, 165, WFGP. The Commerce security officer might have been wrong that Dublin Keyserling was *denied* security clearance, but she certainly had not received it before she resigned.

136. Joseph and Stewart Alsop, "Probe of Hired Informers Urged," *Washington Post*, Jan. 18, 1953. Just as the defense attorneys had, the Alsops emphasized Crouch's inconsistent statements about Leon to the FBI in 1949 and 1951. They also alluded to Crouch's false claim to have told the FBI about a "Mary" before June 1951. Mary and Joe Alsop had worked together at Commerce. Of Crouch's testimony in a Seattle deportation proceeding on Sept. 6, 1950, Leon wrote Fortas, "This latest discovery . . . is perhaps a far more striking proof of the fantastic perjuries of Mr. Crouch than any of the material that we could find last year"; Leon Keyserling to Abe Fortas, Nov. 12, 1953, Keyserling file, Arnold & Porter Papers.

137. Crouch also claimed inaccurately that the Commerce loyalty board had not cleared Mary and that she was only reinstated by executive order; Paul Crouch to Alfred Kohlberg, Jan. 23, 1953, Alsop file, box 5, Kohlberg Papers, Hoover Institution; see also "Statement by Paul Crouch," [Apr. 1954], box 16, Crouch Papers, ibid. Crouch later backed off even further on his story about Parks and Keyserling; "Espionage in the White House, 1934–42," Aug. 1954, Gertrude Parks file, RG 478.

138. J. E. Hoover to Asst. Atty. General Warren Olney III, Jan. 16 and 23, 1953, Dublin Keyserling FBI file; Olney to Hoover, Apr. [date illegible], 1953, ibid.

139. Raymond Farrell, Immigration and Naturalization Service, to J. E. Hoover, Apr. 21, 1954, and Hoover to Farrell, May 5, 1954, Dublin Keyserling FBI file (received separately by FOIA request from the Department of Homeland Security, October 2005).

140. In a last-ditch effort, Crouch asked Hoover to investigate the U.S. attorney general after the latter began investigating him. Ironically, Crouch asked the ACLU for help against the Justice Department's alleged persecution. "Crouch, Accused, Assails his Chiefs," *NYT*, July 9, 1954. See also Pearson column, Apr. 11, 1954; Alsop columns, Apr. 13 and 19, 1954; and Statement by Paul Crouch, all in box 16, Crouch Papers, Hoover Institution. Not long before this, lawyers for the cartoonist Jacob Burkus, who faced deportation based on Crouch's charges, produced affidavits from numerous prominent people to show that Crouch had falsely claimed to know them; Cedric Belfrage, *The American Inquisition, 1945–1960* (Indianapolis: Bobbs-Merrill, 1973), 181–82, 227–28.

141. On McCarthy's threat, see L. B. Nichols to Clyde Tolson, Nov. 9, 1954, Dublin Keyserling FBI file.

142. Commerce loyalty board hearing, Aug. 18, 1952, p. 1386, Dublin Keyserling file, RG 478.

143. For Mandel's economic insecurity, see, for example, a letter in which he worried that as a result of Truman's victory he would be unemployed; Mandel to Ben Stolberg, Nov. 3, 1948, box 6, Stolberg Papers. Crouch often complained of unemployment and high medical bills.

144. Memo in Leon Keyserling file, box 615, Matthews Papers, n.d. but post-1958.

145. Mandel to Sourwine, July 8, 1963, Dublin Keyserling file, SISS Records. Mandel offered an inaccurate reprise of the case, claiming she had been told to face a loyalty board or resign and so resigned.

146. First quotation from Senator Milward Simpson (R-Wyo.), *Congressional Record*, Senate, 88th Cong., 2d sess., Apr. 10, 1964, p. 7552. Abe Fortas to Jack Valenti, Feb. 20, 1964, quoted by Wehmeyer, "Mary Dublin Keyserling," 240. Fortas wrote about twenty letters on behalf of her nomination, according to Mary and Leon Keyserling interview with Laura Kalman, 19, in author's possession.

CHAPTER 5

Secrets and Self-Reinvention: The Making of Cold War Liberalism

1. This scholarship is discussed in notes 105–9 below.

2. Pages are missing from the appointment books for 1928, 1932, 1934, and 1936, and no books survive for 1931, 1933, 1935, 1937, and 1942; otherwise the set is complete from 1927 through the late 1980s. In unprocessed 1996 accession, MDK Papers. Dublin Keyserling died in 1997.

3. Appointment books, 1929–47, MDK Papers; Nathaniel Weyl interview with author, June 18, 2003.

4. Weyl testimony, Commerce loyalty board hearing, June 5, 1952, Dublin Keyserling file, RG 478; 1938 appointment book, unprocessed 1996 accession, MDK Papers; "Mexico 1938 conference" file, box 87, Mary van Kleeck Papers,

Smith. On the January 1940 controversy about Edwin Smith's 1938 speeches in Mexico, see James A. Gross, *The Reshaping of the National Labor Relations Board* (Albany: State University of New York Press, 1982), vol. 2, p. 140. Investigators did not discover Dublin Keyserling's connection with Dorothy Douglas (who soon would mentor Smith undergraduate Betty Friedan). Dublin Keyserling and Douglas worked together in the LWS and NCL, and in December 1939 Douglas invited Mary to participate in the Institute of Labor Studies, a pro-labor research venture Douglas founded with Lumpkin; Landon R. Y. Storrs, *Civilizing Capitalism: The National Consumers' League, Women's Activism, and Labor Standards in the New Deal Era* (Chapel Hill: University of North Carolina Press, 2000), 236.

5. Appointment books, unprocessed 1996 accession, MDK Papers; FBI Reports of Marcellus Meyer, Sept. 17 and Oct. 25, 1982, and John McCarthy, Jan. 13, 1953, Dublin Keyserling file, RG 478; Commerce loyalty board hearing, testimony of Elisabeth Marshall, Nov. 15, 1951, George Marshall, May 26, 1952, and Nathaniel Weyl, June 5, 1952, ibid. Guy Alchon, "Mary van Kleeck and Social-Economic Planning," *Journal of Policy History* 3, no. 1 (1991).

6. Appointment books, unprocessed 1996 accession, MDK Papers; Dublin Keyserling to Trimble, Aug. 6, 1948, Dublin Keyserling file, RG 478, and Arnold, Fortas & Porter, "Analysis of Record and Testimony on Appeal," Sept. 1952, p. 57, ibid.

7. Appointment books, unprocessed 1996 accession, MDK Papers. On the significance of *Pins and Needles*, see Michael Denning, *The Cultural Front* (New York: Verso, 1996), 295–309. On Angelica Balabanoff, see Paula E. Hyman and Deborah Dash Moore, eds., *Jewish Women in America: An Historical Encyclopedia* (New York: Routledge, 1997), vol. 1, p. 115.

8. These calendars exemplify the "importance of social bonds in the creation of political consciousness and political community" on the twentieth-century left; Kathleen A. Brown and Elizabeth Faue, "Social Bonds, Sexual Politics, and Political Community on the U.S. Left, 1920s–1940s," *Left History* 7, no. 1 (2001): 7–42, quotation 11.

9. Appointment books, unprocessed 1996 accession, MDK Papers.

10. Military intelligence officer quotation from 1947, cited by Ellen Schrecker, *Many Are the Crimes: McCarthyism in America* (Boston: Little, Brown, 1998), 510n23.

11. She also attended meetings of the National Committee on the Cause and Cure of War. See appointment books, unprocessed 1996 accession, MDK Papers; Eastern Institute of International Relations flyer (American Friends Service Committee, 1937), and Dublin Keyserling, "Japanese Aggression and American Labor," handwritten 1937 speech, both in carton 2, MDK Papers.

12. Mary's brother Thomas found these letters among their father Louis Dublin's papers. In 1999 Thomas deposited those letters with the rest of Dublin Keyserling papers at Schlesinger Library. Thomas D. Dublin interviews with author, May 21, 1999, and June 17, 2000.

13. "Dad hasn't had a first-class, well-matched bout since you left. We all miss the excitement and fun"; Augusta to Mary, Oct. 13, 1931, carton 1, MDK Papers.

"Life would be sweeter for an old man if you were around to talk or even scrap with"; Louis to Mary, June 3, 1932, ibid. On Mary as her father's favorite, see Augusta to Mary, July 12, 1932, ibid.

14. Quotations from Mary to Mother, n.d, and Mary to her parents, July 5 and 11, 1932, unprocessed 1999 accession, MDK Papers; Dublin Keyserling to Loyalty Board, Oct. 20, 1951, Dublin Keyserling file, RG 478; Mary to her parents, June 30, 1932, unprocessed 1999 accession, MDK Papers.

15. Louis to Mary, Apr. 26, 1932, unprocessed 1999 accession, MDK Papers. Elisabeth to Louis, n.d. [1934], in possession of Thomas Dublin, State University of New York at Binghamton.

16. Dad to Mary, Feb. 6 and May 24, 1932, carton 1, MDK Papers. Mary joked with her father, possibly at her sister's expense, about playing the stereotypical young radical. Mary once teased her father that they should "stage" an argument by mail: "I might tell you I was very sympathetic to communism . . . and wait for you to bite—or write a little blurbily about a capitalistic system being on its last wobbling legs. Well, what about it?" Mary to Dearest Dad, Oct. 29, 1931, unprocessed 1999 accession, MDK Papers.

17. Louis and Augusta letters to Mary, May–June 1932, carton 1, MDK Papers.

18. Augusta to Mary, May 17, 1932, ibid. See also Augusta to Mary, Oct. 13, 1931, ibid.

19. Augusta to Mary, March 9, 1948, ibid. She referred to Leon's "Deficiencies of Past Programs and Nature of New Needs," in *Saving American Capitalism: A Liberal Economic Program*, ed. Seymour Harris (New York: Knopf, 1948).

20. Appointment books, unprocessed 1996 accession, MDK Papers. On evenings at Morris Cohen's, see Weyl interview with author, June 18, 2003. On the Wallings, see James Boylan, *Revolutionary Lives: Anna Strunsky and William English Walling* (Amherst: University of Massachusetts Press, 1998). Louis Marshall, a distinguished Republican lawyer who was a negotiator at the Paris Peace Conference, was president of the American Jewish Committee from 1916 to 1929 and also a longtime board member of the NAACP; see his papers at American Jewish Historical Society, New York City. Thomas Davidson's New York Society for Ethical Culture and the *New Republic* were major points of intersection for the elder generation, many of whom were nonobservant Jews; Thomas D. Dublin interview with author, June 17, 2000.

21. Field secretary Paul R. Porter to Clarence Senior, Jan. 23, 1931, Russian State Archive of Social and Political History (RGASPI), 515-1-2290 (I thank Svetlana Chervonnaya, Moscow, for sending me this document). Porter distinguished between those savvy young militants and the "erratic" Donald Henderson, whom he correctly predicted was about to "join the Communists."

22. Mary to Liz and George, n.d., unprocessed 1999 accession, MDK Papers. This is one of very few surviving letters between the sisters.

23. See Augusta to Mary, 1929–53, carton 1, MDK Papers; quotations from Aug. 6, 1929, Nov. 6, 1931, and Augusta-Mary correspondence 1957–58, latest accession, MDK Papers.

24. Elisabeth had two abortions; Elisabeth to Louis, n.d. [1934], in possession of Thomas Dublin, State University of New York at Binghamton.

25. Mary to her parents, Apr. 17, 1932, unprocessed 1999 accession, MDK Papers; Mary to Dad, May 11, 1932, ibid.

26. See Storrs, *Civilizing Capitalism*, 97, 237; quotation from Helen Hall, "The Field as We Found It," funding application, Mar. 15, 1945, file 5, box 60, Helen Hall Papers, SWHA.

27. Dublin Keyserling address to New Jersey State Assembly in support of state wage-hour bill, Jan. 21, 1940, microfilm reel 96, NCL Papers, LC.

28. Under the changed legal and political circumstances of the early 1970s, Dublin Keyserling reversed her position and worked for the equal rights amendment. See Storrs, *Civilizing Capitalism*, 46–59, 76–90, 249.

29. Mary to Darlings, July 16, 1932; Mary to Mother, Oct. 29, 1931; and see Mary to parents, July 5, 1932, Mary to Mums, June 24, 1933; all in unprocessed 1999 accession, MDK Papers. The letter to Mary from Weyl has not survived.

30. Paul A. Porter of Arnold, Fortas, & Porter, defense counsel for Dorothy Bailey, Fourth Regional loyalty board hearing, Sept. 13, 1948, p. 14, Dorothy Bailey file, Arnold & Porter Papers, Washington, D.C.

31. "An Interview with Paul M. Sweezy," *Monthly Review* 51 (May 1999): 38. Sweezy, who founded the socialist journal *Monthly Review* in 1949, knew Dublin Keyserling but did not respond to my query. He died in 2004.

32. Leon Keyserling testimony, SISS executive session, June 13, 1951, pp. 129–30; June 14, 1951, p. 153, SISS Records.

33. Ferguson accused Leon of submitting unrepresentative excerpts and of trying to hide the Tugwell connection by omitting the book title from his list of writings; SISS executive session, Oct. 18, 1952, SISS Records. Leon wrote that American universities reflected the nation's subservience to "the doctrines of individualism and laissez faire"; the university's football worship and fraternity system rewarded the values of the 1890s, which led to "poverty and war." Keyserling, "Traditions of a Liberal Education," in *Redirecting Education*, ed. Rexford Tugwell and Leon Keyserling (New York: Columbia University Press, 1934), 117–19. In May 1952 the columnist Fulton Lewis Jr. had quoted that article to demonstrate that Leon was "un-American."

34. Leon to Father, Apr. 22, 1932; Leon to Mother and Father, Feb. 27, 1926, and Feb. 21, 1929, Keyserling Family Papers, College of Charleston. Emphasis in original (last quotation). Leon was in sympathy with his professor Felix Frankfurter's turn to "sociological jurisprudence" and legal realism, which included the idea that "freedom of contract" does not exist between unequal parties.

35. Leon to Father, Feb. 13, 1930, Oct. 11, 1932, Nov. 8, 1932, Keyserling Family Papers, College of Charleston. The Socialist Party received about 900,000 votes in 1932. This was not the last of Leon's predictions to be proven wrong: in 1934, he declared that "our anti-lynching bill will certainly pass." After Truman's victory in November 1948, Leon predicted he would be able to make "the lucrative shift to private sector just as well in 1952" because the liberals probably would win again; Leon to Father, Nov. 5, 1948, ibid.

36. Both quotations from Leon to Father, July 15, 1933, ibid.

37. Leon to Father, Feb. 5, 1934, ibid.

38. Leon to Father, June 25, 1934, ibid.

39. Weyl interview with author, June 18, 2003, and Weyl e-mail to author, Oct. 3, 2003.

40. Although William Keyserling had prospered, his wife's institutionalization was expensive; both his daughters had marital troubles and needed financial support; hurricanes devasted his business; and his youngest son contracted malaria in the military service and was unable to succeed as a doctor until well after the war; Leon-William correspondence, Keyserling Family Papers, College of Charleston.

41. Leon to Father, Feb. 13, 1935, ibid. The purge at the Agricultural Adjustment Administration usually is attributed to Frank's antagonizing of southern landowners with his advocacy of sharecroppers (not his conflict with Chicago meat packers).

42. Leon to Catherine, Sept. 25 and 29, 1936, and see also his letter of Sept. 3, all in Bauer Papers, Bancroft. Keyserling scholars have been unaware of his relationship with Bauer. More than one hundred letters from him are in her papers. In 2005, her letters to him were donated to the College of Charleston as part of a large accession to the Keyserling Family Papers.

43. Leon to Father, June 11, 1936, Keyserling Family Papers, College of Charleston.

44. Leon to Father, Mar, 6, 1937 (court packing), Apr, 13, 1937 (labor movement against fascism) and Jan. 16, 1937 (Ed Smith), ibid. See also Leon to Father, Apr, 1934 (on antilynching bill); Feb. 7, 1936, ibid. William was a racial liberal, at least in South Carolina terms; he supported black education and employment programs but may not have favored social integration.

45. Leon to Father, Apr. 13, 1937, ibid., discussing a farmer-worker fight in Hershey, Pa.

46. Leon to Father, Aug. 31, 1938, ibid.

47. Crouch described what he recalled Leon saying in 1937; SISS executive session, June 13, 1951, p. 87, SISS Records.

48. Leon to Father, n.d. [January 1937], Keyserling Family Papers, College of Charleston. Wagner was the new chair of that committee.

49. Leon to Father, Dec. 8, 1937, ibid.

50. Leon to Father, Aug. 30 and Sept. 13, 1945; Jan. 1946, ibid.

51. Leon to Father, Nov. 5, 1948, ibid. Expecting Truman to lose, Leon had been preparing to start a private practice.

52. Father to Leon, Jan. 3, 1949, and Leon's reply, ibid.

53. Leon to Father, Aug. 2, 1950, ibid.

54. Leon certainly believed he was under surveillance. He told his sister-in-law that his phone was tapped, and he upbraided her for doing things that might get him in trouble, such as giving him a membership to a liberal book club. Harriet H. Keyserling conversation with author, Dec. 7, 2007, Charleston, S.C.

55. Leon to Father, Nov. 5, 1950, Keyserling Family Papers, College of Charleston. Emphasis in original.

56. Father to Leon, Sept. 24, 1951, ibid. Torquemada was an official of the Spanish Inquisition.

57. Father to Leon, July 23 and Aug. 24, 1940, ibid.

58. Mary shared that view, to judge by her description of her work with the U.S. delegation to UNRRA; Dublin Keyserling to William Keyserling, Aug. 5, 1945, ibid. Nathaniel Weyl recollected that in about 1946 Leon expressed skepticism of the Cold War, deploring the exaggeration of the Soviet threat. Weyl interview with author, June 18, 2003, and Weyl e-mail to author, Oct. 3, 2003.

59. Leon concluded that U.S. policy toward Russia was not guided by "imperialistic motives." It was the American people, he corrected his father, not American business interests, who were shaping international policy. Leon to Father, July 5, 1947, Keyserling Family Papers, College of Charleston.

60. SISS executive session, June 14, 1951, pp. 226–27, SISS Records. Leon wrote many articles in the 1930s, but some were published under the names of Rexford Tugwell and Robert Wagner. His papers at the Truman Library include many talks he gave in the late 1930s and 1940s, but those would not have helped him before SISS: a 1939 address to the National Lawyers' Guild; a 1945 address to the National Council of Jewish Women in which he blamed U.S. high-tariff policy as a major cause of war; and a 1948 address to the socialist League for Industrial Democracy.

61. My research on Dublin Keyserling's loyalty case originated in 1991 while I was completing research for my doctoral dissertation in the Consumers' League of Massachusetts Papers, SL.

62. Author conversation with Harriet H. Keyserling, Dec. 7, 2007, Charleston, S.C.

63. My dissertation's characterization of Dublin Keyserling as a leftist in the 1930s did not square with Sklar's firsthand impression; Kathryn Kish Sklar to author, Aug. 3, 1995. Thomas Dublin recalled dinner-table arguments with Leon and Mary about the Vietnam War; Thomas Dublin phone conversation with author, July 19, 1998. Both scholars then provided invaluable assistance in locating privately held family papers and photographs.

64. Thomas D. Dublin interview with author, June 17, 2000. The interrogatory was in the late 1940s; the epidemiologist trip was in 1955. In 1953 Thomas D. Dublin became prominent for his work on the Salk polio vaccine. His sister's case file was loaned to officials who reviewed his applications for employment or promotion; see circulation card in Dublin Keyserling file, RG 478.

65. On Elisabeth's request that Mary's letters be destroyed, Thomas D. Dublin interview with author, June 17, 2000. Author telephone conversation with George Marshall's daughter Nancy Shultz, June 16, 1999. Elisabeth died in 1993, and George died in 2001.

66. Augusta to Mary, Feb. 18, 1952, carton 1, MDK Papers. Augusta grumbled that HUAC should be paying attention to real problems such as Ku Klux Klan activities in South Carolina. Her daughter's troubles were not with HUAC, so that comment is another indication that Mary did not reveal exactly what was going on. Augusta's 1948 letters suggest she was unaware of the first stage of Mary's case, not least because she tried to organize a family Thanksgiving dinner at the Marshalls' house even as Mary was facing hearings about her relationship to them; Augusta to Mary, Nov. 22, 1948, ibid.

67. Augusta to Mary, Oct. 2, 1952, carton 1, MDK Papers (the worst headlines about the case appeared on Oct. 1 and 2, 1952). Dad to Mary, Nov. 19, 1952, ibid. Mary's letters to her parents in this period have not survived.

68. Father to Leon, July 6, 1951, Keyserling Family Papers, College of Charleston.

69. Father to Leon, Sept. 21, 1951, ibid.

70. File 1.5, box 2, ibid.

71. On the planned visit, see Leon to Father, Oct. 22, 1951, ibid. William was speaking at the United Jewish Appeal. William Keyserling obituary, *Beaufort Gazette*, Nov. 1, 1951.

72. Dublin Keyserling testimony, July 20, 1951, pp. 4–5, Dublin Keyserling file, SISS Records.

73. Appointment books, 1951, 1952, unprocessed 1996 accession, MDK Papers.

74. SISS executive session, Oct. 18, 1952, p. 119, SISS Records. Leon explained that a new offensive against Crouch had not seemed necessary until word of Mary's suspension from the Commerce Department was leaked to the press in early October.

75. Leon Keyserling to SISS staff, Dec. 1 and Dec. 29, 1952, Leon Keyserling file, SISS Records; Leon Keyserling to Abe Fortas, Nov. 12, 1953, Keyserling file, Arnold & Porter Papers.

76. Leon did write an affidavit for Bauer, just as she had written one for him a few years earlier, but it is not clear that she used it. Leon Keyserling to Catherine Bauer Wurster, Aug. 14, 1953, box 26, Bauer Papers, Bancroft; Mary to Catherine, Sept. 15, 1953, ibid.

77. On fighting with Leon, see Augusta to Leon, May 15, 1951, and Augusta to Mary, May 17, 1951, carton 1, MDK Papers; Thomas D. Dublin interview with Storrs, June 17, 2000. Augusta's letters frequently mention Mary's health problems.

78. Augusta to Mary, June 11, 1950, carton 1, MDK Papers.

79. FBI Report of [name redacted], July 25, 1951, Leon Keyserling FBI file. As noted in chapter 4, the White House loyalty board shared some FBI reports with Leon during his investigation.

80. Willadee Wehmeyer, "Mary Dublin Keyserling: Economist and Social Activist" (Ph.D. diss., University of Missouri–Kansas City, 1995); Kathleen Laughlin, *Women's Work and Public Policy: A History of the Women's Bureau, U.S. Department of Labor, 1945–1970* (Boston: Northeastern University Press, 2000).

81. SISS executive session, June 14, 1951, pp. 220–26, SISS Records. SISS asked for earlier writings, and Leon said he did not have any. In fact Leon did have his earlier writings, but SISS would not have liked them; see note 60 above.

82. Within the Truman administration, rival factions disagreed on whether to militarize the response to the Soviet Union; that debate intersected with a conflict over the federal budget. Leaders of the pro-NSC-68 faction included State Department officials Paul Nitze and Dean Acheson; on the other side were George Kennan from State, Secretary of Defense Louis Johnson, and William Schaub of the Budget Bureau. NSC-68 was declassified in 1975. See Fred M. Kaplan,

"Our Cold-War Policy," *NYT*, May 18, 1980; Lester H. Brune, "Guns and Butter: The Pre–Korean War Dispute over Budget Allocations," *American Journal of Economics and Sociology* 48, no. 3 (1989); Benjamin Fordham, "Domestic Politics, International Pressure, and Policy Change: The Case of NSC 68," *Journal of Conflict Studies* 17, no. 1 (1997); Robert Collins, *More: The Politics of Economic Growth in Postwar America* (New York: Oxford University Press, 2000), 24–25.

83. Leon became acting chair of the Council of Economic Advisers in November 1949 and chair in May 1950. George Marshall was in jail from June through September 1950. For a claim that Leon lost influence during the Korean War mobilization, see Collins, *More*, 42. For a report that Truman was heeding Stuart Symington, chairman of the National Security Resources Board, more than Keyserling, see *Wall Street Journal*, Sept. 29, 1950, box 73, Keyserling Papers, HSTL. At a November 1950 National Security Council meeting, Keyserling and Symington both supported Acheson in calling for a bigger military effort than the Pentagon recommended; Melvyn Leffler, *A Preponderance of Power* (Stanford: Stanford University Press, 1992), 373.

84. Leon Keyserling, "We Can Have Butter and Guns," *Opportunity*, Feb. 1951, box 30, Keyserling Papers, HSTL.

85. Contrast Dublin Keyserling speeches of Mar. 3 and May 13, 1948, with her speech of Nov. 26, 1951, carton 2, MDK Papers.

86. Leon H. Keyserling to Harry S. Truman, Nov. 2, 1951, folder 1, box 1, Keyserling Papers, HSTL.

87. Leon Keyserling letter to editor, *Washington Post*, Dec. 14, 1951, copy in Leon Keyserling file, SISS Records.

88. *Fortune*, Feb. 1952, *U.S. World Report*, April 1952, clippings in box 73, Keyserling Papers, HSTL. Leon Keyserling to Charles Sawyer, May 14, 1952, box 111, Sawyer Papers, HSTL.

89. Collins, *More*, 42.

90. Progressives wanted universal programs, but conservative pressure killed them or whittled them down to veterans' benefits such as the GI Bill. Leon had advocated a bill whose benefits to rural dwellers would "significantly include farm workers, sharecroppers, migratory labor, and . . . those on public lands under the Department of Interior." The latter referred to Native Americans. LHK, "Homes for All—and How," *Survey Graphic* (Feb. 1946): 37–41, 63. The article promoted the Wagner-Ellender-Taft bill because it would "consider people's incomes before we start to build houses, and then tailor the product to the actual need."

91. Leon to Father, Aug. 31, 1938, and Jan. 22, 1946, Keyserling Family Papers, College of Charleston.

92. Dublin Keyserling to Bauer, Sept. 28, 1957, describing Leon's talk to the Federation of Metal Workers in Lugano, box 26, Bauer Papers, Bancroft.

93. Edmund F. Wehrle, "Guns, Butter, Leon Keyserling, the AFL-CIO, and the Fate of Full Employment Economics," *Historian* 66 (2004), quotation 737.

94. Americans for Democratic Action (ADA) was founded in 1947 as an alternative to the Progressive Citizens of America, on the basis that the latter's tolerance of Communist participation was politically and morally wrong. The ADA

appears once in Dublin Keyserling's 1948 appointment book (in February) and more frequently thereafter The ADA's historian says that Leon joined the ADA after leaving the Council of Economic Advisers in 1953, but Leon told SISS he had joined sometime not long after the ADA's inception; SISS executive session, June 14, 1951, pp. 185–88, SISS Records; Steven Gillon, *Politics and Vision: The ADA and American Liberalism, 1947–1985* (New York: Oxford University Press, 1987), 112.

95. Gillon, *Politics and Vision*, 112–14, 29. The collection was Quincy Howe and Arthur Schlesinger, eds., *Guide to Politics* (1954). In the late 1950s, Keyserling became a spokesperson for the "traditionalist" faction within the ADA, butting heads with a faction led by Arthur M. Schlesinger Jr. and John Kenneth Galbraith, who favored a more overtly partisan role for the group.

96. See, for example, Leon Keyserling letter to the editor, "Can't U.S. 'Afford' Superiority?" *Washington Star*, Sept. 9, 1958; Leon Keyserling letter to the editor, *Washington Post*, Dec. 17, 1958; Leon Keyserling letter to the editor, *NYT*, Oct. 2, 1959; "Democrats Hit Unused Plant, Men," *Washington Post*, Apr. 7, 1960; all in Leon Keyserling file, SISS Records.

97. In 1957 the Russians tried unsuccessfully to blackmail Joseph Alsop with photos of him in a homosexual tryst in Moscow; Athan Theoharis, *Chasing Spies: How the FBI Failed in Counterintelligence but Promoted the Politics of McCarthyism in the Cold War Years* (Chicago: Ivan Dee, 2002), 192–96. For the contrast with Galbraith, see "Democrats Hit Unused Plant," *Washington Post*, Apr. 7, 1960, and "Affluence and Poverty," ibid, Apr. 24, 1962; also Collins, *More*, 45.

98. Dublin Keyserling, "Speech on Peace Program at Smith," handwritten notes, Apr. 21, 1938, and "What Every Democrat Should Know about the Recession," Apr. 1958, carton 2, MDK Papers. For the Al Smith anecdote, see "Tribute to Mary Dublin Keyserling, 1958," ibid.

99. The resistance of Dublin Keyserling and Esther Peterson to public denunciation of the Equal Employment Opportunity Commission led Kathryn Clarenbach and Betty Friedan to organize NOW (the National Organization for Women). Dublin Keyserling supported NOW; the point of disagreement was whether it was appropriate for the U.S. Women's Bureau to criticize another agency. Cynthia Harrison, *On Account of Sex: The Politics of Women's Issues, 1945–1968* (Berkeley: University of California Press, 1988), 175, 186, 193; Laughlin, *Women's Work and Public Policy*, 112, 117.

100. "Keyserling Leaves ADA, Blasts 'Clique,'" *Washington Post*, Feb. 14, 1968; Wehrle, "Guns, Butter." Keyserling complained that the anti-Johnson clique in the ADA, led by Schlesinger and Galbraith, had built a wall between him and the Kennedy administration; Keyserling to Hubert Humphrey, Feb. 21, 1968, box 19, Keyserling Papers, HSTL; Leon Keyserling interview, 46, LBJL. For his critique of Johnson's economic policy, see "Keyserling Blasts Strategy of Poverty War," *Washington Post*, Mar. 25, 1964, and "Keyserling Denounces LBJ's Economic Policy," ibid., Feb. 23, 1966.

101. His father kept Leon's letters to him, however, and Leon's brother Herbert and Herbert's wife Harriet donated the entire family's papers in 2000 and 2005 to the Jewish Heritage Collection at the College of Charleston, Herbert's alma mater.

102. Appointment books, unprocessed 1996 accession, MDK Papers. Note 2 above identifies the missing pages and books. There is no way to know when Dublin Keyserling destroyed these records. On her obsession with her papers and shredding of documents, see Thomas D. Dublin interview with author, June 18, 2000.

103. Leon Keyserling interview, 3, LBJL. Senator Simpson joined Tower in opposing Dublin Keyserling's confirmation; *Congressional Record*, Senate, 88th Cong., 2d sess., Apr. 10, 1964, p. 7552. In her own interview for the LBJ Library, Mary told an anecdote about her appointment that omitted reference to the controversy and implied that she was on the job just a few days after President Johnson surprised her with the public announcement; Dublin Keyserling interview, 4, LBJL.

104. Leon and Mary Dublin Keyserling interview with Laura Kalman, 8, 22, in author's possession. See also Leon Keyserling interviews at LBJL, CCOH, and HSTL, and Dublin Keyserling interviews at LBJL, CCOH, WFGP, and with Arlene Winer, 1989, Barnard College Archives. By the time I interviewed Dublin Keyserling in 1991, Alzheimer's disease had impaired her memory, although she was composed enough to change the subject when I inquired about her alleged radicalism.

105. Wehmeyer, "Mary Dublin Keyserling." For critical accounts, see Harrison, *On Account of Sex*, 175–76, 186, 193–95; Laughlin, *Women's Work and Public Policy*, 95, 108.

106. Alonzo Hamby, "The Vital Center, the Fair Deal, and the Quest for a Liberal Political Economy," *American Historical Review* 77 (1972): 661–62.

107. See, respectively, Meg Jacobs, *Pocketbook Politics: Economic Citizenship in Twentieth-Century America* (Princeton: Princeton University Press, 2005), p. 244, Leon was a "committed Cold War anticommunist"; Alan Wolfe, *America's Impasse: The Rise and Fall of the Politics of Growth* (New York: Pantheon, 1981); Donald K. Pickens, "Truman's Council of Economic Advisers and the Legacy of New Deal Liberalism," in *Harry S. Truman: The Man from Independence*, ed. William F. Levantrosser (New York: Greenwood, 1986); Collins, *More*; Brune, "Guns and Butter"; Fordham, "Domestic Politics"; Wehrle, "Guns, Butter," esp. 734, Leon was an "avowed cold warrior." There has been little scholarship on Keyserling's early career, but see the more progressive Keyserling portrayed in Kenneth Casebeer, "Drafting Wagner's Act: Leon Keyserling and the Pre-Committee Drafts of the Labor Disputes Act and the National Labor Relations Act," *Industrial Relations Law Journal* 11 (1989); Casebeer, "Clashing Views of the Wagner Act: The Files of Leon Keyserling," *Labor's Heritage* 2, no. 2 (1990). Keyserling's obituary made no mention of loyalty accusations; *NYT*, Aug. 11, 1987.

108. Hamby, "Vital Center," 661–62. See also Craufurd Goodwin, review of Robert Brazelton, *Designing U.S. Economic Policy: An Analytical Biography of Leon H. Keyserling*, EH.net, Nov. 2001, http://eh.net/book_reviews/designing-us-economic-policy-analytical-biography-leon-h-keyserling.

109. On the disdain of women's liberation activists for the U.S. Women's Bureau and the National Organization for Women, see Ruth Rosen, *The World Split Open* (New York: Penguin, 2006), 84–88. According to Gillon, in the late 1960s

Leon "still adhered to the Vital Center" and was frustrated to be pushed aside by the "new liberalism"; Gillon, *Politics and Vision*, 210. James Wechsler was another 1930s radical who became a Cold War liberal and criticized the antiwar activists of the 1960s; see Robert Cohen, *When the Old Left Was Young: Student Radicals and America's First Mass Student Movement, 1929–1941* (New York: Oxford University Press, 1993), 321.

CHAPTER 6

"A Soul-Searing Process": Trauma in the Civil Service

1. With the help of Arnold, Fortas & Porter, the cases of Dorothy Bailey and John Peters reached the Supreme Court; *Bailey v. Richardson*, 341 U.S. 918 (1951); *Peters v. Hobby*, 349 U.S. 331 (1955). Johnston headed a subcommittee of the Senate Post Office and Civil Service Committee that held hearings in 1955 and 1956 on the administration of the federal employee loyalty-security program.

2. The Wright Commission was a bipartisan group authorized by President Eisenhower in 1955 in response to a rising chorus of criticism of the loyalty-security program. On the suggestion of Vice President Nixon, it was headed by the conservative former president of the American Bar Association, Loyd Wright. By the time the Wright Commission published its recommendations, court rulings had rendered them obsolete. *Report of the Commission on Government Security*, pursuant to Public Law 304, 84th Cong., as amended, June 21, 1957.

3. Confidentiality instructions to researchers are in folder 3, box 104, FFR Papers. On the lawyers' privacy concerns, see Ernest Besig to Adam Yarmolinsky, July 30, 1956 (quotation), folder 8. On HUAC's request for the names and on the FFR's destruction of records, see folder 4, box 107, especially Hallock Hoffman memo, Sept. 16, 1957. The approximately 100 cases in which former loyalty defendants authorized the FFR to release their names in 1956 to the Wright Commission are in folders 8 and 9, box 104, and the case summaries of 353 unidentified individuals are in boxes 105–7.

4. "Report on work in progress," Mar. 8, 1965, folder 7, box 4, Tillett Papers; quotation from Paul Tillett to Donald Meiklejohn, Apr. 13, 1966, folder 5, ibid.

5. Jacob Fisher, *Security Risk: A Memoir of the Fifties and Some Earlier Decades* (Sarasota, Fla.: Piney Branch Press, 1986).

6. Ibid. Cohen's copy ended up in the University of Texas library and happened to be the one I obtained through my university's interlibrary loan service.

7. Bernice Lotwin Bernstein to Parks Banta, General Counsel, HEW, Aug. 23, 1954, and James Forestel reply, Aug. 26, 1954, box 6, Bernstein Papers, HSTL. She was correct that being the subject of a full field investigation carried a stigma, regardless of the outcome. Loyalty officials held it against Thomas Blaisdell that he had been associated with many people whose activities "were sufficient to require full field investigation," even though those people were found to be loyal; IOELB examiner's report, July 7, 1955, p. 12, Thomas Blaisdell file, RG 478. See also Jean Flexner file, RG 478. On the organization's vulnerability to guilt by association, see Faith Rogow, *Gone to Another Meeting: The National Council of Jewish Women, 1893–1993* (Tuscaloosa: University of Alabama Press, 1993), 185–87.

8. Similarly, in requesting the president of Amherst College to vouch for his loyalty, Walter Gellhorn asked him to "please be a repository rather than a bulletin board. I detest being talked about." Gellhorn to Charlie Cole, May 31, 1949, box 302, Walter Gellhorn Papers, Columbia Rare Book and Manuscript Library.

9. Bernice Bernstein to "Reg," Jan. 17, 1955, box 7, Bernstein Papers, HSTL.

10. First quotation from Esther Peterson, *Restless* (Washington, D.C.: Caring, 1995), 86. Second from Jewell Fenzi, with Carl L. Nelson, *Married to the Foreign Service: An Oral History of the American Diplomatic Spouse* (Boston: Twayne, 1994), 117.

11. Ware probably referred to her friend Thomas Blaisdell, who had defended several accused subordinates. Ware to Helen Lockwood, May 2, 1954, box 130, Ware Papers, FDRL; Anne F. Scott, ed., *Pauli Murray & Caroline Ware: Forty Years of Letters in Black and White* (Chapel Hill: University of North Carolina Press, 2006), 102–4.

12. See Kathryn McHale FBI file; Susan Hartmann, *The Home Front and Beyond* (Boston: Twayne, 1982), 156; Susan Levine, *Degrees of Equality: The American Association of University Women* (Philadelphia: Temple University Press, 1995), 69, 74, 81.

13. Caroline Ware interview, 121N, WFGP.

14. Tex Goldschmidt to Alvin Wirtz, Oct. 23, 1948, American Legion folder, box 8, Goldschmidt Papers.

15. One anonymous writer told the FBI that "the Communist Caroline Ware" and two of her employees "laughed at your investigation last year. . . . Why not give their jobs to real Americans?"; postcard from "An American" to the FBI, Mar. 10, 1942, cited in FBI Report of Robert Welton, Sept. 1, 1953, Caroline Ware file, RG 478. See also Ware reply to interrogatory, Apr. 24, 1954, ibid.; Ware to Lockwood, May 2, 1954, box 130, Ware Papers, FDRL. For another example of vigilantism, see Michael T. Wermer file, RG 478.

16. Baker noted Goldschmidt's enthusiasm for the sharecropper cause and his closeness to the Communist organizer Rob Hall; CSC investigator's report of May 8, 1943, Goldschmidt file, RG 478. By contrast, Baker's 1954 affidavit states that in their twenty-two years of friendship Baker had always been certain of Goldschmidt's loyalty to the nation; May 27, 1954, affidavit of Jacob Baker, ibid. Goldschmidt's draft memoir affectionately describes Baker as a good friend despite their political differences.

17. Files of Arthur Goldschmidt, Mordecai Ezekiel, and Edwin Witte, RG 478.

18. Reply to interrogatory, Oct. 20, 1948, pp. 4–5, Jean Flexner file, RG 478. In 1959, Eleanor Flexner published *Century of Struggle*, a sweeping history of American feminism. See Ellen DuBois, "Eleanor Flexner and the History of American Feminism," *Gender and History* 3 (1991).

19. Department of Labor loyalty board hearing, Nov. 4–5, 1948, quoted in "Results of Investigation," Mar. 1954, Jean Flexner file, RG 478. For Beyer's comment, see FBI Report of July 6, 1948, p. 7, ibid. Flexner's husband Paul Lewinson worked for the Library of Congress.

20. Pauli Murray to Caroline Ware, Jan. 31, 1953, quoted in Scott, ed., *Murray & Ware*, 80–81.

21. See Esther Brunauer to Secretary of the Navy, May 10, 1951, and Stephen Brunauer affidavit, May 1951, Esther Brunauer file, RG 478. Also at issue was that Stephen had lived with Esther before he was divorced from his first wife. Although there were many allegations involved in the two cases, the morals charges were key to Stephen's resignation from the navy, and that resignation in turn was key to State's assessment of him, and thus of her. Case 326, folder 2, box 107, FFR Papers.

22. Case 325, folder 2, box 107, FFR Papers; "The Strange Case of Mrs. Brunauer," unidentified newspaper clipping, Oct. 27, 1952, box 21, Kohlberg Papers, Hoover Institution; "Esther Brunauer," *Notable American Women: The Modern Years* (1980), vol. 4, pp. 114–15.

23. Concerns about insufficient income recur in the private correspondence of Wilbur Cohen, Elizabeth Wickenden, Leon Keyserling, Pauli Murray, and Caroline Ware; see also Peterson, *Restless*. On the financial insecurities of a related circle of New Dealers, see Michael Janeway, *The Fall of the House of Roosevelt: Brokers of Ideas and Power from FDR to LBJ* (New York: Columbia University Press, 2004), 25.

24. One superior of Oliver Peterson's evaluated him as loyal but also recommended saving the agency trouble by finding someone with similar qualifications but less baggage. Ambassador Cummings, FBI Report of Sept. 30, 1954, Oliver Peterson file, RG 478. Another way agencies protected themselves was taking the first opportunity to dismiss employees on "reduction-in-force" grounds (RIF) if their clearance had been controversial. For examples of RIF discharges following loyalty clearance, see case 221, folder 4, box 106, FFR Papers; Lucy M. Kramer file, RG 478; and the discussion of Beatrice Braude's case in Stanley Kutler, *The American Inquisition: Justice and Injustice in the Cold War* (New York: Hill and Wang, 1982).

25. Scholars have not examined the "industrial security" programs, but see Ralph S. Brown Jr., *Loyalty and Security: Employment Tests in the United States* (New Haven: Yale University Press, 1958).

26. See materials in box 79, Emerson Papers, Sterling Library, Yale. Wilbur Cohen survived similar difficulties at Ann Arbor. On the more typical outcome, see Ellen Schrecker, *No Ivory Tower* (New York: Oxford University Press, 1986).

27. See Eleanor Bontecou, unpublished manuscript, box 10, Bontecou Papers, HSTL; Val Lorwin obituary, *NYT*, Dec. 11, 1982. Val's father Lewis Lorwin, a Commerce Department economist, also was threatened with perjury charges, as were Mary and Leon Keyserling and Wilbur Cohen.

28. See Dec. 1952 correspondence in folder 80, box 79, Emerson Papers, Sterling Library, Yale; 1954 correspondence in folder 2, box 3, Charlotte Towle Papers, University of Chicago Library. Other civil servants with passport problems in the 1950s include Walter Packard and Rowena Rommel.

29. John Peters to Dr. Sam R. Hall, May 27, 1953, folder 127, John P. Peters Papers, Sterling Library, Yale. Peters was a consultant to the U.S. Public Health Service as well as a professor of medicine at Yale.

30. Memo from Bureau of Personnel Investigation to Loyalty Panel, Oct. 30, 1970, Paul R. Porter file, RG 478. Gertrude Parks faced more difficulty with the

same process in 1964, although she eventually did get her pension; Gertrude Parks file, RG 478.

31. Leon Keyserling was certain his phone was tapped, as noted in chapter 5. Abe Fortas and other Washington officials operated on the assumption that their lines were tapped, according to Tex Goldschmidt, draft memoir, Kerr.doc., in author's possession.

32. Emerson obtained his own FBI file by FOIA request. It takes up two archival boxes. For photocopies from his 1939 address book, see folder 40, box 76, Emerson Papers, Sterling Library, Yale. Among the names in it were many in this book, including his old roommate Leon Keyserling, Lucy and Felix Cohen, and Margaret Porter Bennett.

33. *Carolina Times*, June 7, 1958, and other materials in folder 12, box 57, Aubrey Williams Papers, FDRL. Morrison Williams had parked in a bus stop while his father was addressing a meeting of the integrationist Southern Conference Educational Fund.

34. Jacob Fisher believed he was just one of hundreds of civil servants who lied on their loyalty forms by not disclosing their former membership in the CP. His rationale for doing so is explicated in chapter 7.

35. See her statement to the FBI, July 14, 1943, Nancy Fraenkel Wechsler file, RG 478; obituary, *Columbia Law School Magazine*, July 27, 2009. In private practice, she became an early expert on birth control law and wrote an amicus brief for the 1973 case *Roe v. Wade*. Her husband wrote for *PM* during the war and became chief editor of the *New York Post* in the late 1940s. Many scholars have written about James Wechsler as a leading liberal anticommunist, but none seem to have been aware of his wife's loyalty investigation or how it might have encouraged him to vocalize his anticommunism. See Kevin Mattson, *When America Was Great: The Fighting Faith of Postwar Liberalism* (New York: Routledge, 2004).

36. Esther Brunauer, "The 'Security Risk' System in the Federal Government," Mar. 1955, pp. 1, 15, folder 2, box 107, FFR Papers.

37. Peters to A. B. Lewis, Jan. 26, 1948, Loyalty Review Board appeal hearing, May 12, 1953, p. 66, John P. Peters file, RG 478.

38. Eleanor Bontecou, *The Federal Loyalty-Security Program* (Ithaca: Cornell University Press, 1953), 44–47.

39. Fourth Regional loyalty board hearing, Sept. 13, 1948, passim, and Loyalty Review Board appeal hearing, Dec. 8, 1949, pp. 49, 5, Dorothy Bailey file, Arnold & Porter Papers, Washington, D.C. The U.S. Supreme Court split 4-4 over Bailey's case (Justice Clark recused himself), which meant that the lower court's ruling against her stood; *Bailey v. Richardson*, 341 U.S. 918 (1951).

40. Peters to Joseph McElvain, Mar. 8, 1952, folder 126, Peters Papers, Sterling Library, Yale.

41. Loyalty Review Board appeal hearing, May 12, 1953, pp. 66–69, John P. Peters file, RG 478. Among the many allegations against Peters was the activism of his wife in the Emma Lazarus Club. Peters died at sixty-five in 1955, six months after the U.S. Supreme Court vindicated him in *Peters v. Hobby*, 349 U.S. 331 (1955). Peters received a flood of donations based on news coverage of his

case, and he generously settled Dorothy Bailey's legal bill; see Thurman Arnold to Peters, Oct. 1955, folder 122, Peters Papers. Meanwhile, an anonymous writer (who had confused the law firm's Paul A. Porter with Paul R. Porter of the Mutual Security Administration) urged conservative senators to investigate Arnold, Fortas & Porter because it hired Bailey; anonymous to Senator Homer Ferguson, 1952, Paul R. Porter file, Ferguson Papers, Bentley Historical Library, University of Michigan.

42. Loyalty Board to Secretary of Interior, Feb. 10, 1954, Ralph Russell file, RG 478.

43. "Low-down worm" quoted in biographical note in finding aid to Dorothy Kenyon Papers, Smith. Next quotations from Kenyon obituary, *NYT*, Feb. 14, 1972. For the headlines, see two folders of clippings, box 2, Dorothy Kenyon Papers. She had served as officer of the League of Women Voters, American Association of University Women, YWCA, Women's City Club of New York, and Consumers' League of New York; she was especially active in the ACLU. She had belonged to the American Labor Party but left when Communists took it over. In 1950 she was a registered Democrat as well an ADA member. Among the organizations McCarthy cited as evidence of her disloyalty, the LWS and Consumers' Union were prominent, along with various Spanish aid, Soviet friendship, and civil libertarian groups.

44. Ben Mandel feared McCarthy's attack on Kenyon would harm the cause: "Of course McC went out on a limb by opening up on Dorothy Kenyon who led the fight against the admission of the [Communist] Women's International Democratic Federation in the UN. . . . Was JB responsible for this mess?" Mandel to Stolberg, Mar. 9, 1950, box 6, Stolberg Papers. Publicly, however, Mandel stayed quiet as J. B. Matthews and Louis Budenz continued to challenge Kenyon's loyalty.

45. Eleanor Bontecou to Dorothy Kenyon, Mar. 10, 1950, folder 5, box 47, Kenyon Papers, Smith.

46. Dewson to Kenyon, May 9, 1950, and Kenyon reply, May 15, box 15, ibid.

47. FBI memo to White House, Sept. 22, 1964, Dorothy Kenyon FBI file (obtained by FOIA request, but a copy now is in her papers at Smith).

48. Kenyon, typescript of unpublished manuscript, "The Nightmare Decade," 3, folder 27, box 47, Kenyon Papers, Smith. Emphasis in the original.

49. Leon Keyserling, SISS executive session, June 1951, pp. 97, 124, SISS Records; notes for Mar. 16, 1950, hearing before Loyalty Review Board, box 64, Isador Lubin Papers, FDRL.

50. Fortas quoted from Fourth Regional loyalty board hearing, Dec. 21, 1950, p. 6, Rhea Radin file, RG 478. FBI Report of [name redacted], Nov. 29, 1949, Jane Hoey FBI file.

51. Scott, ed., *Murray & Ware*, 74, 78.

52. Reply to interrogatory, Apr. 17, 1954, Caroline Ware file, RG 478.

53. Reply to interrogatory, Mar. 18, 1952, Dorothea de Schweinitz file, RG 478.

54. IOELB hearing, July 2, 1954, Rome, 88, Mordecai Ezekiel file, RG 478. See also his obituary, *Washington Post*, Nov. 3, 1974. Supporters of people who were not Jewish but whose names sounded possibly Jewish sometimes delicately clarified the situation, as a hearing witness did for mathematician Constance Coorlim, and as Harold Ickes did for Tex Goldschmidt (see below).

55. Notes for Mar. 16, 1950, hearing before Loyalty Review Board, box 64, Lubin Papers, FDRL.

56. Fanelli recalled that the "degradation of the individual" during the hearings left him with severe headaches and nausea until he got used to it. Joseph Fanelli interview with Paul Tillett, Mar. 1, 1962, box 3, folder 9, Tillett Papers.

57. Bernice Lotwin Bernstein, HEW loyalty board hearing, Jan. 12, 1955, box 7, Bernstein Papers, HSTL.

58. "David Demarest Lloyd," *Encyclopedia of Biography* (American Historical Co., 1966), 414; "David Demarest Lloyd Biographical Material" [1952], Lloyd folder, box 110, President's Secretary's Files, HSTL.

59. Harold Ickes letter to Kerr Committee [1943], excerpted in Goldschmidt, draft memoir, Kerr.doc. Sympathetic witnesses emphasized Jane Hoey's devotion to Catholicism; for example, FBI Report of [name redacted], Aug. 2, 1954, Jane Hoey FBI file.

60. See the anecdote about his 1943 Kerr Committee hearing in Goldschmidt, draft memoir, Kerr.doc.

61. Bernice Lotwin Bernstein, HEW loyalty board hearing, Jan. 12, 1955, p. 201, box 7, Bernstein Papers, HSTL. CSC investigator's report of Mar. 1957, Lucy M. Kramer file, RG 478.

62. Federal Security Agency loyalty board hearing, Sept. 22, 1950, Mary Taylor Montgomery file, RG 478.

63. Military District of Washington loyalty-security board hearing, Jan. 22, 1951, pp. 130–48, file of Joseph Churchill Murray, Arnold & Porter Papers.

64. Notes for Aug. 26, 1953, hearing, "McCarthy-era hearings" folder, carton 19, Bauer Papers, Bancroft.

65. Wilbur Cohen statement, June 2, 1954, Wilbur Cohen file, RG 478.

66. Case 3, folder 2, box 105, FFR Papers. Also see case 198, folder 3, box 106, ibid.; Rhea Radin and Dorothea de Schweinitz files, RG 478.

67. Case 194, box 106, FFR Papers. Catherine Bauer reportedly spent about a year trying to clear her name, and her notes fill many folders. Bernice Bernstein gathered thirty-five affidavits and spent weeks preparing for her hearing; Bernice Bernstein to Frank Langley, Dec. 7, 1954, box 7, Bernstein Papers, HSTL.

68. Charlie to Walter, June 1, 1949, box 301, Walter Gellhorn Papers, Columbia Rare Book and Manuscript Library.

69. As noted in chapter 2, the OPA administrator Chester Bowles estimated that he spent one-third to one-half of his time defending his agency from congressional charges of subversion—and that was before the loyalty program was formalized in 1947; Thomas I. Emerson, *Young Lawyer for the New Deal* (Savage, Md.: Rowman & Littlefield, 1991), 218. On the program's direct administrative costs, see appendix 4.

70. FFR case summaries indicate that the lawyers often donated their time or provided it at drastically reduced rates. Even so, fees of $2,000 were not unusual for complex cases, when $10,000 was a very good annual salary for a government official, particularly for a woman.

71. Fenzi, *Married to the Foreign Service*, 117; Peterson, *Restless*, 89.

72. Case 225 (Esther Brunauer), box 107, FFR Papers.

73. Mordecai Ezekiel to Pierce Gerety, chairman, IOELB, Nov. 23, 1954, and other materials in Ezekiel file, RG 478; box 5, Mordecai Ezekiel Papers, FDRL. See appendix 2.

74. For example, see Leon Keyserling to Catherine Bauer, Aug. 14, 1953, box 26, Bauer Papers, Bancroft.

75. Thomas D. Dublin interview with author, June 17, 2000.

76. Peterson, *Restless*, 87; Esther Peterson, "You Can't Giddyup by Saying Whoa," in *Rocking the Boat: Union Women's Voices*, ed. Brigid O'Farrell and Joyce Kornbluh (New Brunswick, N.J.: Rutgers University Press, 1996), 78.

77. Mary Taylor Montgomery file, RG 478; Donald Montgomery obituaries, Oct. 1957, Vertical Files, Reuther Library, Wayne State University, Detroit, Mich.

78. Reminiscences of Charlotte T. L. Walkup, 75, CCOH. The distinguished English physicist Ronald Gurney died of heart trouble at age fifty-five, just after his investigation was reopened in 1953; Natalie Gurney to Eveline Burns, 1949–53, Burns Papers, SWHA.

79. The Washington metropolitan police put McHale under surveillance that continued until her death in 1956 at the age of sixty-six or sixty-seven. Agents and informants reported that McHale had large quantities of food and alcohol delivered for weekends that she spent in her apartment with three other women. Investigators believed McHale was struggling to hide a drinking problem as well as her sexual orientation; she allegedly discarded liquor bottles in the basement trash rather than her own. Kathryn McHale FBI file.

80. UPWA report, "Thought Control," Mar. 15, 1949, enclosed with Alfred Bernstein to Thomas Emerson, Apr. 22, 1949, folder 554, Emerson Papers, Sterling Library, Yale. Carl Bernstein, *Loyalties: A Son's Memoir* (New York: Simon and Schuster, 1989), discusses his father's career and CP membership.

81. Thomas I. Emerson and David M. Helfeld, "Loyalty among Government Employees," *Yale Law Journal* 58, no. 1 (1948): 142. For Emerson's oblique reference to his own experience, see p. 70.

82. See Emerson's FBI file, box 76, and materials in box 79, Emerson Papers, Sterling Library, Yale. One of those students was Ruth Calvin Goldman of the NLRB, who later became his second wife. See her reply to interrogatory, June 26, 1952, folder 80, box 79, ibid.

83. Walter Gellhorn, *Security, Loyalty, and Science* (1950), and *The States and Subversion* (1952); Bontecou, *Federal Loyalty-Security Program*.

84. Adam Yarmolinsky, *Case Studies in Personnel Security* (Washington, D.C.: Bureau of National Affairs, 1955). Asst. Attorney General William F. Tompkins to George Braden, excerpted in Yarmolinsky to Joseph Lyford, Sept. 30, 1955, folder 5, box 104, FFR Papers.

85. During the investigation, foundation staff lived under the threat of losing tax-exempt status and spent much energy complying with congressional requests

for information. On the Reece Committee investigation, see the "history" section of the finding aid to the FFR Papers. Princeton political scientist Paul Tillett claimed that the Fund for the Republic became more cautious after it was attacked in 1955; draft report, 1964, p. 9, folder 2, box 1, Tillett Papers. The Fund for the Republic funded another influential study, the *Report of the Special Committee on the Federal Loyalty-Security Program of the Association of the Bar of the City of New York* (New York: Dodd, Mead, 1956). Named for committee head Dudley Bonsal, the resulting Bonsal Report catalogued flaws and costs of the program and suggested reforms, but its polite tone and failure to call for reopening disputed cases disappointed program critics.

86. "Adam Yarmolinsky Dies at 77," *NYT*, Jan. 7, 2000; Walter Gellhorn file, RG 478. Given that Bontecou left government service in the late 1940s and was prominent in causes that got others in trouble (such as the fight against the poll tax), it is unlikely that she would have been able to obtain government employment in the 1950s. She never got the acclaim that men like Emerson, Gellhorn, and Yarmolinsky did, but her correspondence in the FFR Papers and elsewhere demonstrates that she was a key figure in the movement against McCarthyism.

87. "Statement by Senator Olin D. Johnston on Federal Security Program," press release, Oct. 7, 1954, Philip Young folder, box 1079, Johnston Committee Records; "Witness Charges 'Shadow-Boxing' in Risks Inquiry," *NYT*, Aug. 31, 1955; "Senators Assail Policy on 'Risks,'" ibid., July 22, 1956.

88. Hearings, June 23, July 7 and 14, 1955, box 1074, Johnston Committee Records; George McDavitt folders, box 1070, ibid. The details were even more lurid than reported in the press; McDavitt's staff claimed that he gave special protection and power to his allegedly bisexual and drug-abusing secretary, while coworkers at McDavitt's previous agency, the Displaced Persons program in Germany, insinuated that his German girlfriend was sexually deviant.

89. Joseph Fanelli interview with Paul Tillett, Mar. 1, 1962, p. 9, folder 9, box 3, Tillett Papers.

90. David K. Johnson, *The Lavender Scare: The Cold War Persecution of Gays and Lesbians in the Federal Government* (Chicago: University of Chicago Press, 2004), 214.

91. See UPWA report, "Thought Control," Mar. 15, 1949, enclosed with Alfred Bernstein to Thomas Emerson, Apr. 22, 1949, folder 554, Emerson Papers, Sterling Library, Yale. See also the joint statement by black, Jewish, Japanese American, and other groups requesting the dismissal of a loyalty official who asked Dorothy Bailey her view on blood supply segregation: Michael Straight et al. to President Truman, Apr. 19, 1950, "CSC: LRB" folder, box 17, White House Official File, HSTL.

92. Cases 331–38, p. A-1, folder 2, box 107, FFR Papers.

93. See Paul Tillett's 1962 notes on the case of agricultural economist Wolf Ladejinsky, taken from Johnston Committee Records; case 74 notes, folder 13, box 3, Tillett Papers. For another claim that the loyalty program discriminated against Jews, see Joseph Borkin interview with Paul Tillett, folder 9, box 3, ibid.

94. Case 288, folder 1, box 107, FFR Papers. I have not found protests of discrimination against Mexican Americans, perhaps because not many held government

jobs or perhaps because of the conservatism of the League of United Latin American Citizens.

95. Case 94 notes, folder 13, box 3, Tillett Papers. The attorney, Charles Lockwood of Detroit, had also represented Milo Radulovich, whose appearance on Ed Murrow's *See It Now* program in October 1953 may have been the first sign of the turning tide.

96. Files of William Pickens, Ralph Bunche, and E. Franklin Frazier, RG 478; Mary McLeod Bethune FBI file. In the 1980s, when archivists sampled about a quarter of the 2,400 "oversize" loyalty case files, they reported a "surprising" number of black loyalty defendants. Unfortunately their report did not give specific numbers or names, and the data sheets have been destroyed; see appendix 1.

97. For a wry account of these events, see Tex Goldschmidt, draft memoir, Kerr.doc.

98. See, for example, Walter White to President Truman, Nov. 26, 1948, White House Official File 252-K, HSTL.

99. "Bunche Inquiry Called a 'Farce,'" *NYT*, May 27, 1954; "Bunche Cleared by Loyalty Board," *NYT*, May 29, 1954. At eight boxes, Bunche's file is the largest in RG 478.

100. Henry S. Waldman, "In re: Frazier," Sept. 14, 1961, Frazier file, RG 478; emphasis added. He concluded, "the moral to be learned from the Bunche case . . . is to avoid headlining, if legally possible, and to treat this case as all others, and to guard against informants of the type we had in the Bunche case." Frazier had been investigated on earlier occasions, most extensively while he was on a short-term assignment for UNESCO in 1953–54; because that job ended before he was cleared, he was "flagged" and subject to full reinvestigation when he applied again in 1961. He also had been called before SISS in 1955. Frazier underwent surgery in 1961 and died in May 1962 at age sixty-seven.

101. Leila Rupp and Verta Taylor, *Survival in the Doldrums: The American Women's Rights Movement, 1945 to the 1960s* (Columbus: Ohio State University Press, 1990).

102. Boxes 1065–73, Johnston Committee Records. One wife did protest the fact that her activism in the Women's International League for Peace and Freedom had cost her husband his job at Shell Oil Co.

103. Malvina Lindsay, "Playing It Safe Trend," *Washington Post*, Mar. 22, 1950.

104. "Suggested Counsel to Employees under the provisions of Navy Civilian Personnel Instructions," enclosure with Adam Yarmolinsky to Dr. Hutchins, Apr. 15, 1955, folder 5, box 104, FFR Papers.

105. In an experiment at one dinner party, Fanelli found that people who eloquently discussed the safe topic of ethical relativism stared at their plates when asked about the wisdom of the NATO alliance. Joseph Fanelli interview with Paul Tillett, Mar. 1, 1962, p. 11, folder 9, box 3, Tillett Papers.

106. Affidavit of Joseph Fanelli, Sept. 1960, p. 5, attached to Leonard B. Boudin to Thomas Emerson, Jan. 27, 1961, in folder 535, Emerson Papers, Sterling Library, Yale.

107. Draft study, 1964, p. 75, folder 2, box 1, Tillett Papers.

108. Commerce loyalty board hearing, Mar. 16, 1949, p. 130, Curtis Warren file, RG 478.

109. Tabulated from 353 case summaries in boxes 105–7, FFR Papers. Loyalty program scholars Adam Yarmolinksy and Walter Gellhorn themselves faced questions based on their mothers' leftism.

110. Magdoff, folder 9, box 3, Tillett Papers. See also Rudolph Gentsch, folder 13, box 3; Alfred Evenitsky, folder 10, ibid. "Wife's laundry earnings" from Tillett's report on work in progress, Mar. 8, 1965, folder 7, box 4, ibid. See also case 137, box 107, FFR Papers, on a physicist who was denied clearance and relied on his wife's work as a stenographer.

111. Elaine Tyler May, *Homeward Bound: American Families in the Cold War Era* (New York: Basic Books, 1988).

112. On scrutiny of Truman "holdovers," see FBI internal memo from Mr. Callan to Mr. Rosen, Oct. 26, 1954, Kathryn McHale FBI file. On Murrow's view, see Reed Harris interview with Paul Tillett, May 1, 1962, folder 9, box 3, Tillett Papers. Walter Salant interview, 81–86, HSTL.

113. She called it an "educational organization dedicated to the principles of industrial and political democracy, and against all forms of totalitarianism including Communism." Reply to interrogatory, Sept. 30, 1950, Lucy M. Kramer file, RG 478.

114. Norman Thomas to Olin Johnston, Sept. 6, 1955, box 1076, Johnston Committee Records. Norman Thomas did once ask President Truman to state publicly his convictions that the SP was not subversive; Truman did not reply directly. Thomas to Truman, Feb. 23, 1951, "Loyalty Program" folder, box 873, White House Official File, HSTL.

115. The cases were *Peters v. Hobby*, 349 U.S. 331 (1955); *Cole v. Young*, 351 U.S. 536 (1956); *Greene v. McElroy*, 360 U.S. 474 (1959); and *Vitarelli v. Seaton*, 359 U.S. 535 (1959). See David Caute, *The Great Fear: The Anti-Communist Purge under Truman and Eisenhower* (London: Secker & Warburg, 1978), 292–93; Kutler, *American Inquisition*, 251n9; Ellen Schrecker, *Many Are the Crimes: McCarthyism in America* (Boston: Little, Brown, 1998), 294–97. Schrecker observes that, in these rulings, the Court relied on narrow, procedural arguments rather than on broad principles.

116. In addition to the general image problem of the civil service, the ninety-day clearance process discouraged many applicants. In 1954 the Bureau of the Budget's personnel director surveyed college professors because he was concerned about a drastic decline in the number of people taking the federal service entrance exam (from 1,400 in 1951 to 500 in 1953). Twenty-five respondents observed that "political attacks upon civil servants" had discouraged their students from pursuing government careers. Tillett notes on interview with HEW Personnel Director, 1962, and other materials in folder 12, box 1, Tillett Papers. For related numbers, see Schrecker, *Many Are the Crimes*, 371.

117. Even a sympathetic Reed Harris, himself reinstated by Murrow after eight years out in the cold (see Reed Harris file, RG 478), was not willing to stick his neck out for his employee Beatrice Braude as late as 1965. In the 1970s, the State Department continued covering up that she had been dismissed in

1953 for security reasons, not on reduction-in-force grounds; Kutler, *American Inquisition*.

118. Economist in 1955 from case 92, folder 13, box 3, Tillett Papers. Esther Brunauer, "The 'Security System' in the Federal Government," Mar. 1955, p. 9, folder 2, box 107, FFR Papers.

119. Benjamin Mandel to Warren Irons, Feb. 28, 1961, Wilbur Cohen file, RG 478; Mandel to J. Sourwine, July 8, 1963, Dublin Keyserling file, SISS Records.

120. "Adam Yarmolinsky Dies at 77," *NYT*, Jan. 7, 2000.

121. Handwritten notation on FBI memorandum from J. F. Bland to A. H. Belmont, July 26, 1960, Mary McCleod Bethune FBI file.

122. Henry Robbins, Alfred A. Knopf, to Eleanor Bontecou, Aug. 23, 1956, and Bernard Perry, Indiana University Press, to Eleanor Bontecou, Oct. 4, 1956, box 7, Bontecou Papers, HSTL.

123. Ironically, it was Adam Yarmolinsky of the now-defensive Fund for the Republic who threw cold water on Fisher's publication hopes. Yarmolinsky to Fisher, Sept. 16, 1957, folder 4, box 104, FFR Papers.

CHAPTER 7
Loyalty Investigations and the "End of Reform"

1. Ellen Schrecker, *Many Are the Crimes: McCarthyism in America* (Boston: Little, Brown, 1998), 368–86.

2. Ware to Dorothy Jackson, Oct. 30, 1943, cited in Grace V. Leslie, "'The Most Improbable Country': Caroline Ware, Puerto Rico, and the Origins of One Transnational Feminism," paper presented at the Berkshire Conference on the History of Women, Amherst, Mass., June 2011.

3. As such they were central participants in the international progressive intellectual networks so compellingly described by Daniel T. Rodgers, *Atlantic Crossings* (Cambridge: Belknap Press of Harvard University Press, 2000). On the continuities between the New Deal and U.S. international efforts during and after the war, see also David Caute, *The Great Fear: The Anti-Communist Purge under Truman and Eisenhower* (London: Secker & Warburg, 1978), 329; Elizabeth Borgwardt, *A New Deal for the World: America's Vision for Human Rights* (Cambridge: Belknap Press of Harvard University Press, 2005), esp. 6, 78.

4. For example, compare the work of the "revisionists" William Appleman Williams, Thomas McCormick, and Walter LaFeber to that of the "postrevisionist" John Lewis Gaddis.

5. Burton Kaufman, *Trade and Aid: Eisenhower's Foreign Economic Policy, 1953–1961* (Baltimore: Johns Hopkins University Press, 1982); David Ekbladh, *The Great American Mission: Modernization and the Construction of an American World Order* (Princeton: Princeton University Press, 2010); Nick Cullather, *The Hungry World: America's Cold War Battle against Poverty in Asia* (Cambridge: Harvard University Press, 2010).

6. Felix Cohen to Joe Lash, Dec. 10, 1943, folder 4, box 51, Lash Papers, FDRL.

7. See, for example, William Appleman Williams, *The Tragedy of American Diplomacy* (Cleveland: World Publishing, 1959).

8. Borgwardt, *A New Deal for the World*, 121, 19.

9. The cases of Lewis Lorwin, Charlotte Lloyd, and Catherine Blaisdell's husband Thomas are discussed below. Another example is labor economist Rhea Radin; see appendix 2.

10. Jack Lait and Lee Mortimer, *Washington Confidential* (New York: Crown, 1951), 103.

11. Michael Hogan, *The Marshall Plan: America, Britain and the Reconstruction of Western Europe, 1947–1952* (New York: Cambridge, 1987); John Bledsoe Bonds, *Bipartisan Strategy: Selling the Marshall Plan* (Westport, Conn.: Praeger, 2002); Greg Behrman, *The Most Noble Adventure: The Marshall Plan and the Time When America Helped Save Europe* (New York: Free Press, 2007), 303.

12. *Congressional Record*, House, 80th Cong., 2d sess., Mar. 29, 1948, pp. 3624–25. For the long list of personnel involved in the European Recovery Plan (ERP), see *Congressional Record*, Senate, 80th Cong., 2d sess., Mar. 11, 1948, p. 2528. For the flagging of Dublin Keyserling, as well as Goldschmidt and Blaisdell, see marked copy of *Interim Aid for Europe: Hearings before the Committee on Foreign Relations of the U.S. Senate* (Nov. 1947), 228, in Marshall Plan folder, box 154, Subject Files, SISS Records.

13. "Contributions to the development of the planning idea," annotated list [n.d.], box 15, Lorwin Papers. One obituary credited Lorwin's 1931 address with anticipating Truman's Point Four Technical Assistance Program; *NYT*, June 7, 1970.

14. Lorwin's major books on planning include *Economic Consequences of the Second World War* (New York: Random House, 1941); *Postwar Plans of the United Nations* (New York: Twentieth Century Fund, 1943); *Time for Planning* (New York: Harper, 1945). His earlier books include *Labor and Internationalism* (New York: MacMillan, 1929), and, with the assistance of Jean A. Flexner, *The American Federation of Labor: History, Policies, and Prospects* (Washington, D.C.: The Brookings Institution, 1933).

15. Edward R. Place, secretary to Congressman Samuel McConnell (R-Pa.), to Garfield Crawford, secretary to Senator W. Lee O'Daniel (D-Tex.), Dec. 17, 1947, and Place to Crawford, Dec. 23, 1947, Marshall Plan folder, box 154, Subject Files, SISS Records. O'Daniel was one of the ultraconservative Texas Regulars who tried to block President Roosevelt's reelection in 1944.

16. Cox also reported van Kleeck's 1931 statement that the goal of the Amsterdam conference was "complete reorganization of the present system into a planned, socialized economic order, creating a classless community." *Congressional Record*, House, 80th Cong., 2d sess., Mar. 29, 1948, p. 3625.

17. Ibid.; Edward R. Place, secretary to Congressman McConnell, to Garfield Crawford, secretary to Senator O'Daniel, Dec. 17, 1947, Marshall Plan folder, box 154, Subject Files, SISS Records. Lorwin told investigators he had changed his name because there were so many other Louis Levines, including a Communist author with whom he did not wish to be confused.

18. The *Chicago Sun* labeled his 1941 book with Random House, which was translated into Swedish and Spanish, one of the five most important of the year, according to "Dear John," May 1967, nineteen-page letter from Lorwin to his grandson, in unmarked folder, box 18, Lorwin Papers.

19. On his early encounters with Marxism and Russian revolutionaries, see ibid.; see also Lewis Lorwin file, RG 478.

20. Eleanor Bontecou, *The Federal Loyalty-Security Program* (Ithaca: Cornell University Press, 1953), 295.

21. Cox went on to fight the admission of displaced persons on the grounds they were "loafers and revolutionists" (Eleanor Roosevelt, My Day column, June 12, 1948) and to investigate alleged Communist influence over the major philanthropic foundations.

22. Lorwin to Secretary of Commerce Charles Sawyer, Dec. 5 and 6, 1951, box 12, Lorwin Papers. Cox's attack on Lorwin was preceded a year earlier by similar accusations, apparently intended to discredit Blaisdell and the Office of International Trade, from Reps. Alvin O'Konski (R-Wis.) and George Dondero (R-Mich.); see Lorwin to Blaisdell, Apr, 30, 1947, read into transcript of Commerce loyalty board hearing, Mar. 2, 1951, pp. 423–37, Lewis Lorwin file, RG 478.

23. Lorwin's support later caused trouble for Flexner; see Jean Flexner file, RG 478. For his admiration of her, see Reminiscences of Lewis Lorwin, 232, CCOH. Memo on Lorwin's recommendation of Dublin Keyserling submitted by Jim Walter to FBI, Mar. 19, 1948, Dublin Keyserling FBI file. On Rose Strunsky, see Commerce loyalty board hearing, Mar. 2, 1951, pp. 543–46, 836, Lorwin file, RG 478.

24. See Jean Flexner file, RG 478. On Val Lorwin's case, see Lucy Kramer Cohen interview, Helen Gahagan Douglas Project, Bancroft, and Eleanor Bontecou, unpublished book manuscript, box 10, Bontecou Papers, HSTL. According to FBI reports, Val was an SP member from 1935 to 1939. The State Department cleared Val Lorwin, but a federal grand jury indicted him for perjury in 1953; that indictment was later thrown out on the grounds that the prosecuting attorney had lied to the jury. Val Lorwin obituary, *NYT*, Dec. 11, 1982.

25. Lorwin to Charles Sawyer, Dec. 6, 1951, box 12, Lorwin Papers. A memo summarizing Lorwin's government service is missing the top section of the first page, disguising the fact that the memo was prepared as a "reply to interrogatory"—a fact only ascertainable through examination of Lorwin's loyalty case file at the National Archives.

26. Lorwin quoting from "Harvard Men March on F.D. with Red Flag," *Washington (D.C.) Herald*, Mar. 3, 1933, Reminiscences of Lewis Lorwin, 229, CCOH.

27. "Dear John," May 1967, nineteen-page letter from Lorwin to his grandson, in unmarked folder, box 18, Lorwin Papers.

28. Paul R. Porter, "From the Morgenthau Plan to the Marshall Plan and NATO: A Memoir Written for the Truman Library in 1984," 6, copy in box 11, Goldschmidt Papers. Also see "Thomas Blaisdell, Marshall Plan figure," obituary, *Washington Times*, Jan. 2, 1989.

29. See thirteen-page untitled career summary, "Personal: ECA" folder, box 8, Blaisdell Papers, HSTL; IOELB examiners' report, July 7, 1955, informant Washington T-15, p. 6, Thomas Blaisdell file, RG 478.

30. Joseph P. Lash, *Dealers and Dreamers* (New York: Doubleday, 1988), 217.

31. See thirteen-page untitled career summary, "Personal: ECA" folder, box 8, Blaisdell Papers, HSTL.

32. Ibid.; see also IOELB examiners' report, July 7, 1955, informant Washington T-15, p. 6, Blaisdell file, RG 478; Thomas C. Blaisdell, Reply to Interrogatory, Mar. 20, 1956, p. 13, ibid.

33. Blaisdell file, RG 478; obituary, *Washington Times*, Jan. 2, 1989. See also Gary May, *Un-American Activities: The Trials of William Remington* (New York: Oxford University Press, 1994).

34. Nathaniel Weyl, the organizer of the Morningside Heights branch of the SP, recalled that his friend and later boss Blaisdell was active in that chapter; Nathaniel Weyl interview with author, June 18, 2003. It is unclear how long Blaisdell remained in the SP.

35. Blaisdell Papers, HSTL; Thomas C. Blaisdell Jr. interview, HSTL.

36. Biographical details from Paul R. Porter file, RG 478. On his disagreement with SP foreign policy positions and resignation, see his correspondence with Norman Thomas, 1939–41, reels 9–11, Norman Thomas Papers, NYPL. As a result of Communist conduct during the Spanish Civil War, Porter regretted having welcomed the CP into the popular front against fascism; Porter to Thomas, June 5, 1940, ibid. On Upton Sinclair and Porter's first wife Eleanor Nelson, see Mary E. Harding, "Eleanor Nelson, Oliver Palmer, and the Struggle to Organize the CIO in Washington, D.C., 1937–1950" (Ph.D. diss., George Washington University, 2002).

37. "Dies Denounces New List of 'Reds,'" *NYT*, Feb. 2, 1943; memo for Board of Appeals and Review, Feb. 10, 1943, p. 5, Paul R. Porter file, RG 478. Not only was Porter's first wife a prominent Communist, but his brother James was a CP organizer in the mid-1930s; Paul claimed he had persuaded James to quit the CP.

38. "Free rein" from FBI Report of G. V. Hemelt, Feb. 17, 1947, Porter file, RG 478.

39. Paul R. Porter to Clarence Senior, copy to Norman Thomas, Apr. 23, 1946, reel 16, Thomas Papers, NYPL.

40. Paul R. Porter to Norman Thomas, Dec. 12, 1946, ibid.

41. Porter to Thomas, June 30, 1947, ibid. In the same letter, Porter hailed the proposed Marshall Plan but hoped the Soviets would not force the creation of a western European bloc; western Europe lacked the resources to maintain living standards, he believed, and might end up on the same course as prewar Germany and Japan, turning to militaristic dictators. He also did not want to see "all of Eastern Europe absorbed into the Soviet sphere."

42. Behrman, *Most Noble Adventure*, 57, 333.

43. Porter believed that the Economic Commission for Europe/Economic Cooperation Administration involved a lot of problems that Clayton did not understand

and did not prioritize. Paul R. Porter interview, HSTL. See also Thomas C. Blais-dell interview, HSTL.

44. Borgwardt overemphasizes the discontinuity between the UN agencies and the Marshall Plan, seeing the United Nations as a product of a "multilateral moment" that by about 1946 was supplanted by the Cold War spirit that produced the Marshall Plan. Borgwardt, *A New Deal for the World*, 51.

45. Quoted in Behrman, *Most Noble Adventure*, 303.

46. Ibid., 5. Michael Hogan notes Porter's influence but seems unaware that his advocacy of European integration was inflected by socialist views; Hogan, *Marshall Plan*, 36–42. Bonds, *Bipartisan Strategy*, highlights Republican opposition but does not consider socialist support as a factor.

47. *Congressional Record*, House, 80th Cong., 2d sess., Mar. 29, 1948, p. 3624.

48. The Mutual Security Agency was the successor to the Economic Cooperation Administration. Presumably because Porter's position at that time was beyond the purview of the loyalty program (the IOELB was not created until mid-1953), nothing appears in his RG 478 file about the events that forced his resignation. But see Porter file, box 14, Ferguson Papers, Bentley Historical Library, University of Michigan. For his suggestion that he resigned because he needed a higher salary, see Porter to Clarence Senior, Feb. 24, 1956, reel 30, Thomas Papers, NYPL. Porter may have been under additional pressure to resign because his first wife Eleanor Nelson, the Communist labor leader who remained under FBI surveillance, was in 1953 in the final stages of a losing battle with alcoholism; see Harding, "Eleanor Nelson."

49. On Porter's signing of a pro–Vietnam War statement in 1966, see CSC Report of Investigation, Nov. 1968, p. 6, Porter file, RG 478. When Porter applied for federal retirement benefits in 1970, examiners reviewed his record to see whether it contained loyalty grounds for denial of benefits (they concluded it did not); Bureau of Personnel Investigation to Loyalty Panel, Oct. 30, 1970, ibid. In 1964 Porter attended Norman Thomas's eightieth birthday gala, whose sponsors were attacked by the right; see reels 39, 47, and 81, Thomas Papers, NYPL. On his career as a professor of urban affairs at Cleveland State University, see Porter obituary, *Washington Post*, Apr. 24, 2002.

50. Paul R. Porter, "From the Morgenthau Plan to the Marshall Plan and NATO: A Memoir Written for the Truman Library in 1984," box 11, Goldschmidt Papers. Porter insisted he had "hit it off very well" with big businessmen. As an example he praised Walker Cisler, chairman of the board of Detroit Edison, for having supported a publicly owned power system in Greece; see Paul R. Porter interview, 73–76, HSTL. In fact, Cisler had tried to thwart public power in Greece; see Walter Packard to Abe Fortas, Apr. 20, 1949, box 6, Walter Packard Papers, Bancroft. Porter would have known the story; see Porter-Packard correspondence, box 8, ibid. Senator Ferguson's file on Porter includes a long complaint from an American businessman about MSA policy in Greece; "Dear Mr. Gehle," author unknown (apparently a Greek-American businessman), Aug. 14, 1952, Porter file, box 14, Ferguson Papers, Bentley Historical Library, University of Michigan.

51. The whereabouts of the three series of papers Porter withheld, according to HSTL archivists, is not known; two of his children did not reply to my repeated inquiries.

52. Paul R. Porter Papers, HSTL. Porter shared materials with a scholar of the radical student movement of the 1930s, but he himself is not mentioned in the text or index of the resulting book, presumably because he asked not to be; Robert Cohen, *When the Old Left Was Young: Student Radicals and America's First Mass Student Movement, 1929–1941* (New York: Oxford University Press, 1993), acknowledgments. Porter's 1933–64 correspondence with Norman Thomas is preserved in the Thomas Papers, NYPL.

53. Bauer and Douglas provided affidavits for him when he faced allegations of disloyalty in 1949; see Packard Papers, Bancroft. Packard's respect for professional women is further suggested by his support of the photographer Dorothea Lange, whose dismissal in 1939 he urged the FSA to reverse; Linda Gordon, *Dorothea Lange: A Life Beyond Limits* (New York: W. W. Norton, 2009), 298.

54. On Packard's conflict with senior U.S. officials allied with the Electric Bond and Share Co. of New York, see Packard to Abe Fortas, Apr. 20, 1949, with attached documentation, Fortas folder, box 6, Packard Papers, Bancroft.

55. Fortas to Packard, June 29, 1955, ibid. Packard was seventy when he resigned in 1954, but the Fortas correspondence suggests that loyalty issues, and not just age, may have influenced his resignation.

56. Truman's EO 10422 (Jan. 9, 1953) authorized the IOELB; Eisenhower's EO 10459 (May 27, 1953) set up the machinery. See testimony of Pierce Gerety, IOELB Chair, SISS executive session, Nov. 22, 1954, SISS Records; Caute, *The Great Fear*, chap. 16.

57. On the controversial 1950 statement by an interracial group of scholars working under UNESCO auspices, see Michelle Brattain, "Race, Racism, and Antiracism: UNESCO and the Politics of Presenting Science to the Postwar Public," *American Historical Review* 112 (December 2007): 1386–1413. On one list of 139 IOELB cases pending in the FBI's Washington Field Office, women represent at least 28 percent of the professional employees under investigation; Director, FBI to SAC, Washington Field Office, Aug. 18, 1953, in FBI file of Mildred Fairchild Woodbury, obtained by FOIA request by Ruth Fairbanks, whom I thank for sharing this document with me.

58. Testimony of Pierce Gerety, IOELB Chair, SISS executive session, Nov. 22, 1954, SISS Records.

59. Malvina Lindsay, "The Federal Diary," *Washington Post*, Aug. 11, 1944. Both quotations are from FBI Report of Apr. 8, 1953, Rowena Rommel file, RG 478. For Busbey's comment, the FBI cited *Congressional Record*, House, 80th Cong., 2d sess., Mar. 25, 1948.

60. Testimony of Pierce Gerety, IOELB Chair, SISS executive session, Nov. 22, 1954, SISS Records; Rommel file, RG 478.

61. Rommel file, RG 478, especially FBI Report of Apr. 8, 1953.

62. Mordecai Ezekiel file, RG 478; see appendix 2. The other cases are discussed below. Additional, anonymous examples: a "very important official of UN Secretariat" was cleared in January 1954 but lost $2,000 in fees and two

months' full-time work; a senior economist at the International Bank for Reconstruction and Development, against whom the derogatory evidence included his wife's League of Women Shoppers affiliation, was cleared in 1955 after fourteen months. Case 306, box 107, and case 126, box 105, FFR Papers. The limited scholarship on this episode focuses on the impact on some low-level former Communists in Paris; Caute, *The Great Fear*, 328.

63. Reminiscences of Isador Lubin, 137, CCOH. Lubin headed the Bureau of Labor Statistics under Frances Perkins from 1933 to 1946 before working on the Marshall Plan for the State Department and representing the United States on UNESCO (1946–53). Lubin faced a hearing before the Loyalty Review Board in 1950 but appears to have been cleared without great difficulty. Lubin did not mention that experience in his reminiscences, but see box 64, Isador Lubin Papers, FDRL.

64. See chapter 1.

65. According to his wife, Felix drafted the original bill for the wartime Fair Employment Practices Commission; "Felix S. Cohen," biographical sketch, Sept. 15, 1954, Felix Cohen Papers, Beinecke. On the intentions and defeat of the Alaska Development Plan to create, in effect, reservations for refugees from Nazism, see Dalia Tsuk Mitchell, *Architect of Justice: Felix S. Cohen and the Founding of American Legal Pluralism* (Ithaca: Cornell University Press, 2007), 145–62.

66. Felix Cohen, "Socialism and the Myth of Legality," *American Socialist Quarterly* 4 (Nov. 1935): 3–33. Although Cohen was credited as sole author, Kramer helped him write it. Paul R. Porter sent them a Christmas card congratulating them on their joint achievement; Paul to Felix and Lucy, Dec. 25, 1935, Lucy Kramer Cohen Papers, Beinecke.

67. By 1936, 181 native communities had voted to adopt Indian Reorganization Act constitutions, while 77 had voted not to; Paul C. Rosier, *Serving Their Country: American Indian Politics and Patriotism in the Twentieth Century* (Cambridge: Harvard University Press, 2009), 70. Cohen persuaded his superiors Nathan Margold and John Collier that tribal communities could use existing law to create socialist democracies; Kenneth R. Philp, *Termination Revisited: American Indians on the Trail to Self-Determination, 1933–1953* (Lincoln: University of Nebraska Press, 1999), 3–6. On Cohen's threat to resign, see his undated handwritten letter [unaddressed but apparently to Nathan Margold, 1934], folder 600, Felix Cohen Papers, Addition, Beinecke. Angry that his bill had been changed to keep the Interior Department, rather than Indians, in charge of administering Indian funds, he complained that the revised bill consigned 200,000 citizens to "endure a system of bureaucratic despotism" that was "akin to fascism."

68. The 2005 edition of the *Handbook*, which remains the standard reference work, was dedicated to Lucy, in belated recognition of her contribution; Lucy Kramer Cohen obituary, *Washington Post*, Jan. 5, 2007. See also the documentary film by Nancy Kramer Bickel, *A Twentieth Century Woman: Lucy Kramer Cohen, 1907–2007* (2011); Mitchell, *Architect of Justice*, 166–77, 222–26.

69. Cohen suspected that real estate interests with an eye on Indian land were the ultimate source of pressure for assimilation. Fortunately, he wrote, his colleagues in the Indian office "show a pretty steadfast desire to protect challenged

Indian rights against various forms of capitalist exploitation." Felix Cohen to Norman Thomas, Nov. 8, 1933, box 50, Lash Papers, FDRL.

70. Felix Cohen, "Indian Self-Government," *The American Indian* (Sept. 1949), quoted by Rosier, *Serving Their Country*, 151. On the links between Cohen's Jewish identity, his concern for Native Americans, and his contributions to legal pluralism, see Mitchell, *Architect of Justice*, 145–62.

71. Quotation from draft letter to Hon. Robert W. Kenny, President, National Lawyers' Guild [Sept. 1940], file 489, Felix Cohen Papers, Addition, Beinecke. Cohen explicitly disassociated himself from people who were resigning from the National Lawyers' Guild to distance themselves from the Communists "in the era of Martin Dies." He did not believe Communists should be expelled from the guild, but he was angry at stealth initiatives by Communists to take control, and at the "repudiation of the Popular Front." On the Institute of Living Law, see Mitchell, *Architect of Justice*, 179–83.

72. On the work of Cohen and Kramer in the national and D.C. SP, see boxes 18 and 19, Felix Cohen Papers, Addition, Beinecke. On Felix's resignation "formally but not emotionally" from the SP, see notes on interview with Lucy Kramer Cohen, Mar. 6, 1965, box 50, Lash Papers, FDRL.

73. According to Felix's former colleague Richard Schifter, Felix left when he recognized he would never be made solicitor, because the job was reserved for political appointees; Schifter e-mail to Gene Cohen Tweraser, Apr. 26, 2006, forwarded to author. Truman's sensitivity to charges of harboring radicals would have been a factor in the political reasoning against Cohen's promotion. Accusations of conflict of interest, later proven false, may have been another factor in Cohen's resignation; Philp, *Termination Revisited*, 44; Mitchell, *Architect of Justice*, 258. In 1948 the Department of the Interior honored him with a distinguished service award.

74. Mitchell, *Architect of Justice*, 256–73; Rosier, *Serving Their Country*, 150–59.

75. For Kramer's career, see Lucy Kramer Cohen interview, Helen Gahagan Douglas Project, Bancroft, and Lucy Kramer file, RG 478.

76. Kramer had been close to Gene Weltfish and named her first daughter after her in 1939, but in 1950 Kramer distanced herself from Weltfish and the Communist-influenced organization she headed, the Congress of American Women; reply to interrogatory, Sept. 50, 1950, Lucy Kramer file, RG 478. The State Department turned her down in 1957; ibid. For glimpses of her frantic job search, see Lucy Kramer Cohen Papers, Beinecke.

77. Lucy Kramer Cohen, "Felix S. Cohen," biographical sketch, Sept. 15, 1954, Felix Cohen Papers, Beinecke. After Kramer died in January 2007, her daughters Gene Tweraser and Karen Burke donated additional papers, many of which document the couples' extensive socialist activism into the 1940s. As editor of *The Legal Conscience: Selected Papers of Felix S. Cohen* (1960), Lucy did not select any of his more overtly socialist articles.

78. Lucy Kramer Cohen interview, 158–59, Helen Gahagan Douglas Project, Bancroft. Even the papers that were not deposited until after Kramer's death do not include her reply to interrogatory or other materials on her loyalty

investigation, which is all the more striking because she seems to have thrown out little else.

79. She observed that Secretary of Interior Ickes and John Collier were not socialists and were interested in reforming Indian policy before Felix was hired. Charlotte Tuttle Lloyd Walkup interview with author, June 12, 2006.

80. Ibid.

81. Notes on interview with Charlotte T. L. Walkup, June 18, 1965, box 50, Lash Papers, FDRL. Lash intended to write a biography of Felix Cohen but never did.

82. On their meeting, see Charlotte Tuttle Lloyd Walkup interview with author, June 12, 2006.

83. Ben Mandel, "The Big Shots," May 20, 1941, box 692, Matthews Papers. The right-wing congressman Eugene Cox (D-Ga.) charged in 1942 that Communists had infiltrated the FCC; the Dies Committee too accused several FCC employees. The FCC was trying to avoid oligopoly in the broadcasting industry and ensure that it provided high-quality educational programming. After FCC commissioner Clifford Durr publicized Cox's financial interest in the broadcasting industry, the FBI investigated Durr. Clement Imhoff, "Clifford J. Durr and the Loyalty Question: 1942–1950," *Journal of American Culture* 12, no. 3 (1989); Susan L. Brinson, *The Red Scare, Politics, and the Federal Communications Commission, 1941–60* (Westport, Conn.: Greenwood, 2004).

84. For the claim that the Navy and State Departments had not rated Lloyd eligible, see FBI Report of [name redacted], Nov. 23, 1948, David Lloyd FBI file. On his drafting the ADA constitution, see obituary, *Washington Post*, Feb. 12, 1962.

85. Since 1945, Charlotte had been working part-time for UNRRA in London. Shortly after the White House loyalty board rated David eligible in late 1948, she quit work. She later attributed this decision to the couple's adoption of a second child. But political concerns were a factor as well: after her husband was no longer in the Truman White House, she observed, "I thought I could go back to work." Notes on interview with Charlotte Lloyd, June 18, 1965, box 50, Lash Papers, FDRL.

86. McCarthy did not give Lloyd's name at first in 1950, but the press deduced his identity. See Hansen to Steelman, Feb. 11, 1952; Friedman thirteen-page summary of Lloyd loyalty file, Feb. 11, 1952; and Steelman, Acting Chair of White House loyalty board, memo clearing Lloyd, Feb. 25, 1952 , all in Loyalty Program folder, box 23, White House Confidential File, HSTL. A query about Lloyd's case from the Senate Subcommittee on Privileges and Elections (the Gillette Committee) generated debate within the White House; see Lloyd file, Feb. 7, 1952, box 10, Murphy Papers, HSTL. McCarthy simultaneously attacked Truman aide Philleo Nash, an anthropologist whose sister Jean was organizing an anti-McCarthy campaign in Wisconsin.

87. "David Demarest Lloyd: Biographical Material," Dec. 1952, Lloyd file, President's Secretary's Files, box 110, HSTL.

88. David Lloyd's FBI file describes his investigation up until 1950, but his archived papers do not contain anything to suggest the FBI would have a file

on him. Lloyd's large file of clippings about McCarthy does not include any discussing the attacks on Lloyd himself. Upon Lloyd's death in 1962, the Truman Library news release did not mention McCarthy's attacks; news release, Dec. 11, 1962, "Lloyd" Vertical File, HSTL. A biographical entry provides a genealogy that omits the radicals Henry Demarest Lloyd and Jessie Lloyd O'Connor from David's family tree; "David Demarest Lloyd," *Encyclopedia of Biography* (American Historical Company, 1966), 413–15.

89. The title of this section was inspired by Nancy MacLean, *Freedom Is Not Enough: The Opening of the American Workplace* (Cambridge: Harvard University Press, 2006).

90. Eisenhower appointee Alice Leopold (1953–61) does not seem to have faced loyalty allegations.

91. Annelise Orleck, *Common Sense and a Little Fire: Women and Working-Class Politics in the United States, 1900–1965* (Chapel Hill: University of North Carolina Press, 1995); Jennifer Mittelstadt, *From Welfare to Workfare: The Unintended Consequences of Liberal Reform, 1945–65* (Chapel Hill: University of North Carolina Press, 2005); Kathleen Laughlin, *Women's Work and Public Policy: A History of the Women's Bureau, U.S. Department of Labor, 1945–1970* (Boston: Northeastern University Press, 2000), 113. Cobble recognizes that Red scare politics drove Communist feminists out of labor activism, but she does not appreciate the extent to which the loyalty program ensnared noncommunist leftists at the Women's Bureau; Dorothy Sue Cobble, *The Other Women's Movement: Workplace Justice and Social Rights in Modern America* (Princeton: Princeton University Press, 2004).

92. Laughlin, *Women's Work and Public Policy,* 95.

93. On Friedan's CP affiliation, see Daniel Horowitz, *Betty Friedan* (Amherst: University of Massachusetts Press, 1998). On the voting registrations of Miller and her partner Pauline Newman, see Frieda Miller FBI file. On Peterson, see below.

94. "Frieda Miller," *Notable American Women: The Modern Period* (1980), 478–79; the author relied on an interview with Miller's partner Pauline Newman. Friends who wrote to Miller about her departure from the Women's Bureau assumed that partisan politics were the cause, and she did not dispel that impression. See correspondence in folder 167, Frieda Miller Papers, SL.

95. Frieda Miller file, RG 478.

96. For example, later in 1955, a complaint about Miller's radicalism from a former coworker at the New York Department of Labor led to further investigation; see numerous reports and memos, Aug.–Nov. 1955, Frieda Miller FBI file. Her loyalty case file was pulled about ten more times throughout the decade; Frieda Miller file, RG 478.

97. Brigid O'Farrell and Joyce Kornbluh, eds., *Rocking the Boat: Union Women's Voices* (New Brunswick, N.J.: Rutgers University Press, 1996), 78.

98. Jewell Fenzi, with Carl L. Nelson, *Married to the Foreign Service: An Oral History of the American Diplomatic Spouse* (Boston: Twayne, 1994), 118. Brigid O'Farrell and Joyce Kornbluh, who conducted numerous interviews with Peterson, observed that "her family's experiences with McCarthyism were clearly

difficult for her to discuss even in 1994"; O'Farrell and Kornbluh, eds., *Rocking the Boat*, 286n11.

99. Peterson's papers hold some FBI reports that summarize the allegations against her and Oliver, but they do not include records of the loyalty investigation. Her memoir and numerous oral histories do not mention the American Labor Party, for which she registered to vote from 1939 through 1943; FBI Report of Jan. 18, 1949, Oliver Peterson file, RG 478. The papers she donated include almost nothing on her organization of three New England locals for the left-wing American Federation of Teachers, but papers donated later by relatives provide some insight; see, for example, clipping from *Lowell Evening Leader*, Feb. 17, 1937, in folder 3431, box 146, Peterson Papers, 2005 accession, SL; also Esther Peterson, *Restless* (Washington, D.C.: Caring, 1995), 46.

100. "We never thought we were under any suspicion" until Christmas 1952, she recalled; Peterson, *Restless*, 84. But see Oliver Peterson file, RG 478. The 1949 clearance was made against the recommendation of a dissenting member of the State loyalty board. Esther later asserted, inaccurately, that after 1953 "Oliver was completely vindicated. . . . We had no problem"; O'Farrell and Kornbluh, eds., *Rocking the Boat*, 77.

101. Oliver Peterson file, RG 478. In 1957 Oliver was diagnosed with cancer of the lymph nodes; Peterson, *Restless*, 91.

102. O'Farrell and Kornbluh, eds., *Rocking the Boat*, 77–78.

103. Peterson, *Restless*, 60–61. Compare with "Esther: Disturber of the Peace," p. 25, folder 3409, box 145, Peterson Papers, 2005 accession, SL.

104. Peterson, *Restless*, 60–61.

105. Journal entries for Jan. and Feb. 1953, folder 27, box 2, Peterson Papers, SL.

106. *Women! It's Your Fight Too!* (Brussels: ICFTU, 1956), esp. 4, 9, 27, folder 387, Peterson Papers, SL.

107. During the 1930s, the Petersons had socialized with Charles and Mildred Kramer and with Henry Collins Jr. and his wife Susan B. Anthony III; Charles Kramer and Collins were named by Bentley and Chambers. See "Preliminary Report: The Consumer Movement," n.d., p. 9, file 66, Peterson Papers, SL.

108. Peterson, *Restless*, 130–34; quotation 24. Peterson's work on truth-in-lending legislation also angered the credit industry. Being attacked by the advertisers was the hardest point in her career, she later recalled; Peterson interview with Mary Dublin Keyserling and Caroline Ware, Feb. 16, 1980, p. 40, folder 14, box 2, Peterson Papers, 2005 accession, SL. See also unidentified reports, apparently written by advertising industry representatives between 1965 and 1967, folders 66–76, Peterson Papers, SL.

109. Quotation from Peterson, *Restless*, 131. Veteran consumer activists like Colston Warne urged Peterson to push harder on controversial issues; see Erma Angevine, ed., *Consumer Activists: They Made a Difference* (Mount Vernon, N.Y.: Consumers Union, 1982), 205. See also Esther Peterson interviews, 1968, 1974, LBJL.

110. Peterson, *Restless*, 135; Angevine, ed., *Consumer Activists*, 206.

111. For other cases in the Department of Labor, see Dorothy Bailey, Lucy Kramer, Jean Flexner, and Mary Taylor Montgomery case summaries in appendix 2.

112. Caroline Ware file, RG 478; Ware to Helen Lockwood, May 2, 1954, box 130, Ware Papers, FDRL. The two friends Ware confided in were Helen Lockwood and Pauli Murray. In reviewing the transcript of her oral history, Ware inserted some general remarks about McCarthyism, but she did not discuss her own case; Caroline Ware interview, 121L–P, WFGP.

113. Pauli Murray, *Song in a Weary Throat* (New York: Harper and Row, 1987), 103, 294–97. On Murray's "Lovestoneite" affiliation in 1936 and 1937, see her affidavit for admission to the New York State Bar, May 7, 1948, folder 1246, Murray Papers, SL.

114. MacLean, *Freedom Is Not Enough*, 120–21. Pauli Murray and Mary Eastwood, "Jane Crow and the Law: Sex Discrimination and Title VII," *George Washington Law Review* 34 (Dec. 1965): 232–56.

115. See Glenda Gilmore, *Defying Dixie: The Radical Roots of Civil Rights* (New York: W. W. Norton, 2008), 442. Murray managed to exert pressure on the Equal Employment Opportunity Commission from outside by calling for the formation of a women's equivalent to the NAACP to make the agency do its job. The result was the National Organization for Women (NOW), which Murray helped Betty Friedan organize in 1966. A year later, Murray quit NOW when Friedan insisted that it support the equal rights amendment, which Murray believed would help professional women at the expense of working-class ones. MacLean, *Freedom Is Not Enough*, 128, 150.

116. On the liberal and radical wings of the second-wave women's movement, see, for example, Sara Evans, *Personal Politics: The Roots of Women's Liberation in the Civil Rights Movement and the New Left* (New York: Vintage, 1979); Ruth Rosen, *The World Split Open* (New York: Penguin, 2006). Recent scholarship that challenges that conceptualization, as well as the periodization of "first-wave" and "second-wave" feminism, includes Horowitz, *Betty Friedan*; Landon R. Y. Storrs, "Red Scare Politics and the Suppression of Popular Front Feminism: The Loyalty Investigation of Mary Dublin Keyserling," *Journal of American History* 90, no. 2 (2003); Nancy Hewitt, ed., *No Permanent Waves: Recasting Histories of U.S. Feminism* (New Brunswick, N.J.: Rutgers University Press, 2010).

117. Bauer and Keyserling, the key drafters of the 1937 act, had to accept many compromises to get it passed. Nonetheless, historians generally have agreed with Bauer's assessment of the act's significance. Don Parson, *Making a Better World: Public Housing, the Red Scare, and the Direction of Modern Los Angeles* (Minneapolis: University of Minnesota Press, 2005), 17–18, x.

118. For Bauer's influence on her husband, see ibid., xi.

119. Among the most vociferous opponents of public housing were the U.S. Chamber of Commerce and the National Association of Real Estate Boards. Gail Radford, *Modern Housing for America: Policy Struggles in the New Deal Era* (Chicago: University of Chicago Press, 1996), 180–91, quotation 200. Radford's larger point is that the flawed, two-tier housing policy implemented in the United States was not inevitable. See also Mary Susan Cole, "Catherine Bauer and the

Public Housing Movement, 1926–1937" (Ph.D. diss., George Washington University, 1975), 658.

120. H. Peter Overlander and Eva Newbrun, *Houser: The Life and Work of Catherine Bauer* (Vancouver: University of British Columbia Press, 1999), 252–60. "McCarthy era" files, carton 19, Bauer Papers, Bancroft.

121. Bauer, "Proposed: A Federal-Local Pilot Program"; Leon to Catherine, Dec. 24, 1953, box 26, Bauer Papers, Bancroft.

122. Bauer, "The Dreary Deadlock of Public Housing," *Architectural Forum* (May 1957), discussed in Overlander and Newbrun, *Houser*, 269–71. The latter is the only study to note Bauer's husband's loyalty investigation. The authors interpret Bauer's 1957 article as a surprising reversal in her views, but they do not consider whether the change might have been induced by the investigation.

123. Overlander and Newbrun, *Houser*, 260.

124. See Schrecker, *Many Are the Crimes*, 383–86; Jane Pacht Brickman, "'Medical McCarthyism': The Physicians' Forum and the Cold War," *Journal of the History of Medicine* 49 (1994); Colin Gordon, *Dead on Arrival* (Princeton: Princeton University Press, 2003); Jill Quadagno, *One Nation Uninsured* (New York: Oxford University Press, 2005); Michael Reisch and Janice Andrews, *The Road Not Taken: A History of Radical Social Work* (Philadelphia: Brunner-Routledge, 2001).

125. Edward Berkowitz, *Mr. Social Security: The Life of Wilbur J. Cohen* (Lawrence: University Press of Kansas, 1995); Mittelstadt, *From Welfare to Workfare*.

126. See Shearon file, box 50, Isidore Falk Papers, Sterling Library, Yale.

127. Jacob Fisher, *Security Risk: A Memoir of the Fifties and Some Earlier Decades* (Sarasota, Fla.: Piney Branch Press, 1986), 188, 207.

128. Alan Derickson, "The House of Falk: The Paranoid Style in American Health Politics," *American Journal of Public Health* 87 (1997); Gordon, *Dead on Arrival*, 145. Shearon had interpreted Cohen's and Falk's supplying of factual material to nongovernmental supporters of their national health insurance bill as evidence of a subversive conspiracy. See finding aid to Falk Papers; Falk statement to FBI agents, Dec. 1, 1947, and Cohen statement to FBI agents, Dec. 11, 1947, both in file 335, box 49, Falk Papers, Sterling Library, Yale.

129. Reisch and Andrews, *The Road Not Taken*, 92; Wendy B. Posner, "*Common Human Needs*: A Story from the Prehistory of Government by Special Interest," *Social Service Review* 69, no. 2 (1995). Towle was permanently embittered over Oscar Ewing's failure to back her; Towle Papers, University of Chicago Library. Hoey hung on until 1953, when Eisenhower appointee Oveta Culp Hobby dismissed her; see "Mrs. Hobby Ousts Key Aide from Policy Job," *NYT*, Nov. 4, 1953; Jane Hoey FBI file.

130. Falk left in December 1953, but his resignation was not official until October 1954. He consulted for the World Bank and for the United Steel Workers before becoming a professor of public health at Yale in 1961. The World Bank job brought him before the IOELB; see Falk affidavit, July 7, 1954, file 314, box 48, Falk Papers, Sterling Library, Yale.

131. Fisher, *Security Risk*.

132. Ibid., 224, 27. Derickson does not discuss the post-1948 developments in Fisher's case.

133. Mittelstadt and Berkowitz observe that Cohen's analysis of the causes of poverty became less structural over time; Mittelstadt, *From Welfare to Workfare*; Berkowitz, *Mr. Social Security*.

134. Berkowitz, *Mr. Social Security*, 97–99. Marjorie Shearon, *Wilbur J. Cohen, the Pursuit of Power* (Washington, D.C.: Gray, 1967).

135. Wilbur Cohen file, RG 478.

136. In addition to applying to the United Nations, Cohen applied for academic fellowships and also proposed forming a social security association, headed by him, that would publish Wickenden's book-in-progress. See Wilbur Cohen letters to Wickenden, Mar. 1953–Feb. 1954, folder 5, box 2, Wickenden Papers M99–098.

137. See appendix 3.

138. Wilbur Cohen file, RG 478. Quotation from a former employee of Eloise Bittel, FBI Report of June 2, 1948, ibid. Also see Berkowitz, *Mr. Social Security*, 44.

139. Wilbur Cohen and Michael Wermel files, RG 478; Wermel obituary, http://www.casact.org/pubs/proceed/proceed62/62235.pdf (accessed September 25, 2010). Most of Wermel's associates unequivocally asserted his loyalty, but two anonymous ex-Communist FBI informants declared he had been a CP member; he resigned in exhaustion after multiple rounds of self-defense.

140. Shearon's charges followed Cohen to Ann Arbor and initially made his life difficult there as well; Berkowitz, *Mr. Social Security*, 97. On Cohen's return to government, see Benjamin Mandel to Warren Irons, U.S. Civil Service Commission, Feb. 28, 1961, Wilbur Cohen file, RG 478.

141. "The University of Michigan, 1956–1960," file 2, box 279, Wilbur J. Cohen Papers, SHSW. See also Wilbur J. Cohen interview, 29–33, LBJL.

142. Cohen's son Bruce found materials related to the early phases of investigation in the attic of his father's Ann Arbor house; Berkowitz, *Mr. Social Security*, 344n23.

143. Ibid., 315–18.

144. Ibid., 318–19. Unaware that the loyalty program ensnared Cohen and Wickenden, Mittelstadt argues that until 1946 they favored a comprehensive welfare state, including noncategorical public assistance, but that after 1946 the increased power of congressional conservatives led them to give up on that and work for ADC reform instead. Mittelstadt, *From Welfare to Workfare*.

145. Bernice Bernstein interview, WFGP; Bernice Bernstein obituary, *NYT*, Mar. 2, 1996.

146. Bernard Bernstein interview, HSTL; Bernice Bernstein interview, WFGP; Bernice L. Bernstein FBI file; Bernice Bernstein notes in preparation for HEW security board hearing, folder 3, box 7, Bernstein Papers, HSTL. Another possible factor in accusations against Bernard was his drive to seize Nazi assets in neutral countries and de-cartelize German industry, which brought him into conflict with other U.S. officials; see Martin Lorenz-Meyer, *Safehaven: The Allied Pursuit of Nazi Assets Abroad* (Columbia: University of Missouri Press, 2007), 165–76.

147. Edwin Witte file, RG 478. The detailed finding aid to Witte's papers at SHSW does not suggest that those papers include loyalty-related materials.

148. Wickenden interviewed by Jean Bandler, Dec. 5, 1986, p. 15, box 16, Wickenden Papers.

149. Wickenden was under scrutiny when she left the National Youth Administration. Her boss's response to her resignation seems written to protect her from loyalty allegations. He lauded her for "seven years of incomparable service," during which she "evinced a patriotic devotion to the highest ideals of American life and gave the fullest loyalty to the organization." Aubrey Williams to "My Dear Miss Wickenden," June 29, 1940, box 25, Aubrey Williams Papers, FDRL. Civil Service Commission investigators "flagged" her file on July 3, 1941; CSC form 2462, Arthur Goldschmidt file, RG 478. The next year, however, they rated her eligible for a consulting position to the Office of Emergency Management; see CSC to Wickenden, July 10, 1942, folder 16, box 1, Wickenden Papers M2001–090. Her diary and other unpublished wartime writings suggest she quit out of frustration that as a woman she would not get the promotions she deserved and that as the wife of another federal employee she would not get the salary she deserved.

150. Wickenden later told an interviewer that investigators "knew about her alright" and used her against her husband. Because Goldschmidt had "so much hassle—always got out of it in good shape, but a lot of hassle—I was particularly sensitive." Wickenden interview by Jean Bandler, Dec. 5, 1986, p. 16, box 16, Wickenden Papers.

151. Berkowitz, *Mr. Social Security*, 53–54; Mittelstadt, *From Welfare to Workfare*; Andrew Morris, "The Voluntary Sector's War on Poverty," *Journal of Policy History* 16, no. 4 (2004).

152. John Salmond, *A Southern Rebel: The Life and Times of Aubrey Willis Williams* (Chapel Hill: University of North Carolina Press, 1983), 93.

153. Wickenden diary entry, Jan. 15, 1940, Wickenden Papers M2001–090.

154. Wickenden interview by Jean Bandler, Dec. 5, 1986, p. 13, box 16, Wickenden Papers. See also Wickenden, "Departure from the NYA," memoir draft fragment, folder 17, box 1, Wickenden Papers MS2001–090.

155. Williams's wife treated Wickenden as "the other woman" and later discouraged Williams's biographer from contacting her; Reminiscences of Arthur Goldschmidt , 144, CCOH; see also Arthur Goldschmidt testimony before Subcommittee of Special House Committee on Un-American Activities, Apr. 7, 1943, p. 167, Goldschmidt file, RG 478. "Brilliant and beautiful" is from Salmond, *Southern Rebel*, 67.

156. Goldschmidt, draft memoir, workrelief.doc., in author's possession.

157. Goldschmidt, draft memoir, Dies story doc, in author's possession.

158. Goldschmidt, draft memoir 7 Me and LBJ.doc, in author's possession. Alvin Wirtz was a liberal Texas legislator and organizer of the Lower Colorado River Authority. The last sentence is from a different version of the same story, in Ickes years.doc. Wickenden had a miscarriage in about 1940, and her hard-driving pace during her subsequent pregnancies worried her husband. She had been hospitalized for overwork in 1936; see Wick to Tex, Dec. 1936, box 6, Goldschmidt Papers.

159. See Arthur and Elizabeth Wickenden Goldschmidt interview, Elizabeth Wickenden Goldschmidt interview, Wilbur J. Cohen interview, all LBJL.

160. "Grand design" from Berkowitz, *Mr. Social Security*, 53–54. Fauri was the social security consultant to the pertinent House and Senate committees. Wicken-

den, "Reminiscences on Social Insurance," *Social Insurance Update* (Mar. 1993), folder 18, box 1, Wickenden Papers M2001–090.

161. Wilbur to Wicky, Oct. 2, 1953, folder 5, box 2, Wickenden Papers M99–098.

162. Wickenden, "Reminiscences on Social Insurance," *Social Insurance Update* (Mar. 1993), folder 18, box 1, Wickenden Papers M2001–090. Wickenden memo, "Political Implications of HR 7225," 1956, with explanatory cover note dated Dec. 4, 1985, folder 19, box 1, ibid.

163. See Arthur and Elizabeth Wickenden Goldschmidt interview, Elizabeth Wickenden Goldschmidt interview, and Wilbur J. Cohen interview, all LBJL.

164. Wickenden to Cohen, May 19, 1961 (marked "Restricted), file 5, box 2, Wickenden Papers M99–098.

165. Rickie Lee Solinger, *Wake Up Little Susie* (New York: Routledge, 1992); Gwendolyn Mink, *Welfare's End* (Ithaca: Cornell University Press, 1998).

166. See Lisa Levenstein, "From Innocent Children to Unwanted Migrants and Unwed Moms: Two Chapters in the Public Discourse on Welfare in the United States, 1960–1961," *Journal of Women's History* 11 (2000).

167. On Cohen's embrace of work requirements for AFDC mothers and his important role in 1962, see Mittelstadt, *From Welfare to Workfare*, 102–3.

168. Wickenden, "Social Welfare and the Radical Right," outline for unidentified presentation, Jan. 26, 1962, folder 19, box 1, Wickenden Papers.

169. Wickenden to Abe [Fortas], Nov. 23, 1967, folder 10, box 2, Wickenden Papers M99–098. On Wickenden's defense of welfare mothers against Senator Long at that hearing, see Alice Kessler-Harris, *In Pursuit of Equity* (New York: Oxford University Press, 2001), 273.

170. Elizabeth Wickenden, "Poverty and the Law," Memorandum for the National Social Welfare Assembly, Feb. 25, 1963, folder 7, box 2, Wickenden Papers.

171. Lloyd C. Gardner, *Pay Any Price: Lyndon Johnson and the Wars for Vietnam* (Chicago: Ivan Dee, 1995), 108–10. Angry mayors and congressmen thwarted the initially successful Community Action Programs, notably in Newark and Mississippi. Wickenden regretted that the Economic Opportunity Act of 1964 and the 1967 Social Security amendments repudiated the New Deal principle that public welfare funds should be expended only by public agencies; Morris, "The Voluntary Sector's War on Poverty." At the Office of Economic Opportunity during the Nixon years, Hilda Smith's supervisors were reinventing the wheel. As Caroline Ware reported, Smith found that "ghetto residents are being subjected to professional lectures and academic jargon, in various top-down, manipulative fashions, only by accident of some good local initiative getting at people's needs in their own terms. Undaunted, she cheerfully calls this to her new boss's attention, he finds it a revelation, never of course having heard of any of the things learned long ago in workers' education. He asks her to prepare a manual . . . so here she is ready to pick up again back where we all came in 50 years ago." Caroline Ware to Helen Lockwood, Apr. 2, 1970, box 130, Ware Papers, FDRL.

172. Felicia Kornbluh review of Mittelstadt, *From Welfare to Workfare*, in *Journal of American History* 92, no. 4 (2006): 1517. Mittelstadt describes

Wickenden as nonfeminist based on a misunderstanding of why she declined to be identified as feminist; Mittelstadt, *From Welfare to Workfare*, 136.

173. Robert A. Caro, *Master of the Senate: The Years of Lyndon Johnson* (New York: Vintage, 2002), 240. Johnson waxed eloquent about what electric washing machines meant to Hill Country women like his mother.

174. There were, of course, many public works programs that were not related to public power. See Jason Scott Smith, *Building New Deal Liberalism: The Political Economy of Public Works, 1933–1956* (New York: Cambridge University Press, 2006).

175. Wirtz to Goldschmidt, June 26, 1939, box 6, Goldschmidt Papers. Although Wirtz's wording might suggest otherwise, Texas Power & Light was the opposition. See also Arthur and Elizabeth Wickenden Goldschmidt interview, LBJL. Fortas moved from assistant director of the SEC's Public Utilities Division to general counsel of the Public Works Administration. The three would work together in developing the Lower Colorado River Authority in Johnson's congressional district.

176. In the interim, Fortas was Goldschmidt's boss at the Bituminous Coal Commission, the Power Policy Committee, and the Power Division.

177. Concerned that public policy was enhancing the dominance of California's large growers, Taylor and his allies sought to enforce a provision of the 1902 Reclamation Act holding that an individual landowner could receive only enough water to irrigate 160 acres. Gordon, *Dorothea Lange*, 354–55, 505n26.

178. "Dies Denounces New List of 'Reds,'" *NYT*, Feb. 2, 1943.

179. Goldschmidt, draft memoir, 6 Kerr.doc, in author's possession. Congressman John Kerr (D-N.C.) headed the House committee.

180. Packard to Goldschmidt, Feb. 18, 1943, "Personal Correspondence," box 4, Goldschmidt Papers.

181. Goldschmidt, draft memoir, 6 Kerr.doc.

182. See materials in "American Legion attack 1948" folder, box 8, Goldschmidt Papers.

183. Reminiscences of Arthur Goldschmidt, 398, CCOH.

184. Goldschmidt, draft memoir, Point Four. doc, in author's possession.

185. Reminiscences of Arthur Goldschmidt, 536, CCOH.

186. Goldschmidt file, RG 478. His reply to interrogatory also is in "Loyalty—UN 1954–55" folder, box 10, Goldschmidt Papers. Elizabeth Bentley named Weintraub as a CP member in the late 1930s. An informant alleged that Weintraub hoped Goldschmidt would keep the United States committed to the United Nations' Technical Assistance Administration rather than the State Department's Point Four program. At his hearing, Goldschmidt said that Weintraub had not gotten him any job but also, bravely, that Weintraub should not have resigned.

187. See "Personal letters, 1954," box 2, Goldschmidt Papers. Wickenden to Max Ascoli, Editor, April 30, 1954, folder 1, box 1, Wickenden Papers M2001-090.

188. Goldschmidt, draft memoir, work relief.doc, in author's possession. Unlike most loyalty defendants, Goldschmidt and Wickenden did not later denounce the CP at every opportunity, perhaps because they outlived the Cold

War. On Goldschmidt's leftism at Columbia, see scattered materials in box 13, Goldschmidt Papers. The presence of a blank CP membership card is consistent with his memoir's claim that Rob Hall invited him to join but he declined. Along with CP members Hall and Don Henderson, Goldschmidt headed the Social Problems Club in 1932 (the same club about which Mary Dublin and many others were interrogated).

189. He was director, Programme Division, Technical Assistance Administration (1954–58, on leave 1957 as chief, UN Mission on Resources and Industry to Iran); director, Bureau of Technical Assistance Operations, Department of Economic and Social Affairs (ECOSOC; 1958–59); and then director, Special Fund Operations, ECOSOC (1959–66). Immediately after he became president, Johnson tried unsuccessfully to recruit Goldschmidt to his administration; see Goldschmidt, draft memoir, 7 Me and LBJ.doc, description of Dec. 1, 1963, dinner with the Johnsons.

190. Reminiscences of Arthur Goldschmidt, 781, 786, 789, CCOH. Goldschmidt influenced Johnson's appointment of Goldberg to succeed Adlai Stevenson as U.S. ambassador to the United Nations.

191. Ibid., 780.

192. Ibid., 536–39, 780–81, 787–93. Surprisingly, Mundt did not say a word. The State Department, however, was not happy that Johnson had selected for the U.S. delegate someone who had insider UN knowledge and direct access to the president.

193. Ibid., 790.

194. Wickenden to Fortas, Nov. 23, 1967, folder 10, box 2, Wickenden Papers M99-098. Wickenden earlier chastised Kennedy for his Cuba policy, and Esther Peterson replied to defend Kennedy's position.

195. In 1949 Johnson surprised some public power advocates by Red-baiting Olds to prevent his reappointment as head of the Federal Power Commission. It did not help Olds that he had antagonized the key public power advocates at the Department of the Interior, Harold Ickes and Abe Fortas. Fortas later denied rumors that he was behind Johnson's destruction of Olds. See Caro, *Master of the Senate*, 233–306; Laura Kalman, *Abe Fortas: A Biography* (New Haven: Yale University Press, 1990), 206.

196. Less than two months after Dies called Carmody subversive, Roosevelt asked Carmody to leave the Federal Works Agency for a less visible post as a member of the U.S. Maritime Commission. "Dies Charges," *NYT*, Oct. 20, 1941; John Carmody file, RG 478. The Federal Works Agency eventually was absorbed into the newer and less ambitious General Services Administration; Smith, *Building New Deal Liberalism*, 247.

197. Smith, *Building New Deal Liberalism*, 263.

198. When Dies declared that the Roosevelt administration was harboring over a thousand Communist sympathizers in high-paid positions, Carmody's Federal Works Agency was one of the agencies with the highest numbers of alleged subversives; "Dies Charges," *NYT*, Oct. 20, 1941.

199. Goldschmidt quoted in Smith, *Building New Deal Liberalism*, 250. Goldschmidt had helped write the influential 1938 *Report on Economic Conditions in the South*.

200. Ibid., 254.

201. Goldschmidt, draft memoir, UN@50.doc, in author's possession. On how the early ideals of the Mekong Delta project were harnessed as a tool of U.S. diplomacy, see Ekbladh, *Great American Mission*, 206–7. On Paul Taylor's analogous later career in international land reform, see Gordon, *Dorothea Lange*, 185–86.

CONCLUSION

1. Thomas I. Emerson and David M. Helfeld, "Loyalty among Government Employees," *Yale Law Journal* 58, no. 1 (1948): 142. Helfeld was Emerson's student.

2. Mary Dublin, Handwritten address to Consumers' League of Michigan, Dec. 30, 1938, MDK Papers.

3. Ware's choice of words distinguishes her from contemporaries who emphasized (and often lamented) a perceived "revolution of rising expectations." Caroline Ware, Address to Radcliffe Alumnae Association, 1967, quoted by Anne F. Scott, ed., *Pauli Murray & Caroline Ware: Forty Years of Letters in Black and White* (Chapel Hill: University of North Carolina Press, 2006), 183.

4. Eleanor Bontecou, *The Federal Loyalty-Security Program* (Ithaca: Cornell University Press, 1953), 148.

5. Wickenden's reference to "national privilege" is a reminder that over the course of the 1940s, leftists became increasingly attentive to the international implications of the right's defense of inequality. Wickenden, "Women and the War," unpublished essay [circa 1943], Wickenden Papers M2001–090.

6. James T. Patterson, *Congressional Conservatism and the New Deal* (Lexington: University Press of Kentucky, 1967), 195.

7. In 1969, Kevin Phillips, then a Republican Party strategist, recommended prying white working-class voters away from the Democratic Party by stressing "social issues"—such as abortion rights, the equal rights amendment, and affirmative action. See Phillips, *The Emerging Republican Majority* (New Rochelle, N.Y.: Arlington, 1969); Linda Gordon and Allen Hunter, "Sex, Family, and the New Right," *Radical America*, no. 11–12 (1977); Rosalind Petchesky, *Abortion and Woman's Choice* (Boston: Northeastern University Press, 1990); Thomas Frank, *What's the Matter with Kansas* (New York: Metropolitan, 2004).

8. Nancy MacLean, *Freedom Is Not Enough: The Opening of the American Workplace* (Cambridge: Harvard University Press, 2006), 143.

9. See appendix 1.

10. Mandel at first feared that McCarthy's inaccurate attack on Kenyon would harm the cause, writing to his friend Ben Stolberg, "Of course McC [McCarthy] went out on a limb by opening up on Dorothy Kenyon who led the fight against the admission of the [Communist] Women's International Democratic Federation in the UN. . . . Was JB [Matthews] responsible for this mess?" Mandel to Stolberg, Mar. 9, 1950, box 6, Stolberg Papers. But Mandel remained silent as J .B. Matthews and others continued denouncing Kenyon.

11. For debate on the relative importance of popular values and right-wing elites in explaining "why no social democracy in America," see "Scholarly Controversy: Rethinking the Place of the New Deal in American History," *International Labor and Working-Class History* 74 (2008): 3–69.

12. John Nichols, *The "S" Word: A Short History of an American Tradition . . . Socialism* (New York: Verso, 2011).

13. See Jane Meyer, "Covert Operations," *New Yorker*, Aug. 30, 2010; Sean Wilentz, "Confounding Fathers," ibid., Oct. 18, 2010.

14. Convinced that their country is on the verge of apocalypse, Tea Party activists are possessed by "an almost religious fervor to protect a mythical past"; see "Trouble Ahead," *Financial Times*, Oct. 31, 2010. See also Billy Wharton, Socialist Party of America, "Obama's No Socialist, I Should Know," *Washington Post*, Mar. 15, 2009; "Michelle Obama Keeps Socialist Books in the White House Library," *Guardian*, Feb. 22, 2010.

15. Wickenden, "Social Welfare and the Radical Right," outline for unidentified presentation, Jan. 26, 1962, folder 19, box 1, Wickenden Papers.

Appendix 1

Loyalty Case Records and Selection

1. See two reports by the National Archives and Records Service (NARS), "Analysis and Appraisal of the Civil Service Commission Regular-Sized Investigative Case Files, 1928–1959" (Aug. 1983), and "Analysis of Oversize Civil Service Commission Investigative Case Files" (July 1982), and related internal NARS correspondence at the National Archives, College Park, Md. NARS analysts completed data sheets from large samples of the "thick" and "thin" files. Data collected included demographic information about the defendant, the nature of allegations, and case outcome (where known). Those data sheets were destroyed, but some generalizations drawn from them survive in the reports cited above.

2. In a sample of 529 "oversize" cases, only 13 percent involved "morals" charges, and that category included adultery, promiscuity, alcoholism, and drug use, in addition to homosexual conduct. The total group of roughly 2,400 oversize cases does not include the files of the four lesbian government employees mentioned by David K. Johnson, *The Lavender Scare: The Cold War Persecution of Gays and Lesbians in the Federal Government* (Chicago: University of Chicago Press, 2004).

3. Thomas I. Emerson Papers, Sterling Library, Yale; Eleanor Bontecou Papers, HSTL; Tillett Papers. See also Carl Bernstein, *Loyalties: A Son's Memoir* (New York: Simon and Schuster, 1989); Selma R. Williams, *Red-Listed: Haunted by the Washington Witch Hunt* (Reading, Mass.: Addison-Wesley, 1993).

4. Eleanor Bontecou, *The Federal Loyalty-Security Program* (Ithaca: Cornell University Press, 1953), 76–90. Many scholars have commented on the hazards of using FBI reports. Another FBI motive for gathering personal information was to gain leverage over potential informants, who sometimes cooperated when threatened with embarrassing revelations (about sexual conduct, arrests, or debts, for example).

Appendix 3

Chronology of the Federal Loyalty-Security Program

1. Francis H. Thompson, *The Frustration of Politics: Truman, Congress, and the Loyalty Issue, 1945–1953* (Cranbury, N.J.: Associated University Presses, 1979).

Appendix 4

Statistics of the Federal Loyalty–Security Program

1. Eleanor Bontecou, *The Federal Loyalty-Security Program* (Ithaca: Cornell University Press, 1953), 15.

2. Loyalty Review Board report for the period ended June 30, 1953, in box 12, entry A1 1011, RG 146. The 4.7 million figure is from David Fellman, "The Loyalty Defendants," *Wisconsin Law Review* (1957): 12.

3. Ralph S. Brown Jr., *Loyalty and Security: Employment Tests in the United States* (New Haven: Yale University Press, 1958), 487–88; David Caute, *The Great Fear: The Anti-Communist Purge under Truman and Eisenhower* (London: Secker & Warburg, 1978), 592n15.

4. Bontecou, *Federal Loyalty-Security Program*, 146.

5. Ibid., 56, 72; Caute, *The Great Fear*, 272–73.

6. Bontecou, *Federal Loyalty-Security Program*, 149, 33, 44.

Selected Bibliography of Primary Sources

MANUSCRIPT COLLECTIONS

This book draws on government records, personal papers, and organizational papers. The most important collection for reconstructing loyalty cases is Record Group 478 at the National Archives, followed in helpfulness by the FBI files of loyalty defendants. The records of congressional investigating committees were useful in identifying likely loyalty defendants and in assessing the motives and methods of committee members and staff. See appendix 1.

American Heritage Center, University of Wyoming, Laramie, Wyo.
Oscar Stonorov Papers

Bancroft Library, University of California, Berkeley, Calif.
Gladstein, Leonard, Patsey & Anderson Papers
Walter Eugene Packard Papers
Catherine Bauer Wurster Papers

Bentley Historical Library, University of Michigan, Ann Arbor, Mich.
Homer S. Ferguson Papers

Center for Legislative Archives, National Archives, Washington, D.C.
Record Group 46: Senate Internal Security Subcommittee
Record Group 233: Special Committee on Un-American Activities (1938–44); House Un-American Activities Committee (1945–69)
SEN84A-F13 Records: Senate Post Office and Civil Service Committee: Subcommittee on the Government Employees' Security Program (Johnston Committee)

College of Charleston Library, Jewish Heritage Collection, Charleston, S.C.
Leon Keyserling Papers
Keyserling Family Papers

Columbia University Rare Book and Manuscript Library, New York, N.Y.
Walter Gellhorn Papers
Arthur "Tex" Goldschmidt Papers
Lewis Lorwin Papers
Benjamin Stolberg Papers

Federal Bureau of Investigation Files, Department of Justice,
    Washington, D.C. (by Freedom of Information Act request unless
    otherwise noted)
Bernstein, Bernard
Bernstein, Bernice Lotwin
Bethune, Mary McLeod (in FBI Reading Room)
Douglas, Dorothy
Emerson, Thomas I. (in his papers at Sterling Library, Yale)
Hoey, Jane
Kenyon, Dorothy
Keyserling, Leon
Keyserling, Mary Dublin
Lloyd, David Demarest
McHale, Kathryn
Parks, Gertrude L.
Perkins, Frances (in FBI Reading Room)
van Kleeck, Mary
Ware, Caroline F.

Franklin Delano Roosevelt Library, Hyde Park, N.Y. (FDRL)
Mordecai Ezekiel Papers
Joseph Lash Papers
Isador Lubin Papers
Caroline Ware Papers
Aubrey Williams Papers

Harry S. Truman Library, Independence, Mo. (HSTL)
Bernard Bernstein Papers
Thomas C. Blaisdell Jr. Papers
Eleanor Bontecou Papers
Clark Clifford Files
Oscar Ewing Papers
Leon Keyserling Papers
David Demarest Lloyd Papers
Charles S. Murphy Papers
Philleo Nash Papers
Oliver Peterson Papers
Paul R. Porter Papers
President's Secretary's Files
Charles Sawyer Papers
Stephen Spingarn Papers
White House Confidential File
White House Official File

Herbert Hoover Library, West Branch, Iowa
Westbrook Pegler Papers
Walter Trohan Papers

Historical Collections & Labor Archives, Pennsylvania State University, University Station, Pa.
Harold J. Ruttenberg Papers

Hoover Institution Archives, Stanford University, Stanford, Calif.
Paul Crouch Papers
Alfred Kohlberg Papers
Nathaniel Weyl Papers

Library of Congress, Washington, D.C. (LC)
Communist Party of the USA Papers (microfilm)
George Gershwin Papers
National Consumers' League Papers (microfilm)
Joseph L. Rauh Papers

Lyndon Baines Johnson Library, Austin, Tex. (LBJL)
Wilber J. Cohen Papers
Arthur Goldschmidt Papers

National Archives, College Park, Md. (NA)
Record Group 25: National Labor Relations Board
Record Group 146: Civil Service Commission
Record Group 220: Subversive Activities Control Board
Record Group 478: Oversize Civil Service Commission Investigative Case Files
    Barnes, Joseph F.
    Blaisdell, Thomas C.
    Brunauer, Esther C.
    Bunche, Ralph J.
    Carmody, John M.
    Cohen, Wilbur J.
    Coorlim, Constance
    de Schweinitz, Dorothea
    Ezekiel, Mordecai
    Flexner, Jean A.
    Frazier, E. Franklin
    Gellhorn, Walter F.
    Goldschmidt, Arthur E.
    Harris, Reed
    Keyserling, Mary Dublin
    Kramer, Lucy M. (married name Cohen)
    Lorwin, Lewis L.
    Miller, Frieda S.
    Montgomery, Mary Taylor
    Olds, Leland
    Parks, Gertrude L.
    Peters, John P.
    Peterson, Oliver A.
    Pickens, William
    Porter, Paul R.
    Rommel, Rowena

Russell, Ralph
Siegrist, Marie
Taylor, William H.
Ware, Caroline F.
Warren, Curtis E.
Wechsler, Nancy Fraenkel
Wermel, Michael T.
Weyl, Sylvia Castleton
Wilhelm, Warren
Witte, Edwin E.
Zadin, Rhea Zelda

New York Public Library, New York, N.Y.
Norman Thomas Papers (microfilm)

Sam Houston Regional Library and Research Center, Texas State Library, Liberty, Tex.
Martin Dies Papers

Schlesinger Library, Radcliffe Institute, Harvard University, Cambridge, Mass. (SL)
Consumers' League of Massachusetts Papers
Mary Dublin Keyserling Papers
Papers of the League of Women Shoppers, Washington D.C. Chapter
Frieda Miller Papers
Pauli Murray Papers
Esther Peterson Papers
Hilda Worthington Smith Papers

Seeley G. Mudd Manuscript Library, Princeton University, Princeton, N.J.
Fund for the Republic Papers
Paul D. Tillett Jr. Papers

Social Welfare History Archives, University of Minnesota, Minneapolis, Minn.
Eveline M. Burns Papers
Jacob Fisher Papers
Helen Hall Papers

Sophia Smith Collection, Smith College Archives, Northampton, Mass.
Mary Kaufman Papers
Dorothy Kenyon Papers
League of Women Shoppers Papers
Jessie Lloyd O'Connor Papers
Mary van Kleeck Papers

Special Collections, University of Chicago Library, Chicago, Ill.
Charlotte Towle Papers

Special Collections Library, Duke University, Durham, N.C.
J. B. Matthews Papers

State Historical Society of Wisconsin, Madison, Wis. (SHSW)
Wilbur J. Cohen Papers
Elizabeth Wickenden Papers

Sterling Library, Yale University, New Haven, Conn.
Thomas I. Emerson Papers
Isidore S. Falk Papers
John P. Peters Papers
Henry Sigerist Papers

Vassar College Library, Poughkeepsie, N.Y.
Helen D. Lockwood Papers

Yale Collection of Western Americana, Beinecke Rare Book and
    Manuscript Library, New Haven, Conn.
Felix S. Cohen Papers
Lucy Kramer Cohen Papers

INTERVIEWS AND ORAL HISTORIES

Bancroft Library, University of California, Berkeley, Calif.
Helen Gahagan Douglas Project:
    Lucy Kramer Cohen interview with Fern Ingersoll, 1978
    Arthur Goldschmidt interview with Amelia Fry, 1976
    Mary Dublin Keyserling interview with Fern Ingersoll, 1977
    Elizabeth Wickenden interview with Amelia Fry, 1976

Columbia Center for Oral History, Columbia University, New York, N.Y.
Reminiscences of Eveline Burns, 1965, 1979, 1981
Reminiscences of Arthur Goldschmidt, 1995
Reminiscences of Leon Keyserling, 1969, 1979
Mary Dublin Keyserling interview with Katie Louchheim, June 18, 1981
Reminiscences of Lewis L. Lorwin, 1961
Reminiscences of Isador Lubin, 1957
Reminiscences of Esther Peterson, 1983
Reminiscences of Charlotte Tuttle Lloyd Walkup, 1997 (Columbia University Law
    School Alumnae Project)
Reminiscences of Colston E. Warne, 1971–81

Harry S. Truman Library, Independence, Mo. (HSTL)
Bernard Bernstein interview with Richard McKinzie, July 23, 1975
Thomas C. Blaisdell Jr. interview with Richard McKinzie and Theodore Wilson,
    Mar. 26, 1971
Donald S. Dawson interview with James Fuchs, Aug. 8, 1977
Leon Keyserling interview with Jerry Hess, 1971

Charles S. Murphy interviews with C. T. Morrissey and Jerry Hess, 1963, 1969, 1970
Paul R. Porter interview with Richard McKinzie and Theodore Wilson, Nov. 30, 1971
Walter S. Salant interview with Jerry Hess, Mar. 30, 1970
Walter Trohan interview with Jerry Hess, Oct. 7, 1970

Lyndon Baines Johnson Library, Austin, Tex. (LBJL)
Wilbur J. Cohen interview with David McComb, Dec. 8, 1968, Mar. 2 and May 10, 1969
Arthur and Elizabeth Wickenden Goldschmidt interview with Paige Mulhollan, June 3, 1969
Elizabeth Wickenden Goldschmidt interview with Michael Gillette, Nov. 6, 1974
Leon Keyserling interview with Stephen Goodell, Jan. 9, 1969
Mary Dublin Keyserling interview with David McComb, 1968
Esther Peterson interview with Paige Mulhollan, Nov. 25, 1968
Esther Peterson interview with Michael Gillette, Oct. 29, 1974

Schlesinger Library, Radcliffe Institute, Harvard University, Cambridge, Mass. (SL)
Women in the Federal Government Project (WFGP):
 Bernice Lotwin Bernstein interview with Dulcie Leimbach, 1982
 Mary Dublin Keyserling interview with Jeanette Cheek, 1982
 Caroline F. Ware interview with Susan Ware, 1982
Black Women Oral History Collection:
 Reminiscences of Frances H. Williams, 1977

Interviews by Author
Asho Craine, by telephone, May 19, 1997, Sept. 12, 2004
Donald Dawson, by telephone, Feb. 1, 2004
Thomas D. Dublin in Washington, D.C., May 21, 1999, June 17, 2000, May 19, 2003
Charlotte Tuttle Lloyd Walkup, by telephone, June 12, 2006
Nathaniel Weyl, by telephone, June 18, 2003

Other Interviews
Mary Dublin Keyserling with Arlene Winer, 1989, Barnard College Archives
Mary Dublin Keyserling and Leon Keyserling with Laura Kalman, 1985, in author's possession

Index

Politics and Society in Twentieth-Century America

CPSIA information can be obtained
at www.ICGtesting.com
Printed in the USA
LVOW08s0525010317
525731LV00002B/33/P